D1244613

Edward Sapir

Edward Sapir

Edward Sapir: Linguist, Anthropologist, Humanist

Regna Darnell

UNIVERSITY OF CALIFORNIA PRESS

Berkeley / Los Angeles / London

University of California Press
Berkeley and Los Angeles, California

University of California Press, Ltd.
London, England

Copyright © 1990 by the Regents of the University of California

Printed in the United States of America

1 2 3 4 5 6 7 8 9

Library of Congress Cataloging-in-Publication Data
Darnell, Regna.
    Edward Sapir : linguist, anthropologist, humanist / Regna
Darnell.
        p.   cm.
    Bibliography: p.
    ISBN 0–520–06678–2 (alk. paper)
    1. Sapir, Edward, 1884–1939. 2. Anthropologists—United
States—
    Biography. 3. Linguists—United States—Biography.
    4. Anthropological linguistics—United States. I. Title.
    GN21.S27D37 1990
    306'.092—cd20   89–5016
                                                            CIP

Contents

Preface

Edward Sapir was a man of ideas—the story of his life, therefore, is a story of the interconnection of ideas. The events of his life were largely the events of his career, and they were, in one sense, unremarkable. Sapir was an Eastern European Jewish immigrant, born in 1884. He studied Germanic philology at Columbia University, switching to anthropology (though still specializing in linguistics) under the influence of North America's premier anthropologist Franz Boas. He undertook American Indian fieldwork, held short-term positions at the Universities of California and Pennsylvania, headed the Anthropological Division of the Canadian Geological Survey (1910–1925), was called to the University of Chicago in 1925 and to Yale University in 1931, and died in 1939, after a series of heart attacks, at the relatively early age of fifty-five. He left much of his work incomplete. Sapir was survived by his second wife Jean Victoria McClenaghan, their two sons, and three children from his first marriage to his second cousin Florence Delson (who died in 1924).

These bare bones of Sapir's life shed little light on his continuing status as a revered ancestor in both linguistics and anthropology. He has been consistently labeled as a *genius*—a term that fails to address the range and working style of his mind. Some senior colleagues perceived Sapir as a prima donna, whereas students and close associates recall his extraordinary warmth, modesty, and openness. His writings are still surprisingly modern. His lucid prose, virtually devoid of jargon, remains fascinating; he ties together topics that are, on the surface, quite disparate.

Sapir wrote no single work tying together all the subjects that interested him, although his only book written for a general audience, *Language* (1921), remains a powerful albeit deceptively simple introduction to the study of language. His intellectual descendants tend to be considerably narrower in scope than Sapir himself. Indeed, Sapir has often served as a kind of projective test for the anthropological preoccupations of his colleagues. There sometimes seem to be as many Sapirs as there are linguists and anthropologists claiming continuity with his work. Some know the American Indian linguist, others the theoretician who introduced the concept of the phoneme to North America and pioneered in a process approach to grammar, yet others the anthropologist who emphasized the role of individual personality in culture and protested reification of the culture concept. A few remember that Sapir wrote poetry and composed music. Each of these interests might have dominated the work of a lesser man. But Sapir moved back and forth among them without apparent sense of disjuncture.

Sapir's youngest son, J. David, himself a linguistic anthropologist, suggests (1985) that Sapir was a man whose ideas could not be pinned down to a single topic or focus, whose mind continually jumped to new combinations of ideas. Nowhere is there a single dominating idea. Thus, Sapir's is quite different from the lives and work of other anthropologists of his day. For example, Theodora Kroeber (1970) organizes her biography of her husband around his concept of cultural "configuration," arguing that Alfred Kroeber's life was more consistent and integrated than most, its pattern "deeply cut, cleanly outlined" at an early age. Similarly, Modell (1983) uses Ruth Benedict's model of "pattern" in culture to explore the ramifications of Benedict's personal life. Sapir, however, consistently fails to fit any single categorization in his time or ours.

The development of Sapir's thought was partially chronological. His early career was conventionally Boasian: he wrote grammars and collected texts of American Indian languages on the basis of his own fieldwork and employed both linguistic and ethnological data toward the reconstruction of culture history. But by the mid-Ottawa years, his interests branched out into aesthetics, psychology and psychiatry, and what would later be called culture-and-personality. Nonetheless,

Sapir did not relinquish his earlier interests in Amerindian linguistics. For the remainder of his career, he juggled his increasingly unwieldy commitments, trying to do justice to diverse sets of data, methods, theoretical perspectives, and disciplinary audiences.

Coherent presentation of Sapir's life and work cannot, therefore, proceed entirely chronologically. Each broad topic of his interest is introduced here in biographical sequence and followed to its conclusion even though other matters intervened in time. Despite surface awkwardness, this strategy reflects Sapir's own conviction that his ideas were coherent. He elaborated his major arguments over considerable periods of time.

The content of Sapir's work is, however, only one of the threads unifying his life and career. He spent much of his time and energy organizing and facilitating the work of others. Canadian anthropology retains a direct Sapirian heritage of (Boasian) professionalization, albeit with some ambivalence because—after building up a research team and an institutional base for Ottawa anthropology—he left the nascent national tradition to return to the United States. At Chicago and Yale, Sapir trained a whole generation of students, mostly in American Indian linguistics, just as the discipline of linguistics was itself becoming fully professional. Teaching absorbed much of his energy. His influence on his students was more pervasive than they could easily articulate, even in retrospect.

The institutional structure of both anthropology and linguistics has changed almost beyond recognition since Sapir's time. When he began his studies, linguistics was divided among language departments, particularly Germanics (the discipline within which comparative philology largely arose), and anthropology, which included the study of unwritten languages through fieldwork. The latter was dominated by Sapir's teacher Franz Boas from his appointment at Columbia in 1899 until his death in 1942. Unlike Sapir, however, Boas was a self-trained linguist, whose interests ranged broadly through ethnology (cultural anthropology), physical anthropology, and prehistoric archaeology as well as linguistics. Almost from the beginning of his career, Sapir was recognized as "the linguist" of Boasian anthropology. Moreover, after the founding of the Linguistic Society of America in 1925 he maintained two increasingly discrete professional identities—as linguist and as anthropologist.

Sapir died on the eve of World War II. The interwar period in the social sciences now seems like ancient history. Much of Sapir's energy went into obtaining research funding and training linguists and anthropologists. It is now difficult to evoke the excitement of the period—with its professionalization of linguistics, expansion of American Indian fieldwork, and growing rapport among the social sciences (especially the effort to include psychiatric insights). Edward Sapir was the most articulate prophet of the emerging interdisciplinary social science. Traditional disciplinary boundaries did not confound him. He was a synthesizer who could convince diverse colleagues that they had something to contribute to a common cause.

The institutions that Sapir and his fellow visionaries (particularly psychiatrist Harry Stack Sullivan and political scientist Harold Lasswell) tried to create have not survived the postwar era. Moreover, wartime anthropology moved permanently away from its earlier American Indian focus. Postwar American anthropology became increasingly diverse and specialized, with a simultaneous expansion in positions available and in government research funding. The immediately preceding era is intelligible today only through historical reconstruction.

The network of Sapir's significant others is a virtual roster of anthropology and linguistics in his time. He was one among a generation of intellectual giants—Boas and his first generation of students (including Alfred Kroeber, Robert Lowie, Paul Radin, Alexander Goldenweiser, Leslie Spier, Frank Speck, and Ruth Benedict). Their activities were interconnected with Sapir's, such that their collective stories *are* the history of pre–World War II anthropology and linguistics in North America. Like any other productive scholar who established an intellectual tradition, Sapir was an individual in the context of his two disciplines; his original ideas were linked to their institutional and theoretical development and to his interactions with a network of colleagues.

Biographical subjects encourage different kinds of interpretation. Sapir was an intensely private man. Few documents are available about his early life and what he wrote to others does not lend itself to extensive psychological interpretation. The rationale and consistency of his life rather emerge from the tenor and direction of his work. And that is doubtless how he would have wished future colleagues to approach him. In spite of his sense of privacy, however, Sapir was convinced that both of his disciplines were of potential significance to the general public; he wrote *Language* for the general reader and believed anthropology had as much to offer to the understanding of modern

American society as of the primitive and exotic. His insistence on the symbolic nature of culture, language, and individual behavior goes beyond present-day disciplinary boundaries. His career provides powerful insight into the emergence of the disciplines he practiced. This is an intellectual biography, in which personal relationships are emphasized primarily to interpret Sapir's work and its larger disciplinary context. Nonetheless, his ideas crystallized in relation to the events of his life, the circumstances of his education and employment, his fieldwork, his family responsibilities, the deadlines that plagued him, and the ideas that intrigued him.

In the half-century since his death, there has been no biographical assessment of Sapir, and it is long overdue. Clearly, the passage of time allows greater leeway in treating the complexities of biographical events because the intensity of personal involvements is distanced. The biography which can be written at the time of its subject's death is not the same one which is possible a generation later, nor should it be.[1]

Biography is dependent on the accessibility of documentation. Extensive archival materials have been preserved by others, though Sapir's own correspondence files are available only for the Ottawa period (1910–1925). Documentation is available for many of the institutions within which Sapir's career unfolded. Former students and colleagues offer vivid recollections, as do his five children. There are, thus, many angles from which to view Edward Sapir.

My own perspective toward Sapir is that of a practicing linguistic anthropologist and disciplinary historian. Many colleagues know parts of Sapir's oeuvre better than I do. In addition to archival documents, I have followed the professional networks open to me through my own position within the disciplines Sapir practiced. Though I was born a few years after his death, Sapir has woven in and out of my own career.

I "discovered" his work as a Bryn Mawr undergraduate, studying history of anthropology with A. Irving "Pete" Hallowell (one of the major proponents of history of anthropology as an integral part of the discipline and himself a successor of Sapir in psychological anthropology) and culture and personality with Frederica de Laguna (a later student of Franz Boas whose syllabus was dominated by Sapir and Hallowell). In Sapir as cultural anthropologist I found a potential bridge amongst my often contradictory interests. I was already curious about the mind that could encompass such a diversity of topics and methods.

As a graduate student at the University of Pennsylvania, I met Sapir the linguist, through Dell Hymes, himself a major interpreter of Sapir within the Americanist tradition. My dissertation (Darnell 1969) focused on the developing professional and institutional context of North American anthropology in the late nineteenth and early twentieth centuries. Although Edward Sapir frequently appeared, I approached him not biographically but in terms of his role in the emergence of anthropology and linguistics as we know them today. My initial identification, then, was not with the personality of Sapir but with several of the research traditions to which he contributed.

Also at Pennsylvania, I worked with George W. Stocking, Jr., whose commitment to historians' standards of interpretive history continues to set the parameters for the history of anthropology. Simultaneously, I pursued the Hymesian call for practitioner relevance without sacrifice of historical accuracy. The practitioner sometimes wants to know more about the data than less specialized readers, and only the specialist can pursue ideas "into the nooks and crannies of specialized literature" or oral tradition (Hymes 1983, 21). I came to argue (e.g., Darnell 1974; 1977) that history of anthropology must be both good history and good anthropology.

Many other Philadelphia scholars encouraged my commitment to history of anthropology, but I note particularly Charles Rosenberg in history, Dan Ben-Amos in folklore, John Fought in linguistics, Anthony Wallace and Igor Kopytoff in anthropology; and further, I note Elisabeth Tooker in anthropology at Temple University. The University of Pennsylvania in the late 1960s was virtually unique in its openness to specialization in disciplinary history, to "fieldwork" with archival documents.

I am further indebted to a number of historians of anthropology and related disciplines whose research has dealt with Sapir in various ways. James M. Nyce and Stephen O. Murray have shared documents, argued interpretations, and read drafts with such tenacity that their contributions cannot always be separated fully from my own interpretation. I gratefully acknowledge their long-standing collaboration.

I have drawn extensively on the work of Richard Preston and Robert Allen on Sapir, Wendy Leeds-Hurwitz on Jaime de Angulo, Mary Sacharoff Fast Wolf on Paul Radin, Michael Krauss on Athabaskan linguistics, Bart Jones on Sapir's music, Lawrence Kelly on interwar anthropology, Eugene Brody on incorporation of Sapir's psychology into psychiatric practice, Pierro Matthey on Robert Lowie, and Bennett McCardle on the importance of Canadian archival documents in the adequate interpretation of Sapir. Other influences came largely through published works, particularly Curtis Hinsley on Smithsonian anthropology, Judith Modell on Ruth Benedict, Mary Catherine Bateson on Margaret Mead and Gregory Bateson, Joan Mark on Freud in America, Helen Perry on Harry Stack Sullivan, Dan A. Oren on Jews at Yale, and Jill Morawsky on the Yale Institute of Human Relations.

Scholarly interest in Sapir was intensified considerably by the centennial of his birth in 1984. I have drawn heavily on scholarship initiated in relation to this "year of Sapir." As Stephen Jay Gould noted (1983, 11): "All the world loves a centennial; we can't resist the temptation to celebrate something clean and even in a ragged and uncertain world."

Mouton De Gruyter of Berlin is publishing a sixteen-volume collected works of Sapir. I am grateful for feedback from the editorial board, especially its editor-in-chief, Sapir's son Philip, and Marie-Louise Liebe-Harkort of Mouton De Gruyter, herself a practicing Amerindian linguist. Judith Irvine and I collaborated in editing the culture and ethnology volumes of Sapir's oeuvre. I also acknowledge extensive discussion of Sapir with editorial colleagues Richard Handler, Victor Golla, William Bright, and Eric Hamp.

A conference held at the National Museum of Man in Ottawa in 1984 commemorated Sapir's fifteen years as director of anthropological research for the Canadian government (1910–1925). The three conference organizers contributed much to my own research: Konrad Koerner through his editorial skill and as historian of linguistics, William Cowan about Sapir's poetry and relationship to Ottawa belles lettres, and Michael Foster, with his commitment to the ongoing research tradition in Ottawa and to the historical documentation of Amerindian research. Program chairman Richard Preston has provided a long-standing exegesis of the anthropologist's inherited Sapir. Among Canadian colleagues, I also acknowledge the encouragement of Annette McFadyen Clark, Roy Wright, and Thomas McFeat.

At the American Anthropological Association meetings in 1984, James M. Nyce organized two plenary sessions of the Society for Linguistic Anthropology in commemoration of Sapir, with the encouragement of Jane Hill, also a contributor to the scholarship surrounding the Sapir centennial. In the same year, James M. Nyce also organized a Sapir Memorial Lecture Series at Brown University. Harvey Pitkin organized a session for the American Association for the Advancement of Science; Emmon Bach gave a plenary address on Sapir to the Linguistic Society of America; and Harold Allen described Sapir's summer teaching at the Linguistic Institute in 1937 to the Linguistic Society of America. Although most of these conference materials will eventually appear in print, I have been fortunate to have access to them in manuscript.

My understanding of Sapir in the Americanist tradition owes much to Raymond D. Fogelson, Catherine and Don Fowler, Ives Goddard, and Michael Silverstein. Keith Basso and Harold Conklin were unfailingly supportive.

The following individuals provided interviews and/or correspondence which has added immensely to my portrait of Sapir: John B. Carroll, Helen Codere, Bingham Dai, Leonard Doob, Fred and Joan Eggan, William Fenton, Mary Haas, the late A. Irving Hallowell, Charles Hockett, Dorothy Hoijer, G. Evelyn Hutchinson, the late Theodora Kroeber-Quinn, Weston LaBarre, John Ladd, Ruth Landes, the late Fang-Kuei Li, Yakov Malkiel, the late David Mandelbaum, Ruth Mandlebaum, the late J. Alden Mason, Rhoda Metraux, Ian Michael, the late Stanley Newman, the late Cornelius Osgood, Kenneth Pike, Irving Rouse, William Samarin, Edgar Siskin, William C. Sturtevant, Elisabeth Tooker, and the late C. F. Voegelin.

Sapir was a family man, and each of his five children provided me with recollections, feedback on interpretation, and access to documents. Like their father's professional colleagues, they have sought explanation of the range and continuing importance of his work. They are not, of course, responsible for my interpretations, though they have contributed substantially to them. I want to thank all five and their spouses for their hospitality and cooperation over the last few years: Philip and Marjorie Sapir, H. Michael and Miya Sapir, Helen (Sapir) and Thomas Larson, Paul and Sylvia Sapir, and J. David and Betty Sapir. In addition, I have made the acquaintance of numerous further generations of Sapirs.

I am grateful for research support from the General Research, Course Relief, and Staff Travel Funds of the University of Alberta, the Phillips Fund of the American Philosophical Society, a leave fellowship from the Social Sciences and Humanities Research Council of Canada in 1984–1985, and a Visiting Professorship at Yale University in the fall of 1985. Successive departmental chairmen at the University of Alberta, Michael Asch and Henry T. Lewis, have been continuously supportive. Stanley Holwitz of the University of California Press has consistently maintained that a biography of Sapir was worth waiting for until it reached its own closure.

I gratefully acknowledge permission to cite archival documents, along with the unfailing courtesy of the archivists and executors, particularly Stephen Catlett and Murphy Smith of the American Philosophical Society, Mary Catherine Bateson (Margaret Mead papers), Louise D'Allaire of the National Museum of Man in Ottawa, James Glenn of the National Anthropological Archives of the Smithsonian Institution, Mary Elizabeth Ruwell of the University of Pennsylvania Museum, Lisa Browrer of Vasser College, Gloria Parloff of the William Alanson White Psychiatric Foundation, Patricia Stark of Yale University, and Barbara Narendra of the Peabody Museum at Yale. I have had access to various archival documents through the collaboration of Robert Allen, William Cowan, the late Beth Dillingham, Bart Jones, Michael Krauss, Stephen O. Murray, James M. Nyce, Dan Rose, and Harold Scheffler.

Archival sources consulted are listed, with abbreviations used in the text, following the notes. Archival sources are cited to the original documents even if they have been published (e.g., Mead 1959; Lowie 1965; Golla 1984) because they were so consulted and because of omissions and inaccuracies in various published texts. I have chosen to use the *American Anthropologist* format. Those readers who are not among the many Sapir scholars may easily skip the parenthetical references; those who are will be clear as to the source of particular statements. Some things were told to me in confidence, but no one who talked to me about Sapir refused to be identified. A complete bibliography of Edward Sapir follows the bibliography of references cited.

The manuscript has been read in whole or part by Judith Irvine, Bart Jones, Wendy Leeds-Hurwitz, Dell Hymes, Stephen O. Murray, and James M. Nyce, as well as the five children of Edward Sapir. Press readers William Bright and Raymond D. Fogelson made many useful comments. I have listened gratefully to the responses of each but remain responsible for all interpretations.

Tom King has gone far beyond the obligations of friendship in mediating between me and my word processor. Elizabeth Grimes has provided unfailing moral support. My children—Ian, Kevin, Adam, and Karin Vanek—know a great deal about Edward Sapir and have apparently found it mostly interesting. My husband, Dr. György Ozoray, has permitted Edward Sapir to be a large part of our lives for a long time, with almost unfailing cheerfulness, patience, and encouragement.

Regna Darnell

Edmonton
June 1988

CHAPTER ONE

The Early Years

Edward Sapir was born 26 January 1884 in Lauenberg, Pomerania (Prussia), now Lebork, Poland. The site of his birth was incidental to his father's itinerant career as a cantor. The Sapirs did not remain long in Pomerania and never took German nationality. Of his birthplace, Sapir later remembered only the storks in the village square; he never revisited Europe.[1]

The elder Sapirs were Lithuanian Jews. Edward's father, Jacob David Sapir, was born in Vilkomir around 1861. His wife, Eva Seagal Sapir, came from Kovna, a more rural area. Sapir's native language, although others were certainly spoken around him, was Yiddish. His childhood knowledge of German was probably "slight, if not non-existent" (Philip Sapir, p.c.); he studied standard German in high school. A more significant second language was Hebrew, which he studied through translating the Old Testament with his father from the age of seven or eight (Sapir to Stanley Newman, 12 August 1935). From the age of five, English was spoken around him and he was effectively a native speaker. Family tradition relates that young Edward was slow in learning to speak, talking only at the age of about three. This is characteristic of both intellectually inclined children and those exposed to more than one language.

When Edward was three or four, the family migrated to England. Eva Sapir, Edward, and his younger brother Max remained in Liverpool when Jacob emigrated to America. Jacob Sapir intended to get a job and a place to live, then send for his family. However, he lost contact with his family, who were left virtually destitute in Liverpool until an English social service agency intervened to find Jacob and obtain passage money for the family. Edward was then about six. He attended kindergarten in England and particularly recalled learning to sew (Jean Sapir to Helen Sapir Larson, 4 March 1974: SF).

In 1890, the family settled in Richmond, Virginia, where Jacob Sapir was employed by a prosperous congregation. Edward later recalled this period as a happy one because of its more comfortable style of living. Shortly, however, Max, a sunny child and reportedly his mother's favorite, in contrast to the more somber Edward, contracted typhoid fever and died. After the loss of his younger son, Jacob Sapir so provoked his congregation that he was either dismissed or quit. Subsequent synagogues were of declining respectability, ending on the Lower East Side of New York City, where young Edward attended public school from the age of ten on. Years later, Sapir told his daughter Helen that he could never see New York as a "glamorous" city because of the poverty he had known there.

Although he was a cantor, Jacob Sapir was not personally orthodox; his ties to Judaism were focused around the music of the synagogue. Moreover, his lifelong dream was to sing in the Berlin Opera, for which he tried out twice, once while still in Europe and again after his emigration to America. Such ambitions were unrealistic: Jacob Sapir was a Jew, too short for the public performance standards of the time, and his singing voice was reportedly not outstanding.

Although there was certainly some ambivalence in young Edward's relationship to his father, Jacob Sapir provided his son with a model of intellectual curiosity and imagination independent of formal education. For example, Jacob Sapir was among the first to record Yiddish folk songs; he also composed his own music. Young Edward was exposed to a range of liturgical and folk music, which undoubtedly encouraged him to include music in the scope of his later ethnographic work.

Jacob Sapir spent more time talking with his fellow Jewish intellectuals than earning a living; he was dismissed from a number of positions for arguing with his congregations. The impression of his father's learned discourse on the young Sapir was considerable. In his single volume of published poetry, *Dreams and Gibes* (1917, 20–21), Sapir characterized "The Learned Jew" for whom the Talmud was "his dreamland refuge from the world." To the Gentile, however, this self-appointed scholar was notable only because he sold peanuts on Hester

Street (the heart of the Jewish district of the Lower East Side). The poem reflects considerable ambivalence toward the orthodox Judaism of Sapir's childhood, with the anonymity of Jewish culture in the eyes of the larger American society contrasting to the devout respect for learning of the Hebrew street-corner intellectuals with their lofty disdain for economic realities.

The association of "The Learned Jew" with philology as "a thing of god," symbolically opposed to the well-filled purse, indicates that young Edward identified more easily with the intellectual world of his father than with the practical affairs of shopkeeping personified by his mother, whose small shop provided the family's livelihood during much of his youth.

Eva Seagal Sapir was orphaned at an early age and encouraged by relatives to early marriage and establishment of her own household. Her longing for security was much at odds with her husband's wanderlust. Jacob accepted his bride's lack of family, perhaps even then having no intention of remaining in her small closely knit European Jewish community. Jacob and Eva were not well-suited to meet one another's expectations.

After the death of her younger son, Eva Sapir focused her maternal energies on Edward, to whom she remained devoted throughout her life. Helen Sapir Larson recalls (p.c.): "She intruded herself too much, tried to treat Dad as a child. He pretty much ignored her and went about his business." As Jacob Sapir increasingly failed to provide adequately for the family, marital strain added to Eva Sapir's determination that her remaining son would achieve far beyond his immigrant beginnings. Although Sapir's parents were formally divorced only after 1910, the family was supported much earlier primarily by Mrs. Sapir's shop.

Eva Sapir raised her son without formal religious observance, a position to which he in turn adhered in raising his own children. Sapir's mother was a pragmatist; orthodox tradition had failed to provide her with economic security. Her emphasis on social mobility for her son turned the family further away from Judaism. For the adult Sapir, Judaism involved aesthetics, not religious observance or spiritual commitment.

The adult Sapir had considerable ambivalence over his relationship to his parents, who played "somewhat exaggerated perhaps" Eastern European Jewish husband–wife roles. Sapir told his second wife, Jean McClenaghan Sapir, that "though he understood and respected fully his mother's [concern for] stability and financial responsibility, he nevertheless loved his father for his wealth of ideas and his imagination." He realized that his own intellectual originality came from his father, not his mother (J. David Sapir, p.c.). Helen Sapir Larson (p.c.) does not believe Sapir had a particularly intense bond to his mother, "though he certainly felt responsible for her and appreciative of her help to him in looking after his children" (see chap. 7). Helen's stepmother wrote to her (March 1974: SF): "Your Dad said he used to adore his father when he was young because of all the fascinating things he talked about to him. He felt guilty, he said, because he knew his father didn't deserve to be loved, because of the way he treated [Sapir's] mother, who did deserve to be cherished! at least by her only living son." Helen felt that Grandmother Sapir would have preferred her son to have been a businessman, lawyer, or doctor instead of a scholar: "They had little in common."

Many of Sapir's adult characteristics were apparently established in childhood. Young Edward was purportedly a solemn infant, often a puzzle to his mother. He was intellectually precocious and valued intellectual achievement highly. He felt a strong sense of obligation to live up to his mother's ambitions for him. Sapir sought out the hardest subjects for study and prided himself on performing beyond ordinary standards. Throughout his career, Sapir was proud of his intellectual achievements, although he was disinclined to boast. He often undertook more than he could do, overestimating his energy and capacities. He rarely indulged in play, though there was a dimension of play in his work, particularly in the search for linguistic pattern.

At the turn of the century, New York City high schools were important channels of selection for the brightest and most ambitious immigrant children. Sapir had to obtain a scholarship if he was to continue his studies. At the age of fourteen, then, Sapir began to reap the fruits of his academic diligence, winning a city-wide Pulitzer competition, the prize a four-year scholarship to the prestigious Horace Mann High School. Sapir declined this part of the award, ostensibly because Horace Mann was given over to class distinctions. Instead, he chose to attend Peter Stuyvesant High School, and the remainder of the scholarship financed his Columbia education. Jean Sapir reported (to Helen Sapir Larson, 4 March 1974: SF): "Once that money started coming in, your grandpa [Sapir's father] lost interest in getting a job." This precipitated further discord between Sapir's parents. In any case, Sapir's income supplemented his mother's in this period.

Columbia University

All of Sapir's higher education was at Columbia. He entered his home town university in 1901 and received his bachelor's degree in 1904, that is, in three years rather than the customary four. He obtained a master of arts degree in Germanics, his undergraduate major, in 1905. After two years of coursework, divided between Germanics and anthropology, he left Columbia to do fieldwork in American Indian linguistics, completing his doctorate in 1909. His alma mater awarded him an honorary doctor of science degree in 1929. Columbia and New York City retained great emotional and intellectual importance to Sapir throughout his life.

Columbia was the elite educational institution for the City of New York. Many of its students were children of immigrants, for whom social mobility depended directly on education. An academic degree often involved familial hardship, living at home to save costs, minimal participation in campus extracurricular activities, part-time jobs to cover expenses, and an exemplary scholastic record. Up to 40 percent of the immigrant children entering Columbia were Jewish, somewhat less than for other New York universities but well over the 10 to 12 percent implicit quotas of the elite private institutions of the east coast (Oren 1986, 40). The most blatant effects of American anti-Semitism were, therefore, minimized at Columbia.

Nonetheless, it was a time of change and Edward Sapir represented the new Eastern European Jewish influx, rather than the longer established and more financially secure German Jewish community. The contrast was considerable. For example, Sapir's fellow anthropologist Alfred Kroeber preceded him at Columbia by less than a decade, entering Columbia College in 1892 at the age of sixteen. Kroeber, educated in private schools tied to the Ethical Culture movement, came from a different world. For him, being Jewish was a nonissue (he was not), and German Jews were indistinguishable from other German immigrants. Kroeber might have been describing Edward Sapir when he recalled (T. Kroeber 1970, 26) the respect placed on learning in this tradition:

Not everyone became a scholar, an artist, a practitioner of a learned profession; but everyone lived in an atmosphere of association with them. The most gifted slid easily into the status of such a career; the others maintained the association and attitude . . . a transmuted carry-over of the fetish of rabbinical learning.

A backlash was developing against the economic success of German Jews, however, which would reverberate against the newer, more naive, and more identifiable immigrants from Eastern Europe (Oren 1986, 17). The idealized charms of Kroeber's youth contrasted with the Sapirs' less secure and more poverty-stricken Eastern European heritage. Four million Eastern European Jews fled the pogroms of Czar Alexander II to America by 1925 (Oren 1986, 18). Most came from orthodox homes, accentuating cultural conflict with American society.

The Undergraduate Years

Edward Sapir's Columbia transcript records his preparatory study simply as "public high school." He took a solidly academic program, including virtually every course admissible for university matriculation (excluding only two advanced science options and advanced Spanish). No nonacademic electives were recorded. Columbia required fifteen academic credits for admission; Sapir offered thirty-two. Already it was clear that languages would be Sapir's forte; he had studied Latin (five credits), Greek (four credits), German (three credits), French (three credits), and Spanish (two credits).

Advanced academic studies at Columbia were tending increasingly toward the natural and social sciences (one-quarter of the institution's graduate students in each); one-third specialized in ancient or modern languages, which were given a quasi-scientific character by the newly imported German philological method (Veysey 1965, 173). Literary studies were aligned with philosophy and fine arts and were far from the new trends toward liberal culture, public service, and science.

At the time of his matriculation, then, Sapir had already channeled his ambition into the fields where his greatest talent seemed to lie. His freshman year was necessarily devoted largely to satisfying requirements. Sapir's entrance examination allowed him to exempt English after two semesters. He satisfied the mathematics requirement with some distinction; although Sapir was later interested in mathematical patterning (e.g., to Lowie, 12 August 1916: UCB), he bypassed further study in this discipline. Two years of required gymnasium are the only indication of athletic activity. The debating team was his only extracurricular activity.

In spite of the increasing Columbia emphasis on electives in undergraduate education (Veysey 1965, 119), langauges were still seen as inculcating mental discipline. French, German, and the Classical languages were all considered integral to liberal education. Sapir postponed less compatible requirements to emphasize languages in his first year, obtaining As in all eight semesters of Latin, Greek, and French.

The German department was effectively divided between the history of literature (conducted in German) and linguistics or history of the German language. The college catalogue did not stress conversational skills, although the City of New York was acknowledged to afford ample opportunities for learning the spoken language. This was not the responsibility of the university. The program in philology was a rigorous one: "The philology of the whole Germanic group" of languages was related to the emergence of Germanic philology as a science that included the "comparative grammar of the entire group." The student could obtain exposure to "each and every member of the Germanic group and of the whole group in its inter-relations." In addition to great writers and cultural history, the department offered Gothic, Old, and Middle High German, Old Saxon, Icelandic, modern Dutch, Swedish, and Danish. Sapir completed most of this ambitious program during his Columbia career.

In his sophomore year, Sapir began to specialize in Germanics, receiving As in all six semester courses. Professor William Henry Carpenter, a Germanic philologist trained at Freiburg, quickly acknowledged Sapir's talent for philology and encouraged him to enroll in a primarily graduate course in Dutch.

Columbia did not have an independent department of linguistics; philology was incorporated in each of the language departments. Among these, Germanics was paramount because the methods of Indo-European philology had developed in German academic institutions, although they were later applied to other language families.[2] Among the language-related disciplines, Germanic philology was considered the most "scientific" and academically challenging. Its proponents were German-trained adherents of the new research standards for higher education. They were more concerned to identify nascent scholarly talent than to provide undergraduate education. Carpenter welcomed Edward Sapir as a potential colleague.

Except for one history course, Sapir avoided further requirements. English options in Anglo-Saxon literature, Chaucer, and history of English grammar were useful in Germanics.

It is surprising, however, that Sapir elected three full-year courses in music (harmony, musical dictation, and analysis of musical sound). This gave him a substantially heavier course load than was normal at Columbia, but Sapir's marks permitted this. The music instructor, Leonard McWhood, was a student of the department head, then-popular highbrow composer Edward MacDowell, who was on sabbatical that year. The following year, Sapir signed up for four more semesters of music, jointly taught by McWhood and MacDowell.

Mandelbaum (1949, 489) states unequivocally that Sapir studied with MacDowell. The musician did give private lessons, so Sapir may have audited his course in free composition during his final undergraduate year (Jones, MS). His finances and the constraints of his academic program, however, make special study unlikely. From transcript evidence, it seems that Sapir was encouraged more by Mc-Whood the disciple than MacDowell the master. In any case, it is unlikely that MacDowell would have been interested in a composition pupil, given his escalating conflict with the Columbia administration over time away from campus for concert tours. Eventually, MacDowell turned to the public press with recriminations that art was incompatible with the crass materialism of the university (Burgess 1934, 286–288).

Whatever the precise circumstances of this foray into music, Sapir, later in his life, played the piano with great pleasure, attempted to compose music, and occasionally considered whether he had lost the opportunity for a distinguished career therein. This was the first time Sapir turned to aesthetic pursuits alongside more traditionally academic ones, but this would become a hallmark of his intellectual style. It was perhaps also an implicit acknowledgment of the musical ambitions of Jacob Sapir—an attempted integration of diverse sides of the young scholar's own nature.

During his junior year, the lingering question of requirements forced Sapir to take economics and psychology. There is no indication that introductory psychology intrigued him—certainly it did not lead him, as it did many of Franz Boas's anthropology students, to courses with J. McKeen Cattell (Murray and Dynes 1986).

In Germanics, Sapir continued to receive straight As. He took a semester each of Gothic, elementary Icelandic (Carpenter again), history of nineteenth-century German literature, and Middle High German. The latter three were primarily graduate courses. Sapir was being groomed for a career in Germanic philology. He also took Sanskrit in the Indo-Iranian department with Professor A. V. Williams Jackson. This course was the prerequisite for further courses in Sanskrit, Avestan, and modern Persian which Sapir would take as a graduate student, even after his primary allegiance shifted to anthropology.

At this point, Sapir's academic program took a turn that would redirect his career. He enrolled in an introduction to anthropology with Livingston Farrand which encompassed the scope of that discipline according to Franz Boas, head of the department and already paramount in training American anthropologists. Sapir enrolled simultaneously in an advanced anthropology course, which was not even listed in the catalogue for 1903–1904. The description of Anthropology 5, American Languages, with Franz Boas, read: "Indian myths will be translated in connection with grammatical interpretation. The course extends over two years, allowing time for the consideration of representative types of North American languages." For Boas to allow Sapir into this graduate seminar, he must have known something already about his linguistic abilities. The concurrent introductory work did not interfere with advanced research. Indeed, Boas was characteristically unconcerned about such administrative details as the distinction between undergraduate and graduate students or gaps in student backgrounds.

Oral tradition in anthropology (see also Swadesh 1939, 132) has it that Sapir was converted from Germanic philology to anthropology when Boas confronted him with a counterexample to each of his facile generalizations about the nature of language. Lowie (1965, 6) went so far as to say that: "Intellectually Boas did for Sapir what Hume did for Kant: roused him from dogmatic slumbers." This apocryphal meeting, for which there is no direct evidence, is usually dated after the completion of Sapir's master's degree in Germanics in 1905. Earlier contact with Boas is necessary, however, to account for the Eskimo and American Indian examples in Sapir's master's thesis (Murray 1985). Such citations were, to say the least, unusual for a Germanicist. Sapir's "conversion," therefore, was more gradual than anthropologists have remembered it. He initially turned to Boas's data on unwritten languages to supplement his undergraduate work in Germanics. American Indian linguistics remained, however, a peripheral interest for Sapir until after the completion of his master's.

Franz Boas was a pedagogue of the sink-or-swim school. His courses in anthropometry, statistics, and American Indian linguistics were notorious among survivors of the Columbia graduate program in anthropology[3] for their incomprehensibility. Moreover, Boas acknowledged no grounds for complaint and set similarly high standards for himself. In Germany, Boas had studied physics and geography, not philology. But he taught himself anthropological methods after Eskimo fieldwork made him aware of the relationship between cultural parameters of land use, technology, and environmental determinism (Stocking 1968). His formal education already complete, Boas learned descriptive linguistic techniques to record Eskimo, thereby embarking on a lifelong commitment to collecting native American texts and grammars. Although he never became a "linguist" in the sense that young Edward Sapir was already, Boas believed that any competent student could "do" linguistics, in both field and classroom. Indeed, the urgency of recording dying American Indian languages meant that every novitiate to the discipline was expected to contribute to this enterprise.

Boas's linguistic seminars introduced many potential anthropologists to the discipline. A. L. Kroeber (1964, xvii) (who recalled the "purely intellectual pleasure, as a boy of ten" in recognizing the patterning of classes of strong verbs in English) found this childhood pleasure heightened by analyzing Boas's Chinook texts into grammar. He was fascinated (in T. Kroeber 1970, 46–47) by the process of discovery which came from working with firsthand linguistic data. When Kroeber took the course in 1896, its three students met weekly around the Boas family dining table. In spite of the frustrations of unfamiliar methods and materials, Kroeber recalled a baptism of fire which preceded the ultimate initiation ritual of going to "the field."

Other students were more ambivalent. Robert Lowie (1959, 3), who specialized in ethnology and never devoted much attention to linguistics, characterized Boas's pedagogy as "odd." In planning Lowie's transition from psychology to anthropology, Boas ignored elementary courses and enrolled Lowie in linguistics and statistics. Lowie made sense of this material only by repeating it all the following year. The seminar in primitive mentality was also over his head. It was Livingston Farrand rather than Boas who filled in the gaps in students' backgrounds.[4] Boas encouraged students who responded to the raw data of anthropology and did not waste his time with others.

In any case, Edward Sapir was almost certainly the only student in Boas's American Indian linguistics seminar who was genuinely prepared for it. Although it is no longer possible to establish how explicitly Boas set out to recruit his new protegé from Germanics into anthropology, Sapir's combination of natural aptitude and requisite training would remain unique in American anthropology until his own students began to complete their training two decades later.

Meanwhile, Sapir had yet to complete his undergraduate degree. A summer school marathon of chemistry and physics gave him sufficient credits to graduate in the fall of 1904. The topic of his graduation thesis has not been recorded.

The Graduate Years

The master of arts degree at Columbia was seen as an extension of the bachelor's degree and involved little change in Sapir's program. In contrast, the doctorate was a research degree on the German model. Although Sapir completed the second year of Anthropology 5 with Boas, his major was still Germanics, with a minor in Sanskrit and an extra course in education, in order to teach high school German if Ph.D. funding proved unattainable. His Pulitzer scholarship supported him for this fourth year. He took advanced Icelandic with Carpenter and two full-year courses in German literature.

Sapir's master's degree was duly awarded in the spring of 1905, his thesis being entitled "Herder's Prize Essay 'On the Origin of Language.'" Herder's 1770 essay is a landmark in the Humboldtian linguistic tradition to which both Sapir and Boas arguably belong. Boas had known Wilhelm von Humboldt's disciple Hermann Steinthal in Berlin. The anomaly about Sapir's thesis is not the topic—a likely enough one for a Germanicist—but the inclusion of Eskimo and Indian examples, which must be attributed to two years of study with Boas.

The document contains a number of intimations of the mature Sapir. He argues that Herder is modern in dismissing the question of language origin altogether. Sapir, however, criticizes Herder for retaining a Biblical "time perspective" (Mosaic chronology) insufficient to produce the diversity of "modern, richly organized languages." Sapir would resurrect the term "time perspective" in 1916 to refer to anthropological reconstruction of the cultural history of unwritten languages, again arguing that observable linguistic diversification required greater time depth than had generally been assumed. The same historical processes brought about linguistic change in the Germanic case as in the Amerindian. Sapir's newly acquired Boasian method of historical reconstruction permeates his treatment of the traditional Germanic subject matter.

Sapir expands on Herder's description of the metaphorical character of early language to argue for the aesthetic and functional equivalence of all modern-day languages, primitive or civilized. Americanist examples supplement Herder's Semitic ones to demonstrate the grammatical complexity of all languages. Moreover, literary standardization was unnecessary for fully developed language. Already Sapir, whether consciously or not, was preparing the ground for his later application of Indo-European methods to the study of unwritten languages. Throughout his career, Sapir would continue to use methods from one discipline to infuse the study of intractable problems in another. The Boasian paradigm, Sapir already realized, had a potential applicability beyond the anthropological questions it had been formulated to address.

Sapir dismissed grand theories of human history, preferring to see "linguistic growth" in terms of the individual speaker rather than as inherent in the language itself (1907 [1984], 377). Indeed, reconstruction of culture history led both Boas and Sapir back to the individual, and thereby to psychology. Sapir referred to "the unconscious, or, as we should perhaps say now, largely subconscious, development of speech" (1907 [1984], 356). Boas's notion that the individual is unaware of the meaning of cultural patterns is implicit, although Sapir was apparently already aware of Freudian psychology with its emphasis on latent motivation.[5]

Sapir's summary goes far beyond Herder to call for a remarkably Boasian linguistics (1907 [1984], 388), "a very extended study of all the various existing stocks of languages, in order to determine the most fundamental properties of language." Both Sapir and Boas would apply this empiricist intellectual strategy in their linguistic work.

In 1905–1906 and 1906–1907, Sapir took courses toward his doctorate, holding a scholarship in the first year and a fellowship in the second. His major was linguistics, although there was no department at Columbia with that label. His first minor was anthropology, and the second, German language and literature. In effect, Sapir was still preparing himself to be an Indo-European linguist, although he was also committed to work on data from American Indian languages. Indeed, Sapir was already working on Boas's Chinook data and, between his two years of coursework, Boas sent him to Oregon for a summer of fieldwork.

Boas apparently put little pressure on Sapir to fill in his anthropological background. Sapir did, however, take Farrand's introduction to primitive culture, Boas's seminar in ethnology, and a research course with Boas, presumably in linguistics. Boas's theory course set forth an anthropological model that included geographical distribution of culture and language through time, using historical records, ethnological, and linguistic evidence.

Concurrently Sapir enrolled in Jackson's advanced Sanskrit and three Germanics courses, including Old Saxon and a seminar on Wagner with Carpenter, his long-standing mentor. In 1906–1907, Sapir took Celtic and Swedish. This coursework contributed to his already-impressive data base in traditional Indo-European.

In 1906–1907, Columbia took a major step toward establishing an independent program in linguistics, listing separately in the catalogue relevant courses in philosophy, psychology and anthropology, education, classical philology, Oriental languages, and modern European languages. The introductory course included lectures by fourteen professors. No linguistic area was to be represented by more than one specialist, a policy designed to minimize domination by more powerful personalities and departments. Carpenter, for example, was the only person to offer Germanic and Scandinavian linguistics. Anthropology was unique in having three participants: Boas for American Indian linguistics, Berthold Laufer for Asian languages other than Chinese, and Farrand for physiological psychology. Boas was, therefore, in a position to identify potential students, and possibly to expand anthropological offerings in linguistics. The follow-up course to this survey was on "types of languages," and Sapir took the semester devoted to American and Asiatic languages, taught by Boas and Farrand respectively.

In his final year of courses, Sapir focused on anthropology outside his linguistic specialization. He took Boas's general ethnography course at the American Museum of Natural History, his only archaeology course, and two courses with Sinologist Berthold Laufer.[6] Sapir was permitted to specialize more than most of Boas's students; for example, he refused to take physical anthropology (Haas 1976, 69). He also avoided Boas's statistics, although he took a statistics course in the mathematics department. In addition, Sapir received academic credit for a research seminar with Boas in which he worked up his materials from fieldwork in Oregon the previous summer. His dissertation, "The Takelma Language of Southwestern Oregon," was not accepted until 1909, largely because Sapir's professional work in the interim made it difficult for him to complete it, arrange for its mandatory publication, and return to Columbia to defend it. In Boas's view, however, Edward Sapir was certified as an American Indian linguist by the spring of 1907. The degree itself was but a formality.

This program of courses and research was tailored precisely to the needs of a single student, Edward Sapir. At the same time, however, Boas actively sought out men who fit his broad conception of the discipline of anthropology.[7] Boas began teaching at Columbia in 1899 and focused around three areas: physical anthropology, American Indian languages, and comparative ethnology. The American Museum of Natural History was intended to provide funding for research and fieldwork. Boas (to Columbia President Nicholas Murray Butler, 15 November 1902: APS) wanted both an undergraduate program that would sensitize students to "what is valuable in foreign cultures" and "those elements in our own civilization which are common to all mankind" and a graduate program with a "diverse character"—a careful understatement of the ambitious program Boas already had in mind.

Although he did not slight any area, Boas was particularly adamant that ethnological research "requires a thorough linguistic preparation," making it "necessary for me to give a course of lectures on Indian languages." Boas accurately noted that "all the younger men who study Indian languages have been trained in this course." Graduate training in anthropology was itself still relatively new; formal study in North American linguistics was available nowhere else (see Darnell 1969; 1970). Given collaboration with the American Museum, Boas was optimistic that a major effort could be made to salvage Indian languages and he was eager to recruit suitable personnel. Although Boas's break with the museum in 1905 would cause severe setbacks to his ability to provide fieldwork funding for his students, he was already firmly committed to Edward Sapir as a student.

The key issue in assessing desirability of employment, in Boas's view, was fieldwork (Boas to Kroeber, 8 January 1908: APS). After the break with the American Museum, possibilities for fieldwork were best in California and Chicago. Boas lamented: "If conditions were different here, I should not be so eager to secure positions outside of New York for my best students." In spite of Boas's prestige within the discipline, financial resources were extremely limited and usually depended on collaboration between a museum and a university. Kroeber's position at Berkeley was ideal in this respect. To find such a position for Edward Sapir, under conditions of retrenchment in anthropological resources in New York, would take a little longer than Boas had initially hoped. In the interim, Sapir's apprenticeship was served in fieldwork rather than in teaching.

CHAPTER TWO

Apprenticeship

After completing his course in 1906, Sapir spent several years in the field in various short-term appointments. Although permanent jobs in anthropology were scarce, Boas funded research for his students through the Bureau of American Ethnology or the American Museum of Natural History. Indeed, Boas himself had a rather peripatetic career before his appointment to Columbia in 1899. As a linguist, Sapir's difficulties were compounded because museum funding depended on collection of specimens and associated cultural facts rather than on linguistic descriptions that did not fit easily into public exhibits.

Between 1906 and 1910, Sapir carried out four major field studies: Wishram Chinook in 1905, Takelma in 1906, Yana in 1907–1908, and Ute/Southern Paiute in 1909–1910. He also managed a fleeting exposure to Chasta Costa, Kato, and Catawba (see table 1 for summary of Sapir's field experience). At the age of twenty-six, when Boas engineered his prestigious appointment as the first director of the Canadian government's Anthropological Division in 1910, Sapir was already *the* acknowledged linguist within Boasian anthropology. It was time for him to take his part in the expansion and consolidation of the Boasian paradigm.

Sapir's first publication, in 1906, appeared in a volume dedicated to Franz Boas. He analyzed a text (collected for Boas by his long-standing collaborator George Hunt) on the exchange of coppers by two Kwakiutl chiefs. After performing satisfactorily with Boas's ma-

Table 1: *American Indian Fieldwork*

Date	Language	Location/Informants
July, August 1905	Wishram Chinook	Yakima Reservation, Washington: Louis Simpson, Pete McGuff
Summer 1906	Takelma	Siletz Reservation, Oregon: Francis Johnson
	Chasta Costa	Wolverton Orton (Sundays)
1907–1908	Central and Southern Yana	Sam Batwi
	Northern Yana	Betty Brown
	Kato	Phonetics (with Pliny Goddard)
February 1909	Catawba	With Frank Speck
August–September 1909	Ute	Uintah Reservation, White Rocks, Utah: Charley Mack
1910	Southern Paiute	Tony Tillohash, Carlisle
	Hopi	Joshua, Carlisle
September–December 1910 and 1913–1914	Nootka	Alberni, B.C.: Alex Thomas, Tom Sayachapis, Frank Williams, Dan Watts
1910	Comox	Alberni, B.C.: Tommy Bill
August 1911 (6 days)	Mohawk, Seneca	Grand River, near Brantford: Chief John Gibson
	Mohawk	Caughnawaga, near Montreal
	Tutelo	Six Nations, Ontario: Andrew Sprague
	Delaware	Caughnawaga, near Montreal
	Abenaki	St. Thomas Pierreville
	Malecite	Riviere du Loup
	Micmac	Cacouna
	Montagnais, Cree (Rupert House)	Pointe Bleu, Lac St. Jean

Table 1: *American Indian Fieldwork* (cont.)

Date	Language	Location/Informants
April 1914	Chilcat Tlingit	Louis Shotridge
February 1915	Nass River	Ottawa, 2 weeks: Chiefs Woods, Lincoln, Calder, and Derrick
Summer 1915	Yana (Yahi)	Berkeley: Ishi
April–May 1916	Kootenay	Ottawa: Chief Paul David
	Nass River, Thompson River, Lillooet, Shuswap, Okanagan	
March 1920	Skidegate Haida	Ottawa: Reverend Peter R. Kelly
April 1920	Tsimshian	Ottawa: Two speakers
Summer 1922	Sarcee	Sarcee Reserve, near Calgary: John Whitney
June–August 1923	Kutchin	Camp Red Cloud, Pennsylvania: John Fredson of Venetia and Fort Yukon
	Ingalik	Thomas B. Reid of Anvik
Late 1926–early 1928	Navajo	Chicago: Paul Jones
Summer 1927	Hupa	Hupa reservation, California: Sam Brown, Emma Frank, Shoemaker, Jake Hostler, Mary Marshall
	Yurok	Sundays
	Chimariko	Abe Bush
Summer 1929	Navajo	Crystal City, New Mexico: Albert G. (Chic) Sandoval
1934	Nootka	New Haven: Alex Thomas (with Morris Swadesh)
1934?	Wishram Chinook	New Haven: Philip Kahclamet
1936	Navajo	New Haven: Chic Sandoval

terial, Sapir was sent to Oregon to study Wasco and Wishram Chinook in the summer of 1905. He had just submitted his master's thesis in Germanics. Funding came from the Bureau of American Ethnology, where Boas held the position of honorary philologist and was preparing a series of grammars for the *Handbook of American Indian Languages* (1911; 1922). Boas also contributed to consolidating ethnological information for the *Handbook of American Indians* (Hodge 1906; 1910).

The bureau was more interested in Sapir's ethnological work than in his linguistic efforts. Moreover, financial support had its price. For example, Boas assumed Sapir would not mind collecting Chinookan phonograph records at the request of bureau director William Henry Holmes. This fell through only because the equipment was damaged and could not be repaired in the field (Holmes to Sapir, 19 June 1905; Sapir to Holmes, 30 August 1905: BAE). Both this grant and the one the following year to obtain Sapir's dissertation data on Takelma were for expenses only.[1]

Boas directed Sapir's first fieldwork in detail, expecting him to prepare himself by studying "the myths and traditions" of the Northwest coast (to Kroeber, 5 May 1905: APS). Sapir diligently reported back to Boas on his progress in locating informants and collecting linguistic texts. In the field, Sapir decided to study the Wishram dialect of Chinook at Yakima, rather than Wasco at Warm Springs as originally planned.

The bureau continued to emphasize Sapir's ethnology. Although Sapir (to Holmes, 2 June 1907: BAE) felt himself not "able as yet to write out a well rounded ethnologic account of these tribes," he agreed to contribute to the *Handbook*. Hodge (Sapir to Hodge, 12 November 1907: BAE) accepted Sapir as the bureau's Chinookan specialist.

In spite of the bureau's lack of interest in linguistics, however, Sapir managed to collect a volume of Wishram texts that appeared in 1909 in Boas's American Ethnological Society series. Sapir agreed to include Wasco texts from a previous collector but took for granted that his analysis would supersede Boas's (to Boas, 12 December 1908, 9 March 1909: APS): "If there are any points in the notes that you do not quite understand or are unable to agree with, please let me know and perhaps I can give the reason for my statements more clearly." Sapir's confidence in his own work was growing, as was his realization of Boas's limitations as a linguist. Because Sapir had done the fieldwork and therefore had greater familiarity with the language, Boas raised no objection. In fact, he took the initiative to incorporate Sapir's work on Wishram phonetics into his own Chinook sketch for the *Handbook* (Boas to Sapir, 29 March 1909: APS). The material appeared in 1911 under Sapir's name. Boas was unperturbed that his student's analysis was more elegant and extensive than his own. The point was to record the languages.[2]

Boas was sufficiently satisfied with Sapir's progress to recommend him to Kroeber for a research fellowship in California in glowing terms (24 May 1906: UCB). Boas "should hate to lose" Sapir, who did "first-rate work" on Chinookan. "He is a born linguist, and his work in that direction is about the best that any of my students have done." Although Sapir's ethnology was "very fragmentary," he "picks up knowledge very rapidly, and . . . adapts himself to all kinds of work." Boas hoped to "retain him here at Columbia to relieve me of part of the work of linguistic instruction." That is, Boas was prepared to surrender his own hard-won primacy in the teaching of American Indian linguistics at the only North American university to offer such work to a student who not yet carried out his Ph.D. research! The California position was a second alternative.

Sapir's commitment to Takelma, his field language in the summer of 1906, was considerably greater than to Wishram, partly because he obtained more extensive materials and partly because Chinookan already "belonged" to Boas. Fieldwork established a claim very like ownership, and authorship of materials was virtually equated with their acquisition in the field (Voegelin 1952, 441). Boas congratulated Sapir for "getting such good information out of the few people who are left" (25 August 1906: APS). Sapir was increasingly confident and less frequently reported to Boas in New York. Moreover, he took it upon himself to extend his original mandate to record Takelma. On Sundays, when he followed local custom and did not work, he made notes on Wolverton Orton's Chasta Costa around the kitchen table at his boarding house. Chasta Costa was Sapir's first exposure to an Athabaskan language and led to an exemplary monograph in 1915. Like Boas, Sapir believed in rescuing endangered languages.

Although Sapir published two brief ethnological reports on Takelma in addition to his *Handbook* sketch, he concentrated on a grammar with accompanying texts, conceiving the two as inseparable. He wrote to George Byron Gordon of the Pennsylvania Museum (13 September 1908: UPM): "As you will readily admit, a somewhat elaborate grammatical study of a language in which no adequate text material is available is something of a joke." Gordon, a museum man, was, however, interested in number and length of publications, not in linguistic description per se.

In any case, the Takelma grammar, Sapir's Columbia dissertation, first appeared in a 1912 separate and also in 1922 in the second volume of Boas's *Handbook of American Indian Languages*. Sapir accepted the vagaries of publication but insisted on additional copies for "several people primarily interested in linguistics rather than ethnology" (to Hodge, 24 November 199: BAE). Because of his Indo-European training, Sapir's linguistic network transcended that of bureau ethnology.

Sapir's Takelma grammar did not appear in the first volume of the *Handbook* in 1911 because of a conflict in priorities between Sapir and Boas, who had a very definite idea of the structure of the whole work. It was to provide "a succinct morphological description of all the languages of the continent" which would "classify American Indian languages on a basis wider than that of linguistic stocks" (Boas to Hodge, 22 June 1911: BAE). The 1911 volume was intended to be exhaustive in "analytical study of the morphology of each linguistic family, without any attempt at a detailed discussion of phonetic processes, their influence upon the development of the language, and the relation of dialects." Sapir, as a linguist, considered the latter issues paramount.

For Boas, however, the *Handbook* was the first step in an ambitious program of recording and analyzing all North American languages. It was to be followed by a series of handbooks devoted to the particular linguistic stocks, including "the development of each language, so far as it can be traced by comparative studies." This was, succinctly and in his own words, the "Boas plan for the presentation of American Indian languages" (Voegelin 1952; Stocking 1974). Although Voegelin (1952, 443) characterized Sapir as the "incomparably brilliant exemplar of the Boas plan—when he followed the plan," it was, in fact, the excellence of Sapir's Takelma grammar that constituted its deviation from the plan (Stocking 1974). Most of Boas's collaborators could not compete with Sapir's virtuosity.

Superficially, the problem was one of length. Sapir, not sharing Boas's enthusiasm for a standardized format as a prerequisite to comparing languages, wanted to cross-reference grammar and texts and include multiple texts (to Boas, 31 May 1911: APS). Quality and completeness of each description would produce meaningful comparison in terms appropriate to the language itself, not relying on categories imposed by the analyst (in this case, Boas).

Boas, however, was committed to his own agenda and berated Sapir that "the form of your treatment is so different from that of the rest of the *Handbook*" (31 May 1911: NMM). Boas did not dispute Sapir's conclusions about Takelma, merely his failure to adhere to the "strictly analytical treatment" of the volume:

> . . . if you studied Takelma without any reference to any other language, the form which you would give to your material would be different from what it is now. You have gone into details of probable or possible historical development of forms that are not clear on account of previous historical changes. . . . I fully recognize the propriety of treating the grammar the way you did . . . but I should like to keep the fundamental idea of the *Handbook* as consistent as possible.

Sapir's Takelma sketch appeared as he wrote it, but only in the second volume of the *Handbook*. The first remained as the exemplification of Boas's methods. Conflict was, however, recurrent. When Boas requested a sketch of Ute for the second volume (26 August 1912: APS), Sapir admitted that he did not want to prepare a short sketch: "I confess I believe in rather full treatments, and consider most of the *Handbook* articles inadequate as final presentations." Unsurprisingly, Boas was incensed by the implied criticism, and Sapir (3 September 1912: APS) was forced to smooth his mentor's ruffled feathers, assuring Boas that "most" of the sketches were "interesting and well-done" but that their "scale of treatment" necessarily left out a great deal. Most of the contributors were not primarily linguists and would never present a fuller treatment. Although Sapir did not want to appear "too carping," he insisted that "only a critical standpoint can make for progress."

Sapir failed to address the issue of concern to Boas—a standard format for the writing of grammars which would be useful for investigators with limited training or skill. Because Boas felt himself responsible for salvage linguistics, he could not afford to share Sapir's "purely linguistic" stance. The two had very different priorities at this stage in the development of American linguistics. Sapir was already a "theoretical leader" in American Indian linguistics; Boas was more an "organizational leader," who compromised for the sake of long-range goals and expected his disciples to contribute to the common enterprise.[3]

Boas's annoyance with Sapir produced an uncharacteristic burst of hostility (to Hodge, 7 February 1910: BAE). Sapir "in my judgment, over-emphasizes the phonetic side" and prefers "rather . . . the exhaustive treatment of one stock than . . . the continuation of the work I have in mind." His difficulty "lies in an unwillingness to omit subordinate points and to emphasize the important." What was important to Sapir was to apply Indo-European comparative methods to the reconstruction of language history for unwritten North American languages, a task beyond the imagination and skill of most of Boas's contributors to the *Handbook*. Indeed, Boas himself lacked the training to go beyond synchronic grammar to philological reconstruction of linguistic change. His emphasis always remained on recording the languages.

In retrospect, Sapir's "over-long" Takelma grammar was the first of his exemplars of linguistic description, foreshadowing his later work in formalizing the native speakers' awareness of his/her own language. Indeed, Sapir's Takelma grammar already employed "pseudo-sounds," testifying to an "organic" or "genuine" pattern of sound which would eventually crystallize as the concept of the phoneme; Boas, in contrast, considered native intuition as distortion and sought a single "grammar" that would reflect the shared knowledge of all native speakers. Boas's preconceptions prevented him from responding positively to Sapir's deviation from the established framework. Already Sapir and Boas were set on conflicting courses that would, over the next two decades, result in an increasing divergence of American linguistics from its anthropological roots.

Although Sapir apologized to Boas for the length of his dissertation, hoping it would not prove "unnecessarily windy," he made no move to condense its 400 pages (to Boas, 1 July 1907: APS). He was already in California on a research fellowship and relied on Boas to proceed with commencement arrangements. Boas failed to confirm acceptance of the thesis and responded to Sapir's plaintive inquiry (to Boas, 30 October 1907; to Sapir, 10 December 1907: APS) only in terms of finding a publisher for such a long manuscript. On Boas's advice, Sapir obtained permission from the bureau (to Holmes, 19 June 1907: BAE) to publish part of it separately to fulfill dissertation requirements. Sapir duly left his California fellowship two months early to "take the doctor's examination at Columbia before Commencement" (Sapir to Kroeber, 12 March 1908: UCB). He reported by postcard to Kroeber (20 May 1908: UCB): "The great event has transpired and the upshot is that our noble Alma Mater has earned $35.00 and I a doctorate. Boas was characteristically laconic at the exam." Such was the rather anticlimactic conclusion of Sapir's formal education.[4] Clearly, neither Sapir nor Boas considered the degree significant in itself; nevertheless, Sapir's Harrison fellowship at the University of Pennsylvania starting in October 1908 required that he complete it (Sapir to Kroeber, 20 February 1908: UCB).

California

An unusual employment opportunity, albeit temporary, arose at the University of California in 1907–1908. Alfred Kroeber, Boas's first Columbia Ph.D. in 1901, initially negotiated—on Boas's recommendation—with both Sapir and Frank Speck for a research position to replace T. T. Waterman who was to study at Columbia with Boas that year (Kroeber to Sapir, 23 January 1907: UCB). The offer included round-trip transportation, fieldwork expenses, and a monthly salary of fifty dollars. The incumbent would be supported to write up material from fieldwork. Sapir barely concealed his elation, reporting his "consultation with Dr. Boas" (to Kroeber, 9 February 1907: UCB) and clarifying the terms of employment (which undoubtedly seemed too good to be true).

Sapir proposed to confine both research and writing to the year of the fellowship. He was learning how rapidly field materials accumulated and how long it took to work them up while engaged primarily in new work. He wrote (9 February 1907: UCB): "You will readily appreciate my desire not to have too much dead weight on my hands." Whatever his opinion of the brash young linguist so highly recommended by Boas, Kroeber also wanted the materials written up rapidly for publication in his survey of California languages and cultures.

Sapir readily accepted Kroeber's suggestion of Yana for his field study, suggesting that he would spend "as much time as necessary" to get "an adequate idea" of the language—estimated at three months or less! (At this time, American Indian fieldwork was carried out almost exclusively during academic vacations, making three months an accepted standard.) Kroeber agreed without comment (to Sapir, 18 February 1907: UCB) that he would want to see Yana ready for publication before expecting fieldwork on a second language. By the standards of the time, Kroeber was generous in allowing Sapir leeway to pursue purely linguistic work as well as the more superficial ethnographic mandate of the California state survey, within which Yana was an embarrassing near-blank. Nevertheless, Kroeber was careful to stipulate that he expected "to some extent perhaps the ethnology that you would thereby come into contact with." Sapir, who accepted the Boasian dictum that linguistic texts were useful for both linguistic and ethnographic purposes, willingly agreed.

Sapir almost backed out of the California fellowship, however, because of a more attractive offer. Gordon, of the University of Pennsylvania, after the consultation with Boas which inevitably preceded any job offer in this period, was prepared to offer Sapir a prestigious Harrison fellowship—to include teaching, museum-sponsored research, and potentially a permanent appointment (Sapir to Kroeber, 2 March 1907: UCB). Sapir, elated by the "opportunity of building up . . . an elementary course in ethnography and one in American languages to start out with," assumed Kroeber would rejoice with him in this "chance . . . to establish myself permanently in Anthropology." He proposed to spend the summer in California and write up the results at Pennsylvania. Kroeber (8 March 1907: UCB) graciously agreed. When it transpired that Gordon had been overly optimistic about his department's getting the fellowship, Sapir reverted to the original plan without documented apology to Kroeber. He ignored the administrative constraints on Kroeber.

Sapir was eager to make a good impression in his first official position and was discouraged to learn that California Indians were less enthusiastic about working for anthropologists than those in Oregon (to Kroeber, 15 July 1907: UCB). In a letter written only two weeks after beginning his employment, Sapir apologized to Kroeber for what were in fact the inevitable conditions of such research:

I greatly regret to say that the sum total of my accomplishments up to date is nil. The conditions, though at first glance not unfavorable, are in reality peculiarly adverse. The Indians available for my purposes are strangely independent, largely because of the great scarcity of farm hands hereabouts. . . . Over and above this they are an unusually suspicious set of men. . . . I am sorry to have been forced to waste so great an amount of time in mere canvassing and waiting, but I am sure that little else could have been done.

A few days later, Sapir (to Kroeber, 19 July 1907: UCB) located Betty Brown, "a fairly intelligent informant, though not considered one of the best available." After two days with Brown, Sapir reported enthusiastically: "While much, in fact practically everything, is still obscure, a few points have come out with sufficient clearness." However, "without [extensive text material] a great deal . . . will probably remain obscure." This was, of course, the ideal Boasian procedure for studying a little-known language.

Already Sapir had isolated the essential grammatical differences between men's and women's speech, which are highly characteristic of Yana and which Kroeber had probably asked him to investigate. Sapir's initial explanations of the social constraints on these linguistic phenomena were, to say the least, fuzzy.[5] He wrote to Boas (20 August 1907: APS) that "the most plausible, if entirely unsupported, explanation" was that there were two dialects, one in a state of "somewhat advanced phonetic breakdown." He then postulated that men needed a second dialect in order to obtain wives from another tribe, now "extinct, I suppose." Many women would have retained their original dialect and eventually it would characterize all women. Boas's laconic reply acknowledged the "very peculiar" characteristics of male and female speech and mildly suggested that the explanation was unnecessarily cumbersome. Although Sapir's linguistic skills were unequaled, his ethnological interpretation was rudimentary (28 August 1907: APS):

I think, before assuming the origin of the language as due to admixture of tribes, it might be well to consider whether the mannerism of speech of different social groups may not be a sufficient explanation. . . . Whether it is possible to get satisfactory indication as to this or any other kind of origin of the division of the language into two forms, I do not know; but if you compare the conditions, for instance, to the peculiar phonetic differentiation in Eskimo or to the different mannerism in speech between men and women among the Sioux, I think the possibility of an inner differentiation should be disregarded.

This is a remarkably mild response from a man whose revision of anthropological theory rejected evolutionary reconstruction of previous social conditions. Sapir should have known better.

Meanwhile, Sapir sought Kroeber's advice (30 July 1907: UCB) about whether to pay an outrageous wage to a man who could produce consecutive mythological texts. He decided to continue with Betty Brown, although she was "distinctly poor when it comes to finer points such as discrimination in the exact significance of forms, and apparently unable to give texts of intelligently consecutive narrative."

More seriously, she was inclined to "unconsciously contradict some former statement or implication." After two months in the field, nonetheless, Sapir felt that he had enough material from Betty Brown to return to Berkeley until the slack winter season (to Kroeber, 17 August 1907: UCB). Sapir reported considerable progress in the "elucidation" of Yana, which he saw as "a very queer language" for California, with "the virtually limitless number of verbal suffixes" making "the complete mastery of Yana grammar practically an endless job."

During the winter, Sapir managed to hire Sam Batwi, whose dialect of Yana was new to him but who had served as an informant for Roland Dixon in 1900, the major prior source on Yana. Batwi's knowledge of the myths made him a welcome supplement to Betty Brown (to Kroeber, 6 December 1907: UCB).

A conflict of interest, however, soon developed with Kroeber. Sapir expected to work through his texts in painstaking Boasian manner. Kroeber wanted to establish the place of Yana among California languages (fully crediting Roland Dixon's prior claim to the language, in spite of the superficiality of his linguistic work). Sapir was apparently oblivious to the pressure on Kroeber resulting from the goals of the California survey. Certainly, he was mistaken that Kroeber shared his enthusiasm for extensive linguistic description in the Indo-European tradition (cf. Golla 1986).

Kroeber's priority was to retain firm control of "his" department, in spite of internal factions that culminated in the resignation of Pliny Goddard in 1909. Sapir was too independent and politically naive to be counted on. Moreover, Kroeber, embroiled in his justification of the anthropological research program, did not sympathize overly with Sapir's longing for a permanent position in California. For Kroeber, it was a time of retrenchment, not of expanding less directly practical linguistic researches. Linguistics was included in the California survey as an aid to ethnological classification, not for its own sake. Moreover, the financial support of Phoebe Apperson Hearst, which had established the teaching department, ended in 1908 when the University took over Kroeber's program (Thoresen 1975).

Sapir had again been offered the Harrison fellowship at Pennsylvania, but he preferred California, where the Boasian perspective was already firmly established and he perceived Kroeber as a sympathetic comrade. After stalling as long as he felt decent (Sapir to Kroeber, 15 April 1908: UCB), however, Sapir provisionally accepted Gordon's offer to begin in Philadelphia in October of 1909.

Financial constraints, presented to Sapir as the reason for terminating his appointment, provide insufficient explanation for Kroeber's lack of enthusiasm for keeping Sapir. Indeed, Kroeber wrote to F. W. Putnam (19 February 1908: UCB)

I think that he [Sapir] is not the man we want most . . . because he is no museum man, in spite of his exceptional ability for languages and probably making an excellent lecturer. . . . What we need above all are men of unfaltering loyalty to the Department.

Goddard's position was offered to Speck, who declined, and filled, after a long vacancy, by Kroeber's former student, T. T. Waterman.

There is no evidence that Kroeber saw himself in competition with Sapir. He scrupulously deferred to Sapir's greater linguistic skill and training. Nonetheless, Kroeber's synthesis of California ethnology depended heavily on evidence of linguistic relationship among the various tribes. He wanted to retain control of how linguistic evidence was used in cultural reconstruction.[6] Kroeber further believed that Sapir was not by inclination an administrator or an academic politician and undoubtedly convinced himself that Sapir would be happier in a position that emphasized purely linguistic work.

Sapir felt that he had deserved a permanent position in California. Years later, Kroeber considered it necessary to correct "ancient history," stressing (to Sapir, 21 June 1913: UCB) that California was "too small an institution" to afford a specialist in linguistics (6 December 1918: UCB). Whatever his private assessment, Sapir accepted this reading of the past (to Kroeber, 13 December 1918: UCB): "I am glad, by the way, to realize that you did make a vigorous attempt to keep me at California. Not, perhaps, that it matters so very much, but it *is* nice, after all, to contemplate anything in the way of friendly relations." By this time, the two men were effectively equal in professional status and Kroeber's California position was secure. Both preferred to gloss over previous conflicts.

Unsurprisingly, Sapir was unable to write up his Yana material during the year of his appointment. Kroeber's correspondence with Sapir over the ensuing decade was interspersed with pleas for a completed manuscript. Sapir, who still felt that he would have finished Yana if he had remained in California, procrastinated over this commitment more than any other. Although new work on other languages intervened, Sapir repeatedly assured Kroeber of his scientific interest in Yana. Kroeber reluctantly settled for bits and pieces that could be pried out of Sapir. In Ottawa, Sapir felt constrained to work on Canadian materials and could devote only the occasional evening to Yana or Paiute (also incomplete). He proposed (to Kroeber, 20 February 1911: UCB) the priority of texts, with "grammatical results following at a leisurely pace." Kroeber even stooped to reminding Sapir of his warm ties to the California department, urging him to "keep your connection with the University fresher in the minds of people here" (to Sapir, 26 July 1913: UCB). Sapir, unabashed, noted (21 November 1918: UCB): "you missed your chance when I was your 'research assistant.' I would have been only too glad to stay on at Berkeley. . . . I was full of Yana then and profoundly interested and had made a mighty respectable bite into the collectanea stage." Kroeber responded (6 December 1918: UCB) that even a stem list would be useful: "It would be almost criminal to tie up your data permanently. . . . I realize keenly your reaction to the amount of time that good linguistic work takes but have a feeling that at bottom you will be more anxious than anyone else to do the grammar yourself."

Because of Sapir's financial concerns, he and Kroeber agreed that a California furlough was the only practical solution (Sapir to Kroeber, 21 November 1919: UCB). For Sapir, it was no longer a question of "scientific ideals . . . in which I believe, with moderation, but merely business." In practice, however, the problem was only compounded by Sapir's summer working with Ishi in 1915 (see chap. 4), because this produced data on a different dialect of Yana which Sapir also failed to work up for publication. Kroeber legitimately felt that Sapir had twice failed to meet his commitments to the University of California.

The University of Pennsylvania

Sapir left California early to defend his dissertation, reluctantly accepting the Harrison fellowship. His new superior was George Byron Gordon, the anthropological curator of the University of Pennsylvania Museum and a protegé of university Provost Charles Harrison (Darnell 1970). J. Alden Mason recalled (1964, 2) that Gordon "didn't like teaching but he was rather compelled to." The few students repeated the limited curriculum for the small variations in succeeding versions. Gordon initiated an ethnological publication series, and Sapir was optimistic because linguistics was included (to

Boas, 17 December 1907: APS). The fellowship required Sapir to publish a piece of research annually; in the first year, he offered his Takelma texts (Sapir to Boas, 9 June 1910: APS) and was immediately confronted with the museum attitude that collections were paramount. At California, Kroeber had shielded him from such practicalities of funding for linguistic research.[7]

Sapir enjoyed the presence in Philadelphia of his fellow Columbia graduate student and lifelong friend, Frank Speck. In fact, the two families, including Sapir's father, shared a household for some time (Hallowell, p.c.). Hallowell further recalled (1951, 67): "Sapir once told me how impressed he was by Speck's knowledge of natural history when they were still graduate students at Columbia. As compared with Frank, he felt so much the city-boy and quite inferior." Speck, in spite of Boas's training, was not a linguist (Witthoft 1950, 40), although his career-long concern with the Algonquian hunting groups of the northeastern woodlands was "facilitated" by his "linguistic gifts" (Hallowell 1951, 74). Sapir taught Speck to respect linguistic categorization.

Speck introduced Sapir to the disastrous effects of language loss due to acculturation. In 1909, Sapir joined Speck in a salvage ethnology operation among the Catawbas.[8] Sapir claimed, in spite of overwhelming evidence to the contrary, that "no human being of normal mentality and senses exists or can exist without the full adequate use of a language" (Witthoft 1950, 42).[9]

The two men were so different in personality and research interests that competition did not arise. Sapir was comfortable with Speck, writing to Robert Lowie (16 January 1923: UCB) that he had a wholeness and wholesomeness that other Boasians lacked. Speck was a supportive sounding board for Sapir to articulate his theoretical hunches, particularly on linguistic classification, in advance of public statement.

Just before taking up his first teaching position at Penn, Sapir took his first holiday in some years, writing to Kroeber (19 October 1908: UCB): ". . . the only fieldwork I did was to visit Coney Island once or twice, the rest of the summer being taken up with sweltering and laziness in Brooklyn."

Sapir began his first academic year with six students in a full-year seminar on American Indian linguistics, dealing primarily with Yana and Wasco (Mason class notes: APS) and hoping to work up his field materials. Sapir emphasized that there was "absolutely no resemblance" between the various stocks of American Indian languages. Within a single stock, however, the student might expect to find resemblances of both vocabulary and structure. Phonetics differed considerably "but generally according to definite law." That is, Sapir stressed that the methods of Indo-European philology could be applied without distortion to unwritten languages.

In his American ethnology course the following year, Sapir argued Boas's position that race, language, and culture need not coincide. Linguistic classification, however, was "most convenient because rigid and fixed." Like the neo-grammarians, Sapir saw phonetic laws as unchanging and thereby more amenable to ethnological inference than other parts of culture. The "best piece of evidence of great antiquity of man in America is linguistic diversification rather than archaeological." Language was of methodological preeminence for ethnologists, an argument Sapir would hone to fine precision in his 1916 "Time Perspective in Aboriginal American Culture."

During his second year at Pennsylvania, Sapir continued his linguistic seminar, concentrating on Takelma and Paiute (on the basis of his current fieldwork in Philadelphia). He taught phonetics in the first semester and advanced analysis of a Paiute text in the second (to Kroeber, 16 March 1910: UCB; Mason class notes: APS). He offered American ethnology in the spring of 1910. Throughout, Sapir characteristically berated himself for not catching up with his backlog of linguistic work, noting to Kroeber (7 May 1909: UCB) his "unconquerable disposition to waste time under one pretext or another."

J. Alden Mason was the most prominent of Sapir's students at the University of Pennsylvania. Throughout his life, Mason lionized Sapir's brilliance in a graduate program of far from impressive caliber. Sapir's was "the only good training I ever had—in linguistics." Mason (1964, 3) recalled a less formal, more approachable Sapir than the "famous man he became later."

Sapir was eager to be off to the field after his first year of teaching, writing to Gordon (13 September 1908: UPM): "I confess that I should like to do some purely ethnological research work this year." This duly agreed upon, he and Mason, then a museum assistant, left for the Uintah Reservation in Utah. This was Mason's first field experience (Sapir to Gordon, 19 August 1907: UPM). Sapir located Indians who spoke English fairly well, while Mason reconnoitered for promising archaeological sites (Sapir to Gordon, 24 August 1909: UPM). Although the short first season went well, Sapir wanted to begin earlier the next year to include the seasonal ceremonial round (to Gordon, 4 September 1909: UPM).

Sapir's careful reports to the home office reflect his increasing sophistication in museum politics. Though he stressed the rewarding material culture obtained from the Ute expedition, Sapir quickly arrived at his favorite subject (Sapir to Gordon, 20 September 1909: UPM):

At the end of our season's work, we hope to have gained a fairly systematic idea of the Ute language, information on many ethnological topics, a fairly large collection of myths, and a good set of photographs [by Mason]. The language is rather difficult phonetically, the ethnology seems simple but is well worthwhile.

The pair returned to Philadelphia in late September after they ran out of money. Fortunately, Mason had sufficient funds to get them both home.

Sapir's report—actually a proposal for further research—stressed the decision to "limit ourselves to a few definite topics and work out something substantial, rather than try to cover everything and be hopelessly superficial." Mason collected myths in English while Sapir recorded dictated myth texts in Ute.

. . . a very considerable mass of linguistic material was obtained, and the critical study made of the phonetics and morphology, it is hoped, puts the whole study of the Shoshonean, ultimately of the Uto-Aztekan, linguistic stock on an entirely new and securer footing.

A major research project was in order, in Sapir's view:

The thorough study of the Great Basin tribes, linguistically, culturally, and archaeologically, would demand many years' work and would be most expediently carried on by a small corps, say 4 or 5 men, each taking up some special topic or region. The summer's work among the Utes was undertaken largely as a testing forerunner of the larger field of work just outlined.

The Ute linguistic work would "lead up . . . to a comprehensive study of all the Shoshonean languages." The result, Sapir reported enthusiastically, would be "something quite unprecedented in the study of American languages, a piece of work strictly comparable to the pioneer work of Bopp in Indo-Germanic philology."[10] Unfortunately, however, the Penn Museum did not pursue the Great Basin research program and neither did Edward Sapir.

Sapir wrote to Boasian colleagues rather than to Gordon about his fascination with Ute phonetics, reporting to Lowie (6 September 1908: UCB), for example:

I had always imagined that Shoshonean would prove to be rather simple phonetically, but say, Old Man! If Ute is a fair sample of Shoshonean, I must say that Shoshonean is about the toughest proposition I've yet tackled. At first it is deceptively easy. The difficulties are not in any roughness of phonetics but in the extreme elusiveness of many of the sounds and sound combinations.

To Kroeber, himself a veteran of Shoshonean fieldwork, Sapir mused (7 September 1909: UCB):

I am sure I don't know why Shoshonean linguistics has always been considered so simple. Morphologically, Ute is a rather loose-jointed affair perhaps, though there are many features that are as yet quite puzzling to me, but phonetically it is exceedingly difficult, partly owing to a certain obscurity or slovenliness of pronunciation, partly owing to the subtle character of the phonetic system . . . It seems to be a somewhat gelatinous affair, leaving no decided impression on the mind.

Sapir was optimistic that, after two years of his training, both Mason and William Mechling had some linguistic talent. Although Mason "has not tried his hand at original linguistic research, I know that he has a very good ear and is following all my linguistic work" (to Kroeber, 16 March 1910: UCB). Both Mechling and Mason later worked with Boas in Mexico, but Mason never specialized in linguistics and Mechling ultimately proved disappointing. Yet Sapir continued during his Ottawa years to insist on the success of his linguistic teaching at Pennsylvania (to Boas, n.d.: APS).There is an inevitable element of wistful thinking. These were Sapir's only students until he went to the University of Chicago in 1925.

During the winter of 1909–1910, Sapir worked for four months with a young Kaibab Paiute man from Carlisle Indian School. Although the Museum declined to pursue the Uto-Aztecan program, Sapir wanted to continue his linguistic work. This was the first year since 1905 that he was not in the field. Instead, he worked with Tony Tillohash in a small office in the University of Pennsylvania Museum (Morris Jayne to Sapir, 5 July 1932: UPM).

The choice of Southern Paiute was incidental. Sapir had intended to seek a Hopi informant[11] and worked briefly with Joshua, who later worked for Wilson Wallis (Sapir to Wallis, 10 June 1913: NMM):

I have always been very eager to do some work on Hopi linguistics, as Hopi represents one of the four main groups of Shoshonean, and would undoubt-edly help me immensely in my Uto-Azetakan work. When I was at Carlisle, I got the impression, from the boys whom I got to give me a few words, that the phonetics of Hopi were not exactly the easiest, though perhaps less difficult than those of Paiute.

Sapir "hit on Tony Tillohash at the last moment" and "he proved quite a find." An American Indian language speaker whose English was ad-equate for explicit and consistent glosses but who still knew the tra-ditional language and culture was rare. Tillohash, about twenty-two years old, had completed five years in the English-speaking school at Carlisle. He was of "naturally conservative temperament," had an ex-cellent memory, and a good sense of humor (Fowler and Fowler 1986). He worked as a janitorial assistant at the museum and doubled as informant for Sapir's Indian linguistics seminar. Sapir accepted so-cial as well as academic responsibility for the young man, who was a frequent visitor to Sapir's home and guest at the opera and other cultural events. Jacob Sapir was fascinated by Paiute music; indeed, by this time, Sapir's father was well-established in the ad hoc role of transcriber of music recorded in the field by his son, Speck, and other Boasians.

Sapir initially intended to fill gaps in his Uintah Ute material from the previous summer. In retrospect, however, Southern Paiute far eclipsed Ute in Sapir's oeuvre, partly because of the unusually so-phisticated linguistic intuitions of Tillohash. Indeed, Sapir would im-mortalize the young man's understanding of his native language in his theoretical formulation of the concept of the phoneme in 1925 and 1933. Fowler and Fowler believe that the "phonetic perception" char-acteristic of Boasian linguistics was "severely tested" by Southern Paiute and that the data virtually required Sapir to move toward pho-nemic analysis, however implicitly.[12]

More than any other work, Sapir's Southern Paiute grammar, based on this relatively brief fieldwork in an eastern urban center, would become the exemplar of a method—uniquely associated with Sapir—in which native speaker intuition served to test the adequacy of a grammar. Sapir's treatment of consonantal alternation in Southern Paiute is still a model of analytical excellence. For linguists, if not anthropologists, Sapir's "genius" rests on his ability to intuit the struc-ture of a language from a single speaker. The "structures he intuited were mostly linguistic," and his lifetime oeuvre is solidly grounded in this early intensive fieldwork. Golla (p.c.) refers to the "absolute awe" with which his successors regard "a language which has passed through Sapir's hands."

Because his research was away from the Paiute reservation and because his plan to return to the Ute work was abortive, Sapir was deliberately "thorough" in his treatment of Southern Paiute, not expecting to return to it again (Sapir to Boas, 22 November 1915: APS). Sapir considered "the actual writing the least onerous part of the work" and agonized about the most effective arrangement of the material. Boas, characteristically, given Sapir's record of incompleted work, wanted to see a manuscript, however preliminary.

In spite of Sapir's optimism, however, there were prolonged delays in bringing this material into its classic shape. He worried whether to treat the Ute and Paiute materials together (Sapir to Gordon, December 1910: UPM). After he moved to Ottawa, there was some acrimony over control of materials collected while in Philadelphia. For example, Sapir kept untranscribed musical recordings in his personal possession. Moreover, his expenses for obtaining them had not been reimbursed. Eventually, Jacob Sapir returned 109 records (obtained from his son during his Philadelphia appointment) to Gordon (6 March 1911: UPM) after sending the musical transcript to Sapir for entry of texts. Sapir feared to entrust records to the mails and hoped to accumulate similar material in Ottawa (to Gordon, 21 March 1912: UPM). Indeed, Sapir was sufficiently concerned about the ethnographic value of these recordings that he offered to catalogue them personally for Gordon, although he was no longer under obligation to do so. The records went into storage, and Sapir worked evenings on Paiute texts alongside his ongoing Nootka work for the Ottawa museum (Sapir to Gordon, 20 November 1913: UPM).

The Paiute grammar was initially destined for Boas's *Handbook of American Indian Languages*. But the work proceeded slowly. By 1917 (to Gordon, 26 February: UPM), Sapir explained that he had "systematically arranged" material for "rather an extensive grammar and as complete a dictionary as my material" permits. The interlinear texts were done but the general ethnological sketch and "detailed study of the music" were not. The music would come last because syllables couldn't be fitted to notes without direct access to the records. All materials except the grammar for Boas were to be published by the Pennsylvania Museum. Sapir successfully extracted more money from Gordon to complete the work, pleading pressing family medical expenses.

Sapir also confirmed Gordon's horrified realization that his orthography was not the one recommended by the American Anthropological Association phonetics committee in 1916 (see chap. 5). Although Sapir noted that he "was responsible for the writing of most of it," he did not feel himself bound to it because the grammar, texts, and dictionary had to be written in the same orthography. The standard orthography was merely a convention to facilitate comparison of American Indian languages and aid linguistic recorders with limited training. Sapir reserved the right to choose the best writing system for the unique structure of Southern Paiute.

Gordon wanted to publish the grammar, which Sapir saw as "a quandary" given his commitment to Boas and the bureau (to Boas, 17 March 1917: APS). Boas replied, in toto (19 March 1917: APS): "I fear we will have trouble if Gordon does not give in. According to the rules of the Government, the appropriation will lapse unless you furnish the manuscript. My own relations with Gordon are very friendly. I wonder if you would mind if I write to him." Boas preserved Sapir's dignity but was fully aware of his own greater prestige with Gordon.

Boas wanted an outline of "all the essential parts" of the grammar before the money ran out. He noted, sternly for him: "I have reminded you from time to time of the necessity of finishing this, and I feel that you are under a certain obligation in this matter." During World War I, funds "for carrying on the work" might be lost permanently if they lapsed. Sapir's contribution was part of a larger enterprise, which could be inadvertently jeopardized. Nonetheless, Sapir found Boas's suggestion of a "hurried sketch" to be revised later "impossible" and "highly irksome" (to Boas, 28 March 1917: NMM):

It is precisely the method which I have never followed in any of my writings, and one which is in the most profound manner opposed to my way of doing things. My own habit is always, in both scientific and literary attempts, to prepare the ground thoroughly beforehand and write out the finished manuscript once and for all. In fact, I think that I have never in the course of my whole life written a second or revised version of anything, except where it was a matter of inserts or slight corrections in phraseology that could not be avoided.

Because his card index was in excellent order, Sapir believed he could write the grammar "from cover to cover in a single well-prepared streak." In a spirit of compromise, he proposed an outline of chapter and section headings plus the phonetic description as an alternative to lapsing of the contract:

You must realize that this matter is largely one of individual psychology. I do not write rapidly; in fact the mere mechanical labor of turning out copy is curiously slow in my case as compared with the normal. Where I make up is the extreme care with which I prepare the manuscript, so that comparatively little revision is needed later. Nothing is more abhorrent to me than hastily prepared manuscripts that have to be patched and repatched many times.

Sapir was able to talk to Boas in this tone because of his important position in Ottawa and his established publication record. Boas's first generation of students were rushed into professional maturity because only Boas was senior to them.

At this point, other events intervened. Boas's forced retirement as honorary philologist of the bureau late in 1919—the result of an ill-considered public accusation of inappropriate wartime actions by practicing anthropologists (Stocking 1968; Darnell 1969)—immediately inspired Sapir to inquire (to Fewkes, 8 March 1920: BAE) whether this would affect the publication of his long-promised Paiute sketch. Fewkes replied (20 March 1920: BAE) that the resignation "necessitated more or less readjustment of the work which he [Boas] had in hand." The *Handbook* would be left for "future consideration," though Sapir could publish his material elsewhere if the second volume did not appear. Fewkes willingly released the grammar to Gordon (to Sapir, 19 May 1920: BAE), noting that the actual manuscript was in Boas's possession. By this time, Sapir had convinced himself that the bureau would discontinue the *Handbook*, that the grammar ought to remain with the other Paiute materials, and that publication would be faster with Gordon than with "burying manuscripts in Government files" (to Boas, 28 May 1920: APS). He ignored his own leisurely completion of the manuscript.

This, however, was still not the end of the matter. Gordon declined to publish the enormous mass of Paiute material and Sapir again sought Boas's help in finding a publisher. Gordon (to Sapir, 5 March 1929: UPM) only wanted the grammar, though Sapir had a publication subsidy from the American Council of Learned Societies Committee for Research on Indian Languages and the Carnegie Foundation had also expressed interest.[13] Finally, after the intervention of Carl Buck and Roland Kent, the Linguistic Society of America settled on the American Academy of Arts and Sciences because they would take all three parts of the work (Gordon to Sapir, 1 April 1919: UPM). And thus, in 1930, two decades after the original fieldwork and after his use of Southern Paiute in defining the concept of the phoneme, Sapir's massive study of this language finally appeared in print.

False Starts

During the latter part of Sapir's peripatetic apprenticeship, he negotiated for several more permanent positions. Boas recommended Sapir highly (to Hodge, 29 April 1909: APS) for a position with the Bureau of American Ethnology—clearly the paramount institution in American anthropology for research funding (Darnell 1969; 1971a; Hinsley 1981).

He [Sapir] is by far the most brilliant among the young men. . . . Sapir's primary interest lies so far in linguistic work, but he is also very keen in all general theoretical matters relating to ethnology. I am sure that if he were given the opportunity, he would make something out of an Ethnological Department.

Interestingly, Boas was recommending Sapir to replace him as the Bureau's official linguist. Sapir, definitely intrigued, inquired (to Hodge, 4 February 1910: BAE) whether the position would involve "largely routine work" or "more or less extended field work and the working up of general problems in ethnology and linguistics." He was apparently undisturbed by the absence of teaching opportunities in Washington, but asked about the likelihood of promotion. Hodge replied (7 February 1910: BAE) that the new ethnologist would be sent to the field "as soon as practicable." Publication was not guaranteed, depending on vagaries of Congressional appropriation and current bureau policy; in fact, Hodge's clarification was decidedly ambiguous: "If their respective studies have been along lines which it would be to the advantage of the Bureau to pursue, there is every likelihood that the opportunity will be given to continue them and to prepare the results eventually for publication." Sapir withdrew his application when he received the much more prestigious appointment in Ottawa.

Sapir could have stayed at Pennsylvania. His second year, he held the rank of instructor, with fieldwork guaranteed. But he couldn't judge "what is substantial and what isn't in Gordon's talk" (to Kroeber, 7 May 1909: UCB). Gordon glibly promised rapid academic promotion. Sapir concluded that "the prospects seem reasonable here for me" but distrusted Gordon's lack of expertise outside the museum. He "doesn't know enough about the necessary work in American ethnology and linguistics to know just what he wants." Undeniably, Gordon's enthusiasm for Sapir's linguistic publications waxed and waned over the years of their association. Speck, as Sapir predicted, accepted the same terms.

Sapir believed he had a promising alternative, "an offer that [George Owen] Dorsey made me some time back" to join him at the Field Columbian Museum in Chicago (to Kroeber, 26 May 1909: UCB). Indeed, this possibility precipitated Gordon's salary offer. When Dorsey withdrew his offer, probably a casually offered suggestion taken more seriously by Sapir than intended, Gordon promptly reneged on the salary. Sapir, oblivious to his own contribution to the confusion, concluded: "On the whole, I find that Gordon has such an uncomfortable way of building card houses and then demolishing them that I shall be glad, sooner or later, to paddle my canoe in other waters."

Also during Sapir's two years at Pennsylvania, Boas tried to create a joint appointment for him between the American Museum of Natural History and Columbia University. Although Boas had broken with the museum in 1905, he still saw it as a resource for building up New York anthropology. He hoped Sapir's appointment "would help to reestablish relations between the two institutions" (to Sapir, 22 June 1908: APS).

The museum wanted someone to work in the Pueblo field on a long-term basis. Boas saw no problem, though Sapir would need "a couple of years to fit yourself for work in that region." He admitted, however, that research opportunities were probably better at Pennsylvania. Sapir could teach linguistics at Columbia, but without a permanent staff position. However, "To me your coming here would be very gratifying." Boas's agenda for Sapir in New York was explicit: "The work I should want you to do would be largely an application of your scientific experience of the last few years to graduate teaching." In other words, Sapir would be expected to teach field methods in American Indian linguistics as Boas had done during Sapir's own student days.

Sapir enjoyed having choices. He interpreted potential job offers somewhat naively, dismissing the possibility of other serious candidates. His assessment of the political and financial constraints underlying job offers was less than astute. He continued to resent the perceived California slight, and in various negotiations he ignored obstacles of administrative approval and financial backing, assuming that the quality of his scientific work would ensure his future. For example, he reported Boas's machinations in New York to Kroeber (6 July 1909: UCB) as though events were entirely within his control: "Should I decide to become Assistant Curator of the American Museum, my work will be in the Pueblo region; should I stay here, I do not yet know what field to tackle—possibly the Shoshonean tribes."

Boas was a far more sophisticated politician, but he too was caught offguard by the actions of the American Museum. Because its director, Herman C. Bumpus, disliked Boas, his access to matters of internal politics was limited. Boas wrote to Frederick Ward Putnam (13 July 1909: APS) that Bumpus had "invited" Sapir to come to the museum on the condition "that Sapir should not mention it to anyone." Boas "learned about it by chance," presumably from Pliny Goddard, hired from California in 1909, and professed himself delighted that Bumpus had chosen two men "who are by their training and previous work most strongly committed to the linguistic side." During Boas's tenure, Bumpus opposed linguistic work; but Boas was willing to forgive the past and proceed with urgent research. With museum consent, he arranged a Columbia lectureship. Bumpus then "reared around" and decided he wanted Sapir exclusively for the museum. "When will that scamp break his leg?" commented Boas. Sapir apparently remained unaware of Bumpus's efforts to ensure linguistic work in the Boasian tradition while excluding Boas himself. (Probably Bumpus also hoped Sapir would eclipse Boas.) Sapir (to Gordon, 20 July 1909: UPM) decided to stay at Pennsylvania after a visit to Bumpus, "who was as vague and unintelligible as before." This summary of events was written from Bolton Landing, New York, where the Boas family spent its summers. Sapir apparently expected Gordon, as he had earlier expected Kroeber, to share his enthusiasm for the most impressive available appointment, regardless of convenience to potential employers.

In the midst of the New York negotiations, Boas also recommended Sapir for a position as assistant ethnologist to the Philippine Government Survey, claiming that Sapir, presumably on the basis of his courses with Laufer years previously, knew something about India. Sapir, who was not consulted and assumed the New York position

APPRENTICESHIP   41

was virtually assured, was incensed and ignored Boas's contention (14 June 1909: UPM) that "for your future in the States, a position of that kind might be very helpful." Sapir assumed he would have an academic career studying American Indian languages and found the Philippine proposal thoroughly demeaning.[14] For him, therefore, only New York, San Francisco, Philadelphia, or Chicago—with their established museum and university programs—were acceptable options. Boas, of course, wanted the Philippine work to be done, and was, in any case, less ambitious for individual students than for the overall enterprise of American anthropology as he conceived it.

The job Sapir eventually accepted, as chief ethnologist of the newly created Anthropological Division within the Geological Survey of Canada, housed in the Department of Mines, was arranged virtually behind his back. Boas had inaugurated professional anthropology in Canada with his surveys of Northwest Coast Indians for the British Association for the Advancement of Science beginning in 1888. Although the original mandate of the Geological Survey had included "relics of the native peoples" (Bernier 1984, 397–398), it was 1910 before Reginald Walter Brock, Queens University geology professor and Director of the Survey, approached Boas about a man to build up anthropology in Canada.

Not an anthropologist, Brock took Boas's recommendation of Edward Sapir at face value and dutifully reported to the candidate (3 June 1910: NMM):

I have discussed our plans with Dr. Boas and a number of other specialists and you have been recommended to me as a man who could be relied upon to build up a strong department and to carry on successfully the scientific studies which should be undertaken in this attractive field.

When Brock came to New York to discuss the Ottawa position, Sapir realized the opportunity came "evidently" on Boas's recommendation and immediately wrote (to Boas, 6 June 1909: APS) of his "heartiest thanks for your continued kindness and interest in my welfare." The following day, Boas invited Sapir to dinner, noting his pleasure "that Mr. Brock should have made the offer to you. All that I have done is to tell him about the work that you have had during the last few years."

Sapir was correct that such a recommendation, coming from Boas, was a virtual guarantee of appointment. The success of Boasian anthropology in these early years depended precisely on Boas's ability to push his students, if necessary to create jobs for them. His preeminence in anthropology was such that former students depended on him throughout their careers for this kind of support. Boas was delighted to add Ottawa to the centers for anthropological work as he envisioned it (13 December 1910: APS):

I almost envy you and many of the younger men the possibility of concentrating your energies on research work, on which you start with thorough preparation or, at least, with a good basis to work on, and without the necessity of always stealing the time for research from other work—as I have had to do all my life long; and of the fact that I had to acquire so much of the method of work in philology, physical anthropology, and ethnology myself. I always feel that this unavoidable scattering of energy in different fields in our generation must stop, if we are to make headway.

The scope of the position (Brock to Sapir, 3 June 1910: NMM) would be "pretty much what the man himself makes of it." Brock and his fellow geologists wanted "a thorough and scientific investigation of the native races of Canada, their distribution, languages, cultures, etc., etc., and to collect and preserve records of the same." The new Victoria Memorial Museum building already included an ethnological hall but only a "trained man" could arrange the existing collections. Sapir would be expected to "organize, stimulate, encourage and direct individual [anthropological] efforts" throughout the Dominion of Canada, supported by the British Association and the Royal Society of Canada. The Canadian chapter of the Archaeological Institute of America wanted the new ethnologist as their "leader."

Although substantially behind the United States in progress toward scientific professionalization, Canada was eager to catch up (Darnell 1975; 1976; 1984). Sapir would establish the first Canadian research institution in his discipline. His predecessors were amateurs affiliated with learned societies, in the nineteenth century tradition.[15]

A special vote of Canadian Parliament had already funded the Anthropological Division for the first year, enabling Sapir to build up "a scientific staff . . . as rapidly as possible." Sapir was delighted by the salience of fieldwork in the plans of the Canadian recruiters. He was used to small field appropriations which systematically shortchanged ethnological and linguistic topics in favor of museum interests. To geologists, however, the importance of fieldwork could not be overstated.[16]

Brock acknowledged the urgency of collecting and exhibiting aboriginal cultural materials before they were entirely lost to science; he planned a vigorous publication program. It was a unique opportunity to implement the Boasian program. Edward Sapir, at age twenty-six, already had the self-confidence and the broad experience in fieldwork, museum, and university to structure a national professional anthropology. His apprenticeship was complete when he informed Gordon (5 September 1910: UPM) that he had accepted a position in Ottawa and was leaving immediately for Vancouver Island to begin fieldwork among the Nootka.

CHAPTER THREE

Ottawa: Maturity and Independence

Sapir arrived in Ottawa in the summer of 1910 full of enthusiasm for creating a new scientific institution from scratch—to map the still little-known languages and cultures of the vast Dominion of Canada on the model of the prestigious Bureau of American Ethnology. Nationality was apparently not an issue; after all, Sapir had already been an immigrant once in his lifetime.[1] Rather, his priority was scientific work. Like Boas, he took for granted the internationalism of science. Fieldwork funds were available for a research team to fill in what Sapir himself considered the major gaps in existing knowledge. Already a veteran of competition for scarce research funds, he was eager to administer an apparently extensive budget dispensed by a benign and more or less committed government.

It was the best of all possible worlds. Certainly, Sapir, at twenty-six, had reason to congratulate himself: he had earned a powerful, independent position as the ranking anthropologist in a country with urgent needs for the services of his discipline. After years of short-term fieldwork and demeaning job applications, Sapir embraced a long-range program whose security balanced the financial deprivations of his childhood and educational years. He was, moreover, ambitious to make his professional mark. His new position welcomed specialized linguistic work as the effective handmaiden of ethnology. There was no competition and the future seemed remarkably clear. This euphoria would persist for several years.

A 1913 photograph of Sapir bears this inscription in his unmistakable hand: "Self-satisfied look due to a fancied successful adjustment to all life's demands." Sapir mocked his own smugness without denying its reality. His life had settled into a routine of acclaim and security for the foreseeable future. He was self-righteously content with his apparent lot.

The vicissitudes of Sapir's family life, including financial pressure and parental marital discord, embued him with a strong sense of family obligation. His parents moved to Ottawa, establishing their own household there, although Sapir continued to feel responsible for them. He equated genuine coming of age, however, with the establishment of his own family. It was time to marry. Accordingly, he fell in love with and proposed to a second cousin on his father's side, Florence Delson, whom he had met while a graduate student at Columbia. Florence, born Olga Seidelson, anglicized her name on immigration to America as a teenager. Her family came from Vilna, Lithuania, an important cultural center of Eastern European Judaism. Sapir was not concerned with religious background per se but was delighted by Florence's sophistication and culture, a blend of Europe and America. Florence was considered the "blithe spirit" among her siblings; her "gay and coquettish spirit" first enchanted Sapir and later drove him to distractions of jealousy (Philip Sapir, p.c.). Florence, aided by relatives in the Boston area who understood the importance of education to upward mobility, entered Radcliffe College in 1908, only a few years after her immigration. Radcliffe, like Columbia, had a high reputation but also catered extensively to a local clientele, many of them Jewish (Oren 1986). Florence had few academic ambitions, however, and willingly abandoned her degree to elope with Sapir. From her point of view, it was the coup of the social season. Sapir was securely established in a prestigious position. He had apparently escaped the implicit stigma of Judaism. A brilliant career in his chosen field seemed to lie ahead. The elopement enhanced her sense of optimism and adventure. She apparently expected an active social life to accompany her husband's position.

Neither family was overjoyed. In a kind of reverse snobbery, Sapir's mother—who had someone else in mind for her son to marry (Helen Sapir Larson, p.c.)—rejected the fancy airs of the Vilna Jews. Kovna was a simple country town, whereas Vilna had had a university since 1578 and was a center of Jewish culture in Eastern Europe from the sixteenth century until its devastation by Nazi Germany (Perry 1982, 244). Eva Sapir doubtless recalled with some bitterness that her marriage provided neither security nor social prestige. The Seidelsons, on the other hand, were unimpressed by Sapir's Kovna roots and didn't want Florence to move away from family and community ties. They considered Sapir impoverished and the name of his discipline unpronounceable (Philip Sapir, p.c.).

Sapir, oblivious to family pressure, reported his engagement in a lighthearted letter to Speck (16 January 1911: APS):

> As to your well-meaning attempt to find out whether I am really in love, I suggest that you leave the whole matter in my hands. I shall only say that Florence Delson is *absolutely* penniless, much to my delight. Someday, when you have learned to behave, I may try to have you see her.

Sapir was eager to introduce Florence to his fellow anthropologists. At the Christmas meeting of the American Anthropological Association in Providence, he took Alexander Goldenweiser to Boston to visit her. He reported to Boas (26 January 1911: APS): "She is already being habituated to the anthropological atmosphere," assuring Boas that "I have already spoken to her about you." He even tried to persuade Kroeber and his wife (29 April 1911: UCB) to visit Ottawa on their way east, delighted in his new ability to offer domestic hospitality. Kroeber declined (1 June 1911: UCB) but praised the apparent intelligence, as well as charm (the former quality clearly more important in his mind) of Sapir's wife. He added with apparent amusement: "We are not really at all surprised at your getting married: most men do, and generally to less worthy partners."

Sapir took his marriage very seriously, being devoted to Florence and their children: Herbert Michael was born in 1913, Helen Ruth in 1914, and Philip in 1916. Despite preoccupation with his work, Sapir participated actively, though intermittently, in family social life and the activities of his children until about 1921, when Florence's illness and recurrent hospitalization caused all semblance of normal family life to break down (see chap. 7).

Social life revolved around the family, with many evenings spent around the fireplace with Sapir playing the piano. Various colleagues were frequent guests, especially Harlan Smith, Diamond Jenness, Danish marine biologist Fritz Johansen, and Hu Shi of the Chinese Embassy (with whom Sapir wrote two brief papers on Chinese folklore). There were occasional grown-up parties, with music and dancing. Florence was gregarious and extroverted, "concealing, however . . . a very sensitive and introspective nature" (Michael Sapir, p.c.). She loved dancing, in which Sapir refused to participate. Michael recalls "one big noisy party where I sat transfixed at the head of the stairs watching mother dancing gaily with Fritz Johansen and Barbeau." Sapir was inclined to jealousy on such occasions. The Sapir children particularly remember the wedding of Diamond Jenness and Eileen Blakeney, Sapir's secretary, at the nearby Blakeney home.

Florence used to tell Michael about her life in Russia and teach him Russian folk tales and songs. Her sister Nadya sometimes visited from New York, which always meant good times for the children. Florence would sometimes take Helen and Michael downtown for shopping and an ice cream soda. She took Michael to his first musical play. When, at the age of four, Michael cried at being left behind, Sapir consoled him with his first piano lesson. He taught Michael for a year or two before the child started with a regular teacher. Michael enjoyed playing the piano until he was nine or ten. Sapir also took Michael to his first piano concert. The two occasionally played tennis, though Sapir did not share his older son's interest in sports.

The children felt a proprietary interest in the Victoria Memorial Museum and were sometimes allowed to visit their father in his cubby-hole office there. Sapir always made them feel welcome. Michael re-called (1984, 9):

[A]t the Museum on Saturday mornings, he and his colleagues were frequent lecturers on their subjects to children. I remember with relish my attendance at many of those occasions, but one lecture by Dad on the meaning and significance of "Race" is particularly vivid; he captivated all of us by using, as simple props, three pieces of paper: one white, one black, and one brown or yellow. And in telling myths and stories, he had a terrific way with children.

There were family picnics by trolley car with a packed lunch (where Sapir read a book while the children played), visits to the circus, and "wonderful summer vacations" in the nearby Gatineau Hills (where Sapir gave Michael his first "wading" lesson).[2] These were typical en-tertainments for civil servants of Sapir's rank. Sapir also enjoyed long walks with colleagues, especially Harlan Smith.

With the exception of boys' sports, Sapir knew more about most subjects than his children did. In his diary, entitled "Suggestive Notes," Sapir reported (4 February 1918: SF) his fascination with his children's emerging speech and thought processes. He encouraged their imaginations, writing a series of children's poems entitled "The Streets of Fancifullo." Although his whimsical attitude was somewhat over their heads (Helen Sapir Larson, p.c.), the children were delighted at being the focus of their father's attention. Sapir's children also appeared, in sentimentalized form, in his poems for an adult audience. Energy and noise were his dominant images for childhood.

The family moved several times during the fifteen years in Ottawa, reflecting a balance between increasing family size and financial pressure. Florence was particularly happy in a house near a park with a pond and many birds and was disappointed at a smaller house close to Sapir's office. Helen Sapir Larson (p.c.) recalls that their homes, though often cramped, were always ethnographically interesting, displaying "Navajo rugs, many American Indian crafts (Pueblo pots and beaded work), a Steinway Grand piano, loads of books in glass-doored bookcases, a Samovar (brought from Russia by Florence) . . . , some Japanese prints and Japanese baskets, some Chinese brass vases and enamel work . . . and, I admit, a dearth of good pictures on the walls." In one apartment, however, Sapir's desk was in the living room, presumably taxing his considerable powers of concentration.

Sapir was an indulgent parent, cherishing domestic harmony and orderly routine (though he was inclined to forget birthdays, anniversaries, and appointments unless reminded). Unlike the gregarious and extroverted Florence, Edward had difficulty expressing his emotions verbally. He did so most freely through the romantic poetry fashionable in the period. Florence often felt taken for granted. Nonetheless, Sapir would impose punishments in accordance with the seriousness of the offense. Michael, the oldest and most rebellious of the children, received the most frequent spankings (with a razor strop if the offense was particularly serious).

Sapir's son Philip (p.c., 24 February 1984) recalls his tenacity in the pursuit of linguistic detail: "My God, what a compulsive gatherer, and recorder, of linguistic detail! . . . he would sit up nights, ordering and poring over those yellow-colored slips of his, each with one, and only one, linguistic form written on it, in his precise little squiggles."[3]

Michael Sapir (1984, 11) focuses on his father's "prodigious memory, strong intuitive sense and a sense of the aesthetic aspect of scientific work." Sapir was given by temperament to the rationalistic disciplines of logic, mathematics, philosophy, and science (though the natural sciences never succeeded in capturing his interest). He was minimally interested in application of his models, became easily bored with routine details, especially administrative, and longed for subordinates to shield him from trivia and implement his ideas. In Ottawa, however, he had no students; museum staff were directly responsible for details of cataloguing and exhibits. Sapir preferred to go on to a new idea when he had exhausted the previous one. His sustained attention was held only by his own concentrated and solitary work. He quickly became impatient with the personality foibles and inconsistent thinking he often saw in others. Having an unusual capacity for identifying relevant and pertinent data to support a general point, it annoyed him to explain the obvious. He was, however, always responsible to an alert mind, regardless of intellectual training. He expected associates to acknowledge his intellectual abilities.

Organizing Anthropological Research in Canada

Sapir's model for the Ottawa research program, Boasian in precedent, depended on government and museum funding for professionally trained researchers. He began to mold his Ottawa appointment to this image with a public statement of intent in *Science* in 1911 on "An Anthropological Survey of Canada."

The young director considered his program "a step forward in the development of anthropological studies in America" (1911, 789). The Canadian government gave anthropology a status similar to the one it had held in the United States since the establishment in 1879 of the Bureau of American Ethnology, "the most important body undertaking the study of aboriginal America." Sapir emphasized the roots of his program in the work of the British Association for the Advancement of Science and the efforts to establish a national museum that included ethnology. George Dawson, former director of the Geological Survey of Canada, and Franz Boas had "started the ball rolling" by their researches with Canadian native peoples.

The Anthropological Division already had three staff—Sapir himself; an ethnological assistant, Oxford-trained Marius Barbeau; and former American Museum of Natural History archaeologist and fellow Boasian, Harlan I. Smith—but expansion was planned, particularly in physical anthropology, thereby covering the traditional subfields of physical anthropology, ethnology, archaeology, and linguistics.

Creating an adequate research team was paramount on Sapir's agenda (1911, 790). He had already learned that government funding for scientific research required public justification. He argued that three appointments represented more than "mere mushroom growth" and praised the "clear insight" of the Canadian government about the needs of anthropology; "it was understood at the very beginning that the various scientific interests involved in the term anthropology could not well be successfully undertaken by one man."

Sapir was careful not to restrict the geographical scope of the division to the borders of Canada.[4] To avoid "artificial" circumscription of results, Eskimos had to be studied in Alaska and Greenland; other tribes were distributed arbitrarily between the United States and Canada. It was, therefore, "logically necessary" to follow the boundaries of groups studied.

Race, language, and culture were "interwoven" so that a "reconstructed culture-history" based on one kind of evidence could be "strengthened and even reduced to certainty" by evidence from one or more of the others. Sapir himself was most concerned, however, with linguistic evidence.

Sapir anticipated potential questions about the urgency of anthropological work: "to many it will seem that much has already been done." Existing work, however, was almost trivial in relation to "the standard that must be set for ethnological work" (1911, 790). Knowledge of each of the five Canadian aboriginal culture areas had major gaps. Even the question of culture area itself required skepticism as to whether traits "of fundamental importance" were being used for classification; only further fieldwork could determine the adequacy of the culture area theory. In a footnote, Sapir added (1911, 791):

[A]ll investigation of native mythology, rituals, songs and allied subjects, undertaken without the help of linguistic study, must fail to result in a complete understanding of the native concepts involved. We would not think much, for example, of a student of the history of the Roman Catholic Church that knew no Latin, or of a discussion of German folk songs, even in their purely musical aspect, not based on some familiarity with German itself.

The Athabaskan tribes of the Mackenzie Valley posed the most urgent ethnological problem, because so little was known about them; here "we may expect to find the simplest and most fundamental forms of aboriginal American culture, granted that there is such a thing as a fundamental American culture substratum" (1911, 792). On the west coast, only Boas's Kwakiutl were truly well understood; Sapir himself had begun fieldwork with the neighboring Nootka. Sapir recognized little useful archaeological work except that begun by Harlan Smith.

Of the native languages of Canada, only Kwakiutl, Tsimshian, and Haida were adequately known. With considerable understatement, Sapir noted that existing grammatical and text material was "not generally all that can be desired" (1911, 792). Analysis of "fundamental traits of structure" was hindered by "poor phonological groundwork and a failure to grasp the traits of morphology from a purely objective standpoint." Professional work on Canadian Indian languages needed more than description by untrained recorders. Even Sapir's fellow Boasian anthropologists failed to meet his standards. He explicitly applied to the standards of Indo-European linguistics, according to which no Canadian languages were adequately studied. Stated Sapir: "The time is at hand when purely descriptive linguistic study in America will have to be supplemented by comparative and reconstructive work; it is becoming increasingly evident that such research requires the most minute attention to phonetic detail" (1911, 792).

Sapir recognized that his division could hardly hope "unaided to make the ideally complete survey" he envisioned. Duplication of effort, though unlikely, was welcomed because "the personal equation in the investigation of social sciences" was too rarely addressed. The "cooperation of other institutions and individuals interested in anthropological problems" (1911, 793) was eagerly solicited. In practice, however, it would have to meet Sapir's rigorous standards.

Sapir pleaded, in Boasian terms particular to his public relations goals in Canada, for recording of aboriginal languages and cultures before it was too late (1911, 793):

The Canadian government is to be congratulated on having established a systematic survey of aboriginal Canada. Now or never is the time in which to collect from the natives what is still available for study. In some cases, a tribe has already practically given up its aboriginal culture and what can be obtained is merely that which the older men will remember and care to impart. With the increasing material prosperity and industrial development of Canada the demoralization or civilization of the Indians will be going on at an ever increasing rate. . . . What is lost now will never be recovered.

This article appeared in an American periodical, but its audience was those Canadian politicians and intellectuals whose sense of national pride would be engaged by the foresight with which Canada had embraced anthropology. Sapir also served notice of new research standards to amateur Canadian anthropologists. Government anthropology would espouse professionalization, a process well underway in the United States under Boasian leadership (Darnell 1969).

Response was not universally enthusiastic. Among those slighted by Sapir's obvious allegiance to Boasian anthropology on the American model was Charles Hill-Tout, an amateur ethnologist from British Columbia. He wrote to Sapir (26 February 1912: NMM), minimally disguising his personal pique, that the division might accomplish "the dreams some of us have indulged in during the last twenty years." But the tone of Sapir's article might "alienate the sympathies of some of the earlier students and associations." Sapir should realize "the amount of pioneer work" already done. "You will see that it is indiscreet to start your work by arousing feelings of antagonism to yourself."

Recognizing the underlying threat, Sapir wrote to his British Columbia collaborator James Teit (15 March 1912: NMM) that Hill-Tout "claims that I adopted a 'superior' and 'patronizing' attitude and that I have aroused dissatisfaction among several Canadian anthropologists. I had the bad taste to omit any reference to Hill-Tout in the paper." Sapir was apparently unconcerned about potential repercussions; he perhaps gave too little credence, however, to the power of gossip in the provinces.[5]

Sapir maintained his opposition to Hill-Tout and his fellow amateurs, perhaps more determinedly because of this incident. In 1916, Sapir, as Canada's ranking anthropologist, was asked by President Frank Fairchild Wesbrook of the University of British Columbia (23 June 1916: NMM) whether Hill-Tout would make a suitable head for an academic department of anthropology:

I was afraid that perhaps being self-trained and having undertaken work in a relatively new field of his subject that it would be taking a risk to place him at the head of a department in our University, which, although new, has set itself high standards.

Sapir replied (29 June 1916: NMM) in terms of the long-range academic goals of the institution, emphasizing professional standards over curriculum content:

As to the first incumbent of the new position, should it be established, I should strongly advise that a man be selected who had received thorough training in the science at a University of standing, and who was embued with the university spirit. Many men who have done eminently useful work in anthropology are not thereby necessarily ideally fitted to the charge of an anthropological department in a new and rapidly growing university. . . . To be perfectly frank, I do not think Mr. Hill-Tout would altogether answer the needs of a university.

Sapir preferred to wait to establish an academic program until this could be done in a thoroughly professional manner. Although President Wesbrook may have been surprised at Sapir's hesitancy to enlarge the domain of his discipline on a national scale, he accepted the advice; anthropology at the University of British Columbia began much later.

Sapir and Hill-Tout were, in fact, competitors. Both were authorities on the tribes of British Columbia, and an academic program would inevitably dominate the province's ethnological research. Sapir lacked an academic appointment alongside his museum duties and could not train anthropologists to share his research. During his fifteen years in Canada, Sapir made various attempts to carve out an academic position for himself, first approaching Brock, his superior, to "put anthropological interest in Canada on a somewhat more solid basis" in "at least one of the more solid of Canadian universities" (4 June 1914: NMM). McGill University would be ideal because of its proximity to Ottawa. Brock, however, was content with the existing academically trained staff. The division could not employ more men. Indeed, the argument of urgency in recording dying languages and cultures mitigated against training a self-perpetuating coterie of Canadian anthropologists. McGill, moreover, was located in Montreal where Indian questions were of little immediacy. Even Sapir's willingness to teach one day a week without additional salary, simply for travel expenses, did not make the proposal sufficiently attractive for action.

Sapir then turned to the University of Toronto, also within reasonable commuting distance, where the university was already associated with the Royal Ontario Museum. Although Toronto anthropology was provincial rather than national in scope, President Robert Falconer was supportive in principle, noting that some lectures in anthropology had already been given to arts undergraduates and the public (to Sapir, 10 July 1914: NMM). Sapir proposed a lecture series emphasizing the scope of the discipline rather than concrete facts about particular tribes (to Barbeau, 25 September 1914: NMM). The whole division staff would participate, with Sapir himself covering primitive linguistics. Such a program would have clearly established the scientific preeminence of the Ottawa anthropologists and the scope of Boasian anthropology in Canada. However, implementation was stymied because Toronto was unable to pay travel expenses.

When Sapir again summarized the work of the division in 1912, Hill-Tout was undoubtedly still in his mind. He stressed that the commitment to anthropology had emerged from institutions that preceded him in Canada and portrayed himself not as an innovator but as a civil servant carrying out his duties. Sapir presented his division as the only option to study Canadian aborigines, thereby providing "the necessary background of any comprehensive history of Canada" (1912, 63). The "cultural absorption of the Indian" was urgent beyond the capacities of universities, and required government intervention. The necessary "reasonably high standard in both quality and completeness" of research and publication must go beyond "mere outline sketches of the tribes or culture areas studied."

Exhibits of the Victoria Memorial Museum were not "merely striking or aesthetically effective." Rather (1912, 64), they provided "concrete material" to illustrate aboriginal cultures:

The ideal tribal museum exhibit is not necessarily the one containing a large number of particularly beautiful specimens, but one in which a place is found for every aspect of native culture, where the crude awl or skin scraper is deemed as worthy of attention as the richly ornamented basket or Chilcat blanket.

Sapir insisted that university education was a necessary supplement to government anthropology. He recommended a combination of research and instruction in physical anthropology, philology, sociology, history, and folk psychology as integral to general education. A university should "broaden one's intellectual horizon" and "put one in touch with other forms of thought which are not presented by one's immediate social and economic environment," producing "a critical spirit . . . at the risk, it may be, of demolishing cherished prejudices" (1912, 68).

Sapir explicitly drew upon nationalistic sentiment. Researchers now had to be recruited "from other countries, where systematic attention has been given to this science." But Canadians should prefer anthropologists trained in their own country (1912, 68): "To make science a matter of nationality is, of course, the height of absurdity, but it is natural for a people to want to do its share of the scientific work being carried on within its own territories." Sapir was prepared to develop institutions for Canadian anthropology, emphasizing the ramifications for the concept of Canadian citizenship. Early in his Ottawa appointment, Sapir already stressed communicating with the Canadian intelligentsia, optimistically assuming they would share his priorities for research and education. Sapir was prepared to preach to a whole society on behalf of his program.

Sapir's aspirations received some support within the Geological Survey. Natural science, rather than geology narrowly defined, dominated the survey, which developed specialized branches as its activities expanded (Alcock 1947, 4). George Dawson, director from 1895 to 1901, refused to be constrained by disciplinary boundaries. Next to geology, ethnology was his favorite pastime. He published extensively on British Columbian Indians and was the natural choice of the British Association for the Advancement of Science (BAAS) in 1884 to organize anthropology in Canada (Alcock 1947, 46). Dawson's established reputation in a more developed and highly respected "scientific" discipline permitted him to encourage anthropological work.

Reginald Walter Brock, who hired Sapir, was survey director from 1908–1914 (when he resigned to become a science dean at the University of British Columbia). Brock upgraded the scientific credentials necessary for government service from "natural aptitude" to "professorial qualifications" of a Ph.D. in geology or its equivalent, even if this involved (as it usually did) education abroad (Alcock 1947, 61–63). Brock was responsible for work in botany, zoology, ethnology, and anthropology; "scientists of standing were appointed to these divisions" (Alcock 1947, 64), all of which were held together by their common home in the Victoria Memorial Museum. Under Brock's administration, Sapir knew his work was valued and his values shared.

Public Affairs

As head of the federal government program in anthropology, Sapir frequently found himself a spokesman for native people on a range of social and political issues. Although neither political activist nor applied anthropologist, Sapir, like other Boasians, considered this part of the role of professional anthropologist.[6]

Sapir's first attempt to influence public policy on behalf of Indians followed the death of his interpreter's five-year-old sister in 1914, when he questioned Indian Affairs Commissioner Duncan Campbell

Scott (19 March 1914: NMM) about the quality of medical care available to the Nootka.[7] The local doctor, although told the child's illness was critical, arrived several days later. Sapir, himself a father by this time, was shocked. The long-distance diagnosis turned out to be accurate; the child's tubercular meningitis was not treatable. Although the doctor's cynicism doubtless had realistic roots, Sapir felt he should have tried to help the child.

Sapir accurately noted that the Indians called a doctor only in extreme cases when treatment was unlikely to be of use; nothing "short of active preventive superintendence" would change the situation. Sapir intended no personal criticism of the doctor, who had a substantial white practice as well, but attacked the implicit differential in health care. Sapir thought Scott should take some action. In fact, however, similar conditions prevailed throughout Canada. Scott made no written response to this communication.

Sapir's next appeal to Scott clearly required action. He requested formal procedures to recover eleven treaty belts of wampum, presumably stolen from the Six Nations Iroquois Reserve in Ontario ten years previously (Sapir to Scott, 16 May 1914: NMM). Sapir had learned from Frank Speck that the belts were on display at the University of Pennsylvania in the private collection of George Heye, a trustee of the University Museum where Speck was employed. Sapir stated the evidence legalistically, reflecting prior discussion with Speck about the most effective strategy to return the wampum belts with the least possible repercussion. Sapir was prepared to swear an affidavit that the belts were identical to those illustrated in a scientific paper by William Beauchamp. Beauchamp had traced the belts to a dealer in Chicago known to be "not always very scrupulous about the manner in which he gets or disposes of Indian material." He made several efforts to sell the belts to museums, but "a friend of the Indians" in the New York museum system warned various institutions of the alleged theft. Heye had recently purchased these materials.

Sapir enclosed Speck's letter, including a photo sent to him by the secretary of the Iroquois League at Six Nations. The belts were pictured with the wampum keeper, John Buck, at whose death they had disappeared. Since the Six Nations were not an incorporated body, they could not act on their own behalf to recover their property. Sapir had a signed statement from the chiefs as to the accuracy of the photo and the illegal obtaining of the belts, making the "chain of evidence . . . absolutely complete." Sapir officially requested that Scott, as administrative head of the Department of Indian Affairs, take "the necessary steps" to return the belts. He suggested that Heye be given the facts before any legal action was taken, allowing restitution "without unnecessary unpleasantness to himself." Scott was welcome to use Sapir's name, although Speck could find this "personally inconvenient"—an understatement.

Scott sent Sapir copies of his correspondence with Heye. Sapir's reply (13 November 1914: NMM) noted that the department had been informed of the theft as early as 1900 and had warned the dealer not to dispose of the wampum belts. He offered to obtain evidence of approaches to other museums, making clear his intention to follow through: "I would not be willing to admit that there is the slightest doubt of our full power to recover the stolen property." Heye, a private collector without formal training in anthropology, attempted to forestall action (Sapir to Speck, 11 November 1914: NMM). The belts were returned to Six Nations in 1988 (Fenton, 1988).

This controversy is not unique to the Iroquois or particular museums. There was a considerable market in illegal antiquities in the period and major museums tended to turn a blind eye in the interests of acquiring important specimens for their collections. Successful resolution of such a dispute was, however, extremely rare. Indeed, Scott's willingness to act may have rested on nationalist grounds of recovering Canadian property. Even so, the matter was laborious.

Sapir also became involved in legal issues surrounding the Northwest Coast potlatch[8] ceremony, prohibited by Canadian federal law. Although seldom enforced, the potlatch law threatened government credibility in Indian eyes. As early as 1913, Sapir corresponded with James Teit (18 December: NMM) about scientific support for the efforts of local chiefs to repeal this unpopular law. When Sapir was in Alberni the following year (to Frank Williams, 20 October 1914: NMM), he again attempted action. The local Indian agent preferred to avoid the issue, assuming that the potlatch as an institution would be safer if kept out of the public eye. Sapir, however, was willing to press the Nootka case for cultural autonomy and wrote a statement for the people of Alberni (to Alex Thomas, 14 December 1914: NMM). He agreed to approach the Commissioner of Indian Affairs personally.

Sapir wrote to various colleagues, including Boas, John Swanton of the Bureau, and C. F. Newcombe and Charles Hill-Tout in British Columbia (Sapir to Barbeau, 10 February 1915: NMM): "As a first step in trying to do what I can to see justice done the West Coast Indians, I want to get a number of letters on the potlatch from anthropological experts that have had first-hand experience with the institution."

To Boas, Sapir (19 February 1915: NMM) emphasized the seriousness of his petition and lack of response to date: "I do not know if you are aware that there is a good deal of trouble again about the potlatch law. When I was out in Alberni the Indians were very much disturbed at the renewed rigor with which the old more or less dead letter potlatch law was being applied." Moreover, the Kwakiutl of Albert Bay had appealed to the House of Commons to allow the potlatch exchange of ceremonial coppers. Sapir, because he knew the politicians personally, was "very eager that my Division should, if possible, be of direct practical use to the community." Sapir considered writing a "semi-popular" bulletin; the potlatch could not be "summarily condemned even from the white man's standpoint." From the Indian view, the law involved "unnecessary hardship" and "general demoralization," which Boas himself had "pointed out several years ago." Sapir optimistically concluded: "I have no doubt that a systematic presentation of our point of view, with due regard [i.e., lip service] to the general ideas and needs of the public, would do much to assist the Indian."

Boas responded by return mail (to Sapir, 18 February 1915: NMM) with a letter designed for public use, explaining the meaning of a cultural institution unfamiliar to most white men but fully functional in its natural setting:

[A]n abolition of the potlatch system would mean as great hardship to the Indians as the wiping out of all credits would mean to us. The potlatch is essentially the public pay of contracted debts. . . . For the whites to claim that the copper has no value, and to demand that it be discarded . . . would mean a complete pauperization of the Indians.

It was crucial to "preserve the stimulus inherent in the potlatch system." Unfortunately, politicians were not looking for innovative, culturally sensitive solutions. Neither Sapir nor Boas had any effect on the slow winding down of the cultural discrimination imposed upon Canadian native peoples.

Barbeau, who had worked extensively on the Northwest Coast, was asked his opinion by Commissioner Scott (Barbeau to Sapir, 7 July 1920: NMM): "He asked me to inquire informally and report to him, but not to attract the attention of the Indians as to that, it being his intention not to alter the present law." The intervening five years had not essentially changed the situation. Barbeau personally approved the status quo of nonenforcement. At the same time, however, Barbeau's ethnographic data became involved in public debate over the potlatch law. Sapir (to Barbeau, 16 July 1920: NMM) was more concerned over Indian perception of anthropologists than over the law itself:

I hate to make this role so explicit, but I am afraid that if we do not follow it very literally, we will find ourselves drifting into the position of genteel spies for the Department of Indian Affairs. We cannot afford to be misunderstood by any Indians in Canada.

Anthropologists could not do their research without the conviction of individuals and local communities that they were allies in the often traumatic process of living within a larger white society. Both by professional commitment and personal sense of fairness, Sapir took this stance seriously. He was an elitist, but his elitism was based on intellect rather than financial or social status; to dismiss rights that Edward Sapir enjoyed as a matter of course for any other group of individuals was unconscionable—whatever the associated political circumstances. Sapir was an idealist, and perhaps a better politician for it, albeit not always a practical one.

Sapir urged Barbeau (10 December 1920: NMM) to prepare a pamphlet on the potlatch, based on his prior fieldwork and designed to encourage division input into Department of Indian Affairs policy. Because the department was composed of civil servants rather than scientists, the scientists had an obligation to make accurate information available within the range of their professional competence. Such was dutifully done, though no dramatic effects ensued.

In the winter of 1917–1918, Commissioner Scott approached Sapir with a scheme to introduce a basket industry on the Northwest Coast, in which Indian elders would teach native crafts in local schools. Sapir responded that the project involved far more than "mere sentimentality" (to Scott, 20 December 1917: NMM): "I see no reason why distinctively Indian handicrafts and art work should not be rescued from the category of mere tourists' curios and raised to that of industrially and aesthetically desirable objects." Sapir even urged his local collaborator James Teit (18 April 1918: NMM) to devote his time to this project, and, simultaneously, encouraged Scott to rely on Teit's knowledge of the local situation (18 April 1918: NMM):

His acquaintance, however, with Indian handicrafts is so detailed and accurate, his popularity with the Indians so great, and his sympathy for them so cordial, that I am sure he would very soon develop the necessary business technique for the handling of industrial work.

This would also, incidentally, ensure Teit's continuing employment as an ethnologist and local collector. Sapir's policy placed the scientific skills of his division at the disposal of native communities as well as the federal government. In fact, if anything, the latter was the less comfortable obligation.

Sapir was particularly concerned with the loss of native craft skills, especially when well-meaning school teachers demeaned traditional culture (to Scott, 18 April 1918: NMM):

It is clear that with progressive contact with whites, the Indians tend to lose all respect not only for what is relatively crude or barbaric in their culture, but also for what is of distinct merit and worthy of preservation. It is a particularly melancholy sight to see how rapidly the native handicrafts of the Indians are disappearing.

The proposed project combined "industrial" practicality and moral "heartening" because: "It is the complete cutting off of the younger members from the older generations and what that generation stands for that is largely accountable for the loss of heart among the Indians as a whole. It is perhaps not too late in many cases to teach the Indians respect for what is best in their own culture." Unfortunately, the project was abortive.

The Tribulations of Museum Anthropology

All division fieldwork involved obligation to acquire specimens of material culture and ceremonial life. During his first year, Sapir dutifully catalogued the acquisition of "upwards of 90" Nootka items for the projected ethnological museum. The museum mandate justified fieldwork and Sapir was conscientious in collecting.

By 1911, Sapir attacked the more general question of his curatorial duties. He unpacked all the specimens acquired by the division from various government projects and private donations, sorting them into five culture areas, with physical anthropology and archaeology separate. Sapir personally devised a cataloguing system to reflect the natural classification of ethnological materials, deciding "to renumber the whole collection according to a definitely established scheme" (1912, 379). He catalogued accessions personally since no one else was available to do so.

Sapir immediately tried to balance representation of Canadian tribes. West coast and Eskimo materials were abundant, with little from eastern Canada except the Iroquois (where Chief John Gibson had a standing order for ethnographic material). The greatest gap was Northern Athabaskan. Materials were ready for exhibition whenever exhibition cases arrived. Moreover, lantern slides had been prepared for public lectures related to the specimens. The new director took his duties very seriously.

The annual report for 1912 emphasized that cases and exhibit space were inadequate. The exhibits to be installed in 1913 would have to be restricted to Eastern Woodlands, Eskimo, and West Coast groups, "besides a synoptic survey of the archaeology of the Dominion" (1913, 448). Expected Plains and Plateau-Mackenzie materials would require another exhibition hall. Two totem poles had been installed outside the building, and a high gallery would be needed for the third. Sapir also began his agitation for a museum preparator, preferably also a mechanic, to ensure proper care of existing materials. He noted (1914, 448) that the "purely scientific and office work of the staff" made it impossible for them to continue to do this adequately. In a single year, 1500 specimens had been acquired, largely Iroquoian. A collection of photographs from division fieldwork had been started. Sapir, Barbeau, Goldenweiser, and Teit had collected song recordings, and Jacob Sapir was transcribing these as a supplement to ethnological materials.

The Hall of Canadian Anthropology opened to the public in 1913. Ethnological exhibits were arranged by Sapir's culture area scheme of the previous year. Tribal labels were in place but not specific ones with "scientific knowledge" of use to the public and "the special student." The annual report laboriously recorded the contents of cases and their arrangement in the hall. Canoes were suspended from the ceiling but considerable wall space remained. Sapir started: "No attempt has been made to crowd all of the anthropological material owned by the Survey into the rather limited exhibition at its command" (1914, 358). Rather, material was selected to "give the public a general idea of the culture of the more important tribes of Canada, and of the range of implements and other objects in use among the natives." The balance was carefully stored for exhibit at some future time.

By 1914, there was no space for further exhibits, although (1915, 168): "A number of striking objects of ethnological interest have been placed on top of the cases." A special exhibit on British Columbia basketry now adorned the museum entrance hall and the Iroquois exhibit was fully labeled. Acquisitions continued to be considerable. But the effects of World War I were already being felt. Sapir noted "a falling off due primarily to the necessity induced by the European war of economizing in expenditures" (1916, 265). The situation deteriorated further in 1916 when the museum building was closed to the public so Parliament could meet in it (after its previous building was destroyed by fire). Only a few specimens were purchased.

World War I ended Sapir's active and optimistic museum stewardship. Little has directly remained, although Sapir's inventories, "ingenious" numbering systems for collections, and personally handwritten accession cards reflect the amount of energy he devoted to this aspect of his job (Fenton 1986). Sapir reported to various colleagues that he felt guilty that he did not spend more time on museum work. His own research, of course, was linguistic and ethnological, and only peripherally related to his museum function.[9] Nonetheless, Sapir had a healthy respect for facts, ethnographic and otherwise.

Sapir's principles of museum arrangement and administration were Boasian. Boas had revolutionized the North American notion of the museum as an evolutionary sequence of tool types and cultures arranged without regard for cultural setting. This dispute came to a head with Otis T. Mason of the United States National Museum in Washington (Stocking 1968). Boas argued lyrically that exhibits should be dioramas of material objects in use by appropriately costumed models of native people. Such exhibits were more realistic and comprehensible both to the public and the serious student because the meaning of artifacts was lost if they were wrenched from their context. Although Boas severed his ties to the American Museum in 1905, the legacy of his exhibit principles remains there and is now standard in North American museums.

Boas also emphasized multiple functions of exhibited objects. Although research was a legitimate goal of museum work, closest to the heart of the scientist/curator, entertainment and instruction were also legitimate museum functions. The same exhibit had to answer multiple needs of various audiences. Further collections could be retained for research purposes. The danger was that the museum, especially if not under direct charge of scientists, would dedicate itself to the mere acquisition of material objects, omitting the research necessary to re-construct and preserve their context (Boas 1907). Although Boas of-ten found himself at loggerheads with powerful museum trustees and administrators, he continued to argue that museums were an integral part of the growth of anthropology.

Sapir had imbibed this crusading spirit along with his introduction to anthropology. Many of his Columbia courses had met at the Amer-ican Museum in order to use its collections in teaching. Certainly, Columbia itself had no comparable laboratory facilities. Fieldwork was also a museum resource. Sapir hoped his Ottawa position would en-able him to avoid the conflicting priorities which troubled larger and more established museums. As the "boss," at least for anthropology, he could build up adequate collections, using his staff as a documen-tary team. In principle, of course, this was a near ideal way to pursue anthropological research.

In practice, however, Sapir wanted to concentrate on linguistics and ethnology. He chafed under the restrictions of his museum duties and felt that an academic position would offer better outlets for his special talents. As the euphoria of the initial years declined and Sapir realized that the financial resources available to him were unlikely to keep pace with the program of exhibits and accessions which he envisioned, his disenchantment grew.

Boas, unsurprisingly, found Sapir's attitude unrealistic and inap-propriate to the larger needs of the discipline. After all, Boas had placed Sapir in this position and correctly assumed he would develop a museum devoted to research as well as collecting. Ottawa joined the growing number of North American museums organized according to Boasian principles. There was little likelihood that any successor to Sapir would have enough political power to maintain this policy. Boas was, therefore, understandably prone to lecture his former student that, regardless of his preference for other kinds of work, he was well off relative to many of his peers and unjustified in shirking his ad-ministrative responsibility. Boas's position is explicit in a long letter to Sapir (2 January 1914: NMM):

I heard with concern a few days ago that you are considering leaving the Canadian work and taking a position in a museum, hoping that in this way you may be relieved of administrative duties and give more time to research-work.

I believe that any step of this kind would be the mistake of your life. I do not know whether you have a clear impression of the character of museum work in the United States; but I feel quite certain that I judge it correctly, partly from my own experience, partly from what I see people doing who are employed by museums. The fundamental difficulty that you would find everywhere is that all purely scientific work . . . would have to be done as a side issue, and that the essential interest of the museum is not exploration, but the exhibit, and ordinarily the popular exhibit. . . .

I understand from your previous remarks that the administrative work that you have to do in Canada worries you and is not particularly sympathetic to you; but please do not believe that in any position that you may take, you will be relieved of this kind of work in one form or another, least of all in a museum position. At present you are to a very great extent your own master. You have succeeded in establishing a great many lines of important research; and, as I am inclined to look at it, your success in establishing this work brings with it the responsibility of its future development. . . . I have been happy to think that during all of these years [four] while you were in Ottawa you have gone straight ahead according to what seemed to me sane and safe scientific principles, without yielding unduly to the clamor for premature popularization, which is the bane of our science. For this reason, I should consider it a misfortune for anthropology if you were to give up because the organization of your work entails a certain amount of work which is irksome to you. . . . I envy all you younger men the opportunity for work, which I never enjoyed . . . with ample opportunities for original research, with the possibility of stimulating the research work in many different lines, and with a moderate amount of administrative duties. I can, of course, feel with you that you might like to devote all your time to research work; but there is no position in existence in which this end could possibly be attained. . . . In short, unless you are in a financial position to free yourself entirely from the conditions of remunerative positions . . .

Sapir was, of course, in no such position and Boas knew it. Sapir had a vague idea that a museum position in Chicago with someone else in charge of administration would ease his burdens, allowing more time for writing and providing congenial colleagues to talk to. Boas recognized that this was remarkably naive. That he was so restrained in his admonitions is an acknowledgment of his personal respect for Sapir and sympathy for his frustrations. Nonetheless, Sapir needed perspective to get on with his program. Whatever his immediate reaction to this implicit lecture from his mentor, Sapir did so.

CHAPTER FOUR

The Ottawa Research Team

Sapir had great authority in his new position, which led to considerable curiosity among his Boasian peers. Kroeber, who was forced to contend with vicissitudes of funding from private patrons and conflicts between museum and university priorities (Thoresen 1975), posed a jocular inquiry overlaid with acidity (1 June 1911: NMM): "I am much pleased, by the way, to hear of your multiplying activity and its evidence of resources at your command. Are you running the others, or are you all coordinately taking orders from some non-anthropological authority?" Comparison of their positions was implicit; Sapir had certainly come into his own since his departure from California. Kroeber dominated research in California, but Sapir was in charge of an entire country, with little direct supervision.

The only model available to Sapir was that of the Bureau of American Ethnology, with its emphasis on cooperative projects beyond the scope of a single scholar. Sapir, however, developed a unique administrative style. He was inclined to let the members of his research staff retain individuality in working style and career progression. But membership in the Boasian inner circle also predisposed him to expect loyalty to a social network and substantive disciplinary commitment. Sapir was a laissez-faire administrator, firmly committed to scientific goals but pursuing them through the particular skills and interests of a diverse research team. He demonstrated remarkably little personal ego, confident enough in his own abilities to feel no threat from colleagues or subordinates. Power for its own sake did not interest him.

Sapir saw himself as a member of the research team, as well as its leader. His own researches during his fifteen-year tenure in Ottawa meshed his personal agenda with the need of the division to map the aboriginal languages and cultures of Canada. His annual reports illustrate that the overall plan was far from haphazard. He attempted to familiarize himself with a range of Canadian Indians so that he could supervise more detailed work by others. The role of the chief ethnologist was to relate particular researches to larger goals. Many of the staff were part-time or short-range because of financial constraints and necessarily lacked Sapir's perspective. For all his frustration with day-to-day administrative problems, Sapir excelled at this more abstract portion of his work. The achievements of the division grew directly from his tenacity, long-range planning, and effective public presentation of the division and its program.

Sapir's first priority was to cover the full scope of Boasian anthropology. Harlan Smith was responsible for archaeology, largely on a survey basis. Francis Knowles, the physical anthropologist, suffered from ill health, which eventually led to his resignation. In practice, therefore, the research team concentrated on ethnology, with linguistics tacitly reserved for Sapir himself.

The work of the division was organized primarily according to culture area. Sapir was already a specialist in languages of the Northwest Coast. He inherited a program in Eskimo ethnology and quickly initiated work with the Iroquoian and Algonquian peoples of the Eastern Woodlands. The gaps he hoped to fill were the Plains and the Northern Athabaskans. Various fieldworkers participated in these researches.

The Canadian Arctic Expedition was jointly sponsored by the Geological Survey of Canada, the predecessor and umbrella organization of Sapir's own program, and the American Museum in New York. By 1911, when Sapir's first annual report appeared, the expedition had been in the Arctic for over three years. Sapir, although he had no direct Eskimo experience, became the administrative superior of the project by default. His annual report for 1911 (1912, 390) laconically quoted V. Stefansson's letter, noting that the original ethnological mandate of the expedition was complete. Stefansson sent parts of his unfinished report and remained in the field. Sapir presented the preliminary report without comment (1913, 452).

Privately, however, Sapir approached Roland Dixon, Kroeber's collaborator on California languages, about Stefansson's reputation as a student at Harvard. Dixon (17 November 1911: NMM) reported himself unable to separate the man's scientific work from his character. Stefansson had nearly been dismissed over his marking procedures as a teaching assistant and for borrowing money from fellow students. More seriously, Boas had been astonished at his "ignorance" of the Eskimo language after his first trip. Lack of linguistic training was an inadequate excuse for Dixon or Boas. This candid reference decreased Sapir's enthusiasm for his unchosen bedfellow; unsurprisingly, Stefansson was never invited to join the Ottawa research team.

Stefansson was replaced in the new Arctic Expedition of 1913–1916 by Diamond Jenness, recommended to Sapir by Marius Barbeau, a former classmate at Oxford. Sapir appreciated Jenness's conscientious reports to the home office and acknowledged that the expedition had thrown light on "the problem of the diffusion of the different branches of the Eskimo race" (1915, 174). After three years in Arctic, Jenness returned to the division with a permanent appointment.[1] Sapir was impressed by his work on Eskimo dialects (1916, 270) and willingly allowed this reliable, untemperamental colleague—who became a close personal friend—to pursue his own work.

A systematic research program in eastern Canada was underway in 1911, which would ultimately include work by Marius Barbeau, Alexander Goldenweiser, Cyrus MacMillan, William Mechling, and Frederick Waugh. Sapir himself made a survey field trip with Frank Speck in 1911 to familiarize himself with Iroquoian and Algonquian languages so he could supervise work by his research team in these areas.

Barbeau attempted a salvage ethnography of the Huron and Wyandot, with more impressive results than could have been predicted, given the "widely accredited barrenness of this field of research, owing to the advanced state of civilization prevailing among the few hundred dispersed descendants of the once numerous Huron tribes of Ontario" (1912, 381). Barbeau stressed individual informants because preservation of cultural material was so dependent on their memories. Huron linguistics, however, was not reported "for lack of time . . . notwithstanding that considerable attention has been directed to it" (1912, 385). Under Sapir's direction, linguistic standards were stringent.

Barbeau continued fieldwork and writing on this project until 1914, when he became interested in French Canadian folk tales among the modern Huron and "what influence, if any, European folk-lore has exerted on the content and form of native mythology" (Sapir 1915, 172). Increasingly thereafter, Barbeau, himself French Canadian, worked on the folklore of Quebec. Sapir considered this within the scope of anthropology, though he worried that outside observers might consider the Division to be exceeding its mandate. He, therefore, proposed to Barbeau (7 October 1918: NMM) that "some permanent Canadian organization, such as might well be found in the Province of Quebec, would be the logical development of the work that you have inaugurated." Barbeau took this advice, becoming involved with American folklorists and establishing a folklore archive in Quebec, as well as a separate research division in Ottawa.[2]

Alexander Goldenweiser worked on Iroquoian social organization from 1911–1914, while employed as a lecturer at Columbia. He was primarily a theoretician,[3] and this was the only fieldwork of his long career. Sapir greatly admired "Goldie's" intellectual capacities and held great hope for a more balanced approach (to Wallis, 15 March 1913: NMM): ". . . he may have had the tendency, up till recently, to devote too little attention to mere hard facts, but I believe that he is very rapidly getting over that tendency since he has spent so much time on field work among the Iroquois." Goldie was, however, secretive about his material and unwilling or unable to write up his results as required by the Ottawa appointment.[4] Whatever his virtues as a friend, Goldenweiser was an administrative nightmare for Sapir. The absence of field reports did the program little good in the eyes of superiors who were not anthropologists and valued personal reliability over ethnographic quality or scientific creativity. Sapir was not good at forcing people to do things they did not want to do.

Goldenweiser (along with Paul Radin and Wilson Wallis) provided Sapir with the equivalent of teaching—a constant stream of the brightest young men from the Boasian program. He served them as something between father confessor and administrative facilitator, though he was little older than most of them. He preferred to hire intellectual mavericks whose minds attracted him. Many of them were summer researchers who returned to New York, Boston, Philadelphia, or San Francisco in the intervals between fieldwork, and they helped Sapir maintain contact with the mainstream of his discipline.

Goldie insisted on approaching the Iroquois in his own terms, pronouncing Sapir's efforts to organize team research as "impertinent" (to Sapir, 15 April 1912: NMM). He considered topic boundaries untenable and extended his work on social organization to medicine, dreams, and prophecies. Goldie wanted to study Iroquoian linguistics and Sapir wanted him (28 March 1912: NMM) to use grammar only "to enable you to handle your ethnological material properly." Linguistics was Sapir's jealously guarded prerogative in the division.

The death of Goldie's major informant, Chief John Gibson, in 1912 left considerable incomplete material, especially song texts, and translations.[5] Sapir, under pressure from his own superiors to show "more definite and businesslike" arrangements with his contract staff, preached to Goldie about accumulating unanalyzed material from the field (to Goldenweiser, 6 November 1912; 13 May 1913: NMM). After three seasons of fieldwork without written results, Sapir was hesitant to renew Goldie's contract, realizing that this could jeopardize his entire research program (27 March 1914: NMM). Sapir attempted to shift the onus to Brock, noting that geologists wrote up their reports promptly. He had tried to explain that "one cannot easily finish up a large topic, such as social orgnization, in limited time, but needs to work along several lines simultaneously, trip after trip." The administrative issue was never resolved satisfactorily.

Another researcher was Cyrus MacMillan, an English professor at McGill, who had no formal training in anthropology and who studied the Micmac for the Division in 1911; he was not rehired. He compared his stories to European folklore rather than analyzing them in their own terms. Moreover, MacMillan's work overlapped with that of Wilson Wallis for the University of Pennsylvania. Sapir declined involvement in the dispute between the two (to Wallis, 23 October 1911: NMM), suggesting that they proceed independently to publication. He also solicited Wallis's opinion about MacMillan, noting that he failed to send manuscripts and was unbusinesslike with the survey. Wallis (to Sapir, 18 July 1912: NMM) attempted to give MacMillan the benefit of doubt because he was willing to learn. Unfortunately, he had little rapport with the Indians, and his interest was more literary than ethnographic. Sapir eventually decided not to publish his material on grounds of overlap with more complete work by others (Bernier 1984, 403).

William Mechling, Sapir's student from Pennsylvania, studied the Micmac and Malecite from 1911–1913. He concentrated on songs and trained several Micmac speakers to write their own language. In 1912–1915, Frederick Waugh worked on Iroquois material culture. No systematic summary of the Eastern Algonquian work was ever presented, however.

From 1912–1915, Boasian maverick Paul Radin worked on the Ojibwa, in an effort to fill in major gaps in knowledge of the Canadian

Plains tribes. Radin was Sapir's closest friend among his fellow Boasians. Helen Sapir Larson recalls Radin's generosity, sociability, and humor and that he "turned up wherever we lived." Radin combined joie de vivre, sparkling intellect, and oblivion to the practicalities of the everyday world. Lowie (1965, 70) described him as "one of the most colorful figures in his generation—a gay, intelligent, lovable, civilized wanderer in anthropology and adjoining fields." Radin never held any employment for long, but his association with the Geological Survey of Canada was the most tranquil of his efforts to do so. Sapir, who appreciated the sensitive quality of his fieldwork and his commitment to massive recording of ethnological data, willingly tolerated his haphazard attitude toward the bureaucratic side of his position. Only the financial cutbacks of World War I forced Sapir to terminate his appointment.

Radin, an incorrigible gossip, provided Sapir with an outlet for his less orthodox sentiments about colleagues and the narrowness of disciplinary boundaries. Radin believed that the emerging Boasian paradigm was a dead end because Boas lacked imagination and was too little concerned with history (to Sapir, 27 January 1914: NMM). History, in Radin's view, involved "complete, comprehensive and systematic interpretation" of cultural materials. As Sapir's own interests broadened to include the study of the individual within culture (see chap. 7), Radin provided stimulus and feedback.

Radin, for all his commitment to detailed ethnography, did little to map the languages and cultures of the Plains. Sapir sent Waugh to the Ojibwa in 1916 but this work was never completed; Wilson Wallis visited the Manitoba Sioux in 1914. Wallis found "a conservative people, rich in ethnological data and in material culture" (Sapir 1915, 173). When Wallis had difficulty overcoming factionalism, Sapir (24 June 1914: NMM) recommended hiring "your most bitter enemies" to alleviate their jealousy. He also wrote officially (24 June 1914: NMM) to reassure the Indians that Wallis had the official backing of the Canadian government and that Sapir personally would appreciate their cooperation with him: "We think the Dakota will have as long and complete a story as any other tribe of Indians. There is nothing about it except that [Wallis] wants to get all the story about the Dakota and find out about their ways."

Wallis was trained in philosophy and anthropology under R. R. Marrett at Oxford. While studying philosophy at Pennsylvania from 1911–1914, he attended Boas's seminars in New York, meeting Sapir,

Goldenweiser, Lowie, and Radin (Spencer and Colson 1971: 258), and was drawn into fieldwork for the Ottawa division. Sapir was intrigued by his eclectic and theoretical sociology. Although funding precluded further Sioux work, the two men became friends, and Sapir often used Wallis as a sounding-board for ideas that were unconventional in the Boasian model.

To Wallis, who had no formal training in linguistics, Sapir made his most explicit statement of the need for linguistics in ethnography (10 June 1913: NMM):

It is highly useful, I think, for one making sociological studies among primitive peoples, to know enough about linguistic matters to take down Indian words and even texts with reasonable accuracy. . . . it is always highly important, even from a strictly sociological point of view, to ascertain the native classification. . . . Aside from this special point of relationship terms, there are, of course, many other topics which are not easy to get except through the medium of native terminology. Songs and much of social organization and religion generally can hardly be got at otherwise. I have always been struck by a certain externality about all such studies that were not based on linguistic knowledge. I always have an uneasy feeling that misunderstandings bristle in such writing. . . . to look at it somewhat more broadly, what we are after in studying primitive peoples is, to a large extent, to get their system of classification. This scheme must be more or less reflected in their own language.

I think that one can do a great deal with linguistic material even if one is not out for a linguistic study as such, though one generally finds, on getting into the work, that it is hard to avoid getting into grammatical analysis if one wishes to control the text material adequately.

Sapir realized that his position distinguished his anthropology from that of other Boasians. For example, he wrote to Speck (11 June 1912: NMM): "Oh well, I suppose I'm a crank on linguistics" and to Lowie (26 October 1920: UCB) that ethnology without linguistics produced over-generality—"vague statements worked up schematically make good sociological arguments, but cui bono?" Sapir was determined that the work of the Ottawa division would reflect his own linguistic sophistication or would restrict itself to conventional ethnography.[6]

Very little was known about the Northern Athabaskan tribes of the Mackenzie and Yukon, partly because few anthropologists were willing to brave the climate and cultural impoverishment.[7] In 1912, Sapir obtained the services of James Teit, a former Boas informant who served as an interpreter for Indian delegations to Ottawa. Teit was willing to extend his work on Salish tribal boundaries (Northwest Coast) further north and carry out "what is expected to be a thorough reconnaissance of the comparatively little known" Northern Athabaskans (Sapir 1913, 452).

Although Teit had no training in linguistics, Sapir wanted him to collect vocabularies for comparative purposes (to Goddard, 29 February 1912: NMM). He approached Pliny Goddard, North America's foremost Athabaskanist, for basic vocabulary items likely to have significance for historical reconstruction. Teit could obtain "enough lexical and other comparative material to afford a sound basis for classification of tribes and dialects, rather than to make thoroughgoing linguistic studies for their own sake" (Sapir to Teit, 18 November 1912: NMM). Ethnographic questions were harder to formulate because the basic ethnography was unknown; Sapir suggested (21 December 1912: NMM) that Teit simply adapt his Salish questionnaire. After carrying out a survey of the area, Teit should return to "a more elaborate study of some one typical tribe" (18 January 1913: NMM). Sapir (to Jenness, 5 August 1930: NMM) was convinced that linguistic analysis of continuous texts were the only possible approach to Athabaskan linguistics:

One cannot hope to do serious work with these badly disintegrated Athabaskan tribes of the north unless one uses the linguistic approach. I doubt whether direct questioning on ethnological matters leads to much. One might still be able to obtain something if one followed up the hints given in personal narratives of various kinds.

Teit might be able to do such work after his survey.

Teit defied Ottawa bureaucratic categorizations, falling somewhere between a native informant, to whom the government would acknowledge no obligation for continuous employment, and a scientist on a par with the rest of Sapir's research team. In 1915, Teit took time out from his Ottawa contract to work for Boas, which Sapir considered "impolitic" of Boas (Sapir to Teit, 5 March: NMM). Sapir professed not to care who the material was collected for but noted that Teit's "economic advantage" lay in a continuing contract; the change of employer was "embarrassingly difficult to explain" to his superiors.

Sapir argued (to R. G. McConnell, n.d.; 27 May 1918: NMM) that "it has been understood right along that Mr. Teit's connection with the Survey as an outside service man" would be renewable indefinitely. Teit was "well known in anthropological circles as a careful scientific student." Sapir only gained a small sum for past fieldwork, with the case having to be remade the following year (to Teit, 5 June 1918). Thereafter, Sapir could only purchase completed manuscripts (to Teit, 18 July 1918: NMM).

In 1913, Sapir hired his Pennsylvania student, John Alden Mason, for a "preliminary reconnaissance" at the eastern end of the Mackenzie, supplementing Teit's work further west. Sapir (to Boas, 23 September 1912: NMM) wanted to "get someone who would be willing to stay quite a long time with the Indians, in other words, winter in the country." The Indians were busy and moved frequently during the normal summer field season. Moreover, the simple Athabaskan cultures did not attract collectors of art, artifacts, or folklore. Mason was ideal because of its prior experience with a relatively simple culture, the Southwestern Ute he had studied with Sapir in 1909.

Sapir was pleased with Mason's linguistic results, museum specimens, and phonographic records. Mason was forced, however, to inquire (n.d. 1913: APS) as to the purpose of his trip, noting that Sapir had always taught him that field work should have a specific goal. The tone was humorous, but Sapir declined to share his overview of the Athabaskan survey, as he did with Teit. Nonetheless, he expected this work to "break the back of Athabaskan ethnology" (to Teit, 18 November 1912: NMM).

Sapir's last attempt to cover the Northern Athabaskan area was an informal collaboration with Father Gabriel Morice, a longtime missionary to the Carrier Indians. Sapir was, in fact, more willing to use competent observers without professional training than either Boas or Kroeber. Long contact was important, and language was more impervious to subjective interpretation than other parts of culture.

Morice initiated the relationship, writing enthusiastically to Sapir (13 October 1914: NMM) about his Chasta Costa phonology, based on brief work in Oregon years earlier. Sapir was still modest about his Athabaskanist achievements but appreciated recognition of his generalization from limited data. He expected the full Carrier grammar to be "one of our most authoritative studies" of an Indian language (to Morice, 16 November 1917: NMM). Sapir (21 January 1918: NMM) was eager to aid in completing and publishing the manuscript. Morice (to Sapir, 2 February 1919: NMM) simply wanted his work to appear during his lifetime. Sapir interceded with Boas, whom Morice was hesitant to approach on his own (to Sapir, 14 February 1919: NMM). Boas was offended that anyone should find him unapproachable or less than objective in his evaluation of scientific work (to Sapir,

28 February 1919: NMM): "I do not see why Father Morice should hesitate to write to me." Neither Sapir nor Boas were immediately able to provide publication but both accepted the importance of the work.

Sapir's Ottawa Fieldwork

As head of the Ottawa division, Sapir expected to do almost unlimited fieldwork. The apparent Canadian government commitment to Indian administration based on sound scientific advice from the anthropologists in its employ seemed to reflect a consistent long-range policy. There was no reason to believe that the research team, whatever staff might be added to its ranks, would run out of Indians. This urgency to record disappearing cultures was crucial to Sapir's initial attraction to anthropology. In Ottawa, he could put it into practice.

Moreover, Sapir was enthusiastic about firsthand contact with any new language. Virtually from the first day of any fieldwork, he formulated hypotheses about linguistic structure. He tested and refined these, to be sure, but also had strong and immediate intuitions for the unique structure of each language. He had no standard elicitation format. He took Sundays off to give his informants a rest, but he was happiest with this change of pace when he could work on another language in this otherwise useless "spare time." Sapir enjoyed fieldwork and established excellent rapport, trying to understand how native speakers saw the world. Linguists, of course, necessarily work closely with a few individuals. Sapir preferred informants whose English was sufficient for accurate translation and who themselves had intuition for the structure of their native language. This ability was crucial in teaching Indians to write their language and record additional texts. Without such collaboration, Sapir could hardly have produced such extensive corpora of texts and subsequent analysis in the periods available to him in the field. At the time, an Amerindian linguist might expect to work, as Sapir did, on twenty or more languages during his career. Sapir was unique, not for the number of languages he studied, but for the amount of information he managed to extract from each encounter with a new language.

Sapir's first action in Ottawa was to initiate an ethnological and linguistic survey of the Nootka of Vancouver Island. Just under four months was devoted to this initial effort to fill a major gap in the otherwise well-known Northwest Coast. Although Sapir used the term "survey,"[8] meeting the mapping goals of his general mandate, he immediately delimited his project to a more manageable magnitude (1911, 284). Nootka "life and thought" was exceedingly complex as well as being variable among the Nootka tribes. Sapir visited many villages briefly and thereafter concentrated his study in Alberni, British Columbia.

In his first annual report in 1911, he acknowledged that his primary aim was linguistic. The Nootka language was "one of considerable phonetic difficulty and complexity of structure." Ethnological and mythological texts were recorded phonetically and interpreted word for word with additional grammatical material elicited to clarify them. Sapir wrote: "Such texts are valuable not only from a linguistic standpoint, as they illustrate native speech in actual idiomatic use, but also from a strictly ethnological standpoint, expressing, as they do, the native point of view in matters of custom and belief." This explicit relationship between ethnological and linguistic data would characterize the entire Ottawa research program.

Moreover, only after detailing the methods of his Nootka study did Sapir's first annual report raise the presumable reason for choosing the Nootka—that is, to shed light on the linguistic relationship of Nootka and Kwakiutl, proposed by Boas in the 1890s under the rubric of Wakashan. Adequate description was ideally prior to cross-linguistic comparison.

Sapir explored various ethnological topics and attended native ceremonies, reporting with some smugness (1911, 285) that "during part of the performance I was the only white man allowed to be present," recorded sixty-seven songs (which were being transcribed by J. D. Sapir), and dutifully collected museum specimens. In spite of the productivity of this initial Nootka foray, however, Sapir served notice that his work was merely "a satisfactory beginning . . . of a scientific study of the Nootka Indians" (1911, 285); several seasons of fieldwork would be necessary for "anything like a complete account of these Indians."

In 1911, however, Sapir postponed the Nootka project in favor of "a reconnaissance of several of the more readily accessible Iroquois and Algonkin reserves of Ontario and Quebec" (1912, 380). Six days at Grand River Reserve in Brantford, Ontario, were devoted largely to Seneca and Mohawk (Iroquoian) linguistic work. More Mohawk data was obtained at Caughnawaga in Quebec; unsurprisingly, Sapir identified a separate Mohawk dialect. He was explicit, however, that such limited exposure to these languages could only produce "phonetic insight;" grammar was "quite impossible" in the time available (1912, 380).

Sapir made the somewhat naive assumption that all previous recorders of Iroquoian languages were inadequately trained and therefore inaccurate. His statement that "most, if not all, attempts at recording Iroquois" were "notably lacking in this regard" (1912, 380) considerably exaggerates the importance of his dabbling in a well-established field. Further, there is no evidence that Sapir familiarized himself with existing Iroquoian linguistics, either before or after this superficial fieldwork.

Sapir was quite content to leave Iroquoian linguistics to Barbeau, although he advised Barbeau on his Iroquois radicals paper (where his influence on Barbeau's phonological and morphological treatment is unmistakable) (Michael Foster, p.c.). Sapir did not think highly of Barbeau's linguistic abilities, and Barbeau (1915, 4) undoubtedly understated the case when he acknowledged Sapir's "kind advice on the method followed" in the field and his "collaboration in the study of the comparative phonetics and grammar" of Mohawk, Oneida, and Wyandot. Barbeau had no training to make such comparisons. Although the 1911 field trip gave Sapir confidence in commenting on the Iroquoian work of others, his few published references to Iroquoian are broadly typological and do not reflect his own data.[9]

Sapir also sampled a number of Algonquian languages. An afternoon devoted to Delaware at Grand River Reserve enabled him to generalize about the phonetic specialization of this language. He also recorded some Abenaki, Malecite, Micmac, Montagnais, and Rupert's House Cree, obtaining a useful sense of the relative linguistic positions of Cree and Montagnais (1912, 381): the two were dialects, mutually intelligible from the St. Lawrence Gulf to the Rocky Mountains.

Sapir did not pursue Algonquian interests, although division contract researchers did, especially Mechling. Sapir relied ethnographically on Speck and linguistically on Truman Michelson of the bureau. Indeed, he assured Michelson he wanted firsthand Algonquian exposure only as a baseline for comparative work. When Sapir linked two California languages to Algonquian in 1913, he did not use his own data.

Algonquian was unquestionably the best-known linguistic stock of native North America.[10]

The primary purpose of Sapir's survey, however, was to better supervise the division's planned extensive work in eastern Canada. In practice, Sapir would leave the east to Barbeau, Eskimo to Jenness, and specialize himself in western languages and cultures. Some years later, Sapir explained his philosophy of survey linguistic fieldwork to Wissler (3 October 1920: NMM):

> Of course the linguist may and is likely to want to make a fairly rapid field reconnaissance himself, so as to get a sound phonetic basis and find himself in a position to rightly interpret the published data. My own experience in such matters is that an overhauling at first hand of work done by others is apt to be unexpectedly profitable. (I have only a few hours all told at Haida, for instance, but you would be surprised to know how much of fundamental importance to Na-dene was revealed in those hours. There is, after all, no substitute for direct impressions in linguistics. It is like art. In both fields one may talk a great deal around the subject and, failing direct contact with the source, go far afield.) However, such rapid field reconnaissance . . . would give point of view, perspective, vantage point from which to evaluate what is already more or less adequately recorded.

Men not trained in linguistics missed important points: "A good linguist can find out more, along certain lines, in five hours' honest work than the average ethnologist in six months of weary questioning." Sapir was convinced that linguistics could shed light on ethnology, but was unwilling to let ethnologists do poor quality linguistic work.[11]

In 1912, Sapir's fieldwork was limited to a brief collecting trip in Quebec (1913, 452). James Teit was in Ottawa with an Interior Salish delegation, but Sapir did not use the visiting Indians to expand his repertoire of native languages.

During the fall and winter of 1913–1914, Sapir returned for five months to the Nootka in Alberni, where he was already well known. He taught Alex Thomas and Frank Williams—"two of the more intelligent interpreters" (1915, 172)—to write Nootka phonetically: "This proved of inestimable value, as in this way supplementary text material could be obtained from the Nootka Indians in the absence of the investigator." Sapir could continue his ambitious study without returning constantly to the field. He was, in a sense, the head of another research team of local collaborators guided by his inquiries from Ottawa.

Such collaboration was established Boasian practice. Authorship was held to lie with the anthropologist, the "informant" being understood as a passive instrument for the recording of supposedly objective information. In practice, of course, each individual interpreter had his own axes to grind, a unique point of view toward his own culture.[12] Moreover, since anthropologists often worked at different times with the same native speakers, evaluation of shared informants helped to test the validity and reliability of field results. The personalities and styles of various informants were as well known in the small discipline of anthropology as the cultures they helped to record. Many were, in fact, accorded obituaries in the *American Anthropologist*. By modern standards, the treatment of "informants," a word now considered derogatory by most anthropologists, seems cavalier indeed. By the standards of the period, however, Sapir and his colleagues were scrupulously careful to acknowledge their sources of information. They did not, however, assume a strong native commitment to cultural preservation; that is, they did not expect their consultants to be, or to become, anthropologists. Nonetheless, training of native interpreters by Sapir and other Boasians played a considerable role in the changes that have taken place since.

Characteristically, Sapir's report for 1914 described the Nootka expedition before noting, almost incidentally, "a special investigation of the possible linguistic affiliation" between Athabaskan, Haida, and Tlingit (which he labeled as Na-dene). Sapir considered his comparative papers on American Indian linguistics as part of his division work, although his fieldwork assumed greater importance in his annual administrative reports.

On his second trip to Alberni, Sapir devoted his Sundays to Comox and a few hours to Haida phonetics, to which he hoped to return in terms of Na-dene. In 1915, Sapir organized Nootka texts and worked on the Na-dene linguistic stock (1916, 269).

Sapir entertained four Nass River chiefs in Ottawa, resulting in a fortuitous paper on Tsimshian social organization. He attempted to establish an official policy of regularly using such occasions for anthropological work (Sapir to Scott, 19 February 1915: NMM). In April and May of 1916, for example, two Nass River chiefs and three from interior British Columbia visited Ottawa with Teit. Sapir worked on Nass River, Thompson River, Lilloet, Shuswap, Okanagan, and Kootenay kinship terms. Other members of the division staff also obtained useful results. In 1920, Sapir worked in Ottawa on Haida and

Tsimshian with visiting Indians. Simultaneously, he worked on Nootka texts, many sent by Alex Thomas since his last visit, also reporting laconically (1917, 391) that he "devoted a considerable amount of time to work on various problems of American Indian linguistics."

Ishi: A Brief Return To California

In accord with the mandate of his division, Sapir's fieldwork during the Ottawa years was all related to Canadian languages, with one urgent exception. In the summer of 1915, he returned to California and his long-dormant Yana research (1907–1908) to work with the last surviving member of the Yahi (Southern Yana) tribe. Ishi, named for the word for "man" in his language, was already ill. This was salvage linguistics at its most compelling. Kroeber cabled Sapir (6 September 1911: UCB) that he had "a totally wild" Southern Yana at the museum and Sam Batwi, Sapir's Central Yana informant, could more or less communicate with him. Kroeber offered the services of both Ishi and Batwi if Sapir would come to California. Otherwise, he wanted a list of Yana grammatical elements "for better understanding of language and analyzing of texts." Ishi spoke no English; puzzled local authorities who discovered him were delighted to turn him over to the anthropologists in a kind of protective custody.

Due to misprints in the telegram, Sapir couldn't fully grasp the message but agreed that "the opportunity to work out the dialect thoroughly is not to be neglected. Naturally it is not possible for me to seize the opportunity myself, so I hope that you or someone else in California will take the matter up." He promised to compile a rapid survey of Yana formal [grammatical] elements, though "derivative elements" would take somewhat longer because of their great number. These followed on 11 September (UCB), although Sapir feared Kroeber would have trouble using the stem lists in isolation because he didn't know the grammar. Sapir's opinion of the linguistic talents available in San Francisco was not high. Kroeber (to Sapir, 12 September 1911: UCB) reported that either the dialects were quite different or Batwi had forgotten much of his Southern Yana. Communication between him and Ishi proceeded "only imperfectly." Batwi (Kroeber to Sapir, 7 October 1911: UCB) "is too old to make himself acquainted very readily with a new form of speech" but Ishi would be "delighted to be able to talk Yana with you."

Sapir's enthusiasm increased somewhat as he "had seen quite a good deal about Ishi in newspaper clippings that various friends had sent me." The "almost absolute wildness" intrigued Sapir. He predicted, however, "slow work" until Ishi could provide English glosses (a feat he never mastered).

Kroeber impatiently reported that Ishi learned "no English whatever" in his first two months at the museum and convinced himself that only Sapir could communicate with Ishi in Yana (18 November 1911: UCB):

His language would be an easy matter for anyone half familiar with northern Yana, and I wish that we could put some time at your disposal. He is perfectly tractable. It does not seem to enter his head that a better means of communication between himself and us is called for.

Kroeber continued to send data and progress reports, attempting to further intrigue Sapir. Sapir (27 November 1911: UCB) thanked Kroeber for the "flattering" remarks and agreed to help analytically when his own Yana material was nearer completion.

Waterman was somewhat more forthright about the urgency of Sapir's involvement (to Sapir, 23 December 1911: NMM):

If we could get your name connected with this Yana I wouldn't feel so foolish about the "discovery" of him. I'm sure you would find the material valuable, both linguistically and from the cultural point of view. Sam Batwee, the damned old crank, never got along with this fellow at all, and it's still pretty hard to handle him. But I still have hopes of getting some decent results.

A year later, the work had come to "a complete standstill" until Ishi learned sufficient English to interpret more adequately (Kroeber to Sapir, 16 December 1912: NMM). Kroeber felt that "shipping him to Ottawa" was not feasible, though it might become so. He proposed "a vacation of a month or two on the Pacific coast." Sapir's response (23 December 1912: UCB) is the first instance of serious consideration; but he had prior commitments and needed assurance that California would pay. In 1914, Kroeber and Waterman returned with Ishi to his own country in the mountains of northern California where they obtained "a framework for myths and history" (Kroeber to Sapir, 8 June: UCB). Ishi's English was improving, although "it will be some time before he can attempt even a rudimentary explanation."

Negotiations for Sapir's trip to California took until 1915. Kroeber proposed combining attendance at the American Anthropological Association meetings with fieldwork, noting the urgency of Ishi's health with tuberculosis in remission (to Sapir, 26 April 1915: UCB): "The moral is to get from him what we can while he is well instead of trusting that he will last indefinitely." Sapir took a three-month leave of absence (to Kroeber, 6 May 1915: UCB), much to Kroeber's delight (17 May 1915: UCB): "You will find Ishi bursting with mythological, ethnological, tribal, and geographic information, which he is delighted to impart, but he may need a little training before he will dictate connected texts slowly enough for writing." By the time Sapir actually arrived in California, however, Kroeber had left for a year's sabbatical. The two had not met face-to-face for more than seven years and Kroeber noted (28 November 1915: UCB) that Sapir had "risen in the world since then." Sapir was left to cope with Ishi—and the ghosts of his previous California experience—on his own.

Sapir's initial impression of Ishi was sobering. He wrote to Speck (28 June 1915: APS):

I had my first half-day with Ishi today and am quite discouraged. He speaks very poor English and is very difficult to nail down. However, if nothing else, I can at least get vocabularies as material for comparative Yanan phonetics. He's a fine specimen of an Indian personally and quite affable.

A few weeks later (Sapir to Speck, 17 July 1915: APS), Ishi had learned to dictate texts, though Sapir still complained that "it's a mischief of a job to get them interpreted." The trip, at least, promised not to be a waste of time.

Sapir was forced to devise innovative methods in working with Ishi. He reported to Kroeber after returning to Ottawa (23 September 1915: UCB) that the task had at first seemed "perfectly hopeless, for reasons which you know better than anyone else." Interpretations were "due almost entirely to brute memory of stems and grammatical elements" from other Yana dialects and remained incomplete. Quite a lot still remained obscure: "I think I may safely say that my work with Ishi is by far the most time-consuming and nerve-racking that I have ever undertaken. Ishi's imperturbable good humor alone made the work possible, though it also added at times to my exasperation."

Sapir was particularly delighted with the kinship terms he managed to elicit from Ishi, a "remarkably full and interesting set" (to Speck, 18 August 1915: UCB). He used (to Kroeber, 23 September 1915:

UCB) "different colored paper-fasteners as counters" standing for male and female, laying them out in the form of a genealogical trees supplemented by "long-winded and round-about explanation." Internal evidence confirmed the results. In a paper on Yana dialects (1923, 264) Sapir noted evidence including Ishi's explanations of words, gestures, myth context, and "most important of all, the analogies of the northern dialects." The three dialects could not have been analyzed comparatively without data from Ishi.

Unfortunately, Ishi spent six weeks in the hospital during Sapir's summer in California. Sapir reported (to Kroeber, 23 September 1915: UCB) that "the prospect of a cure seems far from certain." At the first notice of Ishi's illness, Kroeber insisted that Sapir should be told of its seriousness (Kroeber to Waterman, 28 August 1915, quoted in Heizer and Kroeber 1979, 238) and that "the doctors should know Sapir's position. They might be agreeable to let him finish up a few urgent odds and ends." Ishi died early in 1916, an inevitability to which all of his associates seemed reconciled.

Nonetheless, Theodora Kroeber, in her biography of Ishi (1961), recorded that in later years Kroeber, in spite of his realization that Ishi's death was inevitable, could not help feeling that Sapir's insistence on the importance of the scientific work made him partly responsible. Kroeber was emotionally attached to Ishi, in part because of his grief at the death of his first wife, Henrietta Rothschild, in 1913, also from tuberculosis. Moreover, he felt guilty for being away from California while his friend was dying. Kroeber's helplessness against the legacy of white man's disease lashed out at the nearest target—Edward Sapir—whom he had brought back to California to record what Ishi remembered.

World War I and Its Aftermath

World War I brought a period of "retrenchment and disruption" to Ottawa scientific circles, with ethnology low on the list of wartime priorities (Alcock 1947, 69–70). Adding insult to injury, the Parliament Building burned down in 1916, and for the next four years Parliament met in the Victoria Memorial Museum, which was closed to the public. When the Geological Survey regained its premises in 1920, the building was shared with the National Gallery of Art

(Alcock 1947, 72–73). The 1920 reorganization concentrated on making scientific reports more comprehensible to the public and transferring research to provincial jurisdiction (Alcock 1947, 78). There was little ground for optimism as the war took its toll of Sapir's nascent program; losses were never fully regained. Sapir complained to Paul Radin (5 December 1919: NMM):

The atmosphere here is just as unfavorable to anthropology as it was during the war and we are likely to continue to mark time for an indefinite period. I was never so discouraged about the progress of my Division as I am today; even the puny summary reports for our Division that I prepare every year have not been published the last two years. The only real hope for the Division is in a radical change of administration and, though interesting rumors are afloat, there is no great reliance to be put in them. The sad fact is that we have not only not progressed, but have to a considerable extent retrograded.

In spite of setbacks, however, Sapir continued to pursue his program. His annual report for 1920–1921 duly reported that visitors to the newly vacated museum were welcome, though it was still officially closed to the public. A new hall could be utilized as soon as exhibit cases were available.

Sapir was, however, concerned by the continued lack of official enthusiasm for publication. The policy of rigid economy "if continued in its present form, threatens to render all but useless the work of the Division of Anthropology except insofar as the Department allows its anthropological manuscripts to be published by other institutions" (1921, 20). There is no evidence that Sapir's articulate summary of the situation fell on any ears, sympathetic or otherwise. Other agencies and bureaus were in similar circumstances. The position of ethnology, however, was more discouraging relative to prewar levels of support than many other programs simply because the European conflict had catapulted Canada out of its isolationism into the world arena.[13] Indians were of minimal public concern. The immediate problems of reservation settlement were resolved; most Canadians, if they thought about such matters at all, assumed that the Indians would either die out or be assimilated. The defense of a program in ethnology supported by public funds proved a genuine challenge under these conditions, whether or not Sapir was fully aware of the ramifications.

Sapir devoted himself to restoring the previous strength of his program, in museum, fieldwork, and publication. Rearrangement and relabeling of museum collections was completed in 1924–1925, the last year for which he was director of the Anthropological Division. Case labels for museum exhibits were "reduced to a standard form" (1925, 37). An exhibit for the BAAS meeting in Toronto in 1924 proved Sapir was the foremost anthropologist in Canada; colleagues came from many parts of the British empire and Boasians also turned out in full force. Sapir also reported laconically that many ethnological specimens were on loan, some to artists and craftsmen (1925, 37), given the recent increase in popularity of West Coast art.

A clipping from the *Ottawa Citizen* of 7 March 1921 (OPL) reflects the success of Sapir's public education program. Nearly a thousand children appeared on a Saturday morning to hear Diamond Jenness talk about Eskimos, necessitating two separate performances. The police officer on duty was, moreover, unable to keep some of the boys in order, even with "his most severe tones." On Friday evening of the same week, Sapir lectured for "grown up people." Apparently this was a regular feature of Ottawa social and intellectual life. The newspaper report included considerable ethnographic detail about the Eskimo, stressing that the speaker's knowledge came from direct experience. Sapir and his staff eagerly exploited popular interest in ethnographic exotica.

Sapir did not give up on the question of publication, writing to McGinness, director of the Geological Survey, that prompt dissemination of annual reports would "be in harmony with the present efforts of the museum staff to obtain a more explicit recognition as a separate organization" (12 January 1920: NMM).

In his annual report of 1920–1921, the first published since the war, Sapir reported resumption of fieldwork at prewar levels. In the remaining four years of his Ottawa tenure, Sapir emphasized coordinating the results of earlier work. Waugh was sent to the Ojibwa and Naskapi, while Jenness reworked Mechling's Malecite and Micmac material for publication. At the same time, Sapir encouraged Wintemberg's survey of Ontario archaeology, which he hoped would lead to a synthesis of the culture history of the Canadian Indian. Barbeau, Smith, Jenness, and Thomas McIlwraith worked on the Northwest Coast for several seasons. Sapir reluctantly relinquished his own hope for further field sessions with the Nootka. McIlwraith, rather than Sapir, carried out the intensive study of a single tribe, the Bella Coola, emphasizing the "psychological effect" of ceremonies on their participants. Extended fieldwork allowed access to the subjective world of the individual. Moreover, a study of social life took longer than a purely linguistic study. Harlan Smith's Bella Coola work increasingly emphasized native terminology. The influence of Sapir's theoretical position on the relation of the individual to culture was reflected in these studies.

Although Sapir had yet to publish his Nootka texts, he was already eager to get on to new languages. The enforced theoretical concentration of the years without fieldwork encouraged him to concentrate on linguistic classification. He wanted to select new languages in accordance with theoretical rather than solely descriptive questions; the new questions were genetic (historical) ones. Sapir expected his Na-dene stock to link the languages of the old and new worlds. The crux of the matter, in his view, was the tonal quality shared by the Athabaskan languages and Chinese. Sapir trusted no one else to assemble the data to test this hypothesis. He wanted to sample personally the major branches of Athabaskan—not with a view to subgrouping within the stock but for broader comparative purposes. Although each of these languages had its own intrinsic synchronic interest, the same field data applied diachronically.

In 1921, Jenness studied the social organization of the Alberta Sarcee, an Athabaskan group. Although Sapir intended to accompany him for linguistic work, it was not until the following year that he spent two months in "detailed study" of the Sarcee language (1923, 28). His texts of this Athabaskan language were supplemented by "a large body of explanatory grammatical data." Sapir concentrated ethnographically on kinship terms, personal names, and "design symbolism." Although the Sarcee texts were never published,[14] Sarcee was the zenith of Sapir's Na-dene enthusiasm. Its tone system confirmed his prior hypothesis and inspired him to seek further confirmation in other branches of Athabaskan. This question, in one form or another, would preoccupy Sapir for the remainder of his life (see chap. 13).

Sapir's personal research program was back on track. In the summer of 1923, he located, presumably through Frank Speck, two Northern Athabaskan speakers employed at a summer camp in Pennsylvania. The proximity to Ottawa and relative comfort of working conditions (relative to the Mackenzie or Yukon valleys in black fly season) made this an attractive opportunity to add two more languages to his Na-dene repertoire. So Sapir studied two Alaskan languages of the United States for the Canadian government, an indication of the degree of freedom he had to define his own scientific priorities.

Most of the summer was devoted to Kutchin, spoken by John Fredson.[15] Some time was also spent on Ingalik, spoken by Thomas B.

Reid of Anvik. Sapir was disappointed that neither of these Yukon languages had the variety of tone to confirm his Na-dene hypothesis. He continued, however, to assume that data from other Athabaskan languages would settle the matter decisively. The question of Athabaskan tone now eclipsed linking Haida and Tlingit to Athabaskan on Sapir's personal agenda for fieldwork.

Florence Delson Sapir died in April 1924 (see chap. 7 for further details), and Sapir did no fieldwork that summer. By 1925, he had resigned his Ottawa position in favor of a teaching appointment at the University of Chicago. Although he would continue to coordinate his personal research program in terms of questions raised by his fieldwork for the division, Sapir's years of active fieldwork were nearly over, whether or not he realized this. He had become a theoretician, choosing fieldwork sites to answer questions of linguistic relationship rather than simply to record dying languages wherever they were found. Nonetheless, he continued to think of himself as a fieldworker. Even when he did not draw directly on his own data, Sapir's discipline assumed that all primary data was collected by a single observer.

The end of the war did not resolve Sapir's professional disappointments. The years of cutbacks discouraged him and moved his interests away from the mapping of Canadian languages and cultures based on fieldwork by a research team. Nonetheless, he bequeathed to Jenness, his successor, a consistent fieldwork policy, a professionally trained research staff covering the full scope of anthropology, an impressive body of unpublished research, and a great deal of unfinished business. Much had been achieved during Sapir's fifteen years of stewardship in Ottawa.

CHAPTER FIVE

Synthesizing the Boasian Paradigm

The war years curtailed the fieldwork that Sapir considered the essence of his discipline, forcing him to rechannel his efforts into writing up previous results and into more theoretical projects. Although his new priorities were partially imposed upon him by external circumstances, the later Ottawa years were Sapir's most productive in terms of major writing. During these years, he became an articulate spokesman of Boasian anthropology, leading the American Anthropological Association committee that recommended a standardized writing system for American Indian languages in 1916, synthesizing the implicit inferences of Boasian historical reconstruction in "Time Perspective in Aboriginal American Culture" (1916), and writing a general book, *Language* (1921), which presented the conceptual approach of linguistics with reference to a wide range of non-Indo-European languages. In 1921 (see chap. 6), he synthesized the linguistic fieldwork of the previous three decades in a classification of American Indian languages into six great superstocks; this classification would serve as the baseline for anthropologists reconstructing Amerindian culture history until the midsixties. The six-unit classification still provides hypotheses for Americanist linguistics in a more conservative period of comparative reconstruction. In the aftermath of the war, therefore, Sapir synthesized the fieldwork of the earlier part of his career and spoke to a wider audience of anthropologists than in his more specialized grammars, texts, and dictionaries. It is entirely possible that these syntheses would never have been written without the cutbacks in funding of the Ottawa Anthropological Division of the Geological Survey of Canada.

The Phonetics Report

Boasian anthropology consolidated itself as the dominant paradigm in North America during the first two decades of the century. One of the most basic tenets of Boasian anthropology was that all students of American Indians were expected to do a certain amount of linguistic fieldwork, though, for most, this was subordinated to more general ethnological interests. Boas's experience with the *Handbook of American Indian Languages* persuaded him that amateur linguists could do useful work in recording dying languages. These are the same issues of standardization that arose over Sapir's Takelma sketch for the *Handbook*. Amateurs required guidelines that were not beyond their technical capacities. Progress was seriously hampered by the absence of a standardized orthography, because incompatible materials were difficult to compare without linguistic training.

In 1912, Boas established a committee of the American Anthropological Association (AAA) on phonetic transcription of Indian languages. He invited Pliny Goddard of the American Museum and Sapir to join him in this effort.[1] Sapir (to Boas, 9 December 1912: NMM) agreed to participate but reserved the right to devise the orthography "most appropriate to the special problems" of languages he himself studied. He accepted the "quite definite need for much more of a consensus of opinion on methods of transcription" but he was not "a crank" on the subject of standardization, as, by implication, Boas was. Sapir wanted to leave room for the "judgment of the investigator." An explicit phonetic key to guide the reader was the only real necessity. Sapir laconically observed: "Much naturally depends on the particular language."

Kroeber (to Sapir, 18 March 1913: UCB) was less interested in the orthography than in his control over research in California. He favored consensus, and his support was crucial because he was known for his conservative common sense. Not being primarily a linguist, he was perceived as unbiased. Sapir (27 March 1913: NMM) acknowledged that "uniformity in these matters" was only possible with compromise: "You will observe that I am prepared to sacrifice my own preferences on several points." Only the person studying the language could decide what was important; both the structure of the language(s) and the purposes of analysis would, and should, affect the orthography.[2]

John P. Harrington was added to the committee to ensure the cooperation of the bureau, for which he had studied a number of California languages (Laird 1975). That he was not a Boasian added credibility. Unfortunately, Harrington had to be dropped because he was not a member of the AAA and was thus ineligible for its committees (Sapir to Kroeber, 28 May 1914: NMM). During his brief tenure, however, Harrington challenged the basic premises of the committee (to Sapir, 18 April 1913: NMM), arguing the report should be "most undecided in tone." Although discussion might be useful, "variety is delightful. . . . I am glad that various Americanists have various tastes as regards the writing of American languages." Harrington, like Kroeber, insisted that recommendations should be made only if the committee was unanimous. This was, of course, a major setback to standardization. Having asked his opinion, however, the committee was compelled to take his objections seriously.

The committee was, moreover, working to a deadline. They planned to obtain approval of their report at the 1913 AAA meetings and present the new system at the International Congress of Americanists in Washington in 1914 as a symbol of the maturity and consolidation of American anthropology along Boasian lines. Sapir (to Kroeber, 1 January 1913: UCB) apparently did not realize how much contention would emerge, wanting "to further uniformity in America and to bridge over [the] gulf separating American and European usages to some extent."

Kroeber (to Sapir, 6 January 1913: UCB) wanted the committee "to serve as a brake on any extremists." Harrington, for example, had shown "a riotous inclination to indulge in the expressions of fine shades of sounds in the symbols used for them." Kroeber proposed making recommendations "gradually, beginning only with the most absolutely urgent." He also wanted to seek out a wider range of preliminary opinion from nonlinguists, particularly in the bureau and museums.

Sapir responded (27 March 1913: UCB) that the preliminary document was "purposely conservative and undecided in tone." Kroeber (to Sapir, 22 April 1913: NMM) felt he was being pressured and formed an alliance with Harrington that the committee was attempting too much. Compromise wouldn't work if a disgruntled minority ignored the recommendations. Only unanimous recommendations should be presented, "to which all of our members would agree to conform in their own work, except where positively prevented by practical considerations. . . . The slower we go the more we shall ultimately accomplish."

Sapir (to Boas, 28 May 1914: APS) was forced to write an amplified prospectus to get things moving again. This version was acceptable to Boas and Goddard (Sapir to Kroeber, 28 May 1914: NMM). Kroeber (to Sapir, 13 June 1914: NMM) considered the new document good "for its kind," though still "piecemeal." He agreed to accept the majority opinion, although the report was, in his opinion, too "linguistic" for its audience:

I am convinced that the report as it stands will be probably intelligible to and usable by only three or four anthropologists in the country besides yourself, and that everyone else, even with the best intentions, will be baffled by most of it—I am not even sure that it will evoke the good will of many of them. . . . I am afraid that you have not fully realized the prevailing unfamiliarity with even the principles and fundamentals of phonetics . . .

The report could point out that "certain orthographies are preferable to others" without legislating a particular system. Though this "learned and elaborate report" demonstrated that Sapir was "the best equipped man in the subject," Kroeber wanted something "more far-reaching" in practical application.

Unsurprisingly, in spite of the flattery, Sapir's reaction (23 June 1914: NMM) was negative. He agreed in principle that a "general phonetic manual" geared to American Indian sounds would be useful but it would be "a rather bold undertaking" given the present state of knowledge about Indian phonetics. The paradox was the interdependence of theory and orthography: "Until there is more general familiarity with the phonetic basis which should underlie a consistent and well thought out scheme of transcription, there is relatively little use in providing for the latter." Sapir wrote over the heads of his audience to provide "a sort of stimulant" for greater linguistic sophistication. But he professed himself willing to use "sugar-coated methods" if absolutely necessary.

Sapir was tired of the objections to his proposals from colleagues who were, in his view, not competent to decide on linguistic matters. It galled him that the major objections came from Kroeber, who was supposed to be an ally. He wrote to Boas (11 August 1914: APS): "Ah well, what's the use? I have lost interest in it all, because of almost total lack of response." Sapir was pleased with his report and had reached an impasse. Moreover, the time framework of the committee had ceased to apply; the International Congress of Americanists was canceled because of the war in Europe. This removed the pressure "about licking our phonetic report into shape" (Sapir to Kroeber, 1 September 1914: NMM). Boas's interest also lagged when the initial purpose of standardization evaporated.[3] Nonetheless, the third version of the report was eventually approved by Boas, Kroeber, and Goddard (Sapir to Kroeber, 15 March 1915: NMM) and duly published by the Smithsonian Institution in 1916.

Boas suggested a follow-up to Sapir (15 August 1917: NMM). Even when the Smithsonian reprinted the report, however, Sapir declined to revise it (Boas to Sapir, 29 September 1924: APS).[4]

Time Perspective

The phonetics report, for all the collective energy it consumed, was tangential to the main enterprise of codifying the emerging Boasian consensus about the nature of anthropology as a discipline. In that case, Sapir was crucial because he was "the linguist" of Boasian anthropology. The larger impact was nil.

The maturity of Boasian anthropology required the "paradigm statements" of a "normal science" (Kuhn 1961) to lay claim to a theoretical position and a set of methods. From the point of view of potential synthesizers, moreover, "textbook" codification validated their status as core Boasians. Boas's own theoretical writing was inadequate to popularize the perspective, leaving the task to his students by default.[5]

In the years around 1920, Boas's first generation of students provided the syntheses. Sapir's "Time Perspective in Aboriginal American Culture: A Study in Method" in 1916 was rapidly followed by Lowie's *Culture and Ethnology* and Clark Wissler's *The American Indian* in 1917. Lowie's *Primitive Society* and Kroeber and T. T. Waterman's *Sourcebook in Anthropology* appeared in 1920. Sapir's *Language* appeared in 1921, Goldenweiser's *Early Civilization* in 1922, Wissler's *Man and Culture* and Kroeber's *Anthropology* in 1923. The last was most general in scope and ended the intensive period of codification. Although more specialized than any of the others, Sapir was acknowledged as an original theoretician for the emerging paradigm as a whole.

"Time Perspective in Aboriginal America: A Study in Method" established Sapir's reputation as a theoretician. It was written for a symposium on relations between the Pacific area and North America. Sapir seized this occasion to synthesize the Boasian method of cultural reconstruction, using his linguistic perspective to set his own stamp on the method. Sapir (to Kroeber, 2 December 1914: NMM) agreed to speak on "Correlations in Time" for a session on connection of the old and new worlds. He found it "flattering" but could not obtain "a clear idea" of the desired topic.

Kroeber agreed that the topic was "not a happy one" but wanted "something broad enough to allow of wide range" (to Sapir, 7 December 1914: NMM): "What we had in mind was an attempt to grapple with the accumulating but unorganized evidence on the time element in the history of American race and civilization." Asian records went back some distance. Stated Kroeber: "On the American side we have now reached a pretty thorough understanding of the several local types of culture and their interrelations." It might, therefore, be possible to "estimate the length of time involved in these local developments, as well as in such general cultural traits as may be specifically American." These might even be connected to "determinations for the other side of the Pacific." Kroeber urged Sapir to treat the topic in terms of the absence of historical perspective in most American ethnology. Sapir's linguistically conditioned attention to genetic relationship through time made him ideal for the task. Kroeber summarized that

what I had in mind was any treatment of the ethnological material in question which would emphasize its historical bearings more than has been customary. We in this country have been particularly remiss and unimaginative. The average American anthropologist, even if he is an archaeologist, treats his data with the most scrupulous reference to geography, but with an almost punctilious avoidance of the factor of time.

Problems of chronology were, indeed, legion. Native America lacked the written records of the Old World, the sine qua non of traditional historical scholarship. Archaeology was not yet useful for time perspective. The Pecos classification was a decade in the future, though Manuel Gamio had done stratigraphic work in Mexico under Boas in 1911. Kroeber's student, Nels Nelson, had published more sophisticated stratigraphy in 1914. Saville, who taught Sapir Meso-American archaeology at Columbia, had done chronological ordering based on Copan (1907–1910). In 1916, Kroeber pioneered in stratigraphic seriation by collecting surface potsherds at Zuni. Various Boasians were seeking historical inference from ethnographic distribution (Darnell 1977), but Sapir was more interested in genetic relationship of Amerindian languages as the key to time perspective. In 1916, it was reasonable to invite a linguist to discuss time depth.

Sapir's essay pursued "the chronological significance of linguistic differentiation," producing a picture of "a series of movements of linguistically unrelated peoples, possibly from different directions and certainly at very different times" (1916, 77-78). This scenario was "intrinsically highly probable" in spite of being based on inference. Such inference was acceptable precisely because (1916, 452)

linguistic changes proceed more slowly and, what is more important, at a generally more even rate than cultural ones. This means that, particularly where there is abundant comparative material available, we are enabled to penetrate farther back into the past and to obtain a more reliable feeling of relative durations of such linguistic time sequences as are available.

Although Sapir nominally protested his qualifications to tackle the problem, his initial speculations were already quite explicit (to Kroeber, 14 December 1914: NMM):

I think that you are right in your remark about our timidity in grappling with the time element in the history of culture. I think it is historically due to the fact that so many of our men are trained rather in descriptive or psychological comparison than in strictly historical comparative work.

Complex ethnological and linguistic phenomena might be of secondary origin. Sapir developed this argument for linguistic reconstruction most explicitly in his analysis of Subtiaba of Nicaragua (1925); surface differentiation in the present language was trivial compared to the submerged or archaic features that offered tantalizing clues to the historical roots of the language. Sapir was applying the Indo-European distinction between synchronic and diachronic reconstruction to new vistas.

Sapir was less than enthusiastic about the broad questions posed by the symposium topic, considering it "hopeless to correlate type or elements of culture in Asia or Oceania." The question of "absolute time" could not be answered. His paper could only "open up the general question of time perspective in American ethnology, with illustrations here and there based on our specific ethnographic information." Culture areas, whatever the theoretical commitment to "a historical sense," were actually "of a purely descriptive rather than historical value." For example, the buffalo was crucial to Plains culture but not part of its beginnings. Sapir returned immediately to linguistic method: "This type of reasoning is, of course, perfectly familiar to us in linguistic work. In comparing various Indo-Germanic languages among themselves, we are moved entirely by consideration of descriptive resemblances and differences, but we evaluate these historically at every step." Sapir welcomed the opportunity to educate ethnologists about linguistic methods, acknowledging that it was "always more easy to do this in linguistics than in culture anyway." Sapir's essay was self-consciously programmatic, intended to reorient the historical thinking of American anthropologists. In this goal, Sapir was largely successful. "Time Perspective" became a classic for ensuing generations of Boasian ethnologists seeking broader interpretive frameworks for their descriptive data.

Lowie (to Sapir, 4 January 1916: NMM) considered the linguistic argument, not previously made "in definite form," a necessary antidote to Boasian particularism. Sapir's approach, "while perhaps only an adaptation of Indo-Germanic methods to the American field, is most suggestive and ought to have a direct influence on working anthropologists." Lowie's review in the *American Anthropologist* (1919, 76) emphasized the "inferential evidence for a temporal arrangement of cultural events" which "might be expected from the author's special lines of work."[6]

Sapir's colleagues wanted a foolproof method. They got a sophisticated delineation of the theoretical parameters of chronological inference. Sapir assumed that culture areas were arbitrary devices to classify ethnographic data and sought in linguistic classification a historically valid grouping of native American tribes. He cited over fifty different Indian groups, suggesting historical connections to be explored by further research. There was, however, little elaboration about historical documents or archaeological evidence.

Sapir's colleagues were also searching for more adequate historical methods. Radin (to Sapir, 27 January 1914: NMM), who may well have been the foil for Sapir's argument, proposed that chronology would always be "impossible in primitive culture and any attempts to reconstruct one will be artificial or, what is more, vague." Radin turned to the subjective world of the individual in culture as a substitute for history. Sapir was not, however, ready to give up on historical questions; they could be approached rigorously through linguistic methods.

Clark Wissler, involved with Kroeber in arranging the Pacific conference sessions, congratulated Sapir (9 February 1916: NMM) on his time perspective essay. Wissler, who was closely associated with culture area organization of ethnographic data, was eager to encourage any historical inference:

I hope you will develop some of the concrete problems in this field. You could very easily handle some of them as incidental parts of your systematic Canadian field-work. Personally, I should very much like to see linguistic studies demonstrate their usefulness in the solution of more general problems. As it stands now, it is extremely difficult to convince an outsider that linguistic work leads to anything outside of its own special problems.

For Wissler, the geographical classification was "the only real objective thing to which we can look for our point of departure." He missed Sapir's point that linguistic methods provided an alternative to geographical classification and were at least as objective and scientific.[7]

Neither Sapir nor Wissler wanted to emphasize the gulf between their approaches to historical reconstruction. When Sapir read *The American Indian* (1917), he told Lowie (5 September 1918: UCB) it overemphasized material culture and the linguistics was even worse than he expected. Nonetheless, the book had to be praised in public because "it puts our subject on a definite and scholarly basis." Wissler at least attacked "the brass tacks of geography, and, in a preliminary way, chronology." But his synthesis should have incorporated the range of methods set out in "Time Perspective."

The importance attached to "Time Perspective" by his colleagues led Sapir to think about consolidating his academic reputation. Few of his fellow anthropologists actually read his laboriously constructed texts and grammars of Indian languages. Most of the readers of his technical papers were more interested in ethnological implications than in linguistics per se. Indo-Europeanists tended to ignore materials from unwritten languages. Sapir could only establish an audience for his technical work by convincing anthropologists to look seriously at language and linguists to look at a wider range of languages.

Language: The Public Statement

Kroeber contributed to Sapir's self-assessment when he berated him (4 November 1917: NMM) for failing to establish a school of linguistics in anthropology (difficult given that he had no students in Ottawa) and to make his ideas generally known: "The decadence of linguistics is largely your own fault. You're an individualist and haven't built up a school. Do something general in character." Sapir took this advice seriously and sought a format to convey his enthusiasm for linguistic form to nonspecialists, a category including virtually everyone else. He had little patience with the limited linguistic skills of his fellow anthropologists and less faith in their ability to comprehend his vision of language, let alone his specific hypotheses about American Indian culture history. He was equally disenchanted with the Indo-Europeanists' failure to acknowledge the particular problems of fieldwork with unwritten languages.

Language: An Introduction to the Study of Speech portrayed language as an outgrowth of the behavior of members of speech communities. Indo-European linguistics could ignore the cultural foundations of speech because the languages studied shared a basic cultural pattern. As an anthropologist, Sapir removed language from the elitist literary context within which linguistics had developed as a science. Anthropologists knew about fieldwork but not about linguistic methods. Linguists knew the methods but not their application to the full range of human languages. The educated public knew neither. The audience for Sapir's book, therefore, had to be wider than a disciplinary one. In fact, disciplinary boundaries had cut off recognition of the actual creativity of language, which was, in all cultures, a rich and precise vehicle for the expression of thought. Sapir set himself the challenge of producing a book that could be understood by any educated person with an open mind, without elaborate terminology or commitment to particular formalism. Sapir provided no bibliography and few details of his specific researches. *Language* was intended to convey his point of view—solidly grounded in both of his disciplines.

Language was immediately recognized as a Boasian paradigm statement, with its definition of language as a variable human resource inherent in the scope of anthropology, the training of anthropologists, and the commitment to record texts—the actual words of native speakers—for every language currently spoken as an essential part of the record of human civilization. All anthropologists, whether or not they did linguistic work, understood this, and they claimed Sapir's book as their own.

The original edition of *Language* sold only 3,000 copies in the thirteen years it was in print. Yet these were sufficiently influential that it was reprinted in 1939, the year of Sapir's death, and appeared in paperback in 1955. Since then, nearly 180,000 copies have been sold, it has been translated into at least eight foreign languages, and 2,000 copies are still sold annually. No other book in linguistics has attracted such a faithful long-term audience. Moreover, *Language* has always been treated as a general trade book, not as a textbook (*New York Times*, 12 June 1981).

Oral history has it that Sapir wrote the book in a few weeks, in a fit of inspired creativity. This is a myth, perpetuated by Kroeber in 1959 (1984). Sapir had the idea of a general book at least by 1919. Letters to colleagues during 1920 clarify the difficulty with which the manuscript was born and the great care with which Sapir worked on both style and content over a period of at least six months. He was, furthermore, unwilling to devote the necessary attention to his manuscript until a publisher was firmly committed to the project. Negotiations with Harcourt Brace dragged on through the spring of 1920 due to their concern with marketing a technical book on language. Sapir wrote rather querulously to Lowie (25 May 1920: UCB), who had introduced him to Alfred Harcourt (Lowie 1965), that he could not make plans for the next half-year until the contract was finalized: "Indefiniteness makes me rather angry." Having decided that communicating to a general audience was necessary, Sapir wanted to proceed immediately and was disturbed that others did not share his sense of urgency.[8]

Sapir initially thought the book could be completed in two or three months (to Harlan Smith, 22 June 1920: NMM), so he could spend the end of the summer in the field with the Bella Coola; it quickly became clear that this would not be possible. Sapir remained optimistic that the book "will be of some use to linguistic students generally by way of widening their perspective" (to Michelson, 7 August 1920: NMM). He reported to Barbeau (10 August 1920: NMM) that the manuscript proceeded slowly, with only two chapters completed, but that he did not regret the task "in spite of the very considerable concentration that it demands." To Boas, Sapir described the project (25 August 1920: NMM) as "a small introduction to the subject" of language. In spite of the apologetic tone, Sapir intended his book to make the collective program better known:

I hope it may prove acceptable both as a sort of textbook and for general reading. I think it is a crime that you do not write out more of your general ideas. You have done more than your share of detailed descriptive work. I do hope you will continue on your broader anthropological MS. I am sure every one of your students will be disappointed if you do not.

Sapir was not, of course, suggesting that Boas write about language, but rather that the whole approach to culture, history, and psychology needed general treatment for a nonspecialized audience. The relevance of anthropology could only be made clear by its practitioners. Having done his share, Sapir hoped others, especially Boas, would follow suit.

Writing a generalist book also stimulated Sapir to think about the generalization inherent in his more technical work. He noted to Lowie (9 September 1920: NMM) that "this renewed contact with linguistic ideas and data is stimulating me." When Leslie Spier asked Sapir about possible textbooks for a course on language (8 November 1920: NMM), he responded without enthusiasm: "I make it rather a point these days not to read other people's general works on language. I am interested only in source material, that is first hand accounts of specific languages." He also asked Spier for criticism of the first four chapters "from the standpoint of the intelligent public." Spier was a Boasian ethnologist, diligent in recording American Indian cultures, but in no sense a linguist. The "general" audience Sapir apparently had in mind was a fairly sophisticated one.

At this point, Sapir's progress slowed, largely because "the publishers were in no hurry on account of present publishing conditions" with postwar escalation in cost and problematic markets. Sapir berated himself that he would "find myself way behind" if he did not get back to writing.

Sapir also sought a nonspecialist opinion from Wilson Wallis, who fell back on stylistics because the content was "so much beyond my ken" (26 April 1921: NMM). He disputed Sapir's contention that language was inseparable from thought, reflecting his training in philosophy and lack thereof in linguistics. Wallis particularly liked Sapir's "ability to cite from so many languages," which encouraged confidence in the reader that Sapir knew what he was talking about when he talked about language in general. He found the explanations of Indo-European grammatical categories "most enlightening" and admitted he did not understand how linguists grouped genetically related languages. He was drawn to Sapir's discussions of "extra-linguistic" issues about language (language and thought, style and literature).[9]

Sapir's most extensive commentaries on the progress of his manuscript were written to Lowie, who was associated in his mind with the publication arrangements. In *Language* (to Lowie, 8 April 1921: UCB): "I am after ideas . . . not facts for their own sake." He was startled to realize how greatly "language, broadly considered, touches large problems at an astonishing number of points—philosophy of history, psychology, aesthetics." Sapir was stimulated rather than daunted; it was "reassuring" that one "can be sincerely interested in language without being a dry-as-dust pedant." The manuscript was barely complete when he was contemplating a sequel which would "give more facts."[10]

Sapir intended *Language* to present the possibilities of the subject rather than to argue the personal positions of one individual (to Lowie, 19 April 1921: UCB): "Aside from the delicate question of whether originality may fairly be expected from me, I may quite sincerely say that I curbed rather than encouraged the development of my ideas that seemed at all idiosyncratic." He wanted the book to be useful for university students. He realized, however, that the "ideas on classification and drift are really far from orthodox. The teleological taint in the discussion of phonetic law will probably cause eyebrow-raising." Sapir (8 April 1921: UCB) was especially pleased that Lowie liked his discussion of language and thought: "I quite frankly commit myself to the idea that thought is impossible without language, that thought *is* language."[11] Moreover, he realized that his unwillingness to commit himself to any particular form of psychology left the discussion incomplete. But Sapir was a linguist and the science of linguistics did not provide the methodological or theoretical tools to deal with the psychology of language. Nonetheless, he refused to exclude the question simply because it could not be answered based on present knowledge.

In spite of his requests for criticism, Sapir was pleased with most of what he had written. He was, however, unhappy with the discussion of the relation of race, language, and culture as "too negative in result and too much along our continual Boasian lines." Indeed, Sapir did not go beyond Boas's treatment in 1911 (b). Nor did he stress his own position that much could be learned about culture history precisely because language had a different structure from other parts of culture. Sound change assured that similarity between languages was due to common ancestry, not borrowing. Sapir downplayed potential conflict with Boas, who tended to assume that linguistic traits were borrowed in the same way as elements of culture and that the effects of borrowing could not be reliably distinguished from those of genetic diversification (Darnell, in press). But Sapir still agonized over whether he had been too cautious in dissociating himself from the Boasian position. He explained to Lowie (8 April 1921: UCB), who thought he gave short shrift to borrowing, that "possibly Boas and I are poles apart on this point." But he did not modify his text.

Although Sapir usually took style for granted, he commented:

I don't want offensively "drastic" expressions. I have a tendency, I believe, to be snarlingly "clever," but I don't admire this in the least. As I get older, I find I enjoy the "classic" increasingly, though I am afraid if such a dud as myself starts out to be classic he ends up by being tame.

Sapir was fully aware that his concept of "drift" would be dismissed by many as mystical. This was inevitable because "the precise nature (psychological or otherwise) of the sequential process involving accelerated movement to type" could not be specified accurately. Moreover, drift was not restricted to language, but was also found in art, religion, and "social forms." Its determinants were "mathematical and quasi-aesthetic intuitions." In other words, drift, for Sapir, was inseparable from linguistic form as he understood it. He specifically noted that evolution was a different process altogether. The word "drift" was intended to be "non-committal" and was "too innocent to hurt much." In *Language* (1921, v-vi) he put it:

Quite aside from their intrinsic interest, linguistic forms and historical processes have the greatest possible diagnostic value for the understanding of some of the more difficult and elusive problems in the psychology of thought, and in the strange, cumulative drift in the life of the human spirit that we call history or progress or evolution.

Lowie's review of *Language* in the *American Anthropologist* (1923, 43–44) suggested that "theoretically-minded students of culture will view linguistic phenomena with a peculiar interest and must inevitably draw some parallels between the problems arising in this sharply demarcated province of the social heritage and in the grand totality of culture." Because many examples were English, even the novice might gain "new vistas" into the "psychological and historical determinants affecting the growth of speech-forms." However, diffusionists would not be pleased by evidence of linguistic parallels in diverse regions in which "the human mind has arrived at the same form of expression," for example, Chinook and Bantu or Takelma and Greek. Lowie emphasized the "definitely anthropological orientation" of the book, alongside Sapir's masterful philological technique "elaborated and perfected in the Indo-Germanic domain" and applied to fieldwork with American Indian languages. Lowie contrasted Otto Jespersen's book of the same title, which used primitive languages as "only the broader embellishment for the fabric of his philosophy of speech," finding merely "subsidiary exemplification in more exotic spheres." Sapir, the anthropologist, offered an integrated view of language for both disciplines: "Sapir's views . . . are cast in a single mould; they are the outcome of a broad-gauge survey of languages as such, whether spoken by primitive or lettered peoples."

Lowie praised Sapir's explication of the logic of attributing historical genetic relationship to two languages. Linguistics properly led the way in distinguishing the effects of borrowing from those of independent invention. If anything, Sapir did not go far enough for American ethnologists who wanted linguists to give them firm answers to historical questions. But Sapir had wisely chosen not to argue his own positions in a general work (Lowie 1923, 46): "Those who know how definitely he adheres in more technical publications to the view outlined will admire the self-restraint exercised in compressing deep-seated convictions . . . " Sapir's "reverence for the general reader is not common among writers of popular works"; the book "is notably free from crotchetiness."

Sapir took the response to his book very seriously, maintaining a file of reviews and personal letters.[12] He told Wallis (23 November 1923: NMM): "I feel it is rather compact and is likely to withhold some of its contents on a first reading." Some of the initial comments annoyed Sapir (to Lowie, 28 November 1921: UCB); Boas said he hadn't read it yet but knew where his disagreements would fall;[13] Truman Michelson of the bureau restricted himself to a long Fox example on a single point. Radin, characteristically, discussed the book he would have preferred Sapir to write (n.d. 1922: NMM):

This is all right, I suppose, as a presentation of linguistic phenomena from our modern ethnological viewpoint. Now, my dear Edward, write the second volume, telling us what it all means more precisely and imaginatively, particularly in its influence upon the development of literature, religious conceptions, philosophy, etc. Not only what is the relation of language to thought but—far more important—what is its connection with action, etc., etc.

Kroeber (1922, 314) also declined to evaluate the linguistic typology, though he realized professionals might choose to ignore it (as, indeed, most did). He emphasized that Sapir had made a difficult subject accessible to the general reader (1922, 317):

> There is not a diacritical mark in this book, yet its philology is sound; not a footnote or reference, yet it is scholarly; not a page that is difficult for an educated layman, yet it opens new paths of thought. A rare felicity pervades it, a freedom from what is hackneyed; and its balance equals its spontaneity. It is unique in its field, and is likely to become and remain long standard.

To the publisher (15 May 1921: SF), Kroeber characterized the book as "the first treatment of language that will be of interest and utility to other than philologists, metaphysicians, and mystics." Harcourt Brace's announcements of the book referred to Sapir as "one of the most brilliant students of primitive language in America" (Kroeber, who was quoted, actually said Sapir was "the" most brilliant).

Leonard Bloomfield's review in *Classical Weekly* (1922, 142) considered Sapir utterly "dependable" to show the "scientific outlook" toward language. But he wanted a bibliography, to assess how much of Sapir's argument agreed with previous scholars. He singled out Sapir's treatment of the concept of inner or ideal phonetic system, although he felt that both Boas and Ferdinand de Saussure had preceded him. Bloomfield, soon to be Sapir's colleague in the professionalization of linguistics, praised the emphasis on synchronic work as methodologically inseparable from diachronic or historical problems. He extolled Sapir's refusal to depend on the methods of other disciplines, particularly psychology. Interestingly, he then digressed into the behaviorist psychology that underlay his own linguistic theories. He worried, however, that Sapir's fondness for metaphorical speech made the book less scientific; it was "aprioristic speculation . . . in the guise of psychology."

Eduard Prokosch, later to be Sapir's colleague at Yale, emphasized (1922, 355) the "personal" quality of the book and Sapir's "vivid . . . even poetic style." He noted: "It is the style of the inspiring lecturer, of the interesting *causeur*, not of the objective scholar (which Sapir in reality is, to the highest degree." The treatment of phonetic change was "brilliant" (1922, 357). Prokosch was drawn by the "concrete results" of Sapir's "highly subjective, audacious, independent method." To him, there was nothing unscientific in *Language*.

Arthur Remy, who had taught Sapir linguistics at Columbia, noted for the *Literary Review* (6 May 1922) that his experience with "primitive" languages as well as with Indo-European allowed "a more comprehensive view of linguistic phenomena than the average specialist." He was, however, dubious that the general reader could follow it. A. Williams Jackson, Sapir's Indo-Iranian instructor at Columbia (4 March 1922), wrote that he had been inspired to offer a course in linguistics for the first time in many years, with *Language* as the textbook.

In H. L. Mencken's journal, *The Smart Set*, an unidentified reviewer noted that Mr. Sapir was not American but Canadian: "From internal evidence, he seems to have had German training," although "he is not a professor of language at all, but an official of the Canadian government." This reviewer had not done his homework.

Otto Jespersen's book, also titled *Language*, appeared in the same year as Sapir's. Sapir (to Lowie, 14 March 1922: UCB) found it "overgrown, diffuse, ill-proportioned, naive" and concentrating on personal "hobbies" of the author. He reported receiving a copy from the author, with a note that he (Jespersen) no longer worried about repetition after seeing Sapir's book.

Linguists were intrigued by Sapir's treatment of phonetic pattern. Carl Buck, comparative philologist at Chicago and soon to be Sapir's colleague, noted (16 November 1921) that he had "perhaps been vaguely conscious" of this phenomenon before but had never had it "brought so forcibly to my attention." This was a precursor of the concept of the phoneme as elaborated by Sapir in 1925 and 1933. In *Language*, Sapir (1921, 174) referred to "that unconscious sound patterning which is ever on the point of becoming conscious" and noted that a "single sound change, even if there is no phonetic leveling, generally threatens to upset the old phonetic pattern because it brings about a disharmony in the grouping of sounds" (1921, 182). The concept immediately and necessarily implicated native speakers of a language (1921, 183):

It is likely that we shall not advance seriously until we study the intuitional bases of speech. How can we understand the nature of the drift that frays and reforms phonetic patterns when we have never thought of studying sound patterning as such and the "weights" and psychic relations of the single elements (the individual sounds in these patterns)?

The concept of sound patterning was first introduced in Boas's (1889) "On Alternating Sounds." Sapir went further, however, in that the sound patterns of a particular language were interrelated and consistent both in features stressed and their contrastive definition. Boas's point was simply that native speakers heard and spoke a second language according to the phonetic patterns of their native language. He did not elaborate the consequences for the analyst's knowledge of or ability to describe accurately the structure of the native language.

Sapir's earliest statement of the phonemic principle responded (8 September 1916: UCB) to Kroeber's complaints about a speaker who could not learn to write his own language (cf. Silverstein 1985). He suggested that "the trouble may not have been entirely his own," because the difficult sounds were identical "to the native consciousness":

I have had enough experience with teaching Indians to write their own language to know that there is nothing simpler if one has only mastered the organically significant types of sounds. An exhaustive knowledge of all nuances by itself is apt to be more of a hindrance than a help in the teaching of orthography. I would go so far as to say that if one finds that he can make no progress with a native in the matter of teaching him to record a particular class of sounds, that the reason will nearly always, in the wash, be found to be a lack of adequate analysis on the part of the instructor. I am a firm believer in the consciousness, or if you like, the sub-consciousness, in native speakers of the organic phonetic elements of their language. . . . I find that I have written a treatise. I hope you will forgive my "pedantry."

When Sapir published "Sound Patterns in Language" in 1925, he wrote to Lowie (3 April: UCB) that it "amplifies what I hinted about this subject in *Language*." The 1925 version, however, was more explicit in claiming that phonetic process was "unintelligible" in any other terms (1925, 33):

There used to be and to some extent still is a feeling among linguists that the psychology of a language is more particularly concerned with its grammatical features, but that its sounds and its phonetic processes belong to a grosser physiological substratum. . . . the sounds and sound processes of speech cannot be properly understood in such simple mechanistic terms.

Sapir insisted on the need for "the inner configuration" of the sound system unique to each language, "the intuitive 'placing' of the sounds with reference to one another" (1925, 42).

In 1933, Sapir developed the argument still further with reference to field experience of unwritten languages, whose "psychological reality" for their speakers was the sine qua non of analysis (1933, 47):

If the phonemic attitude is more basic, psychologically speaking, than the more strictly phonetic one, it should be possible to detect it in the unguarded speech judgments of native speakers who have a complete control of their language in a practical sense but have no rationalized or consciously systematic knowledge of it. . . . In the course of many years of experience in the recording and analysis of unwritten languages . . . I have come to the practical realization that what the native speaker hears is not phonetic elements but phonemes.

Indeed, Sapir's unabashed preference for the subjective was long-standing. Lowie (1965, 71) noted his early attraction to Rickert's distinction between the natural sciences and those of the spirit (*Geis-teswissenschaften*). The *patterning* of sounds was crucial, not their objective character. As early as 1911, in "History and Varieties of Speech," Sapir had proposed a "common psychological substratum" for the historically attested similarities among languages, reflecting "the unbridgeable distance separating phonetic laws from the laws of natural science" (Malkiel 1986).

Sapir did not consider *Language* a finished product. His planned but never written second edition was needed because it was "too closely packed in its reasoning" (to Lowie, 25 March 1926: UCB). By this time, Sapir was teaching at Chicago and had to reconsider how much could be communicated in general terms: "I am constantly overestimating the ability of students to think abstractly." Students had become his intended general audience.

Sapir's final general statement about language was for the *Encyclopedia of the Social Sciences* in 1933. There is less about poetry and more about modern nationalism in relation to standard languages (Malkiel 1986). Sapir's audience had shifted toward colleagues in a newly independent discipline of linguistics. It lacks the enthusiasm and energy, however, of *Language* in 1921.

Sapir was delighted with the success of his book. He was increasingly depressed by the research situation in Ottawa and longed for an academic appointment in the United States. Popularization of his work seemed the best strategy. Kroeber (17 January 1921: UCB) expressed both Sapir's unquestioned status as the foremost anthropological linguist of the period and the need for him to sell himself to potential employers:

You are wholly right about getting your work out of the anthropological classification. Most of us don't dream of professing anything but abhorrence for languages, and the bulk of the minority are satisfied to claw together raw material. As for a *theoretical* interest, I may be overlooking someone, but when you have named Sapir, Boas, Radin, Kroeber, and Harrington, I think you are through. . . .

At the same time, who is there in this country among the philologists that has enough breadth to make a move in your behalf? They'll *admit* your training with them qualifies you, they'll approve of what you do; but will they care about it? Philologists I have known are a damned inert lot. . . . I think your outlet is in books—books on language. . . . Bank on what you can carve out for yourself. You can do it. That you haven't proves only that you haven't wanted to badly enough to fix every effort on the aim.

Sapir had to prove himself precisely because his work fell between two disciplines, limiting his full participation in either. *Language* allowed him to treat, in a way no one else could do, issues that cross-cut linguistics and anthropology.

CHAPTER SIX

The Classification of
American Indian Languages

From the beginning of his career as a fieldworker with unwritten American Indian languages, Sapir had moved comfortably between synchronic description (texts, grammars, and dictionaries) and diachronic comparative (historical) reconstruction in the Indo-European tradition. Increasingly, as fieldwork funds dried up, the challenge was not so much to describe more languages but to place the native languages of the continent in accurate historical relationship. Forced to spend more time in the office, Sapir consequently spent more time working through data collected by others and comparing it to his own. He was caught up in a vision of the culture history of North America, revealed by archaic traces of the common ancestry of tribes and languages. Sapir had argued for the relevance of linguistics to culture in "Time Perspective" in 1916. Now he sought concrete examples of what linguistic method could suggest about historical relationship.

The established classification of American Indian languages, by John Wesley Powell and the Bureau of American Ethnology in 1891 (Darnell 1971*b*; 1971*c*; Darnell and Hymes 1986), was too shallow in time depth to be useful for historical reconstruction. Powell's staff, with one exception, were not trained in linguistics; related words were identified by surface form, not reconstruction of underlying forms as in Indo-European. Moreover, the bureau classification was designed for practical purposes, for example, the settlement of related tribes on reservations, rather than for historical inference. The fifty-five independent stocks were of vastly different degrees of relationship, ranging from the widespread Eskimo-Aleut of the high Arctic to isolates like Kootenay or Zuni. Most of these linguistic families were not comparable to Indo-European, Semitic, or Finno-Ugric—the major peoples who populated the Mediterranean basin. The Powell classification was, however, a major step forward, codifying the fieldwork of the bureau and filling in, for the first time, the map of native North America. Powell also suggested where further work might reduce the number of independent families. Unfortunately, the classification was received as though written in stone. Ethnologists wanted a temporal framework, and few had the linguistic skills to reassess the evidence themselves.

Sapir was in a position to give North American anthropology an entirely different kind of classification. He had the systematic Indo-European training to relate the isolates to larger stocks. The task dominated his imagination from about 1913 to 1920 when he unveiled his six-unit classification, published in a note in *Science* in 1921, at a Chicago meeting of the American Association for the Advancement of Science.

The six-unit classification was received with consternation by anthropologists—to whom it seemed almost mystical. Sapir did not present his evidence, although his technical papers of the same period argued for its parts. Sapir intended to demonstrate the relevance of linguistic classification as a framework for ethnology, expecting his colleagues to be overjoyed. This was the gimmick to convince anthropologists that linguistics was not dry and technical. Sapir was disappointed and frustrated by the contention his hypotheses aroused. After 1921, he turned away from broad classification, never publishing his evidence linking Na-dene to Indo-Chinese. The better-known 1929 version of the classification virtually repeated the conclusions of 1921.

The six-unit classification, however, is the summary of Sapir's Ottawa years. The mandate of the Anthropological Division was to map the languages and cultures of Canada. Because many of the aboriginal languages and cultures crossed national boundaries, Sapir attacked classificatory problems from the standpoint of the whole continent. Synchronic description recorded dying languages; diachronic comparison, however, shed light on migration, contact, and culture history.

In the 1929 version of his classification, Sapir recognized degrees of certainty within the six units (table 2). He noted twenty-three units, presumably acceptable to most conservative linguists, being based on

Table 2: *North American Linguistic Classification*

Sapir 1929	Sapir (implicit)	Powell 1891
I. Eskimo-Aleut	Eskimo	Eskimo
II. Algonquian-Ritwan	*Algonquian-Ritwan	Algonquian, Beothukan, Wiyot, Yurok
	*Mosan	Wakashan, Chemakuan, Salish
	Kootenay	Kootenay
III. Na-dene	*Tlingit-Athabascan	Haida, Tlingit, Athabascan
	Haida	
IV. Penutian	*California Penutian	Miwok, Costanoan, Yokuts, Maidu, Wintun
	*Oregon Penutian	Takelma, Coos (-Siuslaw), Yakonan, Kalapuya
	*Plateau Penutian	Waiilatpuan, Lutuamian, Sahaptin
	Chinook	Chinook
	Tsimshian	Tsimshian
	(Mexican Penutian)	—
V. Hokan-Siouan	*Hokan	Karok, Chimariko, Salinan, Yana, Pomo, Washo, Yuman, Esselen, Chumash
	*Coahuiltecan	Tonkawa, Karankawa, Coahuiltecan
	*Tunican	Tunica, Atakapa, Chitimacha
	*Iroquois-Caddoan	Iroquois, Caddoan
	Yuki	Yuki
	Keres	Keres
	Timucua	Timucua
	Muskhogean	Muskhogean
	Siouan	Siouan, Yuchi
VI. Aztec-Tanoan	*Uto-Aztecan	Nahuatl, Pima, Shoshonean
	*Tanoan-Kiowan	Tanoan, Kiowa
	?Zuni	Zuni

*Twelve units that Sapir considered to be accepted by most of his colleagues. The reduction of Powell's fifty-five stocks to twenty-three reflected the work of Sapir's generation. The further reduction to six units, he considered his own work.

fieldwork done since Powell's classification of 1891. Of these, twelve were based on Sapir's own work. The six units were more problematic and he expected further work to revise them. In practice, however, the six-unit classification was accepted as a finished product, just as Powell's had been. Anthropologists and linguists had a choice of classifications, and most opted for the conservative or the radical on principle, without attention to the evidence for particular connections. This is perhaps not surprising, because the audience for linguistic classification was a nonspecialized one of anthropologists seeking generalization for cultural description.

The Sapir classification, in spite of quibbles from various quarters, dominated Amerindian anthropology for four decades—as long as linguistics was primarily seen as a handmaiden of ethnology. More recently, linguists, most of whom are no longer ethnologists, have set higher standards of proof for particular connections. Campbell and Mithun (1979) recognize sixty-two independent stocks for the continent, on the basis of detailed sound correspondences; nonetheless, they continue to group their stocks according to Sapir's six units and suggest that further research may again decrease the number of units. At the other extreme, Joseph Greenberg (1987) has gone beyond Sapir in proposing only three units for both of the Americas; although short-range reaction has been skeptical (Greenberg et al. 1987), this effort revives Sapir's contention that linguistic classification properly and uniquely leads to historical reconstruction. It is still impossible to approach American Indian language classification without coming to terms with Sapir's six units. Indeed, many Americanists know Sapir largely, if not exclusively, through this classification. It is, therefore, crucial to understand how Sapir worked his way through existing descriptive data to arrive at it.

The Beginnings of the Classificatory Mania

Sapir did not initiate the effort to reduce the number of linguistic families in North America. Rather, the initiator was Kroeber, faced with the task of classifying the languages and cultures of California, a state that included twenty-two of Powell's fifty-five stocks. Kroeber was eager to group this diversity in some way. He and Roland Dixon of Harvard began with a Boasian model of typological similarity assumed to be a product of diffusion. In 1903 they insisted that genetic relationship was not involved, stating that "we are establishing not families but types of families" (Kroeber and Dixon 1903, 2–3). The classification was not comparable to Powell's because it relied on grammatical similarity rather than lexical content. Kroeber still accepted Boas's assumption that genetic relationship was largely unrecoverable for unwritten languages because the effects of borrowing and historical continuity were indistinguishable.

Eventually, however, Kroeber was forced by the weight of evidence to consider genetic explanation. He wrote to Boas (24 April 1903: UCB) that he was puzzled by the number of lexical resemblances in his data: "it is by no means impossible that many of the languages will turn out to be related." By 1913 (225), Dixon and Kroeber admitted that "the only satisfactory explanation of the resemblances between certain languages was genetic relationship." Both lexical and grammatical similarities were abundant and coinciding; these were more powerful when a number of languages were compared simultaneously.

Kroeber expected Sapir to be sympathetic to his new hypotheses (3 January 1913: UCB):

I could, however, get no intelligible result from our data until finally in desperation I dropped the assumption, under which we had all along been working, that all resemblances were due to accident or borrowing, and assumed genetic relationship. . . . From this time on the skein unwound itself. . . . My wonder now is that we missed the clue . . .

Sapir initially held back from sharing Kroeber's enthusiasm. He distrusted Kroeber's linguistic abilities and still smarted from his perceived rejection in California years before; he may have felt he should have been the one to attack the question of genetic relationships among California languages and may have worried about the reaction of conservative anthropologists, particularly Boas, to tenuous genetic connections. His response to Kroeber (5 January 1913: UCB) was superficially encouraging but reticent about particulars: the results were "extremely interesting" and "rather exciting" with "no theoretical reason" they could not be true when the evidence was examined more carefully. Sapir assured Kroeber (11 February 1913: UCB): "I hope you do not have the idea that I am personally opposed to such syntheses. In fact, I feel strongly that there will be more of them made as our knowledge progresses." He would be "delighted if the total number of linguistic stocks in California should turn out to be very few in number after all"; but this remained to be proved. Sapir was particularly concerned (to Kroeber, 29 February 1913: UCB) that the phonetic quality of the available material was inadequate "for any solid comparative work." He agreed that "once definite phonetic relationships have been worked out, other examples, that at first sight would have seemed far-fetched, fall right into one's hands."

Kroeber tried to enlist Sapir in the California work, because it would be better received if backed by the preeminent linguist of North America. Sapir, however, hesitated to get involved, declining, for example, to link Washo to Hokan in favor of Dixon (to Kroeber, 17 October 1917: UCB). Sapir claimed he had never written down his morphological connections: "There are also a lot of phonetic laws that I have worked out that are implicit in the material." Sapir wanted to retain control of his involvement with Kroeber and his California fiefdom.

Kroeber's success in linking California languages did, however, encourage Sapir to look for similar connections in his own material. He turned, therefore, to demonstration of the genetic unity of the Uto-Aztecan stock, using his own field data on Ute and Southern Paiute. His reconstruction of the phonetic system of Proto-Uto-Aztecan (the common ancestor of the presently-spoken languages) in 1913 was the first systematic application of Indo-European methods to a North American language family. Sapir (to Kroeber, 23 December 1912: NMM) considered his evidence "so peculiar as to defy all interpretation on any assumption but that of genetic relationship." Kroeber had attacked Uto-Aztecan unsuccessfully in his early California years without noting such evidence. Sapir (to Mason, n.d. 1913: NMM) explicitly contrasted the elegance of his reconstruction with Kroeber's more haphazard approach to the Hokan and Penutian stocks in California: "Going some, isn't it? As usual, however, I imagine that Kroeber will guess what is right or almost right and leave it to others to demonstrate." Kroeber's enthusiasm tended to outstrip his evidence.

Kroeber (to Sapir, 24 July 1917: NMM), impressed by Sapir's Uto-Aztecan success, urged him to generalize the argument that technical linguistic work was crucial to historical inference: "By Jove, old man, if I had your knowledge and power of assimilation and skill in handling the damn brute material, I'd have cut you out in reputation as a linguist long ago. At least I'm not afraid to try." Sapir, however, felt that Kroeber's less rigorous efforts compromised the reception of genetic hypotheses.

Sapir encouraged Kroeber to publish the evidence for California Hokan and Penutian. By the time it appeared in print (Dixon and Kroeber 1919), Sapir had already joined the California stocks to even larger units. The hypothesis seemed almost conservative given Sapir's work in the interim. Indeed, between 1913 and about 1917, Sapir came to share Kroeber's enthusiasm for genetic reduction and the two exchanged several letters a week, redolent with new hypotheses. Sapir, however, preferred to work outside Kroeber's domain. Kroeber, although he encouraged Sapir's wider efforts, rarely worked beyond the borders of California.[1] When the classification of California languages was completed, moreover, he turned permanently away from linguistic work, effectively leaving the field to Sapir.

Not everyone shared the classificatory mania of Kroeber and Sapir. Boas was particularly cautious about the amount of evidence required for genetic relationship. He had been more sanguine early in his career, but work with diffusion of cultural elements persuaded him that extensive linguistic similarities were not necessarily genetic. He preferred psychological and typological comparison of languages. Moreover, as Sapir, Kroeber, and a few others proposed increasingly radical unifications of linguistic stocks, Boas's position became increasingly rigid.

Consistent frustration with Boas's inability to comprehend simple linguistic arguments runs through Sapir's classificatory work. Boas, who had no formal training in linguistics, rejected the Indo-European assumption that regular sound change was necessarily genetic in origin. Sapir complained to Radin (10 June 1913: NMM):

[Boas] allows his judgment to be influenced by a preconceived like or dislike. For some mysterious reason he simply does not like to think of an originally small number of linguistic stocks, which have each of them differentiated tremendously, but prefers, with Powell, to conceive of an almost unlimited number of distinct stocks, many of which, in the course of time, become extinct. To me the former alternative seems a historical necessity.

Sapir realized that some of this past history might remain unrecoverable, but to dismiss the possibility of historical inference was inconceivable. To Lowie (15 February 1921: UCB), he acknowledged that compromise with Boas was unlikely:

[Boas's] whole approach is so different from mine and from that of the vast majority of linguistic students that the attempt to argue about the theoretical basis can only result in mutual irritation. . . . His wholesale use of the idea of diffusion must also strike anyone that has any experience with the brass tacks of linguistic history as rather absurd.

Boas went so far as to dissociate himself from the linguistic hypotheses of his former students in the *American Anthropologist* in 1920; only Sapir was identified. Sapir (to Speck, 2 October 1924: NMM) concluded that the problem was unsolvable (Darnell, in press):[2]

At last analysis these controversies boil down to a recognition of two states of mind. One, conservative intellectualists, like Boas, . . . who refuse absolutely to consider far-reaching suggestions. . . . Hence, from an overanxious desire to be right, they generally succeed in being more hopelessly and fundamentally wrong, in the long run, than many more superficial minds who are not committed to "principles". . . . The second type is more intuitive and, even when the evidence is not as full or theoretically unambiguous as it might be, is prepared to throw out tentative suggestions. . . . I have no hope whatever of ever getting Boas and Goddard to see through my eyes or to feel with my hunches. I take their opposition like the weather, which might generally be better but which will have to do.

Boas was particularly incensed when Sapir combined Tlingit and Haida with Athabaskan, into Na-dene. The Northwest Coast was Boas's territory and he considered the similarities Sapir cited as typological rather than historical. Sapir was particularly frustrated because much of his evidence came from Boas's own work, and his former teacher refused to acknowledge its implications.

The acrimony of the polarization is illustrated by Sapir's correspondence with Boas's student, Leo Frachtenberg, over extensions of the Penutian stock in Oregon. Sapir used Frachtenberg's Coos grammar to link Coos to Takelma; Frachtenberg responded (29 June 1914: NMM) that Sapir was "pursuing very wrong methods in dealing with accidental phonetic resemblances among two or more Indian languages." Sapir (2 July 1914: NMM) mildly pointed out that he did not think the similarities were "accidental" because they could be reduced to "definite phonetic laws." Sapir's Uto-Aztecan work showed the potentials, and he now attacked Na-dene, Penutian, and Hokan, attempting to persuade Frachtenberg to join the classificatory bandwagon: "I hope that you have enough feeling for linguistic history to feel as strongly as I do that our present classification of Indian languages into an immense number of distinct stocks has little inherent probability, and must sooner or later give way to tremendous simplifications."

Frachtenberg was impervious to Sapir's arguments and even presumed to tell Sapir how to do linguistic comparisons (20 October 1914: NMM). He assumed that sound correspondences did not prove genetic affiliation and that Indo-European methods were not applicable to unwritten languages. Geographical contiguity and typological classification were the only possible generalizations. Even Boas would not have gone so far in dismissing the historical potential of linguistic classification.

Sapir pointed out to Frachtenberg (8 January 1915: NMM) that Boas had "no personal experience in historic grammar or comparative linguistics." Frachtenberg (to Sapir, 27 January 1915: NMM) persisted in his perceived loyalty to Boas: "I should not for a moment even hesitate in following your method of study if only we had any basis for a historical study of the American Indian languages. And as long as such a basis is wanting, I must perforce adhere to Boas's cautious conservatism." To Boas, Frachtenberg wrote (2 March 1915: NMM) that Sapir's "methods are wrong, and may lead to wrong conclusions"; Sapir was "influenced by the methods applied in Indo-European linguistics which he now tries to apply to the field of American Indian linguistics." This was, of course, precisely what Sapir was trying to do.

Not all of Sapir's critics were Boasians. The conservative establishment in Amerindian linguistics, centered in the Bureau of American Ethnology, was committed implicitly to the Powell classification. Further, each researcher felt territoriality about languages or language families studied. Sapir was unique among American linguists in working on virtually every language family of the continent. Other investigators had missed connections in their own work which Sapir took credit for.

Truman Michelson, the Bureau's Algonquianist, was impressed by Sapir's detailed correspondences for Na-dene but much more skeptical about anything that concerned Algonquian. Pliny Goddard, the established dean of Athabaskan studies, admitted to Sapir (4 November 1920: NMM) that he did not object to his planned comparative grammar of Na-dene but would be hurt if Sapir attempted a comparative statement of Athabaskan itself.

Sapir found himself directly in conflict with Michelson when he linked Wiyot and Yurok of California into a Ritwan family that was in turn linked to Algonquian. Michelson's published critique (1914, 362–363) dismissed the resemblances as accidental because Kroeber would have seen the connection if it existed. Sapir complained to Kroeber (9 September 1914: NMM) that Michelson had never "had to approach a language with complete ignorance of its structure" because he worked only on Algonquian, where "the main structure [was] already completed." Kroeber (15 September 1914: NMM) declined to clarify the gradual emergence of historical connections from field data, suggesting that Sapir ignore Michelson's "puritanical" strictures because "a technical discussion . . . will be regarded as a quarrel between experts of whom one is as likely to be right as the other."

Michelson complained to Boas (26 April 1917: NMM) that Sapir had "fallen another victim to the deplorable tendency to consolidate linguistic stocks without adequate proof." Sapir, in turn, complained to Lowie (15 February 1921: UCB) that Indo-Europeanists like Michelson had a "strictly limited" perspective and that "differences of morphology that seem somewhat minor to us are of staggering importance to them."[3]

Sapir, however, did not retreat from his Ritwan hypothesis. He delayed initial publication in 1913 until he was fully convinced (to Speck, 18 July 1913; to Radin, 18 July 1913: NMM). To Radin, he noted: "When you have that vast expanse of country separating the California stocks from even the westernmost Algonkin tribes, one may well hesitate." To Kroeber (6 August 1913: NMM), Sapir was confident: "This, of course, was one of my strong pieces. It is laughably obvious." Kroeber (21 June 1913: NMM) urged publication: "I am glad . . . you have brought the situation to the point where the question is no longer one of fact as to relationship, but one of working out its circumstances and tracing the history of the individual languages." Sapir, in fact, presented more evidence for Ritwan-Algonquian than for many connections that were more readily accepted.[4] Much of the negative reaction arose from the geographic anomaly of an Algonquian-related family in California.

In 1915, Sapir extended Kroeber's California Penutian to include Chinook ("though you may wink with incredulity") and Tsimshian ("don't faint") (to Kroeber, 24 April 1915: NMM). Kroeber responded (29 May 1915: NMM) querulously that the "perfect definiteness" of the California Penutian and Hokan stocks was lost with these new extensions. Sapir (15 April 1915: NMM) ignored Kroeber's ambivalence and enthusiastically described the likely movement of peoples on the west coast, stating that "you can almost read California history from linguistic geography."

Kroeber (17 November 1915: NMM) was apparently convinced, asking Sapir's permission to cite the unpublished "newer enlarged linguistic families as evidencing movements of population" for his own article on the Pacific coast tribes. Sapir (25 November 1915: NMM) noted that Oregon Penutian and Hokan-Coahuiltecan were already "very probable" and urged Kroeber to publish his evidence (19 December 1915: NMM): "I should be glad not to be alone in this new series of developments."

Surprisingly, there were few objections to Oregon Penutian. Frachtenberg visited California and was impressed by the quantity of Dixon and Kroeber's unpublished lexical evidence. He even insisted to Sapir (17 December 1916: NMM) that he was not dogmatically "conservative," listing several Northwest Coast genetic connections that he intended to demonstrate. In spite of their past relationship, Sapir (9 January 1917: NMM) graciously welcomed Frachtenberg's support: "We are evidently all progressing in the same general direction. After all, the logical facts cannot long be withstood. It is only a question of whether one prefers to be conservative as long as he respectably can, or has a bit more courage than the crowd and is willing to look ahead." Frachtenberg (12 February 1917: NMM) interpreted this to mean that there had never been a conflict between his approach and Sapir's, optimistically predicting that "in the near future you and I will work shoulder by shoulder and show what can be done in American linguistics." Frachtenberg was the only person of the period who attempted to portray himself as Sapir's peer. The collaboration never materialized, however, because Frachtenberg left the discipline (Stocking 1974).

Boas, however, was wary about the Penutian extensions, writing to Sapir (17 July 1918: NMM) that similar stem forms did not establish genetic relationship and citing a counterexample from Siouan. He lectured Sapir (22 July 1918: NMM) on the need to consider other explanations than genetic relationship. Sapir responded (26 July 1918: NMM):

The great psychological differences that you find do not, I am afraid, frighten me quite as much as they seem to yourself. . . . I must confess that I have always had a feeling that you entirely overdo psychological peculiarities in different languages as presenting insuperable obstacles to genetic theories, and that, on the other hand, you are not especially impressed by the reality of the differentiating processes, phonetic and grammatical, that have so greatly operated in linguistic history all over the world.

Boas and Sapir simply had to agree to disagree.[5]

Sapir, stimulated by Dixon's suggestion, then extended the Penutian stock into Mexico. His Hokan work built largely on the work of John Swanton for the bureau. Sapir (to Swanton, 12 April 1918: NMM) went on to speculate about the movement of population in the central part of the continent. Swanton's work was never subjected to serious examination because he was perceived as a conservative. Sapir, however, went on to link Hokan to Subtiaba in Nicaragua, as well as to Siouan and Iroquois-Caddoan. To Speck (11 January 1924: NMM), Sapir suggested that Hokan-Coahuiltecan was "the linguistic group correlating with the earliest and culturally most primitive peoples in California, northern Mexico and the Gulf region." Later movements of peoples scattered the original unity of the stock.

Throughout this period of intensive work on particular genetic connections, Sapir was supported by Kroeber, who accepted connections on Sapir's word before seeing the evidence (13 December 1916: NMM); Kroeber expected Sapir to take responsibility for the majority of the work: "Every nail of proof you drive in absolves me from so much that I haven't got around to doing." Kroeber consistently urged publication and provided Sapir with the feedback few others did (14 August 1913: ALK). Kroeber told Sapir "the prestige of American anthropology will be better maintained if at least some of the claims come with the backing of your critical faculty than if they are all made by people in whom the rank and file of us have less confidence."

The Radin Fiasco

In 1919, Paul Radin, in a paper for Kroeber's California ethnological series, proposed that all North American Indian languages were genetically related. Sapir, who was normally patient with his outspoken colleague, was incensed because Radin's haphazard work jeopardized his own careful effort to consolidate linguistic stocks. Radin doubtless expected Sapir to be annoyed by his challenge to established linguistic classificatory method, but Sapir's vehemence startled him.

Sapir acknowledged the high quality of Radin's descriptive work on American Indian languages. But Radin did not consider himself a linguist and acknowledged no obligation to meet linguistic canons of evidence. He wrote to Sapir (6 August 1913: NMM): "Why do people always look upon me as a linguist, when I have so studiously avoided being associated with them?" Radin wanted to use linguistic data for historical perspective in ethnology rather than as an end in itself.

Radin accepted the proposals of genetic relationship up to 1919 without independent assessment of the evidence. This left him with twelve units, which he argued made his merging of the twelve "hardly so revolutionary" as with a baseline of the Powell classification (1919, 490). Radin used his own fieldwork only for Wappo (a Yukian language) and Winnebago (Siouan). His evidence for continental unity was eight grammatical traits, the most persistent being verb-aspect (hardly unique to Amerindian languages). He cited admittedly inadequate archaeological evidence that migration from Northeast Asia was 15,000 years ago and asserted that linguistic differentiation had postdated the settlement of the continent (1919, 492).[6] Radin then pronounced the unity of all American languages demonstrated to his satisfaction.

Sapir was tempted to review Radin's paper in the *American Anthropologist*, writing to Goddard, the editor (10 June 1919: NMM), that he was "most disgusted" because the paper was "deplorably lacking in method" and "full of all kinds of ignorance besides." Goddard (to Sapir, 13 June 1919: NMM) was delighted that Sapir "offered to attend to Radin" and would "mete out justice." He was unhappy when Sapir had second thoughts (26 June 1919: NMM): Boas could not speak out because his relations with Radin had long been strained; Kroeber was inappropriate because the paper appeared in his series. But Goddard stated: "To ignore it completely seems dangerous because the paper carries with it the authority of the institution." Goddard further noted that Radin was unlikely to remain "permanently angry" with Sapir.

Sapir (30 June 1919: NMM) acknowledged his responsibility but declined because it was "a most wretched performance." A general review of the state of the art would solve the "personal difficulty," but Sapir hoped that Michelson would take on the task. Kroeber "could easily have thrown it out on technical grounds, had he known enough." Meanwhile, Sapir had no objection to his opinion of the paper becoming known privately: "There are some positive points . . . but the task of rescuing them from the mess in which they are embedded is a difficult one, I fear." Sapir no doubt hoped other colleagues would defend the rigorous application of philological methods, but no one came forward.

Kroeber (23 August 1919: NMM) was appalled at the idea that Sapir might respond publicly, which "would only fan the fires of Goddard's sadistic joy." Goddard encouraged "his best friends to wangle undignifiedly" and would particularly enjoy "a dissention in our camp"—that is, among Boasians who wanted to reduce the number of linguistic families. Kroeber professed himself helpless to prevent publication because Radin ignored his warning of the potential reception. Perhaps trying to assuage his own guilt over the debacle, Kroeber claimed to see some possible truth in Radin's proposals: "He is finely organized and his intuitions are good even if not always balanced . . . and I think that we must put up with him." Kroeber did not want to be associated with the paper or to repudiate Radin publicly. A review of the whole situation was overdue, with "Paul's abomination" only part of the picture: "If you attack him he will certainly come back in his childish temper and we should have a squabble. . . . You are irritated now; and that would only help him, or at any rate divert progress."

Kroeber had much to lose. He was attempting to achieve consensus about linguistic classification through the bureau; in his proposal to Fewkes (20 December 1919: BAE), Kroeber linked Sapir and Radin as radicals about classification without distinguishing their methods or training. It was precisely this lack of methodological discrimination which upset Sapir.

Moreover, Radin's paper threatened Sapir's own priority in synthesizing continental linguistic history. In any case, he decided to keep his quarrel with Radin private in order to present his own classification in due time on its own merits. To Radin (25 November 1919: NMM), he pointed out that his own classification was in progress, explaining that he preferred to remain silent because of his "rather unfavorable criticism." Radin would have been better off with "a more modest task," such as connecting Siouan and Muskogean with Hokan. The "real ore" in the paper was "pretty well hidden in the baser mass." Interestingly, Sapir did not insist that Radin's conclusion was wrong, only that his paper did not prove the case: "I cannot honestly say that I believe you have proven your point, though I would not go so far as to say that the point is unprovable." Sapir acknowledged "proto-American elements" that might eventually lead to "much more far-reaching syntheses than most of us have dared to suggest." Indeed, his 1921 classification listed four such features; but he refused to jeopardize his credibility by going beyond what he considered clear evidence.

Radin replied (to Sapir, 23 December 1919: NMM) with the diatribe that Kroeber had wanted to avoid airing in public:

I always knew we were working at cross-purposes, but it never came out so clearly as in your last letter. . . . My interests are primarily historical. . . . The bare fact of the interrelationship of the NA Indian languages is of overwhelming importance to me, for it means so much ethnologically. . . . as soon as I felt convinced of the poetic relationship of the languages of NA I lost the desire to do any more detailed work in linguistics. . . . What is wanted is a person with an historical imagination. . . . But just think of the fun of building these insecure structures!

As a result of Sapir's criticism, Radin associated himself with Kroeber, whom he believed to share his conviction of the importance of history. Radin was unconcerned with the internal philological constraints on historical work, seeking rather a framework for ethnology. Radin's insistence that the data were indeterminate by definition was perceived by his contemporaries as sloppy thinking. Kroeber characterized Radin's intellectual style to Sapir (17 October 1922: UCB): "Paul always loves a clue and is impatient of evidence." His intuitions were "likely to be sound, but equally likely to be unsubstantiable by the material in his possession." Radin "blinks in sunshine and is happiest feeling his way through a fog."

Sapir wanted to reconcile philological method and ethnological necessity and retained his low opinion of Radin's linguistics. Years later, for example, he discouraged Kroeber (28 November 1930: UCB) from allowing Radin to do comparative linguistic work for the Committee on American Indian Languages because "he is best at an unevaluated descriptive record, whether in ethnology or linguistics. He is not critical enough . . . to apply inferential logic to a theoretical problem" (to Kroeber, 5 February 1931: UCB).

The Six-Unit Classification

Sapir considered reading a paper on "The Status of Linguistic Classification in North America" at the AAA meetings in 1919 (to Radin, 5 December 1919: NMM). Radin (12 December 1919: NMM) implicitly took credit for forcing Sapir's hand and urged him to "organize" Amerindian linguistics workers and settle the issue of classification for once and for all. Radin was willing to take on this role if Sapir declined it. Sapir preferred to work alone and did not want to associate his efforts with Radin. He decided to wait with his own classification.

Sapir's own synthesis had been incubating for some time. He wrote to Speck (1 August 1918: APS) that the extended Hokan stock was *"the"* great stock of North America and hinted that the six major stocks might be consolidated further:

Getting down to brass tacks, how in the Hell are you going to explain general American n- "I" except genetically? It's disturbing I know but (more) non-committal conservatism is only dodging after all, isn't it? Great simplifications are in store for us, but we must be critical and not force our evidence. Besides, we must try to work out genealogically degrees of relationship. Only so will fascinating perspectives appear. It seems to me that only now is American linguistics becoming really interesting, at least in its ethnological bearings.

Speck was a safe person to try out far-reaching hypotheses because he did not do comparative linguistic work himself and had no axes to grind, other than his personal loyalty to Sapir.

Sapir revealed his six-unit classification in a letter to Boas (3 September 1920: NMM), explicitly seeking his approval: "But I know you really do feel these things better than anyone else, only you dislike interpreting them in terms of historical perspective." He cited proto-American features, urging Boas not to ignore "fundamental *facts*." Boas (18 September 1920: NMM) reiterated his established position, albeit surprisingly gently:

I don't think our opinions are really as different as they might appear to an outsider. . . . I quite agree with you in regard to the point of view that far-reaching similarities, particularly between neighboring languages, must be due to historical causes. I think, however, that we are not sufficiently familiar with the phenomena of mutual influences of languages in primitive life to decide whether we are dealing with a gradual development of divergence or whether the whole linguistic phenomena ought not to be considered from the same point of view as any ethnic phenomena. . . . If there is disagreement, it seems to my mind certain that the linguistic phenomena must be looked at in the same way as the cultural phenomena.

Sapir remained convinced that comparative Indo-European methods made it possible to treat language differently from the rest of culture. It was inevitable that he and Boas talked past one another.

As Sapir's argument neared its final form, he wrote to Speck (9 October 1920: NMM) about his "far-reaching ideas" that would "send our friends the conservatives by the ears." The six great stocks, "each of which I feel to be a genetic unity," might still be further united. Sapir presented the six stocks to Kroeber (2 October 1920: NMM) as his "present feeling." Kroeber responded (17 December 1920: NMM) that Sapir was "wholly on the right track"; most of his conclusions were "probably true," although some were "hopelessly beyond my depth." Kroeber urged Sapir to put his findings on record without "waiting until you are able to substantiate them in detail, which will be many years. The majority of us won't know what you are talking about, and Boas will think you have turned prophet instead of philologist, but a pronouncement would at least show which way we are tending and emphasize the nature of the problem that lies ahead."

The six-unit classification was unveiled at the December 1920 meetings of the American Association for the Advancement of Science in Chicago; the anthropologists had decided at the last moment to move their meeting to Baltimore. Sapir elected to go to Chicago as originally planned because he wanted to confer with Sinologist Berthold Laufer about possible connections of old and new world languages. There were, therefore, few anthropologists in the audience, making Sapir's presentation something of an anticlimax. The text, entitled "A Bird's Eye View of American Languages North of Mexico," was accompanied by a map.[7] Sapir called for a more "historical and inclusive" classification and presented a typical structural description for each of the six stocks. He noted four potential proto-American features and a possible regrouping of the six stocks into only three. The final sentence of the manuscript read: "Movements of population [are] to be revealed through linguistic research." The word "revealed" was handwritten over "created."

Only three stocks were omitted from the classification: Beothuk of Newfoundland was so poorly recorded that Sapir could not attach it to a larger unit; in 1929, he put it under Algonquian. Waiilatpuan, Lutuamian, and Sahaptin were omitted, later to be attached to Plateau Penutian based on Frachtenberg's long available evidence. Zuni was the most pressing problem. Sapir ignored Kroeber's instinct for a Siouan connection. In 1929, unwilling to accept isolates in the map of American languages, he placed it in Uto-Aztecan. The new inclusions were, therefore, aesthetically rather than linguistically motivated.

Although the 1929 version is better known today and smoother in its argumentation, the 1920 classification is the one Sapir's contemporaries reacted to. Although it was published only as a one-page abstract in *Science* in 1921, it summarized a decade or more of Boasian fieldwork, not all of it done by Sapir, and claimed that genetic relationship provided insight into reconstruction of culture history. The classification appeared amid the most intensive attention to linguistic classification in the history of Boasian anthropology. Because of its inclusive scope, it effectively ended the era of consolidation of linguistic stocks. Sapir went on to other problems, while his colleagues used the classification as an ethnographic baseline or ignored it, as they chose.

After his presentation in Chicago, Sapir was uncertain whether to publish "my map and findings just at present," hoping to work further on Na-dene and possible Asiatic connections "for the next couple of years." Predictably, Kroeber (20 January 1921: NMM) urged immediate publication:

I know how you feel about exposed flanks. Nevertheless if there is any danger you have already incurred it in making your stand public at Chicago. I consider the wisest course therefore to be to put yourself on record and save yourself from misrepresentation. There may not be any great amount of talk about your Chicago presentation, but there is no telling how far it may travel and it is almost certain to be distorted. You can count on the people who are interested in the subject picking up some sort of gossip about it. You will be better protected if their knowledge of your attitude is authoritative. I do not see how publication would lay you open to attack. Since you present no evidence you cannot be charged with misusing it or employing it hastily. . . . To make a confession, I gasped a bit when I realized that you had really presented this outline at Chicago. I was astounded not because your stand seems to me essentially an exposed one, but because I have always been strongly impressed by your cautiousness. I conclude that you must have a lot of ammunition salted away.

Kroeber, clearly, was overwhelmed by the magnitude of Sapir's revisions of the linguistic map of North America. His own linguistic talents were inadequate for the kind of reconstructions Sapir suggested. In any case, Sapir's most recent correspondence had implied that the six-unit classification was still tentative. Moreover, Kroeber was inclined by temperament to conservatism and compromise.

At the same time, Kroeber urged Sapir to publish his hypotheses, he sought consensus in American linguistics. To Sapir (25 November 1919: NMM) he emphasized the need to "find out what we are in substantial agreement about." Kroeber felt that "we have overlooked this common element and are accentuating minor differences so much that our private talk as well as our public discussions are over-disputatious."

In this spirit of compromise, Kroeber prepared a memo for the Bureau of American Ethnology (to Fewkes, 20 December 1919: BAE) suggesting that the bureau should mediate between classificatory extremes. Anthropologists "have a right to demand of the linguists that the latter arrive at definite conclusions as quickly as possible." Sapir and Radin were at one end of the continuum, with Boas and Michelson at the other. Michelson "disclaims theoretical hostility to reductions, but . . . exacts a standard of completeness that would be difficult to attain under the most favorable conditions." Boas assumed that all further reductions were unprovable in principle and refused to look at the evidence for particular hypotheses. Kroeber placed himself, along with Swanton, Dixon, and Harrington, in the middle ground.

Kroeber proposed that Sapir's Uto-Aztecan should be accepted because it had never been seriously challenged. His Na-dene would have to await further evidence: "The recognized specialist on Athabaskan is Goddard. An acceptance by him of the Sapir findings would probably quiet all antagonisms." But this was unlikely, as Kroeber well knew. Swanton's Natchez-Muskhogean and Dixon and Kroeber's Hokan should be accepted as firmly established. California Penutian needed further assessment. Kroeber felt that everyone could agree to this proposal:

Extremists of either wing will never be wholly satisfied; but there is no reason why they should be. Sapir and Michelson would perhaps never agree on just how much evidence constituted positive proof. A radical like Radin would no doubt consider that such findings as won the approval of everyone, or even of the majority, were tame and half-hearted; but he would prefer partial acceptance of his attitude to total rejection. Boas, who deplores all work along these lines as less important than other studies, would nevertheless be likely to welcome a segregation of the more valid and probable reductions from the wildly unsound ones, on the basis that the evil would thereby be limited.

The conference Kroeber proposed for the Christmas meetings in 1920 was never held. It is unlikely that Sapir would have accepted consensus given his opinion of his fellow Amerindian linguists. In any case, he was in Chicago at the time presenting his six-unit classification and talking to Laufer about Indo-Chinese—hardly the conservative consensus Kroeber envisioned.

The Indo-Chinese Hypothesis

Sapir's most dramatic genetic hypothesis was never published. The reception of his six-unit classification undoubtedly inculcated caution. Yet Sapir was personally convinced that his Na-dene stock (Tlingit, Haida, and Athabaskan) could be linked to Asia, clarifying the population movements that produced the present linguistic diversity of native America. Opposition did not modify his opinions but it did cause him to seek further evidence before making a public statement.[8]

At Columbia, Sapir had taken ethnology courses with Berthold Laufer, who shared his enthusiasm for detailed linguistic work as most Boasians did not. Laufer was a German-trained Orientalist who did fieldwork with both written and unwritten languages; he was a veteran of four Chinese expeditions, one of them including Tibet. Early in the century, he was virtually the only Sinologist in North America (Hummel 1936, 101). Sapir stayed in contact with Laufer after he went to the Field Museum in Chicago in 1908. Laufer was only ten years older than Sapir, and the two were collegial early in the latter's career.

Boas highly valued Laufer's work on the Jesup Expedition which studied languages and cultures on both sides of the Bering Strait for the American Museum. Although there were no grand conclusions, Sapir must have absorbed the formulation of compelling research problems from a historical standpoint. Certainly, Laufer was more intrigued by long-range historical inference than most Boasians.[9] Lowie, in contrast, saw Laufer as a "Sinologist who sometimes recorded valuable anthropological data" (1965, 71). Perception of Laufer as fundamentally alien to the Boasian ethnological tradition may, however, have grown out of his encouragement of Sapir's search for Asian linguistic ties.

By 1919, correspondence between Laufer and Sapir focused on linking the languages of the Americas and Asia. Sapir frequently borrowed books from Laufer, complaining (7 September 1920: NMM) that Ottawa was "a desert for literature." Sapir encouraged Laufer's

Tibetan work (28 September 1920: NMM): the language interested him "very much for various reasons":

You may be somewhat amused at my pre-occupation with Indo-Chinese studies, which are in a way out of my line, but the field really interests me very much, and though I fear to hint anything now, it seems to me to vaguely foreshadow certain points of unexpected significance in other fields.

Sapir was particularly concerned about whether Tibetan had tone, as many Na-dene languages did. Sapir hinted to Lowie (9 September 1920: NMM) that his "big comparative study" of Na-dene would require fieldwork with both Haida and Tlingit: "There are so many things I'd like to do in American linguistics that my head swims. A sadly neglected field, yet destined to open up tremendous perspectives." Sapir lamented the absence of good workers for this task. Further, American anthropologists had consistently avoided comparisons to Asian languages and cultures. Sapir commented: "I have no doubt that surprising links will reveal themselves in the fulness of time."

In the fall of 1920, Clark Wissler asked Sapir to comment on his proposal to the National Research Council for anthropological work in Polynesia. Sapir (3 October 1920: NMM) responded, in confidence, that Polynesian might have "a significance we hardly dream of at present." He though that "reconstructed Indo-Chinese, originally a northern language within a stone's throw of certain individuals who were to take a trip to North America, showed significant analogies to Na-dene." There was considerable need for serious linguistic work in the Austronesian area.

In any case, Sapir's unveiling of the six-unit classification coincided with his plans to visit Laufer for discussions of Indo-Chinese. Clearly, he did not consider the two projects different in kind. When the meeting location was changed, Laufer (12 November 1920: NMM) decried the factionalism of the AAA and urged Sapir to come to Chicago "whether there is a meeting or not." Sapir had no difficulty making up his mind; Indo-Chinese was the classificatory priority.

Sapir reported to Lowie (2 February 1921: NMM) "a very delightful visit" with Laufer, who was "as kind and accommodating as he could possibly be." Sapir noted cryptically that they had "a common interest along certain lines which I hope may continue." His next letter to Lowie (15 February 1921: NMM) made the first explicit statement of the Indo-Chinese hypothesis (the discussions with Laufer, of course, were face-to-face):

I no longer believe nor, for that matter, have I ever definitely held that the differentiation of languages in America has taken place entirely on the American continent. On the contrary, I think that the most far-reaching differences of grouping had already taken place on the Asiatic continent, and I believe it goes almost without saying that America was peopled by a number of historically different waves. I am at present of the opinion that the Na-dene wave is the most recent of all. . . . The Na-dene languages are by all means the most "un-American" of all the languages spoken on the northern continent. . . . I am anticipating the most fascinating task in the unraveling of the history of the group.

Meanwhile, Sapir and Laufer returned to the details, with Sapir promising (22 January 1921: NMM) to send him a "selected list of lexical correspondences" between Indo-Chinese and Na-dene.

Sapir's most extensive summary of his Indo-Chinese data came in a letter to Laufer (1 October 1921: NMM, FCM, UCB), with a copy to Kroeber. His enthusiasm was palpable: "My evidence accumulates so fast that it is hard to sit down and give an idea." If the morphological and lexical similarities were accidental, "then every analogy on God's earth is an accident."

It is all so powerfully cumulative and integrated that when you tumble to one point a lot of others fall into line. I am now so thoroughly accustomed to the idea that it no longer startles me. . . . I do not feel that Na-dene belongs to the other American languages. I feel it as a great intrusive band. . . . In short, do not think me an ass if I am seriously entertaining the notion of an old Indo-Chinese offshoot into Northwest America. . . . Am I dreaming?

The chief stumbling block, in Sapir's opinion, was that Na-dene and Indo-Chinese were studied only within their present cultural and typological areas. Without these narrow blinders, the evidence would speak for itself and "the theoretical road to a synthesis" would be clear.

Sapir was preparing to embark on a long-range research program. The Na-dene comparative study would include both actual and reconstructed Athabaskan forms. He would have to tackle Haida and Tlingit as well as Athabaskan proper, with fieldwork geared to obtaining lexical material for comparative purposes. After the comparative grammar of Na-dene, possibly with an Athabaskan etymological dictionary "as a side-show," he would be ready to demonstrate the links between Na-dene and Indo-Chinese. Sapir asked his co-conspirators not to "blab too much" because "99% of one's fellow men are damned fools."

When Kroeber did not respond to the long discourse on Indo-Chinese, Sapir (24 November 1921: UCB) inquired as to his reaction: "I did not expect you to say you believed my preliminary feeler." Kroeber's reply (26 November 1921: UCB) was carefully worded to avoid offense but absolutely without conviction. He professed to have no opinion without seeing the data in detail "and probably following them up with systematic work." This was harder because he knew nothing about the Asian languages: "But in the last analysis, I presume that . . . my opinion contains as its largest ingredient the conviction that Edward Sapir's judgment on such matters is sound." Laufer was more sanguine (1 November 1921: NMM), professing himself "amazed at the wonderful progress you have made in the comparative study of Nadene and Indo-Chinese." But Laufer was already convinced.

Although Sapir continued to accumulate evidence, he found it difficult to devote enough time to his Na-dene work. His correspondence with Laufer continued until he left Ottawa in 1925. Laufer was delighted that Sapir was coming to the University of Chicago and undoubtedly envisioned further collaboration. In Chicago, however, Sapir's interests focused more on culture theory and he increasingly addressed a more linguistically discriminating audience.

The only published report of the Na-dene and Indo-Chinese connection was an unsigned note in *Science* (1925, 1607), apparently motivated by Sapir's appointment to the University of Chicago, described the migration patterns necessary to produce the present distribution of Na-dene peoples. Retention of archaic Chinese prefixes and "tonal peculiarities" were cited as evidence. Sapir sounded more like a magician than a scientist; no details of evidence were stated or said to be forthcoming.

None of Sapir's peers took seriously his contention that the evidence for this connection was of the same kind as that for the six-unit classification and the particular consolidations of linguistic stocks embedded within it.

The article in *Science* brought a response from Arles Hrdlicka, a physical anthropologist at Harvard, who wrote to Sapir (19 November 1926: UC) about his long-standing interest in ties between North America and the Pacific islands. Hrdlicka did not distinguish between Asia and Polynesia and was uninterested in which American languages might have Asian ties. He simply wanted to extend Americanist inquiries beyond the boundaries of the continent. Sapir's reply was not preserved, but it is unlikely that he appreciated such undiscriminating support.

Sapir's linking of the old and new worlds achieved some prominence, however, in 1929 when Sapir and his Chicago colleague Fay-Cooper Cole presented a five-year plan for the work of the department to the Rockefeller Foundation. Frederick Woodward, acting president of the University of Chicago, wrote to Edmund Day of the Rockefeller Foundation (n.d. May 1929) that Sapir's "elaborate comparative work" would "do for a primitive American group what the founders of comparative linguistics did for the Indo-European languages." The results could only clarify the "history of the peopling of the American continent." Such a project had more appeal for funding agencies than technical work in American linguistics. Although Sapir allowed these claims to be made for him, he did not pursue the larger connections. Rather, he focused increasingly on the groundwork that had to precede any serious attempt to demonstrate the Indo-Chinese link.

In fact, by this time, Sapir was much more circumspect in his public statements about linguistic relationship. In 1930, Diamond Jenness, his successor in Ottawa, invited Sapir to speak at the Pacific Sciences Congress in Vancouver in 1932 on the origin and antiquity of the American aborigines (Jenness to Sapir, 19 February 1930: NMM).[10] Sapir, who was to be the only linguist, would speak on Asian connections of American languages. He politely declined (8 March 1930: NMM) on grounds of overcommitment. Ironically, Sapir suggested Boas as the "logical man" to treat the topic. Although Boas was familiar with Asiatic material because of the Jesup Expedition, he was hardly likely to argue for far-reaching genetic relationship or migration. Sapir was no longer willing to associate himself with the lunatic fringes of culture-historical reconstruction. A decade earlier, this invitation would have been his priority.

Sapir did not, however, give up his private interest in an Asian connection. In response to a philological inquiry from Nicholas Bodman of Lake Forest, Illinois, Sapir (21 July 1933: YU) admitted that he had long ago "announced" a relationship of Indo-Chinese and Na-dene:

I still believe this is true but have not so far prepared my notes for publication. There is so much solid reconstructive work to be done in both Na-dene and Sinitic that one naturally hesitates to present the theory in cold print. But I still hope to summon up enough courage to do so one of these days, for I think the lexical and structural evidence is quite good.

He enclosed some examples of cognates but warned Bodman that it was "exceedingly dangerous to compare isolated forms from randomly selected languages." Rather, the emphasis had to be on the phonological patterns of languages as wholes.

Indo-Chinese has received less attention from Amerindian linguists than any other genetic connection proposed by Sapir, although work by Robert Shafer (1952; 1957; 1969), Joseph Greenberg (1987), and Laurence Farget (1986) forms a partial exception. The evidence was limited, the hypothesis was never published, and Americanists were reluctant to look for connections outside the continent. At the Sapir Memorial Conference in Ottawa in 1984, his former student, Mary Haas (in Cowan, Foster, and Koerner 1986, 205–206) acknowledged that Sapir's "far-flung attempts to tie up things that are far apart will continue to excite imaginations for generations to come." She concluded that Sapir was "quite right to know it wouldn't be well received." Firsthand work on the Asian languages, which had to precede the North American link, did not begin until the 1940s.

Sapir's classificatory work was done during the Ottawa years when his primary audience was one of anthropologists looking for historical perspective, only incidentally obtained through linguistic method. After Sapir left Ottawa in 1925, he was in contact with colleagues who were linguists rather than anthropologists. He had already summarized the findings of the Ottawa years, in a systematic effort to extend the theoretical scope of Boasian anthropology, and his colleagues were left to make what they would of the six-unit classification. Moreover, the increasing usefulness of archaeological dating made ethnologists less dependent on linguistics for time perspective. Sapir's own interests moved in other directions. Increasingly, his linguistic work was separated from the anthropological and differentiated from the Boasian model of linguistics as part of anthropology. His theoretical interests in anthropology would move in new directions altogether.

CHAPTER SEVEN

Reorientation Toward Psychology

Sapir reached an impasse in the late Ottawa years. His fieldwork program was effectively curtailed; the Canadian government failed to regain its initial enthusiasm for anthropological research on its aboriginal citizens after World War I; Sapir's writings within the Boasian paradigm reached a kind of closure. He was increasingly motivated by concerns beyond salvage linguistics and ethnology and the established models for linguistic classification and culture historical reconstruction. Moreover, he felt that his colleagues did not adequately appreciate his linguistic synthesis of North America.

From about 1916 on, Sapir was restless. He longed for congenial colleagues with whom to discuss his ideas, students to carry out research and stimulate his own intellect, and new theoretical directions. The potentials implicit in both the Boasian paradigm and the Ottawa appointment had been exhausted. Sapir was left to his own devices to reorient his life and career. He coped with serious family problems, dabbled in poetry, aesthetics, and literary criticism, and explored the interdisciplinary connections of anthropology with psychology and psychiatry. It was a period of intellectual ferment, in which the seeds were sown for his later work in the psychology of culture—a term he always preferred to culture-and-personality. In the Chicago and Yale years, he would become the most articulate spokesman of an emerging interdisciplinary social science; but before he left Ottawa in 1925, he had already worked out the intellectual dimensions of the problems that would dominate the latter half of his career. Although Sapir himself recalled this period as unmitigatedly bleak, his most innovative thought crystallized out of its frustrations and self-doubts.

Family and Personal Problems

Sapir's personal problems, particularly the illness and eventual death of his wife Florence, added to the stress of his professional life during the late Ottawa years. Increasingly, he identified the oppressiveness of Ottawa's climate with his isolation from congenial colleagues. The imagery of his poem "Sun and Snow" (9 December 1919: SF) was that of escape through correspondence with friends in San Francisco (Kroeber and Lowie), New York (Boas and Ruth Benedict), and Denmark (Otto Jespersen): "I flapped my wings And touched three sunny places in the sun."

Florence Delson Sapir was first hospitalized in 1912 in Boston, although Sapir did not then envision long-range effects (Sapir to Speck, 11 June: APS). He had limited faith in the Canadian medical profession and returned to New York or Boston where he and Florence had family ties. Perry (1982, 245) speculates that illness provided Florence with an escape from the routine and social isolation in Ottawa.[1] In 1914 (to Kroeber, 11 February: UCB), Sapir reported that the family's stored household goods were lost in a fire while he, Florence, and infant Michael were in Alberni with the Nootka. This incident worsened Florence's already poor health and Sapir took her to New York for "a thorough examination at the hands of a competent doctor."

Florence's health continued to decline after the birth of her third child in 1916. By about 1918, the strain of a busy household with three active small children was becoming too great to manage, and Sapir felt compelled to ask his mother to come for increasingly long stays to help out. The two women did not get along, and both were upset by their frequent quarrels. Sapir tended to side with his mother, considering his wife "grumpy" rather than physically or emotionally ill (Perry 1982, 245).[2] The situation was further polarized by Michael's dislike of and rebellion against his grandmother. Florence was closest to her elder son, while Sapir aligned himself with his only daughter; Grandmother Sapir became the champion of the baby, Philip. Eva Sapir moved in permanently in the winter of 1920–1921, and Florence, due to her repeated hospitalizations, became further isolated from her family. By this time, Florence had come to dislike Ottawa, especially the winters, but also the relatively dreary social scene and constant tension with Grandmother Sapir. But she also missed her family (Michael Sapir, p.c.).

Sapir was cautiously optimistic about Florence's health during this period, although medical bills compounded the other pressures on him; the lung abscess that would eventually cause her death was of long standing. In 1921, Florence Sapir had "a complete nervous breakdown," diagnosed as severe "melancholia" (Sapir to Boas, 15 September: APS) and involving a number of psychotic episodes. Sapir postponed his Sarcee fieldwork and schemed to find a job away from Ottawa, while Florence went to New York for intensive medical treatment and convalescence.

Sapir began to think in terms of psychiatric help for Florence. Kroeber was then a practicing lay analyst, and Sapir sought his opinion about an appropriate doctor. Kroeber (27 June 1921: UCB) recommended William Alanson White of Washington, D.C., and urged Sapir not to apply his own limited understanding of psychoanalysis, because of his emotional involvement; he counseled a medical doctor as the immediate priority.

Florence returned home in December, much improved, but Sapir continued to seek an analyst. To Lowie (14 March 1922: UCB), he wrote that Boas's son Ernst had recommended the same doctor as had William Alanson White. But "I should have to mortgage my soul for 10 years or more before I got through with him." Florence was admitted to hospital in New York in the spring of 1922, and her convalescence stretched out beyond expectation. Boas (16 September 1922: APS) sent wishes of encouragement that Sapir might soon be able to "resume a normal family life" and mediated Sapir's communication with his wife's doctors. Her mental state improved but her physical health deteriorated. Sapir visited as frequently as possible and Boas (20 December 1922: APS), at Florence's request, made arrangements for Michael to stay with his mother for several months. They lived in a small apartment near Columbia University, across the street from Ruth Benedict. Michael attended public school and enjoyed almost daily walks with his mother and Benedict. Michael also recalls several visits to Boas (who was "like a grandfather") in his office. They frequently visited Florence's sister Nadya and her family.

Florence returned to Ottawa in the spring of 1923, after draining of her lung abscess and removal of all her teeth (a usual treatment for serious infection). Sapir spent the summer chafing under the restrictions of a broken leg, acquired during his brief fieldwork on Northern Athabaskan in Pennsylvania. He was now most concerned about Florence's physical condition. In September, Helen and her mother visited friends in Haverill, Massachusetts; in October, they moved to Brookline, where they had a small apartment close to Florence's relatives. Sapir visited frequently. On the recommendation of her doctors (Sapir to Benedict, 8 April 1924; SF),[3] Florence had her lung abscess drained again. Sapir and all of the children were present. The surgery was successful but infection set in, and Florence died a week later at the age of thirty-four. Antibiotics were not yet available. Sapir wrote to Benedict (28 Mary 1924: SF):

The hereafter does not need an explanation. It had to be invented, or pre-philosophic man would have gone mad. . . . You are right in one thing. Death for myself does not seem such an evil, then why should it for Florence? . . . I had always hoped the future would soften and reinterpret some grievous stretches of the past. That was a selfish motive, like absolution held in reserve. But there was also the feeling that Florence knew so well what to make of life, if only given her due chance. It is difficult for me to believe I know or can ever learn what to make of it.

In retrospect, the precise nature of Florence Sapir's condition cannot be determined. Medical and psychiatric diagnosis were in their infancy, and different practitioners regularly offered contradictory opinions. Lung ailments were usually treated by rest in a warm, dry climate (not, of course, Ottawa). For Florence Sapir, the lung abscess was a chronic debilitating disease. Moreover, severe depression and physical illness were inseparable, the latter increasing "psychiatric vulnerability" (Paul Sapir, p.c.).[4]

Sapir found it very painful to discuss their mother's condition with his children; all three recall the extreme stress of those years. Previous commentators (e.g., Perry 1982) have emphasized Florence's mental condition, probably because it seemed to motivate Sapir's growing psychological interests. Certainly, he devoted considerable agonized thought to possible diagnosis and treatment. But, if anything, Sapir turned away from psychoanalysis as providing no explanation of why this woman was stricken; he suffered pangs of guilt over his own helplessness. In later years he strongly encouraged students and colleagues in personality studies to undergo psychoanalysis. But Sapir never seriously considered doing so himself, because he was unwilling to relive the pain of the later Ottawa years.

Sapir's personal anguish during this period was expressed largely through his poetry.[5] Although many of Sapir's poems from this period were published, these were not. Sapir recognized their cathartic function. His poetic images fluctuated depending on Florence's condition. Grief, loneliness, and failure to accept the loss of a life partner predominate.

Throughout this period, Sapir was beset by financial pressure and lack of time to work. He actively sought professional writing, lectures, and poetry publications to generate income (to Lowie, 29 February 1920: UCB): "Need makes us mercenary, I am afraid." Moreover, Sapir was supporting his father and had his mother in residence. Jacob Sapir had developed paranoid delusions, largely about his musical compositions, and Boas—whom the elder Sapir revered greatly—reported considerable concern (to Sapir, 10 July 1919; 21 October 1920: APS), believing that he should not continue to live alone.

Sapir responded (6 November 1920: APS) that he considered this "knotty problem" virtually "insoluble." His father had lived with the family in the past but was now "more definitely psychotic." The household could not accommodate another disturbed member, especially given that it was run by Jacob Sapir's estranged wife. Sapir did not consider his father a danger to society, and an institution would be needlessly cruel. Sapir supported his father financially, humoring his "absurd requests . . . and try[ing] not to contradict or argue." He was unlikely to change. Boas had no alternative, and Jacob Sapir lived alone in Philadelphia until a fatal heart attack in 1935.

The end of World War I brought further concern over members of Florence's family stranded in Europe. Sapir approached Boas, who was active in organizing Jewish aid for refugees, hoping to borrow money toward emigration. Boas was sympathetic but unable to help (to Sapir, 12 November 1920: APS). Characteristically, Boas turned to professional matters in an effort to ease the pressures on Sapir. He obtained a ticket for Sapir to attend the International Congress of Americanists meetings in Europe in 1924, soon after Florence's death. In spite of Boas's intervention, however, Canadian Deputy Minister of Mines Charles Camsell declined to cover the additional expense on the grounds that he had never heard of the congress and doubted that "its work would appeal to our government" (Boas to Sapir, 20 May, 9 June, 1924: APS).[6]

Throughout this chaotic period, Sapir and his mother tried to provide a normal childhood for the three children. Grandmother Sapir knit clothing for the children, even for Helen's dolls. But she had little understanding of children's feelings and used scare techniques to get them to behave. The period was particularly stressful for Michael, who had been closest to Florence and remembered happier times. Sapir was a conscientious though somewhat preoccupied father. For example, Philip recalls playing hooky and being greeted absentmindedly by his father as he sat on the front porch; Sapir failed to notice that his youngest son should have been in school. Eva Sapir included her son in her frequent admonitions to dress warmly or wear rubbers. The children were embarrassed by their grandmother's thick Yiddish accent (unusual in Anglophone Ottawa civil service circles) and were an unwilling audience for reminiscences about her European youth. Philip Sapir recalls that his father frequently escaped to poetry meetings.

The family outings of earlier years continued, though less frequently. For two summers, probably 1923 and 1924, Michael went to summer camp in Algonquian Provincial Park, which Philip attended after the family moved to Chicago. Sapir gave camp chief Taylor Stattent a Sarcee eagle feather headdress, which he wore at campfires, resulting in reduced fees for the boys.

After Florence's death, Sapir acknowledged to Boas (19 May 1924: NMM) that "it will probably take some time before I can do scientific work with anything like relish. If it were not for my mother and the children I should, I think, be in even more of a stupor." The urgency to find a job away from Ottawa was somewhat abated by Florence's death.

Early Contacts with Psychology

The emerging field of psychoanalysis was part of the intellectual milieu of Boasian anthropology. When Freud lectured at Clark University in 1909, Boas talked on "Psychological Problems in Anthropology" (Mark 1968, 14). His *The Mind of Primitive Man*, published only two years later, asserted the inseparability of anthropology and psychology. Boas acknowledged the influence of socialization on custom, recognized unconscious processes (especially in language), and noted the stress of childhood experience—although his notion of mental process did not emphasize mechanisms or sexual dynamics (Mark 1968, 27). In practice, however, Boas believed that psychological factors could not be assessed until historical factors had been eliminated. Psychology, regardless of its ultimate importance, required a prior base in conventional ethnography. Boas was appalled by Freud's generic psychodramas, such as the Oedipus complex.

Boas's position, however, changed over time. By about 1910, sufficient facts about particular North American cultural histories had accumulated from Boasian fieldwork to turn from cataloguing cultural traits to characterizing the integration of particular cultures (Darnell 1977); moreover, the autonomy of anthropology as a discipline had been established. Benedict and Mead in particular had Boas's tacit approval to modify the inherited research program. Boas nevertheless remained profoundly skeptical about psychology insofar as it adhered to any particular system. He considered psychoanalysis reductionistic and wanted applications to cultural problems; psychology and anthropology remained, for him, separate domains, not sources of cross-disciplinary fertilization.

Sapir's earliest documented contact with psychiatry was his correspondence with F. Lyman Wells of the McLean Hospital in Waverly, Massachusetts, later of the Boston Psychiatric Hospital, which began late in 1915. Wells was a friend of Boas's who, in light of the latter's skepticism about psychiatric use of analogies from primitive societies (Wells to Sapir, 15 December 1915: NMM), approached Sapir for feedback about the relevance of ethnographic data on folklore symbolism to psychiatric treatment, a subject that intrigued most analysts of the period. Wells was a clinician who wanted to demonstrate reversion to the primitive in dementia praecox. Sapir wanted a guide to the psychiatric literature. Because of the established contact, Wells was among the first Sapir consulted about his wife's illness.

Wells relied on secondary sources like Sir James Fraser's *The Golden Bough* for ethnographic information and was delighted that Sapir's firsthand experience of Nootka "mannered speech" was comparable to dementia praecox. He was, however, basically unconcerned with the accuracy of ethnographic data, only with finding clinically useful analogues.

Sapir claimed little knowledge of psychology except of Wilhelm Wundt, which Wells distrusted (to Sapir, 22 November 1915: NMM).[7] He recommended that Sapir concentrate on periodicals since psychiatry was changing rapidly as a result of ongoing disputes between Freud and his major students. Wells, who had only the sketchiest ideas about language, suggested (22 July 1920: NMM) behaviorist psychologist John B. Watson because he had dealt with the "psycho-physics of language." Sapir was not a behaviorist and portrayed language as a symbolic system, noting (24 July 1920: NMM) what he needed from psychology for his writing of *Language*: "My main desire is not so much to communicate psychological information to the readers of the book as to avoid falling into psychological pitfalls myself."

Wells introduced Sapir to clinical psychiatry, which was quite different from academic psychology. Experimental control was impossible; medical training imposed implicit biases toward the physiological, with the psychological as a residual category. Freud himself was trained as an internist and neurologist; cultural variability was not an issue for him because he focused on universal biologically based phenomena. Wells was among the psychiatrists who sought cross-culturally valid concepts of personality in the late twenties and thirties. Sapir's early contact with him set the stage for his later collaboration through interdisciplinary conferences and research projects.

Sapir also discussed his explorations of the psychoanalytic literature with fellow social scientists. He met sociologist William Fielding Ogburn, later to be a colleague at Chicago, in California in 1915 while he was working with Ishi (Mark 1968). Ogburn was in frequent contact with Boasian ethnographers, particularly Lowie (Murray 1987). In 1915, both Sapir and Ogburn were studying Freud in an attempt to incorporate his insights into social science. Sapir (to Ogburn, 30 September 1915: NMM) was indisposed "to take all of Freud's symbols [in *The Interpretation of Dreams*] seriously," while Ogburn (to Sapir, 31 December 1917: NMM) objected to Freudian interpretations of primitive myth: "The psychoanalysts about half the time make fools of themselves when they go into anthropology. They simply don't know enough anthropology." Ogburn doubted psychoanalysis could be integrated with sociology; he used psychological explanations, based in the innate characteristics of the human mind, only when cultural ones were exhausted.[8]

Sapir (to Ogburn, 14 January 1918: NMM) failed to finish Carl Jung's *The Psychology of the Unconscious* because of its "many laughable and amateurish blunders in philology." He found "the psychoanalytic handling of myths and religious ceremonial" to be "suggestive" but withheld judgment because of "a very lively doubt in my mind as to whether these people are just at present properly qualified to undertake the work." Psychoanalysts failed to recognize that psychological phenomena took on new meanings because of historical change: "In other words, the psychoanalysts arrive too rapidly at their goal."

Sapir (5 July 1917: UCB) was convinced, however, that Lowie dismissed psychoanalysis too casually, arguing in terms of the interpretation of contemporary poetry. For literary criticism, psychoanalysis permitted a more "personal" kind of interpretation of the "symptoms of the instinctive life of the creator" (in a 1921 review of Guy de Maupassant and Anatole France). Sapir was less interested in the specific systems of Freud or Jung than in potential uses of "some kind of psychology" for "anthropology, including language." In *Language* (1921, fn. p.157), he noted: "A more general psychology than Freud's will eventually prove [repression and symbolism] to be as applicable to the groping for abstract form, the logical or aesthetic ordering of experience, as to the life of the fundamental instincts."

Goldenweiser also flirted with psychoanalysis and was intrigued (to Sapir, 2 August 1922: NMM) by the resistance of anthropologists to it, saying "after we shed our deep-grained prepossessions, Freud's position tends to become more and more feasible." Freud, "frequently afflicted with the philosopher's itch," was inclined to speculate far beyond his clinical data.

In the early years of his infatuation with "dynamic" psychology (a term common at the time), Sapir reviewed several books on psychoanalysis, psychology, and psychiatry.[9] He (1917*i*, 168) identified the "invaluable core" of psychoanalysis as its proof of unconscious, repressed emotional complexes that "leak out into the consciousness." Freud understood the universal in the human mind but, as perceived by American anthropologists, mistakenly treated unconscious symbols as history. Sapir (1921*j*, 108) noted that anthropologists, "having but lately acquired it," were leery of relinquishing their sensitivity to particular historical developments of culture. He further suggested (1921*m*) that Freud should stick to "pure psychology." However indirectly, Sapir had begun his effort to reconcile the disciplinary models of psychiatry and social science.

Sapir was fascinated by Jung's concept of introvert and extravert[10] as irreconcilable psychological types. Throughout his life, Sapir felt himself isolated from his fellow humans and failed to see why others did not perceive the world as he did. Jung's "explanation" released him from a previously unacknowledged burden of guilt. Moreover,

Sapir believed that he was, like Jung, an intuitive introvert—one who lived the life of the mind. His review of Jung in 1923 (1949, 530–531) referred to Jung's insight as "the stare of a man who has found something, and this something a little uncanny." Sapir's characterization of the introvert is a remarkable self-portrait:

To the introvert the object has always a shade of the inimical. It is not necessarily uninteresting, but it needs to be taken with a grain of salt. The introvert has learned to adapt himself to reality by pruning it of its luxuriance, by seeing and by feeling no more in it than can be conveniently fitted into the richly chambered form of his ego. . . . Where the extravert loses himself in the object, the introvert makes it over in such wise as to master it in terms of his own psyche, leaving much of its individual quality to fall by the wayside—unsensed or unfelt or otherwise undervalued.

Sapir warned his readers to avoid judgment and accept personality as given (1949, 531). Neither type could fully comprehend the other. The introvert was appalled by the apparent vicarious experience of his opposite:

To him, the extravert must ever seem a little superficial, a chronic vagrant from the spirit's home. Nor can the extravert wholly convince himself that behind the introvert's reserve and apparent impoverishment of interest there may lay the greatest wealth of subjective experience and such subtlety of feeling as he may hardly parallel in his own external responses.

Jung's scheme was "uncanny" and "disquieting" because "we are deprived of the serenity of an absolute system of values" (1949, 532). Yet Sapir was hesitant to believe that "the spirit of man will rest content with a schism."

Various Boasians were intrigued by the idea of applying Jungian categories to their friends and colleagues. At the 1924 meetings of the BAAS, Jung was in the air; Margaret Mead (1959; 1966) noted that Sapir and Goldenweiser were the ringleaders of a conspiracy to categorize their fellow anthropologists. Sapir summarized his characterizations in a letter to Lowie (20 May 1925: UCB), although he qualified them by the need to avoid value judgment and hold personality independent of culture—in spite of the practical difficulties of doing so. Sapir contended, in spite of Lowie's skepticism, that the scheme could be applied to individuals "intelligibly and consistently."

Radin and Goldenweiser were extraverts, with the former dominated by sensation and the latter by feeling. Goldie's personality was complicated by an unconscious introvert ideal (explaining his admiration for Sapir). Jaime de Angulo, whom Sapir knew only through correspondence and gossip, appeared to fall in the same category. Frank Speck and Erna Spier were sensation extraverts. This type was apparently a good balance for Sapir's own, since it included a number of his closest friends; these were the "hungry men" of one of Sapir's early poems, who embraced experience with an abandon alien to his own nature. He could experience their sensations only vicariously. However, when extraversion was tempered by feeling rather than sensation, as in Radin, de Angulo, and Goddard, Sapir was frustrated by the subjectivity and rigidity of the style.

Ruth Benedict agreed with Lowie that Sapir was somewhat carried away with his newfound typology (Mead 1959, 72–73). In her diary, Benedict noted that Lowie "quarreled with Edward's classification of him as an extravert—he's an introvert of course and mystic." Lowie's surface poise was carefully controlled. She observed wryly: "That will make us all introverts by auto-definition." Benedict was not impressed with Jung and was probably annoyed at the schoolboy glee with which Sapir and Goldie employed his classification.

Sapir saw some of his colleagues as mixed types. Boas was a feeling introvert whose personal values led him to emphasize thinking over feeling. This accounted for Boas's emotional intensity in intellectual matters and his rigid exclusion of subjectivity from scientific work. It also explained the ambivalence students felt toward Boas's seeming contradictions of character. Kroeber was also a complex type, combining sensation and intuition, but forcing himself into a false extraversion.

Jung claimed that personality traits were inborn, with conscious manipulation of personality causing immense strain, and Sapir was impressed by his argument. Like Kroeber, Obgurn was an introvert with a powerful extravert compensation. Since he knew Ogburn less well, the characterization had less emotional valence. This personality type was apparently common among anthropologists of Sapir's acquaintance.

Wissler, with whom Sapir had never been intimate, was a feeling introvert who managed a culturally successful extraverted and thinking adaptation. Wissler protected his essential self from public view by constructing a distinct scientific persona. Elsie Clews Parsons was a sensation-feeling introvert who insisted on trying to think. Sapir never established much rapport with Parsons, though her sex and financial independence may have complicated the issue for him. Harlan Smith was an intuitive extravert, whose intuition attracted Sapir but whose inability to articulate it disturbed him. They were enough alike to talk but conversation lagged during their long walks. Kroeber's protegé T. T. Waterman was not one of Sapir's favorite people. His sensation-feeling extraversion irritated Sapir, and his jocular assumption of intimacy was highly offensive.

Ruth Benedict was above all "rational," that is, a feeling-thinking introvert. Her surface calm, as Sapir well knew, hid a turbulent personality expressed at this time largely through poetry written under the pseudonym of Anne Singleton. Sapir preferred this side of Benedict to her public persona; rationality impressed him less than sincere emotion.

Sapir's characterizations of his colleagues reveal as much about Sapir as about Jung. For him, dynamic psychology was empirical because it effectively categorized known persons. Interestingly, Sapir avoided categorizing his private relationships—the complexity of his relationship with Mead and the dynamics of his marriage.

Although Sapir did not yet apply these insights to culture, Mead and Benedict (see chap. 9) would soon begin typologizing whole cultures according to personality type. Sapir less often succumbed to this temptation and would construct a culture theory based on individual variability and creativity. None of the three, however, described individual Indians with the complexity of personality that they found in colleagues.

Kroeber: Psychoanalysis and the Superorganic

Kroeber went further than other Boasians in professional exploration of psychoanalysis. In 1917, he undertook a personal analysis of three or four months with Dr. Jelliffe, "one of the original group around Freud in Vienna" (T. Kroeber 1970, 101). Kroeber had recently lost his first wife to tuberculosis and suffered partial deafness as a result of illness. Psychoanalysis was part of his search for renewed psychic balance. Kroeber and Jelliffe became friends, "two scholars in different but related fields engaging in a stimulating give and take conversation." Kroeber turned to Dr. Stragnell, Jelliffe's son-in-law, trained by Anna Freud, for further analysis (T. Kroeber 1970, 102).

Like Sapir, Kroeber wrote book reviews to proselytize psycho-analysis to anthropologists. Reviewing Jung in 1918 (323–324), Kroeber announced that "in some form or another, psychoanalysis has come to stay." Moreover, "the extravagances of some of its followers, and possibly an excessive confidence on the part of all of them" should not detract from the importance of ideas that were already "a per-manent part of general psychology." In other words, anthropologists should not throw out the baby with the bath water, as many were inclined to do. In a 1920 review of *Totem and Taboo*, however, Kroeber debunked Freud's pseudohistory in accepted Boasian fashion (1920, 53).

When Kroeber first addressed the potential relationship of psycho-analysis and anthropology, there was little overt enthusiasm in an-thropological circles (T. Kroeber 1970, 109): "Boas considered Kroe-ber's interest an unfortunate aberration to be borne patiently. Some younger colleagues were less than patient and tolerant." Retrospec-tively, Kroeber (1953, 300) assessed his lay practice, as well as his return to more conventional cultural anthropology: "I did not feel that these insights helped me appreciably to understand culture any better; which was one of the reasons I quit psychoanalysis." For him, the two disciplines remained irreconcilable, although he occasionally applied psychoanalysis to particular problems, for example, Mohave dreams.

Kroeber established his lay practice at the Stanford Clinic through Saxton Pope (Ishi's personal physician) and Henry Harris. He had excellent rapport with neurotic patients but soon realized the need for further training if he were to treat psychotics. He spent two days per week in the clinic (T. Kroeber 1970, 105–106).

Kroeber realized he had to decide which profession to pursue and chose the one of his formal training. Indeed, some of his difficulties in professional identification with psychoanalysis grew out of his an-thropological expectations. The "metaphor" of Freudian transference, for example, contradicted "his ethnological field philosophy, by which the informant-ethnologist relation, if successful, is like a friendship, a growing one, a bond for years, for life" (T. Kroeber 1970, 108).[11]

Kroeber turned to Sapir for feedback in his flirtations with psy-chology, asking him (23 January 1920: UCB) to criticize his unpub-lished literary essays in terms of latent needs, saying "there is a great deal of unconscious in these scribblings." Sapir obliged, with what Kroeber (8 February 1920: UCB) called "your cool, painstaking analysis." Psychoanalysis had not exhausted Kroeber's compulsion to explore his own psyche, and he claimed to learn from Sapir's "unusual combination of acumen with objectivity" (8 February 1920: UCB).

Kroeber thought he had more reason for angst than Sapir because of his age (forty-three), with its consequent "difficulty of cutting out new channels." For all of Sapir's insight into his personality, Kroeber professed himself puzzled by his colleague's psychic makeup, blaming this for his inability to provide truly helpful poetic criticism: "I'm stumped at analyzing you. I see many points in your work, both scientific and verse, that might mean much; but the fundamentals of your personality elude me." Sapir was pleased by his ability to read Kroeber but apparently preferred a one-way analysis.

Kroeber sent the announcement of his analytic practice to Sapir and other Boasians, expecting that Sapir would be supportive (14 July 1920: UCB): "Why are you so silent on the notice of my undertaking? You are the one man in the profession that I had counted on not to take the event either as a slap or as a morsel of gossip." Kroeber felt that his credentials—training analysis and clinical experience—were adequate, at least in America, and was disappointed that he attracted few patients: "I believe it is open to doubt whether this community is ripe for psychoanalysis." San Francisco sometimes seemed as alien to Kroeber as Ottawa to Sapir.

Sapir, however, failed to understand Kroeber's withdrawal from anthropology. Kroeber (29 July 1920: UCB) attempted to excuse his apostasy in terms of emotional traumas that Sapir shared and considered his lay practice no different from Sapir's writing of poetry. Whether or not he accepted Kroeber's motives, Sapir was curious. Kroeber willingly reported his self-assessment (17 January 1921: UCB): his friends kept away and the "educated public is still much more suspicious of the subject than in the East." He enjoyed the work itself: "It's fascinating to watch the symbolism grow bolder and clearer each week."

During Florence Sapir's illness, Kroeber (17 July 1921: UCB) tried to explain the role of psychoanalysis in his personal life: he was glad he had had his analysis but felt that it could only be useful "if you feel the need insistently." Curiosity and indifference were inadequate motivations. Sapir was not convinced to undergo analysis for himself or for Florence.

The difference in the attitudes of Sapir and Kroeber to psycho-analysis was consistent with the substantial divergence in their approaches to anthropological theory. In a classic paper in 1917, Kroeber defined culture as "superorganic," having a structure independent of the individuals composing it. Sapir responded the same year, arguing that the culture of each individual was, in some sense, unique. David Mandelbaum's selection of Sapir's writings in 1949 omitted this critique on the grounds that "the later personality papers make the same points and make them more incisively without the kind of personal reference that this reply necessarily has" (Mandelbaum to Emeneau, Hoijer, Ray, 21 July 1947: SF). Biographically, however, this was Sapir's first effort to redefine the theoretical basis of cultural anthropology along lines also explored in his poetry. He might not have committed his incipient perspective to writing so early without this stimulus.

Moreover, the parameters of this debate are reiterated in correspondence between Sapir and Kroeber, both at the time of publication and near the end of Sapir's life when both men had produced more mature statements about the nature of culture and the individual. Further, this public debate has become a convenient symbol for the range of theoretical positions encompassed by anthropology. For example, Spindler (1978, 15) argues that psychological anthropology has consistently "challenged the culture *sui generis* position head on" using arguments familiar from Sapir's "Why Do We Need the Superorganic?"; Spindler noted "the individual as an idiosyncratic and biographical entity has to be taken into account; culture, as transmissible and accumulative, is based upon psychic and psychological processes that depend upon a self-awareness seemingly unique to humans; and the 'social' or 'cultural' is philosophically an arbitrary selection out of a total mass of phenomena and it is consequently not correct to imply it has a force or life of its own."

Sapir characterized Kroeber's paper to Lowie (10 July 1917: UCB) as "dogmatism and shaky metaphysics." The "excessive undervaluation of the individual" in history was an "abstractionist fetishism," psychologizing at its worst. A series of critiques to the *American Anthropologist* would be "amusing and possibly instructive." He did not, however, want to stand alone in objection, whether to lend force to the argument that not all anthropologists saw culture as Kroeber did or to preserve his friendship with the author.[12]

Kroeber, however, believed Sapir exaggerated the difference between their positions (to Sapir, 24 July 1917: UCB). He considered his argument consistent with Boasian practice, though the abstract statement had not been made previously:

I've left absolutely everything to the individual that anyone can claim who will admit the social at all. . . . What misleads you is merely that you fall back on the social at such occasional times as you're through with the individual; whereas I insist on an unqualified place, an actuality, for the social at all times.

Kroeber believed that the place of anthropology among scientific disciplines depended on the reality of the concept of culture; he urged Sapir to reply in public and stimulate debate on how anthropology related to its sister social sciences. This was, however, an issue Sapir took for granted (to Kroeber, 28 November 1917: UCB); he wanted to refine the anthropological models.

In spite of his public critique, Sapir attempted to stress common cause with Kroeber privately (29 October 1917: UCB), commenting that "our common tendency is away from conceptual science and towards history. Both of us seem to want to keep psychology in its place as much as possible." Sapir "did not expect to convince" Kroeber but to "sharpen" his own views.

The usually phlegmatic Kroeber (n.d. November 1917: UCB) berated Sapir for failing to recognize his defense of all Boasian work from external incursion:

I don't give a red cent whether cultural phenomena have a reality of their own, as long as we treat them as if they had. You do, most of us do largely. . . . If we're doing anything right, it deserves a place in the world. Let's take it instead of being put in a corner. That's not metaphysics: it's blowing your horn.

Like Kroeber, Sapir further explored the question of the relationship between individual and culture. Both continued to formulate their positions in terms of this early debate. For example, Sapir acknowledged Leslie White's use of his critique in teaching a seminar in 1932 (18 January: UM):

The point which I try to make is one which is generally completely misunderstood because it is essentially a philosophical point. I cannot see that cultural data are a new class of data as contrasted with psychological ones in the same sense as that in which psychological data are a new class of material as contrasted with purely organic data. This is not to minimize the importance of cultural data but merely to suggest that the principle of selection or organization of them is not unilinear with principles of selection and organization applicable in the other cases. A failure to recognize this leads to all sorts of perfectly artificial problems on culture or society vs. individuals.

When Sapir was planning his book on "The Psychology of Culture," he wrote to Kroeber (24 May 1932: UCB) expressing his "skepticism about the current point of view" on culture as superorganic:

I am feeling more and more keenly and clearly that the dichotomy between culture as an impersonal concern and individual behavior is a myth—a highly useful one, to be sure, for the preliminary clearing of the ground but very mischievous in the long run because it leads to fatal misunderstandings both about personality and culture.

Very near the end of his life, Sapir wrote to Kroeber (25 August 1938: UCB):

Of course, I'm interested in culture patterns, linguistic included. All I claim is that their consistencies and spatial and temporal persistence can be, and ultimately should be, explained in terms of humble psychological formulations with particular emphasis on interpersonal relations.[13] I have no consciousness whatsoever of being revolutionary or of losing an interest in what is generally phrased in an impersonal way. Quite the contrary. I feel rather like a physicist who believes the immensities of the atom are not unrelated to the immensities of interstellar space. In spite of all you say to the contrary, your philosophy is pervaded by fear of the individual and his reality.

In 1938, as in 1917, Sapir realized that his philosophy of culture was far from dominant in anthropology. The "superorganic" had become, for Sapir, a symbol of the sterility of a narrowly cultural definition of the method and content of anthropology. Kroeber had created an artificial dichotomy.

In "Culture, Genuine and Spurious," completed by about 1918 although published later, Sapir applied the argument for the primacy of the individual in culture to modern national cultures, in a lyrical challenge to individual creativity (1949, 321):[14]

There is no real opposition, at last analysis, between the concept of the culture of the group and the concept of an individual culture. The two are interdependent. A healthy national culture is never a passively accepted heritage from the past, but implies the creative participation of the members of the community. . . . It is just as true, however, that the individual is helpless without a cultural heritage to work on.

Ogburn (to Sapir, 31 December 1917: NMM) admired Kroeber's article as an appropriate model for sociology and failed to understand

Sapir's objection to it. Sapir was not surprised that Ogburn, as a sociologist, sided with Kroeber in the superorganic debate; sociology, after all, was not known for its concern with the individual. But he still attempted to clarify his view of the social sciences (14 January 1918: NMM):

I have certain ideas about the meaning and value of individuality in history that I am afraid are rather heterodox. . . . The attempt to understand history in terms of book formulae that take no account of the individual is, to my mind, but a passing phase of our hunger for conventional scientific capsules into which to store our concepts. When all the experiments in massed action will have brought with them their due share of inevitable disappointments, there will be a very real reaction against this whole way of thinking, but in any event this reaction is not due for some time yet, so you may as well have the laugh on me for the present.

Sapir assumed that the same objections applied to the reification of culture in sociology as in anthropology and criticized Ogburn's exaggeration of the economic motive (to Ogburn, 4 February 1919: NMM).

Although Ogburn had difficulties with Sapir's critique of the superorganic, he was on more familiar ground with "Culture, Genuine and Spurious" (to Sapir, 31 August 1922: NMM):

You created a real atmosphere, and the general tone was elegant. I carried away a real feeling for what was genuine and what was spurious. Somewhat the same idea I have often thought of, but in a different language and a different setting. I phrase it this way: To me culture—as the ethnologist uses the term—is divided into parts. Now there are varying degrees of correlation between these parts. Now where these variables that make up the whole are correlated positively and with high coefficients, to the end that the whole is harmoniously adjusted to the original nature of man, we have what I think you mean by genuine culture. I see it all in terms of varying parts of culture, correlation, original nature, and adaptation.

But Sapir's method was less precise and more "unscientific" than Ogburn would have liked:

You and I seemed in previous talks to understand our meanings of art and science. You say that you like to keep them separate. It seems to me . . . that you have them mixed. I feel that in this article your subjectivity colors your analysis and you almost drift into mysticism. You seem to be struggling to articulate something that you feel emotionally rather than coldly and scientifically.

Ogburn worried that his remarks might seem brief and "impressionistic," as he had accused Sapir of being.

In spite of his failure to convince either Kroeber or Ogburn that the concept of culture required dramatic revision to account for individual variability and creativity, Sapir's interest in psychiatry and psychoanalysis during the late Ottawa years convinced him that this was a priority for the social sciences. Kroeber, Boas, Ogburn, and virtually all of their contemporaries attempted to deal with the new insights emanating from Freud. But only Sapir would attempt a synthesis of social science and psychiatry, of culture and the individual.

CHAPTER EIGHT

Experiments in Aesthetics

Many social scientists of Sapir's day dabbled in belles lettres. Among the many Boasians who wrote poetry, however, only Ruth Benedict—under the pseudonym of Anne Singleton—is remembered by poets. Sapir differed from most of the others in that, during the late Ottawa years, he defined his personal and professional identity in terms of poetry as well as strictly "scientific endeavors." Moreover, his colleagues have remembered that he wrote poetry, though few have read any of it. The ethos of Sapir as humanist remains powerful. For example, David Mandelbaum noted to Jean Sapir (3 January 1956: SF):

Science and art were combined in Sapir in unusual degree. He was a meticulous linguist, disciplined in linguistic detail, capable in the canons of scientific procedure. Yet he was a humanist and artist as well, sometimes predominantly so. He was a poet; upwards of two hundred of his poems and poem translations have published. His essays in music and literature show not only a perceptive, creative intelligence but also reveal the joy he found in those arts.

For Mandelbaum, there was a direct connection between these characteristic aesthetic endeavors and Sapir the scientist:

But the main media for his artistry were ideas. A vivid recollection, shared by more than a few of his colleagues and students, is that of Sapir discussing and developing an idea. He did so lucidly, drawing together many strands of fact and theory to present a coherent, meaningful, and stimulating concept. Sometimes he seemed to be improvising, presenting variations on a thematic idea. But it was the kind of improvisation which comes forth whole and convincing.

Unlike Kroeber or Ogburn, Sapir did not compartmentalize. His responses to his wife's illness, World War I, exposure to psychology, reformulation of Boasian anthropology, and introduction of psychological reality into linguistic theory are inseparable. The late Ottawa years involved intense concentration on aspects of patterning in diverse disciplines.

Music

Sapir grew up with traditional Jewish music; the son of a cantor, he knew the ritual chants of orthodox Judaism by memory. Jewish liturgical music has a different repertoire of diatonic modes and rhythmic patterns than most Western music. In addition, Jacob Sapir recorded folk songs and composed music. When he visited Ottawa, he always carried a black briefcase full of his compositions and asked his son to play them. Said Michael Sapir: "This Dad would do, with some difficulty in reading his father's notations, and with some distaste. He commented a couple of times to me how execrable these compositions were, just awful stuff, he would say" (Michael Sapir to Bart Jones, 17 August 1985).

Sapir's mother was not particularly musical, although she associated music with genteel culture. But Sapir was ambitious; music, no matter how much he enjoyed it, was an unlikely career. Nonetheless, he devoted a surprising number of Columbia electives to music. When he turned to anthropology, Sapir assumed that music was part of adequate ethnography and encouraged his father to transcribe Boasian efforts at ethnomusicology.[1]

In the late Ottawa years, Sapir sought a psychic balance that his career no longer seemed to provide. Although much of his poetry was published and his musical compositions were not, Sapir's most general philosophical reflections on nonprofessional activities come in reference to music, perhaps because a career in poetry, even as a sideline, was always possible for a man who used words well. But music required formal training and years of practice—a full-time commitment. Music, however satisfying privately, was superseded as a realistic option early in Sapir's life. He wrote to Lowie (12 August 1916: NMM): "I do practically no anthropology out of office hours, most of my time being taken up with music—reading and composing." He was writing a sonata for cello and piano and mused about the alternative career[2] that had passed him by, brooding over how much talent he actually had:

It is clear to me that I have more than the average aptitude for music. This does not prove that I could have made a very successful livelihood of it. Circumstances being what they are, it is more than unlikely that I should ever be able to give up anthropology and switch over frankly to music. Still, the impulse tending in that direction is certainly there, and unlooked-for success in some musical venture may someday precipitate a break. However, such a day must at least be quite distant. . . . Even so, to be bluntly sincere, I consider myself already to have been responsible for some *real* music. Some of my happiest moments of late have been due to the pleasure of hitting upon what seem to me to be exquisite bits of melody or rhythm or chordal progressions.

Sapir went on to contrast the aesthetic satisfaction of music with the patterning of language and culture:

Whether or not I have "missed my vocation" is not for me to decide. . . . I somehow feel that in much of my work I am not true to my inner self, that I have let myself be put off with useful but relatively unimportant trifles at the expense of a development of finer needs and impulses, whatever they are. . . . I have no theoretical quarrel with anthropology. The fault lies with me. Being as I am, for better or for worse, the life of an Americanist does not satisfy my inmost cravings. . . . I find that what I most care for is beauty of form, whether in substance or, perhaps even more keenly, in spirit. A perfect style, a well-balanced system of philosophy, a perfect bit of music, the beauty of mathematical relations—these are some of the things that, in the sphere of the immaterial, have most deeply stirred me.

Dissatisfaction with linguistic and ethnographic patterning dominates this melange of impressions. Music satisfied aesthetic impulses, enabling Sapir to return refreshed to other efforts. He did not seriously consider abandoning his successful career. Rather, he wanted to add spice to unavoidable commitments.

Sapir asked Lowie (27 September 1916: NMM) not to advertise his "clandestine ambitions" and disillusionment with anthropology noting that "it may not be altogether politic to advertise dissatisfaction with one's life-work." Sapir's was not a sustained rebellion but a sporadic escape from other pressures. Music allowed Sapir to forget everyday cares. His poem "To one Playing a Chopin Prelude" (20 August

1918) immortalized the efforts of his oldest son Michael at the piano—sweeping away the "strange mistake" of the everyday world and leaving the poet-observer momentarily free. Music enhanced the child's sincerity. Sometimes, however, the piano itself was a source of frustration. In "Hypocrite" (24 August 1918), the personified piano seemed to mock its owner and remain outside his control.

Unsurprisingly, Sapir insisted on musical education for his children. Most of their friends also took piano lessons. Jean Sapir told her stepdaughter Helen that Sapir had once fantasized about having a small family orchestra. None of the children, however, had as much musical talent as their father.

Michael began a decade of piano lessons at age four, not entirely willingly. In the late Ottawa years, Sapir emphasized that Michael had "good touch" and "sensitivity"; Michael (p.c.) noted Sapir "was rather a martinet in trying to keep me practicing and asking Grandmother to check on me too." Having no other musical partner, Sapir tried to teach Michael the simpler bass parts for Beethoven symphonies arranged for four-handed piano. Michael, however, could not keep up with his father's reading speed and finger technique, which greatly irritated and frustrated Sapir. By this time, Michael was taking lessons from a Mr. Saunders, considered one of the best teachers in Ottawa; Michael rebelled against his teacher's insistence on using a metronome and his "pressurized unpsychological approach to teaching kids." Michael stopped playing the piano in Chicago, at about the age of ten.

Helen Sapir Larson recalls that Sapir patiently sat through all of their recitals. On one occasion, when Philip played too slowly, the audience laughed when Sapir yawned. Paul Sapir (p.c.), years later, remembers insisting on violin lessons at the age of eight. A note in the wrong pitch was akin to physical pain and brought Sapir running from any part of the house. He would bang out the correct notes on the piano with considerable frustration. Said Paul: "His anger could be quite frightening." When Paul switched to piano, Sapir was less disturbed by his inevitable errors.

There is no specific record of how Sapir composed; his son Michael speculates that he worked out tunes on the piano, only later writing them down (to Jones, 17 August 1985). Sapir claimed to hear music as he read a score; certainly he had an unusual ability to hold sound in memory. Years later, Harry Hoijer, a former student, noted (to Haas, 8 November 1971) that Sapir "had a strong auditory sense; so much so that he moved his lips when reading. He also greatly enjoyed reading complex musical compositions. Curious, I asked him about this. His answer was that, by reading the score, he heard the music." Sapir responded to the nonverbal and spatial imagery of music, in contrast to the verbal articulation necessary to anthropological analysis. He believed that thought without words was an illusion. In *Language* (1921, 15) he wrote that "no sooner do we try to put an image into constant relation with another than we find ourselves slipping into a silent flow of words." The self-conscious intellectual could escape into music because remembered or anticipated sound depended on pattern relations rather than inherent quality. Jones suggests that the faculties engaged by Sapir's music were closely related to his sense of linguistic patterning (1985, 20):

> Perhaps Sapir extended the music-listening process to other fields, and so became skillful at relating diverse human facts to each other—sometimes even whole spheres of activity which may seen disparate at first. If so, Sapir's auditory inclination may shed light on his insatiable search for pattern and relationship, which we now recognize as one of the most valuable and characteristic aspects of his thought.

Few of Sapir's musical compositions have survived. Michael Sapir recalls that his father rarely played his own compositions and only a few lilting tunes remain in his memory (to Jones, 17 August 1985). "Etude No. 3," examined by Jones, is intended to stretch the player's skills. Its precise directions to the performer, with metronome marking, would require a virtuoso to reproduce. It was "beyond [Sapir's] technical capacity to play it at the speed or with the utter smoothness he scored it for" (Michael Sapir to Jones, 18 September 1985).

Sapir's tastes were broad-ranging, though conservative. Michael Sapir recalls (to Jones, 17 August 1985):

> Although Dad delighted in exploring all kinds of music—George Herzog introduced him to Bartok, he dabbled in Scriabin, he delighted in some of Percy Grainger's lovely melodies, esp. [sic] after Percy visited once with us in Ottawa—I believe that his greatest and most enduring loves were for Mozart, Chopin and Debussy.[3]

For the most part, Sapir's music was intended for personal and family entertainment. In his Chicago years, however, Sapir played the piano in a "casual trio" with colleagues rotating at each other's homes (Michael Sapir to Jones, 5 October 1985). Certainly, his friends always included ethnomusicologists and musicians, especially George Herzog in the Yale years.

Sapir did not entirely appreciate the emerging musical forms of his day. He considered jazz an abomination, although his opposition became less adamant over the years. During Michael's jazz period, however, he played two jazz pieces on the piano ("Kitten on the Keys" and "Dizzy Fingers"). His poem "On Hearing Plaintive Jazz by Radio" (15 June 1924) lacks the elaborate imagery of his poems on classical music, recalling rather the alliterative cacophony of Gerard Manley Hopkins, whose poetry Sapir was among the first to appreciate.

Unlike many of his contemporaries, Sapir appreciated both romantic and classical music. In "On Representative Music" in 1918, he praised the sequence of moods evoked by the romanticism of Beethoven's school (1949, 491). More often, however, Sapir was a classicist, stressing the intrinsic quality of the music—which was much akin to linguistic form. Sapir was fascinated by the interaction of form and emotion (1918 [1949], 491), believing that musical criticism had no absolutes. In his poem "Music" (20 October 1924, published in 1925), Sapir argued that music allowed its listener to forget, apparently a desirable state; it could also transform grief into joy. Michael Sapir summarizes the role of music for his father (to Jones, 17 August 1985):

I think that music was a profound experience for him, most especially closely related to his acute linguistic sense and delicate sense of hearing, of tonal differentiation, etc. . . . Dad felt music to be kindred to linguistic form, tone, etc. and to mathematics in their "autonomy" of function, their universality, and their sheer aesthetic appeal.

Sapir accepted the ethnographic variability of music early in his career. In a 1911 review of Hornbostel on primitive music, Sapir described the patterning of sounds, foreshadowing his later concept of the phoneme. He (1912f, 278) proposed a cross-culturally valid definition of music, startling for the period in its wide aesthetic baseline: "Music is neither purely tone nor purely rhythm. Would it not be more suggestive to think of it in terms of an association of tone production, however it might arise, with the rhythmic impulse manifested in all of man's artistic activities?" Sapir emphasized contrastive pattern rather than rhythm or tone in isolation. Song-texts, dances, and purely musical matters were inseparable in most societies. Many musical peculiarities would prove to have nonmusical causes, for example, a religious mass, lullaby, or bugle call. The "associated cultural features" were the clue to meaning. This was an established Boasian argument about the association of cultural traits, but the application to music was new. In a 1915 review of Percy Grainger's explorations of primitive music, Sapir emphasized "the quite different stylistic peculiarities of the folk-music of different tribes and peoples" (1949, 594). These might be as complex as any modern musical specialization.

Sapir's 1910 paper on "Song Recitative in Paiute Mythology" was his most extensive musical ethnography. Sapir presented eleven tunes—serving functions of characterization, emotional expression, and identification—which characterized the speech of various Paiute myth characters. Jones (1985) notes considerable distortion due to European musical education. Sapir was aware of the existence of different scales but did not hear them accurately in his own material. He emphasized the features selected by the culture (to Helen Roberts, March 1917: NMM): "To distinguish casual from significant variations requires not merely a good ear but . . . the sense of form and instinct for underlying intention." He preferred subjectivity of analysis to mechanical recording of sound.

Sapir's musical theory alternated between pattern thinking and reversion to the more rigid categories of his musical education. He preferred to think his informant made a mistake rather than change his analysis, persuading Tony Tillohash to change "flaws or rhythm" in the song of the Beaver chief (1949, 469). Moreover, Sapir attributed the contrast in the melodically similar songs of the dignified Grey Hawk and his flighty wife Lizard to rhythm rather than melody (1949, 469).

Sapir wanted to work alternately on music and linguistic analysis. Nootka song words were "frequently greatly distorted," forcing him to reconstruct prose forms. Sapir regretted having only free translations of Teit's Tahltan songs (18 November 1912: NMM): "Prose forms are often mutilated according to various stylistic devices to suit the requirements of music."

In musical and literary criticism Sapir first developed a full-fledged pattern analysis. He was concerned both with the relationship of formal constraints to creative process and with the internal (i.e., structural) relationship of musical and poetic units. In "The Musical Foundations of Verse," written in 1918 or early 1919 but not published until 1921, Sapir used music to oppose Amy Lowell's notion of the atomism of free verse (Handler MS). The distinction between prose and poetry was partly arbitrary, depending on the "poetic receptivity of the listener." Sapir approved of free verse, but Lowellian "unitary verse" ignored "the generation of significance (in this case, of appreciable rhythmic patterning) out of the systematic opposition of formal units, in this case, regular time-units foregrounded against the irregular stress units" (Handler MS, 12).

Sapir considered poetry, as well as music, primarily a question of sound (1949, 226): "Poetry does not exist in its symbolic visual form: like music, it addresses itself solely to the inner ear." He illustrated by substituting poetic language with the same rhythm for the rhythmic contour of a prose sentence—thereby proving to his own satisfaction that poetry was latent in all prose. This use of structural opposition preceded Prague School structuralism in literary criticism by a decade.

Sapir (1918, 493) saw language and music as polar categories: music expressed emotion, not concept; both were essential to human expressive life. Music and language were both structured forms of thought, but their patterning was essentially different. Sapir worked out the nature of this difference in music before he applied it to phonemic patterning in language.

An Experiment with the Aesthetics of Design

Although Sapir's aesthetic impulses were expressed largely in music, poetry, and linguistics, he made one foray into visual art. In 1917, he investigated the variability of aesthetic responses to design elements among members of his own society, describing to Laufer (14 November 1917: NMM) one of his "side studies or hobbies that I am just now tinkering with."[4] Sapir sent an American Indian design to colleagues and asked them to develop it: "All I want is a series showing fairly spontaneous reaction, utilizable for psychological study. The problem of artistic conception, or rather of the mode of conceiving a given artistic unit, is what I am after." Sapir's interest in the symbolic and aesthetic complexity of Northwest Coast art styles came from his Nootka work, but he did not try to test aesthetic variability in the field. By using colleagues as subjects, he could ignore the issue of cultural representativeness.

Kroeber, whose dissertation had been on Arapaho design elements, produced a fairly substantial set of designs which (Sapir to Kroeber, 2 July 1918: NMM) had "unusual originality and firmness of artistic conception." Both Kroeber and his sister eliminated one of the three elements in the original design, thereby "developing by simplification." Kroeber's designs (Sapir to Kroeber, 21 November 1918: UCB) "without slavishly copying the original, or treating it as a mere geometric abstraction deprived of subtle particularities, . . . *do* in a mysterious way keep the spirit of the original and idealize that spirit." Paul Radin was predictably intrigued by the "revelations of personality" that were inherent in the designs. The coincidence of approach by Leslie Spier, his mother, sister, and brother (all using repetition to form a complete design) suggested (Sapir to Spier, 13 May 1918: NMM) that the design might strike certain subjects as complete in itself or needing further development. Speck was impressed by "the excellence of the design and the impossibility of doing anything with it that could improve it." Spier's brother didn't like it. The "psychology of aesthetics" might "disclose the somewhat startling thought that completeness of conception pleases some people but displeases others, probably because of its inherent lack of suggestibility."

Sapir intended to pursue this experiment, proposing an Ottawa lecture (to Miriam Finn Scott, 17 March 1919: NMM) on the psychological and linguistic implications of the "spontaneous bent" of various subjects, "selected more or less at random." The thirty to forty sets he had collected showed surprising variability; he noted "there is by all means such a thing as a natural aesthetic bent quite aside from training. . . . The designs show that the average person, while far from aesthetically brilliant, has a certain modicum of individuality," which could be stimulated by appropriate designs. Sapir reported to Kroeber (10 February 1920: NMM) that he had given this lecture several times but not written the paper.

Boas (to Sapir, 23 May 1918: APS) was skeptical, objecting to "ethnologists like myself" as subjects "because we know too much about the theory." Boas's book on primitive art was more careful to identify and control for the effects of "secondary rationalization" or consciousness of cultural pattern. In any case, Sapir never pursued this experiment.

Poetry

Poetry was the primary outlet for Sapir's anguish over his wife's illness and wartime alienation. Its inherent quality is less important than the seriousness with which Sapir took it. He considered poetry part of his intellectual activity and discussed it in his correspondence with Lowie, Kroeber, Radin, and Benedict. For none of the others, however, did poetry contribute substantially to their anthropology. Through his poetry, Sapir approached the psychology of the individual and the nature of creativity—the cornerstones of his culture theory. In retrospect, then, Sapir's poetry is the index and primary symbol for the emergence of his mature intellect (Darnell 1986a).

In Ottawa, Sapir felt isolated from American intellectual life. On his frequent visits to New York, Lowie was his intermediary to the avant-garde world of poetry and art. Lowie also introduced Sapir to editors of literary journals, for which he wrote reviews and poetry. Although not overly impressed by the quality of Sapir's poetry, Lowie (1965, 69) recognized its importance in the late Ottawa years. Sapir's period of intense poetic activity was actually quite short—from about 1917 to 1925. Lowie speculated (1965, 13) that "the more congenial environment" in Chicago allowed Sapir's scientific work to resume its rightful place in his total orientation."[5]

Sapir's earliest dated poem was in April 1917. In the same period, he kept a notebook entitled "Suggestive Notes," in which he recorded ideas for short stories, aphorisms, and poetry critiques. His literary reviews and social commentaries began in 1916, the psychoanalytic book reviews in 1917; between 1918 and 1921, roughly half his publication was literary; in 1922 the aesthetic efforts predominated (Handler 1983, 211). His only volume of poetry, Dreams and Gibes, was published in Boston in 1917; it is likely that Sapir paid part of the cost. The book was dedicated "to my wife"; Florence shared Sapir's love of poetry. Over two hundred poems were published, about half of those that have survived. When Sapir liked a poem, he was eager to have it published and often collected up to a dozen rejection slips before acceptance.[6] He was distressed that Dreams and Gibes received little critical acclaim.[7] An unsigned review in The Dial (23 August 1919) was ambivalent: The book "is seldom of the magic of poetry," though its lines "reveal a free, idealistic spirit." Many of the shorter poems showed a "suggestive turn of thought" but the poetry itself was rarely successful.

Undaunted, Sapir planned a further volume. He actively sought criticism of his poems and accepted it with reasonable grace, acknowledging (to Lowie, 30 June 1917: UCB) that the style might be "slip-shod and rather flippant." However, he objected strenuously to Low-ie's attempt to remove his pronouns of direct address: "Do you believe in impersonal urbanity? Isn't it high time we all recognized clearly that art, criticism and to some extent even science are but expressions of the self? I have no patience with the conventional dodging of the personal."

When Lowie considered starting a poetry journal, Sapir (20 May 1918: UCB) volunteered to write a column of poetry criticism, noting that he would enjoy rejecting poems from "those notables" whose work he considered second-rate. He complained to Lowie (31 October 1918: UCB) of the "priggish pretentiousness" of much current work and professed himself bored by the "owl-eyed and academic" avant-garde. He linked the liberal politics of John Dewey ("a little socio-logical talk goes a long way with me, as you know") and the imagist poetry of Amy Lowell and Ezra Pound (to Lowie, 19 December 1918: UCB). In "Suggestive Notes" (8 January 1918: SF), he remarked that editors "drag the public down to their own supercilious estimate of it."

Sapir subscribed to *The Dial* and *Poetry*, not otherwise available in Ottawa, and corresponded frequently with Harriet Monroe.[8] The so-called "new poetry" was extremely popular around World War I. Mon-roe sought consistent standards, eschewing the "intimate self-revela-tions" and "softness" of many poems submitted to *Poetry* in favor of "hardness combined with passion and intellect" (1920 editorial). Sapir agreed in principle, writing in 1920 (1949, 497–498): "It is precisely the passionate temperament cutting into itself with the cold steel of the intellect" that best utilizes poetic technique. His poem "Blue Flame and Yellow" (15 March 1919: SF) used the same image: "I strove for a blue flame / That would rise like a point of steel." Monroe, however, thought Sapir was careless in his poetic craft. Sapir accepted her ed-iting gracefully, although he rarely allowed revisions in his scientific writing (28 October 1918: UC): "Yes, you are right about my not working hard enough at my verse. I do let things go before I should."

Sapir (14 May 1920: UC) felt that Monroe's choices of his poems "misrepresent me as an extremely sad fellow" and provided "lighter, cynical-frivolous shots." Sapir lacked the confidence to let his poetry stand on its own; his letters to Monroe consistently label it, for ex-ample, as "nostalgic," "facile-pretty," or "impertinent" (30 June 1921:

UC). Sapir thought she overemphasized "anything startling or brusque or cynically clever" and urged her to look for "hardness in the soft-textured stuff" (14 May 1920: UC).

In "Suggestive Notes" (29 November 1917: SF), Sapir mused on how he constructed his poems: "My thoughts are all right—splendid. But they seem to lose their way as they descend from the ink-well to paper." His method was quite different from that of his scientific writing, where he outlined the argument in advance (8 July 1918: SF):

The best way to write a poem is to give up looking for a subject. Grab some phrase or sentence that you hear, if in the least striking, tear it violently from its context, idealize it or whimsicalize or in some other way sketch it on to a remote country, let a new setting grow up out of it at fancy's command (aided by the gentle compulsion of rhyme and rhythms) and, at the end, if necessary, erase the line or phrase that served as stimulus.

More whimsically (28 August 1918: SF): "How does an artist create a character, a psychological study? He polarizes all the souls around him and lets them vaporize. The steam precipitates into a show that his pores absorb. He has material for soap-bubbles." By such a method, trivial content could create a "provocative" form (1917 n.d.: SF): the poet was concerned with "the inner form, the inner circle of relationships and moods."

Art, for Sapir (Handler 1983, 211), united "form and feeling, cultural givens and subjective experience." The aesthetic and affective found too little outlet in the impersonal investigations of the social sciences. Sapir was never successful at incorporating ethnological topics into his poetry. He was more interested in exploring his own nature as observer than in the subjective world of another.[9] Yet, in principle, he credited individuals in primitive culture with the same creative capacity as himself. Ethnography made the exotic commonplace by revealing its meaning for members of the culture—which contradicted the romantic conventions of the period.

Sapir cited Italian philosopher Benedetto Croce in the preface to *Language* (1921). Croce's work confirmed Sapir's growing conviction that aesthetics was essential to both science and art, although "Suggestive Notes" (21 October 1917: SF) was often critical. Although Croce wanted to study how artists and their audiences saw works of art, his concept of intuition ignored cultural variability, thereby leading Croce into subjectivity. Sapir applied the cross-cultural methodology of anthropology, going beyond Croce to suggest that language and art shared problems of creativity. Sapir adapted what intrigued him in Croce and ignored the rest. Croce assumed that intuition had to be conscious for art to exist. Sapir preferred the Boasian position that culture was effective precisely because it was not conscious or rational. Croce and Sapir agreed, however, that intuition was equivalent to art; Croce argued that all sincere self-expression was art. This allowed for individual creativity but made formal definition of art difficult (cf. Handler 1986). Sapir (n.d. 1917: SF) speculated that the effective artist had to "ferret out . . . ideal curves" of expression which would have resonance for many individuals.

In "Suggestive Notes" in 1917 (n.d.: SF), Sapir mused about the aesthetic possibilities inherent in "any intense or extreme form of activity." Although love, patriotism, religion, and art were socially approved forms of the same impulse, murder was also "a very striking form of self-expression." The perfect murder would combine "a venomous impulse with a finely discriminating feeling for form in action." Few murderers, however, brought out the potential of the art form.

The "Suggestive Notes" were private thoughts, rarely developed further. However, Sapir kept up a running correspondence with colleagues about his, and occasionally their, poetry. Radin (to Sapir, 23 February 1915: NMM) argued that valid ethnography captured individual subjectivity and criticized Sapir for avoiding "personal comment of any kind." Radin was puzzled (23 June 1917: NMM) by Sapir's "literary ambitions": "Are you doing it in order to make money or because you like it?" He feared that Sapir might abandon ethnology and philology. As an intellectual, Radin did not want to be left out of the emerging Boasian interest in poetry. He professed surprise (6 December 1917: NMM) that Sapir did not associate him with the new poetry: "I enjoy minor expressions in art. They require so little mental strain to enjoy them." Radin urged Sapir to apply his literary skills to ethnology and abandon poetry (17 August 1918: NMM). Radin's attitude may well have stimulated Sapir to think about the possible parallels of poetry and culture.

Kroeber, whose literary tastes were classical, was not sympathetic to the new poetry, finding Sapir's verse (21 August 1917: UCB) unduly preoccupied with "the trick of composition"; he cautioned Sapir to avoid cliches: "I suspect that when the technique becomes a vehicle instead of the end, you won't be writing about moths and star harmonies. And please, leave out God. I know that's the way it's done, but it's not your way." Sapir (21 November 1918: UCB) responded that he did not want criticism of form "except where a given form seems intrinsically unsuitable to the subject. You must accept all forms as possible." Kroeber (7 December 1918: UCB) insisted that his objection was not to lack of form but "the want of passion": "Your impressions are definite, the moods keen, the expression of them accurate, but all that doesn't make poetry." Sapir, however, wrote poetry to distance himself from strong emotion and missed Kroeber's point. Kroeber (8 December 1919: UCB) preferred Sapir's "relatively commonplace passages" and urged him to cut his imagery "to the bone and your stock of emotion will gain in potency. . . . You have a gift of expression. Don't waste it."

Sapir's poetry, whether or not it was fully successful, fine-tuned his prose style to a precision and elegance unrivaled among his contemporaries. His son Philip recalls an undergraduate class at Yale in which Sapir challenged his students to modify a single word of a passage by John Donne without changing the meaning. Poetry made him aware of style.

Ottawa Intellectual and Social Life

Sapir had little professional feedback in Ottawa. In spite of his complaints about the city's social life, however, he was active in poetic circles. Duncan Campbell Scott, commissioner of Indian affairs, was a poet and occasional critic of Sapir's poetry manuscripts. Correspondence in Sapir's administrative files (NMM) indicates a casual but cordial relationship, maintained until Sapir left Ottawa.

Sapir was a prominent member of the Ottawa Arts and Letters Club. Socialite and romantic novelist Madge Macbeth took him under her implicit patronage, although not until his reputation as a poet was somewhat established. His letters to her[10] are deferential; for example (20 January 1922: OPL): "[Y]our taste is almost uncannily like mine. You have selected certain poems that I have always considered among my best but that I had despaired of getting anyone to see through." Sapir agreed with Mrs. Macbeth (n.d. 1924: OPL) that his poem "The Blind Old Indian Tells His Names," based on his Nootka fieldwork, was not overly successful: "I have not yet the key to the solution of the difficulty inherent in remotely exotic subject matter—probably because my own natural handling of subjects has already something of the remote about it."

Sapir spoke to the Arts and Letters Club on a range of subjects, including his aesthetic design experiment, Indian languages, the state of contemporary poetry, and the arbitrary line between prose and poetry. He served on the executive at various times and as honorary president. With Scott, he was one of three judges for a national literary contest.

Sapir attempted to use his contacts in Ottawa social circles to increase public support for his discipline. In 1920, he established an Anthropological Club of Ottawa. The membership included colleagues from various government scientific departments and anthropologists elsewhere in Canada.[11] Sapir was the president and Harlan Smith the secretary. The club, however, left no record other than a membership list that can be abstracted from the various letters of invitation. Ottawa was apparently not ready for an anthropological society.[12]

In 1921, Sapir was persuaded to teach a course of twenty lectures in English literature from Chaucer to the present for the University of Toronto Extension Department. The 125 students, "nearly all ladies," were from the Workers' Educational Association. Sapir reported to Lowie (28 November 1921: NMM): "Of course, I know nothing about English literature, but that does not seem to matter. I gather that the course is a success." Jenness (1939: 152) recalled this course "before a local Ottawa society" as part of the literary interest that was one of Sapir's "chief distractions" in Ottawa.

That Ottawa society provided more outlet for a poet than for an anthropologist was certainly one of the reasons Sapir pursued his aesthetic interests.

The Effects of War

World War I brought dramatically increased Canadian xenophobia, of which Sapir was apparently little aware. His naivete about Canadian prejudice toward non-Anglo-Saxon immigrants unleashed a strong backlash to his 1919 lecture for the Independent Labor Party. It was only indirectly political, along liberal socialist lines characteristic of the New York intelligentsia. But Sapir was not in New

York and was not a native son with the right to criticize Canada, however implicitly.

The *Ottawa Journal* (28 April 1919: OPL) reported "some rather remarkable statements" about Sapir's opinion of members of Parliament, noting that Sapir was born in Russia, educated in United States, and "said to be a very able man in his line"; his salary was stated. Sapir discussed attitudes of intellectuals toward the labor and employer classes, implying that MPs were selected for "gift of gab" and ability to wear smart clothes. He claimed that the general public refused to acknowledge the existence of classes, including the intellectual, and that a government drawn from the professional and intellectual classes could not represent the people in any literal sense.

An editorial in the *Ottawa Journal* two days later (OPL) carried the headline "A Preacher of Class War" and described "a grand onslaught upon all classes of society" except labor—concluding that Canadian democracy worked very well and if Sapir didn't like it he should return to Russia, as well as condemning Sapir's supporters who claimed he had been quoted out of context. Several open letters to the editor the same day supported Sapir's position. One was signed by six of his fellow civil servants, including Harlan Smith. The editors replied that Sapir had been unable to produce a text for his talk, having spoken from brief notes, and that their impression of his intent was no doubt shared by others; the *Ottawa Journal* was considerably less sympathetic to labor than the *Ottawa Citizen*, which took a more moderate view of Sapir's apparent indiscretion. One of Sapir's defenders, J. M. Macoun (*Ottawa Citizen*, 1 May 1919: OPL) suggested that the words attributed to Sapir were actually used by other speakers. The following day, the *Ottawa Journal* reported that Sapir did not know whether the words were his or not. He clarified that he had referred to "the personnel of government generally," not to the Canadian Parliament.

On the same day, biologist Fritz Johansen wrote a letter emphasizing his friend's scientific ability and that the Canadian government had sought him out to establish its Anthropological Division; he noted that "the Canadian universities do not turn out enough men (if at all) in certain lines of science, to fill certain positions . . . requiring such special knowledge. As a matter of fact, there was no Canadian anthropologist of importance available at the time Dr. Sapir was appointed here." Johansen also noted Sapir's poetic and musical abilities. Sapir was "reticent by nature" and politics, "especially persons, really interest him very little." Johansen accused the paper of attempting "to create a prejudice in the public mind against Dr. Sapir, merely because he was not born in this country" and expressed views "at some variance" with those of the editors.

Sapir found the whole episode acutely embarrassing. The response of his friends demonstrates the seriousness of the issues. Others could be implicated by association. Johansen, for example, was born in Denmark and attended radical meetings, as did most intellectuals in this period.

Sapir believed that the war ended the bright hopes of intellectuals for a better world guided by science and letters. He did not remember Europe and thought of himself as an American and a New Yorker. Ottawa, however, was less cosmopolitan. Sapir was perceived as Jewish. Before the war, Sapir saw no urgency in applying for Canadian citizenship. His application, which may well have seemed a sensible precaution against political harassment and job insecurity, was dated 21 January 1919.[13] In December 1919, after the Armistice, he wrote again to the chief clerk of naturalization asking what happened to his application. The reply (date illegible) claimed that none of the facts on his application could be verified, including his birth, American naturalization, and immigration interview on entering Canada in 1910. Sapir finally received his certificate of naturalization 27 January 1920.

World War I challenged the survival of the British empire; Canada, of course, had much stronger ties to Britain than did the United States. Science was subordinated to the war effort and internal security intensified. For example, the British Columbia postal service refused to forward maps with unfamiliar Indian names which Boas obtained from Sapir to send to George Hunt. Boas (22 July 1918: NMM) hoped that Sapir could confirm that Hunt had been collecting for Boas since 1893, and their correspondence was purely scientific. Boas realized that this might be awkward for Sapir: "If for any reason you hesitate, please don't do it." Sapir replied without repercussions.

Sapir (to Lowie, 19 January 1918: UCB) considered the war "hellishly evil" and beyond the power of individuals to modify. The American draft was "all so stupid" (to Lowie, 27 August 1918: UCB), especially if it might involve his fellow scientists. As the war drew to a close, Sapir considered affiliating with the Independent Labor Party (to Lowie, 12 May 1919: UCB). He was increasingly pessimistic about the postwar political situation, seeing Wilson's harsh peace terms as "a most laughingly vicious circle." But Sapir never acted on his political convictions, as did Radin, Goldenweiser, Lowie, and Boas.

Xenophobic issues arose in the United States as well. For anthropologists, the most obvious case was the dismissal of Leo Frachtenberg from the Bureau of American Ethnology in 1917 for purportedly derogating the president and the country. Sapir attempted to protest (to Hodge, 1 November 1917: BAE), although the Boasians were perceived as German or German sympathizers, and their intervention was unlikely to help. Anti-Americanism was also the implicit issue in the outcry over a 1919 letter by Boas to *The Nation* in 1919 about wartime activities of anthropologists in Mexico (Darnell 1969; Stocking 1968).

Militarism disturbed Sapir. "Suggestive Notes" in 1917 recorded a comedy sketch on the irony of heroism; a man goes to great lengths to avoid military service but is forced by public opinion to enlist and dies in action. Several of the poems in *Dreams and Gibes*, published during the war, articulate Sapir's profound pessimism. The themes include women as fools for encouraging heroism, the futility of academic protest against war, the childishness of diplomats, the concreteness of one individual's death in battle, and a mutilated war hero with a bloodthirsty maiden aunt. That Sapir published such unpopular visions of war testifies to the strength of his pacifism, though perhaps not to his political sophistication. Two later poems, both published, stressed the horror and senselessness of war.

The new poetry movement emphasized the soldier-poet and the effectiveness of war "in sweeping away a stagnant cultural order" (Handler 1986). Sapir did not believe that poets would have a role in rebuilding the social order. In his 1920 essay on the Poetry Prize Contest of the Ottawa Arts and Letters Club, Sapir wrote: "Poem after poem, especially in the class of patriotic efforts, voiced the most distressingly conventional, personally unfelt and unexperienced, sentiments."

Sapir, like Boas, saw patriotism as transcending national boundaries. A renaissance of the entire Western world was overdue. Sapir (1916a) was intrigued by John Dewey's call for American culture to reject outdated European standards of cultural progress. His first statement about the integration of culture was written in this context. "Culture, Genuine and Spurious" lies between social science, social criticism, belles lettres, and aesthetics. "Genuine" culture, integrated for the individual, was virtually impossible in the present state of modern society. Sapir was disillusioned by the false idealism of North American culture; atomization and fragmentation placed a tremendous burden on the individual, whose creativity was stifled because it lacked effective cultural roots. As Sapir longed to integrate his professional work, family commitments, and aesthetic endeavors, modern man floundered in a morass beyond the possibility of individual control.

"Culture, Genuine and Spurious" contains an implicit cultural relativism. The frightening isolation of modern American man from his fellows was not inevitable. Sapir had lived in societies where individual lives, both public and private, were guided by a traditional culture. Modern anomie, therefore, was the price of a particular civilization, not inevitable to the human condition. Sapir did not suggest that civilized man revert to the primitive. The primitive, rather, suggested ways to improve quality of life and create a genuine American culture.

Although "Culture, Genuine and Spurious" was written by 1918 (Sapir to Lowie, 20 May 1918: UCB), it was not immediately published. The first part appeared in *The Dial* in 1919 and the full paper only in 1924, in the *American Journal of Sociology*. The initial audience, therefore, was a popular rather than scientific one. Sapir and others, however, soon brought such concerns into social science. Interestingly, the paper was better received in sociology than in anthropology. Lowie, for example, considered it irrelevant to anthropology because it set aside the technical meaning of culture (1965, 9–10). Anthropologists were unaccustomed to thinking professionally about their own society. But Sapir began with his own society and moved toward revision of social science categories. "Culture, Genuine and Spurious" lies between aesthetics and anthropology. Sapir required of his professional discipline that it respond to the plight of the individual in culture. Much of his work over the next two decades would explore the consequences of this humanist position for cultural description. A further aesthetic dimension of his theory was the "unconscious artistry" of society, elaborated particularly in his class notes during the thirties (Irvine, in preparation); cultural form, for Sapir, was aesthetically integrated.

Sapir's excursions into aesthetics prepared him to seek new cultural models to embody the observed vitality of primitive cultures in anthropological descriptions. Although he had been unsuccessful in adapting poetry to ethnographic description, Sapir would soon embrace the life history as a more congenial medium (cf. Leeds-Hurwitz and Nyce 1986). In his study of personality and the individual, he would attempt a synthesis between Kroeber's superorganic culture and Benedict's psychological patterning of whole cultures.

CHAPTER NINE

Psychologizing Boasian Anthropology

While Sapir was reorienting his personal and professional life, Boasian anthropology was grappling with the integration of culture (Darnell 1977). For some, like Spier, Lowie, or Kroeber, the change was motivated from within the discipline; increasing descriptive knowledge of the variability of Amerindian cultures required explanation of the uniqueness of each. Borrowing made the historical origin of culture traits irrelevant to their present functioning; culture could only cease to be "a thing of shreds and patches" (Lowie 1920) if its integration could be captured in the models employed by anthropologists. For others, reorientation of the Boasian program drew on improved methodological tools from psychiatry. Boas implicitly approved of the changes, particularly in the work of Ruth Benedict and Margaret Mead. In 1911, he had called for ethnographic data before psychological questions could be approached;[1] his own students had provided enough of that data to justify expanding the interpretive models.

But if the availability of data was one strand in the new Boasian anthropology, and psychological analogy was another, the third was poetry. Sapir implicitly believed that the poet might contribute to the poetic style of his/her culture. He was not alone in this fascination with poetic creativity. Benedict and Mead were also active in revising the Boasian model; all were engrossed in literary and aesthetic endeavors during the period their mature thought crystallized. Boas, though oriented more to the natural sciences than the humanities,

171

tolerated the aberrations of the would-be literati among his former students without comment. In fact, he was probably less negative than they feared. The sense of playing hooky from anthropology, however, contributed to the aura of writing poetry. Briefly at the end of Sapir's Ottawa years, he was in frequent and intense contact with Benedict and Mead. Although his later work would diverge substantially from theirs, their feedback was essential to his integration of poetry, psychology, and the role of the individual in culture.

Ruth Benedict

When Sapir read Benedict's paper on the guardian spirit quest in North America, he wrote enthusiastically (25 June 1922: SF)[2] that it was preeminent "among the body of historical critiques that anthropology owes to Boas." He reinterpreted Benedict's argument in terms of his own theoretical interests: "I should like to see the problem of individual and group psychology boldly handled, not ignored, by someone who fully understands culture as a historical entity." Psychological integration would supplement rather than replace Boasian historicism. Sapir was delighted to discover that someone else turned Boasian trait lists into an integrated pattern for each culture—consonant with the aesthetic intuitions of its individual members. Benedict's paper challenged Sapir's lethargy about ethnology, easing his forbodings of impasse in the discipline.

Sapir soon realized that Benedict shared his profound sense of isolation from contemporary American culture. In Benedict's case, the issues were largely feminist. Boas welcomed women into Columbia anthropology at a time when they were otherwise marginal to American intellectual life (Viehman 1985). Later in her career, Benedict claimed that she was drawn to anthropology because World War I "convinced her of the need to pay attention to national character differences" (Modell 1975, 193). More importantly, there was fit between Benedict's personality and the concerns of the discipline. Studying the exotic allowed her to avoid judgments of her own life. Many of her fellow anthropologists were also marginal to mainstream American society. Boas and most of his first generation of students were Jewish immigrants; Benedict apparently associated their marginality with that of American women (Modell 1975, 194–195).

Sapir's father, Jacob David Sapir

Sapir's mother, Eva
Segal Sapir, with her
grandson Philip

Edward and his younger brother Max

Sapir on an early field trip

Paul Radin, Ishi, T. T. Waterman, Sapir, Robert Lowie (1915)

A self-satisfied Sapir
in the early Ottawa years

Florence Delson
Sapir with
Michael (1913)

Edward and Jean McClenaghan
Sapir
in Chicago (ca. 1926)

Sapir at the Linguistic Institute
(1937)

Sapir during the Yale
years

The Impact of Culture on Personality Seminar (1932–1933)—center in white suit, W. I. Thomas; standing on right, Sapir, John Dollard

Hortense Powdermaker rowing Sapir in New Hampshire

Sapir's children at the Centenary Conference, Ottawa (1984)—J. David,
H. Michael, Helen (Larson), Paul, and Philip

The Sapir Centenary Sessions of the American Anthropological Association,
Denver (1984)—back row: Philip Sapir, Edgar Siskin, Richard Preston,
George W. Stocking, Jr., J. David Sapir; front row: James M. Nyce,
Regna Darnell

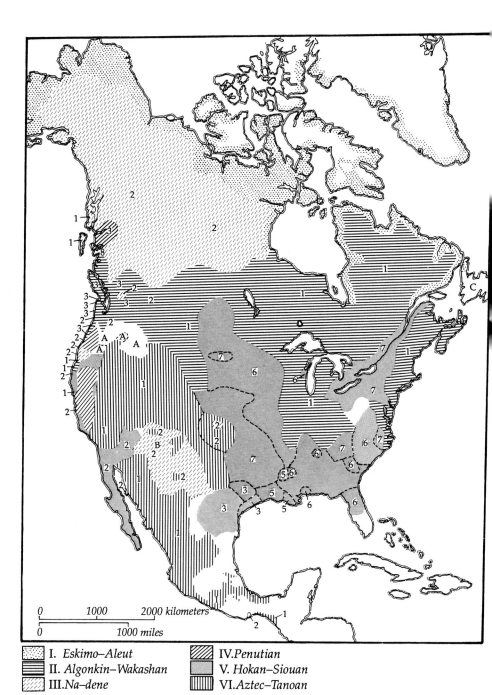

I. *Eskimo–Aleut*

II. *Algonkin–Wakashan*

III.*Na–dene*

IV.*Penutian*

V. *Hokan–Siouan*

VI.*Aztec–Tanoan*

Sapir's six-unit classification of American Indian languages (1921)

Sapir soon identified Ruth Benedict, anthropologist, with Anne Singleton, poet; their correspondence was dominated thereafter by poetry. Mead, in selecting letters from Sapir to Benedict for her Benedict anthology, wrote to Jean Sapir (July 1957: SF):

Edward was more responsible than anyone else for Ruth's developing her minor poetic talent; the constant encouragement, care, criticism, was an atmosphere in which, for the first time in her life, she began to expand as a writer, so that his contribution was not only to her poetry but to her whole writing life.

Benedict was less confident about her verse than Sapir, who published poetry under his own name and hoped for public recognition. Although Mead (1959, xvii) claims that Sapir "relied simply on the pleasant obscurity of the small poetry journals for which we used to carry our friends' manuscripts around in our pockets" to assure his anonymity; in fact, he chafed at the obscurity of the journals that published his poetry. For Benedict, however, her pseudonym and the anonymity of the group of would-be poets centered in New York protected her privacy; many of her poems dealt with childhood experience and intensely personal emotions (Mead 1959, 87–88).

Proponents of the new poetry frequently dedicated their efforts to one another. Sapir wrote "Zuni" for Benedict—her fieldwork experience of the Zuni sense of pattern of repetition and self-control reinforced her own personality. Sapir rarely used ethnographic imagery, but Zuni, for him, was primarily a backdrop for Benedict. The "slow, dreaming ritual" contrasted with the "sharpness of the mesa"; priests "singing softly on the sand" controlled and diluted the vitality of the natural world: "The desert crawls and leaps, the eagle flies. / Put wax in your ears and close your eyes."

"Zuni" was written only months after Florence Sapir's death. Benedict's sympathy eased Sapir's despair, though elsewhere he portrayed her emotional control as a danger to genuine experience. Sapir considered "Zuni" one of his best poems; it appeared in January 1926 in *Poetry* magazine, labeled "To R.F.B." The new poetry strove to transcend the personal in emotions.

Later the same year (23 November 1924) Sapir wrote another poem for Ruth Benedict. "Signal," published in the same issue of *Poetry* magazine, was dedicated to Benedict's alter ego—"A.S."[3] Sapir urged his friend to release her control, to seek emotional experience and indulge latent passions, to acknowledge the inseparability of woman and poet, to "throw fagots on the fire," and "let the maddened cinders dance." The "flame's desire" contrasted sharply with the imagery of Benedict's public personality in "Zuni."

Sapir saw no contradiction in making his analysis of Benedict's personality public. He considered her pseudonym an unhealthy withdrawal from emotional commitment. Mead (1959, 92–93) reported that Sapir "chafed against the concealment as nonsensical." He wrote to Benedict in 1924: "By the way, you mustn't dare to use a nom de plume. No tricks of the protective coloration type." The new poetry movement valued sincerity above all else. In 1925, Sapir pointed out (Mead 1959, 92) that students at Columbia knew she wrote poetry: "It seems absurd to make such an ado about concealment, don't you think?" The following year, he reiterated: "You know how I feel about ever toying with the idea of dissociation of personality. I hate it. Lie outright if you have to, but for God's sake don't stylize the lie into a pretty institution." Benedict eventually began to write poetry under her own name. Her comments on Anne Singleton "became more and more detached" (Mead 1959, 94). Yet she continued in private to dissociate herself from her poetry, using "an older name, 'Sally', for the self who came and went and would 'dictate' lines only when it suited her."

Sapir did not fully distinguish between urging the woman to emotional expression and the poet to more "sincere" verses. Benedict's replies have not been preserved, but there was certainly an element of Pygmalion creating his Paphos. For some time, Benedict allowed Sapir to hold this role in her life. The distancing effect of letters gave her some control over the relationship. Moreover, she intensely admired Sapir as anthropologist and intellect and was flattered by his attention. She undoubtedly felt a certain superiority as he wallowed in his emotional traumas and she held herself aloof. There was little personal risk for her. She could even flirt with the possibility of a more intimate relationship, whether or not she consciously recognized her infatuation with Sapir. Both tacitly maintained a fine line between intimacy and distance. Sapir both needed her aloofness and longed to break through it.

Only Benedict pored over Sapir's poems with a fervor to match his own. They offered mutual encouragement in the period when both were eager to publish poetry manuscripts. Benedict (to Sapir, 4 February 1928: SF) divided Sapir's manuscript into six sections with the first poem in each set giving the "mood or subject matter." This was "a singing sort of verse"—full of sound imagery and phonetic play. Benedict's own imagery was more visual and static.

Sapir stressed psychological content, motive, and mind in action. His poetic muse was analytic, perhaps why psychoanalysis so appealed to him. Benedict, however, attempted self-analysis through poetry. Modell (1983, 140) believes that "confusion lay close to the surface and control tightened into hysteria." Writing was "a duty for her in her therapeutic quest for personality" (Mead 1959, 94). Sapir's poetry, in contrast, attested to "intellectual vigor" and "renaissance virtuosity" (Handler 1986). His confidence could not entirely be transferred to Benedict because they conceived their poetry differently. Sapir, however, assumed that their attunement implied virtual identity of perception of life and career. Benedict valued his emotional support but found his masculine confidence fundamentally alien. She encouraged his therapeutic and occasionally biographical uses of poetry. Sapir's poetry was "wish-fulfilment expression seen against the backdrop of a partly regretted career" (Kroeber 1952; cf. Handler 1986). Kroeber thought this explained Sapir's personalistic theory of culture; Handler applies it only to his poetry. But if the two are indeed related, the poet's creativity as wish-fulfilment carries over to member-of-culture and the one follows from the other. Because Kroeber separated culture and individual, poetry, for him, was unrelated to ethnography.

Sapir agonized over the ideal arrangement of his poems. His personal papers include typescripts with alternative arrangements, indicating that he never entirely made up his mind. Neither Sapir nor Benedict knew much about getting manuscripts published. Sapir intervened on Benedict's behalf with Harriet Monroe (Modell 1983, 186). Both submitted manuscripts to Harcourt Brace, and both were rejected. Sapir received the news first and Benedict wrote to Mead (1959, 91–92) that she was more worried about Sapir's fragile ego than about her own potential disappointment. Louis Untermeyer, the poetry editor for Harcourt Brace, told Benedict that he could only publish one poetry manuscript: she wrote to Mead that "there was nothing to do but tell Edward what had happened. . . . He took the volume away from me and said he'd bury it." Benedict's own manuscript was rejected shortly after, in a letter which did not even contain a signature. Publishing poetry was not a profitable enterprise.

Mead (1959, 93) suggests that this rejection was a transition; Benedict turned away from seeking recognition through poetry. *Patterns of Culture* (1934*b*) would make her famous as an anthropologist, and she was "caught in an unwillingness to trade on her success in one field to bolster up a much more minor success in another." Benedict accepted that poetry would not constitute her claim to fame. Mead reports her observation that the poems "aren't good enough to give one's life to." She assumed that a poet had to be published and shifted her emphasis to other matters, without apparent regret.

Sapir continued to perceive Benedict's poetry differently than she did (Mead 1959, 182): "It's no secret between us that I look upon your poems as infinitely more important than anything . . . you are fated to contribute to anthropology." Benedict, however, increasingly valued her anthropological work. Sapir vacillated between analyzing her personality, which he considered a sign of his friendship, and withdrawing to technical criticism when this became too personal. He also analyzed Benedict's anthropological work; Sapir the theoretician assumed that ethnographers carried their own personality as well as cultural presuppositions into the field. In 1925, he observed that Benedict's writing about primitive religion was "conditioned by your type of personality as a garden surrounded by a fence." Psychoanalysis was perhaps the only way to lessen this inherent subjectivity.

Sapir's analysis caused Benedict increasing strain. He realized she disliked individual psychoanalysis but continued to analyze her. Moreover, he resented her closeness to Boas, which always remained out of reach for him. Columbia anthropology was more intimate in this period than when Sapir was a student. Boas, the paterfamilias, became "Papa Franz" to his later students, many of them women. The New York anthropologists were united by affection as well as intellectual commitment. Benedict increasingly withheld her own thoughts from Sapir, although he did not seem to realize this. His lack of perception caused her to withdraw still further. She increasingly turned aside his efforts to offer personal advice (Mead 1959, 182).

Sapir turned away from poetry after the rejection of his manuscript, but expected Benedict to hold up the aesthetic front for both of them. He considered her talent greater than his (Mead 1959, 181): "Zuni myths are important toys, of course, but your verse, even when you're not pleased with it, is a holier toy." Sapir transferred his own poetic aspirations to Benedict. Early in their friendship, Benedict was reassured, because Sapir was a poet as well as an anthropologist, that self-expression was compatible with a vocation of anthropology. Sapir, lionized among the Columbia anthropologists as a tragic genius (responding to his combination of intellectual power and personal tragedy), valued her poetry, which encouraged Benedict greatly.

The ambivalence of their relationship is unquestionable. Benedict chose a low-key role, similar to that of a maiden aunt, taking responsibility for the children while Sapir took his wife to doctors. Modell (1983, 130) argues that Helen Sapir, especially, served Benedict, whose childlessness had caused her great distress, as a "safe" surrogate daughter.[4] All three children remember Benedict as a familiar presence throughout their childhoods. Sapir presumably appreciated an emotionally calm and undemanding feminine presence during the final years of his wife's illness. Given his family commitments, and Benedict's nominal marriage, there was no urgency in considering possibilities that might never materialize. Neither wanted greater commitment, yet both desperately needed unthreatening emotional stability. Their emotional needs were synchronous.

After Florence Sapir's death, however, the two drew apart. Sapir was reminded of his pain by Benedict, who had shared it, and wanted to leave behind that part of his life. He remarried in Chicago. Never again would he have the same intimacy with Benedict. They had been too intimate to retreat to casual acquaintance. Benedict asserted her personal and artistic independence, and Sapir built a new life in Chicago. Benedict oscillated between "grief at his melancholy and a snappy impatience at indulgent brooding" (Modell 1983, 130). She valued self-control, whereas Sapir alternated between depression and equally intense enthusiasm. During the height of Sapir's personal problems, however, Benedict was invariably patient. Indeed, the whole Columbia group was eager to do whatever they could. Esther Goldfrank recalled (to Robert Allen, 22 June 1971) around 1922: "He came to New York very worn out, almost it seemed in a sort of nervous crisis. . . . I remember one time when Ruth Benedict and I, with sandwiches for us and one for him, went over to visit him in his desolate room. He was very lonely."

A section of Benedict's diary for 1922, published in *An Anthropologist at Work*, records Benedict's immersion in the ups and downs of her relationship to Sapir during one of his frequent visits to New York (Mead 1959, 57–59). On 4 January, Sapir attended the weekly department lunch, and Benedict walked with him to the American Museum afterwards. His wife was physically very ill; they also talked shop. Benedict's infatuation, whether acknowledged or not, was unmistakable: "Bought jam and cards! I must remember afterwards how simple happiness is—I don't want anything more or different at such times—I'm just at ease." The next day, Benedict attended Sapir's lecture and played with his daughter, inviting her for a visit a few days later. Tuesday 9 January was "Helen Sapir's day," involving paper dolls, doll clothes, lunch, swimming, and typewriter. Afterwards Sapir gave a seminar and the trio had ice cream nearby. While Sapir and Benedict talked shop, he also "made fun of Helen which she quite properly resented." Benedict took Helen home and met Sapir again in the evening at a lecture. The next day Sapir lectured and Benedict decided not to have dinner with him, though invited. On Thursday, she met Sapir and his daughter "in the hall, but only in passing." She recorded: "Shall not meet again." On Friday night, Stanley, her long-estranged husband, went to hear Sapir's lecture. He was no doubt curious about the much-touted genius. Benedict spent her weekends at Stanley's Bedford Hills suburban home. Sapir's return to Ottawa resolved the immediate conflict in Benedict's loyalties.

Sapir returned to New York on Friday 9 March when his wife was released from hospital. The following Monday, Benedict met Sapir and Michael in the hall. Sapir said: "At least there's something else to think of besides life and death." Two days later, Sapir sought out Benedict about country boarding places where Florence might recuperate. At his request, Benedict visited his wife in the afternoon. Benedict thought Florence Sapir would be unable to fend for herself in the city, recording that she could not walk a block.[5] Thursday was the weekly anthropology lunch "and I stayed afterwards to talk to Dr. Sapir—who came very late." They spoke of a common acquaintance's tendency to paranoia and Sapir said he understood such sentiments. Benedict ended the day weary and depressed, after buying a birthday present for Stanley. Her use of Sapir's title in the diary was an obvious effort at distancing. On Saturday 17 March, Benedict was on her way home for the weekend: "Saw Dr. Sapir ahead of me at noon, but suddenly I didn't care whether he looked up or not. He didn't and I went on to the train." Stanley's birthday was an anticlimax. By Monday, Benedict had still not heard from Sapir, "though I know he's still here." On Tuesday, she was relieved to receive an invitation to visit. It is unlikely that Sapir realized how much these casual contacts meant to Ruth Benedict. He was preoccupied with his own problems and lacked energy for reciprocity in their relationship. Benedict accepted this. Sapir's presence was emotionally exhausting but invigorating.

Perhaps she expected him eventually to notice the devotion she hid so carefully.

But Benedict was good at hiding her feelings. Steward (1959, 382), reviewing *An Anthropologist at Work*, noted: "Her outward calm, mild demeanor and Mona Lisa smile seemed to indicate a good adjustment to her world. The error of this inference is startlingly disclosed." Benedict could hold herself apart. She was fascinated by death and psychic abnormalities, in ways that Sapir found incomprehensible. Benedict would work out these preoccupations impersonally, through cross-cultural implications of abnormal psychology, which justified her alienation from her own culture and lessened the pressure on her. She had, for example, a vested interest in ethnographic illustrations that her society's taboo against homosexuality was not universal (e.g., 1934*a*).

Some years later, when Benedict was involved with neo-Freudian psychiatry, she took a Rorschach inkblot test for Jungian Bruno Klopfer (Goldfrank 1978, 125–126): "I gave only one answer to each card and each of them was a whole. Quite schizophrenic. . . . Klopfer was amazed at the complexity of my integrations of color and movement." Benedict analyzed her own psychic integration with amused detachment.

As Sapir's problems resolved themselves, Benedict expected him to transcend depression. She reported his state of mind to Margaret Mead (25 September 1925: SF) optimistically:

I spent last evening with Edward, had dinner with his mother and the children and took him off to my hotel where I listened till after midnight. . . . Last night he was tortured by the idea of Nemesis, and I wouldn't let him fall back on it. . . . He is looking a little thin, but alert and well. He's very curious to know how he'll like Chicago. Altogether, I've never seen him when I'd more trust him to meet his problems as they could best be met.

As time went on, however, Benedict was increasingly impatient at Sapir's continued *Sturm und Drang*. Even after his remarriage, he expected Benedict to sympathize with his continuing reflections on the involutions of his relationships. Sapir's emphasis on negative emotions, especially jealousy, seemed childish to Benedict, who had come to terms with her own emotional life and settled for more accepting and supportive friendships with women. She wrote to Mead (21 September 1928) in a tone of superiority to Sapir's vulnerable masculinity:

I've seen a lot of Edward till today when he took a day off. We spent one evening on a bench in a park. It took an hour or two to get him over a discussion of—how would you guess—jealousy. He nearly repudiated me and our conversation because I didn't agree that jealousy was the necessary reverse of any important love and that you measured the size of the love by the size of the jealousy. . . . he bore away the resentment of my lack of understanding of his holy point.

Cross-purposes increased over time. In 1928, Sapir published a paper "Observations on the Sex Problem in America," in which he blamed emergent sexual freedom, separating romantic and sexual love, for the appalling phenomenon of the "modern woman" with her professional ambitions. He described the use of sexuality for therapeutic self-development as "narcissism," while homosexuality was "unnatural." He was particularly irate that popular readers, citing ethnographic evidence of the absence of familiar taboos, overlooked the "coerciveness" of primitive custom. Sapir (1928, 531) considered jealousy integral to genuine attachment. Benedict, to whom Sapir did not send an offprint, took the paper as referring to her—though Sapir protested that he had no particular individual in mind. He also said he didn't expect her to like the paper (29 April 1929: SF): "I do not wish to have our relations unnecessarily muddled by irreconcilable differences, but that you were outraged by a supposed quotation shocked me as few things have shocked me. . . . You were never once in my thought." The same letter contains his lyrical lament for friendship estranged:

Ruth, I don't know why I am writing so much. I had almost convinced myself there was no use writing to you at all, our relations seemed to have become so embittered with misunderstandings, with contrary beats. Oh dear, life is so hard when one tries to be emotionally honest. It's so much better to slip on the kind of spectacles that make one see everything consistently cock-eyed and conventionally intelligible. If I don't write more often to you, it is not because I am not interested—you are one of the very few friends I have ever had—it is because I am too greatly interested and am dead tired of receiving and inflicting useless hurts. This is an age of perfectly terrifying loneliness and no wonder we run to the deceptive anodynes of the mob. I am content to be as lonely as my nature demands and as much more lonely as a profound distrust of the temper of intellectual America condemns me to being. . . . I am too old to learn to be different, too young to be indulgently or wisely indifferent.

This letter, if less than apology, still sought rapprochement.
    When Benedict finally left Stanley, Sapir wrote (4 February 1931:

SF) that his had always been "a ghostly name" and would now remain so. He gave his old friend credit for controlling her own life: "I am sure that you would not allow such a thing to happen if it were not inevitable, as you say."

Sapir was extremely conservative in his attitudes toward women and family, an attitude that may have increased the pressure on Florence (Michael Sapir, p.c.). His poem "Jackals" (Handler 1986) equated these scavengers with prostitutes. Equally, he mocked the "vanity of old-maidishness" and the safe prostitution of the modern feminist. Sapir was a family man. The failure of Florence Delson Sapir to cope with the role cut out for her by husband and society, because of her physical and emotional illness, continued to cause him profound depression. He longed for a woman who attracted him intellectually and who would also accept dependence on husband and children. The professional women of his acquaintance included few such. Benedict was ambivalent about Sapir's traditional notions of male dominance. In *Patterns of Culture* (1934*b*), she identified jealousy as one of the blights of American cultural life. Their positions were essentially irreconcilable.

Benedict, unwilling to risk further intimacy with a man, turned to a close but unthreatening friendship with Margaret Mead which centered around women's issues—particularly the breaking up of both women's marriages and the role of professional commitments in their lives. For Sapir, these issues simply did not arise. For professional men, marriage, personal life, fieldwork, and professional employment were largely unrelated. For women who aspired to nontraditional roles, however, choices had to be made and only women seemed to understand. Mead was a catalyst for Benedict's emerging feminism.

In spite of Mead's frankness in various places, the dynamics of the trio are still not clear, largely because Sapir's position is never articulated and Benedict's only through Mead's report. For Mead, as for Benedict, Sapir was the intellectual giant of Boasian anthropology. She was prepared to attach herself to his retinue and attempted to share the intimacy of Benedict and Sapir—poetic, anthropological, and personal. To a remarkable extent, she succeeded in doing so. Many of the issues that ultimately divided Sapir and Benedict were more explicitly articulated between Sapir and Mead. When Benedict withdrew into herself, Mead stepped into the vacuum.

Benedict felt that Sapir had changed, writing to Mead (29 December 1928: SF) about his bustling immersion in the politics of various granting agencies. She was unimpressed by his newfound sense of self-importance and remained at a rueful distance:

> Out of the evening I spent with Edward there was one hour of free reciprocity and a couple of excellent moments and five hours was on the ogre of THE AGE and the piffle of mental activity. He's singing hymns to the noble businessman. . . . The way for us to follow in his footsteps is to serve on committees and importance will descend upon us. Why, THE AGE has no need of books of verse—that finished off poetry. It was pitiful. The good side of it is his enjoyment of the lectures I heard him give at the meetings—and the charm and assurance he has in them.

Even when Sapir disparaged her fondness for Boas and avoidance of interdisciplinary conferences, Benedict did not condemn him. He had waited a long time for contact with the seats of power. Benedict remembered a more vulnerable Sapir.

Yet, when apparent laziness and self-indulgence emerged in Sapir's public performance, Benedict was judgmental. Whether the jaundiced eye was a product of theoretical disagreement or style of presentation, Benedict's comments were uncompromisingly critical (to Mead, 30 November 1932 in Mead 1959, 325):

> Sapir has been down . . . and it was pretty bad. All his charm couldn't carry him to victory in the face of his thinness of material. . . . Edward's got a new way of freeing himself from the necessity of admitting the role of culture. He analyzed his reactions to football, and he drew the moral that every phase of culture—in all cultures—is all things to all people. . . . All I got out of it was that Edward had satisfactorily phrased his quarrel with the universe again—satisfactorily to himself.

The estrangement between Benedict, Sapir and Mead was crucial to the future of culture and personality. The three were rarely in direct contact during the years when their major theoretical formulations were worked out. Mutual influence, therefore, was restricted to published works and to Sapir's very early efforts at cultural typology. This led to much apparent dissent and personal bitterness. It is unclear whether Benedict understood the influence Sapir had on her culture and personality work. There is no evidence that she understood how Sapir's poetry helped him to formulate the role of individual in culture; largely, he did so after the years of their real intimacy.

Mead, in contrast, shared Sapir's enthusiasm for "imagining what would have been the fate of the very definite personalities I knew—

Franz Boas, Ruth Benedict, [poet] Leonie Adams, Edward Sapir—if they had been born Samoans" (1972, 80). What applied in her own society, applied cross-culturally. Mead shared Sapir's unwillingness to be psychoanalyzed, despite her enthusiasm for applying psychiatric categories to other individuals or cultures. She firmly believed (Howard 1984, 260): "For the upper ten per cent of the upper ten cent, there is no analyst." What she wanted to know about herself, she could find out for herself; what she did not would certainly not be accepted from anyone else. Sapir had a similar need to control his own self-image. Karen Horney, later a psychiatric collaborator in culture and personality, in *Self-Analysis* (1949, 33) noted this common phenomenon. On the one hand, the issue was the need for training analysis for psychiatrists and cross-cultural students of personality; on the other, it was the self-awareness of intellectuals from a range of related disciplines:

A person intending to analyze himself would simply fail to make any self-observations that would lead to insights as yet intolerable. Or he would interpret them in such a way as to miss the essential point. Or he would merely try to correct quickly and superficially an attitude conceived by him as faulty, and thereby close the door to further investigation.

It was perhaps inevitable that those who analyzed one another eventually found themselves estranged.

Margaret Mead

While he shared interests in poetry and anthropology with Benedict, Sapir also was drawn into the more frantic orbit of Benedict's young protegé Margaret Mead, seventeen years his junior. Mead was petite, energetic, and full of enthusiasm for life, anthropology, and—for a time—Benedict's brilliant friend Edward Sapir. Sapir, who was inclined to be somber in those years, perceived her as an elfin sprite and was moved to greater exuberance by her lively presence. He wrote "Ariel" for her 30 December 1924 (published in 1925): her "wild, oblivious" spirit was too "reckless" for safety's sake. If anything, Mead failed to control the emotional expression that Sapir had sought to evoke in Benedict.

Like Benedict, Mead was immersed in the cultural life of New York

City, writing in her autobiography (1972, 90): "I believed that the center of life was here in New York City where Mencken and George Jean Nathan were publishing *Smart Set*, where *The Freeman, The Nation, The New Republic* flourished, where F. P. A. and Heywood Brown were writing their diatribes, and where the theater was a living world of contending ideas." In the early 1920s, the new psychology was inseparable from the new poetry.

Mead was part of a student group at Columbia that called itself the Ash Can Cats and included poet Leonie Adams, whose obvious talent persuaded Mead that her own poetry would never be more than an avocation. Because virtually everyone she knew wrote poetry, she did too. At Barnard, Jung was in fashion and Mead noted (Howard 1984, 43): "I was at one point supposed to be an 'intuitive introvert,' which everybody wanted to be because that was what Jung admired most." A more unlikely introvert could hardly be imagined.

Mead's circle were all feminists, a term that then encompassed a wider range of women's issues than it does today.[6] Like many of her friends, Mead admired intellectual virtuosity and her infatuation led to a brief affair with Sapir. But they wanted different things from their relationship. Older men tended to be conservative; Sapir had three children without a mother. When he proposed marriage and suggested that her proper role in life was to have babies, Mead (1972, 111) wrote "a bitter little verse of feminine protest" because his view would "leave no room for dream." Sapir failed to recognize Mead's professional ambition, leading to an inevitable clash of wills—precisely because of the traits that attracted them to one another. Both were left embittered by the memory. Sapir never in later life spoke of his personal relationship to Mead; she spoke of it often, her regret mingled with bitterness (e.g., Mandelbaum to Darnell, July 1986); she claimed to remember every detail of their relationship; it remained important to her that she had attracted the leading intellect of her youthful generation.

Sapir, in contrast, felt betrayed. His proposal of marriage and family commitment had acknowledged Mead's intellectual attraction. Domesticity was not, in his eyes, a sacrifice but the natural result of intimacy and partnership. He could not comprehend that Mead could be sincerely attracted to him and not want what he wanted. In later years, Sapir would be very negative about Mead's work, which, indeed, she did not do the way he would have done it. Mead in turn resented his inability to accept her as she was. Each belittled the other.

The influence of Sapir's writings on both Mead and Benedict, therefore, centered in the few years when the three were close friends. Sapir developed his ideas about culture and personality in the late twenties and thirties, when their influence was much attenuated. Mead would later attempt to read Sapir out of the history of culture and personality. Moreover, he chose to dissociate himself from that label, partly because he associated it with Mead and Benedict.[7]

In 1924–1925, Sapir was adjusting to the death of his wife and Mead was preparing for her first field trip, determined that she would not be forced into studying yet another dying American Indian culture. Mead met Sapir at the BAAS meeting in Toronto in 1924. Mead noted: "As there were only a handful of us, we saw a great deal of everyone who came" (Mead 1972, 124). Sapir, Canada's ranking anthropologist, was host and in better spirits than in many years. The adulation of Benedict's protegé must have lifted some of his gloom. It was Mead's first large conference and she was intoxicated by the gathering of her would-be peers, each with his or her own "people" from firsthand fieldwork. She particularly remembered Sapir and Goldenweiser for their discussions of Jung's psychological types.

Mead saw a great deal of Sapir during the following year. Her retrospective characterization (1972, 125) stressed the intellectual excitement rather than Sapir's working through of his personal problems:

Sapir was in New York for part of that year, enjoying the poets he met and developing a new interest in pattern, an outgrowth of an interest in Gestalt psychology. I read and lent him Koffka's *Growth of the Mind*. We were all still writing poetry with almost as much intensity as we were working on anthropology.

She wrote to Benedict (8 September 1924: in Mead 1959, 286): "I suppose it's a very bad sign that Sapir has time to write letters, but I do enjoy them. It's such a satisfactory friendship, defaced by no tiresome preliminaries (that's thanks to you) and founded on such sure ground of like-mindedness."

Sapir's letters to Benedict were interspersed with comments about Margaret Mead. He fussed over her delicate health, enlisting Benedict to make her be more careful (23 August 1924: SF), and was impressed that she continued to work in spite of such setbacks (15 November 1924: SF). Sapir was sufficiently confident of the budding friendship to expect Mead to be pleased at his rather brutal criticism of her poetic efforts (to Benedict, 14 February 1925: SF). Sincerity was more important to him than tact. After a weekend at the Mead family farm in Pennsylvania, Sapir wrote to Benedict (18 July 1924: SF): "But Margaret was still more wonderful [than her sister Elizabeth]. She is ever so much bigger than I had imagined her. In that beautiful rustic atmosphere she comes into her own." But he worried about her planned departure for Samoa. Boas was concerned primarily about her physical health, Sapir about "the latent neurotic situation."

When he decided to move to Chicago, Sapir insisted (to Benedict, 22 June 1925: SF): "I shall miss you and Margaret very much. That would have been my chief reason for preferring New York, aside from the obvious advantages of New York as New York, but perhaps you girls can come to Chicago yet or maybe I won't stay there very long." Not long after his arrival in Chicago, Sapir schemed to obtain a position there for Mead (to Benedict, 3 October 1925: SF): "I shall try to do what I can for Margaret. Perhaps an actual offer will appeal to her if it ever comes. But not a word of this to anyone, please!" From Sapir's point of view, this was an ideal solution and he hoped to present Mead with a fait accompli.

Mead, however, did not appreciate Sapir's interference in her life. Behind her back, the three people in anthropology to whom she was closest—Boas, Benedict, and Sapir—all expressed concerns about her trip to Samoa. She believed that Sapir led the conspiracy out of personal motives unworthy of him. Boas wrote to Mead (14 July 1925: APS) about theoretical issues involved in her fieldwork, making it clear that she could still back out without loss of face. Even for Sapir, however, he refused to interfere with her personal or professional autonomy.

Boas was more concerned than he let on to Mead directly. He wrote to Benedict (18 July 1925: APS) that Sapir, his perspective muddled by too much reading in psychiatry, exaggerated the dangers. However, Samoa was an isolated place and Mead was not of robust stature or health. Boas sought Benedict's reassurance that he could leave Mead to her own devices. If he suspected that Sapir's motives were less than altruistic, he did not consider that his business:

Sapir had a long talk with me about Margaret Mead. . . . In my opinion an attempt to compel her now to give up the trip—and that is all Sapir has in mind—would be disastrous. Besides it is entirely against my point of view to interfere in such a radical way with the future of a person for his or her own sake—unless there is actual disease that needs control. Of course, Sapir takes that point of view, but if he were right, then who should not be restrained?

Benedict felt that Sapir overstepped the bounds of both friendship and professional responsibility, reassuring Boas (18 July 1925: APS) that she had already forestalled most of Sapir's objections. Like Boas, she understood, as Sapir apparently did not, that Mead was determined to demonstrate her personal independence and professional competence, regardless of the cost.

Mead apparently felt that domestic decisions could wait until she returned from the field. Retrospectively, she described her feelings (1972, 244): "Edward Sapir's advice that I would do better to stay at home and have a child than to go off to Samoa to study adolescent girls seemed peculiar to me. After all, men were not told to give up field work to have children!" These were the priorities of a modern woman—which Sapir would so bitterly criticize to Benedict a few years later. From the point of view of both women, however, it was Sapir who imposed unnecessary constraints. Mead already had Benedict as a model of a childless woman whose life was far from barren.

In any case, Sapir's plea, in "Ariel," for Mead to remain with him was rejected and she left for Samoa, with a stopover to visit Benedict in the field at Zuni. Mary Catherine Bateson, Mead's daughter, assumes the relationship ended then (1984, 125): "Ruth and Margaret decided that neither of them would choose further intimacy with Sapir, but rather preferred each other." According to Howard (1984, 74): "They talked about Sapir's having fallen in love with Margaret. The only way she could end this affair, Margaret speculated, would be to scheme to have him reject her." Benedict realized how difficult this strategy would be for Mead's direct, honest personality. In later years, indeed, Mead greatly regretted the bitterness of the breakup.[8]

In spite of the agreement between Benedict and Mead, however, Sapir wrote to Mead in the field and she apparently expected some sort of reunion with him on her return. Toward the end of her time in the field, however, he told her that he had fallen in love with somebody else and intended to remarry. Although Mead normally saved all her letters, she "made a bonfire of all [Sapir's] letters on a beach in Samoa and that was the end of that" (Howard 1984, 87). Although she was perhaps unrealistic in wanting to have her cake and eat it too, Mead did not take the relationship lightly. Sapir, on the other hand, began a new life in Chicago and believed Mead did not want to share it with him. The documentation demonstrates cross-purposes, bad timing, and misunderstandings. As a result, Sapir and Mead were never able to communicate about their later, independently developed common interests in culture, personality, and the individual; his estrangement from Benedict was also of long-standing by then.

CHAPTER TEN

Escape from Ottawa

Edward Sapir moved from Ottawa to the University of
Chicago in 1925, thereby entering the center of the North American
academic world as one of its leading lights; he went on to Yale in
1931, where his health declined and anti-Semitism undoubtedly contributed to his premature death in 1939. In retrospect, all this is so
well known to disciplinary history as to seem inevitable. In the early
twenties, however, escape from Ottawa was a mirage that sapped Sapir's energies with its promise of relief for his wife's precarious health
and his own professional disillusionment. He dreamed of New York
and Columbia. After he left Ottawa, Sapir recalled only the bitterness
of his final years there.

Unquestionably, however, the early Ottawa years were as happy as
the latter were painful. A skewed view of the trajectory of Sapir's
career has resulted (Murray 1981, 63):

[He] blamed much of his unhappiness on being [in Ottawa]. His later students, perhaps predisposed to expect life in Canada to be dreary, accepted
that description of the situation. Of course, neither the war nor his wife's
illness were caused by the Ottawa environment, even if both made his life
very unpleasant.

Murray further argues that Sapir realized his problems were "at least
in part intra-psychic." Externalization—blaming the environment—
freed him to work and was, therefore, an effective coping strategy.
Moreover, Sapir assessed possible professional opportunities in polit-

189

ically naive terms, adding to the frustration of his perceived isolation (Murray 1981, 66):

> Sapir's sense of institutional realities—what was and was not possible—was not highly developed. . . . Sapir had misjudged the opportunities at both of the universities [California and Pennsylvania] at which he had held positions prior to going to Canada, and he would find lack of time for research, lack of publication outlets and burdensome amounts of administrative labor problems at the University of Chicago. . . . Dissatisfied at Chicago, he left the protection of sympathetic anthropologists and sociologists for the harsh anti-Semitism of New Haven. . . . What appeared to him to be "greener pastures" were unrealistic expectations. In particular, Berkeley was no more the home of the cultural *avant-garde* than was Ottawa in the teens and twenties.

Many of Sapir's Boasian colleagues were willing, if not able, to help him escape his reportedly intolerable situation in Ottawa. There were no other Boasians in Ottawa to qualify his version of its drawbacks. No more American contract researchers were being hired, and Sapir's colleagues, Barbeau and Jenness, were British-trained.

The Ottawa cutbacks proved to be permanent. Jenness, who succeeded Sapir, focused on making the Victoria Memorial Museum into a national museum rather than a global one like the Royal Ontario under the direction of Thomas McIlwraith (Jenness to McIlwraith, 21 October 1925: UT). The research program, however, lost the eminence it had held under Sapir. Jenness hoped to appoint a young man just out of university, having quickly established that McIlwraith— the only senior anthropologist in Canada not already associated with the Ottawa Division—was permanently settled in Toronto. Jenness looked to a non-Boasian tradition (1 March 1926: UT):

> Personally, I should prefer a Canadian who has been trained in an English university like yourself, or an Englishman with university training, rather than an American. English methods differ from American in many ways and an Englishman coming over here to work would be likely to have a broader outlook than an American.

When Sapir resigned, Duncan Campbell Scott noted the "new paths of usefulness which are absent here," noting wryly that "Ottawa is inured to these changes" (to Sapir, 16 June 1922: UT). Sapir was too elated to feel guilty at abandoning Ottawa anthropology. There is no evidence that he tried to hide his lack of enthusiasm for the city or for his position there. He had to resign, however, from the Royal Society of Canada, when he left the country.

Evaluation of Sapir's role in Canadian anthropology has remained an issue in that country, with many native-born anthropologists denigrating his contribution because he left. That a founding father, already an immigrant, should lack loyalty to the institutions he established was an unpalatable legacy. Moreover, professionalization in universities, along American lines, came very late in Canada. The first academic program began at Toronto the year Sapir moved to Chicago. He left no students to maintain his research tradition. The prestige of the institution declined; ironically, therefore, it did not commemorate Sapir's achievements. In addition, his long-standing opposition to Canadian amateur anthropologists, particularly in the western provinces, had made him enemies.

Professionalization was not a uniquely American phenomenon, although some Canadian anthropologists perceived it as such. Both Sapir and Boas were immigrants to America, criticized as alien upstarts. They also shared a conviction that science was more important than nationality, and that patriotism was a parochial concern. Americans as well as Canadians were incensed by such an attitude, particularly during World War I.

The more recent history of Canadian anthropology has not enhanced Sapir's retrospective reputation. Rapid growth in Canadian academic departments came only in the 1960s. Since Canadians were unavailable for the new positions, mass importation, largely American, characterized the period. By the time Canadian graduates obtained their degrees, the boom was over. Unsurprisingly, anything American was perceived as a threat to Canadian anthropology. Indeed, students of the 1970s were often unwilling to admit that Canadian anthropology constituted a unique national tradition (Darnell 1975). Neither Sapir's achievements nor the continuing role of Ottawa anthropological institutions were accepted as "Canadian."

McFeat (1984) expressed the persistent ambivalence toward Sapir, characterizing him—along with Boas—as one of the "Canadian-associated greats." Jenness was a New Zealander (Collins 1971), part of the British Commonwealth, and not, therefore, comparably alien. Nonetheless, McFeat's enthusiasm was palpable: "Then there was Sapir. But, of course, *he* wasn't a local boy." However, the Sapir Centennial Conference, held in Ottawa in 1984, has encouraged a more realistic assessment of Sapir in Canada—its importance for him as well as his for it. This fifteen-year period was Sapir's most productive in terms of fieldwork and writing, whatever its personal difficulties. He was hired to create institutions for Canadian anthropology and he did so. Sapir encouraged Canadian anthropologists to enter the mainstream of the discipline on an international scale. Professionalization was the dominant trend of early twentieth-century anthropology everywhere, and Sapir ensured that Canadian anthropologists would have to meet the more rigorous research standards that were emerging. Later professional anthropologists in Canada inherited the tradition and standards established by Sapir. Without his sustained effort to develop government-sponsored anthropological research in Canada, the discipline would have remained at a pre-professional level much longer.

During the late Ottawa years, Sapir's disenchantment extended to all institutions. He wrote to Spier (6 July 1920: NMM) that his problems at the American Museum were not unique, that "the best protective device that you can grow is to make up your mind to an absurdly low standard of what you may expect of them. Always be surprised if you get treated half-way decently."

Kroeber tried to arrange for Sapir to replace him at Berkeley for a semester in 1920 (Kroeber to Sapir, 11 February 1919: UCB). Sapir, though intrigued by the possibility of teaching, protested that he had long since forgotten "what little anthropology I ever knew" (18 February 1919: UCB). Neither man took this disclaimer seriously. Even a temporary respite from Ottawa inspired Sapir's promise to "clean up the Yana account as far as possible." The university, however, forced Kroeber to choose between his own promotion and Sapir's leave position; unsurprisingly, he chose the former.

Sapir was increasingly convinced that teaching was the solution to his problems. The publication of his book *Language* was intended, at least partly, to aid in obtaining an appropriate university position (Sapir to Lowie, 28 November 1921: UCB):

It is high time I got on to a univ. job if I am not to die without feeling that I spent my whole life as a square peg in a round hole. This place is getting confoundedly on my nerves. What the hell do I care about exhibits? To be sure, I spend precious little time on exhibit work, but then I always feel that I ought to. . . . I cannot say just how I should actually feel about taking up mainly anthropological work at a university, but I may have to do it to get back to semi-civilization. Of course, a strictly linguistic position would please me rather more.

But the choice of "being a mere philologist at an American university" was not open. Anthropologists working with unwritten languages were peripheral to philology, and Sapir had not published in Indo-

European since leaving Columbia. Anthropology departments couldn't afford a full-time linguist. A joint appointment, which Sapir held at both Chicago and Yale, was the most realistic compromise.

Lowie also tried to get Sapir a job at Berkeley, though the latter feared Kroeber did not really want him there (to Lowie, 19 April 1921: UCB). Lowie also proposed fieldwork in the Pacific for the Bernice Bishop Museum and the National Research Council. Sapir was "most seriously" interested, because the Bishop Museum link to Yale might lead to university work.[1]

In 1922, Sapir approached Dixon about possible paid lectures in Boston, where his wife was receiving medical treatment. Dixon, a peripheral Boasian and Kroeber's ally in classifying California languages, responded (6 February: NMM) that Harvard "most definitely" needed "a man to handle general linguistics" but had no money. He was sympathetic to Sapir's wish to devote himself "to linguistics alone." But universities in this period had no funds for guest lecturers (to Sapir, 10 April 1922: NMM).

Laufer wanted Sapir in Chicago so they could collaborate on Sino-Tibetan. In 1920, Sapir had considered a position as assistant curator at the Field Museum, a substantial demotion, because it might lead to a joint position at the University of Chicago (to Laufer, 28 September: NMM). Laufer sounded out the possibility of funding for a Department of American Languages at the university (to Sapir, 17 January 1921: NMM). Nowhere in the world was there such a department. But anthropology at Chicago was still dominated by Frederick Starr, an evolutionary anthropologist hired by William Rainey Harper when the university opened in 1892; his retirement in 1923 was a precondition for reorganization of anthropology along Boasian lines (Darnell 1969; Miller 1978). Philology was still taught largely in language departments and Amerindian work found no place therein. Laufer found no institutional support to combine ethnology and linguistics. His efforts, however, brought Sapir's name to the attention of Chicago administrators, to be recalled when local conditions changed, as they soon did.

Boasian Machinations at Columbia

Sapir still considered New York his home and Boas his mentor, writing (25 August 1920: NMM): "I should give so much to be in contact with people who are genuinely interested in linguistic research. It would give me the stimulus I so badly need." By this time, Boas apparently accepted that Ottawa was not destined to remain a center of Boasian anthropology. Similar financial cutbacks had crippled the Bureau of American Ethnology a few years earlier, and Canada had no resources for training Boasian anthropologists. For at least one more generation, Boasian anthropologists would have to do Canadian Indian fieldwork without an institutional base in Canada.

Sapir felt that he could advance in Ottawa only as head of the new museum, a civil service position that would preclude his own research (to Boas, 23 September 1920: NMM): "Let me be brutally frank. . . . I am hopelessly out of touch here." Sapir's "real sphere of usefulness" was linguistic and he lacked "the proper stimulus for the kind of work I can and should do." New York should be able to accommodate "at least one general student of language"; he excluded both Boas and Goddard from this category, also noting that Goddard, a rival in Athabaskan linguistics, might oppose his appointment. Sapir urged Boas to keep him in mind even if nothing was immediately available.

Boas (to Sapir, 26 September 1920: NMM) had always wanted Sapir to return to Columbia to carry on the Amerindian linguistic work there; moreover, he had reached normal retirement age. It was time to take action, although conditions were "not by any means encouraging." Boas was now the only anthropologist at Columbia, the American Museum was cutting back, the New School for Social Research was dropping theoretical courses in anthropology, Columbia's classics program had dismissed its only linguist, and only Boas's personal insistence retained the elementary course in anthropology at Barnard College.

In light of these discouraging facts, Boas thought Laufer's efforts at the Field Museum might be more productive for Sapir than his own. He warned, however, that Chicago was "an exhibition museum," so research "has to be done after office hours." This was not the scientific freedom for which Sapir yearned. Boas emphasized the drawbacks of all positions: "I can appreciate your lack of congenial people with whom you can talk over your scientific interests and your other more general interests, but we all have to put up with that condition." Boas assured Sapir that he would do whatever he could but was no longer confident of controlling the course of the discipline, even at Columbia: "There are a good many points about the anthropological situation that worry me very much." Sapir's professional impasse was not unique among the Boasians, although his personal anxiety perhaps was. However he may have wished to help, Boas was powerless.

Sapir, however, did not give up on the idea of Columbia, approaching the matter indirectly through Ogburn, recently appointed to the Department of Sociology. Ogburn (to Sapir, 20 November 1923: NMM) was flattered that Sapir thought he might be useful, but his comments rapidly diffused into an assessment of his own career. He might replace Franklin Giddings as chairman on his retirement, but this would not be for several years. Ogburn confirmed the rumor that anthropology and sociology might be combined—but only after the retirements of both Giddings and Boas. Boas was, in his opinion, likely to remain about eight more years. Literature might be an alternative niche for a linguist. Ogburn reiterated that his own influence was "to a certain extent potential and problematical." He also reported an abortive scheme of Boas and Giddings, possibly involving Sapir.

In 1925, Boas was able to offer Sapir a summer school appointment to teach two ethnology courses (14 October 1924: NMM); he was unsuccessful in adding a third in linguistics (22 October: NMM). Boas reassured Sapir that he had not forgotten the long-range needs of his former student: "There is some interest which leads me to hope that perhaps in a few years a department of linguistics may be established. I wish I could give you better news."

Sapir wanted to structure his ethnology courses around topics of interdisciplinary theory, foreshadowing the approach he would take at Chicago (to Boas, 25 October 1924: NMM): "I wanted to review a number of the more basic points of method, overhauling fundamental concepts, in a way that might be of interest to students interested in psychology, sociology, and history." Sapir continued to remind Boas that he wanted "so badly to get away" from Ottawa (13 April 1925: NMM).

Sapir's Appointment at Chicago

Boas kept his word to inform Sapir of any vacant position, writing (n.d. 1923: APS) that Starr was about to retire from Chicago. He wondered if Sapir had "some way" of presenting his name, presumably other than a direct application. Boas had limited power in Chicago circles, having failed to obtain an appointment there in 1894 because of the prior commitment to Starr. He wanted to obtain the position for a sympathetic ally. Sapir, apparently unaware of these complexities, simply expected Boas to act on his behalf. He reported that he had met Carl Buck, Chicago's most distinguished philologist, through Laufer in 1921 and believed him "favorably impressed." Sapir offered to lecture on any combination of ethnology and linguistics, pressing Boas for details of Chicago intentions to which the latter was clearly not party.

By the fall of 1924, Sapir was sufficiently optimistic about a forthcoming offer from Chicago to remind Boas (2 October: APS) that he still preferred Columbia: "I am very eager not to take a false step. If it is possible for me to get started in New York, I feel that that is the proper place for me to go." He would accept a more "modest" start "because I know so many more people there and would feel so very much more at home." Sapir frankly acknowledged personal as well as professional motives. Only obligations to his children had prevented him from resigning after his wife's death, "even without any definite position promised anywhere." He even asked if Boas could use the Chicago situation to bargain on Sapir's behalf at Columbia, citing the "greater suitability of the New York background" for his mother and children:

[My mother] is a stranger here and likely to feel one in Chicago as well. It would be difficult for her to make a new start. You can easily understand how eager I am to seize upon what elements of homeliness are still left in a difficult situation. . . . Ottawa is going to be impossible for the children as they grow up.

As an afterthought, Sapir asked Boas not to share his ambivalence with Fay-Cooper Cole, who was acting in good faith to finalize an offer to Sapir at Chicago.

Meanwhile, Cole was occupied with the internal politics surrounding the offer to Sapir. During the first year of his appointment (1924–1925), Cole taught seven courses in anthropology. He assured Albion Small, chairman of the joint Sociology and Anthropology Department, that another instructor was needed (12 November 1924: UC). Moreover, physical anthropology and linguistics were essential "in order that our graduate students may secure all their training in Anthropology at this institution." Cole was a Boasian and it was inconceivable to him that anthropology should be taught in less than its full scope.

After his long prelude, Cole got around to his candidate: "I have seen this situation developing" and approached, without any commitment, "the man I believe to be the best fitted for our needs." With remarkable understatement, Cole noted that "he is willing to join us if we can make him a satisfactory offer." In primitive linguistics, Sapir was "the outstanding worker in America." In Cole's opinion, he had been "the shark of the lot" in Boas's seminars at Columbia. Cole assured Small that Sapir would attract a range of students to the joint department.

To Dean J. H. Tuft (23 December 1924: UC), Cole stressed that Sapir would need assurance of rapid promotion if appointed below the rank of professor. Sapir also wanted his title to reflect his specialization in linguistics as well as anthropology. Moreover, special arrangements would have to be made for secretarial services (including specialized typing) in order to obtain "one of the best men in America" in the study of "primitive linguistics and psychological problems in anthropology." The latter emphasis was designed to capture support from the interdisciplinary social science research program emerging at Chicago under Rockefeller Foundation auspices. The dean, unable to assess the quality of Sapir's work, focused on prior teaching experience, extensive fieldwork, and administrative experience directing a research program.

Sapir remained unaware of Cole's machinations with his superiors, continuing to stress Chicago's indecision and his own ambivalence (to Benedict, 27 February 1925: SF): "As yet I am ignorant of whether a favorable decision will stimulate me or deject me." Of course, whether or not he preferred to go to Chicago, a rejection would have profoundly depressed him.

Negotiations proceeded so slowly that Sapir considered applying for the museum directorship in Ottawa after all (to Boas, 15 April 1925: APS). He had been told that funds for his initial salary at Chicago were assured but was "not as sanguine" as before because he did not "exactly understand" the implications in terms of Chicago academic politics. Sapir had not communicated directly with anyone except Cole, and it now seemed to him that Cole had misrepresented the position:

[He] did not make it clear at first that my work would have to come under Anthropology and that, presumably, I should be teaching under his direction. He emphasized complete freedom of work for me and it was to be linguistics only. Now it appears that I am to take part in their Seminar, give a course in something like the Psychology of Culture, and my title could not be named for "General Linguistics" because that would interfere with Buck and others. You see, he was not absolutely frank at the outset.

Unaccustomed to academic decision-making processes, Sapir was oblivious to the constraints on Cole. He did not actually object to working under Cole, but focused on the full professorship as the key to the value Chicago placed upon his services.

Boas's reply (21 April 1925: NMM), however, brought Sapir back to the reality that he badly needed a job. Boas "made some inquiries" and learned that the Chicago expansion was likely to be postponed until 1926, a scenario he considered "not unlikely." The funding drive to which Sapir's appointment was apparently tied would take time. Boas advised Sapir to apply for the Ottawa promotion, resigning a year later if necessary. He did not enlighten Sapir as to his sources: "I have no way to approach Chicago directly without endangering the whole situation, and so far I have not found anyone who can do it for me."

Sapir took the situation at face value, thanking Boas for his help (13 April 1925: APS): "But you have always taken such a lively interest in my progress that it seems natural I should bother you." As details of the Chicago position were clarified, Sapir was reassured (to Benedict, 14 June 1925: SF). The Spelman Memorial of the Rockefeller Foundation would pay his salary for the initial three years; the university would do so thereafter. He worried, however, about formal committee approval:

But until I actually get a black and white offer, I shall not count the cup as having attained the lip, nor shall I have the family's pictures taken for the use of the immigration authorities nor pay my fees for copies of the children's birth certificates nor advertise the furniture nor any of the other things demanded by a decent respect for the accumulated wisdom of society.

Sapir's rush of prose is that of a man who at last begins to believe that his dreams are about to become reality. He assured Benedict that he had "quite ceased to speculate" on the relative advantages of New York (although he expected Chicago's famous factory grime to be hard on white collars).

By his next letter to Benedict (22 June 1925: SF), he had accepted the Chicago position and mapped out his first year's courses. His elation was only superficially masked by complaints about "immigration nonsense." He was "not buoyantly pleased . . . yet not depressed—

quietly expectant about expresses it. I'm prepared to like the change
and also prepared for some disappointment, so I can't be hugely disappointed." Unable to handle more emotional distress, Sapir instinc-
tively protected himself from vulnerability. Already, however, he had
shifted into a new frame of mind, in which Cole, rather than Boas,
was the supportive authority figure:

> For years, I've been placing my hopes in Columbia and Boas, but it seems
> fated not to be. Boas wants me, but I can't help thinking that he doesn't want
> me enough to really wrestle. I suspect he merely goes through a few innocent
> motions and comes away thinking he has moved heaven and earth! It's always
> been that way with all his work for years and years. So that I decided there
> was no use waiting any longer.

It was essential to Sapir to feel in control of his life, that his career
did not progress merely by accident. For all his protestations that he
wanted to leave Ottawa at any cost, Sapir was ambitious and wanted
his peers to value his abilities.

After his arrival in Chicago, Sapir learned Cole's version of Boas's
role in his appointment (Sapir to Benedict, 3 October 1925: SF).
Apparently, Boas had supported Goldenweiser, who was unacceptable
to the sociologists "partly because they thought his anthropology was
not different enough from their sociology" and "partly because the
tale of his not having paid his Columbia Faculty Club bill years ago
has gotten around Chicago and made him taboo." Boas then "flatly
contradicted himself," arguing that anthropology should affiliate itself
with biology, again in the person of Goldenweiser: "At this point the
Chicago people got sore with Boas and felt he was butting in too
much." Boas then supported Michelson of the bureau, a linguist of
considerably less stature than Sapir and only peripherally a Boasian.
Sapir was incensed at what he interpreted as betrayal:

> Meanwhile, I had taken Boas into my confidence about Cole's tentative of-
> fer . . . a confidence which he never reciprocated! I never made the slightest
> move, as you know, in the Chicago affair. Cole wanted me to help out his
> budding anthropological department with work in primitive linguistics and
> cultural psychology and insisted on me. He won out *against Boas*! So I have
> the curious and somewhat amusing satisfaction of knowing that when Boas
> roots for me at Columbia he can't have his way, but when he roots for others
> at Chicago I can slip in.

Benedict apparently attempted to explain Boas's action in terms of his
efforts to bring Sapir to Columbia. He may have envisioned an ex-

change between Sapir and Goldenweiser at the New School for Social Research in New York. Sapir (19 October 1925: SF) accepted this as plausible, but was stymied by Boas's effort to place Michelson over himself. Benedict's "little analysis of Boas's antics" implied that Boas had not mentioned this plan.

Sapir's version of these events depended exclusively on Cole, who had considerable motivation to insure Sapir's loyalty to himself and to Chicago. Unsurprisingly, Cole emerged as the heroic champion of Sapir, and Sapir was suitably grateful; although Cole's "view of life" differed from his own, he was "perfectly congenial in practice." Moreover, Sapir was deeply wounded by Boas's apparent defection, though he tried to gloss over this to Benedict:

What I have learned from the whole Boas episode is not to take Boas too completely into my confidence and to expect nothing, simply nothing, from him. I admire and respect him, of course, but I find myself drifting away from him . . . I do not actually dislike . . . I merely grow indifferent. Should I ever try to get entree into Columbia I should certainly not bother Boas again to work for me but should use other channels of access.

Later, realizing that Benedict's personal loyalty to Boas placed her in an awkward position, Sapir (27 October 1925: SF) hoped she did not feel "too intensely about the Boas incident." He assured her that there had to be another side to the story.[2] Sapir was most offended by his "intuition" that Boas had not been entirely "frank" with him. He speculated that Boas had ignored his wish to leave Ottawa and regretted his own openness:

[Boas] is willing to sacrifice quite all of his friendship for me for other motives, whatever they are. . . . I not only cannot count on Boas's scientific backing . . . but his friendship is not intense enough to amount to anything when it comes to a show-down. Naturally, I object to being nothing *but* a tool in Boas's personal scheme of things anthropological and linguistic. You must not imagine for a moment that I am truly bitter . . . I find myself quite little stirred and very firmly emplanted on the bedrock of a somewhat humorous indifference.

It is characteristic of Boas that he did not explain his actions, even to those directly involved. For Sapir, however, the issue was that the position was tailor-made for him (as a result of Cole's efforts), and Boas tried to force "a linguistic opening for me into an anthropological opening for others." Boas presumably feared that Sapir would not accept the Columbia offer when he was finally able to make it.

The Continued Lure of Columbia

Sapir attempted to put the matter behind him (to Benedict, 27 October 1925: SF). During the early Chicago years, however, he still longed for New York and eventually learned that Boas was still working toward an appointment for him at Columbia. He reported to Boas (14 December 1925: APS) that he liked his new position: "I am interested to find that student contacts interest me over and above the work itself. And then, of course, I was brought up in an urban atmosphere." He professed himself "very much moved" at Boas's continued efforts. Although he would be "a little shamefaced about leaving Cole in the lurch," a full professorship at Columbia had a "superior attractiveness" to which Sapir was far from immune.

Reassurance that Boas had not abandoned him was no doubt equally important to him. Indeed, Sapir discussed the pros and cons of each position with Boas in the same tone as his letters before the move from Ottawa to Chicago. Although the Columbia position was not yet a reality, Sapir was delighted at the first prospect in his career to be solely a linguist.[3]

Unfortunately, however, Boas again miscalculated Columbia's power struggles (to Sapir, 18 March 1926: APS). An Oriental Languages appointment in linguistics precluded further action in 1926. Boas's sympathy ("I wish, for myself, that I could give you better news") makes it clear that his motives related to the Columbia program more than to Sapir's malaise in Ottawa and relative contentment in Chicago.

Sapir was not overly disturbed, writing to Benedict (23 March 1926: SF): "I'm constantly surprised to see how little matters of ambition of that sort concern me. . . . I have a hunch I'm here for good." Already he was becoming increasingly caught up in Chicago social science, which, with its wide-ranging Rockefeller funding, provided opportunities not available at Columbia. Boas, indeed, would soon have nothing to offer. Sapir's anthropology would become less Boasian and more interdisciplinary, relying on the humanities and psychiatry rather than the natural sciences for models. Although he would never abandon linguistics, Sapir would go far beyond the traditional issues of Boasian ethnology. This was the last point at which Sapir might have remained within the anthropology of his Boasian training.

CHAPTER ELEVEN

The University of Chicago: A New Start

Sapir was optimistic about his new position in Chicago, writing in the midst of his packing (to Lowie, 29 August 1925: UCB): "It was high time I cleared out of here and I consider myself a lucky dog to have got the Chicago offer." In fact, he was so eager to immerse himself in the new intellectual environment that he devoted minimal attention to household affairs. Helen Sapir Larson recalls (to Darnell, 22 June 1984) that he bought a whole apartment full of "God-awful" furniture so he could concentrate on his teaching. Sapir was grateful to leave the practical household details of the move to his mother.

Once Sapir had escaped from Ottawa, he was more sanguine about its good points. To Diamond Jenness (22 October 1925: NMM), he lamented his "abysmally small" office and the lack of bookcases; it was "hardly possible to settle down to research work yet." He liked his classes, with students "not very numerous," and the "varied" contacts of the academic community. His children seemed "quite well adjusted."

Sapir almost immediately missed the resources of the Anthropological Division and presented Jenness with his shopping list. He wanted to borrow records of Kutchin songs so a colleague in Romance linguistics could test their phonetics in his lab. Sapir wanted to borrow his lantern slides on the aesthetics of design. Though this project was peripheral to his work in Ottawa, he found his new colleagues in sociology and psychology intrigued by the research design. He was

shocked when Jenness felt compelled to charge him for the slides because he was no longer employed by the Canadian government. Jenness willingly lent library books, sympathized with lack of secretarial
services, and considered Sapir "an unofficial member of our Museum"
(7 January 1927: NMM). When Sapir complained that he had no
time for scientific work, Jenness (15 March 1926: NMM) gently reminded him that he had longed for the "great joy" of "directing able
students to fertile lines of investigation."

The continued friendship was not, however, one-sided. Sapir punc-
tiliously urged Jenness to put himself forward as Canada's premier
anthropologist (15 April 1927: NMM). He encouraged Jenness's
work on Eskimo dialects and experimentation with ethnographic genre
and individual personality (7 June 1927: NMM) and continued to
read his manuscripts (Jenness to Sapir, 15 July 1928: NMM). Sapir
even attempted to acquire Jenness's psychological material for the
American Journal of Sociology, housed in the Chicago Department of
Sociology and Anthropology.

From the beginning, Chicago was a different social milieu than
Ottawa. Grandmother Sapir was hard put to keep up with her distinguished son's guests. Until Sapir's remarriage nonalcoholic teas were
the norm. Chicago sociologists Louis Wirth and William Ogburn, and
economists Henry Schultz and Jacob Viner[1] were occasional dinner
guests, as were Sapir's students. Helen Sapir Larson recalls that Morris
Swadesh was "so bashful" that he would never greet the family but
simply "scoot up to Dad's study." Charles Blooah, the Liberian informant for Sapir's linguistic seminars, was also often around the
house.

Sapir's closest friend among the economists was Frank Knight, later
to be a guest speaker for the Yale "Impact" Seminar (see chap. 17).
Knight used Sapir's work in his courses, citing language as the "purest
most autonomous form of human institution" (Michael Sapir, p.c.).
Michael attributes his later graduate assistantship in economics to the
friendship.

In addition to academic contacts, Sapir quickly became a popular
public lecturer in Chicago. Through ethnomusicologist George Herzog's wife Betsey, Sapir was introduced to Chicago's wealthy North
Side Jewish community, where he basked in the company of the powerful. In fact, Sapir went out in the evenings so often that his children
were quite resentful. For the first time, he felt himself fully appreciated.

He gave a popular lecture course in ten evenings on the Psychology of Culture, modeled on his course at the university, to a group headed by Clarence Darrow, whom he "got to know rather well personally. He's a lovable man and chums a lot." Through Darrow's second wife, Sapir had unearthed ties to mutual friends of Jaime de Angulo and Paul Radin in Berkeley and was delighted to find that "the world is quite small" (to Lowie, n.d. 1926: UCB).

Sapir entered into a series of radio debates with a Chicago rabbi on Jewish assimilation. Chicago was generally accepting of Jews, who were well represented in the university. Sapir argued that Judaism was a cultural tradition comparable to that of any other ethnic group and would gradually die out as each generation's observance became more perfunctory and symbolic. European examples, particularly in Germany, suggested that anti-Semitism would decline as Jews became culturally less distinct from their neighbors. Sapir addressed the concerns of the individual Jew escaping from immigrant poverty and orthodox ritual practice rather than those of Jewish communities isolated in a hostile larger society. Jewish academics were rare in this period; most of Sapir's generation found it advisable to keep a low profile, even in an atmosphere of superficial tolerance.[2]

Sapir was overwhelmed by the range of intellectually stimulating activity available to him in Chicago (to Lowie, 25 March 1926: UCB): "I like it here very well indeed, both at the University and outside. I'm getting infinitely less time for real work than I had expected, but I imagine I shall find myself in time and know how to avoid distractions." Sapir had never before had enough social life to learn how to manage his time. At Columbia, his limited social contacts had been related to his studies; in Ottawa, work had been his priority. Sapir was an introvert, moreover, and social interaction, however stimulating, tired him. The solitude and equanimity which were his preconditions for serious work were now threatened by other distractions, each of which Sapir very much wanted to pursue. He had never learned to manage competing scientific obligations effectively and was unable to make the brutal decisions that would organize his conflicting commitments.

The most dramatic change in Sapir's life in Chicago was his remarriage in September 1926 to Jean Victoria McClenaghan. Michael Sapir (1984, 9) recalls "so vividly his evident greater sociability and happiness at Chicago. There he met his second wife (curiously, a girl from Ottawa)," made personal friends in various disciplines, frequented the Faculty Club, gave public lectures, and joined poetry and music circles. "Those years . . . always seemed to me to be 'golden years' of his life."

As with his first marriage, Sapir wrote eagerly to various colleagues of his great fortune. To Boas (5 October 1926: APS) he explained: "I knew her slightly in Ottawa and got to know her very well last year in Chicago." He emphasized that Jean was working at the Institute for Juvenile Research in Chicago. To Jenness (21 November 1926: NMM), Sapir described his marriage as "a somewhat unexpected event." He appreciated Jean's profession and was optimistic that it could be balanced with family responsibilities. Jenness (22 December 1926: NMM) was "delighted by the youthful effervescence that spar-kled in [Sapir's] pages, even to the extent of real bad English which I never saw you use before." Characteristically, Sapir expressed his light-hearted exuberance, often absent in Ottawa, through words.

The McClenaghans were Scottish-Irish Loyalist immigrants to the Ottawa valley. Jean's father was a minor civil servant. The family could afford to educate only one of their three children. Tuition money was freed for Jean when her brother Vivien received veterans' education benefits after World War I. She obtained bachelor's and master's de-grees in history from the University of Toronto in 1922 and 1924. Jean's parents were unhappy because Sapir was older and had children from his previous marriage, and possibly because he was Jewish. The civil ceremony was repeated in a church for their benefit (Philip Sapir, p.c.). The family, however, soon became reconciled, recognizing Sa-pir's success in his profession and reassured by the presence in his household of numerous Bibles in a variety of languages (presumably attesting to his piety).[3] Jean's middle-class background had not pre-pared her for her family's initial negative reaction to Sapir's Jewish-ness.[4]

Jean, a student in the Master of Science program at the Smith College School of Social Work, was on a nine-month practicum at the Chicago Institute for Juvenile Research between two summers of course work. She and Sapir were engaged when she returned to Smith to write her thesis in the summer of 1926 and were married shortly afterward. Helen Sapir Larson recalls that her father and Jean returned to the Chicago apartment with their witnesses, a Mr. and Mrs. Water-house from the IJR. "They were laughing and having fun and carrying huge bouquets of flowers. I only much later learned what went on that day. The flowers came from a large wedding immediately pre-ceding theirs."

There are two versions of how Sapir and Jean met. He himself (to Jenness, 21 November 1926: NMM) noted Harlan Smith's daughter Elizabeth, a family friend, as the initial connection. Jean came to Sapir in Ottawa as an undergraduate, to discuss either poetry or psychiatry; she apparently knew nothing about his reputation as an anthropologist and linguist. Among Sapir's Chicago associates, the poetry version is substantiated by Stanley Newman and Cornelius Osgood (p.c.). In contrast, Paul Sapir reports that his mother was not overly fond of poetry and presumably influenced Sapir's retreat from it after the early Chicago years. She sought out Sapir in Ottawa as one of the few people from whom she might borrow a book on psychoanalysis.[5] Sapir was impressed that a girl sixteen years his junior was interested in the topic. In any case, the two met again during Jean's social work in Chicago—apparently as a result of deliberate effort on her part.

Sapir was lonely, harrassed by family burdens, and on the rebound from a disappointing affair with Margaret Mead. Characteristically, his feelings were expressed in poetry. In "Love After Bitterness" (12 March 1925: SF), he wrote of the healing of a "desolate wound" by "incalculable love."

The Institute for Juvenile Research offered Sapir a "job" doing the research of his choice at a thousand dollars for three months (Sapir to Benedict, 28 March 1927: SF): the director was "too impatient to stop to find out just *what* research I can, should, or will do. He says he trusts me! . . . Everyone is so good to me these days." The IJR was more interested in Sapir's reputation than in his research, though he was officially associated with IJR personality studies only in 1927–1928. His collaboration with experimental psychologists L. L. Thurstone and Heinrich Kluver was less than successful. As Sapir became more accustomed to the scramble for foundation funding that dominated the Chicago social sciences during these heady pre-Depression days, he found more congenial sources of funding and collaboration.

Soon, however, Sapir reported to Jenness (15 April 1927: NMM) that Jean "was finding it rather fatiguing to carry on both Institute work and household duties." To Benedict (29 September 1927: SF), he noted with cheerful equanimity: "Jean, poor girl, has resigned so she may contemplate at closer range the different types of complex-formation of her husband and his three children." Jean was twenty-six, young to be a stepmother, and had to win the affections of the three children. Philip in particular missed his grandmother, who moved to Massachusetts after the remarriage (although Sapir contin-

ued to support her). Nor was Jean welcomed with open arms by Sapir's students, many of whom were her age. She was from Ottawa,
moreover, a city known to most of them only through Sapir's dis-
paraging comments. Helen Sapir Larson recalls (p.c.) that Jean was
an awkward hostess, although red wine—made in the bathtub because
of Prohibition—was now served at parties; the children were paid a
dollar bribe to disappear when there were dinner guests. There was
never much liquor in the Sapir household, but in this period it was
part of a newfound capacity for sociability.

Jean Sapir did not work in her profession again until after her
husband's death, although his work kept her in touch with the interface of social science with psychiatry. Paul Sapir (p.c.) suggests that
she had intellectual curiosity but lacked rigorous mental discipline and
professional ambition; her intellectual style depended more on intuition than logic.

Sapir's favorite photograph, of himself and Jean standing and smok-
ing, carries the inscription, in Sapir's hand: "Major complex: treatment: a colossal indifference should be developed toward your own
feelings. You create situations which seem insoluble or 'ticklish' when,
as a matter of fact, a little 'flouting' of your own feelings would precipitate them into quite cheerful normalcy." Sapir saw himself as the
leader in their shared intellectual pursuits. This was the domestic stability he had always craved. The birth of Paul Edward Sapir in 1928
cemented this reality.[6] In Chicago, the children remember Sunday
morning walks en famille, Sapir's acquisition of initially troubling bi-
focals, and his teaching them to play chess.

Sapir took his parental responsibilities seriously. Michael graduated
from high school in 1929, and Sapir (to Lowie, 18 March 1929; to
Kroeber, 22 March 1929: UCB) sought advice from colleagues about
his further education. After his summer on the California Hupa reservation in 1927, Michael became interested in anthropology. Sapir
arranged for him to spend a summer at Cole's archaeological dig at
Quincy, Illinois, in 1929 (Cole to Sapir, 19 September 1929: UC).
The following summer, Sapir sent Michael to the Southwest with Paul
Martin (Edward to Jean Sapir, 18 August 1930: SF). A plan for Michael to accompany a Chicago expedition to South America in 1931,
however, fell through (Edward to Jean Sapir, 28 June 1931: SF). Sapir
wanted Michael "oriented in a tangible position" without forcing him.

In the summer of 1929, Michael intended to register at the University of Illinois at Urbana. But in late August, both father and son

were "fascinated" by discussions with a Chicago neighbor's son about the Meiklejohn Experimental College associated with the University of Wisconsin (M. Sapir, 1984, 11). The college was very anthropological; its program focused on the study of two distinct civilizations, fifth-century Athens in the first year and modern American capitalism in the second. In the intervening summer, students were to prepare a regional study of their hometown. Michael spent most of the summer with Jean's brother Vivien and his family and wrote about Ottawa. He was much impressed by Meikeljohn's research design; the text, *Middletown*, by sociologists Robert and Helen Lynd, would later be an important part of Sapir's Yale seminar for foreign students of personality (see chap. 17). Meikeljohn must have been equally impressed by Sapir, because he was invited to talk to weekly group sessions both years that Michael attended. In retrospect, Michael (1984, 11) found the two men comparable—with ideas ahead of their time and now fashionable:

Both men loved teaching and students, and were greatly loved, even "adored" by their students (but not so much by fellow faculty!); both had the power to exalt, uplift and stir up their listeners; both had a love of poetry and things aesthetic, and how these also related to things intellectual and analytical. Both were, in the fullest sense, Humanists.

Sapir (to Cole, 23 September 1929: UC) was pleasantly surprised by Michael's absorption in Greek (to Jenness, 17 October 1929: NMM). Jenness (29 October: NMM) responded: "It probably gives you a special jolt to think of Michael as a classical scholar because you always used to smile at a classical education." Sapir himself had been preoccupied with adding a "scientific" point of view to the study of languages through philology.

Sapir had difficulty reserving time for his family life. His letters to his wife when she visited her parents during the summer of 1930 illustrate his hectic schedule. In three consecutive days (15 August: SF), Max Radin (noted jurist and brother of Paul) had come to dinner, Ralph Linton had taken Sapir to dinner (and returned "home, where we had music and poetry. I liked him quite well"), and George Mohr had dined with the family. In the afternoon, he had talked to a student just returned from the field: "Kirchoff blew in today and we had an Athabaskan seance." A letter from George Herzog in the field in Africa forced Sapir to find supplementary funds for him. He professed himself tired, depressed, and "very lonesome."

Three days later, Sapir sat in on doctoral examinations in sociology and Germanics. Political science chairman Charles Merriam had asked him to examine his young colleague Harold Lasswell's manuscript on psychopathology and politics; Lasswell soon would become a close friend and collaborator in interdisciplinary social science. The secretary who was to begin typing Sapir's Navajo texts had been offered a better job. Mrs. Alice V. Morris, a socialite and enthusiast for international language planning, wanted Sapir to visit her home in Bar Harbor, Maine, after the Social Science Research Council meeting in Hanover, New Hampshire (for which Sapir was preparing to leave). Sapir was looking forward to getting away, even at the price of "a lot of palaver and concern." He assured his wife that he would not let anything interfere with "our little vacation." Indeed, he planned to seek "a tip" about good vacation spots from colleagues (whose opinions he clearly valued, even on nonprofessional matters) (Edward to Jean Sapir, 28 August 1930: SF).

The following spring, on the verge of moving to New Haven, Sapir again wrote his wife (25 June 1931: SF) from the conference circuit of which he was by then an established member:

We're out on the eastern end of the island here and face the open Atlantic. So far I've not tried the water but perhaps I shall after a while. Meanwhile, I'm spending most of my time sleepily listening to not too brilliant talk about such things as consumption and leisure (when a mother takes her children to the zoo, is that to be classified as "work" or "leisure?") and how to make social science as attractive to brilliant college students as physical science or law.

Privately, at least, Sapir smiled at the antics of the academic elite. Although the formal sessions were only "mildly interesting, . . . as usual, the best part is the chance to talk things over with some people."

Sapir used the free Sunday of the conference to catch up on his work. By this time, he was adept at the art of bustling busy-ness. Robert Redfield described his erstwhile colleagues at Hanover in 1929 (to his wife Margaret Park Redfield, daughter of Chicago sociologist Robert Park) (Stocking 1978):

The place is overrun with pedants and potentates. The potentates are the executive secretaries of the big foundations. Collectively they represent huge—staggering—sums of money. . . . There are now about seventy here in all. The Social Science Research Council pays their fares, and boards them, and feeds them and washes their clothes and gives them cards to go to the golf club, and then expects them to produce Significant Results. . . . Sapir and Lasswell kept it up till midnight. How those two can talk! . . . They are so wise in the ways of the academic world. . . . It is rather amusing to watch the Effective Minds in action. . . . The principal psychiatrist present is Harry Stack Sullivan . . . another one, like Sapir and Lasswell, with the gift of tongues. When the three of them get together the polysyllabic confluences are amazing.

Sapir had come a long way from Ottawa. He reveled in the sheer intellectual pleasure of working out ideas through conversation with some of the most powerful minds of his generation. Lasswell and Sullivan were closest to his own ideas and personal style, but the possibilities in Chicago seemed almost limitless.

The University of Chicago

When Sapir arrived at the University of Chicago, the role of American universities was in flux. The older tradition of "private and avocational learning," dependent on local societies without disciplinary specialization (Shils 1978, 160), competed with a recently imported German model emphasizing research and graduate education rather than undergraduate teaching as the core of the university (Veysey 1965, 12). Unlike their German models, however, American universities lacked in-house research funding. Therefore, the new academic research programs emerged under philanthropic sponsorship, first by individuals and later by the emerging large foundations like Rockefeller or the Carnegie Institute. The federal government entered research funding only after World War II.

Not all universities could adopt the new model. Liberal arts colleges retained their independence by avoiding research almost entirely (Shils 1978, 165). Strong university presidents dominated the scramble for funds that culminated during the interwar period (Shils 1978, 167). Three universities were founded primarily to pursue graduate research—Johns Hopkins, Clark, and Chicago. Traditional institutions such as Harvard and Columbia were stirred to competitive action. A generation of "German-returned" presidents and professors collaborated to create a new kind of institution (Shils 1978, 174), using teaching to advance research. Loyalty to the institution of training was expected; graduate education provided a lifetime disciplinary network. This, of course, fostered "parochial traditions" and "institutional ambitions" (Shils 1978, 165). A few institutions came to dominate American intellectual life, and their graduates moved among them (Shils 1978, 166).

It was the age of the academic superstar. The accomplishments of a single individual could catapult a department into national prominence. Four or five in a branch of science (e.g., social science) or eight to ten in a university created a major center of learning (Shils 1978, 177). Universities sought out the best men in a field and vied with one another to obtain their services. Academics, in turn, learned to value their own achievements. As the university became a self-perpetuating system, the new breed of professors concentrated on graduate students and research. One consequence was that other colleagues were potential competitors with incommensurable research programs and claims to limited resources (Veysey 1963, 142).

Anthropology, particularly given the small size of the discipline, played a major role in this realignment of science toward the university. Boas was trained in Germany in the natural sciences and already took the research emphasis for granted in the late nineteenth century, when the ideal form of institutional support was still a moot question for other American anthropologists. Boas, therefore, got a head start. By 1920, his first generation of students virtually controlled the discipline, because Boas had placed them in the few available academic positions (Darnell 1969, 1971a).[7]

At Columbia—one of the few truly outstanding academic institutions—Franz Boas "towered above all others" because of his "steady stream of publications" and "distinguished research students" (Shils 1978, 179). Kroeber, Lowie, and Sapir were among those "each of whom in his turn became a point of crystallization of anthropological study." Boas was not always appreciated at his home institution, but his national network increasingly dominated the discipline. Columbia's other superstars included John Burgess in political science, H. L. Moore and Seligman in economics, John Dewey in philosophy, Morgan in genetics, Charles Beard and James Harvey Robinson in history (Shils 1978, 179). The clustering of superstars guaranteed a power base for each.

Research superstars at the University of Chicago included Moore in mathematics, Manley in English, Michelson and Millihan in physics, Loeb in physiology, W. I. Thomas and Robert Park in sociology, Freund and Charles Merriam in political science, and Shorey in classics (Shils 1978, 179). In such an intellectual environment, interdisciplinary collaboration made sense. Faris's history of Chicago sociology

(1967, 34) lists related work by James Westfall Thompson in history, George Herbert Mead and Edward Scribner Ames in philosophy, Harvey Carr in psychology, H. D. Lasswell in political science, Charles Judd in education, and Edward Sapir in anthropology.

This senior faculty was assembled by the systematic machinations of Chicago's first president, William Rainey Harper, selected by John D. Rockefeller to build from scratch a great university in the Midwest. Harper assembled a "stellar group" by raiding longer established eastern institutions (Karl 1974, 39), doubling the usual salaries, with promotion promised for research. His greatest coup came when Clark University disintegrated after interference from its philanthropist founder. Although Harper's estimates of who would be the superstars were not invariably accurate, his faculty was unique in its quality and institutional ambition.

There were, however, residual tensions in Harper's university. Until 1923, undergraduates outnumbered graduate students; teaching obligations conflicted with research (Karl 1974, 43), creating a tier-system in which senior faculty did graduate research and junior staff taught undergraduate courses. Only the superstars had access to funding. Harper, moreover, devoted little attention to the internal harmony of programs and departments, being "more concerned with the individual intensities of the stars than with their relation to one another" (Karl 1974, 39).

Chicago Sociology

The joint department of sociology and anthropology which Edward Sapir joined in 1925 was already the premier department in the country, housing the *American Journal of Sociology* to disseminate its research results. Sapir was expected to function as a star among stars. Among the excellent social science departments of the university, sociology was paramount and tacitly lent its prestige to the others (e.g., Karl 1974).

During the 1890s, Albion Small brought German sociology, with its emphasis on science and professionalism, to the attention of American scholars (Faris 1967). The theoretician of the early department was William Isaac Thomas, who dominated it until his dismissal in 1918 and led sociology away from speculative evolutionary reconstruction. Like anthropology, sociology was moving toward empirical behaviorism.

The classic Chicago department was the second generation of the 1920s, dominated by Robert Park and Ernest Burgess (Janowitz 1984, 2-3). The tone was "more urban, even cosmopolitan . . . and more professionalized" (Coser 1971, 312-313). Park was a former journalist and Burgess one of his early students at Chicago. Their 1921 textbook, known as "the Green Bible" in local circles, provided a theoretical framework for the new sociology and called for empirical research (Bulmer 1984, 95). Park and Burgess were the first sociologists to utilize concepts from psychoanalysis. Their empirical research identified Chicago as the ideal type of "a modern urban, industrial, expanding city" (Faris 1967, 55) and used it as a laboratory for social science research.

Ellsworth Faris became chairman of the joint department of Sociology and Anthropology in 1925, the year of Sapir's arrival. As a missionary in the Congo, Faris had considerable exposure to so-called primitive peoples. After earning a doctorate at Chicago in psychology with John Dewey, G. H. Mead, and James R. Angell (later president of Yale), Faris ostensibly replaced Thomas as the theoretician of the department. He was the most "anthropological" of the sociologists. Faris was interested, moreover, in how the individual related to his culture (1937, 238).

After 1927, Sapir's old friend Ogburn, a Columbia student of Franklin Giddings, introduced statistics and scientific method to the Chicago department. Although his methods were alien to Sapir's, Ogburn was also interested in ethnography and psychoanalysis. Sapir debated the same issues about qualitative methods and the role of the individual in culture with Kroeber over the concept of the superorganic.

Sapir and the Chicago Sociologists

The seemingly homogeneous Chicago sociologists were divided into three camps: the urban ethnographers, the social psychologists, and, later, the quantifiers (Murray 1987; 1988). Sapir's appointment was designed to strengthen sociological interests in culture and the individual. He was immediately incorporated within the network of Chicago sociology. From 1923 on, the department sponsored summer institutes for present and former department members. Sapir participated in the 1926 institute on personality (Bulmer 1984, 116).

In retrospect, it is difficult to identify specific influences of the Chicago sociologists on Sapir. Mutual citations are virtually nonexistent, as they are in most social science writing of the period. Sapir adopted a number of ideas for an anthropological audience as though they were his own—a frequent result of interdisciplinary collaboration. Indeed, even among the Chicago sociologists, it is sometimes impossible to identify the originator of an idea. Sapir, for example, wrote an article in 1930 for the *American Mercury* discussing the institution of the family in terms familiar from Ogburn's 1928 argument about the shift from production to companionship (Murray 1986). Although he did not adopt the formal apparatus of Ogburn's theory of culture change, the issues Sapir raised were familiar to Chicago sociologists; he had no special expertise.

The Chicago sociologists were more interested in Sapir's culture theory and psychology than in his linguistic work. Park and Burgess's textbook, nonetheless, took the speech community as the unit above the family in complexity, thereby giving some importance to language if not to linguistics per se. A number of their points are compatible with Sapir's *Language*, though almost certainly independently. Sapir would, however, have been appalled by their rejection of Grimm's law, the basis of comparative Indo-European philology, on grounds of Tarde's imitation theory. There is no evidence that Sapir attempted to explain the inadequacies of this view (Murray 1986). The psychological writings of the Chicago sociologists, moreover, shared Sapir's influence from psychiatrist Harry Stack Sullivan. Indeed, Chicago sociologists were "too psychological for the rest of the country" and potentially constituted a congenial atmosphere for Sapir (Murray 1987).

The inviolability of each individual's research domain was the unstated precondition enabling research superstars to coexist. Sapir may, however, have intended an indirect reply to Park and Burgess's overfacile evolutionism in his 1931 application of the comparative method to Bloomfield's Algonquian linguistic data for an interdisciplinary volume on methods in social science edited by Ogburn and Goldenwesier.

W. I. Thomas, although no longer employed at Chicago, remained part of its sociological network and included Sapir in a 1928 inter-disciplinary conference on the Freudian notion of the unconscious. Sapir argued that social behavior reflected "unconscious patterning" at both individual and cultural levels. Such patterning could be deciphered only with a "cultural key" for the interpretation of individual action (1928, 120). Sapir implicitly challenged Watsonian behaviorism, in line with his anthropological field experience of alien cultures. He identified language as the most accessible form of unconscious patterning. This paper was a self-conscious methodological statement directed to the Chicago sociologists.

Several sociology students who were at Chicago during Sapir's tenure have shared their remembrances of collaboration between the two departments with Stephen Murray. Although there is considerable danger in retrospective self-report, they acknowledge Sapir's status but not his actual influence.

Robert Faris, son of Ellsworth Faris and himself a product of the interwar department, says that many sociology students continued to take anthropology courses after the department split in 1929 (to Murray, 2 April, 13 May 1984). Faris regarded Sapir with "a touch of awe," heard him lecture, perhaps read some of his work, but felt Sapir no more relevant to his sociological interests than, for example, geology. He perceived Sapir (mistakenly) as a "convinced and pious Freudian." Faris acknowledged that the interaction of culture and personality was a subject for lunchtable conversation in the late 1920s but failed to realize that the interdisciplinary atmosphere of Chicago may have blurred the disciplinary boundaries of pervasive ideas. Sapir was "a scholar too profound for me to learn from and a man I never visualize as smiling, but gloomy and tense." According to Faris's father, when Sapir was angry about being left out of a meeting, he said that "anyone who knew anything about psychoanalysis knew that the oversight was not accidental." Sapir "had a tendency to break with people who offended him."

Faris recognized more influence on his thinking from Sapir's colleagues Cole and Redfield. He came to "distrust" ethnological data "as more ethnologists came to visit people earlier studied by others, and revealed differences of perception that were to me shocking." In this, Faris was no doubt typical of 1930s sociologists. Methods were becoming more important in sociology, anthropologists were studying "our society," and replicability became a realistic criterion (Murray, MS).

Edward Shils (to Murray, 25 October 1984) recalls no obvious quarrels among the sociologists during his graduate training. He emphasizes, however, that students did not have access to the private opinions of their teachers: "I think that close relations did not exist among the various senior members of the department." Sapir, as far as Shils knew, was highly esteemed in the department. Park, in his opinion, should have been responsive to the kinds of work Sapir did; anti-Semitism may have caused hostility toward Sapir.

Other Chicago students of the period, however, have exaggerated their contact with Sapir retrospectively. Herbert Blumer (to Murray, n.d. June 1984) professed to have taken two courses with Sapir and "remained in close academic touch with him." University records fail to confirm the course enrollment (Murray 1986). Blumer assumed that the split of the two departments was sufficient cause for few students enrolling in both sociology and anthropology courses. In his own case, Sapir's ideas had "considerable influence" (unspecified) but did not "contribute to my central thought."

These sociological reminiscences ignore the personal and interactional effects of Sapir's presence at Chicago. They are concerned with published research results rather than with the working out of ideas in conversation. To the extent that the methods of social science disciplines are reflected in the writing of their history, it is interesting that anthropologists have been much more inclined than sociologists to present personal and interactional data in support of theoretical and institutional arguments (cf. Hallowell 1965, Darnell 1974).

Among Park's students, only Louis Wirth studied with Sapir (Murray 1986). Ellen Winston (to Murray, 4 April 1984), a Park student who took no courses with Sapir (Murray 1986), was encouraged by Ogburn to acquire from Sapir "a broader approach to social services" than Park's "really precise objectives" could provide. She mused that her career path might have veered toward anthropology had she met Sapir earlier.

In spite of the proximity of Sapir to the Chicago sociologists, there is no evidence of intensive personal interaction. Indeed, Sapir most often met his sociological colleagues—insofar as documentary evidence is available—at various interdisciplinary conferences in which he quickly joined them as a regular participant. W. I. Thomas, Ernest Burgess, and Louis Wirth were most active in the conference circuit.

Sapir apparently shared the sociologists' assumption that the disciplines were separate in their core methods and audiences. He wrote to Cole (24 July 1933: UC) that Redfield, the one man who moved easily at Chicago between sociology and anthropology and would soon become Chicago's dean of the social sciences, had interests "just a bit too marginal to anthropology, as ordinarily understood, to make him seem quite the logical man" to edit the *American Anthropologist*. Sapir believed, however, that "some form of integration" of the Chicago type would attract outside funding (to Redfield, 14 May 1934: UC).

The terms of Sapir's appointment at Chicago alienated him from interdisciplinary collaboration. The Laura Spelman Rockefeller Memorial broke its precedent against providing funds for academic salaries in paying Sapir's for three years. In 1927, however, the policy was changed to allow for research professorships (Bulmer 1984, 146), lacking the onerous teaching obligations that so plagued Sapir. Chicago used the new funds to hire L. L. Thurstone in psychology, Simeon Leland in public finance, and Henry Schultz in econometrics (Bulmer 1984, 178). The heavy quantitative bias of these appointments could hardly have reassured Sapir that his kind of social science was valued by the University of Chicago.

Sapir and Ogburn were next-door neighbors, building on an established friendship (Sapir to Lowie, 3 October 1927: UCB). But Ogburn's statistical sociology, in spite of his continued interest in psychoanalysis, polarized the Chicago department. Dissent culminated over the choice of quotation for the front of the Social Science Research Building donated by the Rockefeller Foundation and opened in 1929. Sapir argued that lettering in architecture intruded on building design; any quotation would be outdated in a generation (to Ogburn, 25 October 1928: UC; Karl 1974, 154-155). Sapir, along with Park, resented the quantitative definition of social science implied by Ogburn's choice of quotation.

Paul Sapir (p.c.) believes that his father never acknowledged the inherent competitiveness of academic life, preferring to focus on the fantasy (shared by many academics) that truth is sought for its own sake. Michael Sapir recalls his father's diatribes "about how no politics could equal in viciousness and vituperation the politics of academic life." Sapir wanted to be a team player. In Cole's department, he could maintain this self-image. Chicago, however, was an upstart place and must have frequently offended Sapir's sensibilities. He tended to isolate himself when others might have welcomed him. The only exception appears to have been his students—who recall quite a different person than do colleagues. Sapir functioned best when his ideas could be developed rather than defended. Even in the interdisciplinary conferences, his typical role was not to argue for a personal position but to seek a mutually acceptable statement that would incorporate a diversity of viewpoints. His academic model was Columbia, moreover, with its more subdued intellectual tradition than Chicago.

Rockefeller Foundation Funding in Chicago

The Rockefeller Foundation played a crucial facilitating role in the development of Chicago social science. Monies were channeled through a bureaucracy of professional administrators trained in the sciences they supported. The trustees simply wanted "reliable and if possible quantitative data, collected by methodical, first-hand observation" and emulating "the rigour of the natural sciences" (Bulmer and Bulmer 1981, 347).

The foundations (of which Rockefeller was the largest and most significant for the social sciences) were interested in applied science. Based on the success of psychological testing during World War I mobilization, Presidents Hoover and Roosevelt increasingly sought scientific advice in formulating public policy (Bulmer and Bulmer 1981, 348). Only 8.8 percent of the Rockefeller monies dispersed went to social science, but an influx to anthropology of $2 million over a decade (Stocking 1985) had an unparalleled influence on the training of anthropologists and the growth of the profession.

The University of Chicago was the foremost beneficiary of Rockefeller generosity. From 1917 to 1929, George Vincent, who had taught in Small's sociology department, was president of the Rockefeller Foundation (Bulmer 1984, 135). Beardsley Ruml, director of the Spelman Memorial, earned his doctorate in sociology at Chicago (Stocking 1985). Chicago social scientists advised the foundation bureaucrats what trends to encourage in each discipline.

At the University of Chicago, Rockefeller money allowed ad hoc support of projects. Sapir's appointment at Chicago did not, therefore, automatically lead to full support for the department program. Rather, Cole and Sapir's proposal for fieldwork in the Southwest was channeled to the Committee on Local Community Research. A policy decision awaited the 1929 consideration of the department's five-year research program.

Impressing the foundation bureaucrats became an increasingly important skill. At the annual Hanover (New Hampshire) Conference in 1926, sponsored by the Social Science Research Council, Wissler and Malinowski offered programmatic characterizations of a "new anthropology" (Stocking 1985). Malinowski and Radcliffe-Brown (who spent six years at Chicago) led the American historical tradition toward the study of still-functioning cultures. Africa and Oceania began to replace North America as favored research sites. For a brief period, the exotic subject matter of anthropology seemed to promise "an otherwise inaccessible knowledge of the generic impulses underlying human behavior" (Stocking 1985).

But anthropology did not fulfill its apparent promise in the interdisciplinary social science. Fieldwork was, for most anthropologists, an end in itself. Generalizations would come later. Fieldwork was expensive and replicability a greater issue than for the other social sciences. The Rockefeller Foundation, moreover, was cutting back on social science support, particularly in cultural anthropology.

Boas, throughout the Rockefeller-dominated era, was peripheral. The foundation took the view that he was "no longer an innovative force in the discipline"; moreover, too many of his students were women (Stocking 1985). Disciplinary elders were deliberately bypassed in favor of younger scholars who wanted to revamp their disciplines. Wissler and Sapir were the Boasians who presented themselves to the foundations as representatives of the new trends.

Rockefeller money was not specific to anthropology but was channeled into it through Chicago sociology, which served, during the interwar period, as a worldwide model for integrated social research. Sapir's ability to move in this league in spite of the size of his discipline and his esoteric linguistic specialization testifies to his genuine understanding of the interdisciplinary nature of the emerging social science. Sapir became a major spokesman for the new approach and, consequently, increasingly addressed a nonanthropological audience.

The context of anthropology changed dramatically after the mid-1930s as foundation support dwindled and disciplines became more specialized. There is a tentative, programmatic quality to Sapir's pronouncements in the Chicago and Yale years. Continuing support to test the programmatics was simply not available, and the reasons were beyond his control.

To the extent that foundation funding produced a new social science, it was channeled more through institutions than through individuals—with Chicago leading the pack. Small had long envisioned a "super–graduate school" which would do group research (Bulmer 1980, 51–52). Until the early 1920s, however, social science was a matter of individual research even at Chicago. On the verge of his retirement, Small proposed (3 November 1922: UC) to President Judson that $10 million could be put to immediate use in the social sciences and that the ends might even justify "a Czaristic reorganization of the whole outfit." Departments would have to cooperate. Park and Burgess immediately responded to inquiries about their funding needs in terms of urban research already underway (Bulmer 1980, 64–65).

In this period, interdisciplinary scope and administrative organization were not clearly distinguished. Many scholars crossed discipline lines in their teaching as well as research. Applied research, encouraged by the foundations, also made interdisciplinary projects feasible (Bulmer 1980, 66–67). But how to go about this had to be determined by trial and error.

As the director of the Laura Spelman Rockefeller Memorial, Beardsley Ruml "helped to underwrite the conquest of the academic world by . . . [the] 'behaviorist' school" (Collier and Horowitz 1976, 143). Ruml was the "ideas man" of the Rockefeller Foundation during its active social science involvement. The Spelman Memorial, established in 1918 in memory of the elder Rockefeller's wife and amalgamated in the Social Science Division in 1929, distributed over $50 million during this brief period. Ruml reoriented the memorial from social welfare of women and children to social science research (Bulmer 1980, 70–72). Ruml was adept at the rhetoric of philanthropy. Anthropology, however, was peripheral to his conception in that "remote times and places would not be of central concern" (Bulmer and Bulmer 1981, 364). But his "openness towards intellectually outstanding persons" (Bulmer and Bulmer 1981, 497) left room for creative scientists like Sapir to make themselves indispensable.

Ruml was in a hurry. A time span for the memorial of ten to twelve years had been expected from the beginning. He committed over half of his funds by 1927–1928 and tried to postpone as long as possible the reorganization of Rockefeller boards that was pending in the late 1920s. Edwin Embree noted (quoted in Bulmer and Bulmer 1981, 397): Ruml "succeeded in giving away $25 million before he could be stopped." Though the memorial ceased to exist in 1929, Edmund Day followed Ruml's policies until the 1934 reorganization (Bulmer and Bulmer 1981, 398).

Rockefeller support accentuated trends that were already present in the universities, whose development depended on funding. Professors with grants became more important because they ran committees, spoke at conferences, and had access to trustees (Bulmer and Bulmer 1981, 400–401). The system rewarded initiative and excellence.

Chicago political scientist Charles Merriam, Park, and Burgess obtained Rockefeller funding for an interdisciplinary Committee on Local Community Research (LCRC) in 1923 (Bulmer 1980, 75–80). Sociology got 40 percent of the funds, used mostly for salaries of research assistants on a variety of projects in the city of Chicago. The grant was increased in 1924, and a five-year renewal approved by the Spelman Memorial in 1927. At Hanover in 1926, Park argued that interdisciplinary collaboration would emerge from the cumulative effect of many small-scale studies. Local research projects would use material collected by students and train new researchers (Bulmer 1980, 6). Academic instructors would become research directors.

The University of Chicago Press was funded for Studies in Social Science in 1924; from 1927 on, titles appeared regularly. The Rockefeller Foundation also funded a social science building whose use favored LCRC research with first priority. The building, "1126" [East 59 St.], was arranged by research interest not department, leading to considerable esprit de corps among the researchers who were "mostly young and unattached" (Janowitz 1984, 61).

The memorial also provided seed money for the Institute for Juvenile Research, established by William Healy as a child guidance clinic in 1909. Clifford Shaw and Henry McKay carried out classic studies of adolescents, and psychiatrist Herman Adler became director in 1917. All of these men participated in the interdisciplinary conferences of the period. The clinical emphasis of research institutes made them an ideal source of empirical behavioral data for the academics.

The LCRC attempted to study culture and personality, though Faris, Thurstone, Merriam, and Lasswell were more integral to this scheme than Sapir. This personality project was the only LCRC effort that actually involved several disciplines. The research was "weakly coordinated, but the individual projects were being pursued by unusually able men" (Bulmer 1980, 104). Difficulties arose, however, because departments were unwilling to subordinate their interests to the LCRC. Research organization often meant little more than support for graduate students in various disciplines. In 1927, the LCRC attempted to eliminate smaller, less interdisciplinary projects and focus research around experienced project directors. The subcommittee for interdisciplinary cooperation—consisting of Merriam, Thurstone, and L. C. Marshall of economics—could not, however, agree and disbanded itself (Bulmer 1980, 101–102).

The problem was that active researchers, trained in particular disciplines, pursued their own interests. Sapir was a rare exception. Foundation officials assumed that the "desire for cooperative research which would give a great impetus forward to social science" would emerge spontaneously and would, by definition, be preferable to individual, disciplinary scholarship. When L. D. White retired as chairman of the LCRC in 1929, he attempted to leave behind an explicit plan for more integrated research; his proposal was, however, toned down considerably by Merriam (Bulmer 1980, 107).

In spite of the foundation's enthusiasm for integrated programs, however, the diffuse organization of the LCRC remained the model at Chicago. Rockefeller internal files include a summary of the impasse (Schlesinger to Day, 18 March 1930: RAC):

It's amazing the amount of interest there is in research in general throughout the social science group. . . . Very little attempt has been made to develop a coordinated program out of the mass of requests that keep coming in. However, that is no discovery of mine. The L.R.C. Committee is just as much aware of it, and has reorganized into a smaller, non-departmental group with the express purpose of getting formulated a comprehensive, long-term program.

Because it failed to meet the interdisciplinary aims of the foundation, Chicago received less funding as time went on, as Rockefeller funding for the social sciences declined generally. Ruml made a final, unsuccessful bid to renew anthropology funding in 1933, after the expiration of the five-year program (Redfield to Cole, 16 October 1933: UC). The diffuse Chicago model had reached an impasse. Remaining Rockefeller funding shifted increasingly to Yale, where the Institute of Human Relations was willing to pursue a more integrated research program. Sapir was one of the few Chicago superstars offered the opportunity to follow the funding, although the narrow behaviorism of the IHR would prove essentially alien to him.

CHAPTER TWELVE

Chicago Anthropology

The University of Chicago program in anthropology began when President William Rainey Harper hired Frederick Starr in
1892. Starr, a geologist, was a popular undergraduate lecturer but
failed to tie Chicago anthropology to the emerging Boasian discipline.
"Coming upon anthropology just before its intellectual transformation, Starr's efforts at self-professionalization had the effect of rooting
him permanently in late nineteenth century evolutionism. . . . [He
had] little awareness of the linguistic and textual approaches which
Boas was using to move anthropology from the museum to the academy" (Stocking 1979, 13). Harper preferred museum specimens to
fieldwork, and Starr wanted anthropology reclassified as a natural science (Miller 1978, 54). Starr, moreover, could not attract graduate
students. Although he produced two Ph.D.'s in 1897 (Merton Miller
and David Barrows, later president of Berkeley), the program lan-
guished outside the anthropological mainstream.

Because of Starr, Boas was passed over at Chicago when Harper
hired other dissatisfied faculty from Clark University. Chicago anthropology was further isolated by its association with sociology, although both W. I. Thomas and Albion Small attempted unsuccessfully
to redirect Starr's program. Boas taught summer school at Chicago
in 1908 but declined to leave Columbia permanently (Miller 1978,
55; Stocking 1979, 15). Starr retired in 1923, and the next Chicago
doctorates in anthropology, Leslie White in 1927 and Robert Redfield
in 1928, reflected total discontinuity from his program. In 1923,

Ralph Linton lectured in anthropology. In 1924, Small hired Fay-Cooper Cole, a "thoroughly Boasian" Columbia graduate who was already at Chicago's Field Museum. Cole, a "genial, self-effacing man of no great intellectual pretensions" (Stocking 1979, 17), created a graduate research department.

Cole needed a superstar to bring Chicago to the forefront of American anthropology and urged Small (12 November 1924: UC) to hire Edward Sapir, "the brilliant linguist–anthropologist" and the "shark of the lot" in Boas's seminars. Cole "rebuilt" the Chicago department around Sapir: "at this period Sapir was easily the most influential figure in American anthropology" (Hooton 1940, 158). Lowie (1965, 4) cited the Chicago years as the "peak of [Sapir's] career, when he had gained a following of devoted disciples, had assumed a dominant role in learned societies, and was hobnobbing with the heads of great foundations." Chicago lent "full scope to his extraordinary gifts as a teacher and lecturer," with students to carry on "the researches which he himself had not time to continue" (Jenness 1939, 152). Margaret Mead (1966) emphasized the "great excitement" and "real freedom" of Chicago; Cole "brought Sapir there and he gave him his head and Sapir was to be the great brilliant decoration at Chicago, and students were very excited about his lectures and people went there to study with him and he had a lovely time."

Cole maintained "harmony in personal relationships," partly by not putting himself forward as a scholar (Eggan 1963, 644). Sapir was perceived as more of a prima donna—popular with colleagues who had "a quick mind" but "abrupt and even rude" to those who bored him (Hoijer to Haas, 8 November 1971). Cole allowed Sapir to concentrate on students and research.

Sapir shared the emphasis of Chicago sociology on "the cultural assimilation of immigrant groups in contemporary America," on human behavior rather than on artifacts (Stocking 1979, 17). Although his early work on reconstructed culture history and his Ottawa museum position qualified him to talk to museum anthropologists, he was increasingly interested in the psychological reality of language and culture for individuals—the forefront of the emerging interdisciplinary social science, in which Boasian cultural anthropology outside Chicago had a surprisingly minor role.

Kroeber (1954; 1959a) argued the Boasian position that anthropology had its roots in natural science (physical anthropology and ethnology) and in humanities (linguistics and archaeology). In his mind, the association of anthropology with the social sciences was an uncomfortable overlay (1954, 767). Kroeber argued (1959a, 399–400) that anthropology differed theoretically from sociology only in its emphasis on primitive ethnography. Sapir, rather than Kroeber, Lowie, Spier, or Boas, chose to work at the interface of the old anthropology and the new, with its ties to sociology and other social sciences. These trends came together at Chicago.

The Anthropological Fiefdom

Cole was hired on the assumption that anthropology and sociology would become separate departments. His formal request to Acting President Frederick Woodward (26 November 1928: UC), however, reiterated the cordiality of collaboration. Ellsworth Faris had always shown "lively interest" in anthropology, and "nothing of a personal nature is involved."[1] Cole emphasized the ties of cultural anthropology to psychology, political science, and economics as well as to sociology; of archaeology to history, geology, and paleontology; of linguistics to psychology and various language departments; and of physical anthropology to biology and zoology. Fieldwork linked anthropology to the methods of the Oriental Institute. In an independent department, students could seek specialized training in various directions.

The Chicago linkage of anthropology with sociology was an anomaly. Anthropology was independent at other American universities, including Columbia, Harvard, Pennsylvania, Minnesota, California, and Washington. To obtain jobs for graduates, Cole had to explain that anthropology was taught, in spite of the sociological umbrella. In practice, separation was already in effect, with different requirements for students: "We are, in fact, maintaining a fiction rather than a fact when we call it a joint department, for aside from our chairman and a luncheon once a week, we have little more in common than we would have if separate." Separation was already in place in library budgets, space in the new Social Science building, national associations, publications, and representation on the Social Science Research Council. Anthropology was represented in the National Research Council and the American Association for the Advancement of Science, both of which omitted sociology. In sum, anthropology had come of age as an independent professional discipline and the University of Chicago was behind the times.

Cole was sanguine about funding for a potential research program without equal in North America, citing the formation in 1927 of a Citizen's Committee on Anthropology that included "some of the leading citizens of Chicago." Interchangeability of professional competencies was an unrealistic expectation: "Sociology and Anthropology are so different that we in Anthropology are not competent to judge or to act intelligently on many matters relating to Sociology, nor is it possible for them to pass on matters strictly anthropological."

The independent department was officially approved on 18 February 1929, without protest from sociology. Almost immediately, Cole, Sapir, and Redfield forwarded to Edmund Day of the Rockefeller Foundation a five-year plan to fund anthropology at the University of Chicago (26 March 1929: UC).

They stressed that introductory courses would provide "a broad cultural background for students in the social sciences" to "bridge over the gap between the social and natural sciences." The chief emphasis, however, would be on "fundamental research." Anthropology differed from the other sciences because its studies of "human society and the human mind" required firsthand analysis of "the simpler cultures and the more primitive languages." Immigrant groups, furthermore, had to be studied in relation to their homelands in order to implement adequate policies in urban America. Although anthropologists worked far from campus, they were "cooperative" with the other social sciences. The expenses of anthropological fieldwork were fully justified because of this larger theoretical relevance and because of the "rapidly disappearing cultures and languages" studied. The needs of anthropology were "both peculiar and urgent."

The proposed research was largely American Indian, with quite diverse studies already underway. Cole's program in Illinois archaeology had, in three years, trained a number of graduate students. North American ethnology, reflecting Sapir's interest in Na-dene linguistics, had focused on the Athabaskan tribes of the United States and Canada, although the department hoped to add work on the Central Algonquians of the Great Lakes.[2] Work in Mexican ethnology, focusing around Redfield's studies of social change in Mexico, was well underway. Each research area reflected the interests of one of the faculty.

Sapir's research in American Indian languages was described separately from ethnology. His Na-dene work would result in "an elaborate comparative work which, it is hoped, will do for a primitive American group what the founders of comparative linguistics did for the Indo-European languages." The "technical studies" were expected to lead to "some very interesting and specific conclusions" about the peopling of North America; Sapir "suspected" that Na-dene was connected to Sinitic or Indo-Chinese. That is, Sapir was willing to obtain funding on the basis of the nonlinguistic implications of his work, which would appeal to the Rockefeller Foundation. Sapir also asked for funding for native American informants in the city of Chicago, necessary for the training of advanced graduate students.

Funds were also requested for various ad hoc projects: Blooah and Herzog on Gweabo, Cole's work in Malaysia, and immigrant studies in Chicago, "an unusual laboratory" for students to learn method. Fieldwork training in "our" society was uncharacteristic of anthropology in this period but commonplace for Chicago sociologists. The Rockefeller Foundation was also asked to provide for secretarial help and publication through the University of Chicago Press. The single gap in a traditional Boasian program was physical anthropology, an area conceived as "primarily in the biological field."[3] The proposal suggested a laboratory for studying individual and racial change, citing Boas's work on immigrant head form to tie this to theoretical issues in anthropology as defined at Chicago. Cole taught physical anthropology without enthusiasm until he could hire a specialist.

The anthropologists requested $128,000 over five years. University president Frederick Woodward forwarded the proposal to the Rockefeller Foundation (1 May 1929: UC) with his full approval. Cole (to Day, 8 May 1929: UC) reiterated past successes in anthropology, especially in providing field experience and job placement for students.

Just as everything appeared to be going smoothly, however, Redfield was offered a job at Stanford. Cole (31 July 1929: UC) considered this "a real calamity to Chicago" and urged Redfield to stay to establish "the outstanding department in America, if not in the world." Redfield declined the offer to continue his studies of folk culture in Mexico, oriented toward showing sociologists how urban civilization originally developed (Hughes et al. 1976, 60–63). His continuum of acculturation rejected the traditional anthropological assumption of the isolation of so-called primitive communities from the larger society around them (Leslie 1976, 155). The Redfield project involved several communities and researchers over a period of years, constituting a substantial commitment of Chicago fieldwork resources.

Sapir was involved through his support for Manuel Andrade, the project linguist (to Cole, 7 March 1930: UC).

In the spring of 1930, Chicago hegemony in Mexico was challenged by Kroeber, who planned an ethnological survey. Sapir was shocked by the tone of Kroeber's letter and asked Cole's opinion before responding (29 April 1930: UC). Cole (2 May 1930: UC) assured Sapir that he was not "at all in favor of our giving up the field simply because he has made a reconnaissance or because they have laid out plans for that region." He proposed telling Kroeber that Chicago's Mexican research was part of the five-year plan presented to the Rockefeller Foundation the previous year; the foundation might, however, be impressed by "cooperative work" between the two institutions. Accordingly, Sapir, acting chairman while Cole was in Washington for the National Research Council, wrote to Kroeber (5 May 1930: UC) that there was sufficient work for everyone. Kroeber, however, backed off when confronted with the established Chicago commitment. Although Sapir was not personally involved in the Mexican research program, he realized its importance to the reputation of Chicago anthropology and defended departmental territory.

Cole's overview of Chicago research sometimes troubled Sapir, who wanted to know how his linguistic work "which, as you know, is rather demanding technically" would fit (14 October 1929: UC). He agreed to submit plans for a linguistic exhibit at the Chicago Fair but insisted that this did not do justice to his work: "I must confess that the prospect of making tenses and glottal stops seem picturesque to the public rather appalls me for the moment." Sapir thought he had left such constraints behind in Ottawa. Cole (21 October 1929: UC) was equally nonplussed but hoped Sapir could suggest the "proper place" of linguistics. Sapir wanted to increase the professionalization of linguistics, not to make it palatable to a larger public. After his summer school experience with ethnology graduate students trying to do Navajo linguistics for the Southwest Laboratory of Anthropology in 1929, Sapir stressed "the inadvisability of having unprepared or inadequately prepared men try to do research work in linguistics." Cole (9 October 1929: UC) argued that a linguistic exhibit might lead to equipment funding; the Rockefeller Foundation would be watching them to decide on further anthropological support, at Chicago and elsewhere.

Sapir needed institutional support to train a nucleus of American Indian linguists. He was willing to label his work in whatever discipline would fund it. He wrote to the president's office (10 June 1930: UC) seeking affiliation with the new Humanities Project, on the grounds that the affiliation of primitive languages with anthropology was "after all, rather a convention than a necessity." In a June 1931 summary of research to the Rockefeller Foundation, Sapir argued that the "systematic study of linguistic facts" contributed more to science than "substantive knowledge" of particular languages. He emphasized the testing of linguistic methods with primitive languages:

The prevalent conception of linguistic change has been derived chiefly from the comparative study of one linguistic family—the Indo-European. Its universal validity cannot be asserted until tested in other regions where the languages differ widely. The Athabaskan and Maya stocks offer such a test.

In spite of his insistence on rigorous philological method, Sapir had learned that linguistics had to be presented to nonspecialists in terms of its implications for livelier subjects.

The American Indian linguistics program, in fact, proceeded apace. Sapir reported it (to Cole, 18 November 1930: UC) as "fairly active," including work by Stanley Newman on Tanoan and Yokuts, Walter Dyk on Wishram Chinook, Harry Hoijer on Navajo and Apache, Morris Swadesh on Nez Perce, Victor Riste on Creek, and Sapir on Navajo. Sapir also worked with Mark Hanna Watkins on Chewa, a Bantu language in Nyassaland.[4] In addition, Sapir noted research in linguistic psychology by Newman and general linguistics by Swadesh (funded by the International Auxiliary Language Association).

Given Sapir's Americanist reputation, his foray into African linguistics is particularly interesting.[5] Charles Blooah, a Gweabo speaker from Liberia, was working at a local bowling alley to pay his expenses at University of Chicago (Eggan, p.c.) when Sapir recruited him as a linguistic informant. The four tonal registers of Gweabo provided a phonetic challenge to Sapir (who hummed Navajo tones in teaching it), musicologist George Herzog (who had perfect pitch), and Fang-Kuei Li (who spoke seven or eight Asian tone languages) (Eggan 1986). Sapir (to Jenness, 15 April 1927: NMM) was delighted that the tonal pattern corresponded to "the theory of the West African drum languages," noting "one of the joys of university work—to initiate work among enthusiastic students in a rather intimate way."

Blooah obtained a Rockefeller fellowship to study sociology and began to write out ethnological texts. He and Herzog went to Liberia in 1929–1930 to study Gweabo ethnology and music. Sapir (Report to the Rockefeller Foundation for 1929–1930: RAC) was delighted that the four tones identified through linguistic analysis in Chicago were also found in the drum language and there were "actually... native terms to refer to them." Although Sapir envisioned ten volumes of reports, funding was only obtained for a volume on Gweabo proverbs. Blooah was, however, a less satisfactory informant when seen in his own culture (Sapir to Leslie White, 23 March 1931: UM). Herzog had to recheck most of the ethnological material in the field. Sapir concluded that the limitations of informants could be overcome only by linguistic methods, "personal ethnographic accounts in native texts with interlinear translation. A *systematic* ethnological survey is hardly possible."

Another informant for Sapir's classes was Dr. Hastings Kamuzu Banda, later president of Malawi. Banda was studying history and political science as part of his medical training. He remained proud of his association with Sapir, being more positively inclined toward linguistics than anthropology (Ian Michael to Darnell, 13 March 1987).

In his report to the Rockefeller Foundation at the end of the five-year grant, Cole (to Day, 17 July 1936: UC) justified departmental funding in both research and professional training. All twenty-five students from the fieldwork program were regularly employed in universities or museums. Eleven more had temporary or supervisory posts, three were permanently attached to government projects, and two were fellows of the Social Science Research Council. Nine were present or former members of the department staff. This was, indeed, a unique record. Although Sapir left Chicago early in the granting program, he was instrumental in establishing its fieldwork and training focus and in including linguistics within it.

Sapir's Teaching at Chicago

In 1924–1925, just before Sapir arrived in Chicago, the joint department of Sociology and Anthropology was included within a Social Science Group with philosophy, psychology, education, political economy, political science, and history. The university catalogue listed related courses in law, theology, social economy (social work), religious education, and comparative religion. Cole was an assistant professor of anthropology and Frederick Starr an emeritus professor. Of the senior sociologists—Albion Small, Ellsworth Faris, Robert Park, and Ernest Burgess—only Faris was interested in primitive society. The interdisciplinary approach was expected to lead to "the final interpretation of all the different analyses of human experience." Anthropology had no special status among the social science disciplines. According to the catalogue, the union of anthropology and sociology was "merely provisional." Courses emphasized "the earlier stages of human progress," "a survey of the races of mankind," "the beginnings made by primitive man in times before history," and "necessary methods of research." Fieldwork was not mentioned as a possible method. Courses included primitive culture, American race, primitive religion, ethnography of Malaysia and Africa, prehistoric archaeology, physical anthropology, and primitive languages. Not all of these were given in 1924–1925, unsurprisingly given Cole's sole responsibility.

The course description of primitive languages was presumably written by Sapir in expectation of his appointment. It would include: "phonetics, linguistics, psychological problems in anthropology, methods of recording and analyzing primitive languages." Sapir included in a single description all of his linguistic interests. He would soon break this down into a series of courses. Sapir was so eager to teach that he even liked the idea of "learning something about . . . Fundamental Problems in the Study of Human Culture." He wrote to Lowie (21 March 1925: UCB): "It is an uncharted sea, I am afraid. . . . I am going to try in it to crystallize some ideas about culture that have been emerging in my consciousness from time to time."

During 1925–1926, Sapir taught the advanced course in primitive languages in three successive quarters. In addition, he taught six other courses, rapidly developing an inventory of alternating offerings. His phonetics course, designed for the recording of primitive languages, was intended for both general linguists and prospective fieldworkers. The "theoretical survey of sounds" was followed by "practice work in dictation from a number of languages." A survey course entitled Types of Linguistic Structures focused on "varieties in form of linguistic expression rather than detailed information on particular languages." This was presumably based on the typological sections of Sapir's *Language*. Sapir also regularly taught a General Introduction to Linguistics. Its description included the relationship of language to race and culture and "languages spoken by primitive peoples."

Sapir was expected to teach ethnology as well as linguistics. In addition to American Indian Languages, he offered Northwest Coast Indians, which included economics, social organization, religion, mythology, and art and focused on "the native philosophy of life." Primitive Religion, presumably closely related, included "the psychological bases of religion; characteristic religious expressions among primitive peoples; individual variability of religious experience; the religious life of a number of selected primitive societies."

Psychology of Language and Psychology of Culture were listed as separate courses, although their content doubtless overlapped considerably. The latter, presumably less technical, became Sapir's most popular course and was the title of the book he contracted to write for Harcourt Brace. The course included:

An inquiry into the shifting connotations of the term "culture"; the patterning of human conduct; the relationship of the individual to society, and the meaning of the concept "psychology and culture." Psychological and anthropological points of view will be combined and, so far as possible, reconciled.

Here Sapir worked out his mature position about the relationship of culture and individual.[6]

Morris Opler (1986) provides a summary, based on his class notes, of Sapir's thinking about the integration-of-culture theory during the Chicago years. Although Opler was interested in Apache ethnology, he took all of Sapir's courses in 1930–1931; Cole had told him Sapir might leave the following year. Opler was most impressed by Sapir's linguistic analysis of the social and religious values symbolized by Northwest Coast totem poles. Sapir stressed patterning over ethnographic detail per se:

[T]he challenge is to discover the pattern of any specific lifeway. In such quests, one will find similarities and overlappings as one moves from culture to culture, but rarely identities. Even the formal likenesses become more tenuous when such factors as meaning and weighting are considered.

Sapir clearly distinguished meaning systems internal to a culture from universal cultural patterns based on analyst categories (which confused form and function). In line with his linguistic position, Sapir stressed form.

Because Sapir was accustomed to working with linguistic texts in the words of particular informants, he "wondered whether the influence of dominant personalities or favorably situated individuals might not give a culture a 'slope,' and over time contribute to culture change." It was "a mischievous absurdity" to separate culture and the individual analytically. Sapir encouraged Opler to use life history techniques to capture both cultural pattern and individual variation.

Sapir attacked overreliance on the quantitative techniques that were the rage in Chicago sociology because they couldn't capture underlying meaning. "Only more intimate and detailed studies could reveal the satisfactions and strains that lay behind the formal categories." Increasingly, Sapir used simple everyday examples from his own society—in which native-speaker or member-of-culture intuition for pattern substituted for the painstaking and often incomplete understanding of behavior acquired by the field ethnographer in an alien society.

Sapir, unable to conceive any single index of cultural validity, was uncomfortable with any ranking of cultures into developmental hierarchies. "He wondered whether we counted the losses as well as the gains . . . along this particular cultural path [that of our own society]." In addition to Boasian bias against evolutionary thinking, Sapir insisted on an aesthetic dimension in the assessment of culture based on its meaning for individuals. He wanted to identify the "overriding motifs that permeate, knit together and give character to a culture." Opler would later call these "themes."[7]

In addition to courses in his specializations, Sapir periodically participated in team-taught introductions to ethnology. He was always listed for Research Work in Comparative Indian Linguistics, that is, supervision of graduate students working on his or their own field data. This teaching load quickly came to seem burdensome. For example, in 1929–1930, the first year of the independent department, Sapir got teaching credit for Indian linguistic research by running the (first) Southwest Laboratory of Anthropology field school in Santa Fe; Sapir himself worked on Navajo (see chap. 13). Besides research supervision, he taught two more courses in each of the other three quarters.

These were typical teaching loads at the time, but Sapir—like many of his colleagues—found it difficult to reserve time for his own research. Although students were presumably equally pressed for time, course registration records indicate that graduate students, regardless of specialization, took Sapir's linguistic courses.[8] Archaeologists Paul Martin and James Griffin and physical anthropologist William Krogman enrolled in these alongside ethnologists Fred Eggan, Ruth Bunzel, C. W. M. Hart, Leslie White, Robert Redfield, and Cornelius Osgood—as well as the specialists in linguistics who worked specifically with Sapir. All but the latter were far out of their depth. Eggan (1974, 9), for example, took Sapir's course in Navajo: "If I had had any native skills in language, I would have become a linguist, but with graduate students such as Mary Haas, Stanley Newman, Morris Swadesh, Harry Hoijer and Walter Dyk, the competition seemed too great." Although Eggan did not pursue linguistic interests, he enjoyed seminars at the Sapir home which extended "beyond the allotted hours" over a bottle of wine (Eggan 1986): "Sapir provided cognate Athabaskan forms for the Navajo verbs he discussed in a display of virtuosity which I have never experienced since." In his candidacy examination, moreover, Eggan (1974, 9) was asked to write a sketch of Navajo grammar.

The linguistics students, in contrast, did not enroll in Sapir's ethnology courses and were permitted to specialize, although their degrees were in anthropology. Hoijer recalled (to Haas, 8 November 1971) that Sapir discouraged students from specializing in linguistics because there were no jobs for them.

Students were much impressed by Sapir's lecture style. Hoijer observed (to Haas, 8 November 1971) that he rarely used notes, except an occasional card with a few linguistic forms. Although he "invariably had to look up his telephone number" to call his wife and forgot appointments unless he wrote them down, Sapir's prodigious memory for linguistic forms was legendary. In a seminar at his home in 1930–1931, Sapir responded to a question by quoting "examples from ten or more Indian languages from memory." Hoijer wrote them down and looked them up: "All were pertinent and all were accurate."

The department program grew substantially during Sapir's Chicago years. The catalogue for 1929–1930 listed Cole's Archaeological Survey of Illinois, the Committee on Research in Indian Languages, the Southwest Laboratory, a project in African language and culture, the Field Museum of Natural History, and cultural groups in the city of Chicago (a heritage from the sociology days). Linguistic students were encouraged to take appropriate courses in the various language departments and in Comparative Philology. Cole, though an ethnologist, taught archaeology and physical anthropology, while Sapir concentrated on linguistics and ethnology "with excursions into culture and personality" (Eggan 1974, 6). Redfield, the youngest member of the department, maintained continuity with sociology.

Sapir's office was soundproofed with stucco to allow phonetic work

(Eggan, p.c.). He became so discouraged with his teaching burdens, however, that he applied for eight months' leave by pooling his vacation credits. He noted (to Cole, 17 January 1930: UC) that he had "either been in actual residence or done fieldwork for the University of Chicago every single quarter" since 1925. Sapir felt he needed "a long breath" and wanted the university to provide an adequate replacement. Adequate replacement "would depend somewhat on whether you think it wiser to stress the linguistic side of my work or that part of my work which is concerned with theoretical problems and ethnology." No one could replace Sapir in the full scope of his interests. It would take at least two people, preferably students trained by him.

Sapir, unsurprised when Cole protested his intentions (22 January 1930: UC), reiterated that he was "tired of the continuous routine and inability to concentrate on research work" and that personal responsibilities forced him to seek more money. Cole (to Sapir, 25 January 1930: UC) proposed that definite office hours be closely adhered to to leave time for personal research. "If you will remain in residence I will do all in my power to see that your time is kept as free as possible." Sapir had been invited to run a Rockefeller-sponsored seminar in culture and personality at Yale the following year. He remained another year at Chicago because the seminar was postponed; he had not yet received a permanent offer at Yale.

When Sapir left in 1931–1932, Cole hired Manuel Andrade and Harry Hoijer to cover Sapir's linguistic work until some more permanent arrangement could be made. On the cultural side, he was replaced by British anthropologist A. R. Radcliffe-Brown. Even after Sapir accepted the Yale offer, however, Cole kept his Chicago position open as long as possible in hope that he would reconsider. Colleagues at Chicago predicted anti-Semitism at Yale and hoped Sapir would return to a more congenial academic environment. Chicago was unable, however, to match Yale's terms. Backing from the Rockefeller Foundation involved resources beyond the capacity of a single university. Sapir appreciated Cole's effort (10 November 1931: UC), although he realized the die was cast: "I can say with all sincerity that I have been happy in both places and that there is no question in my mind of a simple opposition between the two." Sapir was committed by the Rockefeller decision to hold its seminar at Yale's Institute of Human Relations. When Cole reiterated his offer in the spring (25

May 1932: UC), Sapir stressed that his reasons for moving to Yale were still valid, though he thought of Chicago "with mingled pleasure and regret" (2 June 1932: UC).

Hoijer, in some regards, maintained a Sapirian approach to linguistics at Chicago. However, his definition of the discipline was narrower than Sapir's and reflected the increasing autonomy of linguistics from anthropology. In cultural anthropology, Sapir also continued to influence the Chicago program after his departure. Although many of his students, particularly in linguistics, went to Yale with him, the work he had supervised in ethnology—particularly in the Southwest—continued at Chicago, though without a superstar to supervise.

The addition of Radcliffe-Brown to the Chicago department was a genuine discontinuity. Cole (to Sapir, 6 November 1931: UC) quickly recognized that the tone had changed thereby: ". . . it is no longer the very intimate group with like interests in the building of the department." Radcliffe-Brown was "delightful" and could "doubtless have a large personal following but it remains to be seen whether he can and will do team work." Cole missed Sapir's combination of personal charisma and departmental loyalty. Sapir responded (10 November 1931: UC) that he was unsurprised by Radcliffe-Brown's "personal following" and expected him to be "a delightful companion." But he was not one of the Boasian in-group: "I don't imagine that he is exactly the sort of person that fits easily into our American departmental framework and . . . I have always felt that he ought, perhaps, to be encouraged to undertake the direction of some more or less self-contained Institute."

Most Boasians were ambivalent toward Radcliffe-Brown. His "Edwardian Cambridge style" was distrusted in North America; moreover, he had "a more narrowly focused intellectual personality than Sapir, and his undeniable charisma tended to polarize response" (Stocking 1979, 21). Sapir personally resented Radcliffe-Brown, because he redirected the Chicago program. Other Boasians also emphasized Radcliffe-Brown's perceived "condescension" (e.g., Benedict to Mead, 28 December 1932: UC):

If only he held to a high standard of achievement and required language control, intimacy with total culture, fundamental understanding of kinship, I could understand his scorn of work so far done in America. He could scorn work in broken cultures too. . . . I know my [North American] material and Brown doesn't. It's nothing against him, but it's silly of him to take such a line with me.

Radcliffe-Brown presented his functional perspective as something new and rejected the North American (Boasian) establishment. Only at Chicago was this possible. Indeed, the first generation of Chicago students exposed to British social anthropology in the person of Radcliffe-Brown developed a synthesis rather than a polarization, in their own view at least (Eggan, p.c.). Whether Sapir and the other first-generation Boasians so perceived the matter is less clear.

CHAPTER THIRTEEN

Sapir's Commitment to Athabaskan

Sapir began his work on the Athabaskan language family in 1906 and continued it through 1938. Through Athabaskan, he put into practice his commitment to Boasian text collection and worked out his position on aesthetics and personality variations in cultural tradition. Athabaskan was the linguistic side of Sapir's mature culture-and-personality position. Krauss, in his definitive discussion of Sapir's Athabaskan (1986), finds it "fair to say that Athabaskan was his favorite language family." His comments on Athabaskan are recurrent: "Dene is probably the son-of-a-bitchiest language in America to actually know" (to Kroeber, 21 November 1918: UCB); "the most fascinating of all languages ever invented!" (to Kroeber, 4 October 1920: UCB); Na-dene was the most recent language family in North America; "I have a big Nadene program ahead" (to Lowie, 15 February 1921: UCB); "The more one looks at the thing, the more fascinating it seems and the more one is convinced that published material is merely raw material and nothing else" (to Lowie, 28 November 1921: UCB). Sapir's enthusiasm persisted despite skeptical response to his Na-dene and Indo-Chinese hypotheses. He was "a *believer*, a *passionate* believer; that was both his strength and his weakness" (Krauss 1986). Among the Athabaskan languages, Sapir's greatest commitment was to Navajo. In 1926, while working with Paul Jones in Chicago, Sapir wrote to Harrington (28 December 1926: BAE) of his planned comparative phonology and dictionary of the entire Athabaskan stock:

"These new Navaho data will assist materially in the reconstruction of the Athabaskan prototype terms."

The following year, Sapir summarized his "attitude and plans" about Athabaskan for Boas and the American Council of Learned Societies Committee on Indian Languages (12 May 1927: APS). His Sarcee and Kutchin materials were on hand. The summer would cover Hupa and one other Pacific dialect (to be studied by Fang-Kuei Li). He or his students would study other dialects, particularly Chipewyan. "My main objective is a thorough comparative study of Athabaskan." Existing materials, however, were so inadequate that considerable fieldwork would be necessary before a definitive statement could be made. With tonal data from these languages and "the full, if somewhat inadequate" materials on Carrier, Chipewyan, Hare, Loucheux, and Navajo, Sapir felt that even the most appalling data could be interpreted comparatively. Sapir wanted to work on Tlingit and Haida personally. He warned Boas that he would be recommending "within the next few years considerable work in Athabaskan to be carried on by a number of people trained to do this work." In other words, the program was too large for any single person, even Edward Sapir. Additional work had to be done by Sapir or someone he had trained to ensure adequate quality.

Fang-Kuei Li was an ideal collaborator for Sapir because he spoke several Asian tone languages and had "a remarkable interest in the Sinitic field" (Sapir to Jenness, 21 November 1926: NMM). Li (to Haas, 12 November 1971) was however, "not convinced" of Sapir's connection of Na-dene and Indo-Chinese. Li used Sapir's Sarcee field material for a master's thesis on Sarcee verb stems.

In the summer of 1927, Sapir worked on Hupa,[1] and Li (to Haas, 12 November 1971) "went off tracking the Mattole Indians" whose language was close to disappearing. Li presented a grammar of Mattole as his doctoral thesis in 1928 and worked up texts and grammar for Wailaki, obtained during the same field trip (Sapir to Boas, 18 October 1929: APS).

Sapir then turned to northern Athabaskan. Because he considered Chipewyan "about the most important Athabaskan dialect to know about" (to Jenness, 7 June 1927: NMM), Li devoted the summer of 1928 to that language. The work was sponsored by the ACLS because Jenness felt the Canadian government would object to fieldwork by a Chinese national (to Sapir, 21 November 1927: NMM).[2] Funding available from Ottawa went instead to Osgood for Hare ethnograhic work.[3] In the summer of 1929, Li studied Hare in Fort Good Hope. Sapir emphasized (to Boas, 18 October 1929: APS) Li's success with recording tone in both Chipewyan and Hare.[4]

After his summer on the Navajo Reservation in 1929, Sapir decided that Navajo would stand for all of Athabaskan in his oeuvre (to Kroeber, 2 August 1930: UCB). He wanted to "prepare a really definitive and detailed grammar of this complicated language." He thought "we ought to have at least one Athabaskan language adequately described." A comparative grammar and dictionary would follow. This stress on Athabaskan persisted to the end of Sapir's life. To Boas (12 April 1938: APS) he wrote: "I consider my Navaho work by far the most important and extensive linguistic research I have ever undertaken."[5]

The verdict about Sapir as an Athabaskanist is further complicated because he was mistaken on what he considered the most fundamental trait of the superstock—tone. His hypothesis was formulated on the basis of Sarcee. Sapir (1925) considered Sarcee tone so basic as to make it "inconceivable that it should not be shared by other Athabaskan dialects." After Sarcee, Sapir did not modify his Proto-Athabaskan phoneme inventory. Krauss (1986: 193) notes that Sapir was slow to modify his position in light of "disappointing or contradictory" evidence. This should, however, be viewed "in the context of Sapir's relations with mediocre and often hostile colleagues. Goddard, for example, could not hear tone, nor would he admit of its importance. Sapir's isolation, exasperation, and often basically defensive position had their cost."

In the summer of 1923, Sapir worked in Pennsylvania with Kutchin and Ingalik. Kutchin tone agreed with Sarcee. Ingalik, however, was not a tone language. Sapir (to Boas, 2 July 1923: APS) was inclined to blame the informant who had "proved disappointing" and "unreliable." He also failed to revise his affricate series on the basis of evidence common to Kutchin and Ingalik, a difficulty compounded by his failure to take account of Boas's 1924 Tsetault data (Krauss 1986: 194). Even with his own Chasta Costa, Sapir preferred to assume he had failed to attend to tone rather than modify his emerging theoretical stance (to Barbeau, 10 August 1920: NMM): "There are so few people that can distinguish pitches adequately. . . . As Goddard had not noticed pitch in Hupa I paid no particular attention to it myself." In fact, however, Pacific Coast Athabaskan lacks tone (Krauss 1986).

In the summer of 1927, Sapir, encouraged by his preliminary Navajo work to expect Sarcee tone throughout Athabaskan, hoped that Hupa would be the missing link (to Jenness, 15 April 1927: NMM): "When Hupa is done, I shall be in a position to write real comparative Athabaskan studies." This time, however, Sapir had to believe his own evidence (to Kroeber, 28 June 1927: UCB): "It's disappointing to find that Hupa has *no tone*! Evidently not all Athabaskan dialects possess it. I had noted its absence in Anvik Ingalik but thought that it might be due to my informant's incomplete knowledge." Sapir, however, still did not give up, noting (to Harrington, 21 July 1927: BAE) that Hupa had "certain interesting remnants" of a tonal system, although it was "very archaic" in most other respects. Sapir was not prepared to modify his theory. He acknowledged that Goddard was right in not hearing Hupa tone (to Harrington, 26 September 1927: BAE) but continued to insist on other inadequacies of his work.

Li's data on Hare and Chipewyan, moreover, unearthed a tonal pattern the reverse of what Sapir's theory predicted. Sapir considered Li's phonetic ability "as accurate as his power of analysis" (to Kroeber, 10 December 1931: UCB); tone reversal was "conservatism of pattern versus complete inversion of external form." Li never disputed, privately or publicly, Sapir's analysis of Athabaskan tone; "the difference in the cultural backgrounds, age, academic position, and the personalities" of the two men mitigated against explicit debate (Krauss 1986). Hoijer likewise declined to comment on Sapir's reconstruction of Athabaskan tone, even after his death (Krauss 1979).

Sapir continued to be interested in Athabaskan tone, although his Athabaskan ledgers include little of his own Hupa material or Li's Chipewyan. Newman obtained Carrier data (Sapir to Jenness, 7 October 1932: NMM) which agreed with Kutchin. Sapir continued to interpret this as reversal. Other potentially definitive evidence came from Eyak, which Sapir was aware of through Frederica de Laguna in 1935 (Sapir to Boas, 26 April: APS). He recognized its importance but did not pursue it. Li recorded Eyak tone in 1952, although Eyak is not a tonal language; he avoided comment on Proto-Athabaskan tone (Krauss 1979).

In any case, Sapir increasingly retreated from comparative Athabaskan to Navajo. His students at Yale were interested in comparative problems, but Sapir taught Athabaskan more on demand than from personal involvement (Haas, p.c.). Presumably Sapir was at least subconsciously aware of the difficulties of his reconstruction and retreated to assemble the descriptive baseline for a more extensive reconstruction, not repudiating his previous hypotheses because he had no systematic alternative. Krauss (p.c., January 1986) believes that "Sapir would go no further than *solid* comparative Athabaskan, if that far" in spite of the enthusiasm of his students for classificatory issues. Even the subclassification of Athabaskan dialects[6] received little attention in lectures.

Collaboration with Father Berard Haile

Sapir's Navajo work was facilitated by his comfortable collaboration with Franciscan priest Berard Haile. Sapir discouraged Haile (17 April 1929: SWL) from taking a doctorate at Catholic University, where the priests were influenced by German diffusionist theories, and was "delighted" when Haile decided to come to Chicago instead (4 September 1929: SWL).

Sapir obtained money for Haile from Elsie Clews Parsons (to Cole, 8 October 1929: UC) so that he "need not worry any further about missionary work and can devote himself entirely for the remainder of his days to Navaho linguistics and ethnology."[7] In fact, however, Haile had no intention of choosing between his scientific and religious vocations. His order allowed him to concentrate on linguistic work and on teaching priests Navajo, although in 1932 it appeared briefly that Haile might be reassigned to active missionary work. Sapir commented (7 April: SWL): "I suppose that there is nothing that you or I could do about that but whatever happens, I hope that it will always be possible for you to devote a large part of your time to the collecting of scientific Navaho materials." In 1938 the issue was finally resolved by Haile's retirement in the Southwest as missionary emeritus (Haile to Sapir, 25 July: SWL).

Haile's status was ambiguous. He was not a student because of his age and professional experience; nor was he a colleague, because he was not an academic; he was not an informant because he was not a Navajo, though Sapir questioned him on many points about his own work and was able to proceed without returning to the field because of Haile's availability. Sapir, "curiously unable to get down to real work on Navaho," toyed with the idea of writing "a definitive grammar of Navaho" with Haile (6 December 1929: SWL). He initially envisioned the rapid production of a Navajo manual (to Haile, 29, 30 June 1930: SWL). Simultaneously, he tested his 1929 Navajo material against Hoijer's, seeking a single orthography for all of the Navajo work under his influence (to Haile, 25 June 1931: SWL).[8] In 1932, Sapir wanted to publish a Navajo stem list useful for both comparative Athabaskan and Navajo per se (to Haile, 26, 28 January: SWL). But he was unable to "drop everything" and urged Haile to compile their joint data.

Haile was greatly distressed when Sapir moved to Yale (to Sapir, 6 February 1931: SWL): "Darn it! if you could only stay at Chicago!" He approached Sapir about transferring his own work to Yale, but Sapir cautioned that Yale did not have sufficient funds for anthropological research and reassured Haile that "the mere matter of where you are officially located is really of small importance" (23 December 1931: SWL). In spite of Haile's enthusiasm, Sapir felt "the time is not ripe as yet and we must use Cole's department and good will for a bit yet" (28 January 1932: SWL). Sapir brought Herzog to Yale to work on Navajo songs on a temporary appointment funded by Mary Wheelwright, a wealthy Southwestern amateur ethnologist, and acknowledged the appeal of a team project on Navajo (to Haile, 4 February 1932: SWL): "It would certainly be nice if you, Harry Hoijer, Herzog and myself could be permanently linked in a serious study of Navaho language and allied subjects."

In 1934, Sapir made an abortive effort to interest David Stevens of the Rockefeller Foundation in funding linguistic and anthropological research at Yale, as they had previously done at Chicago; Sapir continued to feel obligated to Haile since "you and I have linked our work together" (21 September, 3 October 1934: SWL). Foundation policies had changed, however, and Sapir was unsuccessful in organizing a major project on Navajo.

The Southwest Laboratory of Anthropology

The Southwest Laboratory of Anthropology in Santa Fe was a strange amalgamation of local amateur and semiprofessional interests in ethnology, academic interests in regional fieldwork programs (particularly by the University of Chicago), and philanthropic support for social science research (Stocking 1982). Spheres of academic influence had long been established in the southwest, with Harvard dominating in ethnology as well as linguistics. In addition, the southwest had a large contingent of northeastern artists, poets, and intellectuals, many of whom dabbled in ethnology. In the early 1920s, Edgar Lee Hewett came to dominate the New Mexico state museum scene. Hewett, however, was unsuccessful in capturing the attention of John D. Rockefeller, who vacationed in the area with his family. Rockefeller consequently involved the northeastern establishment, thereby allowing a Boasian wedge. Many Boasians were "fringe members of the Greenwich Village community" and attracted to the southwest as an area for research (Stocking 1982, 6).

Southwestern archaeology, moreover, was beginning to provide chronology through pottery sequences from Pecos, excavated by A. V. Kidder. Cole had been running an archaeological field school in Illinois, while serving as head of the National Research Council Division of Anthropology and Psychology. As a result, the NRC executive became "sensitive to the inadequacies of fieldwork training available for graduate students" (Stocking 1982, 6) and turned to the southwest to provide a convenient "laboratory"—much as the city of Chicago had provided a laboratory for the empirical studies of the Chicago sociologists.

It was Kidder rather than Hewett who approached the Spelman Memorial to fund a field school in anthropology. Although Kidder did not want to "undermine existing social institutions" or compete with Hewett's School of American Research, local interests felt themselves losing control of their own ethnological and archaeological resources. Hewett succeeded in postponing the first field school from 1928 to 1929. Land was donated; Rockefeller supplied a building and five years' support, although not a full endowment. The building was dedicated in 1931 in the midst of the Depression (Stocking 1982, 9).

The Rockefeller Foundation was more interested in the aesthetic side of the program than in professional training for anthropologists. Conflicts between artists, archaeologists, amateur philanthropists, and ethnologists plagued the brief heyday of the Southwest Laboratory. Nonetheless, the summer school ran from 1929 to 1934, with three teams of three to five graduate students spending six weeks in each field session. Supervision involved (Stocking 1982, 11)

many of the elder and emergent luminaries of the discipline: Sapir, Jacobs and Hoijer in linguistics; Shapiro and Krogman in physical anthropology;

Kidder, Cole, Roberts, Strong, Haury, and Kelly in archaeology; and Kroeber, Spier, Benedict, White, Linton and Lesser in ethnology.

Eighty-five students received their first field training through this program. Cutbacks in Rockefeller spending, however, resulted in a reduced program in 1935 and 1936, with only matching funds thereafter (Stocking 1982, 11). Efforts were made to revitalize the Southwest Laboratory of Anthropology around Indian crafts, public education, local archaeology, and applied science for the Bureau of Indian Affairs (Stocking 1982, 13–15). Sapir's former student Scudder McKeel, who also had experience with the Bureau of Indian Affairs, was director briefly until it became obvious that anthropological research would not be the focus of the laboratory. The institution lacked a national academic base at a time when universities were also squeezed for funds; locally it was perceived as a snobbish Rockefeller project. So it flourished during the peak of "romantic curiosity" about Indians and became a modest regional institution thereafter (Stocking 1982, 16).

Both Sapir and the University of Chicago were integrally involved in the development of the Southwest Laboratory, in their view an offshoot of Rockefeller support for the department's academic program. Sapir served on the advisory board and Cole on the board of trustees (1938 brochure). The permanent staff were supposed to develop "the larger implications of their own field by coordinated work on a series of common problems." Field training of students and cooperation with government and educational institutions were additional goals. The earliest descriptions of the project include "primitive linguistics"; attracting big names was at least as important as research specialization—Sapir could attract funding. The foundations were asked to support a series of independent projects.

Sapir was the first choice to lead a summer field session. When he agreed to do so, he negotiated with Berard Haile to join the party; "It would be great fun to work with you" (Sapir to Haile, 23 January 1929: SWL). Other participants included Hoijer and Victor Riste (University of Washington) in linguistics and Albert Sassaman in ethnology. The emphasis on linguistics reflected Sapir's own expertise. A Chicago linguistic graduate student, David Lillywhite, and Rockefeller fellow in ethnology Paul Kirchoff were attached. The field school counted as a credit course at the University of Chicago. Fieldwork was expected to test a student's potential in the discipline (Cole to

Sapir, 19 September 1929: UC): "Your remarks concerning the students with you in the field are very interesting and emphasize the value of this sort of training for the purpose of finding out the true character of the man far more clearly and quickly than is possible in the classroom."[9] Sapir mapped out his strategy to Haile (17 March 1929: SWL):

My present plan is to take a week of intensive work at Santa Fe, probably 4 hrs. a day, lecturing to all the students on Navaho phonetics and morphology. Then we are to proceed to the reservation and, before long, work with three main informants—one to dictate texts to you, one to dictate text to me, and one to give Sassaman ethnological data. Outside of regular working hours we can all be discussing problems which are of general interest to us.

Sapir had never been to the Navajo reservation before; he was unaware of local conditions and concerned about the varied backgrounds of his crew (to Haile, 17 April 1929: SWL).

[It is] quite a big party, some of whom have had no experience whatever in Navaho or indeed in any kind of linguistic fieldwork, so that it will not be so very easy to arrange things for the best good of all. . . . We will hold our plans subject to all kinds of changes on the spur of the moment, according to such topics as we get when we actually arrive on the scene.

This was to be Sapir's only effort at directing team fieldwork as well as his only trip to the southwest.

Sapir wanted Navajo data for his own research begun in Chicago with Paul Jones. He was quickly drawn into the life of the reservation. His primary informant, Albert (Chic) Sandoval, was a member of the tribal council, and linguistic work was not his only priority (to Haile, 4 September 1929: SWL):

. . . so when he invited me to come along in his car, I thought I might as well. So now my ears are buzzing with land matters, allotments, stallions, booze, marketing blankets and silverware, and . . . the Navaho speeches. I'll be glad to get back to our humble task of doing Navaho texts.

After returning to Chicago, Sapir sent various inquiries to Chic by way of Haile. For example, he emphasized pottery because of Kidder's interest in it (21 October 1929: SWL). Sapir also inquired whether Haile had followed up on his largely unsuccessful efforts to teach Chic to write Navajo. This was to be a recurrent theme in the collaboration among the three men over the next decade.

Haile also worked briefly on Jicarilla Apache at the insistence of

Elsie Clews Parsons, whose financial support of southwestern field-work gave her considerable authority. Sapir (to Haile, n.d. 1930: SWL) was "very eager that she should feel bound up with our field projects in the Southwest." Although Mrs. Parsons had a doctorate in sociology from Columbia and had done considerable ethnological work herself (Spier and Kroeber 1943), it would be easy to kill her interest "by too bare and technical an exhibit." Sapir stressed the ethnological bearings of the text material but also wanted "some systematic word material" to compare with Navajo (to Haile, 2 June 1930: SWL). Hoijer used the resulting material for comparison to his Southern Apache dialects (Haile to Sapir, 12 December 1933: SWL).

In 1930, Sapir was chairman of the school fieldwork committee and attempted, unsuccessfully, to interest Boas in leading the work (3 January 1930: APS). Over many years, Hoijer arranged his dialect surveys around the summer school (Cole to Sapir, 25 February 1935: US). Sapir (to Cole, 19 February 1935: UC) stressed the usefulness of Hoijer's linguistic knowledge to Benedict's Apache field group the previous year and was eager to repeat this husbanding of expertise for Alexander Lesser in 1935.

Sapir also continued to seek funding through small favors to Mary Wheelwright, Mrs. Parsons, and other local patrons of southwestern ethnology.[10] Although he insisted (27 October, 7 November 1932: SWL) that Haile not allow such efforts to "seriously interfere with our larger understanding," he simultaneously characterized Miss Wheelwright as "our Navaho patroness all around." His main concern, however, was more of methodology than of wasted time in meeting Wheelwright's "whims" (to Haile, 23 September 1933: SWL): "she is not at bottom interested in the severely technical work that we have been doing. She is, like most people, irritated by linguistics and tries to persuade herself that she can get genuine Navaho materials in English translation." For Haile (to Sapir, 12 December 1933: SWL) the problem was that Wheelwright overpaid her informants and forced him out of the market for texts. Moreover, she was sloppy in checking accuracy and authenticity of texts.

Publishing Navajo Texts

Even in academic circles, publication of linguistic texts was far from ensured. In spite of Sapir's commitment to linguistic texts in the native language, he was sometimes forced to resort to ethnological materials in translation. For example, he asked Haile (1 May 1930: SWL) for the myth explaining the figures in a sand-painting rug; in a later paper, he used the changes between sand painting and rug design "as an indication of the Navaho point of view" and tied this to the mythology.

Sapir planned his own volume of texts with both free and interlinear translations but thought that Haile's, after the first volume, might manage with "close but free" translations only (Sapir to Haile, 18 March 1931: SWL). Haile had more materials than he could possibly use and finally decided to concentrate on "material which can be explained by the informant" (to Sapir, 30 March 1931: SWL). Sapir was sympathetic (23 December 1931: SWL): "accumulating a vast mass of raw material in the field is not necessarily a gain in the long run."

When it came to publication, however, even Cole, "with the great majority of Anthropologists, is not interested in linguistic material as such." He preferred "nice-sounding, smooth-flowing English versions which would appeal to a larger clientele and which might help him to get more support for his department" (Sapir to Haile, 28 January 1932: SWL). By this time, Sapir was already at Yale, and Haile's Navajo texts were at Chicago. Sapir agreed that ethnological notes and introductory material would increase the interest to ethnologists. Nonetheless: ". . . all of these Navaho sources, when properly published in adequate English translations, will make a model exhibit of American Indian ritualistic literature." Sapir realized that every native language could not be described in such detail. Haile (18 July 1932: SWL) had the impression that "our text material is rated very low" at Chicago. Haile had agreed to Cole's modifications of the original plan (never carried out for any American Indian language on the scale Sapir and Haile dreamed of) but felt considerable resentment. He acknowledged, however, that the audience for the Navajo texts would be a small one.

A further problem was raised by the songs that accompanied verbal texts. Herzog was working on this material, but getting the two parts transcribed together was an overwhelmingly time-consuming job (Haile to Sapir, 18 September, 20 October, 12 December 1933: SWL). Haile was startled at the lack of connection between song words and chant legend. Ritual variation was also more rampant than he had realized. Neither Haile nor Sapir was pleased when variation in the same materials made it difficult to select a canonical form of traditional material—in spite of Sapir's theoretical emphasis on the importance of the individual as a unique perceiver of culture. Sapir worried that Haile's texts were hard to follow (19 March 1938: SWL): parts sounded like they were addressed to Navajo specialists "rather than to anthropologists in general."

Sapir urged Haile to get the material ready for publication before worrying about mechanics and funding (19 March 1931: SWL), assuring him (23 March 1932: SWL) that Cole was negotiating with University of Chicago president Robert Hutchins over publication. Haile agreed to add ethnological notes and introductory matter (Cole to Sapir, 11 July 1932: UC). Cole wanted to force a policy decision on publishing all the results of departmental research (to Sapir, 5 March 1932: UC); he had the president's support. Sapir responded (9 March 1932: UC) that publication had always been "the least satisfactory element of the scientific situation at Chicago."[11] The function of a university press "should be the making available in as cheap a form as compatible with good taste and readableness the results of the researches carried on by the various departments of the university." Father Berard's material should be presented as

far more than technical linguistic material. It is, as a matter of fact, a first-hand record of an invaluable native document. Long after the culture of such people as the Navaho is gone, these first-hand documents will continue to be of the greatest possible value to students of primitive religion.

Cole was uncertain that the time was ideal for pushing the issue but Sapir (to Cole, 5 January 1932: UC) thought it "a great practical mistake" to repeatedly postpone publication in hope of better revisions: "I have sinned too much in that respect myself to have any faith left in the method."

At this point, a challenge to the Boasian text method of linguistic analysis came from Chicago's new British social anthropologist, A. R. Radcliffe-Brown. In an undated memorandum in May 1932 (UC), he purported to be thoroughly perplexed:

What are such texts as these for? I wish Sapir had enlightened me on this. I read his letter over without finding out just what one does with such texts. . . . Authoritative it will certainly be. But just what will be done by scholars with these texts? I am in the position of one who has never used such texts to contribute to wider problems, either historical or scientific [the opposition of the two is characteristic], and would like to be shown just how. I am clear on this: that if they are to be treasured merely because they are disappearing, and because they are accurately transcribed . . . their publication would then be supported by mere antiquarian sentiment.

Sapir replied to Cole (22 May 1932: UC) that he did not trust Brown. The texts were "a priceless linguistic document" on both ethnological and linguistic grounds. Sapir was incensed by Brown's attitude of "cavalierly sneering" at the text tradition:

Not to speak of the narrowness and short-sightedness of his view, one can only marvel at his coolness—coming from an alien land, with entirely different interests in his head, presuming to tell us where to get off at on all points without taking the trouble to study the ground here and acquaint himself with what has been done and what are the understandings.

Haile's work would be "a definitive thesaurus of Navajo ritual (in the form of carefully recorded origin legends)." The "tidy" volume apparently envisioned by Brown would amount to willful destruction of scientific evidence. If Chicago was unable to respond appropriately, Sapir himself would try to do something rather than "see a beautiful piece of work made hash of because of the hostility of a supercilious gentleman."

Cole, horrified at the intensity of Sapir's reaction, insisted that he exaggerated Radcliffe-Brown's position (to Sapir, 25 May 1932: UC) and emphasized that Hoijer thought enough Navajo material was already on hand for purely linguistic purposes. Moreover, Cole found the present volume "chiefly linguistic," that is, there was "little to indicate what the ritual means to the Navaho." Haile could add such material easily.

Sapir responded (2 June 1932: UC) gracefully to the "very temperate and reasonable tone" of Cole's letter, but protested that Brown wanted to turn Father Berard's texts into a general monograph on Navajo ritual:

You see, from my standpoint that meant not only was the priceless linguistic material as such to be disregarded but that no adequate provision was ever to be made for the publication of Navaho texts, that all my own Navaho field work was, by implication, judged a waste of time, that I might, so far as he was concerned, never have trained Father Berard . . . , that nobody cared for elaborate accounts of specific Navaho rituals, anyway, and that we in America had better get busy and learn something from functionalism as to how a truly readable volume should be prepared. . . . It was all as if some Smart Aleck were to put the proffered texts of the Homeric poems aside with a supercilious remark. . . . I do not like this high and mighty method of passing quick judgment on matters that are necessarily alien to one's own interests and training.[12]

Getting down to "brass tacks," however, Sapir carefully explained to Cole that there was room for Haile's material in spite of his own work on Navajo, which would be "the primary basis for linguistic study. But Navaho is such an extraordinarily cranky language that the comparatively small body of text material which I have in my hands is not enough to serve as a completely satisfactory point of reference for future work in Athabaskan linguistics." Moreover, ethnographic and linguistic goals were, in practice, inseparable, and much ethnological misunderstanding arose from the unavailability of source materials. In spite of the law of diminishing returns, no good Navajo texts existed.

The altercation went on for years. Cole attempted to convince Sapir (18 April 1938: UC) that to publish translations and ethnological notes would not distort Haile's data. In a note on Cole's letter, Sapir proposed that one more ceremony should be recorded with the Navajo text and proposed that Mrs. Parsons might help defray the costs. He also clarified for Cole (25 April 1938: UC) the text method that he adhered to as strongly as did Haile:[13]

I'm not particularly interested in "smoothed-over" versions of native culture. I like the stuff in the raw, as felt and dictated by the natives. When enough such genuine stuff is on hand, a general description for the less technically minded reader is, of course, most desirable, but we should not make the mistake of skimping on native documents. . . . The genuine, difficult, confusing primary sources. These must be presented, whatever else is done. It is the duty of the universities to hold up a high standard of presentation of anthropological source materials. There are too many glib monographs, most of which time will show to be highly subjective performances. We need to develop in cultural anthropology that anxious respect for documentary evidence that is so familiar to the historian, the classical scholar, the Orientalist. We'll *have* to do this, willy nilly, if we are to keep the respect of our colleagues. . . . If we're not careful, thoughtful and essentially not unfriendly colleagues will be getting more and more restive and saying, "Yes, all this is most interesting and I admire the beautiful synthesis that you have made, but where is the raw evidence? I can't tell whether a given statement is common native knowledge or is merely your interpretation of one man's say-so."

Sapir realized that Cole did not share his passion for texts.

Sapir wrote to Haile (30 April 1938: UC) that he wanted him at Yale but did not want to "antagonize" Cole. In any case, the potential funds did not materialize, and Sapir advised Haile (7 May 1938: SW) to "hold onto Chicago." Negotiations to publish the Haile texts dragged on until after Sapir's death, largely due to the expense of typesetting and the small audience of interested scholars.

The Bureau of Indian Affairs

John Collier became commissioner of Indian affairs in 1933 and began a systematic reorganization of the priorities of Indian administration. Collier first met Indians in the context of southwestern romantic idealism in the early 1920s (cf. Southwest Laboratory); his interests in progressive education were encouraged by Mabel Dodge Luhan (who brought D. H. Lawrence to the southwest). Collier's policies were based on political action for Indian self-determination (Kelly 1983). He publicized the commitment of Indians to their traditional culture, particularly religious, and made it clear that assimilation was an inadequate solution to the "Indian problem" (Kelly 1983: 347).

The weight of Indian administration bureaucracy was tremendous, and Collier needed both political and academic allies in his revisions of the system. Among the anthropologists who responded with alacrity were A. L. Kroeber and Fay-Cooper Cole. The latter had considerable experience with Dutch colonial administration in Indonesia and, early in 1934, proposed—along with Radcliffe-Brown (whose British tradition was closely linked to colonial administration—ways in which "the Indian Bureau might make use of Anthropology" (Stocking 1979: 37). Collier's approach to social change on Indian reservations was backed by the philosophy of the New Deal. Cole was eager to cement Chicago ties to the BIA and Southwestern research.

Although Sapir made no institutional bid for ties to Collier's bureau, he favored training in anthropology for all Indian agents (to Cole, 9 March 1932: UC). His Canadian experience had convinced him of the need for change in administrative attitudes toward Indians. Collier's plans overlapped Sapir's both in terms of the Navajo being the largest and most articulate tribe in the country and in his concern for native language education. Sapir met with Collier in Washington (to Haile, 6 June 1934: SWL) to discuss "teaching the Navaho to write their own language." Although Boas's former student, Gladys Reichard, was to teach a summer training course, Sapir initiated a supervisory committee with Haile as chairman and Sapir and Chic

Sandoval as members. The committee would sponsor Reichard, and Haile would instruct her. The BIA wanted Sapir

to prepare a simple introduction to Navaho, such as could be used by traders, teachers, and others interested in the Indian. Of course, this will not take the place of the technical, detailed and scientific grammar of Navaho which I hope to write one of these days on the basis of our materials. In spite of the fact that I am not primarily interested in pedagogical matters, I thought it would be a good stroke to take on this task.

Sapir wanted Haile to compile lists of useful words and phrases for the grammatical material or its appendix. Haile should write to Collier and make it clear "that they need you in their Navaho administration." Sapir also wanted Chic to come to New Haven to "polish up" his own materials.

Sapir was flattered that the Collier administration sought out his expertise on Navajo and was delighted that the skills of linguists were appreciated. In addition, the BIA was a good source of research funding, for Haile if not for himself. Haile was already "in the field" to set up the program, so Sapir would only have to supervise. The BIA clearly intended, moreover, to employ anthropologists; Sapir considered himself more competent than any other contender, particularly Reichard.

Both Sapir and Haile had long-standing difficulties with Reichard. In 1924, she attacked Sapir's classificatory work on Algonkian-Ritwan. He had "made up [his] mind some time ago to avoid all polemic writing" but responded privately (to Reichard, 23 March 1924: via Voegelin) with a statement of his principles for linguistic reconstruction:

The spirit and method which you follow would make it quite possible to disprove the relationship, say, of English and Russian. . . . It all boils down largely to one's intuitive evaluation of cumulative evidence and one's tendency to be inhibited more or less by negative factors. . . . I have considerable doubt if you fully realize in every case how much specifically Algonkian work went into my reconstructions; I could not stop to write an Algonkian phonology.

Reichard had worked on Wiyot (a Ritwan language) and was incensed at Sapir's expectation that his judgment be accepted without evidence on controversial matters. Sapir (to Haile, 22 September 1936: SWL) considered it "poor policy to get her sore, as I suspect she may be— at least toward me, though I hardly know on what ground, as I've helped her all I can whenever she's asked me things." Reichard, however, felt that Sapir patronized her.[14] Sapir advised Haile (6 February, 2 June 1930: SWL) to help Reichard in a practical way without taking her "too seriously." He himself had "coached" her on Navajo and sent her "a rather detailed account of Navaho phonetics." Initially at least, Reichard deferred to Sapir's linguistic judgment and Haile's practical knowledge of Navajo, writing to Haile (13 April 1934: SWL) that she had presented a tentative alphabet to the Indian Bureau, although they were more interested in printing and typesetting problems than in scientific accuracy. The goal should be "a system we can all, laymen and scientists alike, use." Reichard did not include herself among the "scholars" but insisted she could teach the system once it was established.

Sapir asked Reichard to come to New Haven and discuss "the standpoint of the native speaker" (30 April 1934: SWL). He had already written Collier that "the orthography recommended to the Indians must be a simplified form of the scientific alphabet which is gradually coming into use among the few people who are qualified to speak on the subject." Most people exaggerated the difficulties of writing one's own language with a phonetically adequate system. Reichard had already acknowledged (to Haile, 13 April 1934: SWL) that native speakers easily learned to write:

> The whites have always gone on the basis that it would be as difficult for the Navaho as for ourselves to write the language. Perhaps your experience has taught you what mine has, namely, that they learn very quickly once they have been given a symbol for a sound, since they already know the sounds and do not have to struggle with them. I taught a Navaho girl who is here at Barnard to write in four lessons. She makes mistakes because neither she nor I have time for the proper practice, but her mistakes are not with the difficulties we have ourselves.

Reichard considered her alphabet an adaptation of Sapir's.

Sapir did not realize the implications of the phonetic orthography for BIA politics, although he had "personal doubts about the possibility of the average person picking up enough Navaho from a grammatical introduction" and proposed stressing useful phrases learned by rote, with grammar as a supplement (to Haile, 18 July 1934: SWL). Haile considered a handbook of Navajo culture, but Sapir (21 September 1934: SWL) preferred "to give less rather than more and to make that little as lucid as I possibly can. The serious student will then be able to go ahead and enrich his knowledge by personal contact with the Navaho."[15]

Haile was immersed in the practicalities of teaching the language without making it "too dry." He developed a technique for reading out loud to train the ear to Navajo sounds (to Sapir, 6 October 1934: SWL); he also worried that Reichard presented no report on her summer's teaching. Meanwhile, Sapir was in New Haven working with Chic Sandoval at a more theoretical level. He responded (2 November 1934: SWL) that Haile's lessons would be useful "when I get to the more practical aspects of my work." Sapir and Chic had discussed the possibility of bringing a small number of young Navajo to Yale (to Haile, 2 November 1934: SWL): "I have nothing definite in mind but . . . if we had possible candidates we might get Collier interested. This move might be of considerable importance strategically." Partly this responded to Chic's difficulties in writing Navajo, despite training.

Sapir considered himself in control of the scientific quality of linguistic work on Navajo, assuring Haile that he would explain to Collier, if absolutely necessary, that Reichard's "actual knowledge of Navaho is a trifle at best." She had "some inordinate ambitions of her own" about the work.

Haile, increasingly concerned about the direction of the program, wrote to Collier (16 November 1934: SWL) that Reichard was unable to record dictation correctly, failed to emphasize the language itself, and paid Navajo to study their language. Moreover, Reichard did not encourage Navajo pride in the beauty of their language. Navajo should be taught in the schools and should focus on "folk stories in the vernacular."

Sapir also responded to Collier about Reichard's report (19 November 1934: SWL), which he found "a curious blend of enthusiasm, energy, unfairness [to Father Berard] and ignorance." Reichard did not acknowledge that he and Haile had given her a simplified orthography. Moreover, it was "difficult to form a clear idea of what Dr. Reichard's work has been all about." The project ought to be put "on a much higher level." After talking to Collier, Sapir assured Haile (26 November 1934: SWL) that the two of them would continue to decide "all moot questions of orthography." There were, however, some details to be agreed upon before they could "legislate" the final system. Collier appointed Haile as Navajo language consultant and proposed (Sapir to Haile, 15 December 1934: SWL) that he spend the summer in the southwest "and take a hand in the language program." Although he sometimes professed to be "homesick" for the Navajo country, Sapir's previous plans to "revisit you all out there" had been "merely a fantasy, not a plan" (to Haile, 12 December 1933: SWL). But now he seriously considered the matter.

Late in 1934, however, Sapir made what ultimately proved to be the fatal error in his practical Navajo program. "Inspired by the excitement over phonemic theory and the unit-symbol per phoneme orthographic principle so fiercely stated in the *American Anthropoloist*," Sapir gave up the digraphs he had previously used in writing Navajo (Krauss 1986, 198). The new system was more alien in its appearance on a printed page. Moreover, Sapir—to whom orthography was always arbitrary and essentially trivial—underestimated the effect on Chic, his prize exhibit for the interpreter training program, of switching writing systems in midstream (to Haile, 19 January 1935: SWL): "I am particularly eager to learn if Chic continues to make progress. I hope you are not going to tell me that he has been hopelessly confused by our change of systems." Haile (24 February: SWL) simply responded that Chic still preferred to teach under Haile's supervision but that his confidence was increasing.

Sapir was relieved by the report, since he had always questioned whether Chic could be "trusted with the nicer points of Navaho orthography" (to Haile, 6 March 1935: SWL). If Chic could do it, there must be "at least a few Indians" with "a superior natural ear." The new system was "the most suited to Navaho yet devised." Practical simplifications might eventually be made but only "as the result of a massive collective pressure of the Indians themselves." Long-term, native-speaker "instinct" could be trusted. Haile reported (9 March 1935: SWL) that "the natives very much favor this new phonemic system" and that he was adapting a typewriter keyboard to it.

Sapir continued to stress (15 March 1935: SWL) the need for a "nucleus" of Navajo "to carry on the work [of literacy] properly among the whole tribe." He also wanted an elementary manual of Navajo ethnology intended for Navajo schoolchildren more than for whites and "complied from the directly recorded statements of older men and women in the tribe." Giving credit to the elders and having Navajo illustrators would involve the whole tribe in the interpreter training program, thereby ensuring continued BIA support. The texts had to be "entirely clear to Navaho children" (to Haile, 15 May 1935: SWL). In spite of Sapir's lack of practical pedagogical experience, these caveats are now axiomatic in Indian language education. Sapir was a pioneer in the application of Boasian linguistic and ethnographic concerns to native community concerns.

The BIA, however, increasingly favored the Reichard simplified alphabet. Haile's appointment was not renewed. Sapir's planned summer course in Navajo was postponed. Sapir rationalized (to Haile, 5 June 1935: SWL) that the summer in New Hampshire would be preferable because he could work on the grammar. Haile (15 July 1935: SWL) was sufficiently discouraged to propose transferring his work to Yale and bypassing the government administration.

Meanwhile, practical decisions had to be made. Chic felt Haile's revisions of the lessons for white students were "too 'deep' [too theoretical]" (to Sapir, 25 March 1936: SWL). He was concerned (6 June 1936: SWL) that "popular pronunciation" included a "decided tendency of shortening vowels," which made it hard to write sounds as actually heard. Variation in Navajo pronunciation had long disturbed Haile (to Sapir, 30 March 1931: SWL): "Sometimes I do wish that the informants would be more careful in pronunciation and follow some system which would conform to theory. . . . Apparently no excuse, excepting that informants are too lazy to use it correctly." Sapir responded (6 April 1931: SWL) that—at least in collecting texts—it was "not absolutely necessary to have the same words spelled in exactly the same way every time." The issue was somewhat different in 1935, however, because of the conflict over which orthography best reflected the way Navajo was actually spoken. Variability, however real, made the Sapir–Haile system seem inadequate to untrained observers.

Meanwhile, Reichard picked up support for her effort to "reduce our alphabet to an Anglicized form" (Sapir to Haile, 27 June 1936: SWL) from Harrington, the bureau linguist. In spite of Sapir's insistence that the alphabet was inadequate, Collier accepted Harrington's system, and Sapir was left to hope that "there will be a demand for our own alphabet in the field." Sapir's surface acquiescence salvaged Haile's grammar project, but the BIA wanted Sapir to rewrite it in the new system. "The attitude of these men is that of conceited ignoramuses. They seem to think that anything and everything will do." Sapir hoped administrative changes would allow return to the old system.[16]

Collier's education director, Willard Beatty, allowed Haile to prepare sample texts in both orthographies. Haile (to Sapir, 30 August 1936: SWL) was elated when the Navajo preferred the Sapir–Haile system. Beatty promised to try Haile's materials but continued to oversimplify the linguistic issues. He sponsored a course for white students in which no phonetic system was introduced and none of the students could read their own recording of Navajo forms (Haile to Sapir, 22 August 1935: SWL). Haile, convinced that few people had the ear to learn the language, was further appalled that Beatty expected every employee the Navajo service to study spoken Navajo. Haile's problems were further complicated when Chic, after a meeting on orthographic simplification with Beatty, decided that Navajo-speaking students did not need to write tone (Haile to Sapir, 4 October 1936: SWL). Haile acknowledged that "a native with some training" might infer tone from context fairly accurately but remained to be convinced that it should not be written (partly on the theoretical ground that tone was phonemic in Navajo).

Sapir continued to work on the elementary manual of Navajo even after concluding that "government politics and serious scholarly work were never meant to be on speaking terms" (to Haile, 20 January 1938: SWL). Sapir had trouble realizing why anyone would support the Harrington scheme: "I imagine there's an irrational element in it all. Some people are so wedded to our accidental alphabet of 26 letters that they think it's a holy and mystically necessary thing. . . . You just can't argue." Sapir was more philosophical than Haile because he could retreat to his technical linguistic work on Navajo. Meanwhile, Sapir was pleased to find that new works by Reichard, Kluckhohn, and others did not agree fully on Navajo ethnology and urged Haile to get his own material into the fray (4 February 1938: SWL):

Anthropologists tend to fail to see the many subjective factors that enter into the process of recording ethnographic data and I think we ought to have demonstrations from time to time of how different can be the understanding of the same culture conveyed to different students.

Sapir's position grew from his culture theory based on potential individual variability. Relativity of linguistic texts and the influence of the fieldworker on data collection would recur in his work on personality in culture.

Sapir urged Haile to get credit for his lifetime work (16 February 1938: SWL), to worry less about a "definitive account of the classification of Navaho ceremonials" and publish the "fundamental native questions of how ceremonials and ritualistic features are viewed . . . before your broad hints give others ideas." Sapir recommended his own favorite strategy: to "publish a brief account covering the main points first, then amplify and correct it in later contributions."

Even after his heart condition became acute, Sapir continued to work on Navajo, for example, sending Haile (12 May 1938: SWL) a table of his "complete conjugation of a transitive verb." He also produced a title page, table of contents, and the beginning of a chapter on alphabet and pronunciation (to Haile, 20 May 1938: SWL). In view of his "present cantankerous psychology of delay" Sapir proposed that the two be "jointly responsible" for the manual, with Haile producing most of the actual text. Sapir would outline grammatical points and revise Haile's materials.

Haile continued to test his methods in Navajo classes, now primarily to members of his own order. Sapir's organization of the manual fit "splendidly" with practical techniques from teaching experience (Haile to Sapir, 25 May 1938: SWL). Haile invented what would now be called visual aids ("a stone, dolls, drawings of a hogan, bridges, pots and pans, as occasion may require, to visualize my point") and tried to present Navajo ideology without using foreign concepts. Linguistic theory was introduced "imperceptibly" and "in small doses."

Sapir proposed (15 July 1938: SWL) to "scrap the handbook as such" in favor of Haile's "practical lessons"—which he could still "help you sponsor." As completion grew closer, Sapir became more aware of fundamental cross purposes:

I, frankly, am primarily interested in Navaho structure as such and in comparative Athabaskan. So perhaps I'd better plan to do the Navaho job in a strictly formal (and, I fear, very extensive) grammar which would probably frighten the wits out of any normal student and content myself with cheering from the sidelines whenever you send me a new lesson and, if I may, adding stuff which you are to use as you see fit.

Sapir realized that his health precluded sustained work on the larger grammar and released Haile from collaborative obligation.

Increasingly, Sapir became frustrated by the practicalities of applying the Navajo work. For example (27 July 1937: SWL):

You really discourage an intelligent understanding of Navaho *grammar* by holding onto this pitiable straw of simplicity. Why shouldn't students be cudgelled into respect for a crucially important phoneme (') [glottal stop] by writing it even when they don't want to do so. Navaho is *not* English.

Sapir wanted the Navajo work to be definitive on linguistic grounds. He shared Haile's concern over dialect differences, which he considered "barely possible" (to Haile, 19 August 1938: SWL). Alternative forms could not be dismissed as dialect difference, because speakers felt differently about the forms in question and that required explanation, not evasion. "Perhaps isolated forms are too ambiguous to have the informant help much. He may need more carefully worked out contexts to decide which form he would naturally use." That is, spontaneous speech was the standard for adequate description. For Navajo, as opposed to Indian languages where only a few speakers remained and their knowledge was often fragmentary, such a standard was realistic.

Pronunciation of tones, whatever the explanation of its variability, could be clarified by having the informant hum syllables (which Sapir did in his own Navajo classes at Yale): "At first, he'll find it silly and impossible, then he'll tumble to it. In this way you can hear melodic contours more clearly . . ." The important thing (23 August 1938: SWL) was not to allow students to develop "a lazy, dawdling attitude toward the problem of accurately defining the scope of Navaho sound units." Glottalized consonants were not "mysterious."

Sapir's death early in 1939 ended the longest and most productive collaboration of his scientific career. Haile was left to complete the pedagogical tasks and to bring out his extensive Navajo ceremonial texts (Haile 1941–1948). Hoijer was charged by Sapir with completing the scientific grammar of Navajo, a task that was completed only late in his own career.

Another would-be inheritor of Sapir's Navajo mantle was Clyde Kluckhohn of Harvard. When Kluckhohn was unable to attend Sapir's phonetics course in 1936, Sapir offered to go over his material (25 September 1936: HU). Kluckhohn participated in Sapir's spring 1937 Navajo course. Because of Sapir's kidney stones (1 May 1937: HU), the course was "frequently interrupted" and did not achieve "as systematic a close as I had wished for."

Sapir asked Haile (20 May 1937: SWL) to help Kluckhohn, who "has had some work with me in Navaho." Sapir's enthusiasm declined rapidly, however (to Haile, 4 February 1938: SWL). With tongue-in-cheek, Sapir chided Haile about a paper by Kluckhohn and Wyman (16 February 1938: SWL): "Your standard is too high. What you really demand is loving absorption in the language for years before one ventures to interpret native custom and belief."

Sapir wrote to Boas (4 October 1938: APS) about a statement in the ACLS final report that Kluckhohn was teaching linguistics at Harvard: "I do not know what he is doing there, but merely wish to call attention to the improbability of this entry being correct." In spite of Sapir's skepticism, however, Kluckhohn considered himself a Sapir student and a proponent of serious linguistic work. Kluckhohn was one of the people Leslie Spier wrote to about Sapir's death (5 February 1939: HU), and he was a contributor to the memorial volume for him; Spier (30 May 1939: HU) asked him to stress "cultural rather than individual aspects of Navaho behavior" because most contributors seemed to favor psychological topics. Kluckhohn never claimed to share, however, Sapir's interests in the place of Navajo within the Athabaskan stock or its possible connections to Na-dene and even Indo-Chinese. He is remembered as an ethnologist and psychological anthropologist rather than as a linguist.

CHAPTER FOURTEEN

The Professionalization of Linguistics

During the first half of Sapir's career, linguistics lacked an institutional and disciplinary base, being based in language departments, particularly Germanics, and in anthropology, largely American Indian. Sapir was the only American scholar with a firm base in both camps. Leonard Bloomfield was primarily a Germanicist, and Boas lacked the philological training to do linguistics for its own sake. Increasing professionalization of linguistics, however, allowed Sapir to choose colleagues to talk to and audiences to write for. He quickly became a central figure in the emerging linguistic profession in a way that he could not in anthropology because of Boas's continued dominance and the marginality of Sapir's own specialization to the discipline as a whole (which increased in proportion to the independence of linguistics from its anthropological roots).

The professionalization of linguistics was very rapid; since other professional sciences were well established, models were available. The watershed year was 1925, in which the Linguistic Society of America (LSA) was founded, concurrently with its journal *Language* and its program of summer institutes. Sapir's move to Chicago in the same year facilitated his participation. He and Bloomfield quickly came to dominate anthropological linguistics in the LSA. Sapir's Chicago contacts involved him with the International Auxiliary Language Association, a more European and less anthropological audience than he was accustomed to. Along with Boas and Bloomfield, Sapir encouraged American Indian linguistic fieldwork; and increasing professionalism of linguistics facilitated funding from the American Council of Learned Societies through the Committee on American Indian Linguistics. These developments, taken together, gave Sapir a new professional identity, relatively independent of anthropology.

The Linguistic Society of America

The majority of the founders of the LSA were philologists. The anthropologists, however, balanced conservative trends within the language-oriented segment of the emerging profession. Hermann Collitz became the society's first president by virtue of being the oldest of the signers of the founding call (Joos 1986). The first issue of *Language*[1] contained a foreword by Bloomfield titled "Why a Linguistic Science?" which flatly contradicted the views of the presidential address in the same issue. Collitz emphasized prescriptive pedagogy and excluded unwritten languages from linguistics. Joos (1986) identifies Bloomfield's brief credo as a prognosis for the future:

The tradition is that Bloomfield had to be persuaded by the combined eloquence of at least Bolling, Edgerton, Sapir, and Sturtevant, who prevailed upon him to write "an expansion of the Call" detailed enough to counterbalance certain archaic messages and implications in the senior man's presentation, lest the younger recruits give up in discouragement.

Explicit concern with attracting new blood to the profession is characteristic of new societies and disciplines. Bloomfield implied that future linguists would be trained rather than self-taught, and that institutions to train them would be developed.

The call for papers for the first meeting of the LSA, signed by Leonard Bloomfield, George M. Bolling, and Roland Kent, noted that no society was devoted solely to linguistics "in any of its phases," including historical, archaeological, philological, and humanistic. The three authors were writing to "a few men who have been most conspicuous for the publication of linguistic work." The LSA would meet concurrently with the Modern Language Association (MLA) and/or the American Philological Association. The founders did not try to exclude anyone "no matter how vague or frivolous his interest might be" (Joos 1986). Sapir was not involved in the initial machinations because his Canadian base gave him an ambivalent relationship to an

American national society. His move to Chicago, however, brought him immediately to the center of the new organization.

A preliminary meeting was held at the American Museum in December 1924, paid for out of Goddard's entertainment budget (Joos 1986). Sapir attended the organizational meeting of 10 January 1925, where he "stated the need of a new Society and moved a vote of approval and that a Society be formed." He was promptly appointed to the committee on constitution and by-laws (Minutes: APS). Of the 69 individuals who attended the first meeting, 60 were among the 214 members enrolled in 1925. Of these, 88 were also members of the MLA, 77 of the APA, 61 of the American Oriental Society, and 17 of the AAA. Eighteen were members of no related society. Given these figures, the pivotal role of anthropologists in the early LSA is remarkable. The prestige of Bloomfield, Sapir, and Boas contributed substantially to this balance of power.

The twenty-nine signers of the Call were not all active in the actual drive for a new society. Bloomfield was the youngest of the signers. Joos (1986) stresses that these men "were not rebels. Their research, teaching and publication continued patterns of linguistic thinking defined in the neogrammarian movement." Most of the founders knew little about anthropological linguistics. Roland Kent wrote to Boas (31 December 1924: APS) soliciting his support for the LSA: "I wish that I had time and energy to study a bit in the American languages for the light which they would throw on Indo-European processes." He acknowledged the relevance in principle but left in it practice to the anthropologists.

In order to ensure anthropological participation in professional linguistics, Boas was invited to serve as an early president of the LSA. He accepted the invitation to do so (to Kent, 3 December 1927: APS) with a perfunctory statement of regret that he had been unable to attend any previous meeting. The 1928 meeting was held in New York, and Kent (2 December 1927: APS) stressed that elements in the LSA wanted closer ties to anthropology and psychology. They unanimously chose Boas to signal this intent "because of your distinction in your field."

Unlike Boas, Sapir was perceived as primarily a linguist. In 1927, he served (along with Bloomfield) on the executive committee, as well on the AAAS and American Indian languages committees. Boas, after his presidency, continued to serve as chairman of the American Indian languages committee, which was funded by the ACLS independently of the LSA.

Sapir now had a professional identity with peers in his own field. Increasingly, he wrote for this audience. At Chicago, Carl Buck provided students (e.g., Li and Haas) and intellectual stimulation. At Yale, Sapir established firm ties to Edgar Sturtevant and Franklin Edgerton in linguistics and encouraged his students to base themselves in that department. Sapir's return to Indo-European studies during the last decade of his life may also be seen in terms of changing disciplinary audience.

The Linguistic Institutes

Perhaps the important institutional innovation of the LSA was the Linguistic Institute held each summer (with a four-year gap between 1931 and 1936). The institutes (LIs) altered the normal pattern of academic years and identification with a single home campus. This "improved self-confidence and mutual respect among linguists, and between the old and the young within their community, henceforth seen as a continent-wide community." Moreover, it encouraged "a swift burgeoning of talents in those recruits who profited from such concentrated work" (Joos 1986).

In 1927 and 1928, Edgar Sturtevant organized the first LI's at Yale, on the analogy of Woods Hole as a national center for biology. The first LI had sixty-five participants (Joos 1986). Goddard was scheduled to teach "linguistic anthropology" defined in Boasian terms. Examples were "chiefly from Indo-European and American Indian languages." The emphasis on areal and diffusional phenomena came from Boas, the treatment of typology and genetic classification from Sapir. Goddard's "Methods of Studying Unrecorded Languages" emphasized implications of fieldwork methodology for linguistics per se. The laborious detail of his course description illustrates the self-consciousness of the anthropologists about their position in the LSA and their awareness of the lack of appreciation of their methods among linguists. Linguistic Anthropology was withdrawn because of Goddard's fatal illness. Unrecorded Languages was taught by Sapir's former student, J. A. Mason, with one student.

The 1929 LI focused on the ACLS-sponsored Linguistic Atlas organized by Hans Kurath. Bloomfield, the only anthropologically inclined linguist on the organizing committee, criticized European dialect atlas work for its lack of adequate fieldwork methods (Joos 1986). Sapir was not present at these initial LI's. In Chicago, he lacked ties to Yale linguistics and was immersed in Athabaskan fieldwork in the southwest.

In 1930 and 1931, the LI was held at City College of New York. Boas taught in 1930, but most of the sixty registrants were CCNY students. The 1931 LI included no anthropologists. Sapir negotiated with Sturtevant to teach at City College 1933, also hoping to teach at Columbia; this LI was canceled due to the Depression (Sapir to Boas, 20 October 1932: APS). The next LI was in 1936 at Ann Arbor (where it was based until 1940).

Sapir taught at the Linguistic Institute of 1937. The introductory class, with thirty students, was "so remarkably effective" that it was moved to evening the following year so that everyone could attend (Sturtevant 1950). In 1938 Bloomfield taught the introductory course—also his only summer at the LI—it was again a smashing success. At the time, the succession of Sapir and Bloomfield was seen as complementary, although it has been remembered as marking the transition to Bloomfieldian structuralism as the dominant paradigm of American linguistics (Hymes and Fought 1975; Sturtevant 1950; Murray 1983).

The LI position acknowledged Sapir's role in professional linguistics. He was pleased at attendance in his classes and that there were "some good people" (to Spier, 9 July 1937: YUDA). The eight weeks were "quite fruitful" (to Boas, 13 October 1937: APS): "I was pleased to see how much genuine interest there was in American Indian linguistic work." Sapir did not compete with the English-dialect atlas linguists. Rather, he put his prestige behind anthropological linguistics and gathered around him an "inner circle" of the like-minded which included (John Carroll to Darnell, 24 October 1985) (Henry Lee) "Haxie" Smith, Kenneth Pike, Morris Swadesh, and J [who used no period] Milton Cowan.[2]

Carl Voegelin recalls that Sapir taught Navajo by the "spoon-fed inductive method," using himself as an informant. Sapir, Bloomfield, Charles Fries, Zellig Harris, and Voegelin himself discussed using an informant for future LI's (APS).

Kenneth Pike went to Ann Arbor in 1937 because Sapir was teaching there. Sapir obtained a fellowship for him on the basis of a phonetics manuscript Pike had sent him (E. Pike 1981, 66–67):

Sapir congratulated him on the pedagogy, saying that he had gone into detail about things that other people might have taken for granted. Ken and Sapir had started talking in Sapir's office, had continued at lunch, then gone on to Sapir's room and talked till midnight. Sapir skipped a reception in order to do that. When Ken became aware of it, he apologized. Sapir set him at ease, saying that the reception would have been work, but talking linguistics was restful.

Pike (1984, 493–494) had been working on Mixtec without an interpreter for two years. Sapir suggested a solution to Mixtec tone, without knowing the language, in half an hour. Tone had to be analyzed in terms of preceding and following words, not simply pairs of words in isolation, a methodological suggestion that grew directly out of the text-oriented field method. Pike was greatly impressed by Sapir's "gentle personality" and availability to students and faculty alike (1984, 393). Pike enrolled in Sapir's course on field methods as well as the introduction. The latter included "meaning, psychology, and the general make-up of language" and was an amalgam of Sapir's own book *Language* and that of Bloomfield's of the same title (E. Pike 1981, 68). Bloomfield was in Ann Arbor that summer but taught no classes. Pike recalls he did not talk informally to anyone, even about linguistics.

Sapir's role at the 1937 LI was recorded at the time for local publicity statements by Harold Allen.[3] He recalled Sapir as "sharp-tongued" but "approachable," "sometimes imperious," with a singular ability to clarify "the complicated and the obscure." Sapir also gave a public lecture on the implications of Tocharian for the origin of Indo-European. He argued, in lecture discussions, that "we may have gone too far in debunking abstractions." He considered many of the traditional concepts of linguistics unimportant; for example, meaning was determined by usage not by etymology (speakers were not aware of the history of their language). Allen categorized Sapir's laryngeal hypothesis (based on both Indo-European and Amerindian examples) as "the highlight of the summer." For the first time, the anthropologist at the LI was a theoretician respected by the entire profession.

Sapir had his first heart attack at the end of the summer. This was his only opportunity to influence the new generation of linguists. The following year, Bloomfield taught the introductory course, and Allen observes that the balance of the LI was shifting toward descriptive linguistics, particularly Amerindian. Bloomfield was less inclined to theoretical pronouncements than Sapir. Though Sapir was absent in 1938, his version of linguistics was well represented. Allen records Bloomfield's field methods with an Ojibwa informant, Voegelin and Harris's work with a Hidatsa Sioux informant, Swadesh's lectures on English syntax, Pike's discussion of Mixtec tone, and Murray Emeneau's Dravidian research. Bloomfield noted to Boas (3 October 1938: APS) "how well impressed I was this summer at Ann Arbor with the young people," mentioning particularly Charles Hockett whose thesis on Potawatomi (an eastern Algonquian language) was "with Sapir, I think." It was indeed with Sapir.

The next few institutes were dominated by Bloomfield, who came weekly to discuss comparative Algonquian (Allen, MS). Bloomfield taught by collaboration with the class (Voegelin: APS). Voegelin worked with Delaware in 1939 and Ojibwa in 1940. These later-1930s seminars were attended by most of the new generation of American Indian linguists. Many of these, however, were unaware of the pervasive influence of Sapir on their work. Retrospectively, Bloomfield was more salient. Indeed, Sturtevant's obituary of Bloomfield (1950) notes: "many descriptive linguists who got their training from Boas or Sapir have stoutly maintained that they learned their method from Bloomfield." At the time, however, the prestige of the two men was at least equal, probably with an edge to Sapir. But Sapir did not have further opportunity to present his views to the linguists. Professional memory was selective, and the dominance of "Bloomfieldian" structuralism during the 1940s and 1950s has virtually erased collective memory of the earlier period.

Leonard Bloomfield

Sapir and Bloomfield met just as Sapir was leaving for Chicago and Bloomfield was beginning Cree fieldwork under Ottawa auspices; fieldwork was the only way to find out more about this Algonquian language. Bloomfield (26 April 1925: NMM) complimented Sapir on his Southern Paiute grammar, which he found "beautiful, both the language and the work." His own work already focused on the four Central Algonquian languages (Cree, Ojibwa, Fox, and

Menomini), which would remain the basis of his comparative recon-structions. Bloomfield was more conservative than Sapir about genetic hypotheses, preferring to work on demonstrably related languages. In recommending Bloomfield for the "purely linguistic" Cree fieldwork,[4] Sapir (to L. L. Bolton, 29 May 1925: NMM) emphasized that no one in Canada was "in the least qualified to take up this work in the way that we desire." Sapir helped Bloomfield, whose Germanic affil-iations isolated him from the Americanist tradition, to orient himself toward Indian languages.

Both Sapir and Boas were disappointed when Bloomfield moved to Chicago in 1927. Bloomfield realized (to Boas, 22 February 1927: APS) that he would have to concentrate on Germanics but was de-lighted to escape "excessive elementary teaching" and return to a de-cent library. Boas (25 February 1927: APS) was less than enthusiastic about Bloomfield's priorities:

I am very sorry to learn that this may hamper your work on Indian languages. From all you have done it is evident that you are so well prepared for this work that, from a scientific point of view, it is more urgent than the Germanic researches which I presume in this country are, to a great extent, book work.

Sapir was more subtle, noting to Kroeber (13 March 1927: UCB) that he hoped Bloomfield's Americanist work would not suffer unduly "for he is too good a man to lose." There is, however, no evidence for Newman's claim (1984, MS) that Sapir and Bloomfield became "close friends and associates" in Chicago.

Bloomfield admired Sapir's virtuoso intellectual style but considered him a "medicine man" in matters outside language; Sapir, in turn, thought Bloomfield's behaviorist psychology was "sophomoric" (Hockett 1970, 539–540). Moreover, Bloomfield was not interested in cultural anthropology.[5] Unlike Sapir, Bloomfield's primary influence was through his publications. He was personally unassuming and had few students (Bloch 1949, 514). His intellectual heirs codified and rigidified his cautious approach to generalization (1949, 513).

For the discipline of linguistics, the main historiographic question has been the relative influence of Sapir and Bloomfield, with an ele-ment of apologetics apparent in current thought; for example, An-derson (1985) blames the relative eclipse of Sapir in the 1940s and 1950s on his failure to write a major textbook (!) and teaching only once at the LI. The equal status of the two men during the 1930s has retreated before a sense that Sapir was replaced by Bloomfield after his early death. This is partially accurate. For example, Sapir had been invited to serve on the editorial board of Boas's *International Journal of American Linguistics* two years before its official founding (Boas to Sapir, 22 November 1915: APS). Boas organized the journal, but Sapir was the theoretician. At this point, no one would have thought of Bloomfield as an alternative. Less than a month after Sapir's death, Boas invited Bloomfield to join the *IJAL* editorial board (2 March 1939: APS): "I should hope that you might help me particularly in the Algonquian field."

When Mary Haas evaluated the relative contributions of Boas, Sapir, and Bloomfield for the golden anniversary of the LSA, she cited Boas largely as Sapir's teacher. Sapir "expressed the relativistic and holistic approaches of Boas," "clearly savored the nuance of every language he worked on," and worked on an astonishing number of languages (1976, 63). Sapir's pedagogical method was to ask students to "prepare a thumbnail sketch of each of the languages we had been analyzing . . . by making only the most minimal use of actual linguistic forms." Sapir was more interested in generalization than in data per se; texts provided the evidence for generalization. Sapir's students acquired an enthusiasm for language classification that he himself seemed "not to have cared too much about" in the 1930s (1976, 64).

Haas (1976, 64) cites Bloomfield, rather than Sapir, as the source of the technique of fieldwork by immersion in the language, and claims that all three men spoke native languages. Boas learned Chinook jargon. For Sapir, Haas cites only his efforts to communicate with Ishi; Sapir recalled forms in various languages easily, but there is no direct evidence of his conversational skill in any of them. Bloomfield, however, preferred to work without an interpreter; implicitly, Haas takes this as the ideal discovery procedure. The influence of Sapir, Haas's own teacher, emerges as diffuse. Sapir inspired a generation of linguists to rescue dying Indian languages and broadened the scope of linguistics. Haas (1976, 65) cites Bloomfield's *Language* (1933) and general but unnamed works of Sapir and Boas as giving American Indian linguistics "an impact upon general linguistic studies . . . almost as great as that which the study of Indo-European and of classical languages had had in the nineteenth century."

Harris and Voegelin (1953, 62–68) painstakingly contrast the methods of Sapir and Bloomfield; both worked with Sapir first and then with Bloomfield. Sapir obtained texts in the field, published them with very little restoration, elicited single forms to translate his texts, and then made grammatical generalizations on the basis of words elicited in analyzing texts. Bloomfield's grammars were more directly derived from his texts and depended greatly on his personal rapport with an informant. Bloomfield tried to avoid eliciting paradigms so that his informant could not analogize. Sapir used shortcuts of interpreters and directed elicitation, being more interested in results than in methodological consistency. For example, Sapir wrote to Voegelin (17 August 1934; quoted by Hymes and Fought 1975, 957) that "comparative evidence" on Shawnee phonemes "might give one a valuable hint" to "rationalize thus acquired insights as best one can on descriptive grounds."

Hymes and Fought (1975) attempt to reconcile the work of Sapir and Bloomfield, blaming the apparent contrast on short-range disciplinary history. In spite of the "dispersion of Sapir's inner circle" (1975, 905) after his death, Yale during the 1930s produced a Sapir "school" that has been eclipsed in professional memory by the Bloomfieldian "Yale school" that developed later and reached its most extreme expression in Bernard Bloch rather than Bloomfield himself. An overemphasis on discontinuity resulted, as when Harris (1943–1944) restated Newman's classic treatment of Yokuts in his own model.

Hymes and Fought (1975, 974) argue convincingly that the rejection of meaning and the exclusion of historical insight from descriptive grammar had "more to do with conversations in New York City than with experience in the field." What changed was "the establishment of a formal idiom of a certain sort." Bloomfield was not as Bloomfieldian in practice as the method for which he is remembered. In the heyday of Bloomfieldian structuralism, however, "Sapir became almost unintelligible" (Hymes and Fought 1975, 998). Indeed,

in the 1940's and early 1950's there was a downgrading of Sapir on the part of some who admired Bloomfield, although there was no corresponding downgrading of Bloomfield on the part of linguists who admired Sapir. This imbalance in reputation partly defines the period.

Sapir's "First Yale School" shared with Bloomfield adherence to structural methods, commitment to professional linguistics, belief in the urgency of recording Indian languages, interest in historical relationship of unwritten languages, and desire to relate linguistics to other disciplines. The first two were fully shared. Bloomfield, however, was not interdisciplinary in the sense that Sapir was, in spite of his behaviorist psychology.

Little retrospective emphasis has been placed on how Sapir and his students modified Boasian linguistics toward a more Bloomfieldian approach in the 1930s. For example, new orthographic conventions encouraged the development of morphophonemics but left many Boasians behind. Those who continued to define themselves as linguists moved increasingly toward Bloomfieldian structuralism, because that was the direction of professionalism in North American linguistics. Sapir came to seem "remote and isolated" (Hymes and Fought 1975, 1145) from the current practice of linguistics. Linguistics over the last thirty years, however, has reexamined its roots in Bloomfieldian structuralism and returned to a more Sapirian perspective, making him again a revered ancestor (e.g., McCawley 1967; Anderson 1985).

IALA and English Semantics

Sapir met socialite Alice V. Morris, the leading light of the International Auxiliary Language Association (IALA), in New York during the final months of his Ottawa appointment.

IALA assumed that, for practical reasons, an international language needed Anglo-Saxon or Romance roots, "the stream of evolution" of Esperanto and Latin. Speakers could modify structure (grammar) more easily than roots (vocabulary). Because users of the international language would decide on its roots, IALA should focus on structure. Morris assumed that Sapir preferred a criterion of "logic" to one of "naturalness." She wanted to assemble "an impartial analysis and comparison of the structure of different languages and of language itself," resulting in a kind of "universal grammar." Sapir's work would be invaluable (24 February 1925: NMM):

If I grasp your ideas aright, this is akin to what you have in mind, namely to analyze the concept of thought itself and to create a language structure reduced to the minimum number of forms that will furnish every kind of concept with an adequate vehicle of expression. . . . Such a task, namely, the working out of a "world-grammar," should be based on a preliminary study of both ethnic and "made" languages.

Mrs. Morris had begun an outline of possible categories for such a study which she wanted Sapir to comment on before her upcoming trip to Europe in search of support for IALA. She assumed Sapir's interest to be in "practical" psychology as well as philology. To sweeten the request, she offered clerical funds.

Sapir (27 February 1925: NMM) felt it "a pity" that Esperanto had such a headstart over other international language contenders because it was "far too European-based for my taste." Romance or Latin vocabulary was acceptable, but grammar should be as minimal as possible. "A language sounding like, say, Italian, but feeling like an English–Chinese blend would be about the kind of thing I am groping for." But what Sapir found most fascinating was the possibility of adopting categories from more diverse languages, with a "give and take . . . between ourselves and exotic peoples in the basic ordering of concepts and in their symbolic expression." Sapir was adamant that logic was not the primary criterion, being impossible anyway because language grew out of "the helter-skelter of experience." Rather, the international language should be "simple, natural, flexible, self-creative, and, incidentally, logical—with a minimum of conscious machinery." He sent a copy of his book *Language*, noting that his assistance to IALA would be "of a strictly practical and psychological order."

Morris (26 March 1925: NMM) liked Sapir's memorandum on minimum grammatical structure and wanted him to get "a few more signatures from different linguists." She hoped to publish the material without affiliation to the LSA or any other society. Sapir sent the memorandum to Bloomfield, who responded (9 April 1925: NMM) that "men of science" should not be involved in the "political problem of putting over" an international language but that they should be "consulted as to the form of the language." He passed on Sapir's paper to George Bolling, the first editor of *Language*, who was opposed to any international language, particularly an artificial one.[6]

Meanwhile, Sapir attempted to interest Mrs. Morris in the implications of Chinese for grammatical simplicity. She tried to put him in touch with Y.-R. Chao in China and agreed that Chinese would be a "remarkable test of the practicality of an exceedingly simple structure" (26 May 1925: NMM). If Chinese collaboration proved impossible, however, she saw no reason not to try Esperanto roots. Sapir's response has not been preserved.

By the fall, Mrs. Morris recruited another distinguished linguist, Otto Jespersen, who had "promised to be chief advisor to IALA for its linguistic research in the future" (to Sapir, 12 September 1925; NMM). Although he had apparently just been displaced, she wanted

Sapir to come to New York. Sapir responded with amused tolerance. Mrs. Morris wanted him to use his influence with various foundations to support IALA researches (Edward to Jean Sapir, 28 August 1930: SF). Sapir used her visit to Hanover to put Swadesh in touch with European linguists.

Mrs. Morris entertained linguistic dignitaries at her Bar Harbor home (Edward to Jean Sapir, 18 September 1930: SF). Sapir found Dave Morris (a banker and soon to be Ambassador to Belgium) "an awfully good host" with a fine "sailing yacht." The dinner guests had included the former Turkish ambassador, and Sapir was afraid he would "have to become a man of importance, at least of reflected importance," to move in this company.

Sapir tried to explain linguistic concepts to Mrs. Morris (Edward to Jean Sapir, 18 September 1930: SF). Although he always remained somewhat aloof from the IALA social network, he apparently enjoyed the company of various of its members. W. E. Collinson, of the University of Liverpool, wrote to Jean Sapir after her husband's death (9 March 1939: SF) of "long walks . . . to talk over problems with him along the shore of Lake Michigan" in 1929. Collinson also acknowledged Sapir's invaluable contribution to his manuscript on "Indication"; he had critiqued Sapir's "Totality" in the same spirit.

The most intensive period of Sapir's IALA involvement was around 1931 when three of his four publications on international language appeared. The best known of these papers, "The Function of an International Language," appeared in *Psyche*—where language philosopher C. K. Ogden wrote a rejoinder (Mandelbaum 1949, 5). Sapir argued against commitment to any particular international language, stressing the association of native languages with nationalism and identity. No international language yet proposed was adequate (1931, 113). The ideal international language would "serve as a sort of logical touchstone to all national languages and as the standard medium of translation." It should be "as superior to any accepted language as the mathematical methods of expressing quantities and relations between quantities is to the more lumbering methods of expressing these quantities and relations in verbal form." Sapir's enthusiasm for variability of linguistic form comes through the more pedestrian aims of IALA.

IALA brought Sapir into contact with a number of linguistic scholars—especially in Europe—whom he would not otherwise have known. Jespersen, in particular, was an important link between Sapir and the European tradition. He was, however, older than Sapir by more than two decades, and there is an undercurrent of competition in their preserved correspondence. After Sapir's 1925 phoneme paper, his role in uniting American and European perspectives became more significant, even though he never entered the European conference circuit. During the 1930s, however, he had extensive correspondence with Trubetzkoy, who spoke highly of Sapir (Anderson 1985, 220). Moreover, when the International Phonological Association was founded in 1932, Sapir was the only American linguist invited to join its editorial board. He was "the primary link between European and American phonologists until his death" (Anderson 1985, 220).

IALA involved a number of European linguists. By 1940 (IALA letterhead), these included Jespersen, Collinson, Joseph Vendryes (Paris), Nicholas Van Wijk (Leiden), Albert Debrunner (Berne), and William De Cock Buning (The Hague). Collinson, who reviewed Sapir's *Language* in 1924 for *Modern Language Review*, unabashedly sought an eclectic applied model for IALA. Sapir was distinguished by his Canadian Indian fieldwork, "which enables him to view Indo-European languages in better perspective than some who are totally immersed in them" (1924, 253).

Sapir was impressed by Ogden and Richards, whose work he reviewed for *The Freeman*. The two philosophers focused on the symbolic and emotive functions of language, grounded linguistic theory in psychology, and derived meaning from a process of interpretation. The emphasis on intentionality fit with Sapir's interest in the individual as the locus of culture. Malinowski's appendix on primitive languages confirmed Sapir's commitment to an ethnographically based (i.e., cross-cultural) theory of meaning.

Of the three semantics papers Sapir wrote under IALA auspices, two were published in the LSA Monograph Series during his lifetime. "Totality" appeared in 1930 and "The Expression of the Ending-Point Relation" (with Morris Swadesh) in 1932. "Totality" was intended as the first installment of an extensive work to be entitled *Foundations of Language, Logical and Psychological: An Approach to the International Language Problem*. Although the larger work was discontinued, an outline of its projected fifteen sections was included in Sapir's preface. "Ending-Point" was part of a discussion of "Fundamental Relational Notions and Their Linguistic Expression." "Totality" and the posthumous "Grading" were both part of the specification of Quantity. Sapir, Collinson, and Morris brought the project to the LSA, already having the endorsement of the Geneva Congress of Linguists; Jespersen supported "investigating the extent to which natural languages employ similar formal devices" (Joos 1986). The only comparative study resulting from the project was a semantic frequency list for English, French, German, and Spanish published in 1940. Collinson's "Indication" was published in the LSA series in 1936. Morris's elaborate introduction emphasized the "nucleus" of "a stock of symbols and rules adequate to express the most commonly used concepts that underlie all languages."

Sapir may have intended to return to IALA-related work in English semantics. His manuscript on grading, published in 1944 in *Philosophy of Science*, contained a note stating that it was completed long ago and, even in fragmentary form, might induce others "to explore the sadly neglected field of the congruities and non-congruities of logical and psychological meaning with linguistic form." David Mandelbaum included it in Sapir's selected works. Alice Morris obtained ACLS funding, which Sapir used to support Newman and Swadesh between 1933 and 1936. George Trager was an IALA research associate to finance his LSA Monograph on an Old Church Slavonic text. The LSA series was open to IALA publications partly because Mrs. Morris could subsidize the publication. John Carroll also considered working on English grammar along IALA lines (to Sapir, 23 November 1938).

Swadesh worked on relational ideas in English, French, and German (ending-point) (Cole to Rockefeller Foundation for 1930–1931). Newman published on stress and intonation and on English suffixation (in *Word*, a more European-oriented journal than *Language*). Although Swadesh claimed to consider the English grammar project as a way to support American Indian research (Haas, p.c.), his dissertation reflected its influence in the subtitle "A Semantic Study of Word Structure in a Polysynthetic Language" (Hymes and Fought 1975, 972). Whorf worked on the category of aspect during the 1930s, and his speculation on the relation of language and culture draws on IALA's semantic definition of language (Hymes and Fought 1975, 972).

The semantic definition of formal categories was, in fact, integral to the First Yale School that developed around Sapir in the 1930s (Hymes and Fought 1975). Although its suggestions were not followed up at the time, the similarity to case grammar and other recent semantic perspectives is notable. Newman told Sapir's son Philip (P. Sapir to Hymes, 26 April 1986) that there was "never any intention of actually publishing a new descriptive English grammar—only to get out articles on various topics." Philip Sapir, however, recalls Sapir's sustained enthusiasm for the overall project.

Two statements of Sapir's interest are preserved. In an undated report (from the early 1930s: YUDA), Sapir noted the intention to "work out the true form of the language as given by its own usage rather than as projected into it on the basis of Latin grammar or of general logical, or psychological, considerations." The point was one Boas had long made in reference to American Indian grammatical categories: Sapir applied it to grammatical theory and ethnographic discovery procedures, emphasizing that there was "no complete scientific descriptive grammar of English" on an "inductive" basis. Sapir described the team project to the NRC subcommittee on training fellowships (21 December 1935: NRC) in terms of Newman's "original" work on English stress; the "new English grammar" project would "profess complete ignorance of English grammar and take it from the ground up as though it were an unknown language." That is, the anthropologists would use discovery procedures derived from fieldwork to test more conventionally derived linguistic analyses. Sapir saw this semantic work as linking his anthropological interests to linguistic theory.

Hymes and Fought (1975, 967) propose an even more direct connection between the theoretical contributions of the First Yale School and the new English grammar project, resulting in Swadesh's English syllabics, general debates over phonemes versus morphophonemes, and Whorf's model of English phonemics, based on his own dialect of English. Sapir himself accepted the term "morphophonemics" in his 1938 paper on glottalized continuants (Anderson 1985, 233). Because Sapir left no overall statement of his position on either English grammar or morphophonemics, however, this work has been eclipsed in professional memory. Sapir's students, moreover, later reverted to American Indian examples for their theoretical proposals.

The Committee on American Indian Languages

Early in 1926, Franz Boas and an LSA committee spearheaded by Sapir, Bloomfield, and Michelson independently proposed to the ACLS a grant for American Indian linguistics. Boas wrote to

Waldo Leland of the ACLS (14 December 1925: APS) of the "necessity of taking in hand energetically the recording of Indian languages." Only a few of the 350 had been adequately recorded. Boas himself had "collected three languages which have since become extinct." Moreover, Boas's *International Journal of American Linguistics* could publish the results.

Blooomfield (to Sapir, 19 February 1925: NMM) agreed with Boas that the primary concern was the rapid extinction of many American Indian languages. Ideally, there would be "dependable texts for each dialect, plus grammatical and lexical material not covered by the texts," making it possible to "study the larger—or, I should say, the real—problems at leisure." For Bloomfield, immediate fieldwork was necessary if analysis was ever to be possible; it was not an end in itself—as it sometimes seemed to be for many Boasians.

Bloomfield was, however, the silent partner in the committee. Kroeber (to Sapir, 14 January 1937: UCB) described his attitude as "thoroughly cooperative, constructive and self-effacing." He was, of course, junior to Boas and Sapir, particularly in the Americanist field.

The committee covered field expenses, assuming that the grantees had academic positions outside the field season, but universities lacked funds for fieldwork. Salvage of disappearing languages was the priority. Administration was minimal and mainly by correspondence. Publication was reserved for a separate grant. In practice, funds were occasionally allocated for writing up materials when no other employment was available; for example, Mary Haas wrote Boas (21 March 1938: APS) thanking him for the grant: "I am under the necessity of earning a living by some manner, and I was afraid I would have to undertake some new research." Boas was adamant that materials should not languish in manuscript or field notes.

The concerns of the participants were quite diverse. In fact, the Committee on American Indian Linguistics became a tacit battleground for control of Americanist research on a national level, a microcosm for the changing relationship of linguistics and anthropology. Sapir was most concerned with quality of research (to Kroeber, 11 February 1927: UCB): "We *must* have first class quality in our work at the outset, or we may queer ourselves with the linguistic world and fail to get a renewal of our five years grant." The new generation of American Indian linguists should be closer to linguistics than to anthropology. Sapir wanted to redress the disciplinary balance: "American Indian linguistics has always been treated in a somewhat stepmotherly way by both anthropology and the older linguistic disciplines."

Sapir urged Kroeber (13 March 1927: UCB) to professionalize fieldwork methods: individual research should be correlated in order to "Build up a real school of American linguistic research." Needless to say, Sapir envisioned himself rather than Boas as the central figure in that school. He was more confident of Kroeber's support than of Boas's (with his "naive specimens of . . . log-rolling") (to Kroeber, 16 April 1927: UCB): "Boas still has a sublime faith in the adequacy of anybody that happens to have had a course or two with him to do anything from counting beads in Thompson River specimens to making a complete phonetic and morphological analysis of Navaho or Yurok." Sapir returned from a conference with Boas in New York with "a classical fit of the blues" about his relationship to his former teacher. Sapir felt he had earned the right to be a colleague rather than a former student and that his purely linguistic work had gone far beyond Boas's own. Boas, however, was unwilling to resign his self-assigned linguistic preeminence.

Sapir could not challenge Boas directly. He wrote mildly (12 May 1927: APS) that the committee "must not sacrifice vital standards to merely tactical considerations." He reiterated his position to Kroeber (28 November 1930: UCB):

I think we are allowing too many poor or improperly qualified men to do linguistic work that should be entrusted to well-trained persons with a special flair for both phonetics and morphology. Boas still has very much the old pioneering attitude that the main thing is to rescue languages and put a lot of uncritical material on record. . . . I think it is high time that all of the work that we sponsor be of a quality that is high enough to satisfy the requirements of a genuine linguist.

Kroeber was the only survivor of the Boasian insistence on linguistic work by all ethnologists; his linguistic work, however, preceded 1920 and was restricted to California. For the "genuine linguists" Sapir dreamed of, Boas's willingness to support unprofessional work would not be an issue.

Boas willingly acknowledged Sapir's status in the field—as equal to rather than superseding his own. He explained to Edward Armstrong of the ACLS (19 February 1927: APS):

There are two lines of research represented in American linguistics; the one strongly imaginative, bent upon theoretical reconstruction. This is represented by Sapir. The other more conservative, interested in the same problems but trying to reach it going back step by step; in other words, more conservative. This is represented by myself. Both, of course, should be represented in the committee in charge of the work.

Boas proposed a third member of the executive committee and was undecided between Truman Michelson of the Bureau of American Ethnology and Leonard Bloomfield; he found them "remarkably similar." Both were trained in Indo-European, specialized in Algonquian, and were conservative on genetic relationship. The choice of Bloomfield pleased Sapir—who did know the difference between the two men and wrote to Kroeber (13 March 1927: UCB) that Bloomfield was "the real man" for comparative Algonquian.

Sapir favored linking the grant to particular universities, on the model of Rockefeller support for Chicago anthropology (to Boas, 7 January 1928: APS). Chicago already had an American Indian linguistic research program, and Sapir saw the national committee primarily as a supplement to resources already available to him. The ACLS, however, wanted to support the subject of study rather than the institution; a national scope was called for. The advisory board, however, would represent the institutions of the primary researchers. They were the old guard: Boas, Kroeber, Dixon, Speck, Michelson, Goddard, Jenness, Radin (after 1929). Only Sapir, Bloomfield, and Melville Jacobs (a Boas student) were linguists in the narrow sense of the term. The emphasis was on training and on correlating diverse studies.

Kroeber was the most powerful member of the advisory board, because he controlled research in California, where Indian linguistic diversity was greatest. Although no one at California was actively working in linguistics (Kroeber to Sapir, 21 February 1927: UCB), the existence of the committee forced him to reconsider his linguistic teaching. Previous programs had been "too indiscriminate in taking people for training" without background. In fact (to Sapir, 6 April 1927: UCB), the committee should aim to substantially change the discipline. Kroeber worried that Boas wanted to control work done in California. But Boas assured him (30 April 1927: UCB) that the committee would be "entirely guided by your wishes." Kroeber (to Sapir, 9 May 1927: UCB) then agreed to serve on the advisory board: "there is no longer any doubt as to our being able to cooperate . . ."

Over the decade of its existence, the committee supported work by more than forty individuals on seventy different American languages

(Leeds-Hurwitz 1985, 135–136). Annual reports often give conflicting information due to changes in direction of research, completion of manuscript, and publication. The grantees were, however, fairly evenly split between Boas students and Sapir students (excluding the first generation Boasians). Notable among the Sapirians were Broderius, Haas, Hoijer, Li, Newman, Whorf, Swadesh, Riste, Olive Eggan, and Dyk. Boas's linguistic students included several who were primarily ethnologists, e.g., Ruth Bunzel, May Edel, Alexander Lesser, and Gene Weltfish. During the early years of the committee, it was difficult to find trained people. By about 1931, however, choice among possible workers was feasible (Leeds-Hurwitz 1985, 144). Sapir's students were completing their degrees, Boas led a linguistic group in New York, and linguistics itself was becoming more professional. Sapir continued to complain, however, that Boas ruined the natural talent of his students because he "simply never taught them the patterning of sounds. They can learn, of course, like anybody else, though their loyalty to Boas may interfere practically with the proper functioning of their cerebral cortices" (to Whorf, 8 October 1938: YU).

Foundation priorities were interwoven with scientific ones. Sapir initially felt that the proposals to the ACLS should be "not too definite as to objectives and personnel to forestall the criticism of pushing favorite ideas or persons" (to Boas, 12 May 1926: APS). Boas (14 May 1926: APS) countered that the foundations preferred definite budgets, research goals, and "the men that are agreeable to do the work." Sapir worried lest the committee be perceived as legislating individual research or attempting to control the development of the field—as, of course, it was.

A few years later, the committee had to muster its resources to justify further funding. Boas asked Kroeber (20 March 1931: APS) to document the "stimulation" of the grant for "a reestablishment of general linguistics in American Universities," reporting to Sapir (20 March 1931: APS) that the foundations thought "they ought to start things and let other people continue it." Boas thought this was "premature because linguistics is not well enough established at the present time." He wrote to Keppel (22 April 1931: APS) that "an interruption of the work at the present time means that the men whom we have trained would have to drop the subject again and . . . we cannot expect our work to have a deep influence on University life unless a longer period is granted to the Committee."

The tripartite committee decided not to support their own work.

Boas and Bloomfield agreed, and Sapir went along (Boas to Sapir, 7 January 1928: APS). Accordingly, Boas ignored Sapir's request to be paid for completing his Yana manuscripts (Sapir to Boas, 12 May 1927: APS). In 1932, however, Boas channeled committee funds into a publication subsidy for Sapir's long-languishing Southern Paiute texts, grammar, and dictionary.

Paul Radin was a recurrent problem of the committee. In 1927, he refused to serve on the advisory board, only to apply for funds a year later (Boas to Sapir, 12 April 1928: APS). Boas opposed his application on grounds of "general unreliability," by which he meant failure to complete contracted work. For Sapir, the issue was Radin's sloppy classificatory work. Eventually, Sapir (to Boas, 14 February 1929: UCB) pleaded Radin's previous useful work, although Boas continued to feel Radin would produce no results (to Sapir and Bloomfield, 11 April 1929: APS). Finally, Kroeber (to Sapir, 18 November 1930: UCB) intervened on Radin's behalf, arguing that American linguistics owed him something. Radin was eventually paid for manuscripts presented. Sapir (to Boas, 3 May 1933: APS) considered this a "compassionate allowance" that could not be justified in a "strictly businesslike spirit" but which he favored anyway.

Another set of uncertainties surrounded the work of Jaime de Angulo, a California amateur linguist and sometime hanger-on at Berkeley (Leeds-Hurwitz 1983). Kroeber admitted personal disagreements prejudiced his opinion (to Boas, 4 May 1927: UCB); it would be "somewhat embarrassing" if he worked in California. Moreover, in spite of a "faculty of quickly getting the salient outlines of a language," de Angulo lacked "staying power" and would almost certainly fail to "secure an adequate body of text material." Unless he were "pretty rigorously controlled," de Angulo would "do what pleases himself and not what the program calls for." To Sapir (9 May 1927: UCB), Kroeber admitted: "If you can control de Angulo . . . he has the ability to make worthwhile contributions." Sapir acknowledged (to Boas, 12 May 927: APS) a "strong presumption" of moral obligation. Besides de Angulo's Achomawi was "one of the best American studies now in manuscript." Boas thought (to Sapir, 16 May 1927: APS) de Angulo was "very unsafe" for fieldwork. In fact, however, de Angulo worked on six languages for the committee and received over six thousand dollars, more than any other researcher.

Sapir (to Boas, 13 March 1927: APS) wanted de Angulo to work on Karok because of his previous good work on a tone language.

Harrington, who was extremely secretive about what materials he had on hand, complained that de Angulo's work would overlap with his own. Both Boas and Sapir were unaware of Harrington's prior work. De Angulo was switched to a different language, but the issue of coordinating limited resources also had to be resolved.

Sapir had similar problems with Harrington over Chimariko. He took time out from his Hupa work in 1927 to work briefly with this language, believing it to be unstudied (to Harrington, 19 September 1927: BAE). Both de Angulo and Sapir had proceeded in good faith, and secrecy was counterproductive. Sapir claimed to understand Harrington's feelings (26 September 1927: BAE) but insisted "that one must develop a certain attitude of impersonality in these matters." This Harrington never did.

The committee responded to Harrington's protests with a systematic effort to survey American Indian linguistic manuscripts on hand, precipitating a greater coordinating role for the committee. Both the ACLS and the Rockefeller Foundation, however, rejected Boas's argument for publication funding based on the amount of manuscript material available. Boas also made an abortive attempt to extend the mandate of the committee into Mexico on grounds of urgent salvage (to Sapir and Bloomfield, 2 May 1930: APS): "It will remain a reproach to our generation. . . . Without it the picture of the development of human languages will always remain incomplete."

In 1934–1935, A. V. Kidder complained about the allocation of work, and the ACLS arbitrarily revised the committee membership with Kidder as the new chair (Leeds-Hurwitz 1985, 152). Boas was incensed and summarized the work up to that time to vindicate his management of the program. Kroeber and Alfred Tozzer of Harvard mediated behind the scenes. Eventually, Kidder resigned.

Sapir met with Boas and reported to Kroeber (4 February 1935: UCB) that there was no "situation" to worry about. To Lowie (4 February 1935: UCB), he noted that Boas "did not act as though sitting on any such volcano as Kroeber fantasized." On the contrary, Sapir claimed that it was Kroeber who had "considerable willingness to run linguistics in whole or in part." Sapir was careful to protest his innocence of the slight to Boas (to Kroeber, 19 January: UCB): "I do not, as a matter of fact, feel in the least militant, and any ideas that may be afloat as to my desire to wrest power from Boas are utterly unfounded." Indeed, he had tried to keep his "very real and very profound grievances" against Boas to himself. The dispute was "largely the product of Boas's imagination." Sapir did not care whether linguistic work was organized through the committee or particular universities. Both Boas and Kroeber, however, wanted research organized at a national level, cross-cutting institutional boundaries.

In any case, Sapir was worried about how his role was perceived and returned to the theme of his noninvolvement on at least one more occasion (to Kroeber, 2 April 1935: UCB), insisting that he was not consulted about Kidder's appointment and that Boas should have remained the chairman. He assumed that the new committee would not meet.

Kidder was an archaeologist, who worked in the southwest where much of the committee-sponsored fieldwork was done. More significantly, he was tied to the ACLS through Leland, who had proposed him for the committee earlier (Sapir to Boas, 29 January 1929: APS). Sapir, who worked with Kidder through the Southwest Laboratory and was eager to tie up Chicago's interest in the southwest, had no objection, although "Kidder not being a linguist makes the addition of his name . . . irregular." Boas apparently continued to blame Sapir for the confusion, writing to Parsons (4 February 1935: APS) of "the Sapir incident."

Sapir's concern was justified. The balance of power in the committee had subtly shifted from Boas to himself. Boas was increasingly involved in anti-Nazi polemics, and Sapir was more active in American Indian linguistics. By 1934, he began to agitate for a separate Americanist organization. Sapir sought Kroeber's support for "a club or society" to focus interest on American Indian issues, or "primitive linguistics" generally, without prejudice toward affiliations either to linguistics or anthropology.

After reassuring himself that Kroeber was not unamenable to consolidating Americanist linguistic interests, Sapir (17 June 1935: UCB) offered to draw up some alternatives and circularize the potential membership, seeking "an objective way of sensing opinion" that would not seem to allow any group "to impose its preferences on others."

Sapir asked Boas (10 November 1936: APS) to issue a membership call on behalf of the tripartite committee. Roland Kent of the LSA assured Boas (17 November 1936; APS) that he saw "a perfectly definite place" for such a group. He favored a joint membership arrangement that would benefit both groups financially. Boas responded (24 November: APS), as one editor to another, that his *International Journal of American Linguistics* (*IJAL*) could use a subscription boost too.

"I do not think we need to worry particularly about Sapir's plan. . . . I think Sapir's principal object is to bring these people together from time to time to discuss problems of common interest which I think is quite desirable." Only forty or fifty individuals were likely to be involved. Boas reported to Sapir (30 November 1936: APS) that he had reassured Kent and did not think the matter important.

The call for membership, dated 2 December 1936, signed by Boas, Bloomfield, and Sapir, suggested *IJAL* as the official journal of the society. Kroeber (8 December 1936: UCB) congratulated Sapir on the fruition of his idea but remained dubious about adequate personnel and institutional resources. Unfortunately, Waldo Leland of ACLS (to Sapir, 19 December 1936: YUDA) opposed the "multiplication of societies," noting Sapir's extensive involvement in the LSA, where a "nucleus" of twelve active members were Americanists, including "some of the leaders in the field." He proposed a section of the LSA instead.[7]

Sapir did not give up his efforts to consolidate American Indian linguistics. With a number of his students, he published an orthographic note in the *American Anthropologist* in 1934 (Herzog et al.) in which the six authors explicitly identified themselves as Americanists.[8] Although Boas objected that the phonemic transcription lost information, Sapir—backed by a cadre of loyal and well-trained students—now held the initiative in Americanist work. Their recording of Indian languages in the field had led to revision of phonetic transcription into phonemic and was leading to morphophonemic transcription in the Bloomfieldian style.

The group around Sapir at Yale now formed the core of the LSA committee on American linguistics. Roland Kent represented the LSA and Leland the ACLS. Boas was nominal chairman, backed by Sapir and Bloomfield. The others (Whorf, Newman, Hoijer, Swadesh, Mason, and Voegelin) were all Sapir students or associates. The committee planned an introduction to American Indian languages for "general linguistic scholars." Although the plan was conceived much earlier, Swadesh's call for papers was dated a few days after Sapir's death (8 February 1939: YU). *Linguistic Structures of Native America* did not, however, actually appear until 1946, with Hoijer rather than Swadesh as the primary editor. It nonetheless summarized the Sapirian approach to American Indian fieldwork. In his preface, Bloomfield dedicated the volume to Boas, as Sapir had originally intended. Both men had died in the interim. Bloomfield made no reference to Sapir's role, except that he would have contributed a sketch. Boas was "the pioneer and master in the study of American languages and the teacher, in one or another sense, of us all." With the exception of Bloomfield, all of the contributors (Hoijer, Swadesh, Voegelin, Whorf, Trager, Newman, A. M. Halpern) were students of Sapir's at either Yale or Chicago.

In any case, major funding of Amerindian linguistics ended in 1937. Bloomfield (to Boas, 17 February 1937: APS) considered Americanist work "a national duty." The committee had demonstrated that "fairly good" personnel were available. With reasonable financial support, the next generation would be even better: "able persons should be offered a modest living at this kind of work."

Boas had in 1937 proposed to Leland (27 April: APS) a continuing committee of himself, Sapir, Bloomfield, and Swadesh, to prepare a report for the ACLS council, emphasizing remaining gaps in Americanist studies. When the ACLS declined to print Swadesh's report, Bloomfield proposed "another report especially designed to interest foundations in our work." His own brief summary also remained unpublished (Leeds-Hurwitz 1985, 154). Leland (to Boas, 31 January 1938: APS) considered the report "a peculiarly ineffective piece of propaganda" and unreadable.

The ACLS favored joint committees of the LSA and AAA. Sapir chaired the anthropology group and Boas the linguistic one; they plus Bloomfield were the only individuals on both committees (Boas to Leland, 22 November 1937: APS). Sapir considered Boas's report unsystematic (to Kroeber, 4 October 1938: UCB). Kroeber (to Sapir, 11 October 1938: UCB), emphasizing the need for a united front, felt the report would be accepted unanimously if Sapir edited it; he offered to mediate between Sapir and Boas. On the same day, Kroeber wrote to Boas, urging him to satisfy Sapir's objections and threatening to withdraw his approval unless the report was unanimous: "Judging from his attitude in former years," Kroeber believed that Sapir had "a generic sensitiveness on the score of being overridden." His changes would "not prove irreconcilable" in practice.

A brief report, apparently by Boas and Kroeber, eventually appeared in the ACLS bulletin. Boas (1939, 110) reiterated the committee's influence on professional training: "It would be easy to name today a dozen younger workers who are better equipped than were all but a very few leaders of the older generation."

Leland continued to aid Boas with small publication subsidies until

1939, particularly for volume three of the *Handbook of American Indian Languages*, which Boas claimed was largely a result of committee research (to Leland, 16 February 1939: APS). Boas maintained the same editorial policy as with Sapir's Takelma sketch in 1909, asking Mary Haas to condense her Tunica grammar to fit the overall format (Boas to Haas, 16 April 1940: APS).

When Boas gave up his office at Columbia (to Leland, 28 July 1942: APS), the ACLS declined to fund microfilming the materials in his possession, and, in 1946, the manuscripts were deposited at the American Philosophical Society Library.

CHAPTER FIFTEEN

Interdisciplinary Social Science

Sapir's return to academic life in the United States in 1925 coincided with the emergence of institutions for interdisciplinary social science. His own thinking had been moving in parallel directions, from the reconstruction of culture history on the basis of linguistic evidence to the impact of culture on the individual. Increasingly, he used his anthropological perspective to illuminate his own society. His notion of "genuine culture" developed out of his own explorations into aesthetics and psychology. But in Ottawa these ideas had been aberrations. What Sapir wanted more than anything else was people to talk to about his developing thought.

Chicago sociology provided Sapir with an entree into the developing social science but did not offer all the intellectual stimulation he needed. That came, rather, from his collaboration with psychiatrist Harry Stack Sullivan and, to a lesser extent, political scientist Harold D. Lasswell. Armed with congenial allies and connected to the seats of power, Sapir moved into the emerging interdisciplinary network as a theoretician par excellence. The pace was set by the Social Science Research Council, founded by Chicago political scientist Charles Merriam in 1925. Sapir attempted to frame his research program through the SSRC, with partial success. But there were too many conflicting interests within the SSRC, and he looked simultaneously for other institutions where he, Sullivan, and Lasswell could control the kind of interdisciplinary social science that developed (see chaps. 16 and 17).

Harry Stack Sullivan

Harry Stack Sullivan was the closest friend of Sapir's mature years. Their collaboration changed the vocabulary and research direction of both men. Each arrived at his mature position alone and was revitalized by the existence of a kindred spirit. Sullivan's concept of "interpersonal relations" allowed Sapir to reconcile the individual and society and provided an idiom to communicate with interdisciplinary colleagues at Chicago and Yale. Sullivan adopted Sapir's fieldwork methodology, with its variability of personality in different cultural contexts; traditional psychiatry was ethnocentric, crippled by its failure to transcend immediate clinical constraints. For both, their mutual enrichment was the model for interdisciplinary contact.

Sullivan was "more visual-minded than auditory-minded" (Perry 1982, 70), while Sapir used sound to hone his fluency in ideas. Conference transcripts frequently record the two—sometimes enhanced by Lasswell—tripping over their words in a single train of thought, each finishing the other's sentences. Sapir wrote to his wife (16 September 1933: SF):

I have a fancy it would do me some good to see more of Harold and Harry Stack. We three do fit together in a curious and unpretentious way, all of us being willing to see things so seriously that they become frivolous. The two together seem to release me in as healthy and innocuous a way as I can think of.

All three men approached intimacy through the medium of ideas rather than feelings.

Hortense Powdermaker, Sapir's postdoctoral student at Yale, recalled conversations between Sapir and Sullivan at the Sapir cabin in New Hampshire in the mid-1930s (1966):

The thoughts of one man kindled those of the other. My impression was that the remarkable flow of conversation between them was due not only to the high quality of their minds and to their mutual interest in the relationship between the individual and society, but also their personalities—each man seemed to combine within himself something of the scientist and something of the poet.

Sullivan—the genial Irishman—and Sapir—the more somber Jewish intellectual—were on the surface remarkably different. Both, however, felt themselves to be essentially and profoundly at odds with American society.

Sullivan was a loner as a child, escaping farm chores in his books. He never succeeded in joining a peer group, and his clinical practice emphasized the autobiographical tie between failure of male (homosexual) intimacy in adolescence and later schizophrenia. Like Sapir, he was an only surviving child suffering from maternal overprotection and lacking a strong male role model. His mother's nervous breakdown subjected him to the Irish folk belief that insanity was hereditary and caused by sexual sin. Sapir had also dealt with the stigma of mental illness in his first wife and his father—and undoubtedly was much disturbed by its implications for his own and his children's lives. The causes of such illness, of course, were far less clearly understood than at present.[1]

Like Sapir, Sullivan won a scholarship, to Cornell. But he responded negatively to finding others more brilliant than himself and was suspended for some prank, the nature of which is far from clear (Perry 1982, 138, 144–147, 151). He apparently spent the next two years in an institution and later described his "schizophrenic state" during this period. Both Sullivan and his mother considered the episode a disgrace.

Sullivan's career was, at best, irregular. At the Chicago College of Medicine and Surgery, he identified with the "psychiatric tragedies of the dispossessed" (Perry 1982, 161). He received his medical diploma in 1915 and enlisted during World War I. After discharge due to injury from a riding accident, he underwent psychoanalysis for seventy-five hours in 1917. Sullivan changed his name frequently during this period (Perry 1982, 170–171). Disliking surgery, he turned to psychology and anthropology.

Perry (1982, 178) overemphasizes the bond between Sullivan and the Chicago school of sociology. From their point of view, he was always an outsider because he never held an academic appointment. His one indirect contribution (Crowley 1977, 24) was aiding psychiatrist Franz Alexander, whom he had met in Europe in 1928, to emigrate to the United States, a fact hardly appreciated by the University of Chicago in its efforts to exclude Alexander from an appointment in the medical school. Sapir, in contrast, followed a conventional academic career (however he may have felt about the "exile" in Ottawa). His eminent respectability was one of his attractions for Sullivan.

Sullivan moved to Saint Elizabeth's Hospital in Maryland in 1922, at about the same age Sapir was when he went to Ottawa. Sapir was full of self-satisfaction, whereas Sullivan saw himself as drifting, without career impetus or personal intimacy (Perry 1982, 179). William Alanson White (after whom he later named his own institute) gave Sullivan his initial direction.

Sullivan was impressed by White's social science interests and by his "close relationship with significant figures in a wide range of the natural science disciplines" (Perry 1982, 186). White established *The Psychoanalytic Review*, defining psychoanalysis more broadly than Freud. His approach was wider than either Sullivan or his later mentor, Adolph Meyer (Mullahy 1952, 15). White was, however, more important to Sullivan than the reverse. When Sullivan applied for a full-time clinical position in 1922, White wrote that he did not know Sullivan very well (quoted by Crowley 1977, 24): "He is a keen, alert, somewhat witty Irishman, who has a facade of facetiousness which it is a bit difficult to penetrate." Sullivan would eventually come to doubt White's "ability to be candid with him" and realize that "White did not see him as quite belonging to the same elite" (Perry 1982, 188). White's autobiography (1938) does not mention Sullivan or acknowledge influence from any junior colleague.

In 1924, Sullivan moved from Saint Elizabeth's to Enoch Sheppard Hospital in Towson, Maryland, where he had freedom for clinical research until his resignation in 1930. Sullivan developed a therapeutic milieu of working-class males, creating the intimacies patients had not developed in adolescence and resulting in unheard-of recovery rates of up to 80 percent (Crowley 1977, 24). Sullivan was recognized as a "brilliant, eccentric clinician" rather than as a systematic theoretician (Perry 1982, 200). He identified with patients rather than colleagues, and criticized postindustrial Western society as lacking in essential human values. By 1926, Sullivan used the term "interpersonal relations," but most of his own interaction was a substitute for intimacy. With Sapir, he developed something like a patient–analyst relationship but, for the first time for Sullivan, reciprocal (Perry 1982).

Sullivan also established some intimacy with analysts Clara Thompson and Karen Horney. Jean Sapir later recalled (Perry 1982, 335) Sullivan's "pride and delight" at bringing Horney to the Sapir home in New Haven for a weekend. Perry (1982, 210–211) emphasizes that avoidance of marriage was an American intellectual pattern at the time, not a solely personal rejection of intimacy. Sullivan unofficially adopted a (much younger) former patient, Jimmie Inscoe, in 1927. Their homosexual relationship, a not uncommon pattern among intellectuals, was widely suspected, though never publicly acknowledged.

Perry (1982, 224) argues that Sapir, "respected and established as a linguist and cultural anthropologist," was the one exception to Sullivan's attraction to the dispossessed and alienated. There is, nonetheless, an apparent contradiction in her assertion that "hidden beneath the surface of Sapir's brilliance were strands of troubled experience that Sapir would reveal to Sullivan in their first meeting." Certainly, Sapir was an exception to Sullivan's pattern in his conventional heterosexual marriage(s) and large family.

Sapir's academic respectability did not, however, make him boring or unapproachable. Moreover, he served Sullivan as an entree to Chicago sociology. Although Perry (1982, 242) finds this role "curious since Sapir himself stood on the periphery of the whole movement at the time of their meeting," she confuses the length of time Sapir had been in Chicago with his status there. He came as a superstar and was, if anything, more highly appreciated during his early years in Chicago—before his major ties came to be nonlocal. Perry assumes that Sapir's interests in interdisciplinary collaboration were crystallized by his meeting with Sullivan, that previously he had "remained largely a specialist in the life and language of the Indians of the Northwest." In fact, however, the Chicago social science arena contributed to Sapir's articulation of preexisting ideas.

Sapir made an appointment to see Sullivan in Chicago in 1926, soon after the death of Sullivan's mother. Legend (Perry 1982, 243–246, via Jean Sapir) has it that Sapir discussed his emotional turmoil over the illness and death of his first wife. On that initial occasion, the two men talked for more than eight hours. Sullivan elevated Sapir's personal tragedy to a more general level, emphasizing the complex "intertwining of persons and events, the accidents of fate that made a person's experiences different from his contemporaries but completely intelligible to the observer" (Perry 1982, 246). Sullivan helped Sapir to acknowledge his own marginality as a person of "mixed cultures" and to realize that the outcome could have been worse (Perry 1982, 249). Although Sullivan refused to analyze Sapir, the relationship probably had a "therapeutic effect" (Paul Sapir, p.c.); certainly, the emotional catharsis of analysis was present, at least for Sapir. Indeed, Sapir, Sullivan, and Jean Sapir were all well acquainted with psychoanalytic theory and habitually used themselves and their acquaintances as an informal laboratory. Sapir was "one of Sullivan's first intense experiences with a deeply troubled person who was not psychotic" and who had "a developed mind of caliber" (Perry 1982, 246).

Sapir was looking for a psychiatrist he could talk to about the individual and society; that Sullivan filled that need was more important to Sapir than his particular theory (Paul Sapir, p.c.). Sapir was, nonetheless, intensely loyal and did not seek other psychiatric feedback (Philip Sapir, p.c.). Sullivan's idiom worked and he employed it.

Sullivan's other mentor was Adolph Meyer, who avoided exclusive reliance on Freudian doctrine and emphasized symbols more than neural factors; Sullivan, like Sapir, often included "experiences which others do not class as symbolic" to show the functional character of behavior (Mullahy 1952, 14–15). Sullivan met Meyer in 1932, when he was already well on his way toward elevating the "deceptively simple term" *interpersonal* "into the symbol for a whole theory of personality" (Perry 1982, 240). The degree of convergence in the ideas of Sullivan and Meyer would seem to indicate direct and intense interpersonal contact, although they were "a generation apart" and "most of their contacts seem to have been formal."

Sapir enthusiastically took up Sullivan's concept of "interpersonal relations." In the first issue of Sullivan's journal *Psychiatry* in 1938, Sapir noted: "Interpersonal relations are not finger exercises in the art of society. They are real things, deserving of the most careful and anxious study." In his final theoretical paper (1939, 579), Sapir rationalized his extension of the terms psychiatry and psychiatric to social phenomena in terms of excursions by psychiatrists into "basic problems of personality structure, of symbolism, and of fundamental human interrelationships." Sapir was also influenced by Meyer, whose prestige was unquestionable. The choice at the time was whether to espouse psychoanalysis.

In 1930, Sullivan established a private psychiatric practice in New York, which went bankrupt two years later (Perry 1982, 302–304). This is the period of the "Zodiac group," including Sullivan, Clara Thompson, Karen Horney, Billy Silverberg, Jimmie Inscoe, and Erich Fromm (Perry 1982, 354). Originally a social gathering, the Zodiac group crystallized theoretically around Sullivan (Perry 1982, 355). Sullivan moved between Washington and New York, in frequent contact with the Zodiac group and with Sapir in New Haven.

Sullivan, seeking independence for research, founded the William

Alanson White Psychiatric Foundation late in 1933. Sapir became a trustee in 1935 (Sapir to Hadley, 4 October: WAWPF). When the Washington School of Psychiatry was established in 1936, Sapir was proposed as head of the Social Sciences Division (Agenda of Trustees, 8 February: WAWPF). Sullivan also wanted to establish a journal that would circumvent the many "hostilities in psychoanalysis" through "an eclectic editorial policy"; he realized that, in both America and Europe, his position was "dangerously radical" (Sullivan to White, 13 June 1934: WAWPF). Sullivan agonized about the name of the journal (to Ernest Hadley, 6 July 1937: WAWPF), but "interpersonal relations" persisted in all subtitles (Perry 1982, 283). Although the "technical meaning" of the term culture in anthropology was subject to misunderstanding by psychiatrists, it "seemed rather timely to emphasize the relations of personality and culture." The eventual choice of *Psychiatry* distanced Sullivan from Freudian psychoanalysis but retained a medical link.

In the first number of the journal (1938, 135–136), Sullivan promised to "concentrate" research on the "comparative study of personality" with an emphasis on the success or failure of adaptation to society in the age group from fifteen to thirty-five. Personality maladjustments would reveal "the line of collective discontent which furnishes the immediate dynamic of social change." Lasswell's political science and Sapir's cultural variability were combined with Sullivan's preoccupation with adolescence. Sullivan, like the interdisciplinary social scientists he had long been talking to, wanted to understand "each person as an emergent configuration referable to the interplay of factors of native endowment, physico-chemical and biological environments, and personal interaction." Personalities would have to be studied "in culture areas widely divergent from our own" in order to predict "future behavior."

In the same issue, Sapir argued that cultural anthropology needed psychiatric insight for a "method to account for variance" and thereby arrive at "the psychology of cultural processes" (Preston 1984, MS). Sapir presented anthropology and psychiatry as mirror images. Lasswell (1938, 35–36) attempted to define political process in terms of "the symbolic and personality aspects of the context in which [social] rules operate." A synthesis of the three men's ideas dominated the new journal.

Harold Lasswell

Harold Lasswell is remembered in political science (Marvick 1977, 2) as "offbeat, pathbreaking, even deliberately disconcerting." Leo Rosten, brother-in-law of Margaret Mead and Lasswell's student, recalls the Lasswell of 1927 (1969, 1) as "a bit of a freak: pedantic, verbose and quite ill at ease." Lasswell was an intensely private person and oddly shy, "easily seduced by an idea, any idea." He "longed to be a 'participant–observer' in every culture, society, revolution, and laboratory experiment of his time" (1969, 8). Lasswell realigned the discipline of political science toward the study of personality. His new ideas—"gestalt thinking, interdisciplinary frames of reference, development, functional categories and procedures, and . . . the distinction between levels of analysis" (Eulau 1969, 26)—were all shared with Sapir, Sullivan, and much of Chicago social science.

Like both Sapir and Sullivan, Lasswell was an only surviving child, a loner in a conventional WASP household; his high school career was distinguished by debating (Marvick 1977, 15) (this was Sapir's only extracurricular activity at Columbia). Lasswell was considerably younger than Sapir and Sullivan. In 1918, he won a competitive scholarship to the University of Chicago. He remembered the university for the "continuous exposure by able people to comprehensive views both evaluative and analytical" (Marvick 1977, 18–19).

During his first year as a graduate student, Lasswell shared an office with Robert Redfield and Louis Wirth; through them, he met Park, Burgess, Small, George Herbert Mead, and John Dewey (Marvick 1977, 24–25): "the academic environment was benign . . . cross-disciplinary leadership came from men like Park and Sapir." Charles Merriam aided Lasswell's entree to Chicago social science (Marvick 1977, 26).

When Lasswell looked back on his Chicago period (1956, 85, 87), he emphasized that psychoanalysis came to maturity relative to the social sciences in America, not in Europe. In this process, Sapir— among all the Chicago social scientists—stood out: "We cannot overlook the infectious quality of Edward Sapir's speculations on the theme of culture and personality, coupled with his serious concern for creating a band of co-workers knowing psychoanalysis from the inside." Among psychiatrists, Lasswell found Sullivan "the most creative mind" (1956, 87). Lasswell adapted psychoanalysis to studying individual decision makers in a political process. His "sociopsychoanalysis" (1956, 107) emphasized sociopersonal context, ego function, and therapeutic social change.

In 1928–1929, while in Berlin on an SSRC fellowship, Lasswell was psychoanalyzed by Theodor Reik, a first-generation Freudian, and began to explore the political implications of the two great systems of ideas of the time, those of Freud and Marx. *Psychopathology and Politics*, published in 1930 by the University of Chicago, supported by Charles Merriam and read in manuscript by Edward Sapir, summarized his new ideas.

Lasswell maintained close ties to psychoanalysts in both Europe and America, including Freudians and neo-Freudians as well as social scientists. Lasswell, because he lacked medical training, scandalized the Chicago psychoanalytic community by measuring physiological changes in the behavior of volunteers.

Lasswell was preoccupied by the relationship of the individual to society. Like Sapir, he was disturbed by the tendency of social science to abstract the individual out of explanatory statements. The individual's account of himself was but a "natural history" of the attribution of significance to events (1930, 9). Lasswell adapted Freud's notion of free fantasy, suggesting that subconscious intuitions could be brought to conscious awareness, thereby supplying new material for logical thought. This involuted process needed supervision, though not necessarily by a psychoanalyst (1930, 26–32).

Because the authority of the state was modeled on early family relationships, politicians and their constituencies alike drew on basic collective "symbols of the whole" (1930, 172–173, 183–185, 194–198). The dynamics of politics arose from "the tension level of the individuals in society." Like Sapir, Lasswell was interested in the symbolic bonds defining group identity and refused to accept a simplistic stimulus–response psychology. Lasswell was skeptical about progressive political action because of the inevitable manipulation of collective symbols by politicians. Nonetheless, he favored "preventive politics" directed toward reducing the level of social strain and maladaptation. Unsurprisingly, Lasswell was considered a radical by fellow political scientists.

Lasswell believed that training a social scientist was much more complex than training a natural scientist because the former needed direct contact with a variety of social facts (1930, 201–203). Anthropology was important to Lasswell because political process was not restricted to modern American society. He gleefully cited Lowie's argument that all primitive societies have a "state" (1930, 249) because, Lasswell argued, the psychic experiences symbolized in political process were universal. Lasswell was also interested in the methods of the field ethnologist (1930, 149–50). The political scientist should "participate as fully in the daily life of the people as he can, in the hope that presently he will divine such a subjective viewpoint and its characteristic modes of expression [symbols]." Like Sapir, Lasswell assumed the subjective and symbolic to be the only objectives of participant observation. The argument led back to the relation of the individual to culture, to be studied by life history techniques (1930, 261).

Lasswell's career at Chicago, however, was not smooth. University President Robert Hutchins was opposed to political science. In spite of four published books, Lasswell remained an associate professor "with bleak prospects" (Marvick 1977, 32). He spent considerable time abroad or at other American institutions during the 1920s and 1930s (Marvick 1977, 30). Lasswell left the University of Chicago in 1938 without having another job. His collaboration with Sapir and Sullivan was the culmination of his early career; his second career began with his appointment to the Yale Law School in 1947.

The Social Science Research Council

The Social Science Research Council (SSRC) was the brainchild of Chicago political scientist Charles Merriam, who conspired with Beardsley Ruml of the Laura Spelman Rockefeller Memorial to underwrite behavioral research in all of the social sciences. Merriam was more interested in popularization of science than in disciplinary specialization; he freely adopted concepts and methods from various disciplines. He used the term "psychology" in a general sense of human nature and hoped it would extend the traditional boundaries of political science (Karl 1974, 119).

Merriam's lifetime task was to persuade the foundations that "the work of the university was a good investment in reform" (Karl 1974, 122). The American Council of Learned Societies was supposed to link all of the academic disciplines, but, in practice, the social sciences were left out. The natural sciences were represented in the National

Research Council, but psychiatry and social science were peripheral to the hard sciences (Bulmer and Bulmer 1981, 384). The NRC came to the study of personality and culture only through its established interest in racial mental differences.

The annual Hanover conferences of the SSRC were designed to render the social sciences worthy of the standard set by the NRC for the natural sciences. Small peer conferences were among the perks of the natural sciences which Merriam consciously emulated. The training program was a departure from the conventional philanthropic approach of minimizing risk by supporting proven research scholars (Karl 1974, 153). The Hanover meetings "were intended to serve not simply a watchdog function in the screening of applicants for funds but, more importantly, as a continuing opportunity for open discussion and debate . . . among the entire research community" (Karl 1974, 153). National research programs were, therefore, administered by peer evaluation, however ingrown the cliques became in practice.

The SSRC emphasis on research and professionalization threatened the autonomy of universities, which were increasingly dependent on resources and policies outside their control. Initiative shifted subtly from local academic administrations to the individuals who actually did the research (Karl 1974, 153–154). Neither Merriam nor Sapir was always popular back home. Indeed, Sapir abandoned Chicago when funding looked better at Yale.

The SSRC was incorporated in December 1924, with affiliated national societies for political science, economics, sociology, and statistics; the following year, anthropology, psychology, and history were added. Its work proceeded largely by committees in which disciplinary specialists were balanced "with a liberal sprinkling of men working in other fields" who had useful "special knowledge" (Fifth Annual Report for 1928–1929: SSRC). This bureaucratic organization enabled individual researchers to transcend "excessive overspecialization." Foundation bureaucrats were concerned to enhance the public image of the social sciences (Fifth Annual Report for 1928–1929: SSRC), although most of the academic researchers were somewhat aloof from the public. The SSRC's Fifth Annual Report (for 1928–1929) noted that private donors were often college graduates with scientific interest; they expected practical results from research. The SSRC selected projects that "cut across the lines of the single disciplines . . . where the difficulties confronting the individual investigator are obviously great"; interdisciplinary research required "a liberality of financing and . . . planning and patience in the gathering of data of unusual sorts beyond the reach of the lone investigator" (Sixth Annual Report for 1929–1930: SSRC).

The Hanover Conferences

The first summer conference for the interdisciplinary social scientists was held at Hanover, New Hampshire—home of Dartmouth College—in 1926. Hanover quickly became an institution. The arrangements at Hanover were elaborate and the priorities not exclusively intellectual. In 1926, there would be (Arnold Hall to Halsey Edgerton, 26 February 1926: HC): "the very finest kind of entertainment so far as comfort and administering to [the] convenience" of the participants. Hall (to Edgerton, 22 April 1926: HC) was particularly concerned with the quality of the clerk service for guests because "we will be dealing with a group of temperamental men and the success of the Conference depends on dealing with them tactfully and administering to their convenience and comfort in an intelligent and discriminating way." The financial constraints of the SSRC required (16 June 1926: HC) canceling use of the swimming pool, but golf was included.

The following year, Hall (13 February 1927: HC) wanted to improve the lounge by adding overstuffed chairs ("for the men to sink down into after an afternoon of strenuous exercise") and ornamental lamps; refrigerator service for soft drinks would be appreciated; tables in the dining room should seat only four people ("This gives us a greater degree of informality and makes possible more conversation and council during the meal hours").

Present-day conferences of course lack many of these amenities, even in the natural sciences; "temperament" on the part of the participants is strictly a personal problem. But this was the heyday of the great-man theory of scientific research.[2] Many of the guests, however, recognized the absurdity of the "pedants" being pampered by the "potentates." Redfield (n.d. 1930: UC) wrote to his wife from his first Hanover conference, that the SSRC "pays their fares, and boards them, and feeds them and washes their clothes, and gives them cards to go to the golf club, and then expects them to produce Significant Results." Redfield's papers (UC) also include an undated memo or "impressions of Hanover" in which "the savants gather"; Sapir "weaves his subtle web" of wise words and the committees "discuss what will result from their impact. . . . Sapir, Sullivan and Lasswell arouse the sleeping curiosity of the Council and they become a NEW COMMITTEE—Nazdar."

Sapir was also bemused by Hanover, although it was "a welcome interlude" from teaching (to White, 12 August 1926: UM):

I don't exactly know what the conference is all about, but as the Laura Spelman Rockefeller Memorial pays my expenses . . . I shall go and take part in this Oberammergau of social science. To tell the truth, I have even consented to take the lead in one of the evening symposia.

The annual conferences at Hanover were the most prestigious on the conference circuit. Most of the participants, however, met regularly through the auspices of other agencies as well. They were part of a network of elite universities and research institutes which virtually controlled foundation funding. No one who was invited could afford to miss it; and no one who was not invited could get in. Even guests from the Dartmouth faculty required vetting by the problems-and-policy committee (Transcript, 9 August 1926: SSRC).

The organization of the conferences was predictable. Committee meetings were held in the mornings. Afternoons were free because many participants gave up their vacation time to attend. Evenings were spent at group symposia led by various of the participants and followed by extensive discussion (Transcript, 9 August 1926: SSRC). Transcripts of committee meetings and symposia guaranteed confidentiality so top researchers would discuss work in progress.[3] Papers could be published elsewhere, but, in practice, most of the presenters spoke extemporaneously.

The 1926 conference included nineteen presenters, of whom five were anthropologists (Malinowski and four Boasians), seven were from Chicago social science departments, and three were foundation officials. Several were psychologists, but Frederick Wells was the only psychiatrist. Plenary lecturers were given a broad mandate (Transcript, 9 August 1926: SSRC):

We have asked each one of the speakers to come and present the particular research problem that interests him the most and tell us how he got into the problem, what he hopes to do, the problems of methods and of technique that have confronted the pathway of his progress, the difficulties he has had to overcome, and the methods by which he has done it.

In this context Sapir gave his first address at Hanover, entitled "Notes on Psychological Orientation in a Given Society."

In 1927, Sapir did not attend and anthropology was represented by Kroeber, who discussed "The Study of Cultural Phenomena" (Report, August 1927: SSRC).

Discussion in 1928 (Report: SSRC) centered around the "genuineness of the interrelations among the social sciences," a topic on which everyone had an opinion. Ogburn emphasized the need for the social sciences to become more scientific. The foundation bureaucrats also had their agenda. Edmund Day of the Rockefeller Foundation argued that "strategic planning" would lead to identification and encouragement of "desirable developments of social research." Organized research "usually derives from the imagination and competence of some one person." Very few of the social scientists, however, could "convey to the people on the outside the notion that social science, competently conducted, is highly technical."

Sapir challenged Day's "social engineering," defending the necessity for research without immediate practical consequences: "Who knows what is important? What seems most important today may be trivial tomorrow." The engineering attitude was "the dominant note in American culture today and is to be carried right into the very halls of science." Engineering should not be confused with science. Sapir's challenge was disruptive, and the subject was quickly changed.

In 1929, Sapir was in the field with the Navajo and did not attend the Hanover conference, although Cole (19 September: UC) reminded him that departmental interests required someone to take an active interest. "Nothing of particular importance to Anthropology was brought up but our small representation certainly did have an effect on Committee appointments."

At Hanover in 1930, sociologist Robert Lynd talked about "the social science spending of foundation money during the next decade." He had been on the SSRC staff since 1927 and was its first permanent secretary. His warning that the foundations could not continue indefinitely to disperse their principal as well as income, therefore, had to be taken seriously.

Sapir addressed the Hanover conference of 1930 on "The Cultural Approach to the Study of Personality," asserting that the "modern" concept of personality took a cultural dimension for granted, a position not universally shared within any of the relevant disciplines. In spite of surface variations in culture, Sapir insisted on his "intuitive conviction . . . [that] there are always present variations in individual conduct that are roughly parallel to the kind of variations that we consider significant, in a nuclear sense, among ourselves." Culture and personality had to find a middle ground between cultural conditioning and biological determinism. Psychiatrists, however, were not used to considering culture as capable of modifying "the actual persisting personality" and its "private symbolisms." In response to questions, Sapir avoided a single definition of personality in order to focus on individuality independently of commitment to "any particular theory." Variation within any given culture was sufficient to "override all the determining forces of culture itself, even the most subtle ones."

Sullivan, present at Hanover for the first time, noted himself "so sympathetic" to Sapir's position "that it seems almost unnecessary for me to say anything." Though he was "only incidentally a student of culture," Sullivan considered it yet to be demonstrated that psychiatry was a social science. From his viewpoint, cooperation between psychiatry and social science best proceeded by starting in the middle and walking in both directions—a summary greeted by laughter and applause.

Beardsley Ruml, of the Spelman Memorial, took his cue from Sapir's talk in discussing the uniqueness of the various disciplines, noting that fieldwork was rare in social science training, which usually lacked "experiential content" and was "always under suspicion as legitimate academic work."

Sapir's American Indian Acculturation Project

Sapir was active in the SSRC committee on the interrelationship of personality and culture, presenting his proposed research program at Hanover in 1930. Sapir, as the salient theoretician of the proposed research program, attempted to demonstrate that the three projects before the committee were interrelated: first, Lawrence Frank wanted a seminar of foreign students of personality to provide empirical data on their own cultures.[4] Second, W. I. Thomas wanted to study insanity in Scandinavia. Sapir, however, put his faith in a third project—which would draw on the skills of the field anthropologist and provide impetus in funding and prestige to Chicago ethnology.

"The Study of Acculturation and Personality among American Indians" was understood as Sapir's personal project, although, in practice, the work was eventually carried out by others (Linton, Herskovits, and Redfield [1936] at the theoretical level and various students, including Sol Tax, Fred Eggan, and Edward Spicer, at the empirical). Sapir was convinced that social change provided a laboratory, the equivalent of the city of Chicago for his sociological colleagues, for the relationship of the individual and culture. Tribes were selected "to illustrate five rather distinctive American Indian cultures which have made a fairly good adjustment to modern life," in spite of "many problems of social and personal disintegration."

... But the extreme psychological distance between the aboriginal American cultures and the kind of life they are expected to live today should provide an excellent gauge for estimating the possibilities of relatively quick adjustment. It is the essential viewpoint of the proposed study that the individual is seen as the meeting place of contrasting cultures. ... The Indian and his cultures are rapidly passing. The present types of half-way adjustment are also likely to pass in the not too distant future.

The study of culture change would move anthropology beyond the reconstruction of dying traditional cultures. Boasian anthropologists considered present Indian cultures as degenerate and maladaptive. Sapir emphasized that, under conditions of rapid change, the individual had to take an active role in creating a viable culture: "Probably the Indian is involved in a passionate attempt to re-interpret the old ways in terms of the new." The "conflicts considered by psychiatrists" could be observed "in this acute form" at the "cultural margin." Sapir predicted cultural persistence and argued for lessened emotional impact of individual adaptation because every member of the community shared the problem. Sapir was fascinated by Indian cultural resiliency and its alienation from white values.

Sapir's discussion was very theoretical; he still thought in terms of a generalized individual. His SSRC colleagues, however, were seeking methods to study internal variability in culture. Sapir had not done fieldwork along these lines; his understanding of the uniqueness of individual interpretation of culture came through intensive work with a small number of linguistic informants. Redfield provided a more concrete demonstration of the feasibility of acculturation studies, describing his four-communities project in Yucatan. Nonetheless, Sapir was the theoretician whose prestige supported the project. He summarized in terms of a three-pronged procedure: reconstruction of traditional culture (in the standard Boasian mold), study of acculturation itself, and "a more precise personality study." The new program was built on what ethnologists knew how to do.

Redfield and Sapir used Ruth Benedict's classic contrast of Pueblo and Plains Indian cultures to highlight American Indian variability. For example, the Plains emphasis on competition (a theme under exploration by the Yale Institute of Human Relations under SSRC auspices) produced better test performance than other Indian groups. Sapir, thinking in terms of language as the medium of eliciting personality data, suggested that there might also be "important individual differences in verbalization"—that is, not every individual would be equally useful for personality study.

Sullivan, accustomed to the intricacies of interpreting self-report data, noted that the "autobiography is a rationalized document" and suggested that free association or fantasy would be needed to transcend its limitations. Sapir proposed that case studies by an ethnologist should be turned over to a psychiatrist who should then go to the field himself.

Sapir wanted to avoid reification of culture; the others wanted concrete methods that he was not prepared to provide. The SSRC declined to pick up the tab for this massive project; neither the pedants nor the potentates saw it as providing the key to personality study. Because it was backed by Sapir, however, the project was not formally rejected. Sapir realized that the "chances of the project going through are rather slim" but (to Cole, 6 August 1930: UC) that "we should try to keep as many irons in the fire with the SSRC as possible."

Sociologist Robert Lynd supported the acculturation project in an effort to tie anthropology to broader interdisciplinary interests. His 1929 study of a contemporary American community (Muncie, Indiana, renamed "Middletown") used "the prevailing anthropological framework" for its survey data. A 1937 restudy focused on culture change resulting from the Depression.

Sapir urged Kroeber to back the acculturation study as the unique contribution of anthropology to SSRC personality study. He cabled Kroeber from Hanover (10 August 1930: UCB), asking him to join the "nucleus of anthropologists" discussing "personality in relation to changing culture" and discuss "assimilation of and resistance to our culture by American Indians." Kroeber declined (12 August 1930: UCB) but was interested in the apparent infrequency of insanity in Indian cultures and hypothesized that institutions of shamanism and berdache (an ambiguous but highly valued male homosexual role among the Plains and West Coast Indians) drained social stress on the individual. The proponent of superorganic culture concluded that "the ethnological approach has until very recently been too exclusively concerned with culture patterns." Kroeber was ready to study the individual along with Sapir.

Sapir was reasonably satisfied with the outcome: the project would be pursued further by the committee on personality and culture, along with Thomas's insanity project; Hanover discussion had shown "growth of interest on the part of the Council in problems which tie up anthropology with sociology" (to Kroeber, 21 October 1930: UCB).

The SSRC Memorandum on Acculturation and Personality (29 August to 2 September 1930: SSRC) had the enthusiastic support of Ogburn, who cited Margaret Mead as an example that sociology and anthropology could collaborate effectively. Sapir responded that the acculturation study had behind it "the consensus of opinion of the anthropologists of this country." (Kroeber would have been useful here; study of the individual was not his personal hobby-horse.) Sapir argued that "however specifically anthropological in subject matter" the acculturation study was "by no means exclusively or even predominantly so in spirit."

The committee on personality and culture (Minutes, 6 December 1930: SSRC) felt that both the Sapir–Cole and Thomas projects had distinct limitations and did not "involve the concept of personality in any precise sense or in such a way as to make probable the successful application of any of the various techniques of psychiatrists or psychologists in discussing Personality." The committee, with A. M. Tozzer of Harvard as the only anthropologist, assumed that psychiatric techniques would not work on primitive peoples. There was no evidence that the considerable expense would produce "commensurate" results. The committee preferred "relatively restricted and definite research projects." The proposed seminar on the impact of culture on personality had such definiteness. The committee did not, however, reject the contribution of cultural anthropology as one of the "coordinate fields" for personality study.

Sapir continued to discuss the project in the personality and culture committee. After his move to Yale, Sapir (Minutes, 25–26 June: SSRC) argued that Wissler's American Indian studies for the Yale Institute of Human Relations, Klineberg's work at Columbia, and Boas's interest (unspecified) in Germany were all evidence of realignment of cultural anthropology "more and more from the classical group viewpoint toward study of the individual." Sapir invited interdisciplinary students of culture to "review the case histories collected by ethnologists and reinterpret these from their point of view."

The SSRC Committee on Personality and Culture

The personality-and-culture committee envisioned research programs as interrelated prongs of an attack on the study of personality. W. I. Thomas (Report, September 1932: SSRC) argued for a "unitary" relationship of all projects sponsored at both the organizational and implementational levels.

Sapir's memorandum (Minutes, 12 March 1932: SSRC) focused on "what general patterns mean to individuals who participate in them," hypothesizing that "the degree of agreement between the meaning which the individual comes to see in social patterns and the general meaning that is inherent (for others) in those patterns is significant for an understanding of the individual's process of adjustment, as revealing harmony and conflict." He noted the development of programs at several universities and a number of "younger promising students" to carry out such studies. Although this program was not, theoretically, exclusive to anthropology, Sapir's interest in it was.

In an effort to generalize his own interests, Sapir cited (Minutes, 18 February 1932: SSRC) Lynd's study of Middletown as a "model" of the possibilities, although a "more strictly psychological" approach was needed. Many of the problems of the Lynd study could be avoided by turning from sociology to anthropology in method and subject matter. Community studies should "specialize on rather small, relatively homogeneous and self-contained communities that roughly approximate the conditions to be found among more primitive people." Sapir's example was the languishing acculturation study, which he claimed had been initiated at Yale for the Navajo and in Polynesia. He stressed that personnel were available. From the psychological side,

Sullivan and Otto Klineberg were interested in working with primitive data. The Yale Institute of Human Relations was studying "a small urban community in Connecticut" and hoped to link this to the various SSRC projects. Research already underway was more likely to attract funds.

The SSRC increasingly perceived itself as drifting in research policy and commissioned W. I. Thomas to prepare a report on "the organization of a program in the field of personality and culture." In April 1933 (SSRC), Thomas listed a "formidable" number of contributing disciplines, noting that students of culture "claim that profound changes in the behavior patterns of individuals and populations occur rapidly in changed situations." Although Thomas's example was the Institute for Juvenile Research's studies in delinquency, Sapir's acculturation proposal formulated the problem similarly. Thomas called for regional and comparative studies (i.e., sociological and anthropological). The SSRC, however, should develop methodology.

Thomas's report was accompanied by seventy-seven documents— beginning with the definitions of personality prepared by various members of the committees for the American Psychiatric Association colloquium of 1929. Lasswell argued the need for a degree specifically in personality studies. A number of descriptions of life histories and case studies by various investigators were appended. Sapir's note on "the idea-systems of individuals as related to the general cultural patterns" was an excerpt from his 1932 "Cultural Anthropology and Psychiatry." Thomas dealt with "the regional concept" in interdisciplinary terms, including statements by himself, Lasswell, Gordon Allport, and Boas. Ruth Benedict's classic paper on North American configurations of culture growth was appended.

In 1934, when Sapir chaired the personality and culture committee (Minutes, 7–8 April: SSRC), "lack of documentation" was still the problem. Sapir worried that contact with primitive peoples "cannot so easily be made"—at least with the subjective side—and "language difficulties may be practically insurmountable." The techniques of dream analysis, for example, were difficult in one's own society but even more elusive in the primitive. There were still no measures of competition or cooperation. The cross-cultural importance of adolescence in the onset of schizophrenia was still unexplored. No questionnaire had been developed for the psychological traits of an individual because situations with "equal relevance to widely different cultures" were hard to come by. Nonetheless, Sapir grasped at the possibility of characterizing "whole cultures in terms of personality types." The generalized individual might lend insight into the particular individual.

Sapir was fishing for ways to proceed, even suggesting that racial or biological factors might shed light on cultural differences. He didn't want to exclude the physical anthropologists but couldn't help noting that "present techniques" were inadequate. In practical terms, however, cultural anthropology would continue to proceed sui generis.

In spite of Sapir's efforts, however, the SSRC personality program was moving in directions alien to him. In 1934, Mark May chaired the personality-and-culture committee, and the emphasis shifted none-too-subtly to his project on cooperation and competition (Minutes, Problems and Policy Committee, 27–28 October: SSRC). May's report for 1935–1936 (SSRC) elaborated the work of John Dollard on life histories and Margaret Mead on comparative analysis of primitive cases from the literature; both projects had been published and overseen by the Yale Institute of Human Relations. Sapir's inclusive philosophy was thoroughly out of place in this context.

The personality-and-culture committee recommended (Report, September 1934: SSRC) that research be funneled through a small number of institutions where studies were already being carried out. The overall program could begin with the primitive because anthropological methods were already established. Six other degrees of community complexity were defined. Ten to twelve thousand dollars per year for three years would support each research center and experts not available locally would be supplied by the SSRC. Sapir was forced to look elsewhere to support his research programs.

CHAPTER SIXTEEN

Organizing Social Science Research and Training

The SSRC was too unwieldy for the research plans of Sapir, Sullivan, and Lasswell; its range of disciplines defied genuine consensus. Committees, moreover, were often dominated by quantitative and behaviorist approaches essentially incompatible with the collaboration Sapir envisioned between psychiatry and anthropology. Both disciplines were somewhat peripheral to the emerging interdisciplinary social science: anthropology dealt with the exotic and the primitive, and psychiatry lacked an established research tradition independent of clinical practice.

Sullivan's mentor, William Alanson White, was appointed chairman of an American Psychiatric Association committee on the relations of psychiatry to the social sciences in 1927. In 1928 and 1929, the APA sponsored colloquia on "personality organization" that drew in many of the interdisciplinary social scientists from the Hanover conferences. Sullivan, as secretary, argued that psychiatry should adopt social science research standards. In the APA context, Sapir's alliance with Sullivan gave him greater authority than the other social scientists; both Sapir and Sullivan wanted desperately to convince these colleagues of their joint position.

The First Colloquium

The first APA colloquium was held in 1928 and published in 1929. Twenty-one individuals attended the first and seven-

309

teen the second (plus various members of the APA committee). Seven were present at both: Sapir, Sullivan, W. I. Thomas, Ernest Burgess of Chicago sociology, William Healy of the Judge Baker Foundation but formerly of the Chicago Institute for Juvenile Relations, Mark May of Yale's Institute of Human Relations, and Lawrence K. Frank of the Spelman Memorial. Among them, these men virtually controlled the emerging interdisciplinary research on personality. Other Chicago contributors to the first colloquium were F. E. Knight from economics, Robert Park from sociology, Clifford Shaw from the IJR, and L. L. Thurstone from psychology. The Chicago contingent, in spite of disciplinary differences, dominated in numbers and in presenting empirical data for discussion.

Sapir professed himself "only an amateur and dabbler" in personality research (1929, 11) and called for case studies of "a few dozen typical persons, as it were, in our community" (1929, 12). When pressed, however, he was unable to define normalcy, the best form of case histories, or the proper definition of personality. These were the issues he would attempt to work out over the ensuing decade; already, however, interdisciplinary colleagues looked to Sapir for synthesis.

Sullivan wanted specific research to clarify the nature of human behavior. More conservative participants, however, were hesitant to begin without an overall concept of personality. Sullivan worried that participants in the interdisciplinary conferences learned to "converse glibly" (1929, 59–60) without changing their disciplinary point of view. Lawrence Frank noted: "By training and tradition the social scientist is inclined to look for uniformities and by training and professional obligation the psychiatrist is inclined to be more interested in variation" (1929, 26). He wanted to fund research uniting the two views.

Discussion of empirical data from Chicago quickly polarized the quantifiers and the culturologists. Park assumed that delinquency would correlate with cultural areas within the city, but Clifford Shaw (1929, 31) responded that he had no idea what the coefficients of correlation meant: "I get more hunches from the study of specific cases." Sullivan added that statistics sometimes had "no actual validity." Sapir (1929, 32) considered cultural mapping less important than the cultural dysfunction which produced, or at least allowed, delinquency. His example of Blackfoot horsestealing showed the potential variability of the cultural and religious associations of delinquency. The cross-cultural perspective was unfamiliar to the sociologists; but, more importantly, in his own view, Sapir argued for a symbolic definition of culture, for meaning as perceived by its members.

Opinions differed widely as to how many researchers would be needed, and from what disciplines, and how much data they would need to analyze. Sapir favored approaching a limited set of data from as many disciplinary angles as possible. Thurstone and May defended quantitative methods. The rest of the assembled company preferred interpretation to statistics per se. A different kind of consistency, based on the integration of the individual personality rather than the mode for a group, emerged from those with practical experience. Sapir arrived at the same point by way of his theories about the individual and culture.

Sapir articulated the "obvious unwillingness or hesitation of most of us to throw bridges across the chasms which separate our respective disciplines" (1929, 77). Through the range of analytical levels from the physiological to the social, "what we are really talking about is systems of ideas" even "from the very coldest and most objective point of view." Diverse disciplinary perspectives could not be reconciled with a purely behaviorist science; students of the social precluded generalization by treating the individual as "helpless . . . in the flux of culture history." Society (used here as equivalent to culture) "is actually nothing more or less than a system of ideas, or several intercrossing systems." More than any other student of human behavior, the psychiatrist was "the intuitive scientist" interested in human ideas qua system (1929, 78). The psychiatrist "probably commits more sins against common sense and fact than any other known scientist" but with "the most valuable hunch." Society was "simply that external human force that cramps the individual." Both sociologist and anthropologist failed to acknowledge the individual in personality. Sapir assumed, however, no conflict between culture and the individual if the concepts were abstracted correctly (1929, 79): "[E]very individual acquires and develops his own 'culture,' " which "has no psychological meaning until it is interpreted by being referred to personalities or, at the least, a generalized personality conceived as typical of a given society." Sapir was less concerned about particular individuals than with the definition of society itself.[1]

Sapir identified five operative definitions of personality, each of which implied a "slant," with consequences for research.[2] For the psychiatrist, personality had definite form, but that form was obscured by a social mask; removing the mask revealed the essential person behind it (1929, 79). The prenatal and immediate postnatal period of the "subcultural personality" made it possible to distinguish genetic and social factors "of the utmost importance." In Sapir's view, psychiatry emphasized subcultural personality, maintained in spite of cultural conditioning. Sapir saw Freudian developmentalism as the key to the psychiatric point of view and as the counterpoint to his own view of the individual and society. He insisted on the potential relevance of every possible interdisciplinary perspective (1929, 80), "ranging from the purely organismal type of interpretation up to the impersonal and abstract formulations of the theoretical sociologist and the philosopher." Case histories would focus these diverse views. Sapir was perceived as an effective synthesizer because, although his own interests were quite particular to the intersection of psychology and cultural anthropology, he recognized the legitimacy of other approaches.

The colloquium arrived at the unsurprising conclusion that concrete data and a shared method were prerequisite to further interdisciplinary cooperation. The method was life history. Lasswell presented a "proposal" on "adequate personality records" as an appendix to the conference transcript (1929: 93–101). In line with Sapir, he argued that "certain selected individuals" should be studied "intensively... through all known methods."

Lasswell wanted to study normal or near-normal subjects, making it easier to involve nonpsychiatrists. Although no such elaborate proposal was ever carried out, the magnitude of the outline indicates how serious Lasswell, Sullivan, and Sapir were about the need for an empirical data base. Sapir was unenthusiastic about anthropological field studies of personality precisely because methods to study variability were unavailable.

The Second Colloquium

The first colloquium left many loose ends. Differences in perspective had been articulated and methods suggested. The second APA colloquium, sponsored jointly by the APA and the SSRC, tacitly acknowledged the successful claim of psychiatry to a place among the interdisciplinary social sciences. It focused on "work actually in progress." Of the seventeen participants, fewer were elders and theoreticians (e.g., Park and Thurstone were both absent) and more were research institute directors. Personality research was maturing (Kline 1930, 7–8): "Even the splendid isolation of the medical and the social specialties respectively have given way of late, with the appearance of great institutes." Although the participants were specialists: "We are called upon to transcend the psychology of Daniel Boone, and to develop the psychology of the General Staff."·

Each speaker described a concrete research project, followed by discussion and, hopefully, synthesis. Lasswell spoke for the Local Community Research Committee at Chicago (1930, 28). May (1930, 35) wanted to select groups of individuals who were "by more or less consensus" typical of a "standard type of personality." Thomas favored studying behavior in large cultural groups to give methodological control. He wanted to contrast Scandinavian and Italian populations (1930, 41–43), following up on his earlier studies of Polish immigrants. The Mediterranean case would provide a control. Both societies were close enough to Thomas's to use the intuitions of his own culture, an advantage lacking to the field anthropologist.

Sapir's formal presentation was uncharacteristically experimental, presumably in response to the empirical mandate of the conference. Experimentalism further established his legitimacy in the face of the previous year's interest in formal methodology. Sapir categorized himself as "rather an outsider" to the conference because of his primary interest in speech (1930, 37). His entire oeuvre produced only two quasi-experiments about language, and he talked about them both.[3]

For the IJR, Sapir had studied "individual symbolism in the domain of speech" (1930, 37–39), noting how individuals responded to words independently of cultural influence by providing an "artificial context" of nonsense words that could be subjected to phonetic manipulation. The result was a "constellated system" of "intuitively felt symbolic relations between the varied sounds." Sapir felt that such "symbolic sets" could also be isolated for auditory, visual, and kinaesthetic phenomena, though he did not propose specific experiments. He concluded that human subjects have "a tendency to systematization of symbols regardless of overt experience." The study of language led him to a definition of culture in terms of symbol use.

Sapir's second experiment (1930, 39) dealt with the personality implications of the voice. He had isolated four or five "relatively distinct . . . layers of expression" ranging from the physiological to the "highly socialized." Sapir emphasized that "we react to speech keenly in ordinary life," although without consciously articulating its impressions. English vocabulary was, in fact, "strangely limited" in what would now be called paralinguistics. "Almost microscopic study of actual speech records" would develop the necessary vocabulary, although the work was programmatic.

Sullivan studied schizophrenics because (1930, 44) "one finds in almost laboratory simplicity the manifestations of complex processes that are combined in the more fortunate of us in such great complexity that they can scarcely be grasped." In clinical terms, Sullivan argued that simplifying the environment of the schizophrenic to whatever still interested him would lead to something like a normal life. Lasswell interjected an analogy to other "kinds of marginal situations," specifically primitive culture as studied by the anthropologist and the simplified world of the child (1930, 48).

The ensuing discussion was dominated by Sapir and Sullivan, with an occasional question from Thomas. Sapir, choosing an example from his own society, noted that life histories would reflect social evaluation (1930, 50); a successful businessman would gloss "uneasy spells" as "private and irrelevant," whereas an unsuccessful individual would exaggerate their importance. Thomas wanted more exotic examples, asking if climate or behavior determined Arctic hysteria (a "primitive" aberration familiar to most psychiatrists). Sapir (1930, 51) assumed "a socialized form of behavior" persisting independently of "the distribution of personality traits" once it was socialized. Eskimos probably had no more hysterics than any other society but "the real point is that our society has relatively little use for hysterics."

Thomas then asked about severity of stress in the Plains Crazy Dog Society relative to stress in modern life. He wanted Sapir to tell him how to interpret ethnographic reports. Sapir considered this "a rather large order" because "I don't quite see how we are going to measure the strain that society imposes upon us" (1930, 51). Plains Indians need not find the Crazy Dog syndrome stressful. "Much depends, of course, on the social background. You can project your own estimate of strain of course" (1930, 52).[4] The Plains Indian, moreover, would have no comparative basis on which to assess stress.

Sapir believed that the same individual, genetically, would have a different "chance of success or failure" in different societies (1930, 49). Modern America, for example, was less "favorably disposed" toward visions than many primitive societies. Indeed, "the potential psychosis is capitalized by [the primitive] society . . . which makes such an individual less abnormal in his social environment than he would be with us."

Lasswell (1930, 49) was curious about cross-cultural differences in willingness to talk about inner experience. The life history technique "presupposes certain cultural sets." Sapir agreed that expression of individual experience in "fantasy or speculation" was far from universal. He illustrated, without acknowledgement, by Ruth Benedict's contrast of the Pueblo and Plains cultures, with characteristically different reactions to the Ghost Dance and peyote cults. The Pueblos submerged individuality in public rituals, while the Plains encouraged "individualistic and autistic" behavior.

Sapir was not sufficiently confident "about the social psychology of these patterns of behavior" to respond to Sullivan's questions about friendship among males on the Plains, where military prowess was highly valued. He was convinced, however, that individuals differed considerably in the emotional valence of their response to cultural pattern (1930, 53):

Some would follow the pattern very blindly, in a sense unemotionally and unintending, others would realize themselves much more fully in these patterns. It is the same story that we find illustrated among ourselves in religion, for instance. We are all given the opportunity, as it were, for certain typical kinds of religious expression, but few avail themselves of these opportunities.

Sullivan ignored Sapir's modern American example, returning to the rebuff of affection that was critical for many of his male schizophrenic patients. Sapir agreed that different societies would provide different outlets to avoid "schizophrenic debauch." Sullivan noted the clinical effectiveness of separating male and female roles; Sapir responded in terms of sexual confession on the Plains before military action, the function presumably being similar (1930, 53). Both agreed that social acceptance was adaptive. Thomas broke into this dialogue to ask about confession in Plains culture. Sapir, who did not know the Plains firsthand, found response difficult (1930, 54):

The ethnologist is glad to get enough facts together to establish some sort of a case. You can't always get behind the facts and find out the ultimate motivations. Very often questions which are intended to elicit such information are not answered cooperatively, or are not fully understood. Then again you have to deal with the question of tribal rationalization.

Sapir wanted psychiatry to provide better methods for ethnography and rejected the role of purveyor of the exotic for his interdisciplinary colleagues. Thomas, however, returned immediately to Plains confession. Sapir thought it was probably "pretty common" but often "escaped" report. Psychiatry might define it as a feasible ethnological problem. He was uninterested when Sullivan pursued with Thomas the connection between confession and sexuality.

John Anderson of the Minnesota Child Guidance Clinic posed a case of a child who compulsively tied things (1930, 60). Sapir responded in terms of "symbolic consistency" and successive "reorganization of past experiences" (1930, 61, 64). The methodological problem was forcing unitary meaning on complex behavior, a difficulty that arose in ethnology as well as psychiatry (1930, 67):

[W]e are oversimplifying when we think that we can define a certain bit of behavior in purely objective terms. If one first considers the important factor of symbolic meaning of the behavior, one must in each case ask whether or not a given bit of behavior can be the same thing for all individuals. . . . We must learn to see each bit of behavior as not only what it is in measurable terms or as roughly estimated by society at large, but also as, in the individual case, something distinctly other than what it seems to be. There is the necessity of evaluating any type symbolically. I think we should get into the habit of thinking of this as a step in our procedure.

That is, behaviorism could not interpret the symbolic dimension of human behavior. This argument had to be repeated because many of the participants associated behaviorism with empiricism and, by implication, with science. None of the social sciences, moreover, had adequate methods to deal with the symbolic nature of culture. However logical Sapir's argument in principle, no one knew how to proceed in practice—even Sapir. His colleagues, however, continued to press him for ethnographic counterexamples to psychiatric generalizations. He continued to insist that cultural descriptions did not provide data for such speculation. Much of the ethnological literature was based on "reconstruction" from "the statements of a few old men and women." Culture change occurred at variable rates; some things were "absolutely gone, others are kept intact." Therefore, the ethnographer had to "weigh every single fact with reference to its personal, not merely tribal reality." Sapir considered this "a big job" and saw little evidence that it had been done.

In response to a question from Lawrence Frank, Sapir (1930, 86) reiterated that ethnological and contemporary cases were not qualitatively different. The study of "selected primitive groups" would require, however, considerable preliminary work:

[A] great many anthropologists are interested in just these problems, but they don't as a rule get very far, because it takes so very long to get acquainted with the native in other than a superficial sense. There is a very definite wall between you and the average primitive, even if you have got to the state of normal friendliness with them. . . . [It] would be none too easy to get life histories that would be of interest to psychiatrists. . . . I don't think it is possible to sail into an ethnological field with a few generalities in one's mind, ask a few questions and expect to get anything that is worthy of serious consideration. The work will require years of careful approach.

Frank wanted to know if a traditional cultural study would have to precede personality study. Sapir was optimistic, given "a joint enterprise of well trained field ethnologists, primitive linguists, psychologists, psychiatrists, economists, and other social scientists," that significant results could be obtained.

When the conference addressed a program for coordinated research, Sapir proposed a three-tiered approach (1930, 87): first, individual variation should be studied in American society, "remembering that we cannot easily define our own culture objectively." Second, "alien but not too distant cultures" should be investigated. Finally, field ethnologists should approach primitive cultures; although perhaps "the most important," these "parallel studies of the individual in different cultures" were "likely to lead to the most thankless results here and there." Sapir's program had room for everyone.

Human plasticity, for Sapir, was obscured "by the overt character of the materials of culture." Interpreted symbolically, however, the forms of intimacy could vary considerably without effecting its existence. Meaning was more important than external facts. Indeed, the normal person could adapt to "an almost infinite variety of social forms" (1930, 97).

Sullivan focused on "defective training" and superficial understanding of cross-disciplinary jargon (1930, 108), calling for teams of interdisciplinary specialists. James Plant of the Essex County Juvenile Clinic noted (1930, 115) that he preferred to start with psychiatric study of empirical cases already available. Thomas reiterated (1930, 121) the need for subjective materials even without guaranteed reliability and was delighted that Sullivan had agreed to "permit me to see his materials" to provide comparative data for the Scandinavian and Italian studies. For him, the interdisciplinary conferences were useful primarily in light of his own research plans.

Sapir concluded that the problem was "concentration," a need to decide "if we are merely going to dabble here and there within this tremendous terrain" or if there is a systematic program to be endorsed (1930, 122). In a "surgical but not hostile spirit," Sapir suggested that culture and social process per se should be left aside in favor of a focus on the individual. Personality was a good rallying concept, indeed (1930, 123) "the only thing that we really know anything about, inasmuch as we have a conception of ourselves and project that conception into all other bodies that we see about us." The psychiatric focus on personality was equally useful for the social sciences. Statistical data were useful only for "preliminary differentiation" of "types" of personality. The "document par excellence" for clarifying the concept of personality was the life history. Personality could not be isolated from "types of cultural background."

Sapir's typology of cultural backgrounds rationalized his three research foci, involving the daily experience of one's own society, the "friendly feeling" toward a similar culture, and the "remote" background of primitive humans (1930, 124). That is, he distinguished types of relations of the observer to the interpretation of data. Types of psychological adjustment were less easily categorized than the methods of interdisciplinary social scientists. Sapir spoke not as an anthropologist but as a synthesizer of research direction (1930, 124): "Cultural studies of primitive folk in the field" should be subordinated to "the work of studying personality in these given environments." Studies of American society should be of normal or near-normal behavior (though some degree of neurosis was probably necessary to insure a captive population for psychiatric-type study). Similar studies of schizophrenics would clarify the notion of abnormality. The extension to progressively more distant cultures would shed light on the universality or lack thereof of abnormal personality types. The approaches would act as controls on one another. Although no one knew much about the meaning of maladjustment in "the remoter cultures" (1930, 125), Sapir considered "a really profound attack" in two or three cultures "not entirely hopeless."

This statement of research priorities was taken more literally than Sapir had intended. He was nonplussed by the questions. Arnold Gesell wanted to know if he envisioned cross-sectional studies (1930, 125). Sapir was not familiar with the term and protested that he "wasn't thinking of crystallizing a program to quite that extent." He had no particular age group in mind. Challenged to clarify his negative attitude toward statistics, Sapir noted that statisticians chose problems "which would yield or seem to yield to statistical treatment." The "statistical magic circle" so prevalent in social science would not help much in studying individuals. Colleagues who resented Sapir's non-quantitative approach were not reassured.

Thomas shared Sapir's skepticism, noting frequent premature quantification in psychiatry and calling for "masses" of "divergent" life histories (1930, 127). Sullivan (1930, 131) denied "any possible source" for "these innumerable life histories"—although Thomas looked to him to provide them; even five cases would be "a very ambitious program."

Lasswell stressed the inadequacy of training within any single discipline (1930, 132). Thomas (1930, 133) wanted fellowships for social science interns in psychopathic hospitals. John Slawson of the Detroit Jewish Welfare Federation (1930, 134) articulated the fears of many participants, observing naively: "I am just a little bit frightened by Dr. Lasswell's statement that we have to train people as personality students. . . . It means the creation of a new profession, does it not?"

Sullivan jumped to Lasswell's defense (1930, 134), claiming that seven or eight courses would produce "precisely a new profession of people capable of studying their fellow man with some regard to the principles of science and with some aptitude for the securing of data." Lasswell (1930, 135) wanted to create researchers, not mere engineers. Others felt, however, that individuals could work their way into personality research from a number of different directions, as they themselves had done. Lasswell, Sullivan, and Sapir were virtually alone in seeing an integration to the yet-unborn profession which could not be attained on an ad hoc basis. Sullivan (1930, 138) emphasized the rigidity of medical training. Beginning medical students "know so many things that we don't think are right, you see, that we never quite break into each other's universe." Others from the psychiatric side confirmed this.

The conference ended on the "brink of the appointment of a continuing committee" (Lasswell 1930, 142). The APA, however, did not obtain funding for further colloquia on personality investigation and the institutional channel for the envisioned research dried up before it got started.

The National Research Council

Sapir served as chairman of the Division of Psychology and Anthropology of the National Research Council from 1934 to

1936. Although cultural anthropology was more obviously related to the mandate of the SSRC than of the NRC, Sapir had been stymied in his attempts to direct the former into channels of personality research he favored. The APA symposia were abortive, in spite of his enthusiasm for collaboration with Sullivan. He was, therefore, looking for a new outlet to realize their vision.

Sapir believed that disciplinary and subject boundaries were artificial. At Hanover in 1928, he emphasized that many problems in psychology and anthropology were of interest to both natural and social sciences: "You can't legislate in advance as to whether you are going to sheer over into physiology or into social phenomena" (NRC); although "theoretically anomalous," this was also "natural and healthy."

The National Research Council was established in 1916 by the National Academy of Sciences to meet wartime needs for natural science consolidation. Its Division of Anthropology and Psychology[5] was established in 1929. Psychology was considered a natural science because of its experimental character; initially, anthropology meant physical anthropology. The intention—like that of the SSRC and the philanthropic foundations—was "the encouragement of the isolated research worker, and the stimulation of institutions to support their own research" (Poffenberger 1933, 43). Of the anthropologists who served as chairman, Clark Wissler moved between psychology and anthropology, Albert Jenks was a physical anthropologist, A. V. Kidder was an archaeologist, Fay-Cooper Cole was by that time primarily an archaeologist, and only Robert Lowie—prior to Sapir—was a cultural anthropologist.

The scope of NRC anthropology, however, was broadening, with interdisciplinary cooperation between the two segments of the division increasingly salient. Sapir was a logical choice for chairman, because he was already the paramount interdisciplinary spokesman for the emerging personality study.

The NRC Culture and Personality Conference

Sapir, eager to mediate between psychology and anthropology, proposed a conference on personality and culture (Sapir to Marion Hale Britten, secretary to the Division, 8 February 1935:

NRC) to "work out a research program" dealing with "varying human behavior against different cultural backgrounds." He was careful to select "only such men as would be sincerely interested in our work" (Sapir to Britten, 22 March 1935: NRC). The resulting committee was heavily weighted toward Yale, including Wissler and May of the IHR, Francis Blake of the Medical School (where Sapir hoped to develop interdisciplinary collaboration), as well as Sapir himself. Sullivan, Adolf Meyer, and A. Irving Hallowell more explicitly supported Sapir, and their views predominated.

The conference was held at the American Museum, 6 March 1935, with Sapir in the chair. From the beginning, the issue was professional training. Sapir noted that much material "goes to waste in the ethnological field" because anthropologists are taught to select illustrations of group behavior rather than of individual variation. Variations in individual behavior were, however, easier to see in another society because not so "woven into our own lives."

Sapir's longest speech in the conference transcript deals with an issue that had concerned him since his 1917 critique of Kroeber's concept of the superorganic—the meaning of the term culture, as used by anthropologists. He identified three terms: society, culture, and behavior. "Society" was a term more familiar to interdisciplinary colleagues than culture. Sapir, moreover, was increasingly applying anthropological method to modern North American society, where the technical term culture was easily confused with its humanistic counterpart. Although he did not make a fully consistent distinction between the two terms, Sapir used "society" more frequently in interdisciplinary contexts.[6]

Anthropologists were not used to collecting the kind of behavioral data that a psychiatrist could use: "Anthropologists' data, while alluring . . . is a little too vague for someone who is dealing with an individual as an individual." Discussion made it clear that the term culture was understood differently by the participants. No one except Sapir, the only anthropologist present, wanted to confuse the debate by revising the conceptual apparatus of anthropology itself.

Sapir then attempted to switch to terms that had no technical meaning in his own discipline. The "insistence on a definition of unit" seemed to him "sound," although "society" was too large a unit to handle effectively. He thought that the individual, or perhaps the family, might be more useful. Sapir emphasized the meanings of categories in a given culture and whether they could be applied cross-culturally.

Sapir framed the problem of culture in terms of texts in the words of native speakers of a language, "of ideas and cultures in definite individuals." Culture would emerge "as a tendency toward a larger grouping of ideas." This analysis of culture, for Sapir, was prior to the notion of personality. Sullivan responded in terms of the usefulness of the concept of personality. Sapir as chair was forced to conclude that terms were perhaps best left to the individual researcher and topic.

Level of analysis was also a problem. Sapir thought that contrasting "violently different societies" was probably "not very fruitful." His example was taken directly from Benedict's *Patterns of Culture*. West Coast Indians were "the business men of the primitive Americans." Because of differences in use of resources and status attained thereby, however, there was "no direct comparison." And, indeed, Sapir did not compare Nootka rank and status to culturally familiar institutions.[7]

The group agreed to take the individual as its unit of study, though "not to dodge the institution as such." Sapir was encouraged "because I am rather sensitive to the general opinion of social anthropologists who are hard upon this sort of approach." He had long been a voice in the wilderness regarding the study of individuals. The psychologists, however, preferred to accept the existing conceptual apparatus of anthropology.

No progress had been made in training interdisciplinary students of personality since Sullivan's discussion at the 1928 APA colloquium. The 1935 NRC conference, however, established a Committee on Personality in Relation to Culture, with two subcommittees—the chairmen were Sullivan on training and Hallowell on a "handbook of psychological leads for ethnological fieldwork." Sapir sat on both ex officio.

The NRC Subcommittee on Training Fellowships

The Subcommittee on Training Fellowships met at the American Museum, 21 December 1935. Although its proposed program was abortive, it is a remarkable document in elucidating the concrete program Sapir, Sullivan, and Adolph Meyer envisioned. The group wanted to train cultural anthropologists in "personality methods" rather than the reverse. Two candidates were brought forward—

Stanley Newman, Sapir's postdoctoral student, and Morris Opler, a Sapir student at Chicago but more recently at an Apache field school with Ruth Benedict. Sullivan was already involved in Newman's studies of the "linguistic psychology" of vocal communication. A "modified psychoanalytic training" was necessary for either man to continue effectively.

Sapir argued strongly for Newman, describing his grammar of Yokuts as "the most beautiful—perhaps that is not the word some of you might use—story of an American Indian language that has ever been written, beautiful not only because the language is beautiful, but also because the treatment is highly balanced." Newman was "always aesthetic even when he seems most technical and formal." He felt "the relations of things, not merely the facts." Sapir emphasized that Newman's linguistic-psychology work followed up on his own research (Darnell 1989). Newman was eager to undergo training analysis. The only negative thing Sapir could say about him was that he was "thoroughly normal" and possibly lacked neuroses for analysis.

Benedict, although generally silent in subcommittee deliberations, spoke for Opler, emphasizing that Sapir had known him longer and perhaps dismissing Sapir's hyperbole over Newman as excessive: "I don't feel like speaking quite so glowingly about all of his personal advantages . . . but he is an intelligent young man, and if he wants to do this, I expect he would put his best into it." Sapir liked Opler's "fertility of thought and intense seriousness." Opler was "more active externally" than Newman, who "would like nothing better than to be let alone and given something intensely interesting, preferably of an aesthetic type, to do. He wants to understand people." Erich Fromm, one of the proposed training analysts for the project, thought the candidate should be as normal as possible, because the intention was to study normal behavior. Sullivan considered Opler probably no "more neurotic than great numbers of our students."

Other candidates were less seriously proposed. There were, however, a surprising number of people available to work in a field that did not yet exist, including Cora DuBois, Pearl and Ernest Beaglehole, Ruth Bunzel, Ruth Landes, and Walter Dyk. The group then turned to employment after training. Benedict thought the people would be "infinitely valuable" as long as funds were available to keep them in the field. Each should do fieldwork in several societies, to have a basis for comparison. Meyer emphasized that the disciplines would have to change and that the foundations would have to be educated. His goal was to get from "the anecdote stage" to "a basis that would be almost respectable." Wissler thought that one or two cross-cultural students of personality might be successful even if their work wasn't "quite regular."

Sullivan was pleased that none of the potential applicants seemed more interested in clinical work than research. It would be a shame to lose a good anthropologist "to produce a lay psychoanalyst." Sapir "couldn't imagine Newman ever wanting to analyze anybody." The psychiatrists wanted to protect their domain from untrained anthropologists by a clear division of labor. Sullivan clarified that he envisioned "sensitivity to certain kinds of data," not psychoanalysis per se. Kurt Lewin, Sullivan, and Fromm thought fieldwork in American society entirely reasonable. It was Sapir who observed: "Isn't that left to the sociologists to some extent?"

Meyer thought the training should not be exclusively psychoanalytic if the people were to be marketable. His own "commonsense psychiatry" (Lief 1948) was firmly grounded in medicine. At Johns Hopkins University, he argued against the dualism of mind and body and urged social science rapprochement as essential to adequate psychiatric training; he remained, however, profoundly discouraged by the mind set acquired by medical students. (Sullivan shared this position though he was less successful in finding institutional alternatives.) Although Meyer was more physiologically oriented than Sapir or Sullivan, his commitment to change in medical training made him an important ally, as did his professional status.

Sullivan stressed that the greatest gap was in cross-cultural data, which would probably prove at least as important to human behavior as "the biological heritage." For practical reasons, however, psychiatrists weren't going to do fieldwork, so anthropologists would have to learn to study personality.

Both Benedict and Sapir raised methodological issues about fieldwork on personality. Benedict was more optimistic that the training would enable anthropologists to interpret cultural associations encountered, for example, in dreams. She apparently expected subjectivity in fieldwork to disappear as a result of training analysis: "And the cultural anthropologists will have the perfectly beautiful opportunity of allowing psychoanalysts to give a completely impersonal attitude to their chosen students." The complexities of transference seem to have escaped her. Sapir, in contrast, saw the subjectivity of the fieldworker as a serious deterrent to useful work:

I must confess that I would attach very little importance to a personality analysis of a native tribe by a person who had not gone through a pretty careful clearing up process. I think the temptation to project one's own complexes is just too great. . . . I know in my own case I wouldn't dare express judgment with regard to the more intimate personal problems suggested by culture, without preliminary training. I might make interesting observations or suggest interesting leads, but I would consider I had no right to go very far. I think that is true, after all, with most people.

Sapir realized his own transferences and neuroses would interfere with personality fieldwork. He had long ago decided not to be analyzed himself, so others must be trained to do the work.

Sapir was fascinated by Sullivan's emphasis on "the importance of the apparently trivial patterns of behavior"—a "hobby" of his own being "the abolition of the word 'merely.'" The "intuitive person" interpreted small cues. He was less concerned about mistakes in "details of analysis" than in the point of view toward studying the individual in culture.

At a further session the same day, from which Sapir was absent, Benedict was more explicit about her own goals for the training program. The ideal was to make people "more objective." Cultural anthropology did not teach "sensitization . . . to a large number of meaningful constellations in human behavior." Fieldworkers, in spite of their lack of psychological training, had been bringing back "constellations that have never been thought of as fundamental in the behavior of the people." It was necessary to identity these features and their relationship.

Benedict emphasized the life cycle of the individual as an approach to "the life cycle of the culture." Sullivan was "thrilled" by this idea, although the absent Sapir would have been less so. The study of the individual was not, for him, a tool for historical reconstruction; cultures did not have life cycles in the same sense that individuals did.

The subcommittee was optimistic about its training program. Sapir secured explicit personnel commitments in the course of the meeting. Erich Fromm and Karen Horney[8] were to be supervising analysts, with Sullivan as overall supervisor. Meyer would commute weekly from Baltimore to New York.

Meyer wrote to Sapir (23 December 1935: JHU) that he was "particularly fascinated by the necessity of drawing history and linguistics as obligatory considerations into the field of training our own men" (in psychiatry). He had not realized how complex these issues were from a social science perspective and remained firmly convinced that "principles and opportunities for organizing material" would result, without expecting that "the amateur can do any good to the fields [psychiatric] himself." A medical degree and training analysis were prerequisite to personality study within psychiatry, even for Meyer.

Despite the Sapir–Sullivan–Meyer enthusiasm, however, the NRC executive committee rejected the training fellowship program, because it was "overweighted on the side of analysis" and had no checks on the methods used (Minutes, 25 October 1936: NRC): seventy thousand dollars over three years of the program, twenty thousand dollars intended for training analysis of the four students, was too high a price for an experiment. The program included training analysis, work in a mental hospital, and fieldwork in an unfamiliar society.

Sapir made a final plea for the fellowship training program at the executive committee meeting of 16 May 1936 (Minutes: NRC), at the end of his term as division chairman. The division had not found its niche in anthropology and psychology as "a sympathetic guiding body" with an "integrating role." Instead, the council had been perceived as "a mysterious sort of an organization without any very clear purpose." If, however, both disciplines could "put a completely fresh program up to some of the donors or foundations," the programs might still be salvaged.

Sapir's successor, Walter Hunter, felt that the division should support a few specialized projects, citing Rockefeller Foundation policy "to size up the men in the field, plus their projects, and give the money directly to men who have demonstrated ability, on the supposition that money so expended will bring in a return for the science." Sapir protested that good people did not enter a field without encouragement: "psychiatrists and anthropologists are in the grip of prestige, tradition, like everyone else, and tend to shy away from the border line fields." He lamented: "We cannot do anything without some money. We are just picking up crumbs these days." Unfortunately, however, the foundations were resolute in their changing priorities, and Sapir was left without support for his program, from the NRC or elsewhere.[9]

CHAPTER SEVENTEEN

The Impact Seminar: The Call to Yale

Yale News Services announced the appointment of Edward Sapir to the Social Sciences Division of the Graduate School on 12 January 1931, effective the following academic year. Yale president James R. Angell promised that Sapir would "draw these divisions [of the social sciences] together into a single group of studies and research projects" (YU). He would also head a new department of cultural anthropology, previously subsumed under sociology. The plans included additional anthropology appointments, cooperation with the Peabody Museum in New Haven and the Bishop Museum in Honolulu, fieldwork both in America and abroad, and a new division of human geography "to constitute a combined faculty covering the entire range of the Social Sciences."

Angell, a veteran of the great foundations, was excluded from the old-boy networks that dominated Yale politics. Personal ambition and academic experience jointly impelled him to seek a share for Yale of Rockefeller social science funding. Yale needed a superstar, and an SSRC-funded research–teaching program was an important coup for Angell, who was willing to pay a considerable price for his prize.

Sapir would also be a professor in the newly independent graduate department of linguistics; there would be no undergraduate program. The parts of this program were already established in the various departments of languages and literatures. Sapir found congenial colleagues among Yale's linguists, particularly Edgar Sturtevant and Franklin Edgerton. For the first time, he could train students adequately in linguistics. At Chicago, a working collaboration with Carl Buck's philology never developed. But Yale linguistics was more open to anthropology, and Sapir encouraged linguistic students to base themselves in that department. He was able to separate linguistics and anthropology for the first time in his career. He returned to Indo-European studies and developed his English grammar project with Newman and Swadesh partly in response to this new audience.

Though paramount for Sapir, all this was incidental to his appointment, which depended on his prestige in personality studies. The press release noted Sapir's expected collaboration with sociologists and psychiatrists at the Institute of Human Relations in a seminar on "the impact of culture on personality" supported by "a fund for the promulgation of project research." Ambitions for social science collaboration centered in the IHR, where Mark May was already integral to the interdisciplinary conference circuit, and Clark Wissler was an elder statesman of the social science–psychology interface. But they needed a superstar to pull it all together.

Sociology at Yale was dominated by Alfred Keller, student and successor of William Graham Sumner; it was evolutionary, comparative, and generally antithetical to the Boasian historical particularism that, for Sapir, was axiomatic. The Sumner–Keller "science of society" was equally alien to the empiricism of Chicago sociology (Murray 1986b). Sapir's appointment was arranged while Keller was in Europe, and Angell did not consult Keller, doubtless hoping to transcend the limitations of the outdated sociology program he had inherited. Keller would retain the popular undergraduate sociology courses, and Sapir would develop modern, well-funded, graduate research. Angell does not seem to have considered Sapir's welcome under these conditions.

In addition to vested interests in sociology and the Institute of Human Relations, Sapir would operate under subtle prejudice because of the Yale emphasis on undergraduate education. At Chicago, Columbia, and other major universities, graduate research was paramount; at Yale, the reverse was true. Sapir's appointment was to the graduate school; moreover, Sapir was a Jew. Although he did not practice the religion of his childhood, the Yale faculty had few Jews and they were not permitted to teach undergraduates (Oren 1986). Sapir's colleagues at Chicago had predicted these difficulties, without affecting his optimism for the position.

In retrospect, these problems were virtually insurmountable. For Sapir, however, the call to Yale seemed the culmination of his academic

success at Chicago. Chicago, whatever its Rockefeller-induced prestige, was an upstart institution. The prestige of Yale attracted him.
Money, moreover, was always a problem. Sapir supported both his
parents and had four children when he left Chicago; he lost money
in the bank closures at the beginning of the Depression (Edward to
Jean Sapir, 28 June 1931: SF); his older children were of college age.
He gave public lectures to earn extra money. In this context, the almost unheard-of offer of $12,000 salary was both materially welcome
and psychologically satisfying. Sapir felt that Chicago had not tried
very hard to keep him (David Sapir, p.c.); his position was, however,
kept open for more than a year should he wish to return. Chicago
could not outbid Yale because the Rockefeller Foundation was supporting the project that moved him to Yale.

In addition, Sapir was offered five thousand dollars annually for
fieldwork for himself and his students, a group of whom followed him
to Yale. Although Cole at Chicago was not an onerous superior, Sapir
had been in charge of the program in Ottawa, and the independence
of doing so again appealed to him. Promises of departmental expansion, student support, and IHR collaboration were impossible at Chicago where there were already a number of superstars in residence.

The Peabody Museum was the only place where Sapir's appointment did not impinge on vested interests. Dean Edgar Furniss sought
support for Sapir's appointment from its director Richard Lull (7 November 1930: YUPM). Lull replied (6 November 1930: YUPM):
"while he is not known personally to some of us, he is known by
reputation" and would be entirely welcome in the museum. Sapir was
no threat to museum autonomy because of its focus on natural history.
Anthropology there was under the direction of Cornelius Osgood,
Sapir's student at Chicago. Osgood (1985, p.c.) believed himself responsible for bringing Sapir to Yale; Osgood's own appointment,
however, was probably partially dependent on his potential influence
on Sapir (Irving Rouse, p.c.). Certainly, the "impact" seminar was "in
the works" by early 1930 when Osgood was offered his position.

The Call to Columbia

Neither Boas nor Sapir forgot about the linguistic position at Columbia. Sapir was already negotiating his move to Yale

when Boas again raised the issue. Sapir thanked Boas (1 October 1930: APS) for thinking of him "once more" and declined to decide without a concrete offer. But, in sum, "perhaps it would be better for you not to make the recommendation." Sapir's tone was gentle; Boas had lost his chance and both must have realized it.

Boas, however, was finally able to dispense his department to the heirs of his choice. On 17 February 1931 (APS), he wrote to Sapir and Kroeber, offering each a professorship at Columbia. The tone was humble; Boas realized that both men had commitments that might prove more attractive, despite personal loyalties. He played on those loyalties. Sapir (19 February 1931: APS) was "gratified" at the "splendid opportunity" that Boas had been "working toward . . . for several years." He did not imply that the offer was long overdue. Sapir, however, could not have extricated himself from the negotiations to move to Yale. His commitment there was, moreover, long-range. He was "practically certain" to remain at Yale. "In any event, I am looking forward with the keenest interest to working in the East again in the hope of being in closer touch with you." Boas, however, did not give up (26 February 1931: APS): "my wish would be to have you take full charge of the department of linguistics with full liberty to give whatever you like in anthropology." The position was created for Sapir and would not be offered to anyone else. "I am, of course, very much disappointed that the movement on the part of Columbia has not been made a couple of years sooner which would have made everything much easier." Tenacity, however, was no substitute for the momentum of an academic career, and Sapir's was on a different course. Sapir (4 March 1931: APS) reiterated that the arrangements at Yale were particularly attractive, in spite of the "sentimental" advantages of Columbia.

Sapir hoped that Kroeber, at least, would accept Boas's offer (to Kroeber, 20 February 1931: APS), joking that he was "already fantasying a New Haven–New York anthropological club!" The presence of this letter in Boas's papers implies it was written at his request. Kroeber, however, misread Sapir's letter and assumed the Yale situation was temporary. Sapir hastily clarified (26 February 1931: UCB) that he had initially intended a sabbatical but had now accepted a Sterling Professorship. Sapir had given Yale a salary figure he considered nearly ridiculous and "a string of conditions—all accepted." "I am sorry to have to say no to Boas after all these years, but it can't be helped." Kroeber could dictate his own terms: "Columbia needs you badly and you have a strategic position."

Sapir (to Kroeber, 8 April 1931: UCB) was disappointed when Kroeber also declined. Ostensibly, he balked at moving across the country. But California gave him greater independence of the Columbia home base than any other American anthropologist of his generation. That network could not be transferred to New York, and it was late in life to establish a new one.

Whatever the personal cost, Boas gracefully accepted the decisions of both men, remarking wistfully to Kroeber (9 March 1931: APS): "It would have been a great pleasure to have worked with you and Sapir for a few years." Boas was denied, however, the patriarchal satisfaction of spending his last years surrounded by prodigal sons returned. They remained attached to the Boasian network, but Columbia was a place to visit, no longer home. Sapir retained the impulse to go home again longer than did Kroeber, but both developed contexts for their work to which Boas was, at best, peripheral. Ironically, Boas lived long enough that his first generation of students could not succeed him directly, having committed their energies elsewhere.

Kroeber's position was more ambivalent than Sapir's. He was concerned about Boas's role in the reorganized department. The dean (Boas to Kroeber, 18 February 1931: APS) promised Boas he could retain emeritus status indefinitely. "In other words, the present plan is that the three of us would be here at least for some time to come." Although Boas intended to retire as soon as his protegés were firmly in control, Kroeber understood that interference was inevitable. Boas's habit of control was well-established, and Kroeber realized that the length of a continent had sheltered him from it for thirty years. Although Kroeber's personality recoiled from confrontation, he could not accept a nominal role while Boas ran the department.

Boas, however, had planned well. Kroeber was tempted, particularly by the simultaneous offer to Sapir. He wired Boas (26 February 1931: APS) to confirm Sapir's final refusal; Boas tried again to induce Sapir to accept. There was, of course, no potential of conflict between Sapir and Kroeber, who had done little linguistic work since the early California years. Kroeber enjoyed academic administration. Sapir would have been content to be sheltered from it, as he was by Cole at Chicago.

All things considered, Kroeber declined the "larger opportunities" of New York, though with regret. Regret, however, was insufficient to convince him to attempt to succeed the still-active teacher who had virtually created the structure of his discipline, at times seemingly by force of will alone. American anthropology might have been quite different had Boas succeeded in engineering his own succession according to his plan.

The Frank Seminar Proposal

Lawrence Frank's proposal for a seminar of foreign fellows to study the impact of culture on personality in their own cultures was designed to provide an empirical baseline for interdisciplinary personality study. Sapir was the obvious person to lead the project but two institutions were possible—Chicago and Yale. Donald Schlesinger of the IHR wrote to Edmund Day of the Rockefeller Foundation (10 February 1930: RAC) that Wissler was interested in having Sapir direct the project at Yale. Sapir would be able to spend a semester sabbatical at Yale, and "Wissler was under the impression that he would be delighted to come and supervise the project." The SSRC committee would consist of Wissler, Sapir, and W. I. Thomas,[1] who was also "anxious to take part." Schlesinger assured Day that the IHR program would be more integrated than that of the Chicago LCRC.

After a visit to Chicago where he informally sounded out Sapir, Schlesinger reported to Day (28 February 1930: RAC) that Sapir had enough "accumulated vacation credit" for a leave in 1931. Meanwhile, Thomas could work through the Paris office of the Rockefeller Foundation to select the fellows. Moreover (Schlesinger to Day, 18 March 1930: RAC), Angell was "anxious to contribute [financial] services," although "the Chicago group would like very much to have some hand in the game." Schlesinger favored Yale, emphasizing that May, the new executive secretary of the IHR, was "a good psychologist with a keen interest in the personality problem"; Chicago still had no integrated program.

At this point, Sapir became officially involved, through the SSRC problems and policy committee. Frank (to Sapir, 31 March 1930: LC) considered the seminar "a method of advancing the study of contemporary cultures in a systematic fashion simultaneously in a number of different countries." The "leading students of anthropology and sociology" from these countries would formulate "an inventory or schedule" for the "impact of institutional social life upon the individual therein." The Rockefeller Foundation would provide fellowships to the students. Although two universities were interested, "the plan obviously transcends the resources of any single university and involves the participation of individuals in various institutions throughout the country and perhaps abroad"; it was, therefore, crucial to involve the SSRC in coordinating the plan, although the Rockefeller Foundation would be quite directly in control.

When Frank raised the seminar proposal at Hanover in August 1930, fairly detailed plans were already in place (Record: RAC). The "systematic" inventory would be supervised by American specialists in personality study; the fellows would study their nationals in America, participate in a second seminar collaboration, and return to their own countries to study personality there. "The essential desideratum is to develop a pattern of cultural research." At Hanover, Sapir picked up the thread of Frank's proposal, suggesting that American students should be excluded so they wouldn't intimidate the foreign fellows and that the guest lecturers should "act as critics, presenting an organized point of view." He emphasized that Frank had "available personal contacts and institutional machinery" to put the plan into operation; his own role remained tacit.

The following fall, May, acting as a go-between for Angell, followed up Yale's claim with Frank (28 November 1930: YU). Yale offered eighteen thousand dollars for a year's program, "the full-time services of a distinguished anthropologist with whom we are now negotiating," who would "work in close affiliation with your committee, forming the personal link between it and Yale," the part-time services of Wissler "who would doubtless wish to take as active a part in the project as his time will permit," a junior anthropologist as assistant, a seminar room at the IHR, and a dormitory section at nominal cost. There is no record that Chicago made a concrete proposal.

The SSRC committee (Frank to May, 1 December 1930: IHR) "voted unanimously in favor of locating the seminar at Yale and appointed Sapir director and [John] Dollard assistant." The only remaining cost was for the expenses and honoraria of the visiting speakers. Frank felt that SSRC control was crucial to ensure participation: "I do not want anything to be said or done which will compromise that independent status."

Frank's undated memorandum to Day (1930: RAC) emphasized

that the inventory would be used "not only by anthropologists but also by sociologists, psychologists and psychiatrists"; that is, the project was to be genuinely interdisciplinary. Nonetheless, anthropologists had "gradually evolved" useful methods of studying culture "which they use in their fieldwork." The seminar would run like a "prolonged conference," utilizing the "life experience" of the students' cultures and transcending the limitations of experience in any single culture. The students would be young professionals because "outstanding persons" would not be able to spend a year. Sapir would follow up on a "systematic" visiting lecture program to "interpret and unify the individual contributions of the various seminar leaders." The inventory would shed light on mental disorder and crime in a variety of societies, practical results of concern to the Rockefeller Foundation if not to the academic participants. The countries represented were less important than the caliber of the students. Frank clearly expected impressive results.

John Dollard

The decision to appoint John Dollard as the assistant to the impact seminar was apparently Sapir's. Dollard studied sociology with Ogburn at Chicago but did not know Sapir well there (Carey interview with Dollard, 14 April 1972: UC). In 1931, Dollard was offered a job as head of the Paris office of the Rockefeller Foundation, which he felt inspired Sapir's "sudden" invitation to assist him in organizing the Yale seminar. Dollard, in spite of a smaller salary at Yale, preferred "to cast his lot with university work." Dollard was unusual in the Chicago sociology department because of his interest in psychoanalysis, which he had undergone briefly because he was "very neurotic." Dollard's sociological and psychological background balanced Sapir's cultural emphasis; moreover, Dollard had intimate contacts with foundation bureaucrats. Dollard retrospectively described Sapir as a narrow-minded Boasian who failed to comprehend the emerging perspective (Carey interview, 14 April 1972: UC): "He was a strict Boasian and . . . he had these disembodied culture traits walking around. Whereas we in Sociology had something you could recognize as a human community." In any case, Sapir negotiated an assistant professor position for Dollard as a condition of his own appointment (Sapir to May, 19 December 1930: YU). Dollard would teach social psychology and do research through the IHR.

The seminar was postponed until 1932–1933. Sapir was not told the reasons, although he reported to May (9 March 1931: YU): "I have no doubt they are weighty." Day reassured Sapir (18 March 1931: RAC) that the Paris office couldn't get the fellows in time for the fall, and the students needed time for preparation and to practice their English. Dollard would be "even more valuable" with the additional year's experience; the delay involved "no diminution of enthusiasm or confidence." In a further letter (7 April 1931: RAC), Day noted that an SSRC fellowship for Dollard removed "the only commitment which you felt might involve possible embarrassment."

Dollard spent the SSRC fellowship in Germany, considering it "my absolute dream" (Carey interview, 14 April 1972: UC), and was much more committed to psychoanalysis by the time the Impact Seminar actually began. After training analysis, he taught psychoanalysis "from a general social science standpoint." His research combined psychoanalytic and sociological methods in interpreting life histories.

Bingham Dai, the Chinese representative, was more interested in personality than in culture and recalled (to Darnell, 18 December 1985) that Dollard introduced the psychoanalytic approach and influenced Dai's decision to undergo psychoanalysis. Sapir's influence was more diffuse. Dollard had more contact with the students. Sapir was more distant, perceiving his role as master of ceremonies for the visiting dignitaries (Philip Sapir, p.c.); there were, however, a number of social occasions and group meetings at the Sapir home (Michael Sapir, p.c.).

Selection of the Fellows

The selection of fellows was made "in every case" by the SSRC committee, with Dollard as its delegate in Europe. With the exception of the Japanese, Chinese, and Indian delegates, the Paris Office of the Rockefeller Foundation was administratively responsible. In practice, the correspondence was between various Rockefeller Foundation officials in the United States and Sapir as the director of the seminar. Sapir, however, did not contradict Frank's judgment. Dollard reported directly to the foundation. Dollard visited Germany, Poland, and Hungary and proposed various alternative candidates (Tracy Kittredge to Frank, 28 December 1931: RAC). Kittredge (to Frank, 8 February 1931: RAC) emphasized that candidates were most suitable in Scandinavia, Germany, or Poland where research traditions already existed.

Thomas wanted to appoint "a social statistician who was acquainted with Swedish social welfare work and legislation" who would be useful to his own planned study in Sweden; the candidate had no background in personality study (Frank to Sapir, 25 February 1932: RAC). Thomas claimed that no one else was available in Sweden (Frank to Sapir, 29 March 1932: RAC). Sapir (to Frank, n.d. March 1932: RAC) was willing to recommend Thomas's candidate but wanted "something tangible" to present to the SSRC committee. Frank thought (to Sapir, 23 March 1932: RAC): "This was all right from Thomas's point of view, but I don't think it is very good for the Seminar." The candidate was rejected.

Sapir felt that one candidate was too old and that a non-Jewish candidate would be preferable (to Frank, 14 March 1932: RAC): "After all, we cannot afford to have the Seminar criticized for having no less than three Jewish fellows out of a total of fifteen. It seems to me that we cannot very well allow more than two." Sapir would rather eliminate a country than include a primarily literary man (to Frank, 29 March 1932: RAC). Frank responded (30 March 1932: RAC) that a Latin representative other than French was required to balance the Scandinavian and German contingent; moreover, "I am personally much interested in the role of art and aesthetic experience in personality development." Sapir agreed (to Frank, 30 March 1932: RAC), although on grounds of "the difficulty of getting a[nother] candidate from Italy at short notice."

The Program of the Seminar

The Yale Catalogue for 1931–1932 followed Frank's proposal quite literally, advertising "a seminar course on the meaning of culture, its psychological relevance for personality, its value relativity, and the problem of reconciling personality variations and cultural variations. Open only to specially selected fellows under the Rockefeller Foundation grant for foreign fellowships." Frank's intention

(Mead 1966) was "to get very high level, first class people from modern cultures all around the world, bring them here as Rockefeller fellows, put them together and let *them* think out the relationship between the growing field of culture and personality and their own cultures."

A series of undated memos from Sapir in 1932 clarify his planning for the seminar (LC) and represent his thinking about personality research at this time. Preliminary reading would clarify the fellows' picture of contemporary America and introduce the anthropological use of the term culture. Three of the five books recommended were Boasian: Boas's *The Mind of Primitive Man*, Kroeber's *Anthropology*, and Wissler's *Man and Culture*. The Lynds' study of Middletown presented the "everyday cultural status of a typical small town in contemporary America," ostensibly using anthropological methods, and Dewey's *Human Nature and Conduct* presented the pragmatist basis of behaviorist social science. The fellows were expected to practice their English, survey the culture-and-personality literature available in their own countries, and prepare "a rather careful autobiography with particular reference to the psychological factors." Sapir was interested in the "relation of the fellow's own personality to the national culture which he represents . . . so far as the fellow is himself able to make such an analysis." He also wanted "some acquaintance with the background of the fellows before they arrive in New Haven."

Students should not worry about defining culture or personality because the seminar would do that. A "preliminary stock-taking" of personal cultural values would be useful. Sapir emphasized that the definition of personality would be "synthetic," that is, directed to social science concerns and not slavishly Freudian. Sapir's summary of the aims was more anthropological than psychological or psychiatric, emphasizing "the meaning of culture, its relativity and its bearing on personality." Seeds of discord were implicit, since Dollard returned committed to a fairly orthodox Freudianism.

Sapir's syllabus further clarifies his concept of personality research. Boasian anthropology was represented by Boas, Goldenweiser, Kroeber, Lowie, Radin, and Wissler; the only other anthropologists were Malinowski and Edward Tylor, putative father of the discipline. Sapir included his own *Language* and *Time Perspective*, as well as six articles in which he summarized the interdisciplinary perspective;[2] these papers substituted for his unwritten book *The Psychology of Culture*. Sociology was represented by Cooley, Dewey, Kenton, Ogburn, Trotter, and Veblen. Edited volumes by Rice, W. I. Thomas and Ogburn, and Goldenweiser—all including papers by Sapir—attempted interdisciplinary synthesis. Case studies from Chicago sociology were omitted. Psychological works reflected Sapir's own eclecticism: Freud, Adler, Jung, Koffka (gestalt psychology), and Rivers and McDougall (British psychology). Kretschmer and Huntington introduced biological perspectives and Teggart historical ones.

The seminar consisted of two weekly lectures on culture the first semester and on personality (by Dollard) the second semester. The "nuclear course" for the first semester (LC) included: connotations of the term culture, the nature of social science, the difference between culture forms and individual behavior, the race concept, the "supposed psychological causation of culture," and environment and culture. The seminar would then address the construction of a typical cultural scheme that is independent of particular societies, especially in terms of the functions of culture. The reorientation of Boasian anthropology toward pattern, psychology, and configuration was explicit:

... the possibility of studying culture from the point of view of the history and geographical distribution of isolated elements and of elements associated into complexes, some of which are fortuitous, others of which have an inherent functional interrelationship. The value and limitations of the purely objective anthropological viewpoint will be discussed and an inquiry started into the reality and possibility of isolation of psychological patterns in cultural behavior. The configurative point of view will be stressed ... and attention drawn to the multiple interpretation of outwardly similar cultural data.

The second semester would emphasize "the artificiality of the usual contrast between society and the individual"; "the analysis of culture will be put to a side for a while" in favor of personality topics, including early adjustment, personality type, formation of individual symbolisms, "and the relation of these to the impersonal symbolisms of society." Sapir hoped that "something like a typology of culture" would emerge. Psychoanalysis would be handled "both sympathetically and critically." The inventory was "a kind of finder in the investigation of the symbolic significance of different types of behavior in varying societies." Cultural forms had different values in different societies, but underlying meanings were similar. Sapir hoped that at least some of the students would be able to "prepare something like an interpretation of [their] native culture, or at least some significant facet of it."

Every other week, a guest lecturer spent five days giving three talks and consulting with the fellows. The students made periodic reports and prepared a questionnaire about their own cultures (Dai to Darnell, 18 December 1985). Speakers had considerable leeway in subject matter and were not always germane to the seminar topic. Lasswell, in an undated memo to Sapir (LC), suggested that he could discuss the functional approach to American politics "which is the recent emphasis in political science (like hell)," or personality factors in the fate of organizations, or propaganda and political strategy. The invited guests were cronies from the conference circuit, many of them from Chicago, all well known to Sapir.

There are several lists of the guest speakers and topics, some of which reflect intentions rather than actualities. Dai's list, based on his class notes, is taken as definitive. It includes Louis Wirth, Thomas, Frank, Sullivan, Frederick Wells, M. S. Handman, Frank Knight, Lasswell, James Plant, and R. H. Gabriel. Several speakers were locally available without honorarium. Dai's notes record volunteer lectures by Dorothy Thomas, primatologist Robert Yerkes, Florien Znaniecki (Thomas's collaborator in his Polish peasant study), Erik Erikson (on hypnosis), and Thomas (on his SSRC report on personality-and-culture program orientation). May lectured once on personality research and again on the work of the IHR.

The students formed a club to run their own affairs, which entertained the visiting lecturers and occasionally invited the directors to join them (LC). Dormitory life encouraged discussion outside of official classes (Wirth to Sapir, 9 February 1933: UC), although some fellows resented the "paternalistic touch" of the arrangements. Wirth noted that the students were initially shocked by the informality of North American academic style; however, by the end of the year they "were chewing gum in seminar meetings and taking off coats at the conference table on hot days."

The students prepared reports on religion, family life, and etiquette according to a standard format (LC). Because these were not available to other students, however, their effect was only for the authors (and the organizers) (Walter Beck final report, 17 July 1933: LC). Nor were they considered sufficiently systematic for publication; they were designed for "qualitative and exploratory" work rather than statistical comparison (LC). The personal nature of much of the material required specific permission to use it. Students' work was read mainly by Dollard, who taught no other courses; both organizers, however, spent considerable time in consultation with the fellows.

The original plan of collaboration between organizers, guest lecturers, and fellows was not feasible because of gaps in the background of the fellows. A second year would have been necessary to turn the students into bona fide researchers.

The students prepared a set of lecture notes from the nuclear course (LC). These notes are uneven in quality but give some indication of what Sapir presented to the group. Topics included personality types (Jung), anxiety in the modern world, the adjustment of individuals to the requirements of society, signs and symbols, and speech as a symbolic system. Sapir's summary of culture and personality (9, 25 May 1933: LC) was open-ended. He aimed to make the students "feel deeply skeptical about the biological, the psychological or the sociological viewpoints about 'culture' and 'personality.' " Social sciences should study concrete behavior of specific individuals.

During Christmas vacation, each student was expected to observe "scientific work in the U.S." outside New Haven; topics included criminology, race relations, psychiatric hospitals, primitive behavior, and labor relations. The students' first-term reports reflected the reorientation of their thinking but no synthesis. Dai (4 January 1933: LC) summarized his response:

Being a sociologist in my previous training, I have been more or less concerned with the immediate group or cultural reference of an individual's behavior, not quite realizing the role played by the very early experiences of a person and practically ignoring the individual differences due to inheritance. Nor have I been sufficiently aware of the unconscious motivation of behavior.

The seminar had "broken down this professional bias." Walter Beck (31 December 1932: LC) was initially frustrated by the "passivity" of the group in response to lecture materials and the antagonism toward empirical research. He found it difficult to identify scientific method in the "promiscuity of terms and approaches." But he acknowledged the effort to "make the group familiar with the . . . dynamic field, to create a certain vocabulary . . ." Discussion required common background.

For the summer holiday, each student picked a longer project. Clinics and prisons were again popular. Two students returned to Europe, and one compared Cajuns to French Canadians.

Evaluations of the students by Wirth (to Sapir, 9 February 1933: UC), Thomas, Sapir, and Dollard agreed closely. Several of the fellows were out of their depth; they came from countries without research traditions to prepare them for the work. Wirth noted that lack of sensitivity to the cultural background of such students influenced negative impressions.

Dai, the only seminar student to remain in North American academic life, completed a sociology doctorate at Chicago and a medical degree in China, returning to teach psychiatry at Duke University before the Japanese invasion in 1937 (p.c.). He recalled the encouragement of Thomas (to Murray, 3 June 1987), who commented at the time that Dai would be "a first-rate risk if he is not ruined by being drawn into psychoanalysis" (to Stacy May, 13 April 1933: RAC). Wirth expected Dai to return to China with an integrated perspective impossible at any single American university or in any one discipline. Sapir found him "stubborn and independent" and expected much of him. Sapir and Dollard (Stacy May notes, 29 March 1933: RAC) agreed that he was the most promising student "on the personality side." Dai thought the seminar "produced its expected results" only in the case of Andreas Angyal and himself (to Darnell, 18 December 1985). He did not address the question of fellows being expected to return to their own countries and stimulate personality research there.

Max Weinreich, director of the Yiddish Scientific Institute in Vilna, Poland [Lithuania], impressed Thomas as likely to get "more intimate stuff" than most people due to his intense commitment to Judaism; but he was not a really creative mind. Wirth considered Weinreich a "first-rate scholar" who had previously worked "under such great hardship." He would study his own people effectively, with "a vision of the inclusiveness of cultural phenomena and their interrelationships." Weinreich was a linguist, with only peripheral interest in culture and personality. He was the most congenial of the fellows to Sapir intellectually, however, and the two remained friends (Sapir family p.c.).

Robert Marjolin was a social economist, much younger than the other participants, representing France in spite of the distance of his work from the seminar topic. All reporters agreed that he was intellectually outstanding. Marjolin went on to a distinguished career, becoming one of the planners of the early European Economic Community.

Andreas Angyal became director of research at the Worcester State Hospital; the seminar did not direct him toward cultural topics but furthered his prior career direction.

The thirteen fellows represented eight disciplines (psychiatry, psychology, criminology, sociology, literature, education, economics, and linguistics—interestingly, there were no anthropologists) and eleven countries (Germany (two), Poland (two, including Weinreich), Hungary, Sweden, Finland, Italy, France, India, China, Japan, and Turkey. Unsurprisingly, the great synthesis of their diverse backgrounds did not emerge in the single year of the seminar. Nonetheless, all of them wanted to continue related work, making relative assessment crucial.

Results of the Impact Seminar

The direct results of the seminar were disappointing, both to the organizers and the participants. Two of the fellows died soon after its conclusion, one in the course of his summer fieldwork. Ten of the thirteen fellows applied for renewal of their fellowships, but the Rockefeller Foundation ruled legalistically that the applications would be treated as new ones. In an in-house memo to John van Sickle, Stacy May (n.d. 1933: RAC) expressed his belief that "those responsible for the Seminar have not made themselves responsible for the development of a coherent project that urges support . . . upon its inherent merit." The summer programs had no group integration. The foundation was not responsible for "a continuity which they have allowed to lapse." Nothing this explicit was said to the organizers, however. Both Sapir and Dollard tried to obtain further support. Sapir (to Stacy May, 29 March 1933: RAC) supported eight applications and Dollard seven, based on the individual career patterns of the fellows rather than the expectation of an integrated program. One student, oriented toward belles lettres rather than social science, wanted to work on symbolism, and Sapir proposed to direct him "by correspondence." May (to Van Sickle, 24 April 1933: RAC) felt that the literary man, Leo Ferrero, "might do brilliant work by cutting across academic categories." Nonetheless, "our training might spoil a good artist and make a mediocre social scientist." Ferrero died shortly afterward.

Sapir and Dollard submitted a joint evaluation (Sapir to Stacy May, 22 May 1933: RAC). The seminar was "a decided success" because each of the fellows "profited in many distinctive ways" that would show up in their future work. Sapir acknowledged that the SSRC committee may have expected more systematic results, but goals had to be tailored to the needs of the students. Their background made it impossible to "prepare a general outline of cultural patterns from a psychological point of view so as to have something . . . as an authoritative guide for future work in cultural studies." The organizers contented themselves with the "much humbler" task of "providing the students sophistication in the definition and interpretation of culture . . . for the proper understanding of the genesis and development of personality types."

Sapir stressed that the students had very different backgrounds, all unrelated to the integrative intent of the seminar. Sapir and Dollard argued that social psychology could mediate between the formal cultural disciplines and the "segmental studies of human behavior" characteristic of academic psychology. "We believe that it is no mean achievement to have created this common mode of thought." They wanted to continue supervising the more promising students informally for a second year of the program. Stacy May responded (3 June 1933: RAC) that the project as such would be discontinued, though individual renewals would be considered through the Paris office. "There is, of course, not the slightest implication that the work which was done by the Seminar is judged to have been unfruitful."

Sapir wrote to Dollard (10 June 1933: RAC) that "perhaps we can save something." Dollard was apparently quite involved emotionally with the project, writing to May (12 June 1933: RAC) from the Worcester State Hospital where he was doing summer research, expressing his disappointment, not "as a reproach, but [because] I have shared the wishes and hopes of the members of the group so warmly that I cannot escape also being disappointed with them." Indeed, the fellows felt that they were treated unfairly. Walter Beck wrote to Dollard (18 July 1933: RAC): "To be a member of the Seminar seems to be a distinct disadvantage in the considerations of the European representatives." The Rockefeller Foundation was extricating itself from social science research, and Sapir's schemes for implementing his research plans through foundation projects were again abortive.

The Impact Seminar did not meet the promise Frank, Sapir, Dollard, and Thomas had envisioned for it. Margaret Mead (1966) co-opted the seminar records for her cultures-at-a-distance studies in the 1940s but never acknowledged her use of them.[3] Moreover, Mead's version of Sapir's contribution to culture and personality is remarkably minimal. She credits Frank with the idea, and Sapir and Dollard equally with its execution. That Sapir had a particular approach to interdisciplinary social science does not emerge from her inclusion of him only in a list of honored predecessors (introduction to *The Study of Culture at a Distance*: LC).

CHAPTER EIGHTEEN

The Academic Program at Yale: Anthropology

Sapir's prestigious Sterling professorship at Yale was awarded jointly in the departments of anthropology and linguistics; because he was expected to divide his teaching between them, many of his courses were not offered regularly. The number of graduate students was modest, however, and a variety of topics better served their needs. Sapir encouraged his linguistic students to enroll in the linguistics department. His authority there was sufficient to ensure their training; supplementary training was in comparative philology rather than ethnology. More of Sapir's Yale students were linguists than at Chicago; ethnologists in anthropology were supervised by Leslie Spier.

Voegelin and Harris (1952, 323–324) argue that until the mid-1930s linguists trained in anthropology departments were "linguistically weak"; only Indo-European was considered real linguistics. By this criterion, only Sapir, Michelson, Harrington, and Li, among the Americanist anthropologists, were linguists. Paradoxically, anthropologists learned mostly "descriptive analysis of unwritten languages" but were taught to value "sophistication in comparative linguistics." In any case, Sapir compartmentalized linguistics and anthropology during his Yale years. Voegelin and Harris (1945, 324) assert that most of the Yale students would rather have majored in anthropology: "Perhaps Sapir felt that linguists were non-anthropological beings who had to work in a frame of reference of their own." They argue on Sapir's behalf, however, that the new techniques of linguistics (phonemics and

Bloomfieldian avoidance of meaning) were "uniquely fitted to the data of language, rather than to culture in general" (1945, 324–325). Linguistics no longer used the same methods as anthropology.

Sociology had been taught at Yale since 1902 by William Graham Sumner (who retired in 1909) and since 1903 by his protegé Alfred Keller. George Peter Murdock was hired in 1928 as the anthropologist among the sociologists. The Sumner–Keller tradition relied heavily on comparative data from primitive societies for its evolutionary view of the "science of society"—the title of the program. Various sociologists taught courses with apparent anthropological content during the early years of Sapir's appointment. "Modern," that is, Boasian, anthropology was alien to Yale sociology. Keller's power base in undergraduate curriculum and local politics was less important to Sapir than the emerging interdisciplinary social science. In the long run, Sapir was right—but his life was made miserable in the interim by lack of rapport between the supposedly related disciplines.

Keller felt that anthropology as he defined it was integral to sociology; the Yale catalogue for 1929–1930 included in the scope of sociology "both theoretical and applied courses in Anthropology, Ethnology, and the Science of Society. The controlling viewpoint of the Department is evolutionary adjustment." Murdock's ethnology courses were moved to anthropology, but Sapir did not accept him as an anthropologist. Murdock's loyalties were divided between the interdisciplinary network and loyalty to the Yale establishment represented by Keller's science of society. Murdock, moreover, held a grudge against Boasian anthropology before he met Sapir. In an autobiographical statement in 1966, Murdock explained that he "interviewed Boas" who refused to admit him to Columbia as a graduate student because he was "nothing but a dilettante." He eventually returned to Yale, where he had been an undergraduate, and joined Keller's program.

In the preface to *Social Structure* (1949, xii–xiv), Murdock claimed that the new anthropological functionalism of Malinowski was established in American anthropology not by the Boasians but by Keller. Boas had ridded American anthropology of the "intellectual debris" of the older evolution and emphasized fieldwork. But the battle was won by about 1920; thereafter, the Boasian "school accomplished distressingly little . . . toward the advancement of cultural theory." Boas was, moreover, "extravagantly overrated" by his disciples and was an "unsystematic" theoretician and a poor fieldworker. His "respect for ethnographic facts" and "methodological rigor" were best manifested in the work of Lowie, Kroeber, and Spier. In this context, Murdock's less than flattering remarks about Sapir (1949, xv) become less "gratuitous" (Murray 1986):

To Edward Sapir, he is indebted for such linguistic knowledge as he possesses and for his initiation into fieldwork, and he readily acknowledges that the field of culture and personality owes its initial stimulus very largely to Sapir's extraordinary intuitive flair and verbal facility. It becomes increasingly apparent, however, that the permanent contributions of Sapir to cultural theory are relatively slight.

Murdock failed to see how Sapir integrated anthropology and linguistics. Moreover, he did not value intuition.

Murdock and Sapir were "compunctiously correct" (Murray 1986) in dealing with one another at Yale. Sapir, hoping that fieldwork would convert Murdock to the Boasian approach, arranged for him to visit the Haida in British Columbia during the summer of 1932. Sapir's students, however, concluded that Murdock was the "enemy" (David Mandelbaum, Fred Eggan, Weston LaBarre, p.c.). Eggan felt (p.c.) that students were sent to linguistics to remove them from Murdock's influence. LaBarre recalled that Murdock claimed to have had psychoanalysis but was "hostile" to it (to Murray, 21 October 1984).

The graduate catalogue for 1931–1932 described Sapir's hopes for collaboration between cultural anthropology and the other social sciences. Students were expected to have "a general acquaintance with the social science field and with psychological and sociological points of view." The program was not designed to "train technicians" but to explore the nature of culture and "its historical and psychological interpretation." "Reasonable acquaintance" with ethnology, cultural theory, primitive linguistics, and "to some extent" archaeology and physical anthropology was required. Supplementary work in sociology and psychology was recommended. Linguistics courses were available in linguistics and the language departments. Other resources included the Peabody Museum and the IHR. The doctorate was normally based on "first-hand contact with a field project" and would "in no instance . . . [be] a merely factual report." Sapir had long wanted a department of his own (Eggan, p.c.) and thought out the program well in advance of its inception. There was nothing tentative about the 1931–1932 statement—it was a full-blown announcement of a graduate research division.

Existing Yale staff offered courses in the initial year. Osgood, though based in the Peabody Museum, taught prehistoric archaeology and American Indian ethnology. Murdock covered ethnology and physical anthropology. Sociologist Charles Loran offered African ethnology. Sapir listed two courses that were not given in 1931–1932: He taught Primitive Society ("the psychological implications will be stressed") in 1932–1933, thereafter delegating it to Spier, and Primitive Religion and Art in 1932–1933 and 1934–1935, emphasizing "non-material values." During his first year at Yale, Sapir's anthropological teaching consisted only of a "problems" course (shared with Wissler) and a research course in cultural anthropology—that is, supervision of graduate students. Sapir did not offer the problems course in his second and third years; thereafter, he shared it with Spier. Most of the ethnology students (Fenton, p.c.) officially worked with Spier, although Sapir facilitated their arrangements for fieldwork and professional contacts.

Sapir's major course, however, was The Impact of Culture on Personality. It was listed but omitted in 1931–1932 and offered for the Rockefeller foreign fellows in 1932–1933. The course was omitted in 1934–1935 and reappeared the following year under the title The Psychology of Culture, the title of Sapir's course at Chicago and of his unwritten book. The Rockefeller seminar title was Frank's choice, though it agreed with Sapir's predilection for avoiding the simplistic label of culture *and* personality. Sapir taught The Psychology of Culture in 1935–1936 and 1936–1937.

This course load was much lighter than Sapir had carried at Chicago. Administration took much of his time, however. Sapir was delighted when he was elected a fellow of Trumbull College (which included many of Yale's scholarship students) (Leonard Doob, p.c.) and used his office there to escape other routines; the college affiliation also symbolized social acceptance at Yale. He wrote to his wife (20 September 1933: SF):

I must get my key and move the books in. I have a feeling this Trumbull office will be a godsend, if only it gives me a good way to escape from the graduate office. What crazy divinity ever picked me out for an "administrator"? There are so many excellent Herskovits'es and Dollards in the world it seems poor planning to pick on me.

Sapir was more interested in students. LaBarre recalled retrospectively (to Robert Allen, 25 June 1971) a "stupid colleague" (apparently

Murdock) who thought Sapir wasted himself on his students. But Sapir was oblivious to collegial opinion:

Sapir used to go off in some corner of the university to talk with a bright or interesting student, and for hours he would be incommunicado while his secretary frantically sought his whereabouts for some august bureaucratic reason. This kind of thing happened to me once or twice, and I found it immensely ego-enhancing.

During his second year, Sapir increased the anthropology staff: Peter Buck was visiting from the Yale-affiliated Bishop Museum in Honolulu, George Herzog did research on American Indian music, and Leslie Spier became a research associate. Spier was the backbone of the ethnology program throughout Sapir's tenure. Murdock continued to teach courses, but Sapir and Spier still considered him a sociologist.

Sapir's efforts to build up the anthropology program were foiled by lack of funds and their dependence on the IHR—which increasingly moved in nonanthropological directions. President Angell (to Provost Charles Seymour, 19 February 1932: YU), however, was "anxious" to help the anthropologists. Accordingly, Sapir prepared a five-year research plan comparable to the one he, Cole, and Redfield had proposed at Chicago in 1929. But, in 1933, the foundations were withdrawing support from the social sciences and block grants were a thing of the past. Sapir argued to Angell (17 October 1933: YU) that the limited funds of the IHR were intended primarily for "such anthropological researches as bear on general problems of human behavior" and the fields of psychology and sociology. He was concerned about funding for "the strictly ethnographic field." Since Yale compared favorably to Chicago, Harvard, and Columbia in staff and quality of graduate students, he felt that the Rockefeller Foundation should be amenable to comparable support. A total of sixty thousand dollars over five years would ensure fieldwork in two areas of North America (the southwest and northwest, where Sapir's personal interests were centered), South America, and Africa–Oceania–Asia "as opportunity arises," and provide for publication. Sapir emphasized that the department would not "dissipate our energy" by trying to handle all the subdisciplines of anthropology. Osgood would deal with archaeology through the Peabody Museum; linguistic work would focus in that department. Physical anthropology (formerly taught by Murdock) was relegated to the "biological disciplines."

Angell dutifully passed the proposal on to David H. Stephens of the Rockefeller Foundation (29 November 1933: YU), stressing that Yale had the "nucleus of a strong staff in anthropology, ethnology and related subjects." Stephens replied (11 January 1934: YU) that funds were likely to decrease for 1934 and that the priority was studying disappearing cultures. He looked forward to Sapir's opinions on ACLS money for Indian languages. Sapir wrote to Angell (20 January 1934: YU) that he hoped to "squeeze some comfort out of the rather cryptic remark in regard to the future policy of the Rockefeller Foundation." When Sapir wrote Stephens about another matter (18 June 1934: UC), he could not resist raising the "melancholy plight" of anthropology at Yale. Because there was no special fund for research, funds had to be "stolen" from IHR appropriations. There was, however, no important change in Rockefeller policy.

Sapir was on sabbatical in 1937–1938, with Spier as acting chairman. Due to his heart condition, Sapir spent the year in New York rather than in China or Honolulu as planned. In spite of the limited distance, he was in minimal contact with departmental affairs.[1] The first semester, Lowie was a visiting professor, teaching history of ethnology and South American ethnology (Spier to Lohmann, 15 June 1938: YUDA). Senior British anthropologist Charles Seligman held a Bishop Museum fellowship. George Vaillant taught Mexican archaeology. Wissler (culture and environment; Plains culture change), Osgood, Raymond Kennedy (Indonesian ethnography), and Spier continued their previous work.

Arrangements to replace Sapir's linguistics courses were made through anthropology. George Trager taught Phonetics the first term and Benjamin Whorf, Problems in American Indian Languages the second term; Swadesh resigned to go to the University of Wisconsin (Spier to Furniss, 30 June, 12 August 1937: YUDA). Trager was a Slavicist who worked on Sapir's international auxiliary language project and did Tanoan fieldwork, in partial collaboration with Whorf. Whorf was not a regular graduate student, holding the title of "Honorary Fellow in Anthropology" in 1936–1937 (letter of appointment: YUDA).

Sapir obtained initial funds for editing the *Yale University Publications in Anthropology* through a Rockefeller grant for research in language and literature, and "everybody in the department" contributed to the first two volumes (Murdock interview with Denise O'Brien, 4 June 1976). Dean Furniss (to Spier, 24 October 1937: YUDA) considered the outlook for continuing support "gloomy" without matching publication funds from Yale. Sapir and Spier both resigned from their editorship at the end of that academic year (Spier to Mrs. Bernier of Yale Press, 11 June 1938: YUDA).

Spier, however, was optimistic about overall effectiveness of the program (to Furniss, 24 January 1938: YUDA); nine doctorates had been awarded by the independent department. H. Scudder McKeel was director of the Southwest Laboratory of Anthropology. Three were assistant professors: F. G. Rainey at Alaska, W. W. Hill at New Mexico, and Willard Park at Northwestern. William Fenton was an instructor at Saint Lawrence University. David Mandelbaum had an NRC fellowship and expected a permanent position the following academic year. A. E. Hudson was an IHR research assistant and would return to Central Asia for fieldwork before teaching. E. G. Burrows was unemployed, mainly because he wanted to return to Honolulu; "I guess he will have to get over that notion." Spier stressed that "some stopgap job" had been found for everyone. Of the eighteen to twenty current students, three would return to permanent positions (Verne Ray at Washington, W. S. Stallings at the Southwest Laboratory, and Jane Garrettson at Connecticut College).

Furniss (25 January 1938: YUDA) acknowledged the excellent record, noting the "demand for students trained in Anthropology and some kindred subject," especially sociology and psychology; "our students would be well advised to prepare themselves in these lines." Spier responded (24 January 1938: YUDA) that he had no doubt about placing the one or two students who finished each year. He was particularly pleased that, of the three married women who were financially independent and didn't need jobs, Erminie Voegelin "nevertheless will begin teaching at DePauw University in the fall." Spier did not know whether Irving Rouse planned to remain at the Peabody Museum. This impressive hiring record was typical for Yale and better than California, Harvard, or Columbia, the last "rather shocking," with "quantity production" resulting in few permanent jobs.

Spier disagreed strongly with Furniss (24 January 1938: YUDA) about the necessity of the link between sociology and anthropology. He did not oppose interdisciplinary training but wanted students to study other fields out of "real interest in the subject," not to obtain a job. There was barely enough time to train students well in one discipline. The major need of the department was someone to train archaeologists for local museum positions, which "are not to be sneered at." "If we had a first-rate archaeologist here, we would be in a better position to furnish special training for these men and a more rounded training for all." Spier, implicitly speaking for Sapir, defined the department program in terms of traditional Boasian subject matter, not in terms of interdisciplinary collaboration. The research direction of the IHR was incompatible with Sapir's concept of social science collaboration; therefore, somewhat ironically given his nonlocal prestige in interdisciplinary circles, Sapir's program retreated to conventional anthropology.

Sapir wanted Spier appointed permanent chair of the department. When he resigned due to his heart condition, Furniss promised Sapir (15 November 1937: YU) that Yale's adminstration was "eager . . . to relieve you in every possible way of burdensome administrative duties"; Spier would have the official title in the spring "if conditions at that time seem to warrant it." Dean Furniss and President Seymour kept their options open. Without Sapir, anthropological interests had less weight than those of the IHR, which increasingly dominated Yale social science.

Sapir took the threat to his program very seriously, writing to Lowie (17 January 1938: UCB) after his semester at Yale:

Thanks for letting me know about your talk with Dean Furniss. It confirms certain hunches I had had about how that gentleman's mind was working. He seems to have been trying to trap you into saying something which he might construe as indicating a belief that anthropology and sociology ought to combine! Murdock has tried similar insinuations with me in the past.

Sapir was on the defensive, and his precarious health threatened his prestige, at least in local circles.

Murdock (interview with Denise O'Brien, 4 June 1976) felt that Spier had "bungled the job of chairman" to the point where Furniss asked Murdock to take it on; "this was a blow to Leslie and he resigned from Yale in a huff and I did my level best to induce him to stay but he'd thought I knifed him in the back." Spier allowed "personal views" to affect his administration.

The actual reasons for the change of regime remain ambiguous. Spier was "never a gregarious individual" and "eschewed anthropological politics" (Basehart and Hill 1965, 1270). The ethnology students supported him; but Spier had little leverage against established Yale political factions without Sapir to back him. Murdock was aligned with the IHR and interests that Sapir had attempted to counter there, represented by May and Dollard. In this context, it is difficult to take too seriously Murdock's retrospective argument that Spier's resignation was "a blow to me because, of course, I had to make new appointments and fill the gap and remake the department" (to D. O'Brien, 4 June 1976). Nearly half a century later, participants remain reluctant to discuss the recriminations around which Sapir's anthropology program was reorganized. In any case, Murdock rapidly dismantled the program in primitive linguistics and reestablished ties to the IHR; archaeology rather than linguistics became the supplement to ethnology.

Yale Students in Ethnology

Although Sapir was not primarily an ethnologist—his specialization in culture and personality being interpreted at the time as quite different from traditional Boasian cultural anthropology—he was influential in the graduate careers of Yale's ethnology students. As chairman of the graduate program, he had administrative responsibility for all students. Sapir held a weekly open-house (Fenton, p.c.) which was widely attended. Edgar Siskin recalled a ping-pong match on the Sapir porch between Sapir and Malinowski, who was visiting Yale (p.c.); neither was athletic, neither had good eyesight, and both were well endowed with the gift of gab. There was awful ping-pong and excellent conversation—to which it was assumed graduate students would carefully attend.

Sapir followed the Boasian practice of studying all subdisciplines, regardless of specialization. He regularly channeled ethnology and archaeology students into his linguistics courses and insisted on at least minimal training in linguistics as necessary to do adequate ethnographic research.

Sapir's course in Navajo was remembered by Yale ethnology students with the same consternation as Boas's in American Indian languages during Sapir's own student days. David Mandelbaum recalled (to Hymes, 18 May 1981) that "no quarter [was] given to the uninitiated." There was "no pedagogical organization"; Sapir "just threw problems he was working on at students." Mandelbaum (to Darnell, 20 June 1986) was impressed by Sapir's virtuosity even when the content escaped him:

ES was an entrancing lecturer even though I could not always follow his train of thought. He usually sat at a desk or table as he lectured, one hand flat on the surface and the other hand atop it, and though his voice was quiet and his whole manner modest, the flow of his talk was so smooth, his examples so apt, his thinking so relevant, that I always looked forward to attending one of his lectures on general anthropological subjects. But when I sat in on his course in Navaho, I was completely lost. There he spoke to the linguists and I knew so little . . . that I had to bail out of that course after a few, bewildered class hours.

Sapir obtained a linguistic assistantship for Mandelbaum at the Southwest Laboratory, although he applied for ethnology. He worked on San Carlos Apache with Hoijer, "and thereafter ES did not urge me any more in the direction of linguistics" (p.c.).

Irving Rouse, an archaeologist, took Navajo along with ethnologist Weston LaBarre. Everyone else in the course was a professional linguist (i.e., a postdoctoral student). "The discussion was way over the head of one like myself, who had not even learned linguistic notation." At the final session, Sapir remembered that he had two graduate students and "asked each of us a question, which we could not answer." It was much later that Rouse realized how much he had learned (to Darnell, 18 January 1986). LaBarre went to Yale to work with Sapir in linguistics (1958, 280–281) but was intimidated by the competition:

. . . slightly older graduate students already there were Voegelin, Whorf, Swadesh, Newman, Haas and others, and after the culture shock of a course in Navaho with Sapir, I never aspired to compete with these formidable older colleagues in linguistics, though I remained an avid Indo-Europeanist as far as my abilities permitted.

LaBarre switched to personality studies, undergoing psychoanalysis with Dollard, but self-consciously represented himself throughout his career as a Sapir student (1951, 157–158).

Various students used their linguistic training with Sapir to improve the quality of their ethnography. For example, Allan Smith (to Spier, 15 December 1937: YUDA) noted that linguistics was "of no essential importance to my proper study" but it "led to a far more accurate recording of those difficult native words encountered in my ethnographic queries."

The ethnology program was funded through the IHR, which treated American Indian work as interdisciplinary social science. The IHR research fund was a perk of Sapir's appointment, which enabled him to support a number of doctoral and postdoctoral students on a long-term basis. It was easier, however, to convince the IHR, particularly as his relations with it deteriorated, to support cultural research rather than linguistic. The only other source for funding was the Committee on American Indian Languages, which did not include ethnology in its mandate.

Not all of Sapir's students fell clearly into linguistics or anthropology. Walter Dyk was a linguist who continued Sapir's Chinookan work, planning a dictionary and grammar of both the Wishram and Wasco dialects (IHR Annual Report for 1931–1932: YU). But Sapir encouraged his interest in psychology as well. Sapir described Dyk's Navajo life history work to Haile (23 September 1933: SWL) as "under my direction" and focusing on the "dynamic aspects of Navaho life . . . how the various patterns, which have already been described in great part, actually function in the daily life of the people." Sapir's introduction to Dyk's Navajo autobiography was one of the last things he wrote. He praised the personal approach to the events of a culture, one which he himself had attempted with the Nootka; but Sapir never completed a psychological case study of any American Indian group; Dyk's work, therefore, was later cited as the exemplar of Sapir's approach to personality in culture.

Mandelbaum (to Darnell, 20 January 1986) believed that Sapir used methods appropriate to the subject studied, not worrying about whether they were linguistic or anthropological; "his ideas and analyses in linguistic subjects were always informed by his experience and training as an *anthropological* linguist and his broad cultural analyses were always done from the perspective of a *linguistic* anthropologist." Students decided where their focus should lie. Mandelbaum's fieldwork in India (to Department of Anthropology, 6 February 1938: YUDA) emphasized life histories—"sorely needed materials for observations on primitive social psychology from the point of view of psychoanalysis." This was the side of Sapir's thought that appealed to him.

Sapir worked with a few students whose primary loyalties were to the IHR. John Whiting was closely associated with Murdock's cross-cultural survey project. In retrospect, he described himself (to Robert Allen, 27 January 1971) as "a student of Sapir's, although I was never very close to him." Beatrice Blythe, later Whiting, was an ethnology student who got along much better with Sapir. Later, the Whitings (1978, 44) acknowledged Sapir's importance in the development of culture and personality studies for his "more subtle and humanistic point of view," "the importance of knowing the native language for understanding culture," and "suggestions . . . much more subtle and persuasive than the ethnologically naive approach of Freud." In 1987, however, John Whiting explained to Kenneth Pike, in a session of the AAA commemorating Murdock, that Sapir was a poet, not a scientist. By implication, anthropology was a science. Like Murdock, Dollard, and the IHR, Whiting accepted the social learning and imitation theories of Clark Hull. Whiting took his degree in sociology rather than anthropology (Murdock to John Gillin, 4 April 1940: YUDA) to obtain broad social science training; "students in the Anthropology Department at that time were never permitted to take courses outside of the department." Most of his courses were in anthropology, supplemented by psychology with Dollard and psychoanalysis by Earl Zinn.

Cora DuBois's doctorate was from Berkeley, but Sapir encouraged her career in culture and personality, and she acknowledged him as a mentor. But she turned down the position Sapir arranged at the IHR when psychiatrist Abraham Kardiner found money for her to do fieldwork in Alor (DuBois to Lowie, 6 April 1937: UCB). DuBois concentrated on amassing cross-cultural evidence for the relationship of culture and personality. In the preface to *People of Alor*, she noted that "we had talked ourselves out, and only fieldwork could test the procedure." The Kardiner and (Ralph) Linton seminars beginning in 1936 at Columbia established a "pattern of collaboration" between anthropology and psychoanalysis in which Kardiner theorized about "basic personality structure," and various anthropologists provided him with field data for analysis.

Because the IHR controlled fieldwork funding, Sapir's priorities for student support were not always implemented. Pearl and Ernest Beaglehole were ethnologists, although she was interested in personality work. Sapir was adamant in defending them to the Yale-affiliated Bishop Museum in Honolulu. Murdock went over Sapir's head to recommend Clellan Ford, instead of the Beagleholes, for research support before the official committee had a chance to act. Sapir was incensed, particularly with Dean Furniss (to May, 25 June 1935: IHR):

Common sense, let alone courtesy, would have indicated the propriety of the Section of Anthropology being consulted in regard to Yale's preference among the anthropological candidates. . . . I have been ditched by Furniss far too many times for me to keep quiet any longer. If he couldn't manage to see a Section of Anthropology through with dignity and courtesy to the anthropologists themselves he had no right to ask me to come to Yale to be made a fool of.

May responded (23 July 1935: IHR) that he had heard rumors that the Beagleholes had made some bad blunders in Polynesia. Sapir argued (26 July 1935: IHR) that the Bishop Museum had failed to present reasons for its opposition to the Beagleholes; such "insulting insinuations" had to be clarified. They were not.

Hortense Powdermaker, although her work was superficially quite different from Sapir's, was his major protegé at the IHR. Powdermaker was a postdoctoral research associate with a doctorate supervised by Malinowski and field experience in Melanesia. At Yale, she worked with southern blacks at a time when this was becoming something of a bandwagon. Anthropologists were moving toward sociological methods of fieldwork in their own society—with consequent questioning in both disciplines of the validity of anthropological reports by necessarily subjective observers. Powdermaker was in the fighting line of this tradition, holding to a nonquantitative, essentially Sapirian emphasis on the cultural world as structured by individuals.

Powdermaker obtained an SSRC grant in 1932–1933 to study a Negro community in the Mississippi delta. In her autobiography (1966, 131–134), Powdermaker stressed that Sapir encouraged her to apply to the SSRC and backed her proposal. Sapir was convinced that anthropologists could study modern societies, using their own fieldwork methods rather than quantitative sociological surveys. He noted to May (13 December 1932: YU): "It is not often that a properly trained anthropologist, who has a genuine interest in contemporary negro problems in America, comes our way." Powdermaker spent the summer before her fieldwork in New Hampshire with the Sapir family, reading about the American South. She (to May, 27 September 1933: YU) proposed to do a similar study in New Haven under IHR auspices and publish the two comparatively in the "borderline field lying between social anthropology and sociology."

Powdermaker's work was affiliated in the IHR with sociologist Maurice Davie's Negro research project in 1934–1935. Previously, it had been classified as ethnic psychology under the direction of Wissler. The advisory group for the Negro project included Sapir, a Yale historian, and Charles Johnson (IHR report 1934–1935: YU). The intention was to include "a psychiatrist, a social statistician, and perhaps others, at least for special aspects." Sapir (to May, 25 June 1935: YU) wanted the study funded by sociology rather than anthropology to conserve his own funds for American Indian work. May would have preferred to absorb the anthropology budget into his cooperative research program, particularly since the anthropologists' field studies did not cooperate with other social sciences in the IHR.

Powdermaker returned to the field in 1934, still under IHR sponsorship, and introduced John Dollard to fieldwork. Their descriptions of the same community were highly diverse. Dollard emphasized caste and class. Powdermaker dedicated her book, which emphasized community, to Sapir; it was well received by the two most distinguished race relations sociologists of the period, W. E. B. DuBois and Robert Park (Murray 1987, 1988a). Sapir and Davie both wanted Powdermaker's book published by the IHR (Powdermaker to May, 6 January 1936: YU), but May, who was already committed to Dollard's version of the American South, turned down the manuscript on the basis of reader comments, all internal to Yale (12 February 1936: YU). Sapir was the only positive reviewer. May informed Powdermaker (27 April 1936: YU) that she had one year to finish her Negro study under IHR auspices. Dollard's description to Margaret Mead clarifies the lack of affection among the principals (7 June 1937: LC): Powdermaker, he told Mead, "has been doing some unpleasant yammering" about Dollard's book, published by the IHR; she was leaving the IHR, which, "by the way, is one of the reasons why Sapir is so sore." Powdermaker tried to salvage the situation by revising her manuscript (9 March 1938: YU) but eventually withdrew it in favor of a more amenable publisher. Sapir failed to influence the movement of the IHR away from the configurationalist approach to personality.

CHAPTER NINETEEN

The Academic Program at Yale: Linguistics

Sapir's teaching load centered in linguistics; he had less administrative responsibility in that department, and all students interested in "primitive" linguistics depended on him for their specialized training. The linguistics department had a core staff of four: Edgar Sturtevant (the chairman and only member listed solely as "professor of linguistics"), Franklin Edgerton (Sanskrit and comparative philology), Eduard Prokosch (Germanics), and Sapir ("professor of anthropology and linguistics"). Members of various language departments were affiliated, including Miles Hanley in English and Charles Torrey in Semitics. The label "linguistics" carried considerable status at a time when disciplinary autonomy was tenuous; most "linguists" were compelled to teach language and literature.

Mary Haas (Murray interview, 26 July 1978) emphasizes that the Yale linguistics department was "planned" and believes that it became the best in the country with the addition of Sapir. Each student had to "familiarize himself with certain aspects of each language field." No other linguistic department at the time offered serious work in primitive languages.

The linguists who preceded Sapir at Yale were remarkably compatible colleagues. Sturtevant discovered Hittite, the earliest language to split off from Indo-European, in 1906, although World War I delayed publication (Emeneau 1953: 367–368). He explored the "revolutionary effect" of the Hittite material through Sapir's laryngeal hypothesis, discussed with the Yale Linguistics Club in the early 1930s (and at the LI in 1937). Sturtevant wrote "in great excitement" that twenty-six problems of Indo-European grammar were cleared up by Sapir's presentation (Hahn 1953, 380). Sturtevant, moreover, was open to anthropological approaches. He taught phonetics, useful for potential fieldworkers, even before the linguistics department became independent (Emeneau 1953, 366). He was trained in classics and comparative philology at Chicago by Carl Buck and determinedly kept literature out of his linguistics. Like Sapir, he was inclined to try out preliminary ideas and revise them later; as a result, he was sometimes "severely criticized, by the cautious German scholars [who dominated comparative philology], for publishing prematurely" (Hahn 1953, 379). Sturtevant supported Sapir's appeal to Dean Furniss (27 November 1934: YU) to record various "exotic languages" studied by members of the anthropology department for an IHR archive. The social scientists had more trouble with the validity of this project than Sturtevant did.

Sturtevant opposed technical jargon in linguistics, arguing that the Linguistic Society of America should remain a single unit with everyone aware of all kinds of work (in contrast to the isolated sections of the Modern Language Association) (Hahn 1953, 382). The camaraderie of the linguistics department depended greatly on Sturtevant's openness to informal exchange of ideas (Hahn 1953, 383).

Edgerton studied Sanskrit and comparative philology with Maurice Bloomfield but went beyond his mentor in treating Vedic religion and folklore in an anthropological vein. Folklore was also an interest for Prokosch. With Sapir, the last of the four to be appointed, these men built up a unique graduate program, jointly editing the William Dwight Whitney publication series.

Of nine courses listed in general linguistics in 1931–1932, Sturtevant taught eight. His Introduction to Linguistic Sciences ranged beyond Indo-European to present linguistics as a discipline rather than as a subject matter.

Students wanting to specialize in linguistics needed the approval of the department and the agreement of a supervisor. The catalogue noted that many of the courses would not be taught every year, but the curriculum would be selected "after consultation with students." The department offered Indo-European, Indic, Iranian, Greek, Italic, Germanic, Balto-Slavic [Old Church Slavonic], Hittite, Semitic, Egyptian, Sumerian, and "Primitive Languages" (listed last and clearly having a unique relationship to general linguistics).

Sapir listed, but did not offer in 1931–1932, courses in Phonetics and Psychology of Language. Beginning in the following year, he offered them in successive years for two cycles. Psychology of Language was not taught after that; Phonetics was taught by Swadesh in 1936–1937 and 1937–1938. Although Phonetics was listed in the linguistics department, it was "intended to assist the field anthropologist as well as the linguist"; in practice, most of the students were anthropologists. A survey of speech sounds was "followed by practical work in phonetic dictation." The catalogue for 1931–1932 noted affiliation with the ACLS Linguistic Atlas project; graduate students would be favorably considered as "fieldworkers" for it.

The Psychology of Language course was not directed primarily at linguists either. It included "speech as behavior and as cultural configuration" and "symbolism and the problem of meaning," and was open "only to students who have some knowledge of psychology." Anthropologists and Sapir's linguistic students took this course. Yale psychologists, however, never entered into active collaboration with Sapir's program.

Primitive Languages was offered for the first three and the fifth years of Sapir's appointment. It was taught in 1937–1938 by Swadesh. The course description was succinct: "After a brief survey of fundamental linguistic concepts, a number of primitive languages, American Indian or African, will be studied with a view to understanding the varying possibilities of linguistic expression." The wording makes it clear that Sapir expected students without prior training in linguistics. He insisted that his interest in unwritten languages went beyond American Indian; he had materials on Gweabo from Chicago. In practice, however, the course focused on Navajo, with occasional forays into comparative Athabaskan (Krauss, p.c., on the basis of class notes in his possession). The concern with typology (types of linguistic expression) had characterized Sapir's work at least since his book *Language*; it looked backward to Boas's 1911 *Handbook of American Indian Languages* and forward to the so-called Sapir–Whorf hypothesis.

Native American informants were rarely available in New Haven. But even when Alex Thomas came to New Haven to work with Swadesh on Nootka, Sapir (Haas to Murray, 26 July 1978) did not use him in class; he taught from his Nootka files.

We were all expected to go out and work in the field, and actually there was not too much training in that then. . . . We finally persuaded Sapir to give a phonetics course, a non-credit course. He would dictate himself. He made an informant of himself for us to listen to in the various languages he commanded. He was very good at it, but as for determining the structures of the various languages, he did that by bringing in a sheaf of slips and talking about it.

In 1934–1935 and 1935–1936, Sapir offered Comparative Problems in Primitive Languages, a seminar for advanced students "designed to show how linguistic comparisons and reconstructions can be made with the help of orally recorded data in primitive languages." That is, instead of focusing on particular Indian languages, Sapir talked about historical relationship. Haas (p.c.) recalls that Sapir taught this course largely in response to student demand; his own interests were more descriptive than in the 1920s when linguistic classification for a linguistically naive anthropological audience dominated his thinking. The standards had changed and, although Sapir's students acquired his earlier fervor for classification, he himself was lukewarm, preferring to concentrate on comparative Athabaskan. In 1936–1937, Swadesh offered a course in Indian Languages of North America. Primitive linguistics had grown to the point where it needed two instructors.

During each year of his Yale appointment, Sapir was listed as teaching Research in Linguistics, "A consulting course for advanced students, each of whom is set to work on a special research project in primitive linguistics or linguistic psychology." This included a wide range of students, some of them postdoctoral researchers affiliated with the IHR.

In addition to developing his own research program under the linguistic umbrella, Sapir contributed to the team-taught survey courses that integrated the offerings of the department. For several years, he taught one quarter of the introductory course. In addition, Languages of the World was taught by Sturtevant, Edgerton, Prokosch, and Sapir for four years, beginning in 1933–1934. Sapir's share included "Hamito-Semitic, Sino-Tibetan, other languages of Asia, the languages of the South Seas, Africa, and America." The first reflected his awakening interest in the cultural and linguistic history of the Mediterranean basin. Sapir knew the Asian languages because of his earlier interest in linking them to Amerindian languages; in the 1930s, however, he concentrated on genetic units at less remote time depth, with evidence that could be accepted by colleagues trained in Indo-European. Sapir was automatically assigned any unwritten or "primitive" language, the two being understood as identical.

In 1932–1933, the Yale catalogue stressed that students could only enroll in linguistics if their work was more general than any contributing departmental program. There was no M. A. in linguistics. "Students who plan to combine linguistic work with a considerable amount of literary, archaeological, or historical study should enroll in the appropriate department." The list of possible departments included "Social Sciences (Anthropology)." Apparently, none of the other social sciences at Yale saw any need for linguistic training; anthropology, of course, did so primarily because of Sapir.

In 1936–1937, Sapir taught Tocharian (an ancient Indo-European language of Northern Tibet), surveying the existing literature and relating the phonology and morphology to other Indo-European languages. "The importance of Tocharian for problems of Indo-European reconstruction will be stressed." Students were expected to know something about Indo-European grammar. The course was listed but not taught for the remaining two years of Sapir's life and reflected his "return" to Indo-European during this period. Murray Emeneau, a student at this time, recalled (to Mary Haas, 4 December 1971) Sapir's Tocharian as the classic application of Boasian methods for studying areal influence coexisting with genetic diversification of languages. "Emeneau audited some of Sapir's classes and liked him and Sapir really liked him and got into the Dravidian field" (Haas to Murray, 26 July 1978). Emeneau assumed that Sturtevant and Edgerton "disapproved" of Sapir's foray into comparative–historical work along anthropological lines. Tocharian had only recently been identified as a divergent Indo-European language, and Sapir was intrigued by Tibetan influence (through long-term borrowing) on the Indo-European base.[1] Sapir was convinced (to Kroeber, 27 July 1934: UCB) that Tocharian was closer to the pre-Greek roots of Indo-European than any other language; he had "great fun working out the phonetic laws which explain the peculiar changes which have taken place."

Yale's biologist–ecologist, G. Evelyn Hutchinson (p.c.) returned in 1932 from the Yale North India expedition with a photograph of a Tocharian inscription from northern Tibet which the natural science research team could not decipher; he was sent to Sapir, who analyzed it as "Tibetanized Tocharian B, as might be expected geographically," presumably reflecting the diffusion of Nestorian religion in Tibet between the eighth and tenth centuries. Sapir's interest in Tocharian may have dated from this incidental contact; Hutchinson (p.c.) recalls that Sapir did not read the alphabet when he first saw the inscription.

In 1936–1937, Swadesh, Sapir's most outstanding postdoctoral student in linguistics, taught Phonetics and Advanced Phonetics and Phonemics. Although Sapir had defined the phoneme for North American linguistics in 1925, his course description for phonetics never focused on the difference. He considered it more important to teach students how to record languages in the field; the theoretical difference between phonetics and phonemics was subsidiary (although he certainly discussed it in his classes). Swadesh, however, was part of a new generation, with a primary identity in linguistics and a commitment to descriptive treatments with theoretical sophistication. His phonetics course description retained phonetic dictation but added "phonemic method" and "the analysis of actual phonetic systems." The advanced course included "the theoretical basis of phonemics, structural phonemics, morpho-phonemics; the phoneme in its psychological aspect." Only the latter was explicitly Sapirian in terminology, although Swadesh learned his linguistics from Sapir. The structural and morphophonemic approaches were Bloomfieldian. Counter to disciplinary oral tradition, Sapir was interested in the morphophonemic work of the 1930s (Haas, p.c.). Nonetheless, Swadesh brought it into the Yale curriculum.

In 1937–1938, Sapir was on leave, and Swadesh taught the primitive-languages portion of the linguistics program. In 1938–1939, Sapir was scheduled to teach Phonetics and Phonemics, accepting the reorientation toward theory introduced by Swadesh.

In 1939–1940, after Sapir's death, Tocharian and primitive languages were omitted from the catalogue. Bloomfield was hired the following year. He contributed to Languages of the World and taught Menomini (one of his four Central Algonquian languages) under the title Language Structure. Although not as flagrantly anthropological as Sapir's American Indian linguistics courses, Bloomfield covered approximately the same material. Bloomfield also offered two courses in Germanics. He did not separate out the study of unwritten languages from the rest of linguistics. Bloomfield made no move to establish ties to anthropology or continuity to the Sapirian research tradition. The "Yale School" of linguistics that grew up around Bloomfield coalesced through dialect atlas and wartime work quite different from Sapir's Americanist focus. Sapir's students chose to maintain their primary professional identity in anthropology; indeed, the Americanist emphasis isolated them still further because of increasing anthropological work overseas in response to the wartime breakdown of American isolationism. Sapir was not around to take his linguistics into the new era.

Sapir's Return To Indo-European

In the later years of his life, Sapir returned, for the first time since he left Columbia, to Indo-European. He built up a substantial library on the ancient Near East, including Semitic, Hittite, and Tocharian. The Sapir family recalls his enthusiasm for this linguistic work and believes that he "would have reverted more and more into his linguistic studies" had he lived longer; linguistic work was, in Sapir's own metaphor, like "getting out into an open sunny field" (J. David Sapir 1985).

Zellig Harris (to Philip Sapir, 20 July 1942: SF) spoke of a letter from Sapir "giving a very interesting suggestion for the original sound-system of Semitic." In addition to linguistic problems, Sapir was intrigued by the history and archaeology of the Near East, in part related to his revived interest in Judaism in this period. But his favorite genre was a "gleeful return" to "exploratory etymological vignettes"; these "finger exercises of genetic reconstructions" allowed Sapir to move beyond the virtually exclusive focus on Indo-European of his training (Malkiel 1986). Malkiel emphasizes that these "exquisite cameos" might eventually have added up to a systematic treatment of the Mediterranean culture area; "conceivably, [Sapir] felt that he could indulge in esthetically appealing vignettes for some time before reaching a binding decision." Ill health and decreasing energy perhaps made it necessary for Sapir to concentrate on limited projects (Paul Sapir, p.c.).

The First Yale School of Linguistics

Sapir's linguistic teaching was geared to the advanced student or practicing linguist. His only undergraduate (noncredit) course was on the structure of the English language (Philip Sapir, p.c.). Sapir rationalized the course to President Angell (19 November 1934: YU) in terms of "lack of continuity between graduate study in linguistics and cultural anthropology on the one hand and the undergraduate course of study." The English department was amenable, but only presidential intervention could contravene Yale structure.

Haas (to Murray, 26 July 1978) describes the experience of studying linguistics with Sapir, in a manner reminiscent of the puzzled frustration of ethnology students:

> His method was to throw you into the water and let you swim to shore. You had to swim by yourself, more or less. He didn't have a "methodology" in any of the senses you might think of ordinarily today. . . . Probably Bloomfield didn't either, but Bloomfield didn't have any students at all at any time—in linguistics, I'm not talking about German or Gothic. Sapir was a very popular teacher and had a lot of students. . . . He was inspiring, always inspiring. He made you fascinated by language and how it worked. And of course he talked about large numbers of languages, especially American Indian, but he was well versed in many other languages as well. . . . Now at that time that was very shocking to traditional philologists, because you really shouldn't mention Greek and Navaho in the same breath. . . . It was a very strong taboo. As a matter of fact, Buck [at Chicago] didn't like Sapir very much; he thought he was ruining everything and was amazed at what Sapir was doing.

Sapir influenced many Yale linguists. Trager emphasized (to Robert Allen, 26 July 1971) that Sapir's students were important in determining his own thinking. Trager used the term "student" very broadly, "to include almost everyone he had contact with, and not only the few formal students he trained." Certainly, both anthropologists and linguists considered themselves Sapir's students on the basis of quite minimal exposure.

Some of what Sapir was trying to do was in the Boasian tradition and he willingly acknowledged Boas's efforts to "raise the standard of American Indian linguistic work during the last couple of decades" in relation to "the tradition which you have founded" (to Boas, 29 September 1932: APS).

Sapir planned a volume of grammars that would be "more condensed, and, if possible rounded out in form" for the "general linguist" who usually ignored American Indian material "because of the unobviousness of the field from a corporate standpoint" (Sapir to Kroeber, 25 September 1934: UCB). He emphasized (to Kroeber, 17 June 1935: UCB) that Yale linguists wanted such a volume for the William Dwight Whitney publication series. Sapir envisioned a "rough sketch map tracing representative languages," although he did not insist on full genetic classification as he had attempted in 1921 and reiterated in 1929. Swadesh's *Eskimo* was already in hand and exemplified "The Sapir Plan for the Study of American Indian Languages" (cf. Stocking 1974; Voegelin 1952*a*); Kroeber was invited to contribute on Yuki. "I should like to dedicate the volume to Boas and I should not like to have the plan come to his ears prematurely." Sapir wanted to avoid antagonizing Boas by the implication that this work superseded his four-volume *Handbook of American Indian Languages*.

Sapir continued to stress the continuity between his Indian linguistic work and Boas's, partly because he depended on ACLS funding. The New York group trained by Boas met frequently with New Haven Americanists to discuss ongoing work (e.g., Emeneau to Whorf, 31 January 1939: YU), presenting an apparent united front of American Indian linguists to linguistics and anthropology.

The students around Sapir at Yale were his legacy to the discipline of linguistics. They remained a recognizable group within linguistics and anthropology throughout their careers. Hymes (in his obituary of Swadesh, reprinted in Hymes 1983; Hymes and Fought 1975) argues that these students constituted a "First Yale School of Linguistics," which coalesced around Sapir, as the classic Yale school did around Bloomfield.

Mary Haas met Sapir when she was studying comparative philology at Chicago. During his last year there, she married Morris Swadesh and went with him to Vancouver Island for fieldwork (Haas to Murray, 26 July 1978). Sapir wanted Nitinat data to compare to his own Nootka (Haas, p.c.). "Almost at once I heard so much about Sapir that I got interested not in the traditional Indo-European thing but into a comparative sort of thing." Her commitment to the "anthropological perspective" increased after she and Swadesh followed Sapir to Yale in 1931.

Haas believed (to Murray, 26 July 1978) Sapir was always "dominated in some ways" or at least "overwhelmed" by Boas—an effect he had on all his former students. No one "really bucked the old man," because they would find themselves without jobs. Haas was puzzled and somewhat repelled by the constant "little rivalries" among the former Boas students who clustered around Columbia; these were largely women, who "got a very raw deal." It was not an easy period in which to be a female student. When Sapir recommended Swadesh for a job at Berkeley (to Kroeber, 17 July 1935: L UCB), he emphasized that Kroeber could get two linguists for the price of one (the second being Swadesh's wife, Haas). Haas did not consider this chauvinistic (to Murray, 26 July 1978): "[Sapir] told us that he had said it. He didn't think it was being derogatory. . . . Unfortunately it didn't help a bit with Kroeber, because Kroeber was always envious of linguists. The idea of getting 2 probably overwhelmed the man." Although, maintained Haas, Sapir was "always very good to me," he thought it "hopeless" to find jobs for women. In addition, "Sapir had these psychiatrist friends and you know how they have a Freudian perspective on women."

Sapir's attitude toward Haas changed with her increasing linguistic sophistication; her divorce from Swadesh meant that she had to earn a living. Haas became enamored of fieldwork, particularly hunting down the few remaining speakers of southeastern U.S. languages. Haas preferred to work up her materials in the field and was peripheral to Yale politics. When Sapir learned that the Swadeshes were splitting up (to Spier, 25 June 1937: YUDA) he described Haas as "by no means to be sniffed at." She was a better phonetician than Herzog or Whorf and a better Americanist than Herzog or Trager (who weren't Americanists at all). Sapir recommended Haas independently to Kroeber for his California survey, after Swadesh went to Wisconsin (5 August 1937: YUDA): "She is not as brilliant as Morris but more interested in historic problems and fully as accurate in her field methodology."

Haas recalls (to Murray, 26 July 1978) that Sapir trained an amazing number of people given the relative brevity of his teaching years—which she blamed on the long and regrettable isolation of Ottawa. Although he was powerful in institutional terms during the Chicago and Yale years, the time was so short that "he couldn't have had much effect." His "power came rather suddenly. . . . As long as he didn't have an established position in an American university, he couldn't be put on any of those committees. Once he had that, he was put on them."

Sapir took seriously the obligation to find fieldwork funding for his students. He was less successful in finding permanent jobs, though most of the students were still quite junior at the time of his death. Hoijer stayed at Chicago, and Li obtained his position independently. The others were unemployed during Sapir's lifetime except for the hand-to-mouth grants—similar to Sapir's own apprenticeship before Ottawa. Haas "had little fellowships and grants with which he helped me, but the big thing never came along—not for anybody really."

The Sapir family recalls that Sapir was inclined to be critical of his students; the best were Newman, Swadesh, and Li. The first two were associated in most people's minds because of their collaborative work on English grammar and various other enterprises that funded their postdoctoral work at Yale.

Swadesh came to Yale with Sapir and immediately began IHR-sponsored fieldwork with Nootka and Nitinat on Vancouver Island, expecting to complete Sapir's long dormant Nootka texts and grammar. He also worked on Nootka music with Helen Roberts (Roberts to Sapir, 20 June 1936: YU). Other priorities were attacked on an ad hoc basis; in the summer of 1935, Sapir urgently wanted someone to work on Iroquoian; Newman and Swadesh agreed to do this on their vacation if the IHR would pay the field expenses (Sapir to May, 26 July 1935: YU). Swadesh stayed at Yale because of Sapir, but he blamed New Haven's anti-Semitism for many of his personal problems (Haas to Murray, 26 July 1978): "He identified very strongly with Sapir, too; he felt that Sapir wasn't properly appreciated. He was angry at Boas for not accepting Sapir's classification and he tried in various ways to prove that . . . Sapir was absolutely right."

Sapir hoped to place Swadesh at Berkeley and assured Kroeber (17 June 1935: UCB) that there was "no better linguist in the country." His "keenness of analysis," "actual knowledge of linguistic data," "accuracy" of ear, "grasp of methods and principles," and "sheer capacity to do work" were "unparalleled." His surface "asperity of temperament" was not a problem to those who actually came to know him:

I've done all I can for him with fellowships, assistantships, and projects, but there's an end to that sort of thing, and there's no position in sight for him here. . . . I've only had perhaps a couple of students to whom I would apply the dangerous term "genius." He is one of them . . .

Swadesh went to Wisconsin, but this proved temporary. Bloomfield wrote to Boas (7 January 1939: APS) that he felt responsible "in view of Sapir's illness." He was impressed by Swadesh's Menomini texts and organization of young Oneida men to write their own language. But he couldn't find Swadesh a permanent job either.

Haas (to Murray, 26 July 1978) felt that Swadesh "was a good theoretician but he would get bored with it and wouldn't develop his ideas. He wanted some simple way of doing things—fast, like how to phonemicize a language in one night." Swadesh also found himself out of step with developments in American Indian linguistics. He was interested in "linguistic geography," language classification, and other problems that Sapir had left aside as linguistics became increasingly professionalized. Swadesh, however, defended Sapir's classificatory positions as based on ample evidence (1961, 667):

The indications are that Sapir actually examined material for every language or language-family in his [six-unit] scheme, and made no groupings without having found specific items of evidence to support them. He frequently penciled comparisons in the margins of works in his library ... or wrote out lists of cognates, and his students know that he could cite cognates in support of many relationships from memory.

Hoijer fell at the opposite pole of conservatism toward new connections; he edited the sketches planned by Sapir in honor of Boas and his conservatism set the tone for later work.

George Trager was a Slavic linguist who did fieldwork at Taos Pueblo through Sapir. Kiowa and Tanoan (on which he later published with Whorf) shared "fundamental phonetic laws" that reflected ancient genetic connection. In the course of his linguistic work, Trager acquired "in passing, bits of ethnological data ... volunteered by informants."

Carl Voegelin was a late Sapir student who became a self-appointed spokesman for Sapirian linguistics during the 1940s and 1950s, as an alternative to Bloomfieldian structuralism. Sapir inherited Voegelin from Kroeber (17 June 1930: UCB), who recommended him in spite of limited training in linguistics, via anthropology, because of his sustained interest. Sapir penciled a note on Kroeber's letter that Voegelin would be attached to Melville Jacobs's Southwest Laboratory field school to test his capabilities. Sapir put Voegelin to work on Shawnee in Oklahoma (to Kroeber, 13 September 1933: UCB), hoping that he would use linguistic data to reconstruct early population movement. Sapir envisioned Voegelin as straddling the two disciplines rather than as a linguist and expected him to learn linguistic theory from contact with practicing linguists and their field data. For the Tubatulabal morphophonemics of Swadesh and Voegelin, published in 1939, Voegelin explained (to Ted Lightner, 6 October 1970: APS):

Sapir ordered me to write it when I first came to Yale, and assigned Swadesh to me as a tutor since Swadesh knew morphophonemic theory, so far as Sapir had then developed it, while I did not. ... Swadesh put in so much tutorial time that I insisted he be listed as senior author—he was certainly my senior in terms of linguistic knowledge. Sapir told us that he put in much more time than he had anticipated; what he did was to find exceptions to what we would today call rules (e.g., his uncanny sense for anticipating what would occur in

Tub. from his knowledge of Southern Paiute on which he was then reading galley proof). Sapir insisted that we reformulate until there were no remaining or apparent exceptions. (Hymes and Fought 1975, 986)

Swadesh noted to Whorf (3 September 1937: YU) that a group had coalesced in the midwest: Voegelin, Bloomfield (then at Chicago), and Hoijer met once a month. There was no competition between the home institution and the newly mature Sapirians. Nonetheless, the influence of Bloomfield on Swadesh and Voegelin as they began to develop morphophonemics independently of Sapir had important consequences for American linguistics. In many ways, the young Turks were more successful in working up enthusiasm for linguistics than Sapir, whose efforts centered around his new phonemic orthography. Sapir sent his draft to Boas for *IJAL* as a reflection of "something of progress in the appreciation of 'phonemes' as distinct from 'sounds' " (15 August 1934: APS). Boas (28 September 1934: APS) did not "think most of the recommendations that you make are desirable." Bloomfield, caught in the middle, wrote to Boas (4 October 1934: APS) that he had "mislaid Sapir's manifesto." But "general pronouncements on this subject do not excite me. . . . All I want is a few dozen symbols and the privilege of making them mean whatever I choose in any one discussion, or in any one paragraph." Standardization was not an issue for him, and he ignored the implications for professionalization. "The signers are pupils of Sapir who would in any case agree with him." Kroeber (to Boas, 9 October 1934: APS) was opposed to the new phonemic orthography on practical grounds: "When the phonemes have been indubitably determined in a language, the letters chosen for them become of minor importance. Until then . . . premature phonemic considerations are likely to mislead all but exceptional workers." Sapir wanted categories with cross-linguistic validity; Kroeber and Boas, however, remained within the older view of linguistics as handmaiden to ethnology. The orthographic recommendations were published in the *American Anthropologist* rather than in Boas's *IJAL* (Herzog et al. 1934).

Sapir tried to implicate the Columbia group around Boas in his phonemic reform of American Indian linguistics, writing to Boas (8 October 1938: APS) that he wanted two or three New York people to discuss "sound systems and sound alternations" for "our linguistic meeting." Whorf would deal with general issues; Li, who was in New Haven in the fall of 1938, would discuss Sinitic phonemes. Boas did not attend but Sapir (1 November 1938: APS) wanted to follow up.

"It was proposed that we emphasize the relation between phonetics and phonemics by showing what the difference of treatment would mean for specific languages." This was the beginning of structural restatement, which culminated within Bloomfieldian structuralism.

During the 1930s, Sapir, not Bloomfield was the mentor of morphophonemics. Voegelin and Voegelin (1963, 30) claimed that Sapir's Southern Paiute grammar "had the effect of tempting field workers to transcribe texts of preliterate languages phonemically." Boas wrote to students in the field warning that "if they transcribed phonemically, phonetic detail of the languages which they were recording would be lost to posterity."

Zellig Harris met Sapir at the LI in 1937 and was close to both Bloomfield and Sapir. He was a Semiticist, who made brief forays into American Indian linguistics, although Haas (to Murray, 26 July 1978) noted that "fieldwork bored him." Harris would later try to reconcile the Bloomfieldian position with his personal admiration of Sapir (e.g., Harris 1951).

Charles Hockett came to Yale in 1936–1937 and worked with Sapir in psychology of culture and Swadesh in linguistics. Sapir was his dissertation supervisor when he died. Sapir (Hockett to Murdock, 30 July 1938: YUDA) had proposed a descriptive grammar of Potawatomi "with extensive historical and comparative notes," but the material was inadequate for "a stiff dialectology of the Ojibwa group." Hockett then decided he preferred to do Kickapoo ethnological fieldwork. Sapir wrote to Murdock (8 August 1938: YUDA) that the descriptive grammar might encourage Hockett to "extend his Algonquian interests to a dialectic survey of the Ojibwa–Ottawa–Potawatomi–Algonquian group":

My feeling in matters linguistic is never to force the pace. The work is minute and, to most people, soon becomes boring and the returns are relatively slight. So, as soon as a man, like Hockett, shows the least sign of preferring ethnological work, he should by all means be encouraged to go ahead with that because such an interest is far more likely to be rewarding in terms of his career.

Murdock (to Hockett, 15 August 1938: YUDA) accepted Sapir's belief that "a man does best what he wants to do." Sapir would accept the Potawatomi descriptive grammar without the comparative notes for the dissertation, and Hockett could begin Kickapoo work with department money. Hockett then proposed to Murdock (1 October 1938: YUDA) working in psychiatry with Meyer at Johns Hopkins. Instead of a full year in the field, Hockett proposed "shorter bits over a longer period of time." Murdock responded, calmly under the circumstances, that the funding was only for Kickapoo (14 October 1938: YUDA). Sapir commented mildly (to Murdock, 8 October: YUDA) that Meyer, "whom I know and whom I like very much, seems intelligible enough, but I don't yet see what specific proposal Hockett is making, if any." Hockett elected to continue his fieldwork.

After the Kickapoo study, Hockett obtained funds from Boas to spend six months in the Queen Charlotte Islands checking the latter's Haida texts from 1898 (to Murdock, 19 April 1939: YUDA), "since more recent developments in linguistic methodology have rendered much of it unsatisfactory," especially in the phonetics. Boas's acquiescence implicitly acknowledged the effect of Sapir's phonemics on the way fieldwork should be done.

Hockett's thesis was defended only after Sapir's death. Bloomfield was the external examiner (Bloomfield to Murdock, 21 April 1939: YUDA).

Murdock considered Hockett a reasonable product of the department, recommending him as an ethnologist (to Willard Park at Oklahoma, 17 May 1940: YUDA): Hockett's interests, Murdock stated, were "sociological and scientific" and "he habitually views present day social and economic problems from an ethnographical perspective." From Murdock, this was higher praise than Sapir's comment that he regarded Hockett highly as both linguist and ethnologist.

Sapir insisted on bringing Stanley Newman to Yale with him for "psychological work" already underway (on phonetic symbolism) (to May, 14 December 1930: YU). Newman took mostly linguistic courses from Sapir and pursued "linguistic psychology" through Sapir's collaboration with Sullivan. Sapir was unable, however, to obtain funding for interdisciplinary speech studies along psychiatric lines. Newman has been remembered primarily as an American Indian linguist, making this earlier work problematic in retrospect (Darnell 1989). Sapir evaluated Newman more broadly than most of his linguistic students, writing to Kroeber (n.d. 1937: UCB): "Newman is as good a technician as Swadesh," although less committed to fieldwork per se. In linguistic psychology, "his fundamental drive is to understand the patterning of behavior and language happens to be his preferred approach." Sapir responded to Newman's intuitive sense of pattern as he had not to any other of his students. But this made it difficult to place him in a position defined by disciplinary boundaries.

Newman's 1932 dissertation was a grammar of Yokuts that represents the single-best exemplar of Sapirian process grammar, alongside Sapir's own Southern Paiute. Newman and Sapir defended its abstract morphophonemic analysis to Edgerton (Silverstein, p.c.), and the grammar was published as the two men conceived it. When Zellig Harris reviewed Newman's Yokuts for *IJAL*, he characterized it as "aesthetically elegant as well as scientifically satisfactory." The detail was sufficient for the reader to "construct correctly his own statements about the language." Material from six dialects gave comparative perspective (time depth) that was unusual in Americanist work (1943–1944, 196). Harris praised the phonemic perspective not for its contribution to understanding of Yokuts but as providing a "complete common language" for linguistics (1943–1944, 197–198):

> [T]his grammar takes on special methodological importance as perhaps the fullest example of Sapir's mature linguistic methods. Sapir had a consistent and very productive way of handling linguistic material. The fact that he left his Navaho grammar unfinished means that we have no study which can fully reveal his methods. One of the merits of the Yokuts grammar, written when Sapir was alive and by one of his chief students, is that it follows the general lines of Sapir's work.

Language was a pattern of elements, phonemes or morphemes, yielding process or "moving systems" (1943–1944, 199). Words like "pattern" and "configuration" took on a mystical quality to Bloomfieldian structuralists, who increasingly dominated the discipline. Configuration even led to diachronic generalization (1943–1944, 201). Harris insisted that "process" was a method, not simply a term; the relation between two forms involved nonrandom change (1943–1944, 203). Although Harris thought the same generalizations could be stated in terms of Bloomfieldian distribution or "arrangement," the dynamism of Newman's grammar stood in stark, though only implicitly acknowledged, contrast to more "modern" structuralist works. Harris assumed that Newman and Sapir could be understood in terms of the new models and ignored inadequacies in structuralist handling of language change, meaning, and "process." In assuming that "intuitive" field methods should not be dismissed because of their subjective origin (1943–1944, 205), Harris was more influenced by Sapir than he was prepared to admit.

Whorf and the Linguistic Relativity Hypothesis

Benjamin Whorf was the most anomalous of Sapir's Yale coterie. He never held a permanent academic position, although he replaced Sapir during his 1937–1938 sabbatical. His training in chemical engineering and lifetime employment as an insurance investigator were unrelated to his linguistic avocation. Although Whorf carried out professional-quality descriptive studies (two appear in Hoijer 1946), he never obtained an advanced degree in an era of rapid professionalization. Yet, his linguistic relativity hypothesis—that linguistic structure virtually determines thought—still sparks debate among linguists, anthropologists, and philosophers of language. There are tantalizing hints of such a position in the work of Sapir, though coupled with other statements implying the autonomy of purely linguistic structure from culture; Sapir accepted both positions, depending on the problem he was working on.[2] Whorf developed his controversial hypothesis during Sapir's illness and elaborated it after his death, so Sapir never had a chance to comment. Whorf died in 1941 at the age of forty-four, leaving less-sympathetic colleagues to pursue the implications of his work.

In this context, it is important to note what Sapir thought of Whorf before he came to be associated almost exclusively with the linguistic relativity hypothesis. Sapir wrote to Kroeber (30 April 1936: UCB):

Whorf is an awfully good man, largely self-made, and with a dash of genius. He is sometimes inclined to get off the central problem and indulge in marginal speculations but that merely shows the originality and adventuresome quality of his mind. . . . [He] is one of the most valuable American Indian linguists that we have at the present time.

Sapir did not distinguish Whorf from other linguistic students he trained. Moreover, the Whorf papers (YU) indicate that Whorf had a central role in the communication network of the First Yale School as its members dispersed for fieldwork and employment. When Sapir's illness made it more difficult for him to draw the group back to its center, Whorf—who remained in the New Haven area—increasingly filled this role.

Whorf accepted Sapir's expansion of the narrow Indo-European basis of linguistic theory (1956, 218): "We shall no longer be able to see a few recent dialects of the Indo-European family, and the rationalizing techniques abstracted from their patterns, as the apex of the evolution of the human mind." Whereas Sapir's argument was specific to grammatical categories, Whorf was more interested in the philosophical implications of linguistics. Close examination of Whorf's affiliation to the First Yale School of linguistics is necessary to a historically accurate reading of his "hypothesis." Rollins (1980, 47) argues that Whorf's motives for doing linguistics began and ended in philosophy, specifically theosophy, and cites Whorf's nonlinguistic writings as evidence of continued motivation outside his adopted discipline. Carroll (1956), in contrast, suggests that his infatuation with the romanticism of Antoine Fabré d'Olivet was merely "an eccentricity which Whorf outgrew."

Whorf was initially attracted to the study of languages and later to Sapir's version of linguistic science because it shed potential light on philosophical questions. But he learned to formulate these questions in terms of evidence acceptable to linguists—for example, in his grammars of Hopi and Nahuatl and his specifically linguistic papers. That Whorf's stance was "mystical" and Sapir's "secular" (Rollins 1980, 62) is an oversimplification, especially in that Rollins sees Sapir himself as "delicately poised between science and art" (1980, 66).

Whorf studied Hebrew, Aztec, and Maya (Carroll 1956) and received encouragement from Meso-American archaeologists Herbert Spinden, Alfred Tozzer, and Sylvanus Morley of Harvard. None of them were knowledgeable in linguistics, but they valued Whorf's apparent ability to translate linguistic texts useful for archaeological interpretations. Spinden encouraged Whorf (16 March 1928: YU) to present a paper at the Congress of Americanists in New York and meet "other men" working in the field; it is unclear whether Sapir attended. Whorf (to Sturtevant, 20 July 1928: YU) also visited the Linguistic Institute at Yale that summer, establishing a long-term friendship with J. Alden Mason, who taught primitive linguistics. Tozzer encouraged Whorf (18 October 1928: YU) to formulate a "fairly definite problem" and apply for an SSRC fellowship to Mexico; Mason wanted him to compare Nahuatl and Piman (Whorf to Tozzer, 20 October 1928: YU)—that is, to enter the comparative Uto-Aztecan field sketched out by Sapir's early work on Ute and Southern Paiute. Whorf used his grant during his vacation (John Van Sickle to Whorf, 5 January 1929: YU) and thanked Sapir (11 January 1929: YU) for supporting his application. Whorf again visited the Yale LI in 1929 (to Sturtevant, 8 July: YU) and was disappointed to find no work in American Indian linguistics. He was self-consciously building up professional contacts, especially through the LSA.

Tozzer and Spinden encouraged Whorf to send his paper on Nahuatl tone accent and day signs to Sapir. Sapir considered it an "important paper" (to Tozzer, 14 December 1930: YU), and Tozzer noted to Whorf: "This is high praise from a severe critic. I am very glad for you." Whorf sent Sapir (24 February 1931: YU) a Maya paper with "a number of beautifully regular sound-shifts."

Whorf was delighted when Sapir came to Yale, close enough to allow commuting to graduate classes at Yale beginning in the fall of 1931. Carroll (1956) dates Whorf's linguistic career from his "contact with a small but earnest band of Sapir's students" at Yale, but this only intensified his professionalization.[3]

Sapir wrote to Mason (11 October 1932: APS) of "an enthusiast" in Uto-Aztecan named Whorf. Mason responded (9 November 1932: APS) that he knew Whorf and had thought back in 1928 that "some institution ought to grab that lad so he could put in all his time on linguistics and not so much on fire insurance."

Whorf made no secret of his interest in the "fundamental" problem of meaning (to Sapir, 6 July 1932: YU). Although he was not writing for psychologists, he read in a "somewhat desultory" way "the concepts of ordinary psychology"; but this was "no help toward making an analysis, or any sort of scientific approach." Whorf tried unsuccessfully to organize other Mayanists along Sapirian lines (to Oliver LaFarge, 3 January 1933: YU), wanting a "coordinated group" to attack "the whole Mayan stock from a comparative viewpoint, as Sapir is doing with Athabascan and I am with Uto-Aztecan."

Whorf increasingly associated himself with Sapir's group at Yale and with anthropology, entering into correspondence with Kroeber on Uto-Aztecan and Parsons for financial support of his work with Ernest Naquayouma, a Hopi Indian living in New York City. Fred Eggan approached Whorf (10 January 1934: YU) for information on Hopi phonemes to aid in his ethnological work. Eggan (to Whorf, 8 October 1940: YU) hoped for a working knowledge of Hopi and wondered how it fit into Uto-Aztecan. Whorf (10 December 1940: YU) suggested ties of Hopi to northern Paiute and Mono-Paviotso. Eggan (14 December 1940: YU) replied that he needed "historical control" of ethnological material.

Kroeber (5 June 1935: YU) urged Whorf to resist the temptation to wait until all evidence was in. The "delay of a generation or two" left the ethnologists "high and dry." Kroeber was "quite appalled" at the way his thirty-year-old classification had been "accepted and built upon merely because it was the only one available." Internal differentiation of Uto-Aztecan—"even a bare formal classification"—would help "drawing inferences as to ethnic and cultural movements." If such a classification could be supported by "even some signposts of evidence, that much the better." Whorf, however, remained cautious about classificatory work (20 August 1935: YU): "there are still too many little-known languages lying around and perhaps concealing facts that might materially affect my views." Kroeber (30 October 1935: YU) thought Whorf had taken Uto-Aztecan philology "a long jump beyond Sapir's fundamental paper" and had "reconstructed the basic structure while [Sapir] hardly went beyond the phonemic apparatus, except in touches and allusions." Kroeber realized that "ethnological and historical significance" was probably inaccessible by "sound philological technique as such." In other words, he had decided that the great ethnological–linguistic synthesis of the 1910s and 1920s was not only premature but fundamentally impossible! Ethnologists needed "a line of attack" compatible with "the kind of thing that people like Sapir and you are doing."

Bloomfield, starting from quite different premises than Kroeber, congratulated Whorf on his Uto-Aztecan work (7 January 1936: YU) as "a splendid example of how this kind of thing ought to be done." Mason (to Voegelin, 7 November 1939: YU) considered him "clearly the best man we have for the genetic problem," and Haas sent him (20 November 1939: YU) everything she had "about the probable classification of the languages of the Southeast and Texas" in anticipation of his synthesis. The synthesis, however, was a team project (Trager 1946, 3): around 1937, Whorf urged Trager to compile a map of North American languages "using the modification of the Sapir classification that Whorf and I had worked out" and organized by Murdock's outline map of tribes. The map was never published but was used by the Yale group.

Haas (to Whorf, 16 February 1937: YU) assumed that Trager's work on Tanoan would lead to a superstock or phylum classification with Whorf's Uto-Aztecan and "prove to everybody the soundness of Sapir's intuitions along those lines." This Trager–Whorf collaboration "gives me new courage."

In 1937 and 1938, Whorf entered into a complex debate with

Prague School linguist Count N. Trubetzkoy about phonemes in Mayan and Uto-Azetecan. Whorf had reconstructed three vowel lengths for Hopi, and Trubetzkoy (27 July 1937: YU) was convinced there were only two, wanting to use Whorf's data for his counter-argument (18 December 1937: YU). Whorf professed himself convinced (17 January 1938: YU). This is one of the few documented contacts between Sapirian and Prague School linguists in the 1930s. Sapir encouraged Whorf (4 October 1938; YU) to hold his own, reiterating his conviction that phonemic analysis had to be based in native speaker judgment. The issue

should be settled from the standpoint of which of the two modes of presentation seems more apt and economical for Hopi grammar rather than on general principles. If you could follow up with statements such as the one you quote from a Hopi informant, it might help you to solve the problem. The feelings of natives about such matters are extremely important, even if they express themselves amateurishly.

Voegelin (to Whorf, 5 November 1937: YU) praised the one hundred Trager–Whorf reconstructions as "the first application of the proper principle for enlarging or merging stocks." The key was to compare a whole set of languages.[4] Haas (to Whorf, 13 November 1937: YU) articulated similar comparative principles when she reported that her preliminary dictionary of Creek was a basis for "obtaining quickly" considerable material on related languages "as I get around to them."

Sapir's students were redefining American linguistics, self-consciously, expecting to fill classificatory gaps by a concerted assault of fieldwork and analysis. Sapir himself was peripheral, although he was the inspiration. The audience was primarily anthropological. Voegelin wrote to Whorf (2 January 1938: YU) that the linguistic meetings were "not inclined to entertain non-conventional ideas. We are inheritors of a perfect technique, and it is our duty to follow it. . . . There was none of the rapport so common at the anthropological meetings."

Sapir and his students held themselves apart from the Boas group. Sapir noted to Whorf (8 October 1938: YU) that Herzog and Newman were located in New York but not of it. Some of the young Boasians had a good ear, but "Boas has simply never taught them the patterning of sounds." Their chance of learning was not helped by "loyalty to Boas," which might "interfere practically with the proper functioning of their cerebral cortices." Herzog also complained to Whorf (24 October 1939: YU) about the incompatibility of the New York and New Haven groups, proposing discussion rather than silent antagonism. Some had "modes of thought too well established over the decades to change them."

Voegelin organized a symposium for the AAA in 1939, including Bloomfield (linguistic grouping and reconstruction), Andrade (descriptive and historical classification of linguistic forms), Mason (archaeology and linguistics), Voegelin (linguistics and ethnology), Frederick Johnson (Middle American linguistic groups), and Whorf (North American linguistic groups). Voegelin assumed that Whorf was the best person for the genetic question (to Whorf, November 1939: YU), proposing a contrast between "what has been done" and "what has been merely suggested." Sapir's students wanted to make his historical work respectable to the new generation of more conservative linguists.

Whorf favored a linguistic classification intermediate between Sapir's and the established Powell classification and more palatable to the new conservatism than Sapir's. To Robert Spencer, Whorf wrote (10 February 1940: YU) that he recognized seven or possibly eight stocks, separating Iroquoian and Mid-Continental from Hokan (now considered a phylum of stocks) and possibly Mosan from Algonquian. He left Keresan and Yuki as isolates, though the term was not used. The technique for distant phylum affiliation was "more difficult and rigorous than that of comparative linguistics within a stock." Whorf died before elaborating this hypothesis, and Trager went on to other problems. Whorf was arguably the only one of Sapir's students who might have challenged the Bloomfieldian dominance of the next two decades. Because he died prematurely with much of his potential work undone, Whorf's reputation as an American Indian linguist has been eclipsed; he is remembered almost entirely for the linguistic relativity hypothesis.

During Sapir's leave in 1937–1938, Spier, as acting chairman, was concerned to maintain student enthusiasm for technical linguistic work. Although Sapir could teach by the sink-or-swim method, students would be unlikely to tolerate this from a junior visiting lecturer. Ethnology students, moreover, were increasingly restive about requirements in linguistics as that discipline became increasingly nonanthropological. Spier (to Sapir, 30 June 1937: YUDA) thought Whorf was the ideal candidate:

Whorf has a very stimulating way, I think, and I would like to take advantage of his interest in hooking up language and ethnology, for I think it would take with many of our students. They might thus be encouraged to give serious attention to linguistics, when a "straight" linguistics course might leave them cold.

Whorf proposed a North American linguistics course ambitiously covering "a number of languages," including Hopi, Aztec, Maya, other Uto-Aztecan languages, a Penutian language, and a survey of the rest, with comparative treatment of Uto-Aztecan, Azteco-Tanoan, and Macro-Penutian, and general discussion of language classification—the relation of linguistics to anthropology and its usefulness "both as a field technique and as a help to psychological insight and a guide to historical perspectives."

Whorf "would want pay for this" but thought he would come cheaper than anyone else comparatively qualified. He was ready to put himself forward as a professional linguist. He did not propose to leave his other employment, but he wanted the same recognition as Sapir's other linguistic students.

Spier offered Whorf the course in American Indian linguistics (18 July 1937: YUDA), noting that Trager would teach phonetics. He warned that "most of our students are not linguistic specialists" so that "this would be an opportunity for you to engage their interest by giving some breadth to your course." Whorf's response was ready (4 August 1937: YUDA):

I have had for some time ideas about what I should try to teach in a course of this kind. . . . I realize that . . . the students will have, for the most part, only the haziest notions of linguistics, and my idea would be to excite their interest in the linguistic approach as a way of developing understanding of the ideology of other peoples. The keynote, I should say, would be linguistics as bearing on problems that confront the anthropologist, including the fields of ethnology, archaeology and history.

Whorf (to Carroll, August 1937: YU) would focus largely on "a psychological direction, and the problems of meaning, thought and idea in so-called primitive cultures," aiming to "reveal psychic factors or constants" and the "organization of raw experience into a consistent and readily communicable universe of ideas through the medium of linguistic patterns." These documents make it clear that Whorf's famous hypothesis crystallized out of his efforts to translate American Indian linguistics in the Sapirian framework for nonlinguists.

Sapir was interested in approaching the nature of mind through linguistic form. Whorf went further, addressing the mechanisms and forms in a way psychologists could understand. Whorf's position was cultural, in that he assumed these categories to be shared by all native speakers of a language. But this was not the effort to correlate culture and personality which Sapir had developed in his interdisciplinary work.

Whorf explicitly modeled his approach to writing on Sapir's: "This is in a way after the fashion of Sapir, for he always hit the nail right on the head, taking the chance that his reader would use his thinking apparatus." That Whorf was read by his successors in a more rigid fashion does not do justice to his intentions. The Sapir–Whorf hypothesis was tested in rigid scientific fashion in the 1940s and 1950s and largely dismissed when direct unequivocal correlations of language and culture failed to emerge.

CHAPTER TWENTY

The Yale Institute of Human Relations

The Yale Institute of Human Relations was established in 1929 as part of a larger plan to coordinate the "educational resources" of the university around the study of man—thereby making Yale more attractive to foundations supporting research (May 1971, 141–142). The IHR

envisioned the establishment of a large center for professional education, research, and community service, including the Schools of Medicine, Law, and Nursing; the biological and social science departments of the Graduate School; and the New Haven Hospital. . . . [It intended] to promote cooperative research on problems of human welfare and to develop a unified science of individual and social behavior as a foundation for the more effective training of physicians, lawyers, ministers, nurses, teachers, and research workers.

From its inception, the program was more integrated than anything the Chicago LCRC ever envisioned.

Pragmatic philosophy produced a new view of science in this period, stressing "multiple independent causation" in which causes at different levels of structure could not be reduced to one another (Morawski 1986, 219). Diverse disciplines saw themselves as contributing to a synthesis; when all the parts were understood, the nature of the whole would emerge. In Mendelian biology, relativity physics, and Freudian psychology, single overarching paradigms seemed to provide simple answers. Increasing professionalization of disciplines made research more important than undergraduate teaching.

These new goals gave credence to formal and mathematical models (like those Sapir had rejected at Chicago); avoiding the "perplexities" of subjectivity. Psychology was most comfortable with the emerging synthesis (Morawski 1986, 220): "In the end the certainty that had been sacrificed in the newer models for knowledge was (re)located in an orderly methodology—in the procedural rules for conducting scientific work." Interdisciplinary models were drawn from corporate practice, rewarding the enterprising researcher (Morawski 1986, 22). The philanthropic foundations supported what they could understand, that is, businesslike organization and procedure.

Two individuals determined the policy of the IHR: Mark May, an educational psychologist, came to Yale in 1927 and served as director from 1935 until his retirement in 1960; he was passionately committed to teamwork and synthesis as the IHR mandate. Yale president James R. Angell, however, wanted research to establish Yale in foundation eyes; he needed to acquire superstars, along the Chicago model (Morawski 1986, 225): cooperative research programs "would ensure against the cognitive idiosyncracies of individual scientists." May and Angell "challenged the cognitive competency of the individual and derided the individualistic 'fetish' among researchers, though they usually appended an exception for an anomaly, the 'genius.'" Sapir was hired as a superstar—an exception to the corporate rules. And indeed, at Chicago he had never played by the rules. He wanted to train students, judge the research important for them to do, and not worry about funding. He assumed, as head of anthropology, freedom to articulate the program of his choice.

Sapir's definition of psychology had little to do with the experimental laboratory or with Freudian clinical analysis; rather, he favored "a more classical attitude toward human nature" (Karl 1974, 119): mental activity was crucial to explanation of human behavior. Sapir was a convinced antibehaviorist. Chicago social science had its quantitative and behaviorist research, but this was always balanced by a more ethnographic and configurationalist ethos, which Sapir took for granted. Conflict at Yale was inevitable.

In January 1929 Yale requested modest in-house funding for the IHR, arguing that the country had "but two or three universities of major rank at which an integrated plan" for the behavioral sciences was possible. Medical school cooperation was emphasized (3 January 1929: YU). The Spelman Memorial had funded the preexisting Yale

Institute of Psychology, and support was expected to increase proportionately with the reorganization.

There was some internal disagreement over what kind of psychology to emphasize. In January 1929 (YU), Donald Slesinger argued for psychoanalysis, although Dorothy Swain Thomas (n.d. 1929: YU) doubted that "scientific results would emerge through the study of psychoanalysis by psychoanalysts" and thought that students of human behavior should draw on psychoanalysis as needed. At this point, the synthesis was envisioned loosely.

Sapir established an initial program of nine anthropology projects in the IHR by 1932–1933 (Annual Report to IHR: YU): Dollard (abnormal behavior from the sociological point of view), Herzog (Navajo and African music), Scudder McKeel (community survey in Connecticut), Spier (Yuman cultural survey), William Morgan (a medical doctor, Navajo culture and personality), Murdock (Haida), Newman (phonetic symbolism), Hortense Powdermaker (Negro community study), and an unspecified graduate student for Navajo ethnographic work. This was an ambitious program for a new faculty member; its direct connection to anything outside anthropology, however, was minimal.

Wissler, who preceded Sapir at Yale by five years and mediated between anthropology and psychology, was initially eager to accommodate his appointment. Sapir assured May (23 January 1931: YU) that it would be "highly desirable to have the new work in anthropology in close contact with the older work already founded by Wissler." No one suggested that the two programs were related, and Sapir was careful to stipulate that he control his part of the research. Wissler gracefully agreed (to May, 30 March 1931: YU) to provide space for Sapir and his students "so far as we have room to spare." Space would remain a persistent issue between the Wissler and Sapir factions of IHR anthropology.

Graduate Dean Furniss officially notified Wissler (23 December 1931: YU) that Sapir would be in primary charge of the joint budget and space would be rearranged. The pretext was to preserve Wissler's cooperation with the psychologists. Angell (to Furniss, 11 January 1934: YU) was willing to abandon Wissler, albeit as tactfully as possible: "I should naturally want to deal with any readjustment quite considerately and with as little abruptness as possible but I think the present situation is quite unreasonable." May explained the situation to Wissler (2 February 1934: YU) in terms of policy changes in the IHR: "we have been developing gradually a unified program of studies in which practically all of the social sciences and some of the biological sciences are integrated." This required that "from time to time, we liquidate our interests in research started early in the life of the Institute which now appears unrelated to and difficult to articulate with our central core of studies."

Wissler prepared a final report covering the years from 1929–1934 YU): "Having been relieved of all responsibility for the anthropological section of the Institute, the writer attempted to liquidate these projects as soon as possible." The supposed psychological import of Wissler's IHR appointment was not in evidence; culture and personality studies were completely absent. Although Wissler was removed from control of anthropological work in the IHR, his part-time affiliation with Yale continued until after Sapir's death (and his own mandatory retirement). He provided an alternative for anyone who didn't like Sapir's definition of interdisciplinary collaboration.

Initially, the IHR was careful to insist that its integration did not preclude individual research directions. H. S. Burr of the Yale Medical School was among those protesting (18 December 1931: YU) the reorganization of the institute in a more bureaucratic manner: it "was to be a free association of the best minds the University could attract. . . . Opportunities would be given for cooperative, as well as individual, attacks on difficult problems" in "a free association of scholars." Angell (19 December 1931: YU) considered this "a most complete misapprehension" of the intended reorganization, which was "advisory, not mandatory," and involved no "coercive direction" of research. Angell asked if Burr's personal research was restricted in any way; the larger issue of the validity of unrelated and unfunded projects was not addressed. The IHR Annual Report of 15 August 1932 (YU) was explicit as to the direction of the envisioned changes:

We are more and more convinced that the Institute should center its major emphasis on types of research which could not or would not be undertaken without an Institute. At the present time approximately 80% of the funds of the Institute are devoted to projects which are only loosely or remotely related. Many of them do not even fit into a larger pattern. While there is an increasing tendency toward cooperation among investigators in diverse fields, yet these instances are mainly sporadic and accidental.

There was increasing pressure to justify funding. In the early years

(May 1971, 145), "before a coordinated program began to take shape, it was deemed desirable to consider as members of the Institute all individuals who were doing research in the biological and social sciences." This "laudable plan" did not work well, however, because individuals continued to identify primarily with departments rather than with the institute.

The pressure for integration culminated at the halfway point of the ten-year Rockefeller grant of 1929. A report to Angell for the Rockefeller Foundation (29 May 1934: YU), undoubtedly written by May, summarized the internal review process: in its first stage, the institute had acquired personnel and facilities "somewhat like a scientific expedition that recruits a research staff." Only in the second stage was it possible to "determine how far we can go in developing an integrated program" for studying human behavior. Various senior appointments, including that of Sapir, bridged gaps in the previous program. There would soon be "a genuine fraternity of scientists among whom there are no petty jealousies or scientific secrets." The unified program "is being achieved by the simple expedient of using a common research laboratory, namely, the New Haven community." Although it was not yet feasible to "organize all the work of the Institute into one grand program," the directors of the twenty-five research units had begun to meet monthly, creating "a paper program that *looks* quite unified."

Sapir attempted to rationalize his program in terms of the institute plan. His annual report (to May, 15 August 1932: YU) recommended continuing "several projects of a strict ethnographic nature . . . even though they are only remotely related to other social science studies." He also wrote to May (10 December 1934: YU) of work in "social psychology among primitive groups": "I think that it is entirely proper, and quite within the scope of work primarily intended for the Institute, to emphasize behavior studies among primitive groups." Sapir tried, however, to circumvent IHR policy changes through Angell (5 December 1935: YU), requesting ten thousand dollars for each of the next two years because "a number of the younger men in anthropology are very much interested in personality in various cultural groups." Angell had no money with which to respond to this appeal.

The official five-year report, dated 1 December 1934 (YU), optimistically noted: "Traditional departmental barriers will tend increasingly to vanish and more voluntary cooperative and collaborative arrangements will emerge in the interest of common goals." The description of programs was less integrated. A March 1935 memorandum (YU) was more apologetic, stressing that "very few scientists at Yale or elsewhere have had training or experience in cooperative research." The IHR needed greater control of personnel and budgets and a full-time administrator.

Allan Gregg of the Rockefeller Foundation made notes on his interviews with institute personnel (n.d. september 1935: RAC). Opinions were varied. Burr, who had protested reorganization, considered the program "seriously diffuse." Sapir "would hate to see the Institute go." He "would be interested to see studies of individual personalities along the form of clinical work." Sapir was "rather adroit at evading further comments but more because I think he believes the above are the important points than that he is concealing anything." Sapir's lack of enthusiasm for May's synthesis was the underlying issue; that he tried not to jeopardize the institute is clear. In an undated memo about the same time, Gregg (RAC) described Sapir as "a little outside the group; in other respects the Institute is getting along well." Presumably he recognized the inherent collision course. Gregg was impressed with May and thought that Angell's retirement as president would bode well for the institute. Dollard became increasingly committed to the IHR after its reorganization. A note from Edmund Day on a memo from Gregg about a visit to Yale (17 September 1935: RAC) noted that Dollard had "an exceptionally clear idea of what the Institute is about."

At the time of reorganization (Report, 3 October 1935: RAC), the IHR was evenly divided between the biological and social sciences. "Studies extending beyond the New Haven community" included "Anthropological studies of American Indians, and primitive cultures, primitive languages, art and music." Sapir's emphasis on culture and personality was not mentioned. Before 1935, programs were "of a continuing character," with block funds allotted to departments. But by 1935 the liquid research fund could no longer support "new projects of an interdepartmental character" (May 1971, 149). Rockefeller renewals in 1938 were contingent on reorganization, with May's power as director backed by his administration of the liquid research fund.

May sought support, both personal and political, from IHR researchers. For example, he emphasized to Dorothy Swain Thomas (6 August 1935: YU) that the reorganization was "based on the central idea which sold the Institute to the [Rockefeller] Foundation." He had decided that "we must either make a very concerted and even desperate plan to relate our various research programs to this central idea or else we must admit that the idea itself is impractical and that the Foundation was sold on a pipedream." May implied that Thomas's funding was contingent on strengthening her life-history approach "by the more general statistical approaches." Thomas insisted (to May, 10 September 1937: YU) on her "personal loyalty to you and therefore to your program," but its "one-sidedness" was incompatible with "the development of a well-rounded social science program." May interpreted this as rejection of his program and thereafter ignored both Thomas and her research. In spite of her marriage to W. I. Thomas, she was not powerful enough to be tolerated unless she was a fully trustworthy ally.

In 1936, May initiated evening meetings among the senior staff, including Sapir, Murdock, Wissler, and Dollard, to talk about research perspectives (Eugene Kahn to May, 16 October 1936: YU). Erik Homburger (Erikson) (to May, 25 April 1936: YU) was disturbed at the attempt to reconcile Clark Hull's stimulus–response learning theory with psychoanalysis because the latter was not equally systematized. May's synthesis was premature.

Allan Gregg's interview notes of 16–19 November 1936 (RAC) acknowledged that the synthesis was less than complete: "The men so chosen never got together. . . . The leaders that were brought in had points of view, habits of work and personalities . . . which don't favor work in groups." May wanted teamwork, to be achieved through young men, most of them trained at the institute and loyal to it; they "got together with the approval of their professors but not in their company." Dollard was high on the list of team players.

Dollard wrote to Mead (23 November 1936: LC) that the Rockefeller Foundation seemed reasonably impressed: "We had a big seminar meeting . . . where we put on the Institute collaborative stunt." May was "standing his ground very well." Murdock's increasing interest was advantageous "since we do not get much from the anthropologists directly." By the time of Gregg's 18 October 1937 (YU) interviews, May had decided not to ask the Rockefeller Foundation for "support to Sapir's anthropology." The anthropologists had tried to "contribute to the purposes of the Institute" without appreciable result.

Clark Hull's behaviorist psychology was first proposed as an integrating device in the fall of 1935; however, "a majority of the members of the group were not really interested in it" (May 1971, 157). May decided that only the younger men were flexible enough to change. The annual report for 1936–1937 (YU) opposed the "hunches" and "private intellectual interests" of the single scholar to coordinated research planning. Hull's motivation theory would reconcile learning theory with Freudian psychology.

Hull's departmental seminar was opened to IHR staff and offered a "systematic approach to the integration of the social sciences" (Annual Report for 1936–1937: YU). The Monday Night Group began in 1936 with a dozen junior members and expanded to about thirty. Hull brought together "the powerful intellectual tools of logic and mathematics" and "the highly developed experimental and observational procedures of laboratories," and produced "scientific systems on related but over-lapping problems," thereby evolving a broader social science theory.

The new program had three major prongs; learning and behavior and personality development were the two that fascinated May. The first centered around Hull and applied principles of animal behavior to human society, demonstrating "the value of scientific theory as a methodological procedure for achieving a comprehensive and unified social science" (May 1971, 161). Second, Dollard, whose coming to Yale under Sapir's auspices was relegated to a dependent clause, led the personality work. May (1971, 161) argued that psychoanalysis and behavior dynamics had not been integrated because the former was not "academically respectable." Dollard changed all that, with "a series of studies which led not only to the further development and modification of the theory but also to its interrelation with Hull's principles of behavior, on the one hand, and with social structure and culture, on the other." In 1935–1936 (May 1971, 162), Hull, Dollard, and newly hired psychoanalyst Earl Zinn tried to decide whether the "basic generalizations in psychoanalysis could be deduced logically from principles of behavior and learning theory." If not, learning theory would have to be brought into line. The seminar focused on the testing of aggression as a response to frustration and depended heavily on animal behavior models.

The third area of concentration for the IHR was Social Structure and Culture (May 1971, 163–164); May found it difficult to reconcile this anthropological perspective with his interests in learning theory and personality. In 1936–1937, the evening seminars attacked well-known sociological theories with the aim of "relating the cultural ideas and empirical generalizations found in these theories to principles of behavior." Unsurprisingly, given Yale tradition and Sapir's estrangement from the integration campaign, the evolutionary sociology of Sumner and Keller was deemed "the most promising." Murdock brought this work to institute attention through Dollard and "set out to learn psychoanalytic theory."[1] Social psychologist Leonard Doob (p.c.) suggests that Sapir avoided the seminars because they were "over-simplified."

Murdock's Cross-Cultural Survey began in 1937. His Human Relations Area Files were intended "to save time in digging out the answers to questions which were being put to the anthropologists by the other members of the group" (May 1971, 166). Sapir was not included in this synthesis, never accepting an anthropological role in interdisciplinary social science as mere collection of ethnographic exotica. Murdock, in contrast, had long wanted to test theories of social evolution by statistical techniques (IHR Annual Report for 1930–1931: YU); he envisioned "a comprehensive study of the cultural traits in 2,000 primitive tribes," although by 1937 this ambitious goal had been reduced to 400 selected groups. Only the resources of the institute could support this program.

Murdock (n.d. Ca. 1937: YUDA) argued that "conventional anthropology" was unaccustomed to asking general questions ("we can cite only a specific case or two out of our memory or else a vague general impression"). Even descriptively, the data of anthropology remained "undigested and unanalyzed." Anthropology was, moreover, "blissfully ignorant or even scornful of the work of sociologists and psychologists—and therefore could not answer their questions." Murdock was prepared to dismiss the entire Boasian paradigm along with Sapir's department of anthropology. Within the institute, however, Murdock's synthesis was welcome.

The Rockefeller Foundation provided a final ten-year research grant to the institute beginning in 1939; it was one of the few social science institutions to receive ongoing funding. By the end of the 1930s, however, foundations and universities alike no longer expected grand interdisciplinary synthesis.

The Medical School Alternative

Yale's professional schools—law, medicine, and divinity—were in the forefront of Angell's modernization; all were included in the original mandate of the institute. Dean W. P. Ladd of the Berkeley Divinity School (to Luther Wiegle, 19 May 1930: YU) saw the IHR as a way to unite his institution with the Yale Divinity School. Robert Hutchins, dean of the law school until 1930 when he became president of the University of Chicago, was committed to social science orientation in legal training.

Milton Winternitz was dean of the medical school from 1920 to 1935. Under his direction, it explored the role of mind in disease as understood by biology and medicine (Walter Miles to May, 14 January 1936: YU). "Winter ran a one-man show for fifteen years" (Oren 1986, 141–142). Descriptions of him ranged from "genius" to "bastard," and he "ruled with an iron hand" (Oren 1986, 141). His was one of the few medical schools to win the approval of the Flexner Report to the Rockefeller Foundation on American medical education. Winternitz was, however, an anti-Semitic Jew, and Yale could not tolerate him indefinitely (Oren 1986, 150): "The Dean's eccentricities grew too much for the men he had hired. . . . His revolutionary concepts of tying medicine into the social sciences were only begrudgingly accepted." Winternitz was deposed by a faculty coup in 1935 and replaced by Yale alumnus Stanhope Bayne-Jones, whose commitment to interdisciplinary social science was considerably less.

During these years, however, Sapir found more welcome company in the medical school than in the IHR. Winternitz became a personal friend; his functionalist approach to medicine and insistence on the importance of mental phenomena were welcome to Sapir. Winternitz even wanted to teach preventive medicine, based on behavioral studies, to help individuals adjust to the stresses of modern metropolitan life (Morawski 1986, 227–228). Sapir's ideas about the loss of "genuine" culture in modern American civilization were similar enough to invite discussion.

Sapir was also drawn to the medical school because of his collaboration with Sullivan. Clinical practice provided the empirical data base that the interdisciplinary social science needed. Sapir provided his own cross-cultural perspective.

Sapir participated in a series of medical school lectures on the social science perspective. In 1937, he discussed "human beings as defined by culture" and "human beings as personalities" in a series on "Backgrounds of Medical Practice" (Ira Hiscock to Harold Lund, 7 February 1935: YU). Sapir intended to give medical students "a broader view of human society and of the role which medicine plays in it."

He (5 March 1935: YU) favored psychoanalysis as "nearest to dis-covering the terms in which the early experiences can be defined and evaluated." Personality classification (Jung) was much less useful for "throwing light upon the mainsprings of human behavior."

May was also interested in collaborating with the medical school. The IHR attempted, unsuccessfully, to involve Winternitz in the New Haven community study of its social science division (memorandum, January 1932: YU). Medical staff, however, were put off by the im-plication that they did not know their own business. For example, Edwin F. Gildea wrote to May (27 April 1935: YU) that "no one school" of studying human behavior had been "very successful"; he saw no easy route to a "synthesis of the knowledge supplied by various disciplines." May was left with the problem of reconciling "the con-flicting elements" within the IHR.

Sapir knew Bayne-Jones, also a fellow of Trumbull College, before he became dean of the medical school. He presented Bayne-Jones with copies of his own papers to follow up his lectures the previous year (22 November 1935: YU). Sapir was eager to discuss the "general field" of culture and personality, noting that his twelve-member NRC committee on personality in relation to culture included three mem-bers from Yale. Bayne-Jones (30 November 1935: YU) was reading the papers by Sapir, interested in the NRC committee, and eager to talk to Sapir about the "best relations" of the IHR and the medical school.

In 1936–1937, Sapir participated in a lecture series on "Social and Cultural Problems in Psychiatry," speaking on "Why Cultural An-thropology Needs the Psychiatrist," published in 1938 in the first issue of Sullivan's *Psychiatry*. The series also included May, Dollard, and sociologist Maurice Davy. However, communication, though surviving the replacement of Winternitz by a less-sympathetic successor, was too late for Sapir in terms of funding for training programs and research.

Erik Homburger (Erikson) also seemed to promise ties between medicine and social science. May (to Herbert Shenton of the Macy Foundation, 1 February 1936: YU) considered him "the leading child analyst of America" and persuaded him to consult part-time for the IHR. Henry Murray of Harvard recommended Homburger (to May, 6 March 1936: YU) in terms that would have fascinated Sapir and might well have repelled May:

[H]e is an artist by temperament and training. He has thorough knowledge of the Freudian conceptual scheme and can apply it with more intelligence and feeling to the behavior of children than anyone I know of . . . but he has as yet shown very little inclination or ability to devise an adequate experimental situation and to put his theories to the test.

However, Erikson (his name now officially changed) moved to the Berkeley Institute of Child Welfare (to May, 27 March 1939: YU) because his work was not the synthesis that May had in mind.

Dollard's Realignment With the IHR

Although Dollard came to Yale at Sapir's invitation, he soon cast his fortunes with the IHR. Sapir had expected an ally and was bitterly disappointed at Dollard's disloyalty, although he masked this with humor (Osgood, p.c.). Sapir felt that Dollard misrepresented his projects at the IHR (Helen Sapir Larson, p.c.). Dollard was recalled as a difficult personality at Yale, anti-Semitic, WASP, and highly ambitious (Leonard Doob, p.c.). Dollard, with some justification, considered himself the mastermind behind May and the integrated program of the IHR (Doob, p.c.). But Dollard did not get along well with Hull, the supposed theoretical guru of the integration plan.

From the beginning, Dollard was a counterpoint to Sapir. His dissertation (Chicago 1932) on changing functions of the American family used statistical methods that Sapir eschewed. During his year in Europe after the postponement of the Impact Seminar, Dollard wrote to Sapir (21 February 1932: YU) that he wanted to go beyond statistics to social psychology and study the same questions from alternative points of view. This was, of course, entirely consistent with Sapir's own idea of interdisciplinary procedure. "Some form of life history technique" would perhaps have later statistical applications. Dollard assumed, correctly, that this would fit in well with the interests of the working group in New Haven.

Because of the IHR, Yale anthropology was virtually unique in North America in emphasizing research over teaching. When the American Council on Education surveyed anthropology departments in 1933 (R. M. Hughes to Margaret Mead, 5 May: LC), fourteen institutions offered a Ph.D. Yale had granted only two doctorates over the past five years but had eleven staff (including several of the sociologists and Dollard).

In this nurturing environment, Dollard attempted a synthesis of the psychotic person seen culturally, a project initially proposed by Sapir; Lassell and Sullivan were "scientific helps" (1935, 637). In his life history work (1935), Dollard provided a coherent explication of why culture-and-personality students should pursue clinical studies. Although this was consistent with Sapir's views, the two drew increasingly apart.

Dollard recorded his perspective on events at the IHR in his correspondence with Margaret Mead. The two met at Hanover in 1933, and Mead "learned from John Dollard a much firmer way to describe cultural character" (Mead 1972, 221). They worked together on cooperation and competition studies correlated by May in 1934–1935. Mead was impressed by Dollard's ability to sell himself to the foundations that funded social science research.

Dollard was eager to systematize the emerging approach, more in relation to social science than psychology–psychiatry. He wrote to Mead (28 March 1935: LC) about "a training unit for social scientists who want to add personality research techniques to their other equipment." Sapir, at this time, was trying to convince the NRC to support training fellowships, and Dollard may have hoped to undercut his proposal through the IHR. Mead responded (to Dollard, 1 April 1935: LC): "The atmosphere of greed and envy and jealousy which hangs over this C and P research simply sickens me."

Mead was instrumental in organizing a network of neo-Freudian psychologists, including Horney and Fromm (to Dollard, 11, 20, 25 February 1935: LC). She gleefully reported introducing Benedict to Horney and Fromm (20 June 1935: LC). Fromm was "very eager for some kind of further cooperation between us five on defining problems which should be tackled by both ethnologists and analysts." Fromm was instrumental in getting the group of five together to discuss American Indian temperament (3 September 1935: LC). The procedure was collaborative: "once we have thrashed it out among ourselves, [we] call in several field workers . . . and let you and Erich and Horney use them as informants to clarify more details in working out some methodology of approach."

Mead (3 September 1935: LC) reported meeting May at Hanover and finding him "impregnated" with Dollard's ideas: "All of which was very encouraging." Dollard reported (27 September 1935: LC) May's version of the meeting at Hanover, stressing that the IHR was "short of brains" and to have "you and some others here" would be a "luxury." The reorganization, however, was not without its setbacks. May "cannot make much headway against the vested interests, scientific and financial, of the Institute. The thing is laid down like any cultural structure and is impervious to almost anything except revolution."

Revolution, nonetheless, was underway. Dollard persuaded May to hire psychoanalyst Earl Zinn, replacing Eugene Kahn, whose lack of enthusiasm for the institute had long been a thorn in Dollard's side (Leonard Doob, p.c.). Dollard wanted to observe and record actual psychoanalysis for his life history work and needed an amenable clinician. Dollard was convinced that the IHR already had a "small but promising" group to study "the individual in his concrete social setting" and that the project would be "in the dead center of the Human Relations field." Social scientists and biologists had a unique opportunity to cooperate. The time was ripe for "a modest, realistic introduction of psychoanalysis" into the IHR.

Zinn (to May, 12 June 1936: YU) offered a graduate seminar on psychoanalytic theory in the psychology department and undertook an analysis, recorded with permission, of two graduate students (presumably John and Beatrice Whiting). Zinn was willing to associate his work with the IHR model (to May, 14 October 1937: YU) and considered May's frustration–aggression model inherent in the Freudian position.

Dollard (to Mead, 7 June 1937: LC) was also enthusiastic over the IHR program in frustration and aggression. Cooperation with Murdock, moreover, was opening up "the possibility of a real alliance between sociology and psychology" through Leonard Doob. Sapir was outside all of this, objecting to the oversimplified stimulus–response psychology of the Hull synthesis, to May's determination to define what was and was not legitimate social science research, and to Dollard's failure to include him in the research program. Dollard believed that Sapir opposed his work, as actively as he was able, in the power structure of interdisciplinary social science outside of Yale:

One unpleasant result of the realisms of our program is the continued and increased antagonism of Sapir. He has become openly hostile and vituperative toward me, feels that I am trying to undermine anthropology here, that I am arousing the place against him, that I am ungrateful, designing, etc. These opinions he has broadcasted wherever he has been able to find anyone to listen, and his prestige is such that he gets around quite far and wide. I don't think he has gained much ground around here, rather the contrary since most of his accusations are too obvious a cover for his own failure to behave creatively in the Yale [IHR] situation.

Dollard occasionally had his doubts about the imminent possibility of a grand synthesis (to Mead, 8 October 1937: LC). He wanted Mead, who had more field experience than any Yale anthropologist, to tell him "if it is ever possible to do such justice to culture *per se* that it is really legitimate to think along these other lines." Premature or not, however, Dollard stuck to the program. When funding came up for renewal, he hoped that a new integrated scheme would be presented to the foundation, not just "a general grab" for money (to Mead, 10 January 1938: LC).

Dollard consistently criticized the anthropology program for its lack of interdisciplinary focus. He taught in anthropology only after Sapir's death, when Murdock's cross-cultural survey, supported by the IHR, dominated the program. Sapir's anthropology and Yale's version of interdisciplinary social science through the IHR remained parallel lines that never met.

CHAPTER TWENTY-ONE

Dénuement

During the final years of his life, Sapir's chronic heart condition prevented him from completing the work to which he was committed. His dream of interdisciplinary social science receded along with foundation support for research. Yale politics increasingly precluded Sapir's participation in the IHR. Within anthropology and linguistics, anti-Semitism is remembered as the reason for Sapir's unhappiness at Yale, citing his childhood as the son of a cantor, with adult secularism giving way to renewed interest in Judaism at the end of his life, presumably responding to the rise of the Nazis in Europe. All this is true but oversimplified.

Sapir's Relation To Judaism

Judaism was a thread that wove in and out of Sapir's life, as a cultural tradition and a social category applied to him by others. The position he achieved in life was unusual for a Jew of his generation, and ethnic anonymity was not an option.

Sapir's early writings on Judaism were scientific; he was not a practicing Jew. In 1915, he brought his linguistic training and practical experience of Jewish immigrant culture in America to a review of an English–Yiddish dictionary. Later, he was extremely amused by Leo Rosten's *The Education of Hyman Kaplan*, which evoked childhood memories of new immigrants misunderstanding American language and culture (J. David Sapir, p.c.).

Sapir's review of Ludwig Lewisohn's *Israel* in 1926 argued against any single solution to the Jewish problem; Jewish cultural circumstances and individual identities varied widely. Lewisohn's personal commitment to Zionism prevented him from discussing other possibilities, for example, assimilation. Sapir believed that the Jewish problem of cultural conflict was not unique to Jews but was widespread in human history. Lewisohn's emphasis on "the peculiar, narrow, over-intellectualized, yet always intense and vital Jewish culture of eastern Europe" challenged "the more comfortable but also the more flabby and fragmentary culture of Anglo-Saxon America"; the Jewish attitude was "outward deference and an inner awareness of a half-useless superiority" (1926, 216). Sapir's rhetoric reflects his own experience of anti-Semitism; he acknowledged "the necessity of having a cultural background if one is to be oneself" (1926, 217). Sapir the anthropologist pointed out that the Jews were masters of transcending localism, adopting the best from many cultures. This review was written soon after Sapir went to Chicago and reflected his expectation that unobtrusive Jewish identity would do him no harm, personally or professionally.

At Yale, Sapir established pleasant collegial relationships, but he badly underestimated New Haven's conservatism. During his first semester, Sapir gave a public lecture dealing with "free love" which was reported in the *Boston Herald* of 7 December 1931 and set off a public outcry among Yale alumni. The headline announced that Sapir thought free love was better than early marriage. Parents should stress "emotional honesty" and not try to be omniscient mentors. As a scientist, he regarded the concept of sin as irrelevant. Moreover, divorce could be a blessing and was, in any case, a private matter; marriage had declined in social importance. The newspaper clipping was preserved in President Angell's papers.

Sapir (to Angell, 22 December 1931: YU) protested to President Angell of "a complete misunderstanding of the real tenor of my remarks in Boston." He abhorred the term "free love" and had not used it. He referred Angell to his 1929 article in *American Mercury* on the American family for its conservatism. Angell defended Sapir, writing to Dr. William Stone, Yale class of 1888 (19 January 1932: YU), that Sapir was "very greatly distressed" by the misinterpretation of his views:

As Dr. Sapir is a mature scholar of the very highest rank, he is, of course, quite at liberty to voice his views in his own field, which is that of anthropology, . . . in the present instance he has been the victim of sensational reporting—an experience from which I have so often suffered that I feel highly sympathetic.

Angell was also a newcomer to Yale, and his response was probably not very satisfying. Angell was the first nonalumnus president of Yale, and the faculty, who dominated its policy, distrusted him (Oren 1986, 61). The column was apparently syndicated, because Angell also received a letter of protest based on the *Chicago Daily Tribune*. Angell forwarded all letters to Sapir, with the terse comment that no reply was needed: "It simply indicates what you, of course, well know, the price one pays for any public discussion of matters in this field."

Although the surface issue was not Judaism, WASP New England was alien to Sapir. The intellectual stance of German–Russian Judaism was the "anticlerical, antifeudal, experimental and rationalist faith of the French Encyclopedists" (Diamond in Silverman 1981, 69). New Haven lacked a comparable tradition of public debate of social issues; traditional morality was taken for granted, and Sterling Professors were expected to uphold it.

Sapir's friend, Robert Hutchins, president of the University of Chicago and former Yale dean of law, had warned Sapir: "Look, we can't match Yale's prestige, nor salary, nor liberal research budgets, but be warned that you are going into a far narrower society and intellectual tradition and will meet strong anti-Semitism" (Michael Sapir 1984, 9). Sapir ignored the warning.

Yale had few Jews on its faculty when Sapir arrived, and none of them taught the undergraduates who were the backbone of the institution. In 1930, there was 4 Jews among 569 faculty (Oren 1986, 132). Medical school dean Winternitz, was "almost a caricature of the American Jew striving to become part of gentile society"; he was actively anti-Semitic, wanted to buy a house on WASP Prospect Street, and was resented by the local Jewish community (Oren 1986, 136–137, 143). The medical school also included Jews Eugene Kahn (1930–1936) in psychiatry and mental hygiene and Lafayette Mendel (1921–1935) in physiological chemistry—both Sterling Professors. Detractors assumed that hiring one Jew meant others would follow; indeed, Sapir brought Spier and Herzog into the anthropology department. When Spier was not appointed permanent chairman, many students and faculty blamed anti-Semitism (Mandelbaum to Darnell, 20 June 1986).

Angell was apparently oblivious to the difficulties of Yale's Jewish faculty. His problem was to upgrade the research reputation of the institution by attracting the leading scholars in a number of fields, many of whom were Jews (Oren 1986, 131–132). Mendel and Sapir were both hired as "ornaments to a great university" but were not permitted to become central to the institution (Oren 1986, 261).

Among Yale's Jewish faculty in the 1930s, Sapir is remembered primarily because he was denied membership in the Graduate Club. Oral tradition has it that it was the Faculty Club, but that institution was unimportant at Yale, where academic business was conducted by senior faculty at the Graduate Club rather than in their offices. It was unheard of that a Sterling Professor could be blackballed. In fact, however, the incident had little to do with Sapir personally; several Jews were members, but the membership committee included considerable anti-Semitic sentiment. Sapir was the person over whom the issue arose (Oren 1986, 360). Mandelbaum (Oren 1986, 360) believed that "Sapir's candidacy was not helped by his sponsor's being a 'tactless' and 'difficult to deal with' member of the graduate school faculty." The "impolitic anticipation" of anti-Semitism by "button-holing members" in advance may have precipitated the rejection (Mandelbaum to Hymes, 18 May 1981). Sapir's sponsorship came, moreover, from linguistics rather than from the anthropology department he headed.

The sociology department, out of whose territory Sapir's program was carved, was actively anti-Semitic (Doob, p.c.). Murdock, however, minimized this "unfortunate accident" (to Denise O'Brien, 4 June 1976). He claimed that he and others had advised Sapir to wait a few months for a new committee chairman, but Sapir "was sensitive as so many Jews are about discrimination and some of his associates were infuriated to the extent that they thought they ought to make a fight out of it." Murdock, Furniss and May resigned, and Murdock (1976 interview) said he never went there again. At the time, however, Murdock was perceived as anti-Semitic by anthropology students and faculty.

Retrospective discussion of anti-Semitism at Yale has failed to recognize that such an attitude was relatively respectable in the 1930s and was closely related to nationalism. It was less respectable to envy Sapir's achievements than to reject him because he was a Jew. John

Ladd (1984, p.c.), son of Berkeley Divinity School dean William Ladd, who befriended Sapir among other "oppressed radicals," stressed the hierarchial social structure of the Yale community. Being Jewish only became respectable after World War II when Jewish refugees fled to America. Sapir's difficulties with academic politics in sociology and the IHR were expressed in terms of anti-Semitism, though the motivations of his detractors were, in fact, anchored in more mundane issues. Moreover, Sapir's apparent flippancy maddened some colleagues (Paul Sapir, p.c.).

In any case, Sapir's rejection by the Graduate Club in 1932 "sent shock waves through the university" (Oren 1986, 132). Liberal opinion on campus recoiled that someone of Sapir's status could be denied access to an institution vital to his administrative functioning. The admissions committee debated the matter further, and Dean Furniss lodged a strong protest; there is no evidence that Angell took any action (Oren 1986, 133).

Edgerton later engineered Sapir's election to the "less popular" Faculty Club, of which he was the first Jewish member, but he never set foot in it (Philip Sapir, in Oren 1986, 133). Sapir was very hurt by the Graduate Club rejection. Rabbi Siskin explained (Oren 1986, 133),

He would speak to me in smiling disbelief of the social pecking order which he discerned among the faculty. . . The caste distinction between professors struck him as *kinderspiele*, unbecoming a community of scholars. The social emphasis on the campus cast Sapir in the role of parvenu, outsider.

Stanley Newman (p.c.) recalled Sapir's shock at the rejection: "New England Brahmins regarded 'Hebrews'—their polite term for Jews—as strange Oriental people who were inclined to be loud, crude and pushy; cultured people couldn't accept them socially."

Sapir found at least one alternative social outlet; G. Evelyn Hutchinson (p.c.) met him through the Connecticut Academy of Arts and Sciences, which brought together the "learned men of New Haven," whether or not they were on the Yale faculty. "Fairly lively" weekly papers were followed by supper. Sapir attended regularly. The group was socially conservative but politically liberal, including many expatriate Russians; some were "ultra-native-born" and "all [were] displaced persons of one sort or another."

Sapir considered religious practice on the part of his children a personal choice, allowing them to accompany Christian friends to church-sponsored activities. He read his children stories from the Old Testament, perhaps to offset Christian influence; but he did not celebrate Jewish holidays. His food preferences, however, excluded shellfish and pork. The family celebrated Christmas, with a tree but no religious significance, from the Ottawa days on. Sapir "loved the present giving, once we changed from giving him hankies to books. We had him leave a list around the house" (Helen Sapir Larson, p.c.).

Sapir enrolled his younger sons in a school in New Haven that was known for its anti-Semitism and excluded Jews from dance classes, attended by most children in the older grades (Paul Sapir, p.c.). Sapir learned early to ignore anti-Semitic jokes, from various colleagues and acquaintances (Philip Sapir, p.c.); on other occasions, however, he could be quite acerbic. Emeneau (to Haas, 4 December 1971) recalled a "rabid Nazi from Germany" who disapproved of Sapir but attended his phonetics class: "Sapir patiently used him as an informant for the clear uvular trill of his local dialect. . . . I admired intensely Sapir and his humane self-possession."

Sapir often discussed Jewish issues with Rabbis Edgar Siskin and Maurice Zigmond, both graduate students in anthropology who were active in Yale Jewish affairs. Siskin (p.c.) recalls that Sapir believed every individual needed a cultural background. He was not interested in "organized Jewishness" but in the "perpetually insoluble" culture of his childhood. Sapir found the orthodox Judaism of his father's household "stultifying" but responded to the "deeper impulses of Jewish culture."

Siskin read the Talmud with Sapir, as did Mandelbaum and Newman (Sapir to Newman, 12 August 1935):

I'm interested to hear you keep up your Hebrew. . . . Hebrew never ceases to fascinate me—perhaps because, as a little boy of 7 or 8, I used to translate the O.T. with my father. Its grammar is a continual delight and the text material generally interesting in one way or another. When we get together again, would you care to read text with me, say once a week? You could get lots of phonology and morphology in a purely inductive way. It's a language full of queer irregularities (as contrasted with Arabic) but not really difficult. I have a hunch you could work out some tidy revisions on phonemic lines.

Sapir approved of the Jewish tradition of respect for elders, responding to a similar quality among American Indians (J. David Sapir, p.c.). He "became a compulsive bibliophile, amassing a large library of Judaica. He began to read the Bible in Hebrew and had several sets of the Talmud" (Philip Sapir, p.c.). Jean Sapir gave her husband a set of the Talmud for his birthday, and the family was regaled with Sapir's sheer delight at his Semitic linguistic work (Helen Sapir Larson, p.c.).

Sapir was also drawn into Jewish activism by his friendship with Weinreich, one of the founders in 1925 of YIVO, an institute for advanced study in the Yiddish of Eastern European Judaism. YIVO was located in Vilna, "the Jerusalem of Lithuania," which already had a tradition of Jewish learning (Gilson 1975, 62). Weinreich taught Yiddish at the Vilna seminary, even translating Freud and Homer into that language (Gilson, 62). He was YIVO's linguist, standardizing the speech, spelling, and grammar of Yiddish and combining philology, history, and literature. Weinreich focused on how to involve Jewish youth in their own cultural tradition, returning to Vilna with new tools from his culture-and-personality study with Sapir.

Sapir agonized over Hitler's rise to power. When the family moved to New Haven, he agreed to send his son Michael to Germany for a year, on the condition that he write a weekly letter home in German. These letters included graphic descriptions of the massing of the Nazis in Munich and the frenzy of Hitler's speeches, which presumably contributed substantially to Sapir's sense of disaster in Europe, especially because Germany had been more congenial to Jewish assimilation than France. Sapir's conversation was increasingly filled with Spenglerian gloom (Michael Sapir, p.c.). The Sapir family followed the radio broadcasts of H. V. Kaltenborn monitoring early signs of World War II (SF: p.c.). Murdock (to Denise O'Brien, 4 June 1976) recalls a change in Sapir's personality. He took his Yale rejection as evidence that anti-Semitism also gained ground in America "following the German model." Murdock (to O'Brien, 1976 interview) claimed that Sapir bought his farmhouse in New Hampshire "with the idea that when the Nazis took over the country, why he'd have a sort of hiding place in the country." The Sapir family, however, considers this nonsense; most Yale faculty had vacation homes. Paul Sapir (p.c.) suggests: "if ES ever did fancifully joke about such an idea . . . he could have done so without Murdock's quite realizing it was a (wistful) joke. . . . [Perhaps] the New Haven Nazis were what ES was alluding to."

Other American Jewish anthropologists, particularly in New York, were also drawn into the political scene, Boas among them. As president of the AAA, Sapir wrote Boas (23 November 1938: APS) about the possibility of major American "scientific bodies" making "a joint protest against the Nazi government and its treatment of the Jews." He felt that a drafting committee should consist of non-Jews, for reasons of strategy. Boas responded (29 November 1938: APS): "From previous experience I consider it very doubtful whether it is possible to get an official expression from any outstanding scientific bodies." *Nature* was about to publish a letter on the subject with thirteen hundred distinguished signatures, which Boas hoped would have some effect. Columbia was instituting scholarships for refugee students. Boas thought these were potentially effective approaches.

Nonetheless, presiding at a AAA meeting late in 1938, Sapir introduced a resolution against Nazi racism. Only a small group of Boasians voted for the resolution (Goldfrank 1978, 30). The majority argued that Germany was a friendly power. "Thereafter Sapir, with his fine sense of humor, said, 'This resolution was proposed by A. E. Hooton of Harvard.' Everyone thought they were voting against a resolution proposed by Boas." During World War I, both Sapir and Boas argued that science and internationalism were more important than patriotism; but World War II was more polarized.

In the late 1930s, Sapir became more involved in politics. He helped to organize the Conference on Jewish Relations, "a national committee of eminent Jewish scholars interested in the scientific evaluation of social trends effecting Jews" (Oren 1986, 132). Morris R. Cohen, also a Yale Jew, was president and Sapir vice-president. The conference established the journal *Jewish Social Studies* in 1939. "East and Central European centers of learning were being systematically destroyed, and men like Cohen, Sapir, Hans Kohn, and Salo W. Baron felt that American Jewry must pick up the slack."

Sapir wrote a form letter to a number of Jewish colleagues on behalf of YIVO (1 May 1933: YUDA), including Boas and Wirth, in which he emphasized the increasing social science direction of YIVO. In practice, this meant the work of Weinreich with Sapir at Yale. An "outline is being prepared for a rather extensive study of the personality of the Eastern European Jew" under conditions of rapid social change. Sapir stressed that nothing was being asked except the use of scholars' names.

Sapir and others established an American Inter-University Committee on Jewish Social Science "for the furtherance of the Work of the Yiddish Scientific Institute." Bloomfield, anthropologist Melville Herskovits, Paul Radin's brother Max (a distinguished jurist), Henry Schultz, and Wirth probably agreed to participate because of Sapir, who chaired the committee. The twenty-two members did not include Boas. YIVO's Honorary Board consisted of Simon Dubnow, Albert

Einstein, Sigmund Freud, Moses Gaster, Edward Sapir, Bernhard Wachstein, and Chaim Zhitlovsky.

An obituary of Sapir, published in the YIVO yearbook in 1939, noted various public talks on behalf of YIVO and claimed him as a Yiddish linguist, citing his 1915 "Notes on Judeo-German Philology" that dealt with the phonetics of his mother's Kovna dialect. At the World Convention of YIVO, Sapir had expressed his enthusiasm for the work of the institution:

When I was a child, Yiddish was looked at rather contemptuously, as a jargon which could not be spoken of in the same breath with Hebrew, Russian, Polish or German. The latter languages were the languages of the emancipated intelligentsia among the Jews of Poland and Lithuania. . . . I cannot imagine a more exalted and a more practical way for bringing the Jewish masses of Eastern Europe and America into strong contact with the world culture than forging a language held in scorn into an instrument of a magnificent, clear, creative expression.

In his review of Radin's book on monotheism for the *Menorah Journal* in 1925, Sapir argued that the spiritual force of a religion was more important than monotheism itself. Monotheism was not a Jewish or ethnic trait.

Mandelbaum (1941, 139–140) summarized Sapir's changing attitudes toward Judaism and its relation to his anthropology in *Jewish Social Studies*:

For a long time Sapir's attitude toward Jewish problems was that of the anthropologist whose training admits him to a seat in the press box of the human universe. He saw Jewish matters steadily and saw them whole, as befits a scientific observer. During his latter years, however, he began to feel that a place at the observation post does not exclude one from a share in the play on the field. He became more and more engrossed in and concerned with the problems of being a Jew and with the turmoil of modern events. . . . To my way of thinking, Edward Sapir expressed the genius of his people in its finest aspect. Jews are, in a sense, born ethnologists. By virtue of their dual participation in two cultural spheres, that of Judaism and that of their environing society, they are often made sensitive to differences in the forms of culture.

Illness and Retreat

Sapir's initial euphoria in New Haven deteriorated rapidly under pressures of local politics, competing research commitments, and anti-Semitism. His retreat from these pressures was a small farm at Place's Pond near Gilmanton Iron Works, New Hampshire. After two summers in rented homes in New Hampshire, the Sapirs bought more than two hundred acres in forced sale. Sapir's retreat was a source of pleasure to him, as no permanent home was. He wrote to Haile (21 September, 9 October 1934: SWL) about "some new developments in our family which point in the direction of my becoming a large-scale farmer" and of a wonderful summer "tinkering up the place." Helen Sapir Larson (p.c.) recalls: "He loved taking guests on long jaunts around the property." In later years, however, his heart condition forced him to be more sedentary. Nature was a pleasant backdrop for reading; Sapir regularly took a book on hikes, canoe trips, and other family outings. To Whorf, Sapir wrote (7 July 1932: YU) that it was "rather a treat to alternate reading, writing and paddling." To May (25 June 1935: YU) he reported: "I have a 'shack' up here, a sort of hinterland office, with mountains, woods, and lake scenery seeping in from its four windowed sides."

Some family memories are less idyllic. Philip Sapir notes that the first rented house in New Hampshire was fancier than the one eventually purchased. Sapir would emerge for a late breakfast and devote evenings to reading by gas lamp. He never shared his work with the family and was not to be interrupted to fix things.

The refuge from "civilization" substituted for many activities Sapir had long enjoyed, fieldwork and conference-hopping being paramount. He wrote to May (20 August 1934: IHR): "I seem to feel the need, as never before since coming to Yale, of drawing in, as it were, trying to heave a deep breath, and going on with the season's work in the fall when the quietness of the country shall have sunk in sufficiently."

Jean Sapir believed (Helen Sapir Larson, p.c.) that Sapir's heart condition slowed him down even before his first heart attack. Sapir tacitly acknowledged that his obligations were out of control when he retreated to New Hampshire. Initially, the farm was intended as a place to work without interruption; it became, however, a place to recuperate from external pressures.

A series of letters written to Jean Sapir in the summer of 1935 (SF) reflect the degree of Sapir's immersion. His first priority was to arrange his books and manuscripts at "the shack," a two-room cabin behind the farmhouse where he and Jean slept and Sapir had his office. The house, with a newly painted red floor in the living room, was "awfully cozy," though the view made it difficult to do any work. "This place augurs well" (19 June 1935: SF). Sapir's priorities were clear (25 June): "One gets so tired evenings and it's so hard to read or write by lamplight. I've not got into my working stride yet. . . . I find it hard to combine physical work and desk work."

Jean Sapir remained in New York in the summer of 1935 to continue her psychoanalysis with Karen Horney. She went into New York twice a week for a year or two (Paul Sapir, p.c.). Sapir felt that one of them should be analyzed and considered Horney "eminently sane." Sapir moved without differentiation between his opinion of Horney's writings and the progress of Jean's analysis. Sapir hoped she would return "in a mood to enjoy this place" (24 June 1935: SF). Whatever its stresses during the Yale years, Sapir wanted to maintain his marriage. When Jean visited her parents in 1933 with the two younger children, Sapir wrote (14, 16 September: SF) that "some heart-aching shaking down" and brief separation might be healthy but that he perceived "no real dislocation." He could not settle down to work without the noise of the children ("Paul's prattle and David's bawling").

Horney was "terribly anxious to curry ES's good opinion because of his status among social scientists she wanted to impress" (Paul Sapir, p.c.). This "clearly interfered with the possibility of an adequate psychoanalysis" of Jean Sapir. Horney, moreover, was disturbed by Jean's articulation of the hostility in her marriage and feared Sapir would blame her for it; she halted the analysis prematurely because of potential negative effects on Sapir's heart condition. Jean Sapir, disillusioned by New Haven and Sapir's illness, needed to differentiate her life from her husband's. Paul Sapir recalls:

In later years, JVS often used to tell how visibly upset and angry Horney often got when my mother would (in sessions) relate things she had said and quoted to ES from the analysis. Horney apparently did not respond to them analytically. . . . Instead, Horney very un-analytically reproached her patient and tried to make her give Horney a better press to ES.[1]

Sapir's Initial Illness

Sapir took a sabbatical from Yale in the fall of 1937 with full salary (Furniss to Sapir, 13 February 1937: YU).[2] He decided, with Rockefeller support, to spend a full year at Yenching University in Peiping,

China; he arranged for Lowie to replace him for one semester (2 March 1937: UCB). The Chinese–Japanese War, however, made this impossible (Paul Sapir, p.c.).

Sapir had been interested in China since his Ottawa days. The Sapir family assumes that his interest in linking Asian languages to American Indian ones was also a motive. Moreover, both adult Sapirs had long wanted to travel. No research proposal has been preserved. The Rockefeller Foundation did rural reconstruction work in Peiping, where sociology had ties to Robert Park, maintained through former Chicago anthropology student Li An-Che (Li to Redfield, 26 February 1936: UC). Bingham Dai was also in China.

When the Chinese plan fell through, Sapir decided to teach at Hawaii, with the agreement of David Stevens of the Rockefeller Foundation; after Sapir's first heart attack in the summer of 1937, this was postponed to the second semester (Sapir to Furniss, 27 September 1937: YU). Yale was affiliated with the Bishop Museum in Honolulu and Sapir had long been on close terms with Peter Buck there. Former Yale anthropology student E. G. Burrows was also in Honolulu.

But Sapir, relying on conflicting diagnoses by different doctors, seriously underestimated the consequences of his condition and had to spend his entire sabbatical in New York City. Yale president Seymour intervened with the Rockefeller Foundation (to Stevens, 7 December 1937: YU) regarding the financial implications of Sapir's grant: "He is worrying, I believe, about this matter and we wish to be placed in a position to reassure him, in order that conditions may be as favorable as possible to his recovery"[3] Stevens reassured Seymour (9 December 1937: YU) that the situation was beyond Sapir's control and "I should be happy to regard his intention as all that can be asked for from our point of view. My own real interest is in seeing him returned to you in good health."

After his return from Ann Arbor, Sapir recuperated in New Hampshire, writing to Spier (20 October 1937: YUDA): "I hate like fury leaving here, it's such a relief to get away from city life, but I'm really too well now to have any pretext for lingering longer and it does mean a lot of work for Jean." He intended to visit his mother on the way to New York for "a medical overhauling" and then proceed to Honolulu. These arrangements had to be changed dramatically. David spent the year in Columbus, Ohio, with his oldest brother Michael and his wife; Paul spent the first half of the year with his maternal aunt in Ontario, joining his parents in New York for the rest of the school year. Paul remembers his father as weak and bedridden during most of this period (p.c.). Jean Sapir used the year to refurbish her skills in psychiatric social work, realizing that she would be likely to need a job in the not-too-distant future. Sullivan visited frequently, sitting with Sapir or reading to him. "Jean Sapir felt that Sullivan was critical of her for absenting herself from the apartment during the day" (Perry 1982, 366) but persisted in her professional efforts.

Sapir's assessment of his condition varied with his mood and physical symptoms. He wrote to Haile (20 January 1938: SWL): "There was quite a serious relapse and I was put back to bed. But now I seem to be definitely on the mend. I move about in my clothes inside the house and hope to be able to get at least a reduced working schedule in a week or two."

Sapir relinquished the chairmanship to Spier and was not consulted on mundane matters (YUDA). Students were encouraged not to bother him with visits or letters; nonetheless, Spier insisted that he would return in the fall of 1938 (e.g., to Henry Silverthorne, 17 February 1938: YUDA). In fact, no one could predict Sapir's health. Boas scheduled meetings in New York so he could attend (e.g., to Whorf, 16 February 1938: YU). Trager reported to Whorf (28 April 1938: YU) that Sapir had attended the Americanist meetings in New York and was "able to get around a bit." Sapir hoped to settle down to serious work, particularly on Navajo, writing to Haile (20, 26 January 1938: SWL) that he was having his Navajo files sent to him from Ann Arbor. He detested his "enforced idleness." By the end of the school year, he realized that "all work that can be avoided" would have to be, and resigned the chairmanship at Yale permanently (to Haile, 30 April 1938: SWL). Throughout his illness, however, Sapir continued to promise work to be undertaken or conferences to be attended, apparently trying to reassure himself that he would recover his previous energy.

Cardiac diagnosis was primitive in this period. Sapir's doctors could not decide whether he had actually had a heart attack or not. He ignored his condition until his series of relapses in 1938.[4] Helen Sapir Larson recalls "the slowness of his pace and his general air of fatigue" before his first heart attack (p.c.):

I do recall that he once said that the doctor had misdiagnosed his case, and that there was nothing the matter with his heart, that the trouble was digestive. Which would show a certain tendency to denial. . . . I think in the family group there probably wasn't much talk about his health, more a worried silence. His cardiologist was a Dr. Lieberman, recommended by Harry Stack Sullivan, who predicted very well the prognosis, telling Jean he knew "those Jewish hearts," whatever that means. I also recall my father reassuring me that he would get well; this was a month before he died and when he was already confined to his bed.

During his illness, Sapir was elected president of the AAA.[5] Cole predicted this before Sapir's first heart attack (to Spier, 20 February 1937: CU), indicating that health was not involved in the decision. Spier responded (5 April 1937: YUDA) that Sapir would be in China only for the first half of his term and could officiate at the annual meeting. Cole pushed Sapir's nomination, writing to Ruth Benedict (28 October 1937: UC) that Sapir would have been nominated at least three years earlier had there not been conflicting obligations to the NRC and SSRC. "We have already gone into a younger age group and I think that he would feel it very keenly if we were to pass him by." Sapir was duly elected at the New Haven annual meeting in December 1937. His presidential address was delivered by Boas a year later, only a few weeks before Sapir's death. Voegelin described the AAA proceedings to Lowie (n.d. 1939: APS):

Boas, younger than ever, spoke on the topic which Sapir had chosen—after the banquet. He did not mince words, but said that an anthropologist who was not also a linguist was superficial. He cited as examples of men who had successfully combined ethnography and linguistics Edward Sapir and Leonard Bloomfield.

Sapir's students planned a festschrift with Spier as editor, assisted by Newman in linguistics and Hallowell in psychology of culture. Voegelin failed to convince Li (in Ann Arbor in 1937) to remain in America and edit the volume "as Sapir's first and most illustrious student." Sullivan had told the Sapir family in 1937 that his condition was serious, giving him two years to live (Michael Sapir, p.c.). But time was running short (Voegelin to Lowie, n.d. 1937: APS):

Harry Stack Sullivan advised us to telegraph Sapir about the Festschrift, to be sure we beat a third heart attack which was then expected. Sapir replied, and his reply was most heartening to me: highly articulate, using words for their sound in combination as well as for their meaning: —Sapir when happy, I thought.

The Sapir–Sullivan–Lasswell Research Institute

Sullivan tried to convince himself that Sapir's heart condition could be arrested if he did not return to teaching. Sapir apparently also believed that Yale lay at the root of his problems. During his final illness, he asked his wife to write to Hooton at Harvard (where he had taught summer school a few years previously) about the possibility of a job there (David Sapir, p.c.). But jobs were no easier to come by on the brink of World War II than they had been in Sapir's Ottawa years.

Sapir, warned by his physician to slow down in the spring of 1938 (Perry 1982, 366), nonetheless returned to Yale in the fall of 1939 against his doctor's orders (Helen Sapir Larson, p.c.). Sapir and Sullivan agreed that the problem at Yale centered around Dollard, who was "overly ambitious and competitive," and around Yale's anti-Semitism (Perry 1982, 366).

Although Sullivan had long dreamed of his own research institute, the William Alanson White Psychiatric Foundation lacked the financial resources to support Sapir and Sullivan for long-term research. Lasswell suggested intensive efforts to acquire foundation money. Sullivan dutifully traveled about the country seeking contributions, while Sapir, who was reading the Bible in Aramaic, quoted the myth of Balaam and the ass (Perry 1982, 367). Whatever Sapir felt about the desirability of Sullivan's dream, he was unwilling to build up hopes that were likely to be shattered. His recent experience with research funding was largely negative, even when backed by the prestige of Yale. Sullivan had no such resources.

Rumors abounded about what Sapir would do. Dollard wrote to Mead (30 November 1938: LC) that he had heard that Sapir would leave Yale to work with Sullivan in Washington. "In fact, his friends seem to have plastered it pretty well all over the country." Nonetheless, "direct information from him indicates that there has been talk about this but he seems not in the mood to go at the present time." Dollard noted that comparable money or security "could not be offered him" and that Sapir was still quite ill. Sapir reassured Kroeber, who had heard the same rumors (25 August 1938: UCB) that they were "hardly justified":

There has been talk of my joining a unit at Washington but, as far as I can see now, I continue at Yale in 1938–1939. Needless to say, I'm a bit fed up with teaching, for it takes a lot out of me and my health is probably going to be precarious for the balance of my life. And there are many points on this planet that are more attractive than New Haven.

The consensus among Sapir's friends was that "Yale, or a particular department thereof, has let him down at a serious time" (Ernest Hadley to Ross Chapman, 28 March 1938: WAWPF). Lasswell was particularly torn, trying to decide between a deadend though superficially prestigious position at Chicago and a leap into uncertain interdisciplinary possibilities with Sullivan and Sapir. He wrote to Hadley (29 March 1938: WAWPF): "I would much rather cut loose and work with Sapir, Sullivan and you: it is better to start something new and sound."

Lasswell took the lead in a frantic scramble for money, using public relations gimmicks learned in his studies of the American political process. Sapir held himself aloof, although he wrote to Hadley that he would "stall" Yale and hope to resign by 1 April 1938 (Perry 1982, 379). Sullivan's optimism of mid-April was premature, however; he delayed his planned visit to the Sapirs in New Hampshire in August, hoping for more favorable news, and grew increasingly restive over Lasswell's methods (Sullivan to Hadley, 22 August 1938: WAWPF), attributing to Sapir his "disgust at the get-rich-quick" tone of Lasswell's proposals. Sullivan doubted that Sapir would "consider associating himself with anything like what Lasswell seems to have in mind." Sullivan, whose financial problems were pressing, felt increasingly guilty (cf. Perry 1982) over his failure to provide an unstressful position for Sapir and projected his frustrations onto Lasswell. Philip Sapir recalls that much of this machination took place behind Sapir's back (although Sullivan expected Sapir to take the offered escape if it could be arranged) (Philip Sapir to Darnell, 24 February 1984): "Certainly it was Harry Stack's strong desire. I really don't think it was Dad's idea, too—at least in the same way. He went along with HS, certainly, but, as far as I know, never really played an active role at all."

Sullivan resigned himself to medical inevitability, writing to Doctor Wilbur Thomas (8 December 1938: WAWPF): "We are completely disappointed in our efforts to secure funds for the research and fellowship nucleus." Sapir's renewed teaching was "disastrous," and "his life span at best cannot be very much longer." The research institute "would contribute markedly to his very limited chances for survival.

Put very simply. I cannot expect him to survive another heart attack." Although Sullivan realized the situation was hopeless, he wrote to William Blitzsten in Chicago (14 December 1938: WAWPF): "I have for years felt convinced that if Edward and I could get ourselves properly endowed, we would really accomplish something of durable value."

Lasswell went his own way when he came east at the end of 1938. He lost a decade of life history interview files in a moving-van fire. For Sullivan, the urgency of collaboration lapsed with Sapir's death; Lasswell reminded him of the difficulties he had been unable to surmount.

Sullivan responded to Sapir's death with a lyrical obituary in *Psychiatry* in 1939. In the same issue, he wrote an editorial on anti-Semitism, which he considered a "salute to his collaboration with Sapir" (Perry 1982, 375), sublimating his grief into ideas. Neither Sullivan's later work nor *Psychiatry* referred overtly to Sapir after the 1939 obituary, although work by anthropologists was regularly included (Murray 1986*a*). Nonetheless, Sullivan's own thought was so greatly influenced by his contact with Sapir that the product was collaborative, even when not so acknowledged.

The Final Illness

Spier realized well before Sapir's return to teaching in the fall of 1938 that he would "not be able to give so much of his energy as he did in former times" (to Marion Hollenbach, 31 May 1938: YUDA). Sapir attempted to lighten his teaching load, postponing the Psychology of Culture, his "most strenuous lecture course," until the following year (Sapir to Spier, 7 February 1938: YUDA). He would teach American Indian languages in both terms, phonetics and phonemics in the first term, and methods in anthropology in the second (focusing on "the use of language for anthropological purposes"). The light schedule was "inevitable, as I still find that sustained talking is hard on me."

Sapir knew teaching would be a problem but had no choice in days before academic pensions and sick leaves. He realized that his likelihood of serious work was declining and concentrated on making a living for his family. He wrote to Haile from New Hampshire (15

July 1938: SWL): "I find my capacity for sustained work is simply less than it used to be and it looks as though this chronic cardiac condition is a permanent handicap." On the verge of return to New Haven he added (19 September: SWL): "I seem to be all right when I'm very quiet but if I talk energetically I get the heart symptoms, so I guess I'll have to develop a peacefully phlegmatic style of living." This he never succeeded in doing. In fact, he was not well enough to teach and he knew it. Jean Sapir confirmed (to Haile, 29 December 1938: SF): "The truth is the teaching was too much for him almost from the first, and he got sicker and sicker until disaster came."

Correspondence between Murdock and C. G. Seligman catalogues the last semester of Sapir's life from an outsider's view. On 2 December 1938 (YUDA), Murdock wrote, "although his health is not good he is meeting his classes regularly and gives every indication of being able to continue indefinitely albeit at a slightly lowered level of efficiency." Yet, he reported Sapir's "not unexpected" death on 4 February 1939 (8 February: YUDA) "after several months of steady decline."

Yale tried to ease the pressures on Sapir. Emeneau was engaged to teach his courses (Furniss to Murdock, 15 December 1938: YUDA). Although under no legal obligation to do so, the university absorbed the cost. Furniss also reassured Sapir (17 January 1939: YUDA) that at least one of his courses would continue so that his salary would not be affected by the arrangements. By this time, however, it was clear to all concerned that Sapir would never return to his teaching.[6]

Responses to Sapir's Death

Sapir realized the magnitude of his incompleted work and ensured that it would be passed on to his students. Such arrangements preoccupied the final months and weeks of his life. Jean Sapir explained the plans to Harry Hoijer (10 February 1939: SF): "Around Christmas time, he dictated some notes to me suggesting various people who might be asked to take over portions of it. The bulk of the material was to go to you if you felt you cared to take it—all his Athabascan work." Sapir "always considered his Navaho his finest piece of linguistic work." Spier assisted Jean Sapir with the manuscript materials.[7]

Sapir destroyed his personal correspondence before his death (Jean

Sapir to Robert Allen, 1 January 1971; Lowie 1965). Helen Sapir Larson (p.c., 13 November 1984), however, recalls no deliberate attempt to destroy documents:

Maybe he was just "tidying up," knowing his days were limited. During the last couple of years of his life, the family lived in apartments. . . . I imagine he felt that letters he received were meant for him and not for others and since he had an excellent memory he didn't need them around. As for the letters he wrote, he may have regretted some of the frank personal remarks he made on the whim of the moment.

Jean Sapir wrote to Richard Preston (n.d. 1967):

Edward died with the feeling that he had an important point to make that he hadn't managed to get across. He gave up even hoping to get it all written, even before he accepted the fact that he was ill. His work on language was such a pleasure to him that he was able to remain "busy" in that manner, but he did deeply feel that he died without saying his full say!

Dollard wrote to Mead of Sapir's death (n.d. February 1939: LC) that he had "a tragic life." Murdock, who refused for many years to speak publicly about the transfer of power at Yale during Sapir's last illness, told Denise O'Brien (4 June 1976):

Sapir had the keenest mind of anyone I ever met; if I've ever known a genius, it was Sapir. If you follow his career, the tremendous productivity of his early years was simply astounding, but this productivity had ceased by the time he came to Yale. . . . Sapir actually [had an] inability to work which was pitiful to watch.

Murdock considered Yale anti-Semitism incidental to "the whole syndrome of factors that were making him a psychiatric case." At Chicago a famous analyst[8] rejected Sapir, ostensibly because he was too old; Murdock thought "Sapir was so much smarter than the analyst" that he lost his chance to resolve his problems. Murdock, whose disaffection for Sapir clearly colored his remarks, was uncertain whether analysis would have helped him, remarking somewhat gratuitously: "I was never intimate with Sapir because I knew enough about his psychiatric problem to realize that I would be better off [in] my relationship with Sapir if I didn't become too intimate with him." Murdock ignored the physical illness that drained Sapir's energies and failed to acknowledge the research tradition he established at Yale in personality and culture. Paul Sapir (p.c.) suggests that Murdock was "baffled" by Sapir's brilliance and "by the high visibility of some of his neurotic traits

which may, all things considered, have been no more severe than socially 'smoother' people's, but perhaps more grating." After Sapir's
death, of course, Murdock could perpetuate his own views without
contradiction, at least at Yale (where he succeeded Sapir as chairman
and rapidly dismantled his program). This resulted in severe distortion
of Sapir's point of view and possibly exaggerated the unhappiness of
Sapir's Yale years in the memory of his professions.

The obituary letters received by Jean Sapir reflect biographical
events, personal loyalties, and controversies of professional politics.[9]
Few academics have received so many personal tributes or formal obituaries. Even those at Yale who had political quarrels with Sapir were
quick to express their sense of loss. May wrote (6 February 1939):
"While your husband and I differed in matters of policy I never ceased
to admire his intellect and his honesty." Murdock praised both scholar
and man, though somewhat impersonally (5 February 1939).

Whorf spoke for Sapir's students as a group (22 February 1939).
His letter, reading like a single run-on sentence, abounds in religious
imagery: "But the pupils of Edward are not just pupils, we are almost
like a group of disciples, whose master has indeed left them, but part
of whose spirit lives in them." Whorf acknowledged that Sapir's patronage had assured his own career: "If it hadn't been for Edward's
help I would never have got anywhere in linguistics." There were
letters from various former students, expressing their affection for Sapir, his influence on them, and the shock of losing him at such a young
age. Mandelbaum wrote from the University of Minnesota (8 February 1939): "I wonder if you know the thrill of pride that comes
with saying, 'I was one of Sapir's students.' "

Haile wrote (14 February 1939) as both friend and priest: "I don't
mind to say that I have remembered him in my morning's mass and
prayers." The following day, Sapir's long-standing Navajo informant,
Albert "Chic" Sandoval, typed his tribute on Indian Affairs Field Service letterhead from Window Rock. "I am sending my sympathy on
behalf of my family and some of the Navajoes [sic] who had known
him and who thought a great deal of him." Chic was "shocked" on
reading the news in an unidentified newspaper. He signed himself
"sincerely your friend."

Boas expressed (5 February 1939) uncharacteristic emotionalism.
On personal letterhead, he begged Jean Sapir to accept his aid as "a
friend, if you will not forget me." Boas was feeling his own age and
the loss of key members of the group he had built up over forty years

at Columbia: "Can I tell you in any way how I feel that those whom I saw start in life and who have developed to become maturer minds go and I am still here?" Jean Sapir (12 February 1939: APS) responded: "You're meant so much to him ever since his student days."

The formal obituaries of Sapir are remarkable in their number and in the range of periodicals and reviewers included. Boas wrote for the *International Journal of American Linguistics*, Benedict for the *American Anthropologist*, Edgerton for the *American Philosophical Society Yearbook*, Jenness for the *Proceedings of the Royal Society of Canada*, Sullivan for *Psychiatry*, Spier for *Science*, Swadesh for *Language*, Mandelbaum for *Jewish Social Studies*, Voegelin for *Word Study*, Louis Hjelmslev for *Acta Linguistica*, and Ernest Hooton for the *Proceedings of the American Academy of Arts and Sciences*.[10]

In spite of Sapir's many facets, recurrent epithets characterize the reflections of his contemporaries: Boas described him as "one of the most brilliant scholars" in linguistic anthropology, while Benedict considered him "brilliantly endowed." Kroeber noted "an almost incredible felicity" that "I would unreservedly class as . . . genius." Jenness found him "brilliant and inspiring." To Sullivan he was a "genius," albeit frequently misunderstood. Edgerton referred to his "versatility" and "genius," and Spier to his "illumination," "incisiveness," "deftness," "crystalline intellect," and "articulateness." To Swadesh, his mind was "dialectic" and his thinking "integrated." Mandelbaum's adjectives were "brilliant," "gifted," "keen," "inspiring," "sympathetic," "intoxicating"; he had "intuitive hunches" and wielded "the deft scalpel of his wit" expertly. Voegelin identified "a brightness that we associate with youth and poetry and innocence"; Sapir was "extraordinarily brilliant," "exuberant," and "integrative," with "a playful virtuosity." Hoijer stressed his "flair" and "analytical insight," a "provocative and stimulating faculty." For Harris, the key to Sapir was his "complete grasp of linguistics" and "wonderful working of data." Sapir could only be described in superlatives. The writers range from his teacher, Boas, to colleagues in widely different branches of social science, to students—yet their views of Sapir have much in common. He was complex, unforgettable, humane, and, above all, inimitable—particularly in the realm of ideas.

The same adjectives still appear in the reflections of Sapir's intellectual descendants in linguistics and anthropology, although his subsequent reputation is another story. Assessment of his intellectual contribution is ongoing—perhaps the greatest possible tribute to the quality of his mind. Intellectually, his application of Indo-European methods and theories to the study of American Indian languages, his insistence on professionalism in linguistics and anthropology, his consistent elaboration of the consequences of the primacy of the individual as the locus of culture, and the tension between humanism and science in anthropology have provided stimulus for continuing work. Sapir's personal life included both triumph and tragedy, accomplishment and unfulfilled promise, self-promotion and generosity of spirit. His intellectual style as well as his work remains an inspiration to his intellectual descendants.

Notes

Preface

1. For example, Sapir's decision to burn his personal correspondence before his death did not preclude his colleague and friend Robert Lowie from publishing his letters from Sapir. Lowie's sense of responsibility to the future led him to be "chary" of omissions, excluding only the "strictly personal" (1965, 2). Actually, however, omissions from the originals at the Bancroft Library, University of California, are considerably more extensive than Lowie intimates.

One: The Early Years

1. Little is known about Sapir's early life. He rarely spoke of his childhood even to his family. His children were not overly intrigued by their grandmother's recollections. The facts presented here are an amalgam of recollections by Michael, Philip, Paul, and David Sapir and Helen Sapir Larson. I have tied together these observations and related them to concurrent trends in immigration, education, and attitudes toward Jews. Speculations about Sapir's personality are my own.

2. Sapir himself would later extend these methods to the unwritten languages studied by anthropologists.

3. These survivors virtually defined the personnel of the American discipline until after World War I.

4. Ruth Benedict was to do the same for later generations of Columbia students.

5. Sapir did not begin to read Freudian psychology seriously until after 1916. However, Freud's ideas were in the air. Boas had been at Clark University when Freud lectured there in 1908. In *The Mind of Primitive Man* in 1911, Boas would argue that the ultimate problems of anthropology were psychological. Boas rejected Freud's sexual dynamics but accepted the localization of culture in the individual psyche.

6. A decade later, when Sapir began to reconstruct American Indian culture history on the basis of linguistic classification, he turned to Laufer for encouragement in linking the languages of North America to those of Asia. The use of historical and archaeological documents never inspired him, however.

7. The early students were all men. Boas's women students would come later, when the disciplinary identity of anthropology was more secure.

Two: Apprenticeship

1. At least in retrospect, Sapir did not resent this unpaid apprenticeship. A few years later, he explained to his own employee, F. W. Waugh (20 February 1913: NMM): "At the risk of seeming unduly autobiographical, I must say that my first two years of field work . . . were done for expenses only. I do not think you will find that men who have had no specific training in anthropological work are paid for their first season of fieldwork. It is always assumed that a man is willing to go through a little trouble in the beginning in order to accumulate a little experience."

2. Sapir's promised follow-up on his 1907 report of Wishram language and mythology was not completed until his 1930 collaboration with Leslie Spier, *Wishram Ethnography*. Sapir, inundated with other commitments, willingly left the actual work to Spier (e.g., Sapir to Spier, 14 October 1929: UC).

3. See Murray (1983) for discussion of the two types of leadership in science.

4. The degree was not formally awarded, however, until 1909, because of commencement deadlines and vagaries of publication.

5. Sapir's classic paper on this subject was written only in 1929, long after he had dealt with other sociolinguistic phenomena, for example, Nootka abnormal speech types in 1915. In 1907–1908, however, he was unprepared to explain linguistic data in terms of social usage.

6. In any case, Sapir did not move into broad-scale linguistic classificatory work until after 1917 (Golla 1984; Darnell and Hymes 1986).

7. Sapir learned quickly, though not without bitterness. From his Ottawa museum position, he wrote pessimistically to Frank Speck, who stayed at Pennsylvania to develop a teaching program independent of the museum (2 February 1912: APS), that the museum "will want large numbers of specimens and will not be at all interested in ethnological or linguistic results."

8. Sapir and Speck made more such trips during Sapir's Ottawa years. Speck was frequently in the field and Sapir found brief exposure to new languages relaxing. Without guilt for doing no serious work himself, Sapir acquired considerable knowledge of both Algonquian and Iroquoian languages this way.

9. Compare Bloomfield (1929) on Menomini linguistic acculturation.

10. Sapir was correct. His Ute and Paiute data would soon allow him to formulate sound correspondences for the Uto-Aztecan family with Indo-European-like elegance and precision, a first in American Indian linguistics (Sapir 1913).

11. The term "informant" is no longer acceptable in anthropology or linguistics. It is used because it is the term Sapir and his contemporaries used. "Consultant" is now the most common alternative.

12. Phonetic transcription records the physical quality of sounds. Phonemic transcription is less detailed, stressing classes of sounds felt to be identical by native speakers.

13. This was, in fact, an unprecedented committal of funds on the part of the committee, dominated by Boas (Leeds-Hurwitz 1985). The money was intended for fieldwork, not publication.

14. The position was accepted by another Columbia Ph.D. in linguistics, a Fox Indian named William Jones, who was later murdered in the Philippines.

15. In spite of Sapir's efforts, Canada did not initiate academic instruction until 1925 at the University of Toronto.

16. The Bureau of American Ethnology also grew out of a geological survey, when J. W. Powell switched from geology to ethnology. The Canadian choice of the term "anthropology" reflects Boasian influence over the intervening three decades.

Three: Ottawa

1. There was a five-year waiting period for Canadian citizenship. Sapir's application was filed in 1919 and was probably precipitated by the increasing nationalism of the Canadian public service during and after World War I.

2. The Sapirs' New Hampshire home of the 1930s was chosen partly because of its similarity to the Gatineau area.

3. His son Paul recalls the uproar, much later, when, at the age of about two, he removed a number of file slips and put them in the wastepaper basket. Paul Radin confidently attempted to rearrange them, assuming, incorrectly, that he had mastered Sapir's system.

4. This was a persistent awkwardness for the Bureau of American Ethnology, which was effectively restricted to United States territory (Darnell 1969; Hinsley 1981).

5. Maud (1978; 1982), for example, perpetuates the bitterness of British Columbia anthropologists about the alienation of their work from national anthropology because of Sapir's position.

6. A similar approach developed in the British tradition, in a slightly different context because of the administration of the British empire.

7. See Titley (1986) for discussion of Scott's career. His relationship with Sapir was minimal, although they shared interests in poetry and music.

8. The potlatch is a ceremonial exchange of gifts which brings no direct economic benefit and ultimately results in the destruction of valuable property. It was incomprehensible to most white observers and crucial to the social fabric of many Northwest Coast tribes.

9. Sapir was interested in material culture. Fenton (1986) recalls that Sapir asked him to describe the types and distribution of American basketry in his 1934 dissertation defense at Yale. Sapir's interest in native crafts in the field was independent of any museum obligation. For example, he arranged basketry lessons for his daughter Helen on the Hupa reservation in 1927.

Four: Ottawa Research Team

1. He succeeded Sapir as chief ethnologist in 1925.

2. Boas edited the *Journal of American Folklore* but its constituency included literary students of European folklore as well as anthropologists (Darnell 1974; Zumwalt 1988).

3. His Columbia dissertation on totemism went beyond ethnography to the symbolic structures underlying social life.

4. Only in the midthirties did Sapir persuade him to release these materials to William Fenton, then at the beginning of a distinguished career as an Iroquoianist.

5. These were awaiting transcription by J. D. Sapir in Philadelphia.

6. Sapir's colleagues were aware of his linguistic bias. Kroeber apologized for his Yurok notes (17 August 1919: UCB) saying that "the points I am trying to bring out as to individuality, treatment and style would interest you; but the work not being based to any considerable extent on texts or knowledge of the language, I expect you will shrug your shoulders when it is done."

7. The same issues arose when Sapir sent his Chicago student Cornelius Osgood to the Northern Athabaskans in the late twenties.

8. Boas faced similar conflicts between goals of survey ethnography and his own determination to work more extensively on selected groups. Gruber (1967) details his long-standing dispute with the BAAS and the supervision of Horatio Hale.

9. Foster (p.c.) assumes that when Sapir classified all American languages in 1921 he place Iroquoian in Hokan-Siouan on the basis of Latham's mid-nineteenth-century linking of Iroquoian to Siouan and especially Caddoan.

10. It is no accident that Leonard Bloomfield later chose the Algonquian linguistic stock to illustrate the application of Indo-European methods to unwritten languages. While Sapir used the comparative method to search out distant genetic (historical) relationships, Bloomfield preferred the tidier and better-known patterns of recent sound change along neo-grammarian lines.

11. This was a position Sapir held throughout his life. He wrote to Kroeber (28 November 1930: NMM), decrying "the old pioneering attitude that the main thing is to rescue languages and put a lot of uncritical material on record." All work should be able to "satisfy the requirements of a genuine linguist."

12. Compare Cannizzo (1983) on George Hunt's "invention" of Kwakiutl culture.

13. This process began somewhat earlier in the United States, resulting in a rapid decline in the autonomy of the Bureau of American Ethnology and its Congressional support because of its mandate restricting study to native peoples within the national boundaries (Darnell 1969; Hinsley 1981).

14. They will appear in *The Collected Works of Edward Sapir*.

15. The Alaska Native Languages Center published these texts (revised for bilingual teaching); see Fredson (1982).

Five: Synthesizing the Boasian Paradigm

1. The preliminary reports and correspondence on the phonetics report are preserved in the papers of Boas (APS), Kroeber (UCB), and Sapir (NMM). They are reprinted in Golla (1984, 425–448).

2. Sapir acknowledges here that the degree of detail in recording sounds is arbitrary and some variation can be ignored. The distinction between a phonetic (physical) and phonemic (classes of sounds perceived by native speakers) transcription is implicit, although Sapir did not argue the case until 1925.

3. Boas had also encouraged Goddard to prepare a symposium volume to demonstrate Boasian progress in anthropology. The papers were eventually published in the *American Anthropologist*.

4. In 1936, Sapir and several of his students proposed a standard orthography based on phonemic principles (Swadesh et al. 1936), but they did not seek consensus outside their own research group, nor would they have attained it (see chap. 19).

5. Margaret Mead (1959, xviii) noted of *The Mind of Primitive Man* (Boas 1911b): ". . . its polemical character, its awkward and unendearing style, and the lack of reference to any particular primitive man, meant that its importance was successfully concealed from most of the students who were ordered to read it." Boas's work was "so technical that it tempted no humanist within its pages" (1959, xvii).

6. Lowie was not entirely enthusiastic, however. In retrospect (1965, 11), he characterized the essay as a theoretical dead end, "rather a contribution to the *logic* of ethnological research than to ethnology itself." Sapir was "so eminently sane" that he qualified every generalization "beyond the point of practical utility."

7. Wissler also was intrigued by the Sapir-Kroeber work with California

languages, siding "with the progressives" although many of the examples "do not appeal to me as good evidence" (to Sapir, 15 October 1915: NMM). He consistently failed to recognize that linguistics had a method different from and potentially incompatible with the one he used in ethnology.

8. His frustration was doubtless enhanced by a simultaneous effort to publish a volume of his poetry without financial commitment on his part.

9. Interestingly, these are the issues that later commentators have found awkward. For Sapir, they were the raison d'être of linguistics and definitely part of its scope.

10. This intention persisted, at least theoretically. Sapir wrote to Lowie (16 January 1923: UCB): "I only hope that I may have the chance to write a more thorough study of a group of selected languages. But who would want to publish such a book?"

11. Sapir's conviction of this relationship was later elaborated by his student Benjamin Whorf and is still associated with the names of both men (see chap. 19).

12. I have access to these through J. David Sapir.

13. Boas (to Sapir, 20 October 1922: APS) went to some trouble, however, to provide copies of Sapir's book for libraries in Germany and Russia.

Six: American Indian Languages

1. He did, however, relate Seri and Tequistlatec of Mexico to California Hokan.

2. The Darnell paper explores the conflict in basic assumptions between Boas and Sapir.

3. Years later, Leonard Bloomfield told Sapir (27 May 1925: NMM) that the proof for the Ritwan-Algonquian would have to await reconstruction of Proto-Algonquian. He was then reconstructing the quite regular sound correspondences of Proto-Central Algonquian. Sapir, however, preferred to work with more distant connections for which evidence was necessarily less systematic.

4. The hypothesis was ultimately vindicated by Sapir's student, Mary Haas, in the 1950s. Goddard (1986) conservatively reviews Sapir's evidence, concluding that he was correct about the connection in spite of serious errors in his examples.

5. Boas was not always negative toward Sapir's classificatory work. In 1924, he tried, ultimately unsuccessfully, to fund Sapir for an international conference to read a paper with which Boas would disagree (Mead 1959).

6. Sapir, in contrast, envisioned several waves of migration, each differentiating through genetic diversification and areal borrowing in situ.

7. This map is available in a limited edition through the Canadian Ethnology Service of the Canadian, Museum of Civilization, Ottawa, by permission of the Sapir family.

8. Although Sapir never retracted his Indo-Chinese hypothesis, his later work focused more narrowly on Athabaskan per se, and ultimately on Navajo.

9. Interestingly, Kroeber considered him the only alternative to Sapir for an essay on time perspective in 1916.

10. Jenness worked closely with Sapir in the period when he first formulated the Indo-Chinese hypothesis and was much impressed by the possibility of connecting the old and new worlds. He emphasized this issue in his obituary of Sapir for the Royal Society of Canada (1939, 151).

Seven: Reorientation toward Psychology

1. The implication is that prolonged semi-invalidism was an acceptable middle-class phenomenon (cf. Sontag 1977). Sapir's children generally find Perry's speculations unfounded.

2. The Sapir siblings object to this generalization, apparently based on loose interpretation of interviews with Jean Sapir not long before her death in 1979.

3. Many of Sapir's letters to Benedict were published by Margaret Mead (1959). Biographical items, however, were largely omitted. I have had access to Mead's full transcription by courtesy of the Sapir family.

4. Paul Sapir is a practicing psychoanalyst.

5. Sapir's unpublished poems are in the possession of the Sapir family. William Cowan has compiled them consecutively as a prelude to publication of selected poems.

6. Sapir never returned to Europe, although he maintained extensive ties with European colleagues through correspondence.

7. He must have been aware also of the work of William James, which was at the height of its American popularity.

8. Margaret Mead, who studied with both Ogburn and Boas, described the apparent compulsion of social scientists to incorporate psychology (1959, 16): "Without any psychological theory which could both include and supplement cultural theory, the nature of man had to be derived from cultural materials. . . . the alternative seemed to be endless projections of man as he behaved in our own culture onto mankind as a whole."

9. The boundaries among these were then quite fluid.

10. This is Jung's spelling of the term.

11. The sharp demarcation between the personal and professional relationship of analyst and client became more crucial after about 1923. At about the same time, psychoanalysis came to be dominated by medicine. Consequently, the credentials of all lay analysts became unacceptable. Kroeber's lay training was excellent for its time.

12. Goldenweiser's brief note appeared alongside Sapir's.

13. The term "interpersonal relations" reflects Sapir's friendship and collaboration with psychiatrist Harry Stack Sullivan during the late twenties and thirties.

14. "Genuine" culture was defined in terms of its integration and the self-fulfilment of the individual.

Eight: Experiments in Aesthetics

1. This commentary draws on a manuscript by Bart Jones on Sapir's music. Jones explored Sapir's reliance on sound in his linguistic work in response to my biographical inquiries.

2. He once told his daughter Helen that he might have preferred to be a philosopher.

3. The latter was a fairly new composer at the time.

4. At the same time, Sapir was playing with a class of reduplicated words in English represented by counting-out rhymes, which had both historical and psychological roots.

5. The change was gradual, however. In Chicago, Sapir was active in the group around Harriet Monroe, founder of *Poetry* magazine.

6. Sapir kept a detailed record of his poetry submissions and rejections, which is in the possession of the Sapir family.

7. Sapir's second wife (9 January 1955: SF) reported that he later considered publication of *Dreams and Gibes* "one of his most embarrassing mistakes."

8. The papers of *Poetry* are in the University of Chicago Archives. I cite them from Handler 1986.

9. Handler (1986, 3–4) notes: "Sapir tried on different voices in his poetry, characteristically distancing himself from his subject, writing about personalities and states of mind. . . . If Benedict's poetry is confessional, Sapir's is observational—though he himself is often the subject observed."

10. I have access to this correspondence through the courtesy of William Cowan and his thorough documentation of Sapir's social and intellectual activities during the Ottawa years.

11. John Wesley Powell used a similar strategy to build a national power base through the Anthropological Society of Washington, doubtless Sapir's model.

12. Sapir was eager to collaborate with colleagues in other disciplines, although his colleagues Waugh and Smith had more in common with the predominating natural sciences. In 1918, however, Sapir contributed a brief note to the *Ottawa Naturalist* on the origin of the term "whiskey-jack."

13. I have access to these documents through William Cowan.

Nine: Boasian Anthropology

1. Stocking (1974) argues that Boas had completed what, for anyone else, would have been a normal career by 1911 and that it was the end of an era for him.

2. Sapir's letters to Benedict are cited from the full transcript prepared by Margaret Mead (SF).

3. The juxtaposition of the two poems indicates that editor Harriet Monroe had penetrated Benedict's pseudonym.

4. Helen Sapir Larson, however, considers this analysis grossly exaggerated. Michael Sapir agrees, noting that Benedict also took him under her wing.

5. Michael recalls her physical abilities as much greater.

6. Cf. Rosenberg 1982.

7. Mead was bitter that she was not invited to contribute to the Sapir memorial volume (Spier et al., 1941), originally intended as a festschrift (Mandelbaum, p.c.). Sapir's former students, however, did not see Mead as relevant to Sapir's work or close to him personally.

8. Jean Sapir (to Philip Sapir, n.d. 1957: SF) believed that Mead included the Sapir letters in her book about Benedict (Mead 1959) primarily to prove that Sapir, whatever his later criticisms of her work and personality, had once liked her.

Ten: Escape from Ottawa

1. Sapir eventually went to Yale as a result of the culture-and-personality work he elaborated at Chicago.

2. If Boas took anyone into his confidence, it has not been recorded in his papers. It was, however, his custom to recommend more than one person for any available position before indicating his personal preference; this may explain the Michelson issue.

3. Only a few months earlier, Sapir had written to Benedict (9 November 1925: SF) about his difficulties in dealing with the ethnological part of his Chicago responsibilities: "I do wish, Ruth, someone would explain to me once for all why one studies primitive customs. It bothers me not to have discovered it yet. I think I shall die without knowing—at least my bones won't."

Eleven: University of Chicago

1. When Helen babysat for the Viner children, Sapir thought she should refuse "the going rate of 25 cents an hour" and do it "as a friendly gesture."

2. Overt anti-Semitism would become an issue for Sapir only in New Haven, where it was reinforced by his concerns over rising Nazi power in Germany.

3. Linguists collect Bibles because they are often the first texts translated into a given language and are directly comparable across languages.

4. She would react equally naively to the anti-Semitism of Yale a few years later.

5. This version is confirmed by the other Sapir siblings.

6. (James) David, named after his two grandfathers, was born in New Haven four years later.

7. On these grounds, Sapir had excellent cause to resent his relegation to Ottawa where teaching was impossible. Boas, however, always intended Sapir to return to Columbia to carry on the program in American Indian linguistics.

Twelve: Chicago Anthropolgy

1. Leslie White's official obituary (Service 1976, 612) claims that Faris rejected his 1927 dissertation as "not theoretical enough" and that "ensuing disagreements among the faculty helped to precipitate the formation of the separate department of anthropology" over a year later. White, in an interview with Matthews (15 November 1964, UC), stated that Cole threatened to leave the university if the departments were not separated. White's version is undoubtedly oversimplified.

2. Sapir probably hoped to support the Central Algonquian work of Leonard Bloomfield, who was in the German department.

3. Sapir retained his lack of enthusiasm for physical anthropology within anthropology at Yale (Rouse, p.c.).

4. Watkins was the first black Ph.D. in anthropology, and Sapir supervised his work in Africa on his native language until he left Chicago in 1931 (Stocking 1979, 17).

5. At Yale, Sapir served on a master's committee for a South African named Matthews, later a distinguished politician.

6. Only the outline of Sapir's book on the psychology of culture was ever written. An integrated transcription of class notes from a number of Sapir students will appear in *The Collected Works of Edward Sapir*, edited by Judith Irvine.

7. In the class notes, Sapir calls these "master ideas," a position consistent with the idealist definition of culture implicit as early as "Culture, Genuine and Spurious."

8. I have access to these records through Stephen Murray.

Thirteen: Commitment to Athabaskan

1. This was something of a family expedition. Jean, Michael, and Helen accompanied Sapir. Jean expanded her work on child training for the Institute for Juvenile Research in an ethnographic direction (Sapir to Jenness, 13 March 1927: NMM).

2. Problems of prejudice against the Chinese also arose in California.

3. Jenness hoped to persuade Sapir to work for the Ottawa Division of Anthropology personally. By this time, however, Sapir could easily obtain foundation support for his own work. The problem was research funding for students.

4. Li then returned to China and did not work further on Athabaskan until a brief project in 1952.

5. Boas, however, failed to mention Athabaskan in his 1939 obituary of Sapir, presumably because so little of the data were actually published, Krauss (1986) contains an appendix cataloguing Sapir's published and unpublished Athabaskan work.

6. Sapir always preferred the term dialect rather than language within Athabaskan per se, thereby emphasizing the closeness of these languages to one another.

7. This is the spelling Sapir used. "Navajo" is now accepted.

8. Hoijer worked primarily on Apache, closely related to Navajo. But he had training and experience in comparative linguistics which Haile did not. Hoijer rather than Haile was the literary executor of Sapir's Navajo material and devoted much of his own career to completing it (Beals 1977, 107).

9. "Man" was the operative word. Cole opposed a laboratory fellowship application from a woman because of the difficulties of finding positions after training.

10. Sapir obtained long-range support for Hoijer's Apache linguistic field-work through Hoijer and Opler's ethnographic work (Opler MS). Mrs. Parsons also supported the ethnographic work of Leslie White at Acoma, the most secretive of the pueblos.

11. Yale, however, had similar problems.

12. This was a typical Boasian reaction to Radcliffe-Brown. The Boasians equated their methods with professional anthropology and did not take well to any challenge of the urgent need to record native language texts.

13. Sapir's culture-and-personality work would soon develop the life-history method, based for him in linguistic method, into a critique of psychiatric methods.

14. Margaret Mead (1959) notes that at the BAAS meetings in Toronto in 1924 Gladys Reichard was the only person not charmed by Sapir.

15. Sapir's scientific grammars also emphasized pattern rather than detail. This position foreshadows his later methodology in relating the individual to his//her culture.

16. In practice, Morgan and Young returned to a similar system in 1937, but this was too late for Sapir in terms of practical involvement on the Navajo reservation (Krauss 1986).

Fourteen: Professionalization of Linguistics

1. The first issue also contained Sapir's classic paper on the concept of the phoneme, which placed American linguistics in a position to contribute to

European linguistic theory, where Prague School phonology was an independent invention. Bloomfield contributed his reconstruction of the sound system of Central Algonquian, a demonstration of the applicability of Indo-European philological methods to the study of unwritten languages.

2. Carroll did not consider himself part of this group, though Sapir encouraged his work. His tie to Sapirian linguistics came later through Benjamin Whorf.

3. Allen summarized his notes on the LI's of this period in a plenary lecture to the LSA in December 1983.

4. Bloomfield was the only linguist per se whose research Sapir ever supported during his tenure in Ottawa.

5. When David Mandelbaum (1984, p.c.) visited Bloomfield on his way to the Cree, Bloomfield was friendly but not useful.

6. Sapir's memorandum was published in *Romantic Review* rather than in a professional journal.

7. In practice, however, the Americanist linguists now meet in conjunction with the American Anthropological Association.

8. Herzog, Newman, Sapir, Haas(-Swadesh), Swadesh, and Voegelin were listed in alphabetical order to emphasize the consensus in their position.

Fifteen: Interdisiplinary Social Science

1. The facts of Sullivan's early life are taken from Perry's definitive biography of Sullivan (1982); their juxtaposition with Sapir's early experiences is, of course, my own.

2. Arthur Koestler's *The Call Girls* (1972) describes the conference circuit in terms remarkably replicated at Hanover.

3. Participants apparently received copies of the transcripts, since they are included in the papers of several regular attenders.

4. Sapir would soon become involved quite directly in this project by organizing the "Impact of Culture on Personality" seminar at Yale for the Rockefeller Foundation.

Sixteen: Organizing Research

1. Only Leonard Outhwaite of the Rockefeller Foundation realized that Sapir attended to individual variation in meaning rather than to real individuals in a specific social context.

2. This notion was elaborated in Sapir's class notes and in an article on personality in *The Encyclopedia of Social Sciences*.

3. The published versions were "Speech as a Personality Trait" (1927) and "A Study in Phonetic Symbolism" (1929).

4. This assessment of observer subjectivity is very different from "Culture, Genuine and Spurious," in which Sapir projected his own unsubstantiated frustration with modern society into his interpretation of the "genuineness" of the so-called primitive. But his audience then was humanistic.

5. The order of the two disciplines is variable in all documents.

6. Sapir's usage is independent of the distinction between society and culture which arose through the British social anthropology brought to North America by Malinowski and Radcliffe-Brown.

7. In "Psychiatric and Cultural Pitfalls in the Business of Getting a Living" (1939), however, Sapir equated the functions of status acquisition in West Coast and American economic systems.

8. Both were so-called neo-Freudians, who argued that culture differently modified pan-human biological determinants of personality, making studies of differential socialization crucial.

9. The committee on personality and culture existed until 1941, but it never pursued anything like the Sapir–Sullivan personality training program.

Seventeen: The Call to Yale

1. Thomas may have suggested the seminar idea to Frank in the first place. It reflects his emphasis on studying near cultures, largely European. Moreover, he was influential in the SSRC, and his institutional loyalties were outside Chicago. Frank was not otherwise particularly interested in cross-cultural evidence. Mead (1966), however, emphasizes Frank's contribution and minimizes Sapir's; she does not mention Thomas.

2. These were: "Language and Environment," "Do We Need a Superorganic?" "Culture, Genuine and Spurious," "Speech as a Personality Trait," "Cultural Anthropology and Psychiatry," and the *Encyclopedia of Social Sciences* series on "communication," "custom," "dialect," "fashion," "group," and "language."

3. They are included in her papers at the Library of Congress. There is no documentation of the transfer and the Sapir family was unaware of it.

Eighteen: Yale Anthropology

1. Documents for Spier's chairmanship and the early years of Murdock's are in the department of anthropology; I have access to them by courtesy of Harold Scheffler. Sapir's administration is not so preserved, making reconstruction of his program more difficult. IHR files (YU) contain records of student fieldwork.

Nineteen: Yale Linguistics

1. Emeneau's own work in India would follow up on this model, at the borderline between the Indo-European and Dravidian language families. No other Indo-Europeanist at Yale was greatly influenced by this work of Sapir's.

2. Sapir's strongest relativity statement was a brief note titled "Conceptual Categories of Primitive Languages," an abstract of a paper read to the National Academy of Sciences in 1931. This was published only after his death.

3. Hockett (in Hoijer 1954, 2) mistakenly asserts that Whorf began to do speculative work on language and thought only after his association with Sapir. In fact, Sapir provided Whorf with a method to approach his long-standing questions.

4. Greenberg (1987) calls this "multilateral comparison."

Twenty: Institute of Human Relations

1. John and Beatrice Whiting, who were analyzed by Zinn, observed retrospectively (1978, 43) that the Hull synthesis "was quite compatible with the materialism of Sumner and Murdock, the practicality of Spier and the functional approach of Malinowski."

Twenty-One: Dénuement

1. When Jean moved to New York after Sapir's death, Horney declined to resume the analysis. Jean could no longer afford her. More important, Horney presumably "wanted to avoid dealing with the results (to the analysis) of her own professionally and ethically inadequate conduct. In addition, with ES dead, JVS was now less interesting to her (Paul Sapir, p.c.).

2. Yale's leave policy was one year off in seven at half pay or a semester with full pay for full professors (assuming substitution without reducing the program or overloading others); assistant and associate professors got full salary but had to pay a substitute out of that salary (9 April 1939: YU).

3. The file copy of Seymour's letter contains an initialed comment from Dean Furniss that Yale should not imply any liability for Sapir's obligation.

4. Paul Sapir (p.c.) notes that the ventricular aneurism was "hopeless," no matter how Sapir approached his convalescence. The aneurism probably resulted from his second heart attack in the summer of 1937. More sophisticated diagnosis might conceivably have forestalled this.

5. Sapir served as president of the LSA in 1930.

6. Yale also provided posthumous fellowship money, at the urging of Os-

good, for Sapir's son David to attend Yale, as Philip and Michael had done. Faculty sons received preferential treatment at Yale, but this was still irregular and attests to Sapir's reputation at that institution (perhaps also to collective guilt).

7. Manuscripts in the possession of the Sapir family are at the American Philosophical Society in Philadelphia. Many of these will appear in the Sapir *Collected Works* now in progress from Mouton–De Gruyter.

8. This analyst was probably Franz Alexander. Jean Sapir, however, told her son Paul (p.c.) that Sapir's negative opinion of Alexander was influential in the University of Chicago's decision not to collaborate with his psychoanalytic institute. Sapir's negative opinion may have resulted from the incident cited by Murdock.

9. I have access to these letters through the courtesy of J. David Sapir. There are far too many to catalogue in detail.

10. The majority of these are reprinted in Koerner 1984.

Abbreviations

Archival Documents Cited

APS   American Philosophical Society (Franz Boas, J. Alden Mason, Edward Sapir, Frank Speck)

BAE   Bureau of American Ethnology, National Anthropological Archives, Smithsonian Institution

CU   Columbia University

FCM   Field Columbian Museum, Chicago

HC   Hanover Conference transcripts, Dartmouth College

HU   Harvard University (Clyde Kluckhohn)

JHU   Johns Hopkins University, Chesney Archives, School of Medicine (Adolph Meyer)

LC   Library of Congress (Margaret Mead)

MNA   Museum of Northern Arizona, Flagstaff (Gladys Reichard)

NMM   National Museum of Man, Ottawa (now renamed Canadian Museum of Civilization) (Edward Sapir, Diamond Jenness, Marius Barbeau)

NRC   National Research Council, National Academy of Sciences

OPL   Ottawa Public Library (Madge MacBeth)

RAC   Rockefeller Archive Center

SF   Sapir family documents

SSRC   Social Science Research Council

SWL   Southwest Laboratory of Anthropology

UC   University of Chicago (Robert Redfield, Fay-Cooper Cole,
        Louis Wirth, interviews by Fred Matthews and James Carey)

UCB   University of California, Berkeley, Bancroft Library (A. L.
        Kroeber, Robert H. Lowie)

UM   University of Michigan (Leslie White)

UPM   University of Pennsylvania Museum

UT   University of Toronto (Thomas McIlwraith)

VC   Vasser College (Ruth Benedict)

WAWPF   William Alanson White Psychiatric Foundation

YU   Yale University, Sterling Memorial Library (Benjamin Whorf,
        Institute of Human Relations, Presidents' Papers)

YUDA   Yale University Department of Anthropology (Leslie Spier,
        George Murdock)

YUPM   Yale University, Peabody Museum

Institutional Abbreviations

AAA   American Anthropological Association

AAAS   American Association for the Advancement of Science

ACLS	American Council of Learned Societies
APA	American Psychiatric Association
BAAS	British Association for the Advancement of Science
BIA	Bureau of Indian Affairs
IALA	International Auxiliary Language Association
IHR	Institute of Human Relations (Yale)
IJR	Institute for Juvenile Research (Chicago)
LCRC	Local Community Research Committee (Chicago)
LI	Linguistic Institute (LSA)
LSA	Linguistic Society of America
NRC	National Research Council
SSRC	Social Science Research Council

Journal Abbreviations

AA	American Anthropologist
AJS	American Journal of Sociology
AL	Anthropological Linguistics
BBAE	Bulletin of the Bureau of American Ethnology
CRSA	Canadian Review of Sociology and Anthropology
HL	Historiographica Linguistica
HOA	History of Anthropology
HOAN	History of Anthropology Newsletter

IJAL   International Journal of American Linguistics

JAF   Journal of American Folklore

JHBS   Journal of the History of the Behavioral Sciences

JRAI   Journal of the Royal Anthropological Institute of Great Britain and Ireland

KASP   Kroeber Anthropological Society Papers

Lg.   Language

MAAA   Memoirs of the American Anthropological Association

PAPS   Proceedings of the American Philosophical Society

UCPAAE   University of California Publications in American Archaeology and Ethnology.

UCPL   University of California Publications in Linguistics

VFPA   Viking Fund Publications in Anthropology

References Cited

Alcock, Floyd
    1947   *A Century in the History of the Geological Survey of Canada.* Canada Department of Mines and Resources, Mines and Geology Branch, National Museums of Canada, Special Contribution 47.

Allen, Harold
    1983   The Early Linguistic Institutes. Paper read to the Linguistic So-
    MS   ciety of America.

Anonymous
    1919   Review of Edward Sapir, *Dreams and Gibes. The Dial* 67: 174.
    1922   Review of *Language. Smart Set.*
    1925   Note on Indo-Chinese. *Science.*

Anderson, Stephen R.
    1985   *Phonology in the Twentieth Century.* Chicago: University of Chicago Press.

Bateson, Mary Catherine
    1984   *With a Daughter's Eye: A Memoir of Margaret Mead and Gregory Bateson.* New York: William Morrow.

Beals, Ralph
    1977   Harry Hoijer 1904–1976. *AA* 79: 105–110.

Benedict, Ruth
    1923   The Concept of the Guardian Spirit in North America. *MAAA* 29.
    1934*a*   Anthropology and the Abnormal. *Journal of General Psychology* 10: 59–82.
    1934*b*   *Patterns of Culture.* Boston: Houghton Mifflin.

Bernier, Helene
    1984   Edward Sapir et la Récherche Anthropologique au Musée du Canada 1910–1925. *HL* 11: 397–412.

Bloch, Bernard
    1949   Leonard Bloomfield 1887–1949. *Lg.*: 87–98. Reprinted in Sebeok 1966.
Bloomfield, Leonard
    1922   Review of Edward Sapir, *Language*. *Classical Weekly* 15: 142–143. Reprinted in Koerner 1984.
    1925   On the Sound System of Central Algonquian. *Lg.* 130–156.
    1929   Literate and Illiterate Speech in Menomini. *American Speech* 2: 432–439.
    1933   *Language*. New York: Henry Holt.
Boas, Franz
    1889   On Alternating Sounds. *AA* 2: 47–53.
    1907   Some Principles of Museum Administration. *Science* 25: 921–933.
    1911a   Introduction to the Handbook of American Indian Languages. *BBAE* 40.
    1911b   *The Mind of Primitive Man*. New York: Macmillan.
    1920   The Classification of American Languages. *AA* 22: 367–376.
    1939   Edward Sapir. *IJAL* 10: 58–63. Reprinted in Koerner 1984.
Bulmer, Martin
    1980   The Early Institutional Establishment of Social Science Research: The Local Community Research Committee of the University of Chicago, 1923–1930. *Minerva* 18: 51–110.
    1984   *The Chicago School of Sociology: Institutionalization, Diversity and the Rise of Sociological Research*. Chicago: University of Chicago Press.
Bulmer, Martin, and Joan Bulmer
    1981   Philanthropy and Social Science in the 1920's: Beardsley Ruml and the Laura Spelman Rockefeller Memorial, 1922–1929. *Minerva* 19: 347–407.
Burgess, John W.
    1934   *Reminiscences of an American Scholar: The Beginnings of Columbia University*. New York: Columbia University Press.
Campbell, Lyle, and Marianne Mithun, eds.
    1979   *The Languages of Native America*. Austin: University of Texas Press.
Cannizzo, Jeanne
    1983   George Hunt and the Invention of Kwakiutl Culture. *CRSA* 20: 44–58.
Carroll, John B.
    1956   Introduction to *Benjamin Lee Whorf: Language, Thought and Reality*. New York: John Wiley 1–23. Reprinted in Sebeok 1966.
Collier, Peter, and David Horowitz
    1976   *The Rockefellers: An American Dynasty*. New York: Holt, Rinehart and Winston.
Collins, Henry B.

1971   Diamond Jenness: An Appreciation. *Anthropologica* 13: 9–12.
Coser, Lewis A.
1971   *Masters of Sociological Thought.* New York: Harcourt, Brace, Jovanovich.
Cowan, William, Michael K. Foster, and Konrad Koerner, eds.
1986   *New Perspectives in Language, Culture, and Personality: Proceedings of the Edward Sapir Centenary Conference, Ottawa, 1–3 October 1984.* Amsterdam and Philadelphia: John Benjamins.
Crowley, Ralph M.
1977   Harry Stack Sullivan 1892–1949. *Aesculpius*: 23–26.
Darnell, Regna
1969   *The Development of American Anthropology 1880–1920: From the Bureau of American Ethnology to Franz Boas.* Doctoral thesis, University of Pennsylvania.
1970   The Emergence of Academic Anthropology at the University of Pennsylvania. *JHBS* 6: 80–92.
1971a   The Professionalization of American Anthropology. *Social Science Information* 10: 83–103.
1971b   The Powell Classification of American Indian Languages. *Papers in Linguistics* 4: 70–110.
1971c   The Revision of the Powell Classification. *Papers in Linquistics* 4: 233–257.
1974   The Development of American Folklore Scholarship 1880–1920. *Journal of the Folklore Institute* 10: 23–49.
Darnell, Regna
1974   *Readings in the History of Anthropology.* New York: Harper and Row.
1975   Towards a History of the Professionalization of Canadian Anthropology. *Proceedings of the Canadian Ethnology Society*: 399–416.
1976   The Sapir Years at the National Museum. *Proceedings of the Plenary Session of the Canadian Ethnology Society*: 98–121. Reprinted In Koerner 1984.
1977   Hallowell's Bear Ceremonialism and the Emergence of Boasian Anthropology. *Ethos* 5: 13–30.
1984   The Sapir Years in the Canadian National Museum, Ottawa. In Konrad Koerner (ed.), *Edward Sapir: Appraisals of His Life and Work* (Amsterdam and Philadelphia: John Benjamins, 1984).
1986a   The Emergence of Edward Sapir's Mature Thought. In W. Cowan, M. Foster, and K. Koerner (eds.), *New Perspectives in Language, Culture, and Personality* ... (Amsterdam and Philadelphia: John Benjamins, 1986), pp. 553–588.
1986b   Personality and Culture: The Fate of the Sapirian Alternative. *HOA* 4: 156–183.
1989   Stanley Newman and the Sapir School of Linguistics. In Mary Ritchie Key and Henry Hoernigswald (eds.), *Essays in Memory of Stanley Newman.* Berlin: De Gruyter.

In press Edward Sapir and the Boasian Model of Cultural Process. In
James M. Nyce, (ed.), *Proceedings of Sapir Memorial Symposia*,
Brown University.

Darnell, Regna, and Dell Hymes
1986   Edward Sapir's Six-Unit Classification of American Indian Languages: The Search for Time Perspective. In T. Bynon and F.
Palmer (eds.), *Essays in the History of Western Linguistics*. (Cambridge: Cambridge University Press), 202–244.

Diamond, Stanley
1981   Radin. In Sydel Silverman (ed.), *Totems and Teachers: Perspectives
on the History of Anthropology*. New York: Columbia University
Press.

Dixon, Roland B., and A. L. Kroeber
1903   The Native Languages of California. *AA* 5: 1–26.
1913   New Linguistic Families in California. *AA* 15: 647–655.
1919   Linguistic Families of California. *UCPAAE* 16: 48–118.

Dollard, John
1935   *Criteria for the Life History*. New Haven: Yale University Press.

DuBois, Cora
1944   *People of Alor*. Minneapolis: University of Minnesota Press.

Eggan, Fred
1963   Fay-Cooper Cole 1881–1961. *AA* 65: 641–645.
1974   Among the Anthropologists. *Annual Review of Anthropology* 3: 1–
19.
1986   An Overview of Edward Sapir's Career. In W. Cowan, M. Foster,
and K. Koerner (eds.), *New Perspectives in Language, Culture, and
Personality* . . . (Amsterdam and Philadelphia: John Benjamins,
1986), pp. 1–16.

Emeneau, Murray
1953   Edgar Howard Sturtevant 1875–1952. *American Philosophical Society Yearbook* 1952: 339–343. Reprinted in Sebeok 1966.

Eulau, Heinz
1969   The Maddening Methods of Harold D. Lasswell. In A. Rogow
(ed.), *Politics, Personality and Social Science in the Twentieth Century* . . . (Chicago: University of Chicago Press, 1969), pp. 15–
40.

Farget, Laurence
1986   *Na-Dene and Sino-Tibetan: Historical Linguistics and New Data Towards Establishing Genetic Relationships*. Master's Thesis, University
of Lyon, France.

Faris, Ellsworth
1937   *The Nature of Human Nature*. Chicago: University of Chicago
Press.

Faris, Robert E. L.
1967   *Chicago Sociology 1920–1932*. San Francisco: Chandler.

Fenton, William

1986   Sapir as Museologist and Research Director 1910–1925. In W. Cowan, M. Foster, and K. Koerner (eds.), *New Perspectives in Language, Culture, and Personality* ... (Amsterdam and Philadelphia: John Benjamins, 1986), pp. 215–240.

1988   Keeping the Promise: Return of the Wampums to the Six Nations Iroquois Confederacy, Grand River. *Anthropology Newsletter*: 3, 25 (October).

Fowler, Catherine S., and Donald D. Fowler

1986   Edward Sapir, Tony Tillohash, and Southern Paiute Studies. In W. Cowan, M. Foster, and K. Koerner (eds.), *New Perspectives in Language, Culture, and Personality* ... (Amsterdam and Philadelphia: John Benjamins, 1986), pp. 41–66.

Fredson, John

1982   *John Fredson Edward Sapir Haa Googwandak* (stories told by John Fredson to Edward Sapir). Fairbanks: Alaska Native Languages Center.

Gillin, John, ed.

1954   *For a Science of Social Man: Convergences in Anthropology, Psychology and Sociology*. New York: Macmillan.

Goddard, Ives

1986   Sapir's Comparative Method. In W. Cowan, M. Foster, and K. Koerner (eds.), *New Perspectives in Language, Culture, and Personality* ... (Amsterdam and Philadelphia: John Benjamins, 1986), pp. 191–214.

Goldenweiser, Alexander

1910   Totemism: An Analytical Study. *JAF* 23: 1–115.

Goldfrank, Esther S.

1978   *Notes on an Undirected Life as one Anthropologist Tells It*. New York: Queen's College Press.

Golla, Victor, ed.

1984   The Sapir–Kroeber Correspondence: Letters between Edward Sapir and A. L. Kroeber, 1905–1925. Survey of California and other Indian Languages 6. Berkeley: Department of Linguistics, University of California.

1986   Sapir, Kroeber and North American Linguistic Classification. In W. Cowan, M. Foster, and K. Koerner (eds.), *New Perspectives in Language, Culture, and Personality* ... (Amsterdam and Philadelphia: John Benjamins, 1986), pp. 17–40.

Gould, Stephen J.

1983   *Mare's Eggs and Hen's Teeth*. New York: Norton.

Greenberg, Joseph

1987   *Language in the Americas*. Stanford: Stanford University Press.

Greenberg, Joseph et al.

1987   Current Anthropology Review of *Language in the Americas*. *Current Anthropology* 28: 647–667.

Gruber, Jacob

1967   Horatio Hale and the Development of American Anthropology. *PAPS* 3: 5–37.

Haas, Mary
1941   Tunica. In Franz Boas (ed.), *Handbook of American Indian Languages*, vol. 4. Washington, D.C.: Bureau of American Ethnology, 1–143.
1976   Boas, Sapir and Bloomfield. In Wallace Chafe (ed.), *American Indian Languages and American Linguistics: The Second Golden Anniversary Symposium of the Linguistic Society of America*. Lisse, Holland: Peter de Ridder, 59–69.

Hahn, E. Adelaide
1953   Edgar Howard Sturtevant 1875–1952. *Lg.* 28: 417–434. Reprinted in Sebeok 1966.

Haile, Father Berard
1941–   *Learning Navaho* (four vols.). St. Michaels, Arizona: St. Michaels
1948.   Mission.

Hall, Robert A., Jr., ed.
1987   *Leonard Bloomfield: Essays on His Life and Work*. Amsterdam and Philadelphia: John Benjamins.

Hallowell, A. Irving
1951   Frank Gouldsmith Speck, 1881–1950. *AA* 53: 67–87.

Handler, Richard
1983   The Dainty and the Hungry Man: Literature and Anthropology in the work of Edward Sapir. *HOA* 1: 208–231.
1986   The Vigorous Male and Aspiring Female: Poetry, Personality and Culture in Edward Sapir and Ruth Benedict. *HOA* 4.
MS   Significant Form: Sapir's Phonemic Poetics. Read at the American Anthropological Association, Denver, 1984.

Harris, Zellig
1943–   Yokuts Structure and Newman's Grammar. *IJAL* 10: 196–211.
1944
1951   *Methods in Structural Linguistics*. Chicago: University of Chicago Press.

Hanis, Zellig, and C. F. Voegelin
1953   Eliciting in Linguistics. *Southwestern Journal of Anthropology* 9: 59–75.

Herzog, George, et al
1934   Some Orthographic Recommendations. *AA* 36: 629–631.

Hinsley, Curtis
1981   *Savages and Scientists: The Smithsonian Institution and the Development of American Anthropology, 1883–1911*. Washington, D.C.: Smithsonian Institution.

Hockett, Charles, ed.
1970   *A Leonard Bloomfield Anthology*. Bloomington: Indiana University Press.

Hodge, W., ed.

1906,   *Handbook of American Indians*. Washington, D.C.: Bureau of
1910   American Ethnology.
Hoijer, Harry, ed.
1946   Introduction to *Linguistic Structures of Native North America*.
        VFPA 6: 9–29.
Hooton, Earnest A.
1940   Edward Sapir. *Proceedings of the American Academy of Arts and
        Sciences* 74: 157–159.
Horney, Karen
1942   *Self-Analysis*. New York: Norton.
Howard, Jane
1984   *Margaret Mead: A Life*. New York: Simon and Schuster.
Hughes, Everett, et al
1976   Discussion: American Ethnology: The Role of Redfield. In John
        Murra, ed. *American Anthropology; The Early Years*. (St. Paul:
        West Publishing Co.), 139–145.
Hummel, Arthur
1936   Berthold Laufer 1874–1934. *AA* 38: 101–103.
Hymes, Dell
1983   *Essays in the History of Linguistic Anthropology*. Amsterdam and
        Philadelphia: John Benjamins.
Hymes, Dell, and John Fought
1975   American Structuralism. In T. A. Sebeok (ed.), *Current Trends in
        Linguistics, 10: Historiography of Linguistics*. The Hague: Mouton,
        903–1176.
Janowitz, Morris
1984   Foreward. In Lester R. Kurtz (ed.), *Evaluating Chicago Sociology:
        A Guide to the Literature with an Annotated Bibliography*. Chicago:
        University of Chicago Press.
Jenness, Diamond
1939   Edward Sapir. *Transactions of the Royal Society of Canada*: 151–
        163. Reprinted in Koerner 1984.
Jespersen, Otto
1922   *Language: Its Nature, Development and Origin*. London: Allen and
        Unwin.
Jones, A. Bart
1985   Edward Sapir's Music.
MS
Joos, Martin
1986   *Notes on the Development of the Linguistic Society of America, 1929–
        1950*. Ithaca, New York: Linguistica.
Jung, C. G.
1923   *Psychological Types*. New York: Harcourt, Brace.
Karl, Barry D.
1974   *Charles E. Merriam and the Study of Politics*. Chicago: University
        of Chicago Press.
Kelly, Laurence

1983   *The Assault on Assimilation: John Collier and the Origins of Indian Policy Reform*. Albuquerque: University of New Mexico Press.

Koerner, Konrad, ed.
1984   *Edward Sapir: Appraisals of His Life and Work*. Amsterdam and Philadelphia: John Benjamins.

Koestler, Arthur
1972   *The Call Girls*. London: Hutchinson.

Krauss, Michael
1979   Athabaskan Tone.
MS
1986   Edward Sapir and Athabaskan Linguistics. In W. Cowan, M. Foster and K. Koerner (eds.), *New Perspectives in Language, Culture, and Personality* . . . (Amsterdam and Philadelphia: John Benjamins, 1986), pp. 147–190.

Kroeber, Alfred L.
1920   Review of Freud, *Totem and Taboo*. AA 22.
1922   Review of *Language*. *The Dial:* 314–316. Reprinted in Koerner 1984.
1954   The Place of Anthropology in Universities. *AA* 56: 764–767.
1959   The History of the Personality of Anthropology. *AA* 61: 398–404.

Kroeber, Theodora
1961   *Ishi: The Last of the Yahi*. Berkeley and Los Angeles: University of California Press.
1970   *Alfred Kroeber: A Personal Configuration*. Berkeley, Los Angeles, London: University of California Press.

Kuhn, Thomas
1961   *The Structure of Scientific Revolutions*. Chicago: Phoenix.

LaBarre, Weston
1958   Family and Symbol. In Wilbur and Munsterberger (eds.), Psychology and Culture. . . . (New York: Universities Press), 156–167.

Laird, Carobeth
1975   *Encounter with an Angry God*. Bauning, Calif.: Malki Museum Press.

Lasswell, Harold D.
1930   *Psychopathology and Politics*. Chicago: University of Chicago Press.
1938   What Psychiatrists and Political Scientists Can Learn from Each Other. *Psychiatry* 1: 33–39.
1956   The Impact of Psychoanalytic Thinking on the Social Sciences. In Leonard White, ed. *The State of the Social Sciences*. Chicago: University of Chicago Press, 84–115.

Leeds-Hurwitz, Wendy
1983   *Jaime De Angulo: An Intellectual Biography*. Doctoral thesis, University of Pennsylvania.
1985   The Committee on Research in Native American Languages. *Proceedings of the American Philosophical Society*.

Leeds-Hurwitz, Wendy, and James M. Nyce
1986   Linguistic Text Collection and the Development of Life History in the Work of Edward Sapir. In W. Cowan, M. Foster, and K. Koerner (eds.), *New Perspectives in Language, Culture, and Personality*... (Amsterdam and Philadelphia: John Benjamins, 1986), pp. 495–432.

Leslie, Charles
1976   The Hedgehog and the Fox in Robert Redfield's Work and Career. In Murra, ed. *American Anthropology: The Early Years.* St. Paul: West Publishing Co., 146–166.

Lief, Alfred, ed.
1948   *The Commonsense Psychiatry of Dr. Adolph Meyer.* New York: McGraw-Hill.

Lowie, Robert H.
1919   Review of Edward Sapir, *Time Perspective. AA* 21: 75–77. Reprinted in Koerner 1984.
1923   Review of Edward Sapir, *Language. AA* 25: 90–93. Reprinted in Koerner 1984.
1959   *Robert H. Lowie Ethnologist: A Personal Record.* Berkeley and Los Angeles: University of California Press.

Lowie, Robert H., ed.
1965   *Letters from Edward Sapir to Robert H. Lowie.* Berkeley, Calif.: mimeo.

Lynd, Robert, and Helen Lynd
1929   *Middletown: A Study in Contemporary Culture.* New York: Harcourt Brace.
1937   *Middletown in Transition: A Study in Cultural Conflict.* New York: Harcourt Brace.

McCawley, James D.
1967   Sapir's Phonologic Representation. *IJAL* 33: 106–111. Reprinted in Koerner 1984.

McFeat, Thomas
1984   Cons, Marks and Stings in a Land of Strange Outcomes. Canadian Ethnology Society Plenary Address on the History of Canadian Anthropology.
MS

McIlwraith, Thomas F.
1948   *The Bella Coola.* Toronto: University of Toronto Press.

Madge, John
1962   *The Origins of Scientific Sociology.* New York: Free Press.

Malkiel, Yakov
1986   Sapir as a Student of Linguistic Diachrony. In W. Cowan, M. Foster, and K. Koerner (eds.), *New Perspectives in Language, Culture, and Personality*... (Amsterdam and Philadelphia: John Benjamins, 1986), pp. 315–340.

Mandelbaum, David
1941   Edward Sapir. *Jewish Social Studies* 3: 131–140. Reprinted in Koerner 1984.

Mandelbaum, David, ed.

1949   *Selected Writings of Edward Sapir*. Berkeley and Los Angeles: University of California Press.
Mark, Joan Te Paske
1968   *The Impact of Freud on American Cultural Anthropology*. Doctoral thesis, Harvard University.
Marvick, Dwaine, ed.
1977   *Harold David Lasswell on Political Sociology*. Chicago: University of Chicago Press.
Mason, J. Alden
1964   Anthropology at the University of Pennsylvania. *Philadelphia Anthropological Society Bulletin*.
Maud, Ralph
1978   *The Salish People: The Local Contribution of Charles Hill-Tout*. 4 vols. Vancouver: Talonbooks.
1982   *A Guide to B.C. Myth and Legend: A Short History of Myth-Collecting and a Survey of Published Texts*. Vancouver: Talonbooks.
May, Mark A.
1971   A Retrospective View of the Institute of Human Relations at Yale. *Human Relations Area Files* 6: 141–172.
Mead, Margaret, ed.
1959   *An Anthropologist at Work: Writings of Ruth Benedict*. London: Secker and Warburg.
Mead, Margaret
1966   Neglected Aspects in the History of American Anthropology. Yale University lecture, 8 December 1966. Tape via Harold Conklin; transcribed by R. Darnell.
1972   *Blackberry Winter: My Earlier Years*. New York: William Morris.
1974   *Ruth Benedict*. New York: Columbia University Press.
Mead, Margaret, and Rhoda Metraux, eds.
1953   *The Study of Culture at a Distance*. Chicago: University of Chicago Press.
Michelson, Truman
1914   Two Alleged Algonquian Languages of California. *AA* 16: 361–367.
Miller, R. Berkeley
1978   Anthropology and Institutionalization: Frederick Starr at the University of Chicago 1892–1923. *KASP* 51: 49–60.
Modell, Judith
1975   Ruth Benedict, Anthropology. In T. Thoresen (ed.), *Toward a Science of Man* (The Hague: Mouton, 1975), pp. 182–203.
1983   *Ruth Benedict: Patterns of a Life*. Philadelphia: University of Pennsylvania Press.
Morawski, J. G.
1986   Organizing Knowledge and Behavior at Yale's Institute of Human Relations. *ISIS* 77: 219–242.
Mullahy, Patrick

1952   *The Contributions of Harry Stack Sullivan*. New York: Heritage House.

Murdock, George P.
1949   *Social Structure*. New Haven: Yale University Press.

Murray, Stephen
1981   The Canadian Winter of Edward Sapir. *HL* 8: 63–68.
1983   *Group Formation in Social Science*. Edmonton: Linguistic Research, Inc.
1985   A Pre-Boasian Sapir? *HL* 12: 267–269.
1986   Edward Sapir and the Chicago School of Sociology. In W. Cowan, M. Foster, and K. Koerner (eds.) *New Perspectives in Language, Culture, and Personality* . . . (Amsterdam and Philadelphia: John Benjamins, 1986), pp. 241–292.
1987   The Postmaturity of Sociolinguistics: Edward Sapir and the Chicago Department of Sociology. *History of Sociology* 7: 75–108.
1988   The Reception of Anthropological Work by American Sociologists. *JHBS* 24.
1988   W. I. Thomas, Ethnologist. *JHBS* 24.

Murray, Stephen, and Wayne Dynes
1986   Edward Sapir's Coursework in Linguistics and Anthropology. *HL* 13.

Newman, Stanley
1944   The Yokuts Language of California. *VFPA* 2.

Ogburn, W. F., and Alexander Goldenweiser, eds.
1927   *The Social Sciences and Their Interrelations*. Boston: Boston University Press.

Ogden, C. K., and I. A. Richards
1930   *The Meaning of Meaning*. London: Kegan-Paul, Trench, Trubner.

Opler, Morris
1984   Edward Sapir, Ethnologist, at Chicago. Paper read at American
MS   Anthropological Association.

Oren, Dan A.
1986   *Joining the Club: A History of Jews and Yale*. New Haven: Yale University Press.

Osgood, Cornelius
1985   Failures. *AA* 87: 382–387.

Park, Robert, and Ernest Burgess
1921   *Introduction to the Science of Sociology*. Chicago: University of Chicago Press.

Perry, Helen Swick
1982   *Psychiatrist of America: The Life of Harry Stack Sullivan*. Cambridge, Mass.: Belknap.

Pike, Eunice
1981   *Ken Pike: Scholar and Christian*. Dallas: Summer Institute of Linguistics.

Pike, Kenneth

1984   Some Teachers Who Helped Me. *HL* 11: 493–495.

Poffenburger, A. T.
1933   The Division of Psychology and Anthropology. In *A History of the National Research Council 1919–1933*. Washington, D.C.: National Research Council.

Powdermaker, Hortense
1939   *After Freedom: A Cultural Study of the Deep South.* New York: Viking.
1966   *Stranger and Friend: The Way of an Anthropologist.* New York: W. W. Norton

Powell, J. W.
1891   Indian Linguistic Families North of Mexico. *Seventh Annual Report, Bureau of American Ethnology, for 1885–86: 7–39.*

Preston, Richard J.
1986   Sapir's Psychology of Culture Prospectus. In W. Cowan, M. Foster, and K. Koerner (eds.), *New Perspectives in Language, Culture, and Personality*... (Amsterdam and Philadelphia: John Benjamins, 1986), pp. 533–552.
1984   Sapir, Sullivan, and Lasswell Collaborations: Real and Imagined.
MS   Paper read at American Anthropological Association.

Prokosch, E.
1922   Review of *Language. Journal of English and Germanic Philology*: 353–357.

Radin, Paul
1919   The Genetic Relationship of the North American Indian Languages. *UCPAAE* 14: 489–502.

Remy, Arthur
1922   Review of *Language. Literary Review.*

Rogow, Arnold, ed.
1969   *Politics, Personality and Social Science in the Twentieth Century: Essays in Honor of Harold D. Lasswell.* ... Chicago: University of Chicago Press, 1969, pp. 123–145.

Rollins, Peter C.
1980   *Benjamin Lee Whorf: Lost Generation Theories of Mind, Language and Religion.* Ann Arbor, Mich.: Popular Culture Association.

Rosenberg, Rosalind
1982   *Beyond Separate Spheres.* New Haven: Yale University Press.

Rosten, Leo
1935   *The Education of Hyman Kaplan.* New York: Harcourt Brace.
1969   Harold Lasswell: A Memoir. In A. Rogow (ed.), *Politics, Personality and Social Science in the Twentieth Century: Essays in Honor of Harold D. Lasswell* (Chicago: University of Chicago Press, 1969), pp. 1–13.

Sapir, H. Michael
1984   Tributes Given to Famous Dads: Edward Sapir. *Meiklejohn Education Foundation Quarterly* 3: 3, 9–11.

Sapir, J. David

1985   Edward Sapir. *Language in Society* 14: 289–298.
Sebeok, Thomas A., ed.
1966   *Portraits of Linguists: A Biographical Sourcebook for the History of Western Linguistics, 1746–1963.* 2 vols. Bloomington: University of Indiana Press.
Service, Elman
1976   Obituary of Leslie White. *AA* 78.
Shafer, Robert
1952   Athabaskan and Sino-Tibetan. *IJAL* 18: 12–19.
1957   Note on Athabaskan and Sino-Tibetan. *IJAL* 23: 116–117.
1969   A Few More Athabaskan and Sino-Tibetan Comparisons. *IJAL* 35: 87.
Shils, Edward
1978   The Order of Learning in the United States from 1865–1920: The Ascendancy of the University. *Minerva* 16: 159–195.
Silverstein, Michael
1985   Sapir's Psychological and Psychiatric Perspectives on Culture. Paper read at American Association for the Advancement of Science.
Spencer, Robert, and Elizabeth Colson
1971   Obituary of Wilson Wallis. *AA* 73.
Sontag, Susan
1977   *Illness as Metaphor.* New York: Farrar, Strauss and Giroux.
Spier, Leslie
1939   Edward Sapir. *Science* 89: 237–238. Reprinted in Koerner 1984.
Spier, Leslie, et al., eds.
1941   *Language, Culture and Personality: Essays in Memory of Edward Sapir.* Menasha: Sapir Memorial Fund.
Spier, Leslie, and A. L. Kroeber
1943   Elsie Clews Parsons 1875–1941. *AA* 45: 244–255.
Spindler, George, ed.
1978   Introduction, *The Making of Psychological Anthropology.* Berkeley, Los Angeles, London: University of California Press. Pp. 1–38.
Steward, Julian H.
1959   Review of Margaret Mead, *An Anthropologist at Work. Science.* 129: 322–323.
Stocking, George W., Jr.
1968   *Race, Culture and Evolution.* New York: Free Press.
1974   The Boas Plan for the Study of American Indian Languages. In Dell Hymes (ed.), *Traditions and Paradigms in the History of Linguistics* (Bloomington: Indiana University Press, 1974), pp. 454–484.
Stocking, George W. Jr., ed.
1974   *The Shaping of American Anthropology 1883–1911: A Franz Boas Reader.* New York: Basic Books.
1978   Pedants and Potentates: Robert Redfield at the 1930 Hanover Conference. *HOAN* 5: 10–13.

1979   *Anthropology at Chicago: Tradition, Discipline, Department*. Chicago: Joseph Regenstein Library.
1980   Sapir's Last Testament on Culture and Personality. *HOAN* 7: 8–11.
1982   The Santa Fe Style in American Anthropology: Regional Interest, Academic Initiative, and Philanthropic Policy in the First Two Decades of the Laboratory of Anthropology, Inc. *JHBS* 18: 3–19.
1985   Philanthropoids and Vanishing Cultures: Rockefeller Funding and the End of the Museum Era. *HOA* 3: 112–145.

Sturtevant, Edgar
1950   Leonard Bloomfield 1887–1949. *American Philosophical Society Yearbook* 1949: 302–305. Reprinted in Sebeok 1966.

Sullivan, Harry Stack
1938   Psychiatry: Introduction to the study of Interpersonal Relations. *Psychiatry* 1: 121–134.
1939   Edward Sapir. *Psychiatry* 2: 159.

Susman, Warren I.
1973   *Culture as History: The Transformation of American Society in the Twentieth Century*. New York: Pantheon.

Swadesh, Morris
1961   Linguistics as an Instrument of Prehistory. *Southwestern Journal of Anthropology* 17.

Thomas, William I., and Florien Znanieki
1918–   *The Polish Peasant in Europe and America*. 5 vols. Boston: Gorham.
1920

Thoresen, Timothy
1975   Paying the Piper and Calling the Tune: The Beginning of Academic Anthropology in California. *JHBS* 11: 257–275.

Trager, George L.
1946   Changes of Emphasis in Linguistics: A Comment. *Studies in Philology* 43: 461–465.

Veysey, Laurence R.
1965   *The Emergence of the American University*. Chicago: University of Chicago Press.

Viehman, Martha
1985   Women in Columbia Anthropology. Yale University.
MS

Voegelin, C. F.
1952   The Boas Plan for the Presentation of American Indian Languages. *PAPS* 96: 439–451.

Voegelin, C. F., and Zellig Harris
1945   Linguistics in Ethnology. *Southwestern Journal of Anthropology* 1: 465–465.
1952   Training in Anthropological Linguistics. *AA* 54: 322–327.

Voegelin, C. F., and Florence M. Voegelin

1963   On the History of Structuralizing in 20th Century America. *AL* 5: 12–37.

White, William Alanson
1938   *The Autobiography of a Purpose*. Garden City, N.Y.: Doubleday, Doran.

Whiting, John, and Beatrice Whiting
1978   A Strategy for Psychocultural Research. In G. Spindler (ed.), *The Making of Psychological Anthropology* . . . (Berkeley, Los Angeles, London: University of California Press, 1978), pp. 41–61.

Whorf, Benjamin
1956   *Language, Thought and Reality*, New York: John Wiley.

Wilbur, George B., and Warner Muensterberger, eds.
1951   *Psychoanalysis and Culture: Essays in Honor of Geza Roheim*. New York: International Universities Press: 156–167.

Witthoft, John
1950   Frank Speck. *Pennsylvania Archaeologist* 19: 38–44.

Zaslow, Morris
1975   *Readings of the Rocks: The Story of the Geological Survey of Canada 1842–1972*. Ottawa and Toronto: Macmillan.

Zumwalt, Rosemary Levy
1988   *American Folklore Scholarship: A Dialogue of Dissent*. Bloomington: Indiana University Press.

Complete Bibliography of Edward Sapir*

1906   The Rival Chiefs, a Kwakiutl Story Recorded by George Hunt (edited, with synopsis, by Edward Sapir). In *Boas Anniversary Volume*. New York: G. E. Stechert & Co.: 108–136.

1907a Herder's *Ürsprung der Sprache*. *Modern Philology* 5: 109–142. Reprinted in *Historiographica Linguistica* (1984).

1907b Notes on the Takelma Indians of Southwestern Oregon. *American Anthropologist* 9: 251–275.

1907c Preliminary Report on the Language and Mythology of the Upper Chinook. *American Anthropologist* 9: 533–544.

1907d Religious Ideas of the Takelma Indians of Southwestern Oregon. *Journal of American Folk-Lore* 20: 33–49.

1908a Luck-Stones among the Yana. *Journal of American Folk-Lore* 21: 42.

1908b On the Etymology of Sanskrit àsru, Avestan asru, Greek Dakru. In Modi, J. J. (ed.), *Spiegel Memorial Volume*. Bombay: 156–159.

1909a Characteristic Features of Yana (abstract). *Science* 29: 613; *American Anthropologist* 11: 110.

1909b Review of Frank G. Speck, *Ethnology of the Yuchi Indians*. *Old Penn Weekly Review* (Philadelphia), December 18: 183.

1909c *Takelma Texts*. University of Pennsylvania, Anthropological Publications 2, no. 1: 1–263.

1909d *Wishram Texts, together with Wasco Tales and Myths collected by Jeremiah Curtin and edited by Edward Sapir*. American Ethnological Society Publications 2. Leyden: E. J. Brill.

---

* This bibliography of Sapir follows that compiled for the *Collected Works of Edward Sapir* by Victor Golla.

1910a   An Apache Basket Jar. *University of Pennsylvania Museum Journal* 1 (1): 13–15.

1910b   Review of C. Hart Merriam, *The Dawn of the World*. *Science* 32: 557–558.

1910c   Some Fundamental Characteristics of the Ute Language (abstract). *Science* 31: 350–352; *American Anthropologist* 12: 66–69.

1910d   Song Recitative in Paiute Mythology. *Journal of American Folk-Lore* 23: 455–472.

1910e   Takelma. In Hodge, F. W. (ed.), *Handbook of American Indians North of Mexico*. Bureau of American Ethnology, Bulletin 30, pt. 2. Washington: Smithsonian Institution: 673–674.

1910f   Two Paiute Myths. *University of Pennsylvania Museum Journal* 1 (1): 15–18.

1910g   Takelma. In Hodge, F. W. (ed.), *Handbook of American Indians North of Mexico*. Bureau of American Ethnology, Bulletin 30, pt. 2. Washington: Smithsonian Institution: 917–918.

1910h   *Yana Texts* (together with *Yana Myths*, collected by Roland B. Dixon). University of California Publications in American Archaeology and Ethnology 9: 1–235.

1911a   An Anthropological Survey of Canada. *Science* 34: 789–793.

1911b   The History and Varieties of Human Speech. *Popular Science Monthly* 79: 45–67.

1911c   The Problem of Noun Incorporation in American Languages. *American Anthropologist* 13: 250–282.

1911d   Review of R. B. Dixon, *The Chimariko Indians and Language*. *American Anthropologist* 13: 141–143.

1911e   Some Aspects of Nootka Language and Culture. *American Anthropologist* 13: 15–28.

1911f   *Summary Report of the Geological Survey, Department of Mines, for the Calendar Year 1910*. Anthropological Division: Report of Field Work. Ottawa: 284–287.

1911g   Wishram Chinook (Incorporated in F. Boas, Chinook). In Boas, F. (ed.), *Handbook of American Indian Languages*. Bureau of American Ethnology, Bulletin 40, pt. 1. Washington: Smithsonian Institution: 578, 579, 625–627, 638–645, 650–654, 673–677.

1912a   The Indians of the Province. In Boam, H. J. (comp.), and Ashley G. Brown (eds.) *British Columbia: Its History, People, Commerce, Industries, and Resources*. London: Sells, 135–140.

1912b   Language and Environment. *American Anthropologist* 14: 168–169.

1912c   The Mourning Ceremony of the Southern Paiutes (abstract). *Science* 35: 673; *American Anthropologist* 14: 168–169.

1912d   Review of Franz Boas, *Kwakiutl Tales*. *Current Anthropological Literature* 1: 193–198.

1912e   Review of A. A. Goldenweiser, *Totemism: An Analytical Study*. *Psychological Bulletin* 9: 454–461.

1912*f*   Review of Carl Stumpf, *Die Anfänge der Musik. Current Anthropological Literature* 1: 275–282.

1912*g*   *Summary Report of the Geological Survey, Department of Mines, for the Calendar Year 1911.* Anthropological Division: Ethnology. Ottawa, 379–381.

1912*h*   The Takelma Language of Southwestern Oregon. Extract from Boas, F. (ed.), *Handbook of American Indian Languages.* Bureau of American Ethnology, Bulletin 40, pt. 2. Washington: Smithsonian Institution, 1–296. (Also published 1922*d*.)

1912*i*   The Work of the Division of Anthropology of the Dominion Government. *Queen's Quarterly* 20: 60–69.

1913*a*   Algonkin p and s in Cheyenne. *American Anthropologist* 15: 538–539.

1913*b*   A Girls' Puberty Ceremony among the Nootka Indians. *Transactions, Royal Society of Canada.* 3d series, 7: 67–80.

1913*c*   A Note on Reciprocal Terms of Relationship in America. *American Anthropologist* 15: 132–138.

1913*d*   Review of Erich von Hornbostel, *Über ein akustisches Kriterium für Kulturzusammenhänge.* Methods and Principles. *Current Anthropological Literature* 2: 69–72.

1913*e*   Review of Karl Meinhof, *Die Sprachen der Hamiten. Current Anthropological Literature* 2: 21–27.

1913*f*   Southern Paiute and Nahuatl, a Study in Uto-Aztekan, Part 1. *Journal, Société des Américanistes de Paris* 10: 379–425.

1913*g*   A Tutelo Vocabulary. *American Anthropologist* 15: 295–297.

1913*h*   Wiyot and Yuruk, Algonkin Languages of California. *American Anthropologist* 15: 617–646.

1914*a*   Indian Tribes and Customs. In Boam, H. J. (comp.), and Ashley G. Brown (ed.) *The Prairie Provinces of Canada: Their History, People, Commerce, Industries, and Resources.* London: Sells, 146–152.

1914*b*   Indian Tribes of the Coast of British Columbia. In Shortt, Adam, and Arthur G. Doughty (eds.) *Canada and Its Provinces,* vol. 21. Toronto: Glasgow, Brook and Co., 315–346.

1914*c*   *Notes on Chasta Costa Phonology and Morphology.* University of Pennsylvania, Anthropological Publications 2 (2): 271–340.

1914*d*   *Summary Report of the Geological Survey, Department of Mines, for the Calendar Year 1912.* Anthropological Division: Ethnology and Linguistics. Ottawa: 448–453.

1914*e*   *Summary Report of the Geological Survey, Department of Mines, for the Calendar Year 1913.* Anthropological Division: Ethnology and Linguistics. Ottawa: 358–383.

1915*a*   *Abnormal Types of Speech in Nootka.* Canada, Department of Mines, Geological Survey, Memoir 62, Anthropological Series 5.

1915*b*   Algonkin Languages of California: A Reply. *American Anthropologist* 17: 188–194.

1915c Corrigenda to Father Morice's *Chasta Costa and the Dene Languages of the North. American Anthropologist* 17: 765–773.

1915d The Na-dene Languages, a Preliminary Report. *American Anthropologist* 17: 534–558.

1915e Notes on Judeo-German Phonology. *The Jewish Quarterly Review* 6: 231–266.

1915f *Noun Reduplication in Comox, a Salish Language of Vancouver Island.* Canada, Department of Mines, Geological Survey, Memoir 63, Anthropological Series 6.

1915g *A Sketch of the Social Organization of the Nass River Indians.* Canada, Department of Mines, Geological Survey, Museum Bulletin 19, Anthropological Series 7.

1915h The Social Organization of the West Coast Tribes. *Transactions, Royal Society of Canada,* 2d series, 9: 355–374.

1915i Southern Paiute and Nahuatl, a Study in Uto-Aztekan, Part II. *American Anthropologist* 17: 98–120, 306–328; *Journal, Société des Américanistes de Paris,* 11 (1914): 443–488.

1915j *Summary Report of the Geological Survey, Department of Mines, for the Calendar Year 1914.* Division of Anthropology: Ethnology and Linguistics. Ottawa: 168–177.

1916a Culture in the Melting Pot, comments on John Dewey's article, American Education and Culture. *The Nation Supplement* (December 21), 1–2.

1916b Letter to the editor: The Woman's Man. *The New Republic,* Sept. 16: 167.

1916c Nootka (phonetic orthography and notes). In Boas, F. (ed.), Vocabularies from the Northwest Coast of America. *Proceedings, American Antiquarian Society* 26: 4–18.

1916d Percy Grainger and Primitive Music. *American Anthropologist* 18: 592–597.

1916e Review of Paul Abelson, ed., *English–Yiddish Encyclopedic Dictionary. The Jewish Quarterly Review* 7: 140–143.

1916f *Summary Report of the Geological Survey, Department of Mines, for the Calendar Year 1915.* Division of Anthropology: Ethnology and Linguistics. Ottawa: 265–274.

1916g Terms of Relationship and the Levirate. *American Anthropologist* 18: 327–337.

1916h *Time Perspective in Aboriginal American Culture: A Study in Method.* Canada, Department of Mines, Geological Survey, Memoir 90, Anthropological Series 13.

1917a Do We Need a "Superorganic"? *American Anthropologist* 19: 441–447.

1917b Letter to the editor: International Philippines. *The New Republic,* Nov. 3: 23.

1917c Letter to the editor: Ireland's Debt to Foreign Scholars. *The Dial* 62: 513.

1917d   Linguistic Publications of the Bureau of American Ethnology, a General Review. *International Journal of American Linguistics* 1: 76–81.

1917e   *The Position of Yana in the Hokan Stock.* University of California Publications in American Archaeology and Ethnology 13: 1–34.

1917f   Realism in Prose Fiction. *The Dial* 62: 503–506.

1917g   Review of Henry T. Finck, *Richard Strauss, the Man, and His Word.* A Frigid Introduction to Strauss. *The Dial* 62: 584–586.

1917h   Review of Sigmund Freud, *Delusion and Dream.* A Freudian Half-Holiday. *The Dial* 63: 635–637.

1917i   Review of Oskar Pfister, *The Psychoanalytical Method.* Psychoanalysis as a Pathfinder. *The Dial* 62: 423–426.

1917j   Review of Romain Rolland, *Jean-Christophe.* Jean-Christophe: An Epic of Humanity. *The Dial* 62: 423–426.

1917k   Review of C. C. Unlenbeck, *Het Passieve Karakter van het Verbum Transitivum of van het Verbum Actionis in Talen van Noord-Amerika. International Journal of American Linguistics* 1: 82–86.

1917l   Review of C. C. Uhlenbeck, *Het Identificeerend Karakter der Possessieve Flexie in Talen van Noord-Amerika. International Journal of American Linguistics* 1: 86–90.

1917m   The Status of Washo. *American Anthropologist* 19: 449–450.

1917n   *Summary Report of the Geological Survey, Department of Mines, for the Calendar Year 1916.* Anthropological Division: Ethnology and Linguistics. Ottawa: 387–395.

1917o   The Twilight of Rhyme. *The Dial* 63: 98–100.

1918a   An Ethnological Note on the "Whiskey-Jack." *The Ottawa Naturalist* 32: 116–117.

1918b   Kinship Terms of the Kootenay Indians. *American Anthropologist* 20: 414–416.

1918c   Letter to the editor: Miss Farrar's Singing. *The Ottawa Citizen,* Jan. 14.

1918d   Representative Music. *The Music Quarterly* 4: 161–167.

1918e   Review of Benigno Bibolotti, *Moseteno Vocabulary and Treatises. International Journal of American Linguistics* 1: 183–184.

1918f   Review of Samuel Butler, *God the Known and God the Unknown,* God as Visible Personality. *The Dial* 64: 192–194.

1918g   Review of G. K. Chesterton, *Utopias of Usurers and Other Essays.* Sancho Panza on His Island. *The Dial* 64: 25–27.

1918h   Review of James A. Montgomery, ed., *Religions of the Past and Present* (Faculty Lectures, University of Pennsylvania). A University Survey of Religions. *The Dial* 65: 14–16.

1918i   Tom. *Canadian Courier,* Dec. 7: 7.

1918j   *Yana Terms of Relationship.* University of California Publications in American Archaeology and Ethnology 13: 153–173.

1919a   Civilization and Culture. *The Dial* 67: 233–236. (Also published as 1922c and as pt. 2 of 1924b.)

1919*b*   Corrigenda and addenda to W. D. Wallis's *Indogermanic Relationship Terms as Historical Evidence. American Anthropologist* 21: 318–328.

1919*c*   Corrigenda to "Kinship Terms of the Kootenay Indians." *American Anthropologist* 21: 98.

1919*d*   Data on Washo and Hokan. In Dixon, R. B., and A. L. Kroeber (eds.) *Linguistic Families of California.* University of California Publications in American Archaeology and Ethnology 16: 180, 112.

1919*e*   A Flood Legend of the Nootka Indians of Vancouver Island. *Journal of American Folk-Lore* 32: 351–355.

1919*f*   Letter to the editor: Randolph Bourne. *The Dial*, Jan. 11: 45.

1919*g*   Letter to the editor: Criticizes Labor Gazette. *The Ottawa Citizen*, March 31.

1919*h*   Letter to the editor: Concerning Hilda Conkling. *Poetry*, Sept.: 344.

1919*i*   A Note on French Canadian Folk-Songs. *Poetry* 20: 210–213.

1919*j*   Review (unsigned) of Cary F. Jacob, *The Foundations and Nature of Verse. The Dial* 66: 98–100.

1919*k*   Review of R. Tagore, *Lover's Gift, Crossing, Mashi and Other Stories.* The Poet Seer of Bengal. *The Canadian Magazine* 54: 137–140.

1919*l*   Review of C. Wissler, *The American Indian.* The American Indian. *The New Republic* 19: 189–191.

1920*a*   The Heuristic Value of Rhyme. *Queen's Quarterly* 27: 309–312.

1920*b*   The Hokan and Coahuiltecan Languages. *International Journal of American Linguistics* 1: 280–290.

1920*c*   Nass River Terms of Relationship. *American Anthropologist* 22: 261–271.

1920*d*   A Note on the First Person Plural in Chimariko. *International Journal of American Linguistics* 1: 291–294.

1920*e*   The Poetry Prize Contest. *The Canadian Magazine* 54: 349–352.

1920*f*   Preview of R. H. Lowie, *Primitive Society.* Primitive Society. *The Nation* 111: 46–47.

1920*g*   Review of R. H. Lowie, *Primitive Society.* Primitive Humanity and Anthropology. *The Dial* 69: 528–533.

1920*h*   Review of R. H. Lowie, *Primitive Society.* Primitive Society. *The Freeman* 1: 377–379.

1920*i*   Review of J. Alden Mason, *The Language of the Salinan Indians. International Journal of American Linguistics* 1: 305–309.

1921*a*   A Bird's-eye View of American Languages North of Mexico. *Science* 54: 408.

1921*b*   A Characteristic Penutian Form of Stem. *International Journal of American Linguistics* 2: 58–67.

1921*c*   A Haida Kinship Term among the Tsimshian. *American Anthropologist* 23: 233–234.

1921*d*   *Language: An Introduction to the Study of Speech.* New York: Harcourt, Brace and Co.

1921*e*   The Life of a Nootka Indian. *Queen's Quarterly* 28: 232–243, 351–367. (Reprinted as 1922*y*.)

1921*f*   Maupassant and Anatole France. *The Canadian Magazine* 57: 199–202.

1921*g*   The Musical Foundations of Verse. *Journal of English and Germanic Philology* 20: 213–228.

1921*h*   *Report of the Department of Mines for the Fiscal Year Ending March 31, 1921.* Ottawa, 18–20.

1921*i*   Review of *The Mythology of All Races,* vol. 9 (Latin American, by Hartley Burr Alexander). Myth, Historian, and Psychologist. *The Nation* 112: 889–890.

1921*j*   Review of *The Mythology of All Races,* vol. 3 (Celtic, by J. A. Macculloch, and Slavic, by Jan Machal), vol. 11 (Latin American, by Hartley Burr Alexander), and vol. 12 (Egyptian, by W. Max Muller, and Indo-Chinese, by J. G. Scott). The Mythology of All Races. *The Dial* 71: 107–111.

1921*k*   Review of Robert Bridges, ed., *Poems of Gerard Manley Hopkins.* Gerard Hopkins. *Poetry* 18: 330–336.

1921*l*   Review of W. A. Mason, *A History of the Art of Writing.* Writing as History and as Style. *The Freeman* 4: 68–69.

1921*m*   Review of W. H. R. Rivers, *The Instinct and the Unconscious.* A Touchstone to Freud. *The Freeman* 5: 357–358.

1921*n*   Review of J. M. Tyler, *The New Stone Age in Northern Europe*; Stewart Paton, *Human Behaviour*; E. G. Conklin, *The Direction of Human Evolution.* The Ends of Man. *The Nation* 113: 237–238.

1921*o*   A Supplementary Note on Salinan and Washo. *International Journal of American Linguistics* 2: 68–72.

1922*a*   Athabaskan Tone. *American Anthropologist* 24: 390–391.

1922*b*   Culture, Genuine and Spurious. *The Dalhousie Review* 2: 358–368. (Also published as pt. 1 of 1924*b*.)

1922*c*   Culture in New Countries. *The Dalhousie Review* 2: 358–368. (Also published as pt. 2 of 1924*b*.)

1922*d*   *The Fundamental Elements of Northern Yana.* University of California Publications in American Archaeology and Ethnology 13: 215–234.

1922*e*   Language and Literature. *The Canadian Magazine* 59: 457–462. (Chap. 11 of 1921*d*.)

1922*f*   *Report of the Department of Mines for the Fiscal Year Ending March 31, 1922.* Ottawa: 22–25.

1922*g*   Review of *More Jataka Tales,* retold by Ellen C. Babbitt. A Peep at the Hindu Spirit. *The Freeman* 5: 404.

1922*h*   Review of Maxwell Bodenheim, *Introducing Irony.* Introducing Irony. *The New Republic* 31: 341.

1922*i*   Review of Maxwell Bodenheim, *Introducing Irony*. Maxwell Bodenheim. *The Nation* 114: 751.

1922*j*   Review (unsigned) of Arthur Davison Ficke, *Mr. Faust*. *The Dial* 73: 235.

1922*k*   Review (unsigned) of Selma Lagerlöf, *The Outcast*. *The Dial* 73: 354.

1922*l*   Review of John Masefield, *Esther and Berenice*. *The Freeman* 5: 526.

1922*m*   Review of John Masefield, *King Cole*. The Manner of Mr. Masefield. *The Freeman* 5: 526.

1922*n*   Review of Edgar Lee Masters, *The Open Sea*. Mr. Master's Later Work. *The Freeman* 5: 333–334.

1922*o*   Review of Edgar Lee Masters, *The Open Sea*. Spoon River Muddles. *The Canadian Bookman* (April): 132, 140.

1922*p*   Review of Edgar Lee Masters, *Children of the Market Place*. *The Dial* 73: 235.

1922*q*   Review of Gilbert Murray, *Tradition and Progress*. *The Dial* 73: 235.

1922*r*   Review of E. C. Parsons, ed., *American Indian Life*. A Symposium of the Exotic. *The Dial* 73: 568–571.

1922*s*   Review of Frederick Pierce, *Our Unconscious Mind and How to Use It*. Practical Psychology. *The Literary Review, New York Evening Post* (July 1): 772.

1922*t*   Review of Edward Arlington Robinson, *Collected Poems*. Poems of Experience. *The Freeman* 5: 141–142; published also in *The Canadian Bookman* (August): 210–211.

1922*u*   Review (unsigned) of George Saintsbury, *A Letter Book*. *The Dial* 73: 235.

1922*v*   Review of Edward Thomas, *Collected Poems*. *The New Republic* 32: 226.

1922*w*   Review of Louis Untermeyer, *Heavens*. Heavens. *The New Republic* 30: 351.

1922*x*   Review of R. S. Woodworth, *Psychology: A Study of Mental Life*. An Orthodox Psychology. *The Freeman* 5: 619.

1922*y*   Sayach'apis, A Nootka Trader. In Parsons, E. C. (ed.), *American Indian Life*. New York: B. W. Huebsch, Inc., 297–323. (Published earlier as 1921*e*.)

1922*z*   The Takelma Language of Southwestern Oregon. In Boas, F. (ed.), *Handbook of American Indian Languages*. Bureau of American Ethnology, Bulletin 40, pt. 2. Washington: Smithsonian Institution, 1–296. (Published earlier as 1912*a*.)

1922*aa*   Vancouver Island Indians. In Hastings, James (ed.), *Encyclopaedia of Religion and Ethics*, vol. 12. New York: C. Scribner's Sons, 591–595.

1923*a*   The Algonkin Affinity of Yurok and Wiyot Kinship Terms. *Journal, Société des Américanistes de Paris* 15: 36–74.

1923b Archaeology and Ethnology (bibliography). *Canadian Historical Review* 4: 374–378.

1923c A Note on Sarcee Pottery. *American Anthropologist* 25: 247–253.

1923d The Phonetics of Haida. *International Journal of American Linguistics* 2: 143–159.

1923f *Report of the Department of Mines for the Fiscal Year Ending March 31, 1923.* Ottawa: 28–31.

1923g Review of Edwin Björkman, *The Soul of a Child. The Double Dealer* 51: 78–80.

1923h Review of A. E. Housman, *Last Poems.* Mr. Housman's Last Poems. *The Dial* 75: 188–191.

1923i Review of Johannes V. Jensen, *The Long Journey.* The Epos of Man. *The World Tomorrow* 6: 221.

1923j Review of C. G. Jung, *Psychological Types, or the Psychology of Individuation.* Two Kinds of Human Beings. *The Freeman* 8: 211–212.

1923k Review of Truman Michelson, The Owl Sacred Pack of the Fox Indians. *International Journal of American Linguistics* 2: 182–184.

1923l Review of C. K. Ogden and I. A. Richards, *The Meaning of Meaning.* An Approach to Symbolism. *The Freeman* 7: 572–573.

1923m *Text Analyses of Three Yana Dialects.* University of California Publications in American Archaeology and Ethnology 20: 263–294.

1923n A Type of Athabaskan Relative. *International Journal of American Linguistics* 2: 136–142.

1924a Anthropology at the Toronto Meeting of the British Association for the Advancement of Science, 1924. *American Anthropologist* 26: 563–565.

1924b Culture, Genuine and Spurious. *American Journal of Sociology* 29: 401–429. (Pt. 1 previously published as 1922b, and pt. 2 as 1919a and 1922c.)

1924c The Grammarian and His Language. *American Mercury* 1: 149–155.

1924d Personal Names among the Sarcee Indians. *American Anthropologist* 26, 108–119.

1924e Racial Superiority. *The Menorah Journal* 10: 200–212.

1924f Review of *The Novel of Tomorrow and the Scope of Fiction,* by Twelve American Novelists. Twelve Novelists in Search of a Reason. *The Stratford Monthly* (May).

1924g The Rival Whalers, a Nitinat Story (Nootka Text with Translation and Grammatical Analysis). *International Journal of American Linguistics* 3: 76–102.

1925a Are the Nordics a Superior Race? *The Canadian Forum* (June), 265–266.

1925b The Hokan Affinity of Subtiaba in Nicaragua. *American Anthropologist* 27: 402–435, 491–527.

1925c   Indian Legends from Vancouver Island. *Transactions, Women's Canadian Historical Society of Ottawa* 9: 142–143.

1925d   Let Race Alone. *The Nation*: 211–213.

1925e   Memorandum on the Problem of an International Auxiliary Language. *The Romanic Review* 16: 244–256.

1925f   Pitch Accent in Sarcee, an Athabaskan Language. *Journal, Société des Américanistes de Paris* 17: 185–205.

1925g   *Report of the Department of Mines for the Fiscal Year Ending March 31, 1924.* Ottawa: 36–40.

1925h   *Report of the Department of Mines for the Fiscal Year Ending March 31, 1925.* Ottawa: 37–41.

1925i   Review of F. G. Crookshank, *The Mongol in our Midst*; H. W. Siemens, *Race Hygiene and Heredity*; Jean Finot, *Race Prejudice*; J. H. Oldham, *Christianity and the Race Problem*. The Race Problem. *The Nation* 121: 40–42.

1925j   Review of *The Complete Poems of Emily Dickinson*. Emily Dickinson, a Primitive. *Poetry* 26: 97–105.

1925k   Review of H. D., *Collected Poems*. An American Poet. *The Nation* 121: 211.

1925l   Review of A. Meillet and Marcel Cohen, eds., *Les Langues du monde*. *Modern Language Notes* 40: 373–375.

1925m   Review of Paul Radin, *Monotheism among Primitive Peoples*. Is Monotheism Jewish? *The Menorah Journal* 11: 524–527.

1925n   Review of Edwin Arlington Robinson, *Dionysus in Doubt*. The Tragic Chuckle. *Voices* (November): 64–65.

1925o   The Similarity of Chinese and Indian Languages. *Science* 62 (1607), supplement of 16 Oct.: xii. (Report of an interview.)

1925p   Sound Patterns in Language. *Language* 1: 37–51.

1925q   Undesirables—Klanned or Banned. *The American Hebrew* 116: 286.

1926a   A Chinookan Phonetic Law. *International Journal of American Linguistics* 4: 105–110.

1926b   Philology. In *The Encyclopaedia Britannica (Supplementary Volumes, 13th ed.)* 3: 112–115.

1926c   Review of Leonie Adams, *Those Not Elect*. Leonie Adams. *Poetry* 27: 275–279.

1926d   Review of George A. Dorsey, *Why We Behave Like Human Beings*. *American Journal of Sociology* 32: 140.

1926e   Review of Knight Dunlap, *Old and New Viewpoints in Psychology*. *American Journal of Sociology* 31: 698–699.

1926f   Review of Father Berard Haile, *A Manual of Navaho Grammar*. *American Journal of Sociology* 32: 511.

1926g   Review of Otto Jespersen, *Mankind, Nation and Individual from a Linguistic Point of View*. *American Journal of Sociology* 32: 498–499.

1926h   Review of Ludwig Lewisohn, *Israel*. *The Menorah Journal* 12: 214–218.

1926i   Speech as a Personality Trait (abstract). *Health Bulletin*, Illinois Society for Mental Hygiene, December. (Also published as 1927*h*.)

1927*a*   Anthropology and Sociology. In Ogburn, W. F., and A. Goldenweiser (eds.) *The Social Sciences and Their Interrelations*: chap. 9. Boston: Houghton Mifflin Co.: 97–113.

1927*b*   An Expedition to Ancient America: A Professor and a Chinese Student Rescue the Vanishing Language and Culture of the Hupas in Northern California. *The University of Chicago Magazine* 20: 10–12.

1927*c*   Language as a Form of Human Behaviour. *The English Journal* 16: 421–433.

1927*d*   Review of F. H. Hankins, *The Racial Basis of Civilization*. A Reasonable Eugenist. *The New Republic* 53: 146.

1927*e*   Review of Jean Piaget, *The Language and Thought of the Child*. Speech and Verbal Thought in Childhood. *The New Republic* 50: 350–351.

1927*f*   Review of Paul Radin, *Crashing Thunder: The Autobiography of an American Indian*. *American Journal of Sociology* 33: 295–296.

1927*g*   Review of A. Hyatt Verrill, *The American Indian: North, South, and Central America*. *American Journal of Sociology* 33: 295–296.

1927*h*   Speech as a Personality Trait. *American Journal of Sociology* 32: 892–905.

1928*a*   The Meaning of Religion. *The American Mercury* 15: 72–79. (Published also as 1929*f*.)

1928*b*   Observations on the Sex Problem in America. *American Journal of Psychiatry* 8: 519–534.

1928*c*   *Proceedings, First Colloquium on Personality Investigation; Held under the Auspices of the American Psychiatric Association, Committee on Relations with the Social Sciences*. New York: 11–12, 77–80.

1928*d*   Review of Clarence Day, *Thoughts without Words*. When Words Are Not Enough. *New York Herald Tribune Books* 4: xii.

1928*e*   Review of Sigmund Freud, *The Future of an Illusion*. Psychoanalysis as a Prophet. *The New Republic* 56: 356–357.

1928*f*   Review of Knut Hamsun, *The Women at the Pump*. *The New Republic* 56: 335.

1928*g*   Review of James Weldon Johnson, ed., *The Book of American Negro Spirituals*. *Journal of American Folk-Lore* 41: 172–174.

1928*h*   Review of Roland G. Kent, *Language and Philology*. *The Classical Weekly* 221: 85–86.

1928*i*   A Summary Report of Field Work among the Hupa, Summer of 1927. *American Anthropologist* 30: 359–361.

1928*j*   The Unconscious Patterning of Behavior in Society. In Child, C. M., et al. (eds.) *The Unconscious: A Symposium*. New York: A. A. Knopf: 114–142.

1929*a*   Central and North American Languages. *Encyclopaedia Britannica* (14th ed.) 5: 138–141.

1929*b*   The Discipline of Sex. *The American Mercury* 16: 413–420. (Also published as 1930*a*.)

1929*c*   A Linguistic Trip among the Navaho Indians. *The Gallup Independent* (Ceremonial ed., Aug. 23, Gallup, N.M.): 1–2.

1929*d*   Male and Female Forms of Speech in Yana. In Teeuwen, St. W. J. (ed.), *Donum Natalicium Schrijnen*. Nijmegen-Utrecht: N. v. Dekker & van de Vegt: 79–85.

1929*e*   Nootka Baby Words. *International Journal of American Linguistics* 5: 118–119.

1929*f*   Religions and Religious Phenomena. In Brownell, Baker, (ed.) *Religious Life* (Man and His World, vol. 11). New York: Van Nostrand: 11–33.

1929*g*   Review of Franz Boas, *Anthropology and Modern Life*. Franz Boas. *The New Republic* 57: 278–279.

1929*h*   Review of R. L. Bunzel, *The Pueblo Potter*. Design in Pueblo Pottery. *The New Republic* 61: 115.

1929*i*   Review of M. E. DeWitt, *Our Oral Word as Social and Economic Factor. American Journal of Sociology* 34: 926–927.

1929*j*   Review of Waldo Frank, *The Rediscovery of America. American Journal of Sociology* 35: 335–336.

1929*k*   Review of Bertrand Russell, *Sceptical Essays*. The Skepticism of Bertrand Russell. *The New Republic* 57: 196.

1929*l*   The Status of Linguistics as a Science. *Language* 5: 207–214.

1929*m*   A Study in Phonetic Symbolism. *Journal of Experimental Psychology* 12: 225–239.

1929*n*   What Is the Family Still Good For? *Winnetka Conference on the Family* (Oct. 28): 331–34. (Also published as 1930*g*.)

1930*a*   The Discipline of Sex. *Child Study* (March): 170–173, 187–188. (Also published as 1929*b*.)

1930*b*   *Proceedings, Second Colloquium on Personality Investigation; Held under the Joint Auspices of the American Psychiatric Association and of the Social Science Research Council*. Baltimore: 37–39, 48–54, 67, 84–87, 96–97, 122–127, 153–156, 166.

1930*c*   Review of James Truslow Adams, *Our Business Civilization: Some Aspects of American Culture*. Our Business Civilization. *Current History* 32: 426–428.

1930*d*   *Southern Paiute: A Shoshonean Language*. Proceedings, American Academy of Arts and Sciences 65 (no. 1): 1–296. *The Southern Paiute Language*, pt. 1.

1930*e*   *Texts of the Kaibab Paiutes and Uintah Utes*. Proceedings, American Academy of Arts and Sciences 65 (2): 297–536. *The Southern Paiute Language*, pt. 2.

1930*f*   *Totality* Linguistic Society of America, Language Monographs 6.

1930*g*   What Is the Family Still Good For? *The American Mercury* 19: 145–151. (Also published as 1929*n*.)

1931*a*   Communication. *Encyclopaedia of the Social Sciences* 4: 78–81.

1931b   The Concept of Phonetic Law as Tested in Primitive Languages by Leonard Bloomfield. In Rice, Stuart A., (ed.) *Methods In Social Science: A Case Book.* Chicago: University of Chicago Press: 297–306.

1931c   Conceptual Categories in Primitive Languages. *Science* 74: 578.

1931d   Custom. *Encyclopaedia of the Social Sciences* 4: 658–662.

1931e   Dialect. *Encyclopaedia of the Social Sciences* 5: 123–126.

1931f   Fashion. *Encyclopaedia of the Social Sciences* 6: 139–144.

1931g   The Function of an International Auxiliary Language. *Psyche* 11: 4–15; also in Shenton, H. N., E. Sapir, O. Jespersen, *International Communication: A Symposium on the Language Problem.* London: 65–94.

1931h   Language, Race, and Culture. In Calverton, V. F., (ed.) *The Making of Man.* New York: 142–156. (Chap. 10 of 1921a.)

1931i   Notes on the Gweabo Language of Liberia. *Language* 7: 30–41.

1931j   Review of Ray Hoffman, *Nuer-English Dictionary. American Anthropologist* 33: 114–115.

1931k   *Southern Paiute Dictionary.* Proceedings, American Academy of Arts and Sciences 65 (3): 537–730. (The Southern Paiute Language, pt. 3.)

1931l   Wanted, A World Language. *The American Mercury* 22: 202–209.

1932a   Cultural Anthropology and Psychiatry. *Journal of Abnormal and Social Psychology* 27: 229–242.

1932b   Group. *Encyclopaedia of the Social Sciences* 7: 178–182.

1932c   Review of James G. Leyburn, *Handbook of Ethnography. American Journal of Science,* 5th series, 23: 186–189.

1932d   Two Navaho Puns. *Language* 8: 217–219.

1933a   The Case for a Constructed International Language. *Actes du Deuxième Congrès International de Linguistes, Genève, Aout 1931.* Paris: Librairie d'Amérique et d'Orient, Adrien Maisonneuve, 86–88.

1933b   Language. *Encyclopaedia of the Social Sciences* 9: 155–169.

1933c   La Réalité Psychologique des Phonèmes. *Journal de Psychologie Normale et Pathologique* (Paris) 30: 247–265. (Also published in an English version, 1949.)

1934a   The Emergence of the Concept of Personality in a Study of Cultures. *Journal of Social Psychology* 5: 408–415.

1934b   Hittite *hepatis* "Vassal" and Greek ὁ παδός. *Language* 10: 274–279.

1934c   Personality. *Encyclopaedia of the Social Sciences* 12: 85–87.

1934d   Review of Melville J. Herskovits and Frances S. Herskovits, *Rebel Destiny: Among the Bush Negroes of Dutch Guiana.* The Bush Negro of Dutch Guiana. *The Nation* 139: 135.

1934e   Symbolism. *Encyclopaedia of the Social Sciences* 14: 492–495.

1935a A Descriptive Grammar of English: Report of Progress, 1934. *American Council of Learned Societies Bulletin* 23 (June 1935): 125–127.

1935b A Navaho Sand Painting Blanket. *American Anthropologist* 37, 609–616.

1935c Review of A. G. Morice, *The Carrier Language (Dene Family): A Grammar and Dictionary Combined. American Anthropologist* 37: 500–501.

1936a The Application of Anthropology to Human Relations. In Baker, N. D., C. J. H. Hayes, and R. W. Strauss (eds.) *The American Way.* Chicago and New York: Willett, Clark, 121–129.

1936b A Descriptive Grammar of English: Report of Progress, 1935. *American Council of Learned Societies Bulletin* 25 (July 1936): 775–778.

1936c Greek ἄτύζομαι, A Hittite Loanword, and Its Relatives. *Language* 12: 175–180.

1936d Hebrew 'argáz, A Philistine Word. *Journal of the American Oriental Society* 56: 272–281.

1936e Hupa Tattooing. In Lowie, R. H., (ed.) *Essays in Anthropology Presented to Alfred Louis Kroeber.* Berkeley: 273–277.

1936f Internal Linguistic Evidence Suggestive of the Northern Origin of the Navaho. *American Anthropologist* 38: 224–235.

1936g κύββα: A Karian Gloss. *Journal of the American Oriental Society* 56: 85.

1936h Kutchin Relationship Terms. In Osgood, Cornelius, *Contributions to the Ethnography of the Kutchin.* Yale University Publications in Anthropology 4: 136–137.

1936i Review of D. Westermann and Ida C. Ward, *Practical Phonetics for Students of African Languages. American Anthropologist* 38: 121–122.

1936j Tibetan Influences on Tocharian. I. *Language* 12: 259–271.

1937a The Contribution of Psychiatry to an Understanding of Behaviour in Society. *American Journal of Sociology* 42: 862–870.

1937b Hebrew "Helmet," a Loanword, and Its Bearing on Indo-European Phonology. *Journal of the American Oriental Society* 57: 73–77.

1937c The Negroes of Haiti, review of Melville J. Herskovits, *Life in a Haitian Valley. The Yale Review* 26: 853–854.

1937d Review of James A. Montgomery and Zellig S. Harris, *The Ras Shamra Mythological Texts. Language* 13, 326–331.

1938a Foreword to Walter Dyk, *Son of Old Man Hat.* New York: v–x.

1938b Glottalized Continuants in Navaho, Nootka, and Kwakiutl (with a Note on Indo-European). *Language* 14: 248–274.

1938c Hittite *siyanta* and Gen. 14: 3. *American Journal of Semitic Languages and Literatures* 55, 86–88.

1938d Review of Thurman W. Arnold, *The Folklore of Capitalism.* *Psychiatry* 1: 145–147.

1938e   Why Cultural Anthropology Needs the Psychiatrist. *Psychiatry* 1: 7–12.

1939a   From Sapir's Desk: Indo-European Prevocalic *s* in Macedonian: The Indo-European Words for "Tear" (edited by E. S. Sturtevant). *Language* 13: 178–187. (Also published in part as 1939b.)

1939b   Indo-European Prevocalic *s* in Macedonian. *American Journal of Philology* 40: 463–465. (Also published as part of 1939a.)

1939c   Psychiatric and Cultural Pitfalls in the Business of Getting a Living. *Mental Health*, Publication of the American Association for the Advancement to Science 9: 237–244.

1939d   Review of Zellig S. Harris, *A Grammar of the Phonecian Language*. *Language* 15: 60–65.

1939e   Songs for a Comox Dance Mask (edited by Leslie Spier). *Ethnos* (Stockholm) 4: 49–55.

1942   *Navaho Texts, with Supplementary Texts by Harry Hoijer* (edited by Harry Hoijer). Philadelphia: Linguistic Society of America.

1944   Grading: A Study in Semantics. *Philosophy of Science* 11: 93–116.

1947   The Relation of American Indian Linguistics to General Linguistics. *Southwestern Journal of Anthropology* 3: 1–4.

1949   The Psychological Reality of Phonemes. In Mandelbaum, David G., (ed.) *Selected Writings of Edward Sapir in Language, Culture and Personality*. Berkeley: University of California Press, 46–60. (English version of 1933c.)

Coauthored Publications and Publications Based on Sapir's Materials

Barbeau, Marius, and Edward Sapir
    1925   *Folk Songs of French Canada*. New Haven: Yale University Press.
Freeland, L. S.
    1930   The Relationship of Mixe to the Penutian Family (with notes by Edward Sapir). *International Journal of American Linguistics* 6: 28–33.
Golla, Victore (ed.)
    1984   *The Sapir–Kroeber Correspondence: Letters between Edward Sapir and A. L. Kroeber, 1905–1925*. Survey of California and Other Indian Languages, Department of Linguistics, University of California, Berkeley, Research Report 6.
Hockett, Charles F.
    1946   Sapir on Arapaho. *International Journal of American Linguistics* 12: 243–245.
Lowie, Robert H. (ed.)
    1965   *Letters from Edward Sapir to Robert H. Lowie*. Berkeley: privately printed.
Mandelbaum, David G. (ed.)

1949   *Selected Writings of Edward Sapir in Language, Culture and Personality.* Berkeley: University of California Press.

Mead, Margaret (ed.)
1959   *An Anthropologist at Work.* Boston: Houghton Mifflin.

Newman, Stanley S.
1948   English Suffixation: A Descriptive Approach. *Word* 4: 24–36.

Roberts, Helen H., and Morris Swadesh
1955   *Songs of the Nootka Indians of Western Vancouver Island.* Based on phonographic records, linguistic and other field notes made by Edward Sapir. Philadelphia: American Philosophical Society.

Sapir, Edward, and Charles G. Blooah
1929   Some Gweabo Proverbs. *Africa* 2: 183–185.

Sapir, Edward, and Harry Hoijer
1967   *The Phonology and Morphology of the Navaho Language.* University of California Publications in Linguistics 50.

Sapir, Edward, and Hsü Tsan Hwa
1923a   Humor of the Chinese Folk. *Journal of American Folk-Lore* 36: 31–35.

1923b   Two Chinese Folk-Tales. *Journal of American Folk-Lore* 36: 23–30.

Sapir, Edward, and Albert G. Sandoval
1930   A Note on Navaho Pottery. *American Anthropologist* 32: 575–576.

Sapir, Edward, and Morris Swadesh
1932   *The Expression of the Ending-Point Relation in English, French, and German.* Edited by Alice V. Morris. Linguistic Society of America, Language Monographs 10.

1939   *Nootka Texts: Tales and Ethnological Narratives with Grammatical Notes and Lexical Materials.* William Dwight Whitney Linguistic Series, Linguistic Society of America. Philadelphia.

1946   American Indian Grammatical categories. *Word* 2: 103–112.

1953   Coos–Takelma–Penutian Comparisons. *International Journal of American Linguistics* 19: 132–137.

1955   *Native Accounts of Nootka Ethnography.* Bloomington: Indiana University Research Center in Anthropology, Folklore, and Linguistics (= *International Journal of American Linguistics* 21, no. 4).

1960   *Yana Dictionary.* Edited by Mary R. Haas. University of California Publications in Linguistics 22.

Sapir, Edward, et al.
1916   *Phonetic Transcription of Indian Languages* (with F. Boas, P. E. Goddard, and A. L. Kroeber). *Smithsonian Miscellaneous Collections* 66 (6). Washington, D. C.: Smithsonian Institution.

1934   Some Orthographic Recommendations (with others). *American Anthropologist* 36: 629–631.

Spier, Leslie, and Edward Sapir

1930   *Wishram Ethnography.* University of Washington Publications in Anthropology 3: 151–300.

Swadesh, Morris

1949   Salish–Wakashan Comparisons, by Edward Sapir. In Smith, Marian W., (ed.) *Indians of the Urban Northwest.* New York: Columbia University Press, 171–173.

1964   Comparative Penutian Glosses of Sapir. In Bright, William, (ed.) *Studies in Californian Linguistics.* University of California Publications in Linguistics 34: 182–191.

Index

Acculturation, 303
Adams, Leonie, 184
Alexander, Franz, 290, 416n
Allen, Harold, 267
Alternating sounds, 104
American Council of Learned Societies, 277–287, 297
American Museum of Natural History, 40, 63
American Psychiatric Association, 309–319, 320
American Society, 317, 318, 321
Andrade, Manuel, 235
Angell, James R., 327, 328, 332, 333, 349, 384, 385, 386, 388, 399–400, 402
Angulo, Jaime de, 142, 283–284
Angyal, Andreas, 341
Anti-Semitism, 189, 204, 328, 394, 399, 400–402, 412, 416
Athabaskan ethnology, 50
Athabaskan tone, 85–86, 240, 260

Banda, Hastings Kamuzu, 230
Barbeau, Marius, 49, 58–59, 67–68, 76
Bayne-Jones, Stanhope, 392, 393
Behaviorism, 139, 215, 269, 316, 384
Benedict, Ruth, xi, 10n, 134, 142, 143, 151, 169, 172–183, 187–188, 304, 307, 315, 322–325, 395

Blake, Francis, 321
Bloch, Bernard, 271
Blooah, Charles, 203, 229–230
Bloomfield, Leonard, 77n, 102, 116n, 214, 226n, 262–268 passim, 268–272, 273, 277–286 passim, 364, 366, 371, 373, 378, 405
Boas, Franz, 104, 136, 142, 159, 167, 168, 172, 176, 186–188, 211, 223, 264, 266, 269, 270, 277–287 passim, 306, 337, 366, 367, 379, 404–405, 411, 417–418; American Museum of Natural History, 62–63; diffusion vs. genetic relationship, 99–100, 113–115, 117–118, 122; finding jobs for Sapir, 20, 24, 38–43 passim, 63–64, 137, 193–200, 329–332; *Handbook of American Indian Languages,* 36–37; professional standards, 67; psychology, 12n, 137–138, 144; teaching at Columbia, 9–11, 13–15
Boasian paradigm, 91–92, 96, 171–172, 346–347, 391
Bolling, George, 263, 273
British Columbia, University of, 52–53
Brock, Reginald Walter, 41–42, 53, 55
Buck, Carl, 37, 103, 196, 265, 328, 360, 366
Bumpus, Herman C., 40

475

Designer:	U. C. Press Staff
Compositor:	Auto-Graphics
Text:	10/13 Galliard
Display:	Galliard
Printer:	Haddan Craftsmen
Binder:	Haddan Craftsmen